HORROR and SCIENCE FICTION FILMS III

by Donald C. Willis

THE SCARECROW PRESS, INC.
Metuchen, N.J., & London 1984

Library of Congress Cataloging in Publication Data

Willis, Donald C.
Horror and science fiction films III.

Bibliography: p.
1. Horror films--Catalogs. 2. Science fiction films--Catalogs. I. Title.
PN1995.9.H6W54 1984 791.43'09'0916 84-13885
ISBN 0-8108-1723-3

Manufactured in the United States of America

To Bill Warren,
for assistance above and beyond...

INTRODUCTION

Horror and Science Fiction Films III: 1982-1983 includes, in addition to complete-as-possible coverage for the years 1982 and 1983, end-of-year releases from 1981 (Volume II covered new releases up to October 31st of that year) and updatings of entries from earlier volumes, plus rediscoveries from every decade. The cutoff date for films for this third volume in the series was December 31, 1983. To qualify, a film must have either been released theatrically or to TV (inside or outside the U.S.), or have been completed and screened at a film market, festival, etc. (such trade and ratings-screenings usually being the earliest sure sign of a movie's completion)--by that date. There are approximately 760 titles in the main list; approximately 475 of those titles are critically annotated.

Retrospective entries in this volume focus on the Fifties, though due to the demands of the current product, I was not able to return to as many movies from that period as I would like to have....Key titles: The ALLIGATOR PEOPLE, The ATOMIC KID, CREATURE FROM THE BLACK LAGOON, The CREATURE WALKS AMONG US, EYES WITHOUT A FACE, The INVISIBLE BOY, IT CAME FROM OUTER SPACE, KILLERS FROM SPACE, The MAN FROM PLANET X, The MAN WHO COULD CHEAT DEATH, The MOLE PEOPLE, The MONOLITH MONSTERS, PHANTOM OF THE RUE MORGUE, REVENGE OF THE CREATURE, RIDERS TO THE STARS, RODAN, SHE DEMONS, The SPACE CHILDREN, TARANTULA, VERTIGO, WHEN WORLDS COLLIDE, and, yes, WILD WOMEN OF WONGO.

Other key entries in Volume III: BLADE RUNNER, CREEPSHOW, The DARK CRYSTAL, E.T., The EVIL DEAD, The FALLS, GALAXY EXPRESS, HALLOWEEN III, The HUNGER, JUDEX, LEGEND OF THE BAYOU, MS. 45, POLTERGEIST, RETURN OF THE JEDI, SOMETHING WICKED THIS WAY COMES, The STALKER, STRANGE INVADERS, TWILIGHT ZONE--THE MOVIE, VAMPYR, VIDEODROME, and ZELIG.

The key names in film horror and science fiction the past few years have been, most probably, Steven Spielberg and Stephen King--Spielberg as director (E.T. and the "Kick The Can" segment of TWILIGHT ZONE--THE MOVIE) and producer (POLTERGEIST); King as scriptwriter (CREEPSHOW) and source author (CUJO, CHRISTINE, The DEAD ZONE). King has now either worked with or provided material for almost all the other key personnel in the sf-horror-film field--Stanley Kubrick, David Cronenberg, John Carpenter, George Romero, Brian De Palma, Tobe Hooper--except Spielberg. Oddly, King's one direct collaboration (with Romero) for the screen--CREEPSHOW--seems atypical for both King and Romero. In it, they both seem to be on holiday--one would not, at least, normally associate either of them with a "fun" movie. Second-hand, but more recognizable, King hit, arguably, both a new high (CUJO) and a new low (CHRISTINE) in 1983, while David Cronenberg--who might have made the definitive King movie-adaptation, but was perhaps daunted by the commercial and critical failure of VIDEODROME--reined in his imagination for The DEAD ZONE, a decent, even-dramatically-ambitious film, but also a cautious, no-"untoward"-surprises one.

Spielberg continues to be one of the more exciting forces in American film--in any genre--though he still (especially with POLTERGEIST) seems to be as much an Idea factory as an artist. ("He has an idea about every thirteen seconds," one of his co-partners, Frank Marshall Jr., has noted.) Entertaining as the stunts and effects in POLTERGEIST (and, to a certain extent, E.T.) are, they overwhelm the people, and reduce the latter almost to reaction shots. In POLTERGEIST and E.T., the fantasy element more or less doubles as the subject of the movie; Spielberg's unstated goal seems to be to show us, simply, how may tricks these ghosts/aliens can do...a lot of them, it transpires, and some verily wonderful ones....Conversely, in Spielberg's section of TWILIGHT ZONE--THE MOVIE, Mr. Bloom (Scatman Crothers) does only one trick--he makes old people young. The story, then--the subject--is the people, and their responses to the magic-making: exhilaration, amusement, surprise, enforced reflectiveness. (One "girl" finds the prospect of losing "all the people that I loved again" a dismaying one.) Only one idea here, basically--but that's all you need sometimes.

The most exciting thing about Spielberg is that this is still, essentially, just the beginning. As he says, "I haven't made my IT'S A WONDERFUL LIFE yet." That he hasn't is less important than the fact that he realizes that he hasn't. He may never make his WONDERFUL LIFE, but CLOSE ENCOUNTERS OF THE THIRD KIND, E.T., and, now, his TZ-TM contribution suggest that he is, at least, headed in the right direction.

If this is the beginning of the Spielberg saga, the period 1982-1983 also saw the end of an era--"Famous Monsters" magazine ceased publication, apparently for good. ("Stevie" Spielberg's name actually appears in an early FM, or so unverified rumor, or legend, has it.) When FM began operation, in the late Fifties, horror and science-fiction movies were "big," or at least numerous. They were everywhere, both in theatres and (in, notably, "Shock Theatre"-type packages of the classics) on television. Fans, like myself, of these movies found themselves almost preternaturally "in tune" with this new magazine. We didn't just buy it--we were part of it, or it was a part of us. It was not enough, we discovered, simply to see movies like HORROR OF DRACULA and The MUMMY'S GHOST--we had to know more about them, what made them (us?) tick--for the (seemingly contradictory) purposes of, at once, explaining them "away" and keeping them "alive," alive in (clearly, at least in retrospect) more-emotionally-manageable form.

"Famous Monsters" made our search for arcane knowledge enjoyable--editor Forrest J Ackerman kept the tone light. There would, of course, always be those who would say that the tone of FM was too light, that a monster magazine was no place for puns and plays on words, for humor in the captions under photos from The MOLE PEOPLE ("I'm a mole cowhand from the Rio Grande")--but what better place? The fact is that FM did, also, bring us the rare photos; the checklists of Poe films, Chaney films, dinosaur films; the scoops on horrors yet to come. And this whole subject of monsters could, it's also true, be said to be rather...grim, or morbid--the unexpectedly sunny approach was perhaps the best one, the one that made FM outlast all early competitors. FM was at once serious and frivolous--it allowed both for absorption in and detachment from its subject, which subject was, after all, really not that important--or was it? It allowed us our own world--as suggested by the title of FM's short-lived companion magazine, "Monster World"--with the humor functioning as a sort of life line to the real world...as a thread leading out of the labyrinth. One could get lost in FM and yet find one's way back. Like a good movie, it involved us thoroughly, then returned us to the--somehow altered (for the better)--light of day.

+++

"The evidence" (to quote Andrew Sarris) "is visible on the screen"; but it's sometimes conflicting evidence. Effects people and directors like Harry Woolman, Frank X. Carrisosa, Joe Quinlavin, Paul Landres, and Allan Apone may or may not spell their names thus; but the people who compose the credit scrolls for the movies on which they worked spell the above names several different ways. The titlers are especially creative with Harry Woolman. That's the usual spelling. (See END OF THE WORLD, 1977, for instance.) He's aka Harry Wolman (ALIEN ZONE) or Harry Wollman (DR. BLACK; MR. HYDE). Variations on the other names listed above include Alan (Apone), Quinlavian, Quinlivan (at least in one printed source), Carriosa, Carrisusa, and Landers. At the beginning of DESTINATION NIGHTMARE, Paul is "Landers"; at the end, "Landres"--or, to quote Groucho Marx, Who are you going to believe--me or your own eyes?

+++

For their kind assistance in various capacities, I would like to thank Joe Dante, Don Glut, Scot Holton, Mark Kausler, Jim Shapiro, Jonathan Van Landschoot, and Bill Warren; Nancy Goldman, Linda Artel, and Edith Kramer of the Pacific Film Archive; the staff of the Academy of Motion Picture Arts and Sciences Library; and Gold Key Entertainment.

+++

Thirteen-Best (1981-1983):

MS. 45/The EVIL DEAD/SPECIAL BULLETIN/The HUNGER/The FALLS/The DARK CRYSTAL/TWICE UPON A TIME/E.T./WARGAMES/QUEST FOR FIRE/HEARTBEEPS/RETURN OF THE JEDI/GALAXY EXPRESS.

Runners-up: MISS MORISON'S GHOSTS/CUJO/The ROAD WARRIOR/POLTERGEIST/STRANGE INVADERS/VIDEODROME.

More Memorable Shorts, and Parts of Films

NOW YOU TELL ONE(1926)/DANCING ON THE MOON(1935)/The DIABOLICAL TENANT(1909)/The BLACK IMP(1905)/"Kick The Can"(TZ-TM, 1983)/The COOK IN TROUBLE(1904)/IT'S A BIRD(1930)/The INFERNAL CAULDRON (1903)/PALACE OF THE ARABIAN NIGHTS(1905)/"Rude Awakening"(HAMMER HOUSE OF HORROR, 1980)/"It's A Good Life"(TZ-TM, 1983)/the Crystal Spider in KRULL/Lester's dialogue in The LOVE BUTCHER/the pyramid in The DAY TIME ENDED/the hole in ENCOUNTER WITH THE UNKNOWN/the masked ball in JUDEX/the 360-degree tracking shot in VERTIGO/the shadow-world in VAMPYR/the phone wires in IT CAME FROM OUTER SPACE.

And the climactic sequences of DEMENTED, DEATHDREAM, The STALKER, The UNSEEN(1981), and of course DRAGON ZOMBIES RETURN and The 27TH DAY
--the effects sequences in BLADE RUNNER, RETURN OF THE JEDI, The THING(1982), EGGED ON, The HUNGER, TOURIST TRAP, POLTERGEIST, and The EVIL DEAD
--the monsters in DEMON POND, BASKET CASE, The BOOGENS, XTRO, The DEADLY SPAWN, and of course HOLLYWOOD BOULEVARD.

More Memorable Performances

Sue Tyrrell, NIGHT WARNING, ANDY WARHOL'S BAD
Harrison Ford, RAIDERS OF THE LOST ARK, BLADE RUNNER, STAR WARS
Michael Caine, DEATHTRAP, The HAND
Rip Torn, A STRANGER IS WATCHING
Dan O'Herlihy, HALLOWEEN III
Sandy Dennis, SOMETHING EVIL
Ingrid Pitt, COUNTESS DRACULA
Don Opper, ANDROID

Carrie Snodgress, The ATTIC
Nigel Bruce as Dr. Watson
Anthony Perkins, PSYCHO II
Vincent Price, the Poe films
Lon Chaney, The UNKNOWN, The PENALTY, WEST OF ZANZIBAR
Nielsen, Macnee, & Graham, SPACESHIP.

More Memorable Scores

Maurice Jarre's for EYES WITHOUT A FACE, JUDEX
David Raksin's for NIGHT TIDE
James Horner's for KRULL
Jerry Goldsmith's for TWILIGHT ZONE--THE MOVIE
John Williams's for HEARTBEEPS
Georges Auric's for DEAD OF NIGHT
Max Steiner's/Bach's for BEAST WITH FIVE FINGERS.

+++

Sneak previews: following is a non-exhaustive list of titles of films either ostensibly completed and scheduled for release in 1984, or films actually in release (indicated by "#"), already (through May), in 1984.

#AIRWOLF(TV)
AKELARRE(Sp)
#ANGEL
The APPOINTMENT(B)
The ARK OF THE SUN GOD(I-Turk)
The ATLANTIS INTERCEPTORS(I)
#The BLADE MASTER(I/aka ATOR THE INVINCIBLE: THE RETURN)
BLIND DATE
BLOODBATH AT THE HOUSE OF DEATH(B)
BLOODSHED
BOGGY CREEK II
BROTHER FROM ANOTHER PLANET
BYE-BYE, JUPITER(J)
CANNIBAL FURY(I)
The CENTURIONS(I/aka ROME 2072)
#CHILDREN OF THE CORN
#The COLD ROOM(TV)
CONAN II
The CRYSTAL SWORD(I)
DEATHMASK
DEEP GHOST
DELTA SPACE MISSION(Rum)
EVIL JUDGMENT
The EVIL TOUCH(I)
Los EXTRATERRESTRES(Arg)
The FINAL WAR(J)
#FIRESTARTER
The FLIGHT OF DRAGONS
FRANKENSTEIN'S GREAT AUNT TILLIE
#FRIDAY THE 13TH--THE FINAL CHAPTER
GREMLINS
HARD ROCK ZOMBIES
HEALTH CLUB HORRORS
HIDEOUS SUN DEMON: THE SPECIAL EDITION
#The ICE PIRATES
#ICEMAN
#INDIANA JONES & THE TEMPLE OF DOOM
INNOCENT PREY(Austral)
#INVITATION TO HELL(TV)
JUNGLE BOY, KENIYA(J)
LION MEN VS. THE WRATH OF THE WITCH QUEEN(Turk)
LOCKE THE SUPERMAN(J)
LOOSE JOINTS(aka FLICKS)
LOST ON ADVENTURE ISLAND
MURDER ROCK(I)
#MUTANT
NIGHT OF THE REAL DEAD PEOPLE
ONE NIGHT STAND(Austral.)

The OUTING
POSSESSED(I)
RANA--THE LEGEND OF SHADOW LAKE
RATS(I/aka NIGHT OF FEAR)
#RIPTIDE(TV)
ROAD OF THE DUNGEON MASTER
#ROBIN HOOD AND THE SORCERER(B)
#SLAPSTICK OF ANOTHER KIND
SPACE PATROL
SPLATTER
STAR TREK III
STONE BOY(Fili)
SWORD OF HEAVEN
A TALE OF THE EARTH(J)
TALES OF THE THIRD DIMENSION
TEEN DEMON
TEXAS HONEYMOON HORROR
#THEY'RE PLAYING WITH FIRE
THRONE OF FIRE(I)
TO KILL A STRANGER(Mex)
TOKI WO KAKERU SHOJO(J)
2020: TEXAS GLADIATORS(I)
The WARRIOR AND THE SORCERESS(Arg-US/aka CAIN DEL PLANETA OSCURO)
WARRIOR OF THE LOST WORLD(I)
WENDIGO
WIZARD WARS
ZOMBIE ISLAND MASSACRE(aka PICNIC or The LAST PICNIC)
ZOO SHIP

TABLE OF CONTENTS

EXPLANATORY NOTES

The general order of information for entries in the main listing is as follows:

Title/Country of origin/Distribution company (TV distributors of movies originally released theatrically are listed first, in parentheses)/Production companies/Year (in cases where general-release date and completion or copyright date differ, both are given, the latter date in parentheses)/Animation, color, wide-screen, and 3-D indications/Running time (in cases where r.t. here conflicts with that found in other printed sources, it's from a timed theatre or TV viewing)/Alternate titles/Director/Scriptwriter/Source/Photography/Music/Art Direction/Special effects/Makeup/Sound effects/Reference sources/Cast/Synopsis/Comment.

* or (I) - refers to an entry in the 1972 main list.
** - refers to an entry in the 1972 out list.
*** - refers to an entry in the 1972 shorts-and-animated-films list.
2 or (II) - refers to an entry in the 1982 main list.
2P or IIP - refers to an entry in the 1982 peripheral-films section.
(A) - refers to an entry continued in the addenda.
(P) - refers to an entry in the peripheral-films section.
(M) - refers to an entry in the main list.

Underlined words indicate corrections.

A new feature this volume: abbreviated entries for movies with science-fiction and/or horror scenes or minor sf/horror elements.

Variety citations without page numbers generally refer to reviews in Variety's (indexed) Film Reviews section.

ABBREVIATIONS

B - British
Can. - Canadian
F - French
G - German
H.K. - Hong Kong
I - Italian
J - Japanese
Sp - Spanish
W.G. - West German
Cant. - Cantonese-language
Mand. - Mandarin-language

AA - Allied Artists
AI - American International
BFI - British Film Institute
BV - Buena Vista (Disney)
Col - Columbia
FVI - Film Ventures Int'l.
Fox - Twentieth-Century Fox
Indep.-Int'l. - Independent Int'l.
MOMA - Museum of Modern Art, N.Y.
Para - Paramount
QFI - Quartet-Films Inc.
UA - United Artists
Univ - Universal-International or Universal
WB - Warner Brothers

anim - animation
stopmo anim - stop-motion (or object or puppet) animation
ws - wide screen
m - minutes
c - circa (or copyright)
sfa - same film as
aka - also known as
orig t - original title
int t - intermediate title (early title in-between original & release titles)
alt t - alternate title
re-r t - re-release title
cr t - title in film's credits
tr t - translated title

D - director
SP - screenplay
Adap - adaptation
Addl Dial - additional dialogue
Ph - photography
Mus - musical score
PD - production design
AD - art direction
SpFX - special effects
VisFX - visual effects
SpMkp - special makeup
Prosth - prosthetics
Elec - electronic (music) or electrical (effects)
MechFX - mechanical effects
PyroFX - pyrotechnic effects
Roto - rotoscope
Syn or Synth - synthesizer
SdFX - sound effects
Cost - costumes
Exec - executive
Assoc - associate
P - producer
Narr - narrator or narration
Coord - coordinator
Ed - editor
Sup - supervisor
Cons - consultant
Adv - adviser
Asst - assistant
Opt - opticals
Min - miniatures

Ref - reference sources
pb - pressbook
pr - press release
vc - video cassette
vt - video tape
Academy - Academy of Motion Picture Arts & Sciences Library
AFI - American Film Institute Catalog
BFC - British Film Catalog
Boxo - Boxoffice
Cinef - Cinefantastique
FM - Famous Monsters
Glut/CMM - Classic Movie Monsters
Glut/TDB - The Dracula Book
Glut/TFL - The Frankenstein Legend
HR - Hollywood Reporter
HKFFest - Hong Kong Film Festival
IFG - Int'l. Film Guide
JFFJ - Japanese Fantasy Film Journal
LAT - Los Angeles Times
LC - Library of Congress (Motion Pictures)
Lee - Reference Guide...
Lee(p) - Reference Guide (problems)
Lee(e) - Reference Guide (exclusions)
MFB - Monthly Film Bulletin
Maltin/OMAM - Of Mice & Magic
NYT - New York Times
PFA - Pacific Film Archive (Film Notes, Library)
S&S - Sight & Sound
SFChron - San Francisco Chronicle
SFExam - San Francisco Examiner
screen - information obtained directly from the film
TV - information obtained directly from TV showing of the film
TVFFSB - Television Feature Film Source Book
TVG - TV Guide
V - Variety(weekly)
V(d) - Variety(daily)
VV - The Village Voice

HORROR AND SCIENCE FICTION FILMS III

A HAUNTING WE WILL GO WB 1966 anim color 7m. D: Robert McKimson. Ref: Maltin/OMAM: Speedy Gonzales, Daffy Duck. "WB Cartoons." LC. no Lee.
Witch Hazel...haunted house..."weirdo beastie." (WBC)

*ABBOTT AND COSTELLO MEET THE INVISIBLE MAN 1951 (BUD ABBOTT AND LOU COSTELLO MEET THE INVISIBLE MAN--cr t) Story: Hugh Wedlock Jr., Howard Snyder. SpPhFX: David S. Horsley. Ref: TV. Glut/CMM. V 3/7/51. Lee. Weldon. Hirschhorn.
References to Frankenstein (the line, "If that ain't Tommy Nelson, it's Frankenstein") and to Universal's original invisible man (a photo of Claude Rains as Griffin); Arthur Franz as the new invisible man, Tommy Nelson; deja vu (if that's the right term) invisibility tricks with cigarettes and clothes; familiar blustering from Lou. One of A&C's feebler efforts, featuring, at its best, a just-passable pickpocket routine.

*ABBOTT AND COSTELLO MEET THE KILLER 1949 (BUD ABBOTT AND LOU COSTELLO MEET THE KILLER, BORIS KARLOFF-cr t) Mus: Milton Schwarzwald. Ref: TV. V 8/3/49. LC. Hirschhorn. Weldon. and with Harry Hayden.
Lou hypnotized by swami (Boris Karloff) to kill...disguised killer in spooky caverns...dead bodies everywhere. Wan comedy-mystery. Lou's burbling, spluttering, choking, snuffling, and whining is alternately grotesque and charming--and can't possibly be ignored. Bud's straight work can, though he has a few ingratiating moments too. Karloff is pretty much lost in the shuffle of supporting players.

*ABBOTT AND COSTELLO MEET THE MUMMY 1955 AD: Alexander Golitzen, Bill Newberry. SpPhFX: Clifford Stine. Ref: TV. Hirschhorn. Lee. Weldon.
Eight mummies (Eddie Parker and 7 fake ones: Michael Ansara, Bud, 5-mummy band)...bit with giant lizard darting into burial chamber...animated bat...and of course Bud & Lou, with draggy material except for the "pick/shovel" routine, which

gets to be so silly it's amusing. Universal's Egypt is about as exotic as Disneyland East. Lou's "takes" go on and on.

L'ABIME DES MORTS VIVANTS (F) Eurocine 1982 color 95m. (aka The OASIS OF THE LIVING DEAD. Le TRESOR DES MORTS VIVANTS) D: Jesus Franco(aka A.M. Franck). SP: Daniel Lesoeur. Ph: Max Monteillet. Mus: Daniel White. Ref: Ecran F 31:57,43. 36:76. V 5/13/81:283. 5/12/82:268. with Manuel Gelin, France Jordan, Jeff Montgomery, Henri Lambert.
Treasure guarded by Nazi-zombies in the North African desert.

ABSURD--ANTROPOPHAGOUS 2 (I) Filmirage 1982 color D: Aristide Massaccesi(aka Joe D'Amato). Ref: V 5/12/82:196. 5/13/81:160. 9/30/81:16(ad). Ecran F 31:42. with Laura Gemser, Van Johnson.
Man exposed to radiation becomes indestructible "spirit of evil." Sequel to The GRIM REAPER.

ACES GO PLACES II (H.K.-Cant.) Cinema City 1983 color/ws 101m. (aka MAD MISSION PART II) D: Eric Tsang. PD: Nansun Shi. AD: Oliver Wong. SpFX: Gene Grigg? Ref: screen. V 2/23/83. 3/30/83:58(ad). 5/4/83:341(ad),380(ad). IFG'83:153: sequel to ACES GO PLACES(P). with Sam Hui, Carl Mak, Sylvia Chang.
In a prologue, mini-copters crash through the windows of a building and converge inside to form a huge flying robot, BG I, which is operated by remote-computer-control and which shoots rockets at one of our heroes, "King Kong." ("My name's King Kong. What's yours?") Later, near the end of the movie, Kong produces a small, immobile robot from his "magic box" (i.e., a suitcase) and uses it to engage robot BG II in a battle of "super-speed rockets." BG II shoots lasers from its "eyes" and red rays from its "feet," but ultimately proves no match for Kong's fleet of mini-robots (e.g., Bomber Ant, King Kong, Peter Pan, The Man with The Golden Gun)--the latter zap BG II with all sorts of electric and laser rays. (One little robot even produces its own electrical field and cuts through a steel wall.) Plus: a rocket-rifle, rocket-firing cars, stun darts, a one-man flying-or-hovering-harness, etc.
ACES GO PLACES II (like AIRPLANE II) is a science-fictional sequel to a non-sf film, though it's clearly cut from the same basic narrative pattern as ACES I--there's even a "strange interlude," again, in the middle of the film, a full-fledged musical number featuring a silly if catchy tune re: being friends. This time around, the more-or-less incidental villain (White Glove in the original) is a Clint Eastwood-like Filthy Harry (whose "agent" is Henry Kissinger). PART II replaces remote-control model cars with a horde of robots and rays--the opening and closing sf-sequences, in fact, are the movie's highlights, chock-full as they are of effects and stunts with motorcycles and mechanical men. The filmmakers' grasp of comedy, however, is somewhat less sure than their grasp of spectacle, and this movie is, basically, and not-too-fortunately,

a comedy. Here, the authors are, at the least, eclectic, borrowing, sparingly, from Keaton (and COPS) and Chaplin (and CITY LIGHTS--the swallowed whistle), as well as (less sparingly) from The Three Stooges (the bop-and-tweak routines). (One of the three protagonists even observes, at one point, "We're The Three Stooges.") If comedy is more or less dead, the art of mugging certainly isn't....

ADAM RAISES CAIN 1919 silhouette anim silent D: Tony Sarg. Ref: Don Glut: dinosaur comedy. no LC.

ADVENTURES IN THE CREEP ZONE see SPACEHUNTER

ADVENTURES OF BOB AND DOUG MCKENZIE see STRANGE BREW

ADVENTURES OF DAVID GRAY see VAMPYR

ADVENTURES OF FREDDIE see MAGNIFICENT MAGICAL MAGNET OF SANTA MESA

*The ADVENTURES OF SHERLOCK HOLMES 1939 83m. Based on characters created by Sir Arthur Conan Doyle. Ref: screen. TV. LC. V 9/6/39. "The Detective in Film." Weldon. and with Mary Forbes, George Regas(Mateo).

May, 1894. That "very Genius of Evil," Professor Moriarty (George Zucco), provides his nemesis, Sherlock Holmes (Basil Rathbone), with two "toys" to keep the master detective's deductive mind occupied--while Moriarty makes off with the Crown Jewels of England. The more elaborate "toy" to be set in motion concerns the Brandon family, and is wound up with "cryptic warnings of avenging death," sent first to Lloyd (Peter Willes) and then to Ann Brandon (Ida Lupino)--warnings in the form of drawings featuring an albatross, the "angel of destruction." Lloyd lives in fear, but not for long--he dies, "with the back of his head all...," just as, many years before, in South America, his father died. Ann is plagued by the eerily muted strains of an oboe-like, South American wind instrument ("That music gives me the creeps!"), which melody she associates with the night of her father's death ("death in every note of it"). It was "strange music (which) didn't begin and didn't end--it just went on...." It proves to be an "ancient Incan funeral dirge" from the Andes. The instrument of death (or, in Ann's case, near-death) proves to be a bolas....

The sequences of Lloyd's death and Ann's near-death are shot and scored horror-movie style, with fog snaking about trees and fences, and chiller music emanating from that Incan "oboe," or from Twentieth Century-Fox's music department. In Lloyd's case we see nothing--we just hear him scream. In Ann's case we see the shoes of her apparently-clubfooted stalker. There are no monsters or monster-dogs here: the horror effects (aural and visual) are all done in the name of atmosphere--but they help to make this one of the more satisfying Holmes films.

Holmes and Dr. Watson (Nigel Bruce) have some of their most winning I-am-a-genius/I-am-ordinary-but-lovable (respectively) exchanges, and Rathbone makes the most of one or two long, involved, involving speeches in which you can hear the mystery being unraveled by Holmes, strand by strand. As Holmes, Rathbone always seemed to come in third best to Nigel Bruce and to whoever was playing Moriarty, but he is, here, most engaging. The viewer pays, however, for the Rathbone-Bruce "duets": the Ida Lupino-Alan Marshal scenes are garden-variety melodrama, somehow-necessary, banal evils.

ADVENTURES OF SUPERMAN, The see SUPERMAN AND THE JUNGLE DEVIL

ADVENTURES OF THE STARKILLER see STAR WARS

*AELITA 1924 Ref: screen. PFA notes 7/23/80.

A scientist daydreams that he builds a spaceship and journeys to Mars, where he finds a civilization of rulers and workers, and their queen, Aelita, who loves him. (She had, it seems, been observing him with the aid of an apparatus for investigating life on other planets.) An odd mixture, this, of science-fantasy-dream, domestic melodrama, and low comedy. Only the latter element really survives. How the disparate narrative elements were supposed to fit together is anybody's guess now--a guide to the "reading" of AELITA might be helpful.

The AERODROME (B) BBC-TV/Kenith Trodd 1983 color 91m. D: Giles Foster. SP: Robin Chapman, from Rex Warner's novel. Ph: Kenneth McMillan. Mus: Carl Davis. PD: Geoff Powell, Tim Harvey. Ref: V 11/30/83: book's future (the Fifties) now, of course, the past. with Peter Firth, Richard Johnson, Richard Briers, Natalie Ogle, Jill Bennett, Mary Peach.

Fascistic Air Force "gradually takes over every aspect of civilian life" in England.

The AFTERMATH Nautilus/Barkett 1980 color 95m. Story,SP,D, P,Ed,with: Steve Barkett. Story: also Stanley Livingston. Ph: Dennis Skotak, Tom Denove. Mus: John Morgan. PD,Co-Mkp: Robert Skotak. VisFX: The Skotaks;(add'l & with) Jim Danforth. Laser Anim: John Wash. Opt: CFI. Asst D: Scot Holton. Ref: TV: laser gun. Bill Warren. S.Holton. with Lynne Margulies, Sid Haig, Christopher Barkett, Vincent Barbi, Larry Latham, Forrest J Ackerman, Dick Miller(voice).

"What the devil's going on down there?!" Glad you asked. Well, it seems a couple of astronauts return to a world torn by "nuclear blasts" and "biological weapons," and a devastated Los Angeles is stalked by mutants and ruthless killers. Weird storms prevail. Clearly, technology is controlling man. Or as FJA, as the museum curator, puts it, "Destroyed by atoms and germs--what irony!"

The irony of this determinedly, doggedly grim sf-drama is that, in its very attempt to enlist our sympathy for the hero,

Newman (Barkett), and his cause--namely, the methodical extermination of human scum (e.g., "baby-killers" like Haig's Cutter)--it systematically extinguishes any such incipient sympathy. In the movie's badly miscalculated climactic sequence, Newman deliberately and nastily shoots, then slices up one of the arch-vermin, more graphically than the vermin are shown perpetrating their horrors. The director, clearly, wants audience catharsis--what he is more likely to get is alienation. He confuses mere ferocity with heroism....Newman dies for his cause; however, in a quasi-Chaplinesque, down-the-road-and-into-the-sunset parting image, his surrogate son is portrayed as, also, his surrogate avenger. Newman lives! The latter prospect, however, is liable to provoke, in context, not so much the desired surge of viewer excitement, as a feeling closer to dismay. With friends like Newman....

See also: JUPITER MENACE, The.

El AGUJERO EN LA PARED (Arg.) del Plata 1982 color 90m. SP, D: David J. Kohon. Ph: H. Collodoro. Mus: Lito Vitale. AD: M.A. Lumaldo. Ref: V 7/21/82: "Faust" variation. with Alfredo Alcon, Mario Alarcon, Maria Noel.

A man trades his soul--for riches--to a "stranger called Mephi."

AIRPLANE II: THE SEQUEL Para/Howard W. Koch 1982 color 83m. (AIRPLANE 2002! AIRPLANE 2!--both early ts) SP,D: Ken Finkleman. Ph: Joe Biroc. Mus: Elmer Bernstein; Richard Hazard. PD: William Sandell. SpVisFX: Phil Kellison;(sup) Joe Rayner; (min) Coast. SpFX: Robert N. Dawson. SpSdFX: Alan Haworth. Mkp: Monty Westmore. OptFX: Modern, Master. Ref: screen. V 12/8/82. Academy. with Peter Graves, Robert Hays, Julie Hagerty, Lloyd Bridges, Chad Everett, William Shatner, Chuck Connors, Raymond Burr, Richard Jaeckel, John Dehner, Rip Torn, Kent McCord, James A. Watson Jr., Sonny Bono, Jack Jones, John Larch, Sandahl Bergman; Steve Levitt, Steve Nevil(creatures); Herve Villechaize, Patty Dworkin, Mary-Robin Redd, Art Fleming, Leon Askin, Hugh Gillin, Marcy Lafferty.

Commercial flight to the moon via Pan Universe plane is diverted by HAL-type computer toward the sun....lunar base... bits with E.T. and the Starship Enterprise...live monster-vacuum...Godzilla-types on Tokyo newscasts...Death personified in the cockpit...musical references to 2001, BATTLESTAR GALACTICA, etc...man-into-jelly bit...old lady literally bored to death...ROCKY 38 ad...clips from the silent HUNCHBACK OF NOTRE DAME..."metabolic change" which at 0.5 worp (sic) turns all passengers into Richard Nixons.

Paramount, attempting to consolidate the AIRPLANE! and science-fiction markets, comes up here with a rather agreeable-if-messy comedy. The material ranges from plain bad to fun dumb to well-nigh-ingenious, though the laughs don't depend much on actors, on (that is) timing, delivery, or nuance of personality. The cast is pretty much incidental to the visual and verbal wordplay. Example of same: a) shot of pilot Graves looking at plane's instrument panel and deadpanning "That's strange"; b) shot of instrument panel--three squares labeled "Weird," "Strange," and "Bizarre"--middle square lit up. This is editors', not actors' comedy. But the silliness is sometimes so winning, and is so relentless, that you may find yourself laughing at the bad stuff as well as the good--unable, even, perhaps, to tell which is which. The film generates a willing suspension of dismay in the viewer, and the hits make up for a lot of the misses. (Plenty of both.) The film's sense of humor is loopily literal-minded. The line (coming from a photographer in a courtroom) "How about a photo for the Daily News?" generates a quick exchange of items between hands--an 8x10 glossy for a copy of a newspaper. It's not surprising that "Roget's Thesaurus" makes an appearance in this film--the director, obviously, is obsessed with words and phrases. Hardly a line of dialogue goes by, it seems, without having to pass lexicographical inspection for possible double-meaning, for hitherto unsuspected comic potential. The viewer is given, in effect, an "instant replay" of each line, and the replays reveal quirky, silly little ambiguities. (A)

The ALCHEMIST Ideal-Reinberg/Appelbaum 1983 color 84m. D: Charles Band. SP: Alan J. Adler. Ph: A.W. Friend. Mus: Richard Band. PD: Dale A. Pelton. SpFX: Doug White, YF&S;(ph) John Lambert, Paul Gentry. OptFX: Lambert, Guy Marsden. Anim: Gentry, Marsden. SpMkpFX: Steve Neill, Rick Stratton et al; (des) Karen Kubeck. Demons: Tony Abatemarco, Billy Scudder. SdFX: Steve Beach. Title Des: Sam Alexander. Ref: MFB'83:209. Ecran F 29:54. Screen Int'l 7/16/83. V 10/20/82:124(ad). with Robert Ginty, Lucinda Dooling, Bob Glaudini.

1771. A man is cursed by the Alchemist to live as a "snarling beast"....demons unleashed through the gates of hell. (SI)

ALICE IN WONDERLAND(by L. Carroll) see BETTY IN BLUNDERLAND

The ALIEN ORO (Can.) Gold Key-TV/T.A.E. 1973(1982) color 95m. (The STARLOST QUINTOLOGY 3. The STARLOST: THE ALIEN ORO-cr) D: Joseph Scanlon, Francis Chapman. SP: Forer, Walman, A.C. James. Created by Cordwainer Bird. Mus: Score Prods. PD: Jack McAdam. VisFX, Exec Co-P: Douglas Trumbull. Graphic Des: In The Sunrise. Mkp: Carol Davidson. Cons: Ben Bova. Ref: TV: two episodes from "The Starlost" TV series. GKey. TVFFSB. TVG. with Keir Dullea(Devon), Robin Ward, Walter Koenig(Oro), Gay Rowan, Alexandra Bastedo; William Osler(voice).

2791 A.D., aboard Earthship Ark, a giant spacecraft "8,000 miles in character" (and featuring a thermonuclear propulsion system), sent out from a troubled Earth in 2285 A.D. to "seed other planets." Oro, an alien on a salvage mission, takes command of the temporarily crippled Ark, the advanced technology of which his people want to study. He and the hero, Devon, ultimately engage in a robot-moderated debate for possession of the Ark--with their arguments, they score points and build up "force field" power. The robot's bias for its human makers eventually tips the scales in Devon's favor; Oro's dissatisfied superiors destroy his ship by remote control and strand him on the Ark...."window in space"..."iris" doors.

"Truth or Consequences" in space. Oro loses the force-field debate--which glibly pits his logic against Devon's humanism--but the winner spares his life: i.e., See, we're humanistic! There's also soap/space opera in the first half of the film--a human-alien romance stirs up the suds--and fair comedy from a "wildman" named Williams. But the drama is developed in fits and starts, and mostly in dialogue, and the only pressing question proves to be, Is Oro friend or foe? Which question, at that, really isn't too pressing.

2 ALIEN ZONE Boehs(Myriad Cinema) 1978 (The HOUSE OF THE DEAD-alt TV t) D: Sharron Miller. SP: David O'Malley. Ph: Ken Gibb. Mus: Stan V. Worth;(lyrics) Ayn Robbins. AD: Paul Staheli. SpFX: Harry Woolman. Opt: Modern. Mkp: Helen Little. Ref: TV. TVG. and with Ivor Francis(The Mortician), Judith Novgrod, Burr DeBenning, Charles Aidman, Stefanie Auerbach, Gary Willis, John King.

Five tales of the bizarre. 1) Teacher tormented by students' pranks is "bitten to death by children" (or are they children?) with monster-teeth. 2) Camera buff lures women to his apartment, films himself murdering them. 3) World's two "leading criminologists" eliminate each other. 4) Businessman trapped overnight in warehouse is mentally tortured, driven to alcoholism. 5) Framing and concluding story re: "mortician" who displays previous "clients" (all victims of their own weaknesses) to his latest one....The operative word in the title is of course "zone" (as in "twilight"), not "alien," though Gold Key's promotion would have us think ALIEN. And this isn't bad as Serling imitations go. There is a modest amount of wit evident (at least in the first three tales), some decent acting, and a sense of ingenuity-on-a-budget at work. The payoff of tale number one is a wry variation on the charge of the ghoul brigade in NIGHT OF THE LIVING DEAD, and tale two adds some sick-jokey footnotes to PEEPING TOM. The other stories are standard anecdotes, with moments.

ALIENS FROM ANOTHER PLANET ABC-TV/Irwin Allen & Kent & Fox-TV 1967 color 90m. AD: J.M. Smith, R.E. Maus. SpFX: L.B. Abbott. Ref: TV. TVG. "TV Drama Series." with James Darren, Robert Colbert, Robert Duvall, Lew Gallo(alien), Tris Coffin, Byron Foulger, Joe Ryan, Wesley Lau, Ross Elliott; John Hoyt, Vitina Marcus, Fred Beir, Jan Merlin(aliens).

Two spliced-together episodes of "The Time Tunnel" TV series. 1) "Chase Through Time": a saboteur (Duvall) flees into the tunnel (and the Grand Canyon, in the year 1547) after hiding a nuclear time bomb in the complex. Flash-forward to One Million A.D. and the Ultimate Human Society, "an enormous beehive," ruled by the cruel Masters. ("They're like bees.") Here, the time travelers find blue-skinned and gold-skinned people, invisible force-fields, "solar energy conducted by radio waves," and the saboteur, hard-at-work on a teleporter. Back in One Million B.C., our travelers (now five in number) are menaced by finned dinosaurs from Allen's The LOST WORLD. 2) "Visitors from beyond The Stars": the tunnelers land in the year 2268, right in the middle of a spaceship bearing emissaries from Alpha One, "a hungry planet" without protein--the aliens' searches for protein account, it's said, for UFO sightings on Earth. ("We frequently pass through your solar system.") A slight adjustment in time produces a Martians-in-the-Old-West effect in 1885 Arizona, where the aliens demonstrate their "projector" (a disintegrator-gun) and temporarily turn one time traveler into a "zombie"....Two TV shows, simply sporting a new title. The simplistic sentiments of the first story qualify as "humanistic" only in the loosest sense of the word. They should change the title of this "film" again, to "Time Capsule," put it in one, and bury it....

ALL SORTS OF HEROES (B) Manchester Polytechnic 1982? puppet anim SP,D: Rick Megginson, Steve Hughes. Ref: VV 1/11/83: 50: "giant robots."

ALLAN QUATERMAIN(by Haggard) see KING SOLOMON'S TREASURE

2 ALLIGATOR Alligator Inc.(Brandon Chase) 1980 Story: Sayles, Perilli. Mus: Craig Hundley. AD: Michael Erler. SpFxMkp: Robert Short. SpFX:(coord) R.O. Helmer; W.F. Shourt, David Bartholomew et al. Titles: Rabin. SpOptFX: Film FX of Hollywood. Min: Bill Kaufman. Ref: TV. MFB'82:39. Weldon: "sewer worker named Ed Norton." and with Mike Mazurki.

A little of everything: a big, hungry testosterone-stimulated alligator named Ramon...stunts with erupting sidewalks and flying police boats...false alarms...hucksters and opportunists...politics...sewer scenes galore...a hero with a "past" and thinning hair...and a heroine who's into snakes....Conversely, not much of anything. So this time it's an alligator. Next time a wildebeest....

*The ALLIGATOR PEOPLE 1959 SpFX: Fred Etcheverry. Mkp: Ben Nye, Dick Smith. Ref: TV. Bill Warren. Scot Holton. Joe Dante. Weldon. "Horror Film Stars." Lee: Mus: Irving Gertz.

Dr. Mark St. Clair (George Macready), studying the phenomenon of lizard-limb replacement, discovers the "reptilian substance"--a hydro-cortisone hormone--responsible for it. Applying his discovery to humans, he injects a protein chemical--extracted from the anterior pituitary gland of alligators--into the veins of accident victims. Their limbs heal, but a year after treatment they begin to suffer side effects: an "additional secretion" in the gland begins to turn them into alligators. X-ray and gamma-ray energy (the latter from cobalt

60) is directed at the victims, in the hope of finding a way of reversing the process, but fate intervenes, and over-exposure to the rays turns our hero (Richard Crane) into a full-fledged alligator person....

The story is told from the viewpoint of the hero's bride (Beverly Garland), and divides into mystery (first half) and tragedy (second half). Her husband "just disappears" on their wedding night. Eventually, she tracks him to The Cypresses plantation (in the swamps outside picturesque Bayou Landing, Louisiana). Although she is invited to stay the night, noone there seems to know his name, and she's told not to leave her room. She is suspicious: "There was something sinister about The Cypresses." Meanwhile, in another part of the mansion, "number six," a man with his head encased in candy-box-like wrappings, is giving the Doc trouble. "These are people!" he has to remind his aides--his over-emphasis is unsettling, or would be if the title of the movie weren't The ALLIGATOR PEOPLE, and mystery were actually possible. "Who could be playing (the piano) in the dead of night?" wonders the wife. Denseness is her forte--the plot demands it of her; the light must dawn slowly in her since the script is so spare. The husband is turning into an alligator; the doctor is turning (for a cure) to cobalt--that, essentially, is the plot, and it requires a lot of narrative Hamburger-Helper. Said plot does, however, yield two interesting moments: the bride, still on the honeymoon train, has just been deserted by the groom (who has received some bad news from Dr. St. Clair). We see him through a train window--from her point-of-view--as the train departs, leaving him, inexplicably (to her), behind on the station platform. And, in the climactic scene, the image of the now-fully-alligator-headed hero battling an alligator--wrestling, futilely, as it were, with his fate--is at once ludicrous (he is, after all, obviously a man in an alligator-head mask) and oddly evocative. (Where it wouldn't be if he were wrestling, simply, a snake or a dog.) Macready gives the smoothest performance; anti-alligator Chaney Jr. ("dirty, nasty, slimy gators!"--an alligator chewed off one of his hands), the most amusing one.

See also: FALCON'S ADVENTURE, The.

ALLIGATORS see GREAT ALLIGATOR, The

ALL'S FAIR AT THE FAIR Para 1938 anim color 7m. D: Dave Fleischer. Anim: Waldman, Place. Ref: screen. PFA(flyer). Maltin/OMAM. no LC. no Lee.

World's Fair of the future features robot barbers/pianist/dancers, a mechanized beauty parlor, a shake-and-build home-making machine (instant houses!), etc. Fairish Fleischer cartoon seems modeled on the Disney MODERN INVENTIONS(1937).

ALONE IN THE DARK New Line/Robert Shaye & Masada 1982 color 91m. Story,SP,D: Jack Sholder. Story: also Shaye, Michael

Harpster. Ph: Joseph Mangine. Mus: Renato Serio. AD: Peter Monroe. SpMkpFX: Thomas Brumberger, Don Lumpkin;(apparition) Tom Savini. PyroFX: Matt Vogel. Opt: Cinopticals. Ref: MFB '83:125. screen. V 7/28/82. Ecran F 28:8-9. with Jack Palance (Frank Hawkes), Donald Pleasence, Martin Landau, Deborah Hedwall, Phillip Clark(The Bleeder), Dwight Schultz.

The Haven, New Jersey. Four "voyagers" (read: "patients") escape from a country asylum's maximum-security second floor; join looters ransacking a sporting-goods store during a general blackout; terrorize their doctor's family with an assortment of arrows and knives. The besieged respond in kind, with cleavers and baseball bats....monster-at-the-window hallucination...madman's-nightmare intro....All the shock-and-suspense staples, with study notes on the Prevalence of Violence. Palance's institutionalized psychopath (the film seems to be saying) would be right at home in our violent society-as-a-whole, which is represented by the looters and by a punk-rock group performing (with appropriate props) "Chop up Your Mother." "It's not just us crazy ones who kill," he observes, in a moment of convenient lucidity. (Less meaningful, but just as helpful a line is the exclamation "Oh, my God! It's The Bleeder!") In the final sequence, we find Hawkes literally right at home with the new-wavers on the dance floor. No, it's not, suddenly, science fiction...not a teleportation device which whisks him there. It's just a narrative contrivance or two, though the effect is sf. All the characters here are part of a writer's conceit re: violence as a universal common denominator. They all might have been teleported into the movie....

ALS JE BEGRIJPT WAT IK BEDOEL (Dutch) VNF/Hower 1983 anim color 80m. SP,D: Kroon, Geelen, Jensen. Based on M. Toonder's story & comic strip. Mus: H. Schoonderwalt. Ref: V 3/16/83.

Monster from The Black Mountains..."monster fils" Swellbelly.

*The AMAZING MR. X 1948 PhFX: George J. Teague. Ref: screen. V 8/4/48. Weldon. and with Virginia Gregg.

Seances...apparitions (e.g., a "floating" wedding gown)... "dead" man who lures his credulous wife to the edge of a cliff. The latter sequence is quite good: we see him visually distorted, through her eyes, and her against projected backdrops (as if she's effectively lost to the real world). John Alton evocatively lights and shoots the "effects" scenes, and makes the light positively glisten on jewels, eyes, and Richard Carlson's teeth. And Turhan Bey (as a professional spiritualist) has some funny moments. But much of the movie is simply plot, and Cathy O'Donnell's wide-eyed-romantic kid sister (to Lynn Bari's "widow") is a bit hard to take.

AMAZING SPIDER-MAN, The see SPIDER-MAN...

*The AMAZING TRANSPARENT MAN Miller-Consolidated 1960(1959) Sp FX: Roger George. Mkp: Jack Pierce. Ref: TV. and with Red

Morgan, Cormel Daniel.

An "eminent nuclear scientist," Dr. Peter Ulaf (Ivan Triesault), has invented a machine which uses X, alpha, beta, omega, and ultra-violet rays to "neutralize tissue and bone structure in the body," and thus render lab animals invisible. His employer, Major Krenner (James Griffith), plans to use the machine to create "an entire army of invisible men." He breaks ace safecracker Joey Faust (Douglas Kennedy) out of prison, and forces the transparent Faust to steal radioactive x-13 material from government vaults. But the plan backfires, and some fissionable material blows up Krenner and "half the county."

Krenner at one point tells Faust, "You're mean and bitter. You trust noone and you hate everyone." No exaggeration--and Faust is the hero of this movie....For most of it, he's really a heel, a "hero" only by contrast with Krenner, who's callous, sadistic, egomaniacal, etc. At the end, however, Faust learns that he's dying of radiation poisoning, and is convinced (by Ulaf) to take Krenner with him--from Ignoble to Noble in two seconds! Just so does Jack Lewis's script twist and turn, or rather lurch. The editing is jerky, too--in fact Edgar Ulmer's movie is a sort of primer-in-reverse on the art of editing: i.e., Don't do it this way.... It's just "cut!", and you're in some other place with some other actors....The only intended amusement the film offers is the sequence in which the invisible Faust has "flashes" of visibility, at the most inopportune time--while he's robbing a bank. ("Why do I keep appearing and disappearing?!") Otherwise, the invisibility effects are unimaginative and inconsistent (e.g., the ray makes clothes disappear, but not the straps holding down a guinea pig).

*The AMAZING TRANSPLANT Jerand/Mostest Prods. 1970 color 78m. D,P: Louis Silverman. SP: Dawn Whitman. Dial: Titan Prods. Ph: C.D. Smith. Mus: Music Sound Track. SpFX: Eli Haviv. Opt: B&O. SdFX: Emil Haviv. Ref: TV: Electric Video. AFI. with Juan Fernandez, Linda Southern, Larry Hunter, Kim Pope.

"Poor, sick" Arthur Barlen strangles his fiancee; tries to "act natural"; then--via a series of flashbacks featuring various women--is shown shuttling back and forth between "natural" and "maniacal" states. The amazing explanation: "This crazy transplant idea!" Arthur, a virgin, and envious of his (dying) friend Felix's success with women, made, some time back, a strange request of Dr. Cyril Mead: "I want you to put Felix's penis on me!" The doctor tried to explain to him, at the time, that sex is more mental than physical, but Arthur was convinced that he would be more "sexually active" with Felix's penis.... And he is--thanks, apparently, to the "power of suggestion"--or at least he would be, but for catch-122: Arthur proves to be the inheritor of a personality quirk as well as an organ. It seems that, whenever Felix saw a woman wearing gold earrings, he would become "passionately excited." That may, originally, have been the idea, but in Arthur's case it leads to murder....

Not the most plausible of storylines, that. In fact, it's probably the weirdest pretext ever for a simple series of soft-core sex scenes. Donated brain-wave patterns (BRAINWAVES), yes. Donated blood (BLOOD SONG), okay, maybe. But a penis with a memory...? It cannot, after all, be simple "suggestion" which makes Arthur "see gold." He has no prior knowledge of Felix's obsession with gold earrings. He doesn't know--like The Shadow, the penis knows....The earring "trigger" mechanism itself anticipates HANDS OF THE RIPPER(1971) and its gimmick with the jewels, though this is not to suggest that TRANSPLANT was in any way influential. Noone in his right mind would look to this film for inspiration, narrative or otherwise. This was just another of the transplant movies popular in the early Seventies, and likely about the looniest of them all.

AMERICAN CLASS see NATIONAL LAMPOON'S CLASS REUNION

AMERICAN NIGHTMARE (Can.) Mano & Manesco 1981 color 95m. D: Don McBrearty. SP: John Sheppard. Story: John Gault, Steven Blake. Ph: Daniel Hainey. Mus: Paul Zaza. AD: Andrew Deskin. Opt: Film Opticals. Mkp: Miriam Freifeld. Title Des: Paul Lynch. Ref: TV: Media Home Ent.(video). no Academy. with Lawrence S. Day, Lora Staley, Neil Dainard, Michael Ironside, Lenore Zann.

Madman disgusted with "sick degenerates" commits series of brutal murders with knife and razor blade; ultimately plunges to his death in a trash bin....Yes, he does. Film, which takes place in "the gutter you call life," is a sort of half-hearted VICE SQUAD(P), with a trying-to-be-sleazy feel to it. As in VICE SQUAD, the killer's targets are hookers and their "sordid associates"; but NIGHTMARE is angled more towards mystery and suspense-horror than towards action. The madman's identity is not revealed until the climactic sequence, and his murders--particularly a bathtub strangling and the knifing of a transvestite--are staged and scored for horror....The script is so flimsy that it requires three or four separate night-club strip acts for padding.

AMITYVILLE II: THE POSSESSION (U.S.-Mex) Orion/De Laurentiis & Media Technology 1982 color 104m. (La POSESION DE AMITYVILLE) D: Damiano Damiani. SP: Tommy Lee Wallace, from Hans Holzer's book "Murder in Amityville." Ph: Franco DiGiacomo. Mus: Lalo Schifrin. PD: Pierluigi Basile. SpMkp: John Caglione Jr.;(asst) Stephan DuPuis. SpFX:(sup) Glen Robinson; (asst) Gary Zeller. Ref: screen. MFB'82:257. V 9/29/82. 5/25/83:28. with James Olson, Burt Young, Rutanya Alda, Moses Gunn, Andrew Prine, Diane Franklin; Sondra Lee et al(voices).

A pre-quel to The AMITYVILLE HORROR. A demon from the cellar of that same house possesses a teenage boy and drives him to commit incest with his sister and to murder his whole family. At the end, a priest exorcises the demon and is himself possessed by it....The effects this time include imploding stomachs, instant rotting-heads, blood-dripping faucets and holy sprinklers, revolving beds, levitating paint brushes, walls of fire, and self-cracking mirrors....At one point the boy's mother cries "Oh, my God!--what's happening to us?" A better question: "What isn't?" AMITYVILLE II is Evil as Special Makeup Effects--Good, here, is simply a pretext for another effects extravaganza. At the core of the effects display (in this rather extreme version of REBEL WITHOUT A CAUSE) lies a potentially disturbing true-life horror anecdote. The sequence of the massacre itself has, in fact, a certain intrinsic power. The son's ghoul-makeup for the sequence might even be an objective correlative for the horror of the violence therein, though it's also a bit distracting. (In its particular use in the sequence it might also be seen as a lift from DEATHDREAM.) But, basically, this movie is a real mess. It's at once "serious"--in its treatment of the church and the family--and anti-serious--in its grovelling attempts to be ever-so-entertaining-gross. It's not so much lively as ridiculously hyper-active, though its chronic over-eagerness yields, very occasionally, an eerie moment--e.g., the (invisible) demon (indicated by a subjective camera) hanging upside down, monkey-like, from the rafters, smack in front of the face of the boy; his now-dead-sister's phantom voice completing a phone call (to the priest) which was begun while she was alive. (He ignored it and instead went out hunting.) For the most part, however, AMITYVILLE II is just another new dog performing old tricks.

AMITYVILLE 3-D Orion/De Laurentiis 1983 3-D & color 93m. D: Richard Fleischer. SP: William Wales. Ph: Fred Schuler. Mus: Howard Blake. AD: Giorgio Postiglione. SpFX:(coord) Michael Wood;(crew) David Wood et al. SpMkp: Vince Callaghan. SpOpt FX: Gary Platek. SpFX: Al Griswold, Connie Brink. SpPhotos: Benno Friedman. Titles Des: Pablo Ferro. Ref: screen. V 11/23/83. with Tony Roberts, Tess Harper, Robert Joy, Candy Clark, John Beal.

The names of the people are different in this follow-up to The AMITYVILLE HORROR--only the house remains the same. ("Something weird is going on.") The "gateway to hell" is re-opened when the floorboards over the dry well in the cellar give way. The (Indian?) demon within subsequently attempts to take the spirit of a girl with him, but has to make do with a live psychic researcher. The house self-destructs, leaving only a little fly-demon to emerge from the ashes....On another front, a man whose face appears disfigured, or "altered," in photographs taken in the house, proves to be marked for death-by-flies. Enlarged, one photo reveals the image of a demon's head on the man's face. The photos self-incinerate and also incinerate the woman who took them....Plus: doppelganger of dying girl...instant frost, and freezing winds from cellar...haunted elevator...nightmare re: thing-from-well...Institute for Psychic Research probing (a la The ENTITY) the phenomena...fake medium and "balls of light."

A bad thing can get worse--if you doubt it, here's the evidence, the third and easily the worst of the Amityville films. 3-D is just odds and ends from the previous two, and from other, non-Amityville horrors. It has no plot to speak of. It's simply a series of pretexts for getting people into the house, either singly or in small, carefully-selected groups (e.g., a gaggle of teenagers, a lady photographer, a mother and the doppelganger of her daughter). The 3-D process is wasted on the usual comin'-at-ya stunts, though it does add to the atmosphere of exterior shots. The first two Amityvilles seem almost respectable by comparison....

AMUCK! (I) Group 1 1978 color/ws 99m. (aka MANIAC MANSION) D,P: Jurgen Goslar. Ref: TV: Catalina Home Video. VideoSB: "horror." no AMPAS. Weldon. with Farley Granger, Barbara Bouchet.

A secretary, Greta, whose friend disappeared from a Venice mystery villa (and who wrote to her re: the presence there of a "superior force") goes to Venice to investigate and finds herself at the mercy of an author who enjoys "the sadistic pleasure of playing cat and mouse." She discovers that Rocco, a half-wit "giant of a man," killed her friend in a fit of sexual frenzy, and soon finds herself (as the woman who knew too much) ticketed for a similar (premeditated) end....woman who has, or claims to have, ESP, and who, in a trance, predicts the heroine's death...blackmailing butler who's slashed to death...."Cat and mouse" tale winds up as "The Lion and the Mouse," as Rocco rebels and comes to the rescue of our heroine (who earlier played nurse for him when he cut himself). Horror foreplay with chiller music, false alarms, red herrings, and a thunderstorm, climaxed by a brief, Rocco-amuck scene in which he dispatches host and hostess....Thin as mystery, horror, or erotic intrigue. Granger's novelist is amusingly pretentious. ("Lost in a million facades of a doomed city....") The movie isn't even that.

ANDROID Island Alive & New Cinema/SHO-Android 1982(1983) color 78m. D: Aaron Lipstadt. SP: James Reigle, Don Opper. Idea: Will Reigle. Ph: Tim Suhrstedt;(addl) Greg Gardiner. Mus: Don Preston. AD: K.C. Scheibel, Wayne Springfield;(asst) Roger Kelton;(des cons) J.M. Cameron. SpMkpFX: John Buechler; (prosth) Don Olivera. SpVisFX: New World;(coord) Susan McLaughlin;(min des) Jay Roth;(tech d) Julia Gibson;(ph) S.B. Caldwell. Graphic Art: Philip Foreman et al;(des) Sarah Burdick. SpSd FX: John Pospisil. Opt: Image 3, Linda Henry. Arcade: GCE. PyroFX: Roger George. Graphic Anim: January Nordman. Ref: V 10/13/82. screen. PFA notes 3/26/83: orig. New World. MFB'83: 64-5. Academy. Cahiers 355:55-6. SFExam 1/20/84. Berkeley Monthly 3/84. with Klaus Kinski, Brie Howard, Norbert Weisser, Opper(Max 404), Kendra Kirchner(Cassandra I), Crofton Hardester.

October 2036, post-android-revolt-and-prohibition. A scientist (Kinski) planning to dismantle his independent-minded android ("the Munich syndrome") and replace it with the more sophisticated Cassandra I (the perfect working-class-prototype and woman) is himself dismantled, and revealed to be an android....Max 404 used as executioner after "moral governor" removed from head...."target voided" in space, a la video game....clips from METROPOLIS and IT'S A WONDERFUL LIFE... indirect reference (severed, live android head) to AGUIRRE, WRATH OF GOD.

A small charmer, quite unpretentious for an android movie--a pleasant antidote to the lugubriousness of a BLADE RUNNER. You won't find answers, here, to the loftier philosophical questions concerning humans and robots, but you will find smaller questions (such as, What does an android departing a space station for Earth pack?) answered quite wryly. (Spare fingers, eyeballs, hands.) If its action sequences are unremarkable, the movie is laced with humor and a delicate sort of pathos, or wistfulness. The quietest but most surprising scene: Max discovering that his ticket to Earth, Maggie (Howard), is dead. Max is pictured, simply, in longshot, emerging glumly from her room, wearing a now-superfluous fedora and carrying a now-useless suitcase. No more need be (or is) said or done. Opper is a pleasure to watch as the behaviorally-erratic but well-meaning Max. You can all but see his imperfectly-programmed thoughts bumping into each other on their way to fruition, or non-fruition....

ANGEL ABOVE AND THE DEVIL BELOW Martoni 1974 color 80m. D: Dominic Bolla. SP: John Cutaia, Katherine Merlin. Ref: SF Exam 2/18/83. poster. Cinef IV:1:36. with Brittany Laine, Starlyn Simone, Mindy Bryant.

Demonically-possessed vagina.

ANGEL OF H.E.A.T.: THE PROTECTORS--BOOK #1 Pan Imago/Schreibman-Kant 1982 color 93m. (The PROTECTORS, BOOK #1-orig t) D, PD: Myrl A. Schreibman. SP: Helen Sanford. Ph: Jacques Haitkin; Brad Six. Mus: Guy Sobell. Prosth: William Munns;(exec) Gordon Greid. FxEd: David Yewdall, Colin Mouat, Chuck Smith. Opt: Movie Magic. Ref: TV. TVG. V 8/31/83. with Marilyn Chambers, Stephen Johnson, Mary Woronov, Milt Kogan, Harry Townes; Robert Burr, J.B. Bassinger, Justin Smith(androids).

Power-mad scientist fashions a battalion of remote-controlled, camera-eye androids (whose "erotic circuits" are "almost blown" by two humans)...one "android capable of sacrifice...love"... remote-control holograms..."ultimate amplification microprocessor"...high-frequency-sound super-weapon...martial-arts-style quasi-hypnosis..."The Protectors," international vigilantes.... Failed semi-camp. Iffy even as a showcase for Marilyn Chambers--"jaunty" intrigue prevails, as if the filmmakers thought that their narrative inventions could somehow interest us more than Chambers' charms. Bad miscalculation.

ANNABEL LEE(by Poe) see NIGHT TIDE

ANNEES LUMIERES, Les see LIGHT YEARS AWAY

ANTROPOPHAGOUS see GRIM REAPER, The

APARTMENT ON THE THIRTEENTH FLOOR (Sp) Atlas Int'l./Jose Truchado 1972('74-U.S.) color 98m. (La SEMANA DEL ASESINO) D: Eloy de la Iglesia. Ref: Cinef IV:1:33: "horror." Weldon. Academy. V 5/3/72:175. with Vicente Parra, Emma Cohen, Vicki Lagos.

Slaughterhouse worker commits a series of brutal murders; dumps the bodies into a meat pulverizer.

The APE CREATURE Indep.-Int'l./Rialto(Wendlandt) 1968('75-U.S., Hampton Int'l) color 96m. (*The GORILLA OF SOHO. The GORILLA GANG-U.S.; above is TV t) Mus: Peter Thomas. AD: W. Vorwery et al. Ref: TV. Willis/SW. Ginny Moilanen. V 10/25/72. Cinef IV:4:35. and with Herbert Fux, Hubert von Meyerinck, Inge Langen, Eric Vaesser, Maria Litto.

What is the connection between, a) the Love and Peace for People organization, b) the mother superior of the charitable Mary's Home and, c) The Monster and The Gorilla criminal band? Scotland Yard wants to know what after three millionaires who left their millions to Love and Peace are murdered. A white ambulance is always seen at the scenes of the crimes, and dolls bearing clues coded in Arabic (e.g., "The Gorilla is the murderer") are found on the bodies of the victims--The Gorilla proves to be Jack Corner, the earless, "completely disfigured" boss of the Gorillas, who commits his murders disguised as a gorilla. ("Gorillas, gorillas! All I hear about is gorillas!") Solicitor named, apparently incidentally, Dr. Jekyll....No mystery to this mystery. There is a link between the above-named organizations, but that seems pretty obvious from the start. The nature of that link is clarified, somewhat, in the course of the film, but that course is such a meandering one that it's tough to care whodunit or whatizit. Suspense and action scenes, comedy, and music are without distinction. This is your basic, uncomplicated, plain-bad unmovie.

APOCALIPSIS CANIBAL see NIGHT OF THE ZOMBIES(Sp-I, 1980)

*ARTISTS AND MODELS 1955 From the Lessing-Davidson play. SpFX: John P. Fulton. Process Ph: Farciot Edouart. Mkp: Wally Westmore. Ref: TV. LC.

Jerry Lewis dreams out loud, gives Dean Martin ideas for "Vincent The Vulture" space comics...space station...(working) disintegrator-atom-gun...."Bat Lady" model (Shirley MacLaine) for comic books....Fifties-style comedy (i.e., noise, no laughs). Tedious slapstick; vacuous plot, songs. Lewis's outlandish dream-spiels afford the only amusement.

ASSASSINO AL CIMETERO ETRUSCO see CRIME AU CIMETIERE ETRUSQUE

ASTRAL FACTOR New Century/Jordan(Lyon) 1983(1978) D: John Florea. SP: Arthur Pierce. SpFX: Robert Brown, Peter Kuran. Ref: V 9/9/81:28: "sci-fi." 5/17/78:188(ad). 3/23/83:26. Ecran F 22:10.34:70. Willis/SW. with Robert Foxworth, Stephanie Powers, Elke Sommer.

*The ATOMIC KID Mickey Rooney 1954 SP: B. Freedman, Murray. Mus: Van Alexander. AD: Frank Hotaling. SpFX: Howard & Theodore Lydecker. OptFX: Consolidated. Mkp: Bob Mark. Ref: TV. screen. Warren/KWTS! LC. V 12/8/54: "for the Saturday matinee trade." Weldon. and with Hal March, Fay Roope, Stanley Adams, Milton Frome, Don Haggerty, Peter Brocco, Robert Nichols, Paul Dubov, Slick Slavin.

"Destiny awaits" Barnaby "Blix" Waterberry (Rooney)--in the form of "the most powerful atomic bomb yet developed." The latter is detonated just 100 yards from him, at Frenchman's Flat, near Atomic City--thus does "Operation Miracle" turn him into "the only living nuclear chain reaction." Blix's basal metabolism is doubled. At first he talks at twice normal speed and radiates "like pure U-235." Only immersion in heavy water "slows down" his neutrons. A "20,000 volt" kiss from his nurse (Elaine Davis) sets him literally aglow and causes a statuette to melt, logs in a fireplace to catch on fire, and lamps to switch on. Now "short, red-headed, and radioactive," he has only to pass by a row of slot machines in a Las Vegas casino to make them all hit the jackpot, and at one point he uses his arms as antennae for a car radio which his radioactivity has fritzed out. Eventually, he returns to normal and waxes wistful about being "the former atomic kid...."

Or, How We Learned To Stop Worrying And Love The Bomb back in the Fifties. Japan got Godzilla; we got Mickey Rooney. As a sitcom, this movie dates as badly as "December Bride" or "Our Miss Brooks." Politically and scientifically, it is, shall we say, irresponsible, though that's not really quite the word--the word for The ATOMIC KID doesn't exist. It's hard to believe that it exists--and, yet, as late as 1981 we still have (non-ironic) comedies making light of nuclear-waste accidents (MODERN PROBLEMS) and atomic explosions (SUPER FUZZ). Now (after The DAY AFTER, TESTAMENT, and SPECIAL BULLETIN), the next step would seem to be backward, to DR. STRANGELOVE and irony--that last stop before insanity as a response to the prospect of Armageddon. The ATOMIC KID is valuable only as a sort of time capsule--historically, as an indication of what was considered viable by Hollywood as entertainment at a certain point in time; more personally, as a reminder of what ex-non-atomic kids like myself thought (God help us) was funny when we were 10 or 11. At those Saturday matinees (see above), the slot-machine scene was a howl--what can I say...?

ATOMIC MONSTER see IT CAME FROM OUTER SPACE

ATOR THE FIGHTING EAGLE (I) Comworld/Filmirage 1983(1982) color 90m. (ATOR-ad t. ATOR L'INVINCIBLE) SP,D: David Hills.

Ph: F. Slonisco. Mus: Mario Cordio. AD: John Gregory. Mkp: Pat Russel. Ref: screen. V 3/16/83. 12/22/82:4(rated). 10/20/82:46(ad). 5/4/83:296. LAT 3/8/83. Academy. Ecran F 31: 46. with Miles O'Keeffe, Sabrina Siani, Ritza Brown, Edmund Purdom, Laura Gemser, Dakkar.

The Age of Darkness, in The Valley of The Shadows. Hero Ator, of prophecy, ends the 1,000-year reign of "The Ancient One," The Spider King, with an atomizing shield. Plus: a sorceress (Gemser) who conjures up visions, transforms a man into an owl, and turns into a crone when the drape falls from her magic mirror...giant spider (or two)...shadow-warriors-from-shield...bleeding eagle-statue....Competence takes a holiday in this mini-epic-fantasy. A camp-like laxness prevails: heroine: "Now we must pass through The Land of The Walking Dead." Hero: "Well, if we gotta go...." They do, but The Walking don't look very Dead. (Most wear helmets and just walk, then vanish.) Ator is also given to superfluous "Let's get outta here"'s. Noone takes credit for the special effects (e.g., a rather sedentary monster-spider; the system of knotted ropes which comprises its "web"), which isn't surprising. What's surprising is that someone <u>does</u> take credit for writing, directing, etc. Sequel: SWORD OF THE BARBARIANS.

ATTACK FROM OUTER SPACE see MUTINY IN OUTER SPACE

The ATTIC Samuel Goldwyn Co./Atlantic Releasing/Forum & Dryden & The Attic Assoc. 1980 color 95m. SP,D: George Edwards. SP,Assoc P: Tony Crechales. Ph: Gary Graver. Mus: Hod David Schudson. AD: Tom Rasmussen. Mkp: Jim Gillespie. Opt: CFI. Ref: TV. FM 176. TVG. Willis/SW'81. Ecran F 35:61-2. with Ray Milland, Carrie Snodgress, Ruth Cox, Rosemary Murphy, Michael Rhodes.

Wichita spinster tied to invalid father concocts (visualized) revenge fantasies--e.g., her pet chimp as a savage ape throttling him. At the end, the distracted Louise is trapped in an attic with the dead chimp and the decaying body of her fiance, as a storm rages outside....theatre playing DEADLY GAMES (the phone chat re: PSYCHO--a quote within a quote!)....A fairish, very sober and serious closet-drama-with-horrific-overtones. The atmosphere between possessive father (he's faking invalidism and killed her fiance) and repressed daughter is so close that the film is almost as oppressive for the viewer as for the protagonists. There's material and talent enough here for a one-hour TV drama--Snodgress does intense-repressed nearly as well as Julie Harris can, and the pathos-and-horror ending is a quite satisfactory "payoff": it effectively literalizes the family-trap theme, and not incidentally balances the scenes with Louise's friend Emily. (Louise sees to it that Emily escapes <u>her</u> trap.) But the 90-plus-minute running time is achieved only with padding (with "lyrical" interludes) and needless repetition.

2P AXE New American Films/Boxoffice Int'l.(Novak)/Frederick Prods. 1977 color 67m. (LISA, LISA-orig t. CALIFORNIA AXE MASSACRE-B) SP,D,with: Frederick R. Friedel. Ph: Austin McKinney. Mus: George N. Shaw, John Willhelm. Mkp: Worth Keeter. Ref: TV: Best Film Video. MFB'82:196-7. V 3/30/83: "horror." AMPAS. Willis/SW. with Leslie Lee, Jack Canon, Ray Green, Frank Jones, Douglas Powers.

Three gangsters hole up in a country house inhabited by a young woman and her paralyzed grandfather. One of the three attempts to rape her; she slashes him to death with a razor, cuts his body up with an axe, and stores the parts in a trunk. The leader of the gang ends up as a bowl of (red) soup....Portraits in abnormal, and unpleasant, psychology. "Bleak" would be giving poor, traumatized Lisa's situation all the best of it. She goes from slaughtering chickens to slaughtering criminals, and back--small world, isn't it? This isn't so much a slice-of-life as a sliver. Tending her mute, good-as-dead grandpa is obviously a drag for Lisa. She needs a few laughs, a change--not, however, the one she gets. Even the television doesn't work--the TV screen is almost as dead as her eyes.... The authentically lifeless-looking eyes of Leslie Lee, here, provide the movie with, at least, a grim, almost Lewtonesque center--they're a fixed "No Sale," rung up, as it were, on a cash register of the soul. But the script has a contrived, inauthentic feel of hopelessness about it....

BALDIOS see BARUDIOSU

BALLET ROBOTIQUE 1982 7m. D: Bob Rogers. Ref: V 2/9/83:6: at Berlin Film Fest. Filmex: "giant robots."

BARD, The see TWILIGHT ZONE REVISITED

BARON'S AFRICAN WAR, The see SECRET SERVICE IN DARKEST AFRICA

BARUDIOSU (J) Toei & Central/Int'l. Movie Co. 1981 anim Ref: V 1/20/82:53: "sci-fi." JFFJ 14:7: aka BALDIOS.

Feature composed of the last three (never telecast) episodes of the TV series "Space Warrior--Baldios."

BASKET CASE Analysis/Ievins-Henenlotter(Basket Case) 1982 color 87m. SP,D,Ed,Anim?: Frank Henenlotter. Ph: Bruce Torbet. Mus: Gus Russo. AD: Frederick Loren. SpMkpFX: Kevin Haney, John Caglione Jr.;(addl) Ugis Nigals. Titles: Leo Anim. Opt: Image Galaxy. Dedicated to Herschell Gordon Lewis. Ref: screen. V 4/21/82. MFB'83:92-3. with Kevin VanHentenryck, Terri Susan Smith, Beverly Bonner, Robert Vogel, Lloyd Pace.

A man has his Siamese-twin monster-son, Belial (who "looks like a squashed octopus"), surgically separated from his more-normal son. Belial, who can still communicate, telepathically, with his twin, gets stronger after separation, and proceeds to wreak revenge on his father (by buzz-sawing him in half) and on the surgeons (one a vet)....The normal-twin's "nightmare" of a rape scene proves to be a telepathic image of Belial raping and maiming the former's girl friend....An occasionally quite charming, low-budget horror-comedy-drama--the LITTLE SHOP OF HORRORS of 1982. Belial does the most horrible things to people (and finally and inevitably to his twin), but he is, for us, too teddy-bearish in demeanor to be taken seriously. He's the kind of monster-doll a boy might use to frighten and delight his younger sisters. His savagings (of enemies and hamburgers alike) are invariably accompanied by comically-ferocious-sounding noises. It's Belial's tragi-comedy that the women in the movie can't take him seriously either, as a lover at least--only as a monster fit to scream at. And he cannot, it seems, take vicarious, telepathic pleasure in his twin's love life. Episodes in same only send him into jealous, or envious, rages....All the characters here (not just Belial) are comically shrill, louder-than-life, and the "stylization" of character is appreciated. But it's also a bit wearing. Belial might be even more amusing and likable in a quieter, more mundane setting. The brief picture of him (in flashback) snuggled-up in his protective, substitute-mother's arms, as she reads him (and his brother) a bedtime story, is at once absurd and touching. He's obviously only a prop here, but context is all, and this wryly-observed living-room tableau brings Belial to life. This flashback is a mock-sentimental image of happier, vanished times...for a rubber octopus.

*BATMAN FIGHTS DRACULA Lea/Fidelis 1967 color D: Leody M. Diaz. SP: Bert R. Mendoza. Mus: Tony Maiquez. Ref: WorldF'67. Glut/TDB. with Jing Abalos(Batman), Dante Rivero(Dracula), Vivian Lorrain, Ramon D'Salva.

*BATTLE BEYOND THE SUN AI(Filmgroup)/Mosfilm 1959('63-U.S.) color 75m.-U.S. (NEBO ZOWET) D,Assoc P:(U.S.) Francis Ford Coppola(aka Thomas Colchart). SP:(U.S.) Nicholas Colbert, Edwin Palmer. Mus: Jan Oneidas or Y. Meytus;(U.S.) Carmen Coppola. AD,SpFX: Y. Shvets. SpFX: also Francis Selbin, Nelson Lorin, G. Lukashov et al. SpSeqs: Alberto Locatelli. Mkp: Edward Ondine. Ref: TV. Lee. AFI. Weldon.

November, 1997. A post-atomic-war world divided into North and South Hemis...first (aborted) flights to Mars...spacecraft pulled into the sun...monsters on Angkor(sp?), "planet" orbiting Mars (the latter planet observed to "absorb" the sun's rays)...ocean landing-platform...space station....Not Coppola's best. The only added, American footage (apart from the title sequence), however, appears to be the battle between the gourd (with eyes dangling from the ends of its tentacles) and the cucumber (with its toothy mouth sewn on its trunk sideways), two "monsters" guaranteed not to give anyone nightmares, though they do at least provide some badly-needed incidental comedy. A tired "cooperation" theme and stilted heroics prevail.... The movie is bearable only during some of the effects sequences, the "straight" highlight of which is Mars rising splendorously on Angkor: Big Red. The planet lives up to its advance notice: "Mars, Nancy--think of it!"

2P The BATTLE WIZARD (H.K.) Shaw 1976 color D: Pao Hsueh Li. Ref: Shaw Bros. IFG'78:178(ad). with Li Hsiu-hsien, Tanny.

Drinking the blood of the monster, Red Python, gives a young duke super-strength. He fights the Dragon-crocodiles, the Red-Robed warrior, "and other monsters." "Charming girl...who has an army of snakes to fight for her...."(SB)

BATTLETRUCK see WARLORDS OF THE TWENTY-FIRST CENTURY

BE MY VALENTINE, OR ELSE... see HOSPITAL MASSACRE

The BEAST WITHIN UA-MGM/Bernhard-Katzka 1982(1981) color/ws 95m. D: Philippe Mora. SP: Tom Holland, from Edward Levy's novel. Ph: J.L. Richards. Mus: Les Baxter. PD: D.M. Haber. SpMkpFX: Thomas R. Burman;(art) T. Hoerber. SpFX:(foreman) F.J. Cramer; G.J. Elmendorf. SpSdFX: Nieman-Tillar. Opt: Pacific. Ref: screen. V 9/28/81:4(rated). 2/17/82. Weldon. with Ronny Cox, Bibi Besch, Paul Clemens(Michael), Don Gordon, R.G. Armstrong, L.Q. Jones, Luke Askew.

The first were-cicada movie. Man chained up in cellar and fed corpses becomes beast-man; rapes woman, who gives birth to boy who (at age 17) seems possessed by his father's spirit, sheds his human skin, and becomes a cicada-monster....man embalmed alive....A mish-mash of your favorite dumb scenes from werewolf movies. Dramatically, it's back to square one; graphically, this is another step "ahead." The makeup effects here constitute the yukkiest inside-job transformation yet. (Michael sprouts big knobs on his face, a monster-tongue pops out of his mouth, and his back starts unzipping itself--three more of the thousand unnatural shocks that flesh is heir to in horror movies....) The continuity is pre-functional. The "Oh, my God, no!" scene (as Michael strangles his beloved) might be hommage a BEFORE I HANG(1940)--misplaced reverence....

The BEASTMASTER UA-MGM/Leisure Investment/Beastmaster N.V. & ECTA 1982 color 118m. SP,D: Don Coscarelli. Sp,Co-P: Paul Pepperman. Ph: John Alcott. Mus: Lee Holdridge. PD: Conrad E. Angone. SpMkpFX:(des) William Munns;(art) David B. Miller. SpFX: Roger George, Frank DeMarco;(cons) Michael Minor. SpCons: Nikita Knatz. Min:(ph) Cruse & Co.;(models sup) W.N. Guest. Sword: Victor Anselmo. SdFX: The Pro's, Paul Clay, Jeremy Hoenack. Opt: Optrex. Ref: screen. Weldon. V 8/18/82. MFB'83: 93-4. Fangoria 22:17: title from Andre Norton's book. with Marc Singer, Tanya Roberts, Rip Torn(Maax), John Amos, Daniel Zormeier(winged-creature leader); Janet DeMay, Chrissy Kellogg,

Janet Jones(witch-women).

Unborn hero transferred via witchcraft from mother's womb to beast's....monstrous bird-men which crush their victims in their wings...zombie-monsters, men drained of blood and subjected to brain-rearranging...magic ring...magic blue liquid.... Pleasant enough adventure-fantasy, but at two hours even the invention of Don (PHANTASM) Coscarelli wears a tad thin. The story here is the conventional procession of slaughters, escapes, and rescues--periodically enlivened by black magic and monsters, and by bird's-eye-view landscape shots (as the hero "sees" through the eyes of his eagle aide). You'll remember the flailing onslaught of the mailed-fisted zombies, the battle by the burning moat, the cute, funny ferrets, and the bird-men ominously spreading their wings. But you'll probably forget who lived, who died, and who was rescued. (Well, maybe you'll remember that one of the ferrets died--heroically.)

The BEAUTIES OF THE NIGHT (F-I) UA/Franco London & Rizzoli 1952('54-U.S.) 90m. (Les BELLES DE NUIT) Co-SP,D: Rene Clair. Ref: screen. V 10/15/52. Lee

Dream sequence re: a prehistoric age, visualized complete with cavemen and papier-mache stegosaurus and brontosaurus.... Generally droll, amusing fantasy, with some inspired moments.

BEAUTIFUL SCREAMERS see SILENT MADNESS

BEAUTY AND THE BEAST WB 1934 anim 7m. D: I. Freleng. Ref: "WB Cartoons." Lee. Maltin/OMAM. LC.

Dream: monster from cover of "Beauty and the Beast" book.

The BEGINNING (Can.) Gold Key-TV/T.A.E. 1973 color 95m. (The STARLOST QUINTOLOGY 1.) Ref: GKey. TVFFSB. TVG. with Sterling Hayden, Keir Dullea, Barry Morse, Robin Ward.

See also: ALIEN ORO, The.

The BEING Best Film & Video 1983(1980) color 79m. (EASTER SUNDAY-orig t. aka FREAK) SP,D: Jackie Kong. D: also (uncred.) Robert Downey. Ph: Robert Ebinger. Mus: Don Preston. AD: Alexia Corwin. SpFxMkp: Mark Bussen. Ref: Bill Warren. V 2/16/83:24. 11/2/83:4(rated). 11/16/83. with Martin Landau, Jose Ferrer, Dorothy Malone, Ruth Buzzi, Bill Osco.

Holiday horror in Idaho, as nuclear dump spawns monster.

La BELLE CAPTIVE (F) Argos 1983 color 88m. SP,D: Alain Robbe-Grillet. SP: also Frank Verpillat. Title from the Magritte painting. Ph: Henri Alekan. Mus: Schubert, Ellington. PD: Aime Deude. Video: Verpillat. Ref: V 3/2/83. 2/2/83:28: at Avoriaz. FComment 2/84:13. FQ Smr'83:39. Ecran F 33:40-1. PFA notes 4/19/84. with Daniel Mesguich, Gabrielle Lazure(Marie-Ange), Cyrielle, Daniel Emilfork.

Vampire-woman.

BELLES DE NUIT see BEAUTIES OF THE NIGHT

BELLS see MURDER BY PHONE

La BESTIA Y LA ESPADA MAGICA (Sp-J) Aconito-Amachi 1983 (La BESTIA Y LOS SAMURAIS-orig t) SP,D & with: Jacinto Molina. Sequel to *2 MARK OF THE WOLFMAN. Ref: Ecran F 33:71. V 5/9/84: 398. with Julia Saly, Beatriz Escudero, Sigueiro Amachi.
Waldemar the werewolf in Japan.

BETTY IN BLUNDERLAND Para 1934 anim 8m. D: Dave Fleischer. Anim: Crandall & Johnson. Ref: TV. Lee. LC.
Betty Boop as Alice-in-Wonderland...dragon-monster...music from HORSE FEATHERS. Darn cute.

BETTY BOOP'S BAMBOO ISLE Para 1932 anim 7m. D: Dave Fleischer. Anim: Kneitel & Wolf. Ref: TV. LC. Maltin/OMAM.
Betty and Bimbo vs. a horde of demon-ghosts on a South Sea island. Short 'n' sweet.

BETTY BOOP'S UPS AND DOWNS Para 1932 anim 7m. D: Dave Fleischer. Ref: screen. LC. MFB'74:167-8: included in The BETTY BOOP FOLLIES.
Saturn buys Earth, eliminates gravity. Okay cartoon.
See also: BIMBO'S INITIATION. MYSTERIOUS MOSE.

BEWITCHED (H.K.-Cant.) Shaw 1981 color 98m. SP,D: Kwei Chi-Hung. SP: also Szeto On. Ph: Li Sun Ip. Ref: V 10/21/81. 5/12/82:333(ad). Ecran F 22:52. with Ai Fei, Lily Chan, Fanny.
Wizard, curse, possession.

2 BEYOND EVIL Milano 1980 Story,Co-P: David Baughn. Mus: Pino Donaggio. AD: Gordon Rattray; Dana Rheaume et al. SpMkpFX: Ron Figuly. SpFX: Joe Quinlavi(a)n;(ph) James F. Liles. Sd FxEd: Lee Stepansky. Title Des: Rick Westover. Assoc P: Don Edmonds. Ref: TV. Weldon. and with Anne Marisse, Janice Lynde (Alma), Peggy Stewart, Alan Caillou, Verkina Flower, Anne Gaybis.
Casa Fortuna, a "million dollar" haunted house on a "small island" in the Pacific, has been vacant for over 100 years, and for good reason. Alma Martin, the last woman-of-the-house, made a pact with the devil and immersed herself in "crazy weird things" like black magic. By "focusing her energies," she could do virtually anything she wanted to, including return from the dead and break her murderer-husband's neck....In the present, Barbara (Lynda Day George) has visions of Alma, whose spirit is attempting to possess her, and who needs human sacrifices to increase her power. Alma/Barbara psychically makes cars and mechanical cranes kill, and, with green rays from her eyes, atomizes a woman. The crypt which houses Alma's remains and gives her "access" to the world of the living is dynamited, but to no avail. Finally, the restoration to Barbara's finger of her own ring separates out Alma's spirit, which then disintegrates....Straight, no-surprises spirit-possession stuff is neither original nor silly enough to be amusing. The effects

tricks are very familiar, just, perhaps, arranged in a slightly different order. The story itself hasn't really changed much since SUPERNATURAL(1933)--this time they should have called it "Superfluous." Ms. George--who is becoming the new heroine of the horrors--isn't bad. Donaggio's score is generally as tacky as what's on the screen, though the end-credits music is atmospheric.

BEYOND THE FOG see HORROR ON SNAPE ISLAND

BEYOND THE GATE see HUMAN EXPERIMENTS

BEYOND THE STARS see UNEARTHLY STRANGER

BEYOND THE UNIVERSE Gold Key-TV c1981 color 90m. Ref: GKey. TVFFSB. TVG. with David Ladd, Jackie Ray.
Lasers and the occult in the 21st Century.

BIG CAIMANO RIVER see GREAT ALLIGATOR, The

BIG GAME HAUNT WB-7A 1968 anim color 7m. D: Alex Lovy. Ref: "WB Cartoons." LC. Maltin/OMAM. no Lee.
Haunted house...ghost.

BIG MEAT EATER (Can.) BCD 1982 color 82m. SP,D: Chris Windsor. SP: also Phil Savath, Laurence Keane. Dial: Gisele Villeneuve. Ph: Doug McKay. Mus: J. Douglas Dodd. SpFX: Michael Dorsey, Iain Best, Jim Bridge. Mkp: Todd McIntosh. Titles: Aniscope. Ref: MFB'83:327. V 9/22/82. 2/16/83:24. with George Dawson, Big Miller(Abdulla), Andrew Gillies, Howard Taylor.
The Fifties. In their quest for the element baloneum, aliens resurrect Burquitlam's mayor from the dead....radiation-created (temporary) mutation...car-into-spaceship.

BIMBO'S INITIATION Para 1931 anim 7m. D: Dave Fleischer. Ref: Maltin/OMAM. LC. Joe Dante.
Ghostly, hooded figures chase Bimbo through underground maze; all are revealed to be Betty Boop(s).
See also: TWILIGHT ZONE--THE MOVIE.

BIRTH OF THE EARTH see EVOLUTION

BLACK AUTUMN see PSYCHO-MANIA

The BLACK DOLL Univ 1938 60m. D: Otis Garrett. SP: Harold Buckley, from W.E. Hayes's novel. Ph: Stanley Cortez, Ira Morgan. Mus D: Charles Previn. AD: Ralph Berger. Ref: TV: A Crime Club Selection. "B Movies." TVG. FDY. Hirschhorn. with Donald Woods, Nan Grey, Edgar Kennedy, C.Henry Gordon, Doris Lloyd, John Wray, Addison Richards, Holmes Herbert, William Lundigan, Sid Saylor, Arthur Hoyt.
Three men involved in a long-ago murder and cover-up fear

that the victim has returned. ("He's come back to life....It's Barrows, alright--or his ghost!") Black Doll ("La Muneca Negra") from the past seems to herald death....music from BRIDE OF FRANKENSTEIN....Lively, compact mystery-with-a-horror-atmosphere. Or, how Universal got around the British horror-movie ban of the time. Nonstop thunder and rain; screams and attic shadows--the climactic dramatic moment is, in fact, punctuated by a peal of convenient thunder. Woods' calm, deliberate private investigator is played off against Kennedy's eternally-flustered cop. Woods is bearable, even likable; Kennedy appears to be suffering from an acute attack of Una O'Connor. Sufficiently twisty plot.

BLACK FERRIS(by R. Bradbury) see SOMETHING WICKED THIS WAY COMES

The BLACK IMP (F) Famille Melies/Melies 1905 6m. (Le DIABLE NOIR) D: Georges Melies. Ref: screen. PFA notes 11/16/82. Lee.
Imp-devil torments guest at inn with multiplying chairs, burning bed, elusive dresser....The chairs spring up, one after the other, forcing him further and further back. Then, uncornered, he pulls one chair, then another, then another out of one chair....A most imaginative Melies short--on beyond trickery into proto-surrealism. The progression of the appearance of the chairs--only one more at a time--may be arithmetical, but the sense of mystification increases geometrically. The magician here produces his rabbits without benefit of top hat....

BLACK LAGOON see CREATURE FROM THE BLACK LAGOON

The BLACK PLANET (Austral.) Fable 1982 anim color 78m. SP, D,P: Paul Williams. Ph: Russell & Bullen. Mus: Kevin Hocking. Ref: Australian Motion Picture Yearbook 1983. V 5/4/83:420.
Tale of a distant planet, Terre Verte, which is running out of energy.

The BLACK ROOM CI/Ram/Butler-Cronin 1983 SP,D: Norman Thaddeus Vane. D: also Elly Kenner. Ph: Robert Harmon. AD: Yoram Barzilai. SpFX: Mark Shostrum. Mkp: Sylvia Florez. Ref: Bill Warren. Academy. HR 3/13/81. V 6/1/83:4(rated). 2/16/83:24. (d)1/19/81. 10/26/83:113: "horror film." no PFA. with Stephen Knight, Cassandra Gaviola, Jim Stathis.

BLACK SUN, The see JOURNEY THROUGH THE BLACK SUN

BLADE RUNNER WB/Ladd Co. & Shaw/Perenchio-Yorkin/Deeley-Scott (Blade Runner) 1982 color/ws 114m. D: Ridley Scott. SP: Hampton Fancher, David Peoples, from Philip K. Dick's book "Do Androids Dream of Electric Sheep." Ph: Jordan Cronenweth;(addl) Steven Poster, Brian Tufano. Mus: Vangelis. PD: Lawrence G. Paull. SpPhFX:(sup) Douglas Trumbull, Richard Yuricich, David Dryer; EEG;(ph) Dave Stewart;(opt sup) Robert Hall;(min tech) Bob Spurlock;(chief model maker) Mark Stetson. SpFloorFX:(sup)

Terry Frazee;(tech) Logan Frazee et al. Mattes:(art) Matthew Yuricich;(ph) Bailey & Takahashi. Anim: John Wash. ElecDes: Evans Wetmore. SpCamTech: Alan Harding. FxIllus: Tom Cranham. Mkp: M.G. Westmore. Ref: screen. TV. V 6/16/82. FQ W'82:33-38 (M.Dempsey). S&S'82:312. MFB'82:194-5. Weldon. Ecran F 26:10-49(R&J-M Lofficier). with Harrison Ford; Rutger Hauer, Sean Young, Brion James, Joanna Cassidy, Daryl Hannah(Replicants), Edward James Olmos, Morgan Paull, Hy Pyke.

L.A., 2019. Blade Runner Deckard (Ford) vs. renegade, Tyrell Corporation Nexus-6 Replicants--"more human than human" slave-labor robots (or, disparagingly, "skin jobs"), with four-year life-spans (planned obsolescence) and synthetic memories, or "implants." Both human and robots are, it transpires, far-from-emotion-proof. ("Replicants weren't supposed to have feelings--neither were Blade Runners.") Genetic designer (William Sanderson) whose "glands grow old too fast" (his "accelerated decrepitude" making him close kin to the Replicants) and who has a (Pretorius-inspired?) brood of mechanical toys.... living-billboard plugs for a supposedly-utopian Off-World colony...one "special" Replicant (Young) with "no termination date."

A wry, occasionally-touching, "Frankenstein"-themed anecdote all but loses its way in this design-and-effects-minded superproduction. Harrison Ford--definitely your man for the 21st Century--plays a more-Forties-than-Forties (20th Century) movie-tough-guy-type, and his mock-cynicism provides a much-needed counterpoint to the film's willed lethargy, or anomie. If any actor could undercut the visual pretensions here, he could; but he plays a bit part to the technology's starring role. And most of the other actors seem strangely mannered, whether or not they're playing Replicants. Only Hauer's Roy Batty emerges as more character than affectation--and his confrontation with Tyrell (Joe Turkel), his maker, is a vivid paraphrase of the climactic windmill scene in the 1931 FRANKENSTEIN. Though the script's mortality themes "take" in certain scattered sequences--such as Batty's death scene, at the end--they generally seem a pretext...for action, camera movement, eye-pleasing effects.... Those effects/spectacle sequences do achieve, admittedly, an extraordinary sense of melancholy--a technologically-created lassitude--all through the use of music, models, effects, and a very-deliberately-moving camera. The atmosphere is at once intoxicating and hothouse-oppressive. The visual design of BLADE RUNNER is overwhelming, or (from another angle) overbearing--the narrative elements shrivel beside it, or inside it.... The melancholic nature of the characters is achieved with more-conventional means: Deckard's thawing emotional-ice and the Replicants' dawning humanity both seem, basically, sentimental notions (the tough-guy/android/alien with a soft spot), one-dimensional humanism scrambling Forties film noir and Fifties movie-science-fiction. Only Roy Batty here seems an original, not-strictly-movie-bred creation. Robot, human, or in-between, he's unique. He possesses a sense of irony--and a highly-developed esthetic sense--as well as feeling. The other Replicants (and non-Replicants) seem constructs tailored to themes. Batty seems his own tailor, or author, an inventor as well as an invention.

BLADERUNNER(by W.S. Burroughs) see TAKING TIGER MOUNTAIN

BLONDE GODDESS Evart/Planet 1982 color & b&w 85m. SP,D,Exec P: Bill Eagle. SP: also C.T. Cruel. Ph: Misha. PD: Craig Esposito. Mkp: Corrine Parker. SpMechFX: The Wonder Machine. SpFX: Pegasus;(d) Dexter Eagle. Ref: screen. SFChron 9/25/82. Gent 10/82:91-2. with Susanna Britton, J. Ford, Loni Sanders, Ron Jeremy, Jane Kelton.

Comic-book artist fantasizes himself as astrobiologist in the distant future, teleported via "transfer ray" to the realm of a Darth Vader-like warlord, whose spirit unleashes anti-gravity rays....narrated by Karloff-mimic...MAN IN THE MIRROR poster in private-eye parody....At the end, the hero is transported into his fantasy realm....Below-average-of-kind, whether the kind be porn or parody. Ford also sees himself as "Louisiana Smith," in a parody of RAIDERS OF THE LOST ARK, which notion seems rather redundant. And Bill Eagle would be on surer ground invoking Albert Herman than he is invoking Steven Spielberg. (Ineptitude lives!)

*BLOOD BEAST FROM OUTER SPACE Armitage 1965('68-U.S.) (The NIGHT CALLER-B & TV t. NIGHT CALLER FROM OUTER SPACE-TV ad t) SP: Jim O'Connolly. Mus: Johnny Gregory. AD: Harry White. Mkp: Bunty Phillips. Ref: TV. Lee. BFC. AFI. Weldon. Stanley. and with Robert Crewdson(alien), Marianne Stone, Warren Mitchell, Aubrey Morris.

Scientists at the British government's Falsley Park Radio & Electronic Research Establishment are entrusted with an object which has traveled through space at speeds up to 10,000 mph, and which was guided to Earth with "inhuman accuracy." The small, freezing-cold sphere proves to be an "energy valve" with a "selenium shell." (The latter acts as a "thermionic buffer.") In conjunction with a master transmitter on Ganymede, the third moon of Jupiter, it transmutes and receives matter, in the form, specifically, of a "creature of superhuman intelligence and power," with snake-like green eyes, a scarred face (but a well-trimmed moustache & beard), one monster-hand, and a device enabling him to breathe in our atmosphere. As "Mr. Medra" of Orion Ents., he lures young women to his office, hypnotizes them, and, ultimately, takes them back with him to Ganymede, apparently to help restore a civilization destroyed when it "interfered with the laws of the universe."

The title tune ("The Night Caller") promises "mad, forbidden secret thrills," and scientist Jack Costain (John Saxon) sees Medra as a being with a "primordial lust for violence and savagery." Medra does, indeed, eliminate some humans who get in his way. At the end, however, he is allowed to return to Ganymede with his prizes, after smugly noting to assorted on-lookers that his people have solved "that problem." It's indicative of the general dramatic imprecision of the film that the "problem" alluded to remains as vague and elusive as the "solution." It is, perhaps, "violence and savagery," or rampant emotionalism. Whatever message it is that this visitor brings us is, however, garbled, and his credentials are suspect anyway....On the surface, this is a routine, low-budget British sf-er. The script is, however, quietly absurd, in mainly unengaging, non-campy ways. It pretends to be painstaking and "scientific," but seems, merely, to be trying to compensate for its dramatic imprecision with technical detail and precision. Sample involved exchange:

"Well, the base control seems to be the source of a fluctuating magnetic field."

"Then it could act as an automatic monitor, and control the input ratio?"

"Yes, that's why I suggest that it's an energy valve...." The one intriguing touch: references to certain "3-D" photos (taken by Medra) the backgrounds of which "alter"....The acting, at least, is competent--the actors make even the most nonsensical-sounding data sound sensible; and there's some very dry British humor in an interview with the parents of one missing girl.

BLOOD OF THE IRON MAIDEN see IS THIS TRIP REALLY NECESSARY?

*BLOOD OF THE VAMPIRE Artistes Alliance-WNW 1958 Ref: TV. BFC.

A doctor--whose blood disease requires periodic transfusions--experiments in deep-freezing humans and in keeping bodies-without-hearts artificially alive....No story here, just two narrative "questions": will Dr. Kallistratus (Donald Wolfit) find a cure for his disease? Will our hero (Vincent Ball) escape from Kallistratus? Overriding both is a third question: who cares? Tired hero-and-villain stuff.

BLOOD SHACK Program Releasing Corp./Cine Paris(Steckler) 1981 (1980) color 55m. D: Wolfgang Schmidt. SP: Christopher Edwards. Ph,Ed: Sven Christian. Mus,SdFX: Frank A. Coe. P: Carol Flynn. Ref: TV: Intervid(video). TVFFSB. V 10/26/83:322 (ad). with Carolyn Brandt, Ron Haydock(Tim), Jason Wayne, John Bates, Steve Edwards, Laurel Spring, Linda & Laura Steckler.

The Legend of The Trooper is a 150-year history of death--and an old shack haunted by the fiend. ("The Trooper'll git you!") This hooded phantom dispatches his victims with axe and saber. At the end, one "phantom" is unmasked and killed--but there may be another....Horror on a dime, or maybe 11 cents. The celluloid itself may have been the only expense for this glorified-home-movie horror. BLOOD SHACK isn't really a movie so much as it is a few scenes repeated again and again. The film has done all that it's going to do by the end of the first 10 minutes. Oddly, though, the phantom's first attack is well-photographed-and-edited; otherwise, the photography is (at best) undistinguished. The only reason people venture into this haunted house is that they're told not to. ("Stay away from this house!")

BLOOD SONG Summa Vista/Allstate & Mountain High 1982 color 90m. (aka BLOODSONG) D: Alan J. Levi;(addl scenes) Robert Angus. SP,P: Frank Avianca, Lenny Montana. SP: also James Fargo. Story: J.M. Shink, George Hart. Ph: Steve Posey. Mus: Rob Walsh;(lyrics) Monty Turner;(vocal) Lainie Kazan. AD: Robert A. Burns. SpFX: Rick Hatcher. SdFX: Dan Thomas. Mkp: Yvonne Curry. Opt: Freeze Frame. Ref: TV. Bill Warren. V 9/28/83:48. with Frankie Avalon, Donna Wilkes, Richard Jaeckel, Antoinette Bower, Dane Clark, L. Montana, William Cullen, Victor Izay.

Oregon. Madman (Avalon), who as a boy witnessed a multiple murder, escapes state mental hospital, commits series of hatchet murders....Teenager (Wilkes) for whom he was a rare-blood-type donor "sees" his crimes (cf. BRAINWAVES), has psychic flash-forward in which she sees his (stolen) van....dialogue reference to King Kong....A rerun of cliches of young love, unhappy families, psycho-killers. The girl's psychic link with the killer is the only distinguishing feature, and it is a fairly clever suspense ploy, if it's not exactly sound science. It makes it seem as if he is pursuing her, psychically, all through the film. Unfortunately, it's not a two-way link: before he can actually begin to pursue her physically, he must see her see him burying a body. The fulfillment of this dramatic prerequisite involves a few rather large coincidences of time and place. Some fun-suspense in the climactic sequence (set in a lumber yard), but a fizzle of a "coda."

The BLOOD THIRSTY DEAD (H.K.) Shaw 1981 D: Sun Chung. Ref: V 10/14/81:210(ad). 5/13/81:275. JFFJ 14:36: The BLOODTHIRSTY DEAD. with Pai Piao, Lo Lieh.

BLOOD TIDE (B-Greek) 21st Century/Connaught Int'l.-Athon(Raftage) 1982(1980) color 83m. (The RED TIDE or RED TIDE-orig t. aka BLOODTIDE) SP,D: Richard Jeffries. SP,P: Nico Mastorakis, Donald Langdon. Ph: Ari Stavrou; Miguel Gurzon. Mus: Jerry Moseley; James Simpson. AD: A. Crugnola. SpFX: Yannis Samiotis. SpDes: Vince Jeffords. Creative Cons & Co-P: Brian Trenchard-Smith. SpExplosFX: Dick Albain or Albane, A&A. Ref: screen. V 10/13/82. LAT 8/17/80. with James Earl Jones, Jose Ferrer, Lila Kedrova, Mary Louise Weller, Martin Kove, Deborah Shelton (Madeline), Lydia Cornell.

An island off Greece. The monster (which "moves freely between land and sea") responsible, back in 1521 B.C., for the local "blight" is unleashed again by explosives, and begins seeking a virgin sacrifice (although it marks time with some non-virgins too)....ritual with man in monster-mask...woman with psychic link to monster....A pretty bad, but rather fun, old-fashioned monster movie. The monster itself might be the Return of the Giant Claw, and is, wisely, never seen very clearly.

(Clearly enough once, however, underwater, for camp purposes.) The "mysterious" details, this time: ancient coins, an ancient symbol, icons hidden beneath icons, a woman kept (rather loosely) under the monster's spell, a bricked-up hole in a sea cave, strands of seaweed-slime found at the scenes of the crimes. The suspense: will the best actor (Jones) and/or the most attractive blonde (pick one) be killed off too soon for the movie's own good? Jones, fortunately, survives until the end, and our heroine beyond it....

BLOODRAGE Picture Company of America 1979 color 83m. D: Joseph Bigwood. SP: Robert Jahn. Story Cons: Bernhardt J. Hurwood. Ph: Joao Fernandes, Joseph Scherer. Mus: Michael Karp; David Mullaney. AD: John Lawless, George Hayward Jr. SpMkpFX: Dennis Eger. SpFX: Deed Rossiter. SdFX: Roy Valle. Opt: EFX. Co-P: Joseph Zito. Ref: TV: Best Film Video. no PFA. with Lawrence Tierney, Ian Scott(Richie), James Johnston, Jerry McGee, Jimi Keys, Judith-Marie Bergan.

Clean-cut, too-straight, unbalanced young man accidentally kills a hooker; goes to New York City and strangles another one ("Maybe something's wrong with me"); breaks the necks of a neighbor woman and her dog; gets tossed out of a window by the cop-friend of the first prostitute....The sleazy milieu of BASKET CASE, without any of the latter's inverted charm. BLOODRAGE is a genre movie without a genre--it's not quite a suspense-horror movie (although the suspense scenes are, in terms of music, imitation-PSYCHO); not quite a psychological study (although Richie himself narrates); not quite a crime drama/sociological study/TAXI DRIVER. The table is all-too-neatly laid for Richie: New York is thriving in violence mirroring his own "bloodrage," and prospective female victims abound....Such abundance makes it easy for psychopaths <u>and</u> scriptwriters. This is the type of melodrama in which "even-handedness" means <u>everyone's</u> unsympathetic.

BLOODSONG see BLOOD SONG

BLOODTHIRSTY DEAD, The see BLOOD THIRSTY DEAD, The

BLOODTIDE see BLOOD TIDE

2P BLOODY BIRTHDAY Judica 1980 color 85m. SP,D: Ed Hunt. SP: also Barry Pearson. Ph: Stephen Posey. Mus: Arlon Ober. AD: Lynda Burbank, J.R. Fox. SpFX: Roger George. Opt: Rabin. Mkp: Julie Purcell. SdFxEd: Provision. Ref: MFB'82:226-7. Ecran F 22:5,33,77. V 2/16/83:24: sfa CREEPERS? 10/15/80:187 (ad): at Mifed. 9/30/81:32(ad). with Susan Strasberg, Jose Ferrer, Lori Lethin, Melinda Cordell, Joe Penny, Ellen Geer, Ward Costello.

Meadowvale, Calif. Three children, born ten years ago during a solar eclipse, go on a murder spree.

BLOODY PARROT (H.K.) Shaw 1981 Ref: JFFJ 14:36: "gory." Villains fake "flesh-eating monster women."

BLUE DEMON CONTRA CEREBROS INFERNALES (Mex) Cinematografica R.A./ America 1968 color 85m. (**El CEREBRO INFERNAL-orig t) D: Chano Urueta. SP: F. Oses, A. Orellana. Ref: WorldF'68: BLUE DEMON AGAINST THE BRAINS OF HELL-tr t. M/TVM 2/67. Lee. with David Reynoso, Ana Martin, Blue Demon, Noe Murayama.
Blue Demon vs. mad scientists who extract people's brains.

BLUE HOLOCAUST (I) D.R. 1979 color 94m. (BUIO OMEGA) D,Ph: Aristide Massaccesi(aka Joe D'Amato). SP: Fabbri, Guerrini. Mus: Goblin. Ref: Ecran F 22:14,77. with Kieran Canter, Cinzia Monreale, Franca Stotti, Anna Cardini.
The eternal triangle: governess, taxidermist, latter's fiancee's embalmed corpse.

BLUE THUNDER Col/Rastar-Carroll 1983 color/ws 108m. D: John Badham. SP: Dan O'Bannon, Don Jakoby. Ph: John A. Alonzo; (aerial) Frank Holgate;(motion control) Dream Quest;(min) Jack Cooperman. Mus: Arthur B. Rubinstein. AD: S.Z. Litwack; Bernard Cutler. SpFX:(sup) Chuck Gaspar; Jeff Jarvis;(elec) Peter Albiez. VisCons: Philip Harrison. Video:(coord) Rick Whitfield;(displays) Burbank Studios;(sup) Hal Landaker. Opt: Movie Magic. SupSdFxEd: W.L. Manger. Motion Control: Scott Squires et al. Ref: screen. V 2/2/83. SFExam 5/13/83. PSA Mag 7/83:50: "whisper mode" & sound-monitoring technology not extant. MFB'83:211-12. Ecran F 36:51-62(R&J-M Lofficier). with Roy Scheider, Malcolm McDowell, Warren Oates, Candy Clark, Daniel Stern, Joe Santos, Mario Machado.
The showpiece of the U.S. government's Project THOR (Tactical Helicopter Offensive Response) is Blue Thunder, a helicopter with "a few new wrinkles": e.g., an infrared camera, a thermograph, and super-sensitive mikes, which paraphernalia allow X-ray-like penetration of buildings; a computer hooked into virtually every data bank in the U.S.; a "tracer light" (on the pilot's helmet) which aims a 20mm electric cannon; and the no-noise "whisper mode." Plus: dogfights over L.A. with copters & F-16's--Arco Tower hit by heat-seeking missile....
A glorified showcase for a new piece of hardware. The ends, however, (the aerial chases over the streets and through the drainage ditches of L.A.) almost justify the means (a plot built on coincidence and contrivance). Clearly designed to appeal to the viewer's delusions of grandeur and power, Blue Thunder is a virtually-indestructible, mechanical Superman, and the movie itself is a sight-and-sound power trip, the story's moral undercurrents notwithstanding. McDowell is callous; Scheider is sensitive. But the versatility of Blue Thunder is what counts here--it gives the old intrigue a new technological wrinkle. When, at the end, Scheider junks the helicopter, we're supposed to see his act as a moral victory over Big Brother McDowell; actually, it just means the fun's over. Hypocriti-

cally, the script deplores what Blue Thunder represents (a full-scale invasion of privacy) while exulting in what it is and does. If the movie can't have it both ways, however, it does well enough one way: images like that of the silent monster-copter (hovering outside a 30th-floor window in the "whisper mode") suddenly listing and scuttling off, screen right (the spy spied), like an airborne crustacean, are worth a bit of narrative duplicity....film-as-hardware. Good supporting performances (supporting the whirlybird, that is) by Scheider and Oates. Their relationship is a typical individualist-and-boss variation. (It might be star-reporter-and-editor or athlete-and-coach as easily as cop-and-chief.) But Oates revels in sarcastic exasperation, and Scheider, too, will have none of it (i.e., high-handedness, by McDowell or Oates).

BOARDINGHOUSE Coast Films/Blustarr(Howard Willette) 1982 color 100m. D & SpFxMkp: Johnn Wintergate. SP,Mus: Jonema. Ph: Jan Lucas, Obee Ray. Mus: also 33-1/3, Kalassu, C. Conlan et al. Computer Graphics: Balcom. Ref: TV: Paragon Video. V 3/14/84. no Academy. Bill Warren. with Hawk Adley(gardener/Jim Royce), Alexandra Day, Kalassu, Joel Riordan, Brian Bruderlin, B. Kora.

9/18/72. An authority on telekinesis and his wife commit (apparently) double suicide; their house, subsequently, gets a "bad rep" for being haunted: a woman's hand is ground up in the garbage disposal. A woman in a trance hangs herself. Another has an ice pick thrust through her hand. Yet another starts bleeding, then drowns herself. A man's guts pop out. A possessed cop makes a woman's face bleed and her eyes pop out, then shoots himself. Shower tiles bleed....Behind it all: the ex-owner's daughter, Deborah (Day), a "homicidal maniac" with "strong telekinetic ability" who can appear as a red phantom, and who makes a man's heart jump out of his body. ("Now I have it forever!") At the end, two other telekinetic folks battle and defeat her, though her body is never found....

Or, The Videoville Horror. BOARDINGHOUSE has the same uninflected look and sound as those old ABC Late Night video horrors, and its gore and horror effects derive from the last-eight-years'-worth of bad-house movies. Flat-footed, just-pour-it-on shock scenes alternate with scenes of the female boarders lolling around home-and-garden in shorts and swimsuits. The climax, however, in which Deborah reveals herself as the Woman with the Power, and she and her opponents generate gaily-colored swirls of mist, or fog--as well as psychic energy--is loud and garish enough to be rather entertaining. The two nightmare sequences (featuring skeletons, clutching-hands-from-graves, and a pig-headed creature) are also a notch or two more imaginative than the rest of the movie: in the first, the dreamer dreams her bed (as well as herself) into the cemetery, in which setting it seems surreally at-home....

2 BOMBA ON PANTHER ISLAND 1949(1950) PD: Gordon Wiles. Ref: TV. LC: c12/18/49. TVG: 1950 release. and with Harry Lewis.

African natives "believe that the soul of a dying animal sometimes takes refuge in the body of a human being"...in this case, in the body of a woman (Lita Baron) part-French, part-??, whom they believe to be the "taboo cat" or "killer beast...getting even for cutting down the trees" on their island. The woman with the "evil eye," conveniently for the theory, always seems to turn up just after the killer panther has stalked away. She also gets involved in a Simon-Smith-Randolph, CAT PEOPLE-like romantic triangle, pitched at the simpers-and-jealous-pouts level....Yes, a Bomba The Jungle Boy horror movie, sentimentally and didactically pro-jungle and anti-civilization. A third of the movie is simply Bomba (Johnny Sheffield) giving the heroine (Allene Roberts) stock-shot-illustrated lessons on the beauties and beasties of Africa. (Her initial view is that it's just "heat, insects, and superstition.") One of the lesser wake-of-CAT PEOPLE efforts....

BOO MOON Para 1954 anim 3-D & color 7m. (Casper) D: S. Kneitel. Mus: W. Sharples. Ref: LC. Maltin/OMAM: sf. Mark Kausler: re: moon men.

2P The BOOGENS Sunn Classic/Taft Int'l. 1981 color 94m. D: James L. Conway. Story,SP: David O'Malley. SP: also Bob Hunt. Story: also Tom Chapman. Ph: Paul Hipp. Mus: Bob Summers. PD: Paul Staheli. SpFX: Jon Reeves, Doug Kramer. SpMkpDes: William Munns, Ken Horn. Opt: Film FX. SdFxEd: Sound FX. Ref: TV. MFB'81:195. Weldon. V 4/15/81:28(rated). 1/27/82. with Rebecca Balding, Fred McCarren, John Crawford, Peg Stewart, Anne-Marie Martin, Jeff Harlan.

Disaster-plagued mine, closed since 1912, is re-opened and found to be inhabited by huge, tentacled turtle/squid-like monsters....Classically discreet monster-movie saves full-view shots of its nasty centerpieces until almost the end. In the meantime, we see only: a woman dragged-by-the-legs across her cabin floor and into the cellar; a bit of tentacle; a pile of human skeletons beside an underground lake; tentacle-tips ripping open a floor vent; needles-in-tentacles slashing faces.... And these babies move--at a near-Steadicam pace. Their most distinctive contribution to film-monster tradition, however: the sudden, whip-like attacks they mount on human limbs with their all-purpose tentacles. Not since Lash LaRue....Everyone's dialogue here has a wry touch to it--which uniformity makes for undifferentiated characters, but listenable dialogue. Even the dog-mascot is a rather wry little fellow.

BOOGEYMAN II Cinevid(New West) 1983(1982) color 82m. D: Bruce Starr. SP,P,with: Ulli Lommel. Sequel to The BOOGEY MAN, or (Br t) The BOGEY MAN. Ph: Philippe Carr-Forster; David Sperling. Mus: Tim Krog; Craig Hundley, Wayne Love. SpFX: CMI, Craig Harris. Mkp: Shirley Howard. Ref: TV: VC II Video. V 8/24/83. MFB'81:133. with Suzanna Love, Shannah Hall, Sholto von Douglas(Joseph), Ashley Dubay.

Poor Lacey (Love) is prodded into recalling her story--otherwise known as The BOOGEY MAN--to a bunch of shallow Hollywood-types. ("Tell them what happened in the barn.") There follows approximately a half hour of footage from the original film. Then the butler, Joseph, picks up the one remaining fragment of the cursed mirror (Lacey, who carries the fragment around, is, herself, "immune" to it), and it "uses" Joseph as a vehicle to destroy those who would exploit Lacey's experiences. ("Noone's going to make a movie about my mirror.") In some Close Encounters of the Derivative Kind, stuffed animals spring to life in a child's bedroom. Garden hoses and shears, barbecue tongs, a corkscrew, and a toothbrush then come to levitating life and kill; a metal ladder smacks one woman into a suckling position on a car's exhaust pipe; and one victim is apparently suffocated to death by a can of shaving-cream-gone-berserk. Yes, she is. Joseph is drowned, but his hand reaches out from the grave to make an (occupied) car explode....

No question, this is a curious film. In terms of gross-out horror movies, though, it's no competition for The EXORCIST; in terms of social satire, it's not exactly Proust. And as a satire, specifically, on Hollywood and its crassness, it somehow lacks bite. Although this sequel has a Hollywood setting, the original is, oddly, treated here not, simply (and more credibly), as a fantasy film--to which, then, the fictional director in Part II is asked to make a fictional sequel--but as a true story (which the director is asked to film), and Lacey is treated as a real person, while the subtext, of course, is that the fictional director in Part II--Mickey--is played by the actual director of Part I--Lommel. Somebody is exploiting someone, or something, but it's hard to say who or what: Lacey, Mickey, Lommel, the latter's real-life experiences, or her reel-life experiences. Intentionally or not, BOOGEYMAN II qualifies as a modernist conundrum. Its very desultoriness--e.g., the several murder victims are quickly introduced, one after the other (in a strange, backyard-party "lineup" effect), then as summarily dispatched, with little or no get-acquainted time in-between--such desultoriness may be intended, as a comment on the generally mechanical quality of ten-little-victims movies or, from another angle, as a response to industry pressure to make such movies: i.e., as a tacit, insolent "Well, here's what you said you wanted and I hope you're happy." In other words, the slipshod quality here seems achieved. This is a movie which works, or rather which doesn't work, on many different levels, but which was perhaps not really supposed to work, in which case it succeeds famously....

BOOK OF THE DEAD see EVIL DEAD, The

BORN IN FLAMES Iris/Borden-Jerome 1983 color 78m. SP,D,Ed: Lizzie Borden. Ph: Ed Bowes et al. Mus: The Bloods et al. SpFX: Hisao Taya. Ref: screen. V 3/16/83. VV 11/15/83:60-61. with Honey, Jeanne Satterfield, Adele Bertei, Diane Jacobs.

The U.S., 10 years after the Socialist-Democratic War of Liberation. The government is, supposedly, Democratic-Socialist; prostitution and crimes like rape are on the wane. But "economic sex wars" are forcing women out of the jobs which they fought to get; progressive radio stations like Phoenix and Regazza are being hit by arsonists; and the Socialist Youth Review comes under attack for its outspokenness. In response, the Women's Army begins interrupting TV newscasts and Presidential addresses, and calling for a new revolution....Easy ironies (along the lines of "Plus ca change....") and oppressed-of-the-Earth cliches. Future sexism and racism, here, are meant to look like today's, and the climactic call-to-arms is really directed at us, now. The film's depiction of governmental and industrial reactionism, however, is probably too glib and simplistic to get much of a reaction of its own.

BOSKO THE DRAWBACK WB 1933 7m. D,P: Hugh Harman. Ref: "WB Cartoons." LC. no Lee.

The Hunchback of Notre Dame as a football player....

BOYHOOD DAZE WB 1957 anim color 7m. D: Chuck Jones. Ref: "WB Cartoons." LC. no Lee.

Little boy dreams he's fighter-pilot defending Earth from Martians.

BRAINSTORM MGM-UA/JF(Douglas Trumbull) 1983 color/ws 105m. D,P: Trumbull. SP: Robert Stitzel, Philip Frank Messina. Story: Bruce Joel Rubin. Ph & Assoc P: Richard Yuricich. Mus: James Horner. PD: John Vallone. SpVisFX: Entertainment Effects Group;(anim) John Wash;(ph) Dave Stewart, J.R. Dixon; (opt fx sup) Robert Hall;(computer fx sup) Don Baker;(vis fx sup) Alison Yerxa;(min sup) Mark Stetson;(mattes) Matthew Yuricich;(cons) Virgil Mirano. SpFX: Robert Spurlock, Eric Allard, Martin Bresin. SpSynFX: Serafine, Underwood, Manning. SpCons: S.&G. Grofi;(fx) Robert Hickson et al. Video: Greg McMurry. Ref: screen. SFExam 9/30/83. FComment 10/83:76-82. V 9/28/83. Bill Warren. MFB'83:328. with Christopher Walken, Natalie Wood, Louise Fletcher, Cliff Robertson, Joe Dorsey, Alan Fudge, Jordan Christopher, Nina Axelrod.

Scientists working at a North Carolina research institute make a "true, one-of-a-kind scientific breakthrough": a machine which, in conjunction with a helmet, allows the wearer of the latter perfect, complete, vicarious experiences. The sensations of sight, sound, touch, taste, and smell--and even the memories--of one person can thus be transmitted to another, or stored on tape and replayed. The tapes, however, have side, or after-effects: e.g., a "Psychotic Episode" (stored under "Project Brainstorm") triggers same in a boy, and a tape of the death of one of the scientists, Lillian Reynolds (Fletcher), replayed in part, kills one man and alters the personality of her co-worker, Michael Brace (Walken). When, finally, the latter replays the tape for himself--in its entirety--he almost "loses himself" in the stars and joins her in death, but is rescued by his wife, Karen (Wood)....DR. JEKYLL AND MR. HYDE(1932) on TV...cf. the premises of The SORCERERS(1967).

BRAINSTORM is a delicatessen of ESP. You're encouraged to sample a little of everything behind the counter here: happy, romantic memories; erotica; madness; even simian sensations--and "the scariest thing a person ever has to face," death. You can sense the excitement of the filmmakers, here, in their subject--they want to examine all the possibilities of their premise. The problem with the movie is that they don't communicate their excitement through the characters therein. Writers and director seem so agog over this Pandora's-helmet idea that they forget the story. Or should have forgotten it. There is a narrative (the familiar individual-vs.-the-corporation story), but it doesn't develop the premise. The narrative merely develops itself. It, simply, provides the characters with any number of pretexts for donning the helmet, at which times the screen widens, and the audience experiences third-hand what the characters experience second-hand. For us: not-quite-Cinerama; for them: Cinerama-plus, or Instant Proust, as the past is recaptured in visualized memory "bubbles." These vicarious experiences prove to be, generally, little more than Super Panavision stunts, though the romantic episode with Michael and Karen is intriguing: their happier, romantic past really is recaptured. The use of the helmet promotes true empathy between the two, physical empathy, as he sees himself through her, and vice versa....Will this scientific rejuvenation last?--yes, assumes the script, with unsatisfying glibness. The metaphysical uses to which the machine is put are more problematical. In The WALKING DEAD(1936), John Ellman (Boris Karloff) returns from a brief stay in the beyond, and says only that he experienced "peace and...."; BRAINSTORM attempts to elaborate on the "....", but just adds more dots, as Lillian's dying memories (passing through Michael) segue into vistas of abstract butterflies, or winged souls, and other vaguely-positive, over-the-rainbow images. The ambitions of BRAINSTORM are generally more charming than they are realized....

BRAINWAVES MPM/CinAmerica 1982 color 80m. SP,D,P: Ulli Lommel. Dial: Buz Alexander, Suzanna Love. Ph: Jon Kranhouse; Lommel. Mus: Robert O. Ragland. AD: Stephen E. Graff. SpFX: N.H.P. Mkp: Cathy Estocin, Phillip Debbs. Ref: TV. V 9/7/83. 6/1/83:4 & '82(rated): Comworld. with Keir Dullea, Love, Vera Miles, Percy Rodrigues, Tony Curtis, Paul Willson, Nicholas Love(Willy), Corinne Alphen(Lelia), Eve Brent Ashe.

San Francisco. A woman (Love) who has suffered "a traumatic blow to the brain," and is lying in a coma, is the first person to be submitted to "the Clavius process...." Corrective brain-wave patterns are fed from a computer--via electrodes--into the damaged areas of the victim's brain, and succeed in restoring normal electrical activity. The process proves, however, to transmit not only the motor reflexes, but the memories, as well, of the dead donor, a murder victim. The recipient begins to relive, in "flashback" flashes, the murder scene (cf. BLOOD-SONG), and the killer finds himself in danger of being identified--by his victim....

The premise of BRAINWAVES is so new it's old. It's simply a more-scientifically-involved version of the theory (behind such mysteries as Los MUERTOS HABLAN, 1935, The LAST LOOK, 1909, and FOUR FLIES ON GREY VELVET, 1971) that the retinas of a dead person retain the image of the last thing seen before death.... Science and mystery, in BRAINWAVES, seem very arbitrarily yoked together, although the Clavius process is exactly what every detective would love to have at his disposal--if only Clavius (Curtis) knew what he was on to...! But he's a mere stooge for the harebrained inspirations of the plot. Even at the end, he seems about to (unwittingly?) recycle the brainwaves of the deceased murderer. He never learns....BRAINWAVES is competently photographed, acted, and directed, but the script is a frightfully timid blend of more-or-less-incidental pathos and would-be suspense.

BREATH OF AIR, A see DIH

*The BRIDE AND THE BEAST 1958 (aka QUEEN OF THE GORILLAS) Sp FX: Gerald Endler. Mkp: Harry Thomas. Ref: TV. Lee. Weldon. "E.D. Wood, Jr. A Man & His Films": with Steve Calvert(The Beast). FM 66:23: with Ray Corrigan(gorilla).

A dull, extraneous escaped-Indian-tigers subplot (and incidental stock-footage fest) takes up half an hour. But stick around for gems like: (the wife) "I still shudder at the strange sensation I had when the gorilla was trying to be tender." And: (the doctor) "Basically, we're all animals." A must for fans of Bronson Caverns. Featured: a most curious scene in which the gorilla is in the familiar act of carrying off the heroine, and she isn't screaming....Something new under the sun! (Seems she's a gorilla, too....)

BRIMSTONE & TREACLE (B-U.S.) UA Classics/Sherwood/Namara-Salke & Solow(PFH) 1982 color 87m. (BRIMSTONE-early t) D: Richard Loncraine. SP: Dennis Potter. Ph: Peter Hannan. Mus: Sting; Michael Nyman, The Go-Go's. PD: Milly Burns. Mkp: Elaine Carew. Ref: screen. HR 11/9/82: "psychological horror film." V 9/1/82. Academy. S&S'82:262: "horror tale." New Rep 11/29/82: "satanic agent." SFExam 11/19/82. Sacto Union 12/22/82: from banned BBC play. Berk Monthly 3/83: "an angel with an angle." with Sting(Martin), Denholm Elliott, Joan Plowright(Norma Bates), Suzanna Hamilton, Dudley Sutton.

A mysterious stranger invades a troubled English, suburban household; lightens the lives of an unhappy couple; sexually cures their traumatized daughter....nightmare sequence...subjective (Martin's viewpoint?) praying-up-a-storm sequence.... The above one-line synopsis is also, it must be noted, an interpretation. It pre-supposes that the "bombshell" which, at film's end, the suddenly-coherent young lady drops (i.e., that it was a caught-in-the-act episode involving her father and his secretary which led, indirectly, to her trauma) is a salutary, air-clearing disclosure: end of repressed guilt for him; end of paralysis for daughter; beginning of a new life for mother. It's as if, in The OLD DARK HOUSE(1932), the presence of the benighted (def. 2) visitors at Femm Hall had acted on the Femms, rather than vice versa. (In actuality, the frightful, benighted (def. 1) Femms scare their guests straight, morally.) Martin seems, in every way, a positive influence (the pathetic family which we see at the start of the movie certainly doesn't need any more trouble), although Anne Baxter's psychotic troublemaker in GUEST IN THE HOUSE(1944) might, at first, seem to be the role model for Martin. Lines like "You could be the devil himself for all we know" seem to point her way. And there's no denying that there is something diabolical about him; he is, perhaps, a sort of Satan-in-reverse, an accidental angel. His only obvious motivation is sexual--he lusts after the daughter. He might be a horny angel, unwittingly spreading goodness and light. Psychoanalytically-speaking, he makes all the right moves. He flatters the mother into sexual self-awareness; he unblocks the daughter's sexually-triggered psychosis with sex. The identification of Martin with a portrait of Christ is not necessarily ironic, as, initially, it appears it must be. Nor, necessarily, is the mother's line, "Oh, Martin, the angels must have sent you!" He's the answer to a maiden's (and everyone else's) prayer.... The film itself, however, is admittedly little more than a vehicle (for the Martin character), an intellectual puzzle. It's a metaphysical mystery, intriguing exclusively on an abstract level. Its protagonist, Martin, is one of the oddest movie Good Samaritans since Bunuel's Nazarin....

BRITANNIA HOSPITAL (B) UA Classics/EMI-NFFC-British Lion(Film & General) 1982('83-U.S.) color 117m. D: Lindsay Anderson. SP: David Sherwin. Ph: Mike Fash. Mus: Alan Price. AD: Norris Spencer. SpMkpFX: Nick Maley. SpFX: George Gibbs;(tech) Richard Conway, Dave McCall;(addl) Peter Aston. SdFxEd: Alan Pattillo. Ref: screen. MFB'82:104-5. V 5/19/82. VV 3/15/83:41. NYT 3/6/83: character from IF... & O LUCKY MAN! with Leonard Rossiter, Graham Crowden, Malcolm McDowell(Mick), Joan Plowright, Jill Bennett, Marsha Hunt, Frank Grimes(Genesis' voice), Robin Askwith, Dandy Nichols, Mark Hamill, Vivian Pickles, Valentine Dyall, Brian Glover, Roland Culver, Alan Bates.

"Man remade" a la "Frankenstein": Dr. Millar's Genesis Unit (of the Britannia Hospital's Millar Centre for Advanced Surgical Science) constructs a being "neither man nor woman--greater than either" from preserved human limbs and organs. But the head, taken from Mick Travis, is re-severed, and the project scrapped. The doctor's alternative: an electronic human brain. It proves, however, to be, simply, an elaborate "broken record." ("How like a god....How like a god....") Plus: laser surgical-hacksaw...brain-cocktail.

Sputtering satire on British class structure, labor unions, science, technology, what-have-you. The all-too-human factors--compromise, ineptitude, imperfection--are not new to satire. They're even venerable, but the script fails to galvanize its own elements. There are occasional nice ironies--e.g., the man-made machine commenting on man, at the end, both directly, by quote, and indirectly, by breaking down. But they're fairly effectively lost in the hubbub, and the comic tone and structure seem rather staid and old-fashioned in this free-wheeling era of Monty Python and Saturday Night Live. Sherwin's script brandishes its RELEVANCE like a sword of self-righteousness, as if to say, We're not just <u>comedy</u>, you know. BRITANNIA HOSPITAL is as easy a target as most of <u>its</u> targets, and <u>they're</u> sitting ducks....

BRONX WARRIORS see 1990: THE BRONX WARRIORS

BROWNIE see DARING YOUNG MAN, The

BRUCE LEE IN NEW GUINEA (Chinese) 1980 color/ws 90m. D: Kong Hung. Ref: TV. TVG. no Academy. with Bruce Li, Kwong Lee.

Snake Worship Island, off New Guinea, where the local oppressor is The Great Wizard, of the ("real bad!") black-magic Devil Sect. He rules the Snake People and practices snake-style martial arts. Left for dead, at one point, in his own snake pit, he magically leaps right out again and shakes off a slew of snakes....The island's legendary, magic snake-pearl cures a baby under a spell....silly guard-ape...vision in which girl "sees" boy as a snake....More kung-fu inanity. Just a lot of l. & a. (legs and arms). On hero and villain, said appendages are weapons; on our Snake-Princess heroine, they're just decorative, but very. The ape strikes a welcome, fleeting camp-note.

BUD ABBOTT AND LOU COSTELLO MEET THE INVISIBLE MAN see ABBOTT AND COSTELLO MEET THE INVISIBLE MAN

BUD ABBOTT AND LOU COSTELLO MEET THE KILLER see ABBOTT AND COSTELLO MEET THE KILLER

BUDDY'S LOST WORLD WB 1935 anim 7m. D: Jack King. Ref: "WB Cartoons." Lee. LC.

Dinosaurs and cavemen on deserted island.

BUENAS NOCHES, SENOR MONSTRUO (Sp) Frade 1982 D: Antonio Mercero. Ref: V 5/4/83:414. Ecran F 32:70. with Regaliz, Paul Naschy, Luis Escobar, Fernando Bilbao.

Musical-comedy for children features Count Dracula, Frankenstein's monster, Quasimodo, and a werewolf (Naschy, but not as Daninsky).

BUIO OMEGA see BLUE HOLOCAUST

BULLSHOT (B) HandMade 1983 color 88m. D: Dick Clement. Ref: MFB'83:272: bit with paralyzing ray. V 9/21/83: "giant octopus."

BUMP IN THE NIGHT see FINAL TERROR, The

*BUNCO SQUAD 1950 Ref: TV. V 8/16/50. poster. Academy call sheet. and with Vivien Oakland, Dick Elliott, John Hamilton, Harry Lauter, Don Dillaway, Don Kerr, Tol Avery.

Racketeer sets up East Indian-oriented Rama Society in order to bilk wealthy L.A. matron. "Spooky" scenes: a "princess" materializing "spirits" at "services"/seances...magician Dante the Great (as himself) instructing others in the ways of spiritualists, at Rancho Dante...a hood attacked, in the dark, by "phantoms" (i.e., the heroes, dressed in black)....Flat-footed quasi-documentary/quasi-drama, sounding at times like a public-service message re: bunco schemes.

BUTCHER, BAKER, NIGHTMARE MAKER see NIGHT WARNING

CAFE FLESH Caribbean 1982 color 76m. SP,D,Co-P: Rinse Dream. SP: also Herbert W. Day. Ph,Co-P: F.X. Pope. Mus: Mitchell Froom. PD,SpStageFX: Paul Berthell. Mkp: Peter Magaraci; Kenny Detroit. VisCons: Mark Zito. Ref: TV: VCA Video. Velvet 12/82:100. with Andrew Nichols, Paul McGibboney, Pia Snow, Marie Sharp, Robert Dennis, Becky Savage, Angel Selby.

"A mutant universe," in the future, after "the Nuclear Kiss." Ninety-nine per cent of the population are Sex Negatives who have, apparently, either been irradiated, or conditioned to find sex repulsive and physically impossible. "Desire is in chains," and the few Sex Positives are forced to perform for the Negatives on the stage of the Cafe Flesh, which is run by Moms, "the June Taylor of the nuclear set." <u>One</u> female Negative finds herself becoming a Positive....bit with emcee as a "vampire" (complete with vaguely-Lugosi accent)...performer as "baby" with "vampire"-teeth.

Modernist porn which divides its future society into the "haves" and "have-nots," or rather the "cans" and "cannots." This division may be meant to be a metaphor (for porn stars/ audience?) or it may not. It may as well <u>not</u> be, because the movie succeeds, all too well, in disorienting its <u>own</u> audience. It's as intellectually frustrating for the viewer <u>as</u> the stage acts are sexually frustrating for the patrons of Cafe Flesh. Still, an adult film which dares to be disorienting certainly qualifies as, at least, a curiosity, and this <u>is</u>, technically-speaking, a professional job, which most such films emphatically are not.

CAKE-WALK INFERNAL see INFERNAL CAKE-WALK, The

CALIFORNIA AXE MASSACRE see AXE

CALLING, The see MURDER BY PHONE

CALLING ALL G-MEN see YOU MAY BE NEXT!

CAMPSITE MASSACRE see FINAL TERROR, The

CANNIBAL FERROX see MAKE THEM DIE SLOWLY

CANNIBAL HOLOCAUST (I) F.D. 1979 D: Ruggero Deodato. SP: G. Clerici. Ph: S. D'Offizi. Mus: Riz Ortolani. Ref: Prod. Ital. V 5/9/79:320(ad): not sfa 2 The LAST SURVIVOR. 5/7/80. Ecran F 22:47-8. with Francesca Ciardi, Luca Barbareshi, R. Kerman.
Documentary filmmakers goad Amazon tribesmen into acts of "horror and cruelty"; suffer for their outrages.

CANNIBALS IN THE STREETS (I-Sp) Almi Cinema 5/New Fida & Frade 1980('82-U.S.) color 91m. (SAVAGE APOCALYPSE. The SLAUGHTERERS. CANNIBALS IN THE CITY. INVASION OF THE FLESH HUNTERS-alt or ad ts) SP,D: Antonio Margheriti. SP,Story: Jimmy Gould. Ph: F. Arribas. Mus: Alex Blonksteiner. PD: W. Patriarca. SpMkpFX: G. De Rossi. SpFX: Don Shelley. Ref: V 8/18/82. 5/13/81:333: aka VIRUS. Willis/SW'83. Weldon. with John Saxon, Elizabeth Turner, John Morghen, Cindy Hamilton, Tony King.
Returning Vietnam vets infected by virus which turns them into cannibals.

CAPTAIN AMERICA II CBS-TV/Univ-TV 1979 color 96m. D: Ivan Nagy. SP: W.S. Schiller, P. Payne. Ph: V. Martinelli. Mus: Mike Post, Peter Carpenter. AD: D. Snyder. Ref: TV: appar. from "Captain America" series 2-parter. SFExam. "Tous Les Films 1980": theat. release in France. Weldon. with Reb Brown, Connie Sellecca, Len Birman, Chris Cary, Lana Wood, Christopher Lee, Katherine Justice.
Drug which makes man (Lee) age instantly. Tacky stuff.

CAPTAIN HARLOCK IN ARCADIA (J) Toei 1982 anim color (WAGA SEISHUN NO ARUKADEIA or WAGA AOIBA NO ALUCADIA) Ref: JFFJ 14: 9: My Youth in Arcadia-tr of J t. V 10/20/82:229. 8/25/82.
Origin of the Space Pirate. From the "Uchu Kaizoku Kyaputen Harokku" TV series. See also: GALAXY EXPRESS.

CAPTAIN INVINCIBLE (Austral-U.S.) Seven Keys(Mora) 1983 color 90m. (aka The RETURN OF CAPTAIN INVINCIBLE) D: Philippe Mora. SP: Steve de Souza, Andrew Gaty. Ph: Mike Molloy. Mus: William Motzing. PD: David Copping. Ref: V 7/13/83. 1/19/83:4 (rated). Ecran F 36:42-3. with Alan Arkin, Christopher Lee, Kate Fitzpatrick, Bill Hunter, Graham Kennedy, Michael Pate.
Flying super-hero...hypno-ray...weird dwarf-assistant of the evil Mr. Midnight(Lee).

CAPTAIN SCARLET VS. THE MYSTERONS (B) ITC-TV 1982 puppets color 90m. Ref: TVG: Martian invasion. Sequel to 2 REVENGE OF THE MYSTERONS FROM MARS.

*CAPTIVE WILD WOMAN 1943 Story: also Maurice Pivar. Mkp: Jack Pierce. Ref: screen. TV. Lee. FM 66:23. V 4/28/43. Hirschhorn. Weldon. and with Ray Corrigan(ape).

Employing the cerebrum of one woman (Fay Helm) and secretions from the sex glands of another (Martha Vickers), a mad doctor (John Carradine) turns an ape, Cheela, into Paula Dupree (Acquanetta), whose power over lions impresses lion-tamer Milburn Stone: "You know we could use a girl like that around here!" Jealousy, however, causes Paula to revert to an ape-woman, then all the way back to the ape state....Preposterous package of stock footage/music/ideas irresponsibly splices old BIG CAGE footage and new circus-story footage to FRANKENSTEIN-crossed-with-CAT PEOPLE-derived scenes. Stone's physical resemblance to Clyde Beatty (the stock-shot star of the movie) was pretty obviously responsible for getting him his part. (He has no other apparent qualifications.) Carradine's transformation of the scruffy ape into the voluptuous Acquanetta is, unquestionably, the greatest scientific feat of all time. (Those sex hormones really worked.) All this and Evelyn Ankers too!

CARMILLA(by J.S. Le Fanu) see VAMPYR

2P CARNIVAL OF BLOOD Monarch/Kirt 1976(1970) color 90m. (DEATH RIDES A CAROUSEL-orig t) SP,D,P: Leonard Kirtman. Ph, Assoc D: David Howe. Mus: The Brooks Group;(elec) H. Crisman. Sets: Deborah Howe. Mkp: Troy Roberts. Ref: TV: WV Video. Willis/SW. V 5/12/71:203. Weldon. with Earle Edgerton(Tom), Judith Resnick, John Harris(aka Burt Young)(Gimpy), Eve Packer.

A madman--whose mother "hurt" him and his cuckolded father many years ago--covers his fire-scarred face with a rubber mask and kills "mommy" again and again by killing "selfish" and "demanding" women who patronize his Coney Island booth. He severs one woman's head during a horror-house ride; extracts eyes and tongue from another victim; and knifes a third, then pulls out some of her internal organs. (Either that, or she's carrying sausages in her handbag--camera angle and distance allow for some ambiguity.) He stuffs the collected body parts into a teddy bear.

The killer's psychological hangups here are certainly curious enough--this must be the only movie in which teddy bears function as sexual surrogates, and bear the brunt, so to speak, of all manner of human traumas. (One bear--not the madman's--gets painted black, out of spite; another loses its stuffings to anger.) The movie, in short, does not lack for macabre underpinnings--what it lacks is a script. To compensate, the actors improvise like mad and chew up running time nagging each other. Coney Island, here, seems a rather small amusement park: each couple visits the same three attractions. The gore effects, fortunately, are not at all convincing, and seem inspired by BLOOD FEAST--strange inspiration!

La CASA DE LAS SIETE TUMBAS (Arg.) 1981 D: Pedro Stocki. SP: Polverini, Real. Ref: IFG'83: The House of the Seven Tombs-tr t. Ecran F 33:47. with M.A. Sola, Soledad Silveyra.
"Horror and fantasy...lonely dark manor."(IFG)

CASA STREGATA, La see HAUNTED HOUSE

The CASE OF THE STUTTERING PIG WB 1937 anim 7m. (Porky Pig) D: Frank Tashlin. SP: M. Millar. Ref: "WB Cartoons." Lee. LC.
Horror parody..."Jekyll and Hyde formula."(WBC)

CASPER see BOO MOON. FRIENDLY GHOST, The.

CASTLE OF THE CARPATHIANS(by J.Verne) see MYSTERIOUS CASTLE IN THE CARPATHIANS, The

2 CAT PEOPLE RKO-Univ/Fries 1982 color 118m. Ph: John Bailey; (New Orleans) P.V. Brack. Mus: Giorgio Moroder;(lyrics) David Bowie. AD: Edward Richardson; Jack Taylor. SpVisFX: Albert Whitlock. SpMkpFX: Tom Burman;(art) Lance Anderson, Tom Hoerber et al;(wardrobe) Kathy Clark. SpFX: Tom del Genio, Pat Domenico, Karl Miller. VisCons: F. Scarfiotti. SpOptFX: Robert Blalack. SpArtifacts: Ellis Burman et al. Mattes:(art) Syd Dutton;(ph) Bill Taylor, D. Glouner. SpSdFX: Jack Manning. Ref: screen. V 3/24/82. MFB'82:156-7. Weldon. Ecran F 26:56-61 (J.-M.Lofficier),78. and with John Heard, Annette O'Toole, Lynn Lowry, Ed Begley Jr., Ruby Dee, Neva Gage(cat-woman).
The remake of the 1942 classic concerns an "incestuous race" of cat people, originating from human sacrifices to black leopards. The cats, apparently, assimilated the humans (psychically and physically) and are able to mate only with other cat people--or (yet more exclusive) only with closely-related cat people--since they generally revert, in sexual situations (or after tasting blood) to leopard form, and must kill to regain human form. Escape claws: cat people need not, it transpires, kill their lovers--anyone (or, apparently, any rabbit) will do. If any cat person of the opposite sex would do as a "safe" mate (safe for the mate, that is), then Irena Gallier (Nastassia Kinski) could fix up her incest-fixated brother, Paul (Malcolm McDowell), with the cat woman whom she meets in a cafe. But he insists that she is the one for him, whether out of personal whim or racial necessity is left unclear. And what to do when Irena falls for a mere human, Oliver Yates (John Heard)? He cannot kill her, as she begs him to. (Similar romantic-martyr pleas go unfulfilled, as they must, in horror movies from DAUGHTER OF DR. JEKYLL to The BEAST WITHIN.) Author Alan Ormsby has a more charming, mix-and-match idea in mind: the outcome of this sexual circuitousness is predicated on the facts that, a) Irena values pure love over sex and, b) Heard's zoo curator values other animals over humans. Labyrinthine are the ways of love....Ormsby's Arbitrary Rules of Order for Cat People, here, rather clog and confuse the narrative, though there are scat-

tered comic and lyrical moments. A Lubitsch-like comedy of cat manners was perhaps indicated.

Le CAUCHEMAR DU FANTOCHE (F) Gaumont 1908 anim short (aka The PUPPET'S NIGHTMARE. FANTOCHE'S NIGHTMARE) D: Emile Cohl. Ref: Lee. Crafton/BM: "strange hybrid monsters."

CAVEMAN INKI WB 1950 anim color 7m. D: Chuck Jones. Ref: LC. Maltin/OMAM. "WB Cartoons." no Lee.
"Monstrous, sabertoothed lion," caveman, dinosaurs.(WBC)

CAZADOR DE LA MUERTE see DEATHSTALKER

CAZADORES DE CABEZAS see SANTO CONTRA LOS CAZADORES DE CABEZAS

2 CEMETERY GIRLS Int'l. Amusements 1973 (COUNT DRACULA'S GREAT LOVE-TV cr t. DRACULA'S GREAT LOVE-TV ad t) Mus: C. Bernaola. AD: Cubero, Galicia. SpFX: Pablo Perez. Mkp: Emilio Puyol. Ref: TV. Weldon: aka VAMPIRE PLAYGIRLS? and with Julio Pena.
Count Dracula aka Dr. Kargos aka Dr. Marlowe seeks the love of a virgin to restore himself to "human existence," and the blood of an innocent to restore his daughter to life. He stakes an unruly member of his harem, allows the rest to perish in sunlight, and, in a ceremony, sucks the blood from the wound made by a "painless" dagger through the neck of his chosen one. He can materialize at will, and his brides can leap about magically....irrelevant vampire-man....Lively enough, but a real mess. Dracula figuratively goes through hell bringing together the requisite bodies, skeletons, and blood; and Karen still says "No!" (He then stakes himself.) This is a grand framework for a romantic comedy--and Paul Naschy's physiognomy suggests John Belushi-as-Dracula. But the movie yields only several quarts of fake blood and no laughs, although one scene--in which a male vampire and a female vampire attack each other--is either funny/ha-ha, funny/strange, or both. (They don't quite know what to make of the incident, and you may not either.) Violence and decolletage generally and unambiguously prevail.

CEREBRO INFERNAL, El see BLUE DEMON CONTRA CEREBROS INFERNALES

2P The CHAIN REACTION (Austral) WB/Palm Beach & VFC & AFC 1980 color 91m. SP,D: Ian Barry. Ph: Russell Boyd. Mus: Andrew T. Wilson;(elec) Spencer Lee; Chopin. AD: Graham Walker; L. Coote. SpFX: Reece Robinson. OptFX: Ken Hoffman. Mkp: L. Lamont-Fisher. Supertruck: Trick Pick-Ups. Ref: TV. Warren. V 4/23/80. Ecran F 33:67. with Steve Bisley, Ross Thompson, Arna-Maria Winchester, Ralph Cotterill, Lorna Lesley.
1977. A plutonium leak at nuclear power plant WALDO starts a chain reaction of contamination (from water to grass to cows to milk to humans) across the Australian countryside....Eerie enough to look at--ghost towns, headlights-in-the-rain, men in white suits and helmets, "reptilian" villains shot from low

angles. Easy enough to dismiss--everyone speaks in tones of ominous melodrama. You want these guys to take it a little bit easier. It's Armageddon, almost, but the movie needs some laid-back counterpoint. And amnesia is a rather hackneyed plot support....Some hit-and-run-level excitement with confrontations, escapes, chases.

CHAPPAQUA Regional & Minotaur(Rooks) 1966 b&w & color 82m. SP, D,P,with: Conrad Rooks. SpFX: ctr. Mkp: The Pipards. Ref: screen. Lee. AFI. Photon 19:45. with J.-L. Barrault et al.

Scattered fantasy/semi-horror scenes of the director/hero imagining himself as a cloaked, top-hatted, Lugosi-voiced vampire (ritualistically sucking blood from a woman's neck), or as dead and in a coffin, or imagining others as cadaverous-looking gentlemen....A limp series of psychedelic visions, by a moviemaker who seems to be imagining he's Fellini, and featuring what seems like a running parody of Howard Hawks cigarette-motifs.

CHARLIE BOY/THE THIRTEENTH REUNION see HAMMER HOUSE OF HORROR

CHASE THROUGH TIME see ALIENS FROM ANOTHER PLANET

CHATEAU DES CARPATHES(by J.Verne) see MYSTERIOUS CASTLE IN THE CARPATHIANS, The

CHAUDRON INFERNAL see INFERNAL CAULDRON, The

CHEECH AND CHONG'S NEXT MOVIE Univ/C&C Brown 1980 color 96m. (HIGH ENCOUNTERS OF THE ULTIMATE KIND-B) SpVisFX: Albert Whitlock. SpLaserFX: Laser Media;(cons) Linda Livingston. Min: Universal Hartland. Anim: Paul Power. Ref: TV: MCA Video. MFB'83:98-99. V 7/23/80.

Cheech and Chong pulled up on spaceship's light beam.... Cheech (with Chong hanging on) sent literally through the roof by "space coke," into space and an (animated) joint/spaceship.... Chong as Aztec-type god in Cheech's dream of sacrificial ritual (and near-necrophilia)....Another rambling wreck of a C&C comedy. They go into each scene or bit of business so cheerfully, though, that you keep expecting something really funny to develop, and expectation is better than nothing....

CHEECH AND CHONG'S STILL SMOKIN' see STILL SMOKIN'

CHILDREN OF THE FULL MOON/VISITOR FROM THE GRAVE see HAMMER HOUSE OF HORROR

CHRISTINE Col-Delphi/Richard Kobritz(Polar) 1983 color/ws 110m. D & Mus: John Carpenter. SP: Bill Phillips, from Stephen King's novel. Ph: Donald M. Morgan. Mus: also Alan Howarth. PD: Daniel Lomino. SpFX:(sup) Roy Arbogast;(foreman) Bill Lee; D.L. Simmons, E. Hui et al. MkpSup: Bob Dawn. Opt: Modern.

Ref: screen. SFExam 12/9/83. V 12/7/83. with Keith Gordon, John Stockwell, Alexandra Paul, Robert Prosky, Harry Dean Stanton, Roberts Blossom, William Ostrander, David Spielberg.

"What is it about that car?" Well, "her name's Christine," she's a 1958 Plymouth Fury (license number CQB 241), and "she's real sensitive." She responds so well to the love of her owner, a Rockbridge (Calif.) High student (Gordon), that she can wholly regenerate herself. Her "rejuvenation" is complete when her speedometer (which initially registers over 90,000 miles) brings itself back down, at the end, to "0." Christine runs down Arnie's "enemies" (generally without Arnie at the wheel), but becomes jealous of his girl friend, and tries to choke her to death. (Christine, also, plays only thematically-relevant rock 'n' roll tunes on her radio.) She seems to possess Arnie, and her jealousy expresses itself through him in hostility towards everyone. ("I don't think he's Arnie.")

If, physically, Christine is a beauty, psychologically, she's a mess. She's as neurotic--and dangerous--as the house in THIS HOUSE POSSESSED. And this movie is nearly as ridiculous as that one. (Christine also resembles, with her self-healing powers, another monster-house, the centerpiece of BURNT OFFERINGS.) It's getting more and more difficult to see John Carpenter as any sort of serious director. (DARK STAR is a long time ago now, and far, far away.) What self-respecting filmmaker would choose to make CARRIE Meets THE CAR? Here, Carpenter rips off even himself, with this new HALLOWEEN-like unstoppable monster. As in The THING(1982), the only worthwhile scenes involve special effects, and this time even they can't quite salvage the woebegone narrative. On a movie from which most authors might, understandably, want their names removed, Carpenter has his above the title....The script's most puzzling move is the transformation of Arnie into Mr. Hyde. He has already transformed (none too credibly) from schlemiel into Joe High-School. Obviously, the next step in such a weirdly-willed evolution is Monster. A strange fate for a regulation misunderstood-teenager....

A CHRISTMAS CAROL (Austral) (Showtime-TV)/Burbank Films 1982 anim color 72m. Anim:(d) Jean Tych;(sup) Warwick Gilbert. Adap: Alex Buzo, from Charles Dickens's story. Mus: Neil Thurgate. Storyboard: Steve Lumley. Ref: TV. TVG.

Voices: Robin Stewart, Bill Conn et al.

The usual ghosts, including the Death-like Christmas Yet To Come...sequence in which Marley dies, his face becomes a skull, and his spirit leaves his body...all-a-dream ending....Bare-minimum animation, with the characters little-more-animated than manniquins. Their listless "performances" make this one of the least compelling versions of the Scrooge story. And the pathos inherent in the latter is given rather-too-free rein. The score, though, is fair, and some of the artwork--the atmospheric exteriors, Marley's ghost's face--isn't bad.

See also: MICKEY'S CHRISTMAS CAROL.

CHRONOPOLIS (F) PdC-INA-AAA 1982 anim color 70m. SP,D,Des, Anim,Ph: Piotr Kamler. Mus: Luc Ferrari. Narr: Michel Lonsdale. Ref: V 7/28/82: "highly imaginative." Ecran F 40:25.
Immortals in a city-in-space "fabricate" time to overcome boredom.

CIAO MARZIANO (I) PAC 1979 SP,D: P.F. Pingitore. SP: also Castellacci. Ph: Carlo Carlini. Mus: Bocci, Gribanovski. Ref: Prod. Ital. with Pippo Franco, Silvia Dionisio.
Martian in Rome compelled to do as the Romans do.

La CITE FOUDROYEE 1922 70m. (*A CITY DESTROYED) Ph: Daniaux Johnston. AD: Robert Gys. Ref: screen. David Bradley. Lee.
1930. Richard Gallee, "le maitre de la foudre," has perfected an "infernal invention" based on the "conversion of natural electricity." With the backing of an industrialist, he sets out on a "monstrous project" to destroy Paris....As a prelude, he unleashes lightning (from "electrified clouds") on a city 30 miles away from Paris, setting the city aflame. His power proven, he commences to destroy The Eiffel Tower, La Gare du Nord, the Opera, etc....This vision of destruction proves, however, merely to be an illustration of a book; the "electric machine," a printing press....The 14 extant minutes of La CITE FOUDROYEE are more titles than film and are very scratchy and grainy. Even in this truncated version, however, the all-a-book, shaggy-dog ending seems dismayingly "clever."

CITY OF THE LIVING DEAD see GATES OF HELL, The

COBRA (J) Toho-Towa 1982 anim color feature Des: Studio Nue. Ref: V 8/4/82:35. JFFJ 14:11: based on a magazine comic series.
"Space pirate Cobra and his female android...."(JFFJ)

COLLISION COURSE see JOURNEY THROUGH THE BLACK SUN

*The COLOSSUS OF NEW YORK 1958 Mus: Van Cleave. Mkp: Wally Westmore. Process Ph: Farciot Edouart. Ref: TV. Lee. Weldon. with Ed Wolff(robot; voice: Ross Martin).
The eyes of a robot-with-a-human-brain can see everywhere, hypnotize humans, emit death rays....Pathetically-flimsy variation on FRANKENSTEIN and DONOVAN'S BRAIN. This time the monster-making scientist (Otto Kruger) uses a certifiably good brain (that of his genius-son), but it turns bad, as altruism sours and becomes nihilism. (Death, not food, is the son's final solution for the poor, in the script's one, unexpected stroke of perversity.) Why?--Dad, it seems, left out the soul. (The script waxes philosophical in the worst ways.) "Humanism" here is a pretext for horror, with soulless science as the boogey man. Neat titles-that-come-from-beneath-the-sea, though. (Cf. The MOLE PEOPLE and its titles-from-within-the-volcano.) And the "colossus" is pretty impressive-looking. Van Cleave provides frissons-via-piano.

The COMING Int'l. Films/Landsburg 1983(1980) color SP,D,P: Bert I. Gordon. Mus: Arthur Kempel. Ref: V 10/14/81:38(ad). 9/14/83:6: at Sitges. Weldon. with Susan Swift, Tisha Sterling, Albert Salmi, Guy Stockwell.
Spirit possession...evil parasite...time-leaping.

COMPUTERCIDE see FINAL EYE

CON CAPER AND THE CURSE OF RAVA see SPIDER-MAN

CONAN THE BARBARIAN Univ/De Laurentiis/Pressman-Conte 1982 color/ws 126m. SP,D: John Milius. SP: also Oliver Stone. Suggested by Robert E. Howard's "Conan" character. Ph: Duke Callaghan. Mus: Basil Poledouris. PD: Ron Cobb. SpFX:(sup) Nick Allder;(floor sup) George Gibbs;(mkp sup) Carlo de Marchis; (mkp) Colin Arthur;(mattes) Dennis Bartlett;(chief tech) Antonio Parra;(tech) Richard Conway, Ron Hone et al;(min) E.R. del Rio. SpVisFX: Frank Van Der Veer. Anim:(vis fx) Visual Concept, Peter Muran; Katherine Kean et al;(opt) RGB, J.H. Hagedorn. Tech Adv: L.Sprague de Camp. Ref: TV. V 3/17/82. MFB'82: 167-8. with Arnold Schwarzenegger, James Earl Jones, Max Von Sydow, Sandahl Bergman(Valeria), Cassandra Gaviola(witch), Mako(wizard), William Smith, Franco Columbu, Jack Taylor.
"An age undreamed-of...when the oceans drank Atlantis." 1,000-year-old sorcerer/snake-demon Thulsa Doom(Jones)... gigantic snakes...snakes-as-arrows...spell which repels wind-like spirits of death, restores Conan to life...witch-escaping-as-fireball...human stew...vision of the dead Valeria....Moderately-entertaining heroic epic. Revenge, as usual, is the primary motivation. Conan is the hero, out to revenge the deaths of his mother and (later) Valeria; Thulsa Doom is the villain, out to revenge the death of his pet monster-snake and the theft of a gem. "Epic" here seems to be a synonym for "simple," in dramatic terms, though Conan's vanquishing of Thulsa Doom proves a rather somber occasion--the sorcerer half-convinces him that he is (at least figuratively) Conan's father, his motivator. (Cf. the Darth Vader-Luke Skywalker relationship in the STAR WARS trilogy.) But Conan's momentary existential dilemma is ended by a sequel-is-threatening postscript-title. The epic dimensions of CONAN are most fully realized in the music; in some of the photography and effects (the swooping, animated wind-demons prove to be the film's imaginative highlight); and in Jones' performance. He gives lines like "Now they will learn why they fear the night" the authority they deserve. _Other_ actors give _other_ lines (e.g., "Two or three years ago it was just another snake cult") exactly what _they_ deserve too....One of Conan's aides does his crying for _him_; someone should have been designated to do his acting. If Schwarzenegger and Bergman have occasional affecting moments, it's almost in spite of their acting non-presences. If CONAN were a still, the two would be _perfect_....

CONQUEST (Sp-Mex-I) Di Clemente 1983 color 88m. (MACE IL FUORILEGGE) D: Lucio Fulci. SP: Gino Capone. Ph: Garcia Alonzo. Mus: Claudio Simonetti. Ref: Ecran F 36:46. V 10/20/82:115(ad). with George Rivero, Sabrina Siani.
Magician, Ocron, who rules an army of wolf-men...zombies.

The COOK IN TROUBLE (F) Famille Melies/Star 1904 7m. (SORCELLERIE CULINAIRE) Ref: screen. PFA notes 11/16/82.
Slighted sorcerer unleashes horde of devils on cook and assistants; they cook the cook in stewpot. Fast and furious Georges Melies short, with demons popping in and out of stewpots, stoves, and boxes. (They pop in and out of the pots; the cook is only popped in.) Macabre farce so deft and inventive it's exhilarating.

COSMIC PRINCESS (B) Group Three/ITC-TV 1976(1982) color 90m. D: Charles Crichton, Peter Medak. SP: Johnny Byrne, Charles Woodgrove. Two episodes ("The Metamorph" & "Space Warp") from the "Space 1999" TV series. Mus: Derek Wadsworth; Barry Gray. AD: M. Ford, D. Gregg. SpFX: Brian Johnson;(lighting) Nick Allder;(ph) David Litchfield;(elec) M.S.E. Downing. Anim: Dolphin. P: Fred Freiberger. Ref: TV. TVG. "Fantastic TV." with Catherine Schell(Maya), Martin Landau, Barbara Bain, Brian Blessed, Anouska Hempel, Nick Tate.
Moonbase Alpha vs. the ruler of a planet who "feeds" space travelers' minds to a "biological computer." Their zombie-like bodies are then used to work his mines. "Molecular transformation" turns his daughter, Maya, into, variously, a bird, a dog, an ape, a monster, and another, worse monster; turns one creature and several weapons to stone....energy light-bubble... disappearing spaceships..."graveyard of spaceships"..."space warp"...ship with magnetic energy....Old TV shows, unfortunately, in this case, never die. The actors' almost-comically-earnest dramatics are, finally, neither comic nor dramatic--although camp is achieved, briefly, with the spectacle of the ghastly-monster-Maya running about the surface of the moon in slow motion. The latter sequence is pretty certainly not supposed to be comical--her powers of transformation are not controllable and are intended to be werewolf-tragic....

COUNT DRACULA'S GREAT LOVE see CEMETERY GIRLS

COUNTDOWN TO DISASTER (B) ITC-TV 1981 puppets color 90m. SpFX: Derek Meddings, Brian Johnson. Ref: TVG.
Sequel to 2 THUNDERBIRDS ARE GO.

CRACKLE OF DEATH ABC-TV/Univ-TV & Francy 1974 color 94m. D: Don Weis, Alex Grasshoff. SP,Story: Bill S. Ballinger, Arthur Rowe. SP: also Rudolph Borchert. From "The Night Stalker" TV series. Ph: R.W. Browne. Mus: Jerry Fielding, Luchi De Jesus. AD: Raymond Beal. Ref: TV. TVG. "TV Drama Series." with Darren McGavin, Philip Carey, Simon Oakland, William Smith, Elaine

Giftos, Tom Drake, Joyce Jillson, Robert Cornthwaite, Fred Beir.
Two TV shows interwoven: "The Doppelganger": the doppelganger of a dead arsonist attempts to take over the life and/or body of an orchestra conductor; appears to others as an "optical illusion" and causes the bodies of the conductor's associates to ignite. "Matchemonedo": an ancient, invisible bear-god wreaks havoc in Chicago's new Lakefront Hospital, causing earth tremors, cracks in the walls, and soaring temperatures. It appears that the diversion of cold lake-waters has brought Matchemonedo out of hibernation. The plasma of its victims congeals, leaving a "tar-like substance"--this old bear, apparently, "breathes in" pure energy, in the form of either plasma or electricity. Its appearance is captured, accidentally, on X-rays which, when assembled, reveal a huge eye....

Another case of a couple of old TV shows willed into "movie" form. The doppelganger story features "previews" of the hospital story, while dialogue references to the doppelganger are oh-so-subtly cut in to the hospital episode. (McGavin's Kolchak, narrating: "It must be my destiny to die by fire--first the doppelganger and now this Matchemonedo.") The bear-god story is a terrible piece of legend-mongering, a clear cut or two below the level of its companion piece, though in both stories everyone (not just Kolchak) seems to be glib-tongued, or exasperated with glibness, or both. Everyone has the same shtik. The doppelganger itself, however, is both kind of eerie and, in its near-prankishness, amusing. At one point, it appears at several church windows at once, as, in effect, a triple or quadrupleganger.

CRASHER JOE (J) Fuji 1983 anim 120m. Ref: V 4/6/83:37: sf.

*CREATURE FROM THE BLACK LAGOON 1954 (BLACK LAGOON-orig t) Story: Maurice Zimm;(uncred.) Jack Arnold? Mus sc: H.J. Salter. D:(underwater) James C. Havens. SpPh: Charles S. Welbourne. SpMkp: Bud Westmore, Jack Kevan, Millicent Patrick et al. Ref: screen. TV. Jim Shapiro. Warren/KWTS! LC. Hirschhorn.

"There are many strange legends in the Amazon"--the main one concerns "a man who lived underwater," a "gill-man" or "man-fish," a "demon" or "monster." The fossilized hand of just such a link between land and sea creatures is found in a limestone deposit (dating from the Devonian period), in the Amazon jungle, where life is "exactly as it was 150 million years ago." The bulk of the deposit has been washed into the Black Lagoon, where an expedition from the Instituto de Biologia Maritima searches for further fossil fragments....Its members find a live gill-man, who becomes fascinated with one of their number (Julie Adams) and attempts to abduct her....

The original CREATURE feature is still worth seeing for its 3-D effects--in 3-D, underwater bubbles are amazing. The Creature himself (Ben Chapman and, underwater, Ricou Browning) is rather over-exposed in this, his first film. He's onscreen so much that he wears out his welcome. We first see him as a finned claw reaching out of the water...by the end of the movie, this here-comes-the-claw business has become either a motif or a cliche, it's used so often. There's no plot as such: they go after the Creature; the Creature goes after them. His fascination with Kay never really gets beyond the voyeurism stage. There's always a human (with rifle or harpoon-gun) around. The dialogue scenes in this movie are dead long before the Creature is--Richard Carlson pontificates about "the water and its secrets"; Richard Denning talks about money and glory; Julie Adams screams. Salter's score is alternately atmospheric and schlocky; the movie as a whole is generally just schlocky, despite the lyrical-erotic scenes of the Creature making his own "find" (Kay).

See also: CREATURE WALKS AMONG US, The and REVENGE OF THE CREATURE (sequels), and DOS FANTASMAS Y UNA MUCHACHA. OCTAMAN. 2 MUNSTERS' REVENGE, The.

*The CREATURE WALKS AMONG US 1956 Mus sc: Henry Mancini. SpPh: Clifford Stine. Mkp: Bud Westmore;(sp) Millicent Patrick, Jack Kevan. Ref: TV. Warren/KWTS! Jim Shapiro. Hirschhorn.

The Creature from the Black Lagoon (Ricou Browning) is alive & well & living in the Florida Everglades, after surviving REVENGE OF THE CREATURE. Captured by a scientific expedition when his gills are burnt off, he is converted from a sea to a land creature (played by Don Megowan) employing a set of standby lungs with which to breathe....As Bill Warren notes, the science here is rather loopily labyrinthine in its logic, and it's just a means to an end--a semi-allegorical inquiry into the nature of the human condition--an end which proves just as loopy as the means. As geneticist Rex Reason notes, "We all stand between the jungle and the stars." The Creature becomes the Metaphor from the Black Lagoon, representing the jungle in us, while, for their part, the characters themselves make jungle noises associated with jealousy, hate, and violence. The Creature, even, at one highly-significant point, breaks out of its cabin just as Gregg Palmer begins to assault Leigh Snowden. The ending is ambiguous, or simply confused. Jeff Morrow opines that "the beast remains a beast"; but Reason seems to prevail: the Creature returns to the sea, but semi-domesticated in that it kills only when provoked. The irony is that, after all this to-do, the best scenes remain the ones at the beginning with the pre-land Creature. They more or less recapitulate earlier sequences in the series--a "raptures of the deep" "ballet" with Ms. Snowden substitutes here for the underwater eroticism with Julie Adams in CREATURE FROM THE BLACK LAGOON--but for once repetition proves more fruitful than variation. Mancini's lulling, enticing wonders-of-the-Everglades music complements suspenseful play with various-sized, menacing (and non-menacing) blips on the sonar screen. (Three of the blips are divers, but the fourth...?) Even here, however, lines like "You can't bypass nature!" break up the mood above-water, and the Creature's three-note, musical "signature" blare breaks the mood underwater.

CREATURE WASN'T NICE, The see SPACESHIP

CREEPERS see BLOODY BIRTHDAY

CREEPSHOW WB/UFD/Laurel 1982 color 129m. D: George Romero. SP & with: Stephen King. Ph: Michael Gornick. Mus: John Harrison. SpScenicFX,PD: Cletus Anderson. SpMkpFX: Tom Savini; Darryl Ferrucci et al. Anim: Anivision. Art:(spectre) Ron Frenz;(comic) Jack Kamen. FX:(green) Bill Bilowit, Jan Foster; (drowning) Ed Fountain. Des:(graphic) Larry Fulton;(titles) Bob Woolcot, The Animators. Opt: Computer Opticals, Plastrick. Ref: screen. V 5/26/82. MFB'82:260-1. with Hal Holbrook, Fritz Weaver, Adrienne Barbeau, Leslie Nielsen, Carrie Nye, E.G. Marshall, Viveca Lindfors, John Amplas(Nathan's corpse).

"Voodoo doll" vignette (with spectre and doll) framing five stories: 1) "Father's Day": living corpse returns to claim human-head cake; 2) "The Lonesome Death of Jody Verrill": plant-life-form from meteorite overruns man (King), house, yard, etc.; vision in mirror; 3) "Something To Tide You Over": living corpses return from sea to exact revenge on murderer; 4) "The Crate" (from King's short story): ape-monster found in crate leftover from 1834 Arctic expedition; 5) "They're Creeping up on You": warped old man besieged, finally invaded bodily by hordes of cockroaches; cockroach-in-blender _hommage_ to The GIANT SPIDER INVASION.

Handsomely-mounted tribute to Fifties horror comics recalls similar Amicus omnibus horrors of a decade ago, and is similarly pretty vacuous, though there are at least more laughs and gasps this time around. At the center of all segments except, perhaps, the second: the mechanics of revenge. And although the latter are especially ingenious in the first half of story number three, even _there_ they're still just _mechanics_. Revenge is a waiting game for both revenger _and_ viewer--as if aware of this dramatic limitation, Romero and King are always livening things up (in mid-anecdote) with incidental frissons and chuckles. The most desperate (and yet amusing) of these diversionary ploys are Holbrook's professor's Walter Mitty-like revenge daydreams in "The Crate"; while Nielsen, Weaver, and King come up with the best diversionary _actors'_-ploys, and make their stories' non-suspense bearable. Romero and King make little more of their slender tales than did the Amicus people of _theirs_, though the material--hate, frustration, bitterness--would seem, on one level, to be suited to Romero, who seems genuinely drawn to the themes of melancholy and unhappiness. But here he and King make jokes of these themes. Romero--usually too serious for his own good--is here too flippant. CREEPSHOW is more likable than are his other films, but it's also more disposable. MARTIN and The CRAZIES may be rather unpleasant and largely unsuccessful, but they do leave a residue of sadness and regret. Romero seems to keep his sense of drama and his sense of humor in separate containers. (Even when--as in DAWN OF THE DEAD--he employs both in the same film.) The only moments of feeling in CREEPSHOW belong to an aging woman (Lindfors) lamenting over wasted lives beside the grave of the despised uncle she murdered. His moldering arm pops out of the ground (a terrific "bus"), and it's back to mechanics--although this revenging corpse is comically insistent, growling only "I want my cake!" as he dispatches his relatives. The "Jody Verrill" segment offers the movie's only respite from revenging corpses and cockroaches. In it, this grass from outer space simply grows and grows, all over poor, luckless Jody's hands, face, tongue, living room, and porch. Nothing he can do about it. The plant's the thing here. Romero seems to have been carried away by the pictorial potential of the subject, and this odd grass-amok idyll is a real visual curiosity, a vision of a rampant nature reclaiming the land from civilization--not over a period of time, in years or decades, but in hours. This is the vegetable version of The MONOLITH MONSTERS.

CRIES IN THE NIGHT see FUNERAL HOME

CRIME AU CIMETIERE ETRUSQUE (F-I) Leitienne 1982 color 90m. (ASSASSINO AL CIMETERO ETRUSCO) D: Christian Plummer. Ref: Ecran F 36:76. with Elvire Audray, Paolo Malco, John Saxon, Marilu Tolo, C. Cassinelli, Wandisa Guida, Van Johnson.
Immortal Etruscan priestess...eerie cemetery.

La CRUZ DEL DIABLO (Sp) Bulnes 1974 color 97m. D: John Gilling. SP: Jacinto Molina, J.J. Porto, from G.A. Becquer's novels. Ph: Fernando Arribas. SpFX: Pablo Perez. Mkp: Cristobal Criado. Ref: Ecran F 31:56: unofficial fifth in the "Blind Dead" series. with Carmen Sevilla, Adolfo Marsillach, Emma Cohen, Eduardo Fajardo, Monica Randall, Tony Isbert.
A brutal murder at an inn is linked with the Templars (who appear in a dream sequence).

CRY FOR THE STRANGERS CBS-TV 1982 color 92m. D: Peter Medak. SP: J.D. Feigelson, from John Saul's novel. Ref: Cinef XIII:6. TVG 12/11/82. with Patrick Duffy, Cindy Pickett, Brian Keith.
"Lurid legends" and "raging storms" on the coast of Washington.(TVG)

CRYPT OF DARK SECRETS Majestic Int'l.(Jack Weis) 1976 color 71m. (cf. MARDI GRAS MASSACRE) Ref: TVFFSB. Bill Warren. Cinef. Stanley. Ecran 22:55: sfa LOUISIANA SWAMP MURDERS? with Maureen Chan, Ronald Tanet.
2,000-year-old Aztec goddess haunts house in the bayous.

CUJO WB/Taft Ent./Blatt-Singer(Sunn Classics) 1983 color 94m. D: Lewis Teague. SP: Don Carlos Dunaway, Lauren Currier, from Stephen King's novel. Ph: Jan De Bont. Mus: Charles Bernstein. PD: Guy Comtois. SpVisFX:(mkp) Peter Knowlton; Bob Clark, David Nelson et al;(mkp asst) Michael Lavalley. SpFX: Rick Josephsen.

Opt: Modern;(fx) Cinema Research, Peter Donen. Title: Cimarron;(anim) Ruxton. Ref: screen. SFChron 8/15/83. V 8/17/83. Jim Shapiro. MFB'83:301-2. with Dee Wallace, Daniel Hugh-Kelly, Danny Pintauro, Ed Lauter, Christopher Stone, Kaiulani Lee.

"There's no such things as real monsters." There is, however, a monstrous, rabid Saint Bernard terrorizing the community of Castle Rock, Maine, and a mother and her small son become trapped for one day, two days...inside a stalled car outside an isolated house, as the dog lurks, and every little noise upsets it....JAWS reference....You want harrowing, you got harrowing. CUJO is a NIGHT OF THE LIVING DEAD or The TEXAS CHAIN SAW MASSACRE for the masses. Like its eponymous canine, it goes for the jugular. This is not quite a recommendation, not quite a warning, but a bit of both. CUJO is what Parents' Magazine used to call good of kind, the kind here being the siege horror-movie, which may not be everyone's favorite kind of horror movie. This subspecies reduces or (to employ a less prejudicial term) narrows its subject to a situation. What might, in the storyline of another movie, be just one step--a payoff sequence, no more--becomes half the film. CUJO, however, plays fairer than NIGHT or TEXAS. It doesn't depend (like the former) on continually-wrangling protagonists or (like the latter) on an eternally-screaming heroine, to keep the audience on edge in-between onslaughts. Its people even sleep when possible. The horror is concentrated, but the characters are allowed to breathe. (No wordplay--the boy is asthmatic--intended.) The image of the rabid dog is, of course, an objective correlative for family problems--there's even a cut, at one point, from a shot of the trapped-boy's father simmering, to a shot of Cujo festering (after being bitten by the rabid bat). The family problems are, however, unimaginatively sketched. (The boy's fear of the dark is more-satisfyingly described than are they.) It's only with their poetically-licensed metamorphosis into "real monsters"--the quotidian spectres of Cujo's viciousness, the boy's fits, and the rejected-lover's rampage (one horror echoing the other)--that they take on any emotional force. And force meets force, as the mother (Wallace) takes a baseball bat to poor Cujo (bats just don't agree with him): the woman with the bat (see also The SHINING) is becoming the primal Stephen King image, at least in film adaptations of his books....

*2 CURSE OF THE HEADLESS HORSEMAN DLM 1972(1971) 80m. SP,P: Kenn Riche. Ph: Henning Schellerup. SpFX: Harry Woolman. Mkp: Bud Miller. SdFX: Jon Davison. Ref: TV: Cultvideo. and with Don Carrara, Claudia Ream, B.G. Fisher(Solomon), Margo Dean, Lee Byers, Joe Cody.

"The curse begins again": a doctor inherits a ranch located in a valley said to be haunted by a headless horseman. "Soon it will be night. There will be a moon...a special moon," and according to the cadaverous old caretaker, Solomon, the horseman will ride and seek to satisfy his "unending need for revenge" on eight gunmen. He apparently does ride; but two fake headless horsemen confuse matters....At any rate, one of these three rides around splattering people with blood from the severed head which he carries with him. ("Somebody threw some blood at me!") The principal fake horseman dies, but the (apparently) real one rides off at the end....

Rudimentary filmmaking. The script doesn't even make it clear why the horseman is tracking the eight gunfighters--the narrator says something to the effect that they murdered him, but all we seem to see is a shootout in which the eight kill each other off. Nor is it made clear exactly which horseman it is that's splattering everybody. And the feckless plot cancels itself out, at the end, by proffering both supernatural and logical explanations for the mysterious goings-on. The movie is a series of long, virtually unedited takes, with a soundtrack consisting of not-always-audible dialogue, hokey horror-narration, and miscellaneous music and songs. Smoke and reports from gunshots are not even in synch, and some of the end credits are blurry almost to unreadability. (No, the blurriness is probably not intentional, though from the standpoint of incrimination, it certainly ought to have been....)

CURSED MEDALLION, The see NIGHT CHILD

CURTAINS (Can.) Jensen Farley/Simcom & Guardian Trust(Curtains) 1983(1982) color 89m. D: Jonathan Stryker(rn: Richard Ciupka). SP: Robert Guza Jr. Ph: Robert Paynter; Fred Guthe. Mus: Paul Zaza. AD: Roy Forge Smith; Barbara Matis. SpFxD: Colin Chilvers. Prosth: Greg Cannom; Jeffrey Kinney. OptFX: Optical House. Ref: screen. V 4/20/83. MFB'83:212. Ecran F 36:40: 1980? with John Vernon, Samantha Eggar, Linda Thorson, Annie Ditchburn, Lesleh Donaldson, Lynne Griffin, Jo-Anne Hannah.

An actress (Eggar) has herself committed to an insane asylum in order to get "inside" her new role. She gets too far inside....Her director (Vernon) invites six actresses to his estate to audition for the starring role, in her place. They are systematically murdered by someone (Hannah) in an old-hag horror mask....Considered in "classical" thriller terms, CURTAINS is a variation on the relatives-gathering-at-old-house-for-reading-of-old-geezer's-will mystery--"And then there were four," as the director here notes at one point. In more-contemporary terms, this is simply a variation on the six-women-stalked shocker. In neither mode does it offer much new or of interest. It does, however, at least promise something--in the form of "charades." The title is of course a double entendre, literally referring to theatre curtains, figuratively to death; the name of the story's director is also the name of the film's; and there are at least five "scenes" in the film which prove to be characters' acts, nightmares, or auditions. There's also a reversal on this "it's only a performance" trick--an overheard exchange of words, passed off by the exchangers as a scene from a play. And Eggar performs her opening stage-scene for real, later in the film. These elaborate theatre-and-life stunts seem to be preparing us for something more than the triviality of the final revelations....It's just a killer-on-the-loose story after all.

D'ENTRE LES MORTS(by Boileau-Narcejac) see VERTIGO

DIH (Yugos.) Viba 1983 color 113m. (aka A BREATH OF AIR) D: Bozo Sprajc. SP: Zeljko Kozinc. Ph: V. Perko. Mus: Jani Golob. AD: Jani Kovic. Ref: V 8/17/83. with Draga Potocnjak, Ivo Ban, Milena Zupancic.
"Futuristic 1990s....about newly born children dying of a mysterious lung infection....run-of-the-mill scifier...."

DAFFY RENTS WB 1966 anim color 7m. D: R. McKimson. Ref: "WB Cartoons." LC. no Lee.
"Monster giant rat."(WBC)

DAIJOOBU, MAI FURENDO (J) Toho/Kitty 1983 color 119m. SP,D: Ryu Murakami. Ph: Kozo Okazaki. Mus D: K. Katoh. AD: Osamu Yamaguchi. Ref: V 5/25/83. Ecran F 33:71. with Peter Fonda, Jinpachi Nezu, Reona Hirota.
Sf-allegory: superstrong spaceman (Fonda) vs. exponents of the conventional...lobotomized "robot."

The DAMNATION OF FAUST Famille Melies 1903 (*FAUST IN HELL) Ref: screen. PFA notes 11/16/82.
Mephistopheles torments Faust with visions of a huge, monstrous, tentacled head, satan (winged), dancing girls, and demons. A Melies curiosity only, though the appearance on the scene of the monster-head is a startler.

DANCE OF THE DWARFS (U.S.-Fili) Dove & Panache 1983 color 93m. D: Gus Trikonis. SP,P: Michael Viner. SP: also G.W. King, Larry Johnson. From Geoffrey Household's novel. Ph: Michael Butler;(aerial) David Butler. Mus: Perry Botkin;(songs) Snuff. AD: R.A. Nicdao. SpMkpFX: Craig Reardon. SpFX:(sup) Teofilo Hilario; Jun Santiago, Narciso Tolentino, Andy Aturba. ProsthFX: Altered Image. SpSdFX: Gary Chang. Titles:(des) Dan Curry; Modern. Ref: TV. V 3/31/82:34. with Deborah Raffin, Peter Fonda, John Amos, Carlos Palomino; "Turko" Cervantes, Cherron Hoye, Gil Arceo(creatures).
"There are many terrible things out there!" "There" is the Philippine jungle, and the "things" are "dwarfs...devils... spooks...devil's children...." "They come only at night" and "feed on living blood and flesh." The devil-creatures are "possibly prehistoric," and look like gargoyles only Godzilla could love. They have glowing red eyes and rudimentary wings, yet don't fly or climb....Apart from the facts that they're not

dwarfs and they don't dance, the title is dandy. Fonda plays, roughly, Bogart; Raffin plays, roughly, Hepburn, but AFRICAN QUEEN this isn't. It isn't even RAIDERS OF THE LOST ARK, though that movie seems to be the immediate inspiration--action and adventure capped by fantasy. Music and photography aren't bad, but the movie only marks time until the creatures appear, at the end. There seems, then, to be a touch or two of stop motion; mainly, though, men-in-suits effects. But after an hour or so of the Fonda and Raffin characters any sort of monster would be welcome.

DANCING ON THE MOON Para/Fleischer 1935 anim color 7m. D: Dave Fleischer. Anim: Kneitel, Crandall. Mus: Tobias, Mencher. Ref: screen. PFA(flyer). Charles Hopkins. Lee. LC.

The rocket-plane-like "Honeymoon Express to the Moon" takes off from Earth up an ordinary playground-slide, and carries a Noah's Ark-like ship of animal-couples to the moon, for an hour of dancing. (No cover, no spacesuits.) Delightfully silly animated lunacy. On their way to the moon, the honeymooners stick their heads out the rocket windows and sing a chorus of the title tune. Comic pathos is provided by a downcast, top-hatted cat whose sweetheart gets left behind on Earth. He resorts to solitaire, knitting, etc. The combination of foreground animation and vivid-colored background models is enchanting. Top Fleischer.

DANGUARD ACE see SHOGUN WARRIORS: DANGUARD ACE

The DARING YOUNG MAN Col 1942 73m. (BROWNIE-orig t) D: Frank Strayer. SP: Karen De Wolf, Connie Lee. Ph: Franz Planer. Mus: John Leipold. AD: Lionel Banks. Ref: Bill Warren. LC. TV. Maltin/TVM. Academy. V 3/18/43. (d)6/16/42. HR 3/18/43. MPH 12/19/42. with Joe E. Brown, Marguerite Chapman, William Wright, Claire Dodd, Lloyd Bridges, Don Douglas, R.E. Keane, Robert Middlemass, Arthur Lake(Dagwood), Minerva Urecal, Irving Bacon, Philip Van Zandt, Danny Mummert, Carl Stockdale.

"Radio-controlled bowling ball...insures a strike at every toss."(MPH) Typical Joe E. Brown comedy.

The DARK CRYSTAL (B-U.S.) Univ & AFD/ITC/Henson-Kurtz 1982 color/ws 92m. Story,D,P & with: Jim Henson. D & with: Frank Oz. SP: David Odell. Ph: Oswald Morris;(mattes) Neil Krepela. Mus: Trevor Jones. PD: Harry Lange. Concep Des: Brian Froud. SpVisFX: Roy Field, Brian Smithies. MechFX:(sup) Ian Wingrove; (d) Smithies;(ph) Paul Wilson;(des) Leigh Donaldson et al. Creature Devel:(des) Froud;(sup) Sherry Amott. Chief Modeller: Allan Moss. SpSdFX: Ben Burtt. OptFxD: Richard Dimbleby. WireFX: Bob Harman. Mattes: Mike Pangrazio, Chris Evans, Industrial Light & Magic. Narr: Joseph O'Conor. Ref: screen. V 12/15/82. VV 1/11/83:50. MFB'83:39-40. Hirschhorn. with Kathryn Mullen, Dave Goelz, Brian Muehl;(voices) Stephen Garlick, Billie Whitelaw, Lisa Maxwell.

Another world, another time: the good Mystics and bad Skeksis become one at the Great Conjunction of the three suns--1,000 years after the Dark Crystal lost a shard and tore the world asunder....Adam-and-Eve-like Gelfling couple...beetle-crab-like Garthim monsters...Podlings...round, dog-like pet...dream-fasting (i.e., memory-stimulation by touch)...living "dessert" at Skeksis feast...slaves, creatures drained of their living-essence through exposure to the reflection of the Crystal--the liquid residue then offered as a drink to the Skeksis emperor...old hag with removable eyeball and mechanical scale-model of the heavenly bodies...landstriders...little crab-creatures, scamperers, dragonfly-whirlybirds, carrot-bunch creatures...huge, caterpillar-like bog creature (friendly)...crystal bats (spies, unfriendly)...living trees...living roots...various animals-in-and-out-of-cages.

The DARK CRYSTAL is, by all odds, the most densely-and-delightfully-populated other-universe of creatures since Starevitch's The MAGIC CLOCK, and _that_ takes us back to 1926. It is, in effect, an unending roll call of unearthly Muppets, and, as such, constitutes one of the more imaginative deployments of men-(and hands)-in-suits creations in fantasy films. (_Pace_, Godzilla.) The range of creation encompasses all kinds of animal fur, animal noises, modes of locomotion and flying, and miscellaneous flora, fauna, and points in-between. The powerful but rather indiscriminate _Garthim_ (assigned to capture Gelflings, they succeed in bagging everything but) invariably loom up, en masse, along the whole width of the wide screen. They are Imposing. At the other end of the pictorial scale are the various _scurriers_, scamperers, and whatnot, which scoot by, almost unnoticed, in the background, or around the edges of the screen. They are Unobtrusive, and yet very endearing. These incidental Muppets give this world visual depth. They make you wonder what's in _back_ of the background. The _caged things_ which haunt the shadowy recesses of the Skeksis' detention room are only glimpsed, tantalizingly, just long enough to make you wonder if forms so diverse could all come from this one world. (Perhaps some are imported....) Even when these creatures manage to break out (at the mystic summons of the winged, female Gelfling) they move so quickly that you can't quite pin them down, morphologically-speaking. The _Skeksis_ are more problematic. They look like overdressed vultures and are, graphically, so complicated that they tend towards becoming, simply, large blurs. The _Gelflings_ are simpler and sweeter. And yet _all_ of the main characters, or creatures--Gelflings, Skeksis, and Mystics--are onscreen long enough both to _absorb_ and _dispel_ our fascination. They are not quite engaging enough, visually, to compensate for their dramatic mere-adequacy; they're stronger on design than personality. They lack the emotional, or expressive, range of good actors, and, in truth, figure in a narrative which is, for the most part, stuck at the good-against-evil level. The DARK CRYSTAL is eminently satisfying as spectacle; only passable--although devilishly inventive--as narrative. It takes a ton of Muppets to shore up weak points in the story. The prevailing mood is almost somber--as if the idea of myth were holy, and this myth's component parts icons. And yet the movie is generally a joy to watch--it need not be taken as seriously as it perhaps yearns to be.

DARK EYES see SATAN'S MISTRESS

DARK NIGHT OF THE SCARECROW CBS-TV/Wizan 1981 color 93m. D: Frank De Felitta. Story,SP: Julius D. Feigelson. Story: also Butler Handcock. Ph: Vincent Martinelli. Mus: Glenn Paxton. AD: C.M. Zacha Jr. SpFX: Cliff Wenger. Mkp: Jeremy Swan. Opt: CFI. Ref: TV. TVG 10/24/81. with Charles Durning, Lane Smith, Robert F. Lyons, Jocelyn Brando, Larry Drake(Bubba).

Murdered man (Drake) returns as avenging scarecrow; uses thresher, silo, tractor, and pitchfork as weapons against his killers. Witless, overheated revenge melodrama. Poor-to-reprehensible.

A DATE WITH THE FALCON (UA-TV)/RKO 1941 63m. D: Irving Reis. SP: Lynn Root, Frank Fenton, based on Michael Arlen's "Falcon" books. Ph: Robert DeGrasse. Mus: Paul Sawtell. AD: Albert D'Agostino, Al Herman. Ref: TV. TVFFSB. LC. with George Sanders, Wendy Barrie, Allen Jenkins, James Gleason, Mona Maris, Frank Moran, Hans Conried, Victor Kilian, Elizabeth Russell.

An inventor creates perfect synthetic diamonds, in this generally shrill comedy-mystery. Sanders has a few amusing scenes as The Falcon, but is, basically, painfully impish. And with Jenkins, Barrie, and Gleason all feigning comic exasperation with him, it gets a bit wearing.

The DAWN EXPRESS PRC/M&A 1942 63m. (NAZI SPY RING-alt t) D: Albert Herman. SP: Arthur St. Claire. Ph: Eddie Linden. Mus D: Lee Zahler. Sets: James Altwell? Ref: TV. "B" Movies. no FDY. V 6/10/42. Academy. LC. with Michael Whalen, Anne Nagel, William Bakewell, Constance Worth, Jack Mulhall, Hans von Twardowski, Kenneth Harlan, Robert Fraser, George Pembroke.

Chemist's formula-3-11 chemical compound, when added to gas, doubles the latter's effectiveness; formula 3-b-11 (one half of 3-11), mixed improperly, explodes....nightmare sequence....The Herman touch--familiar to fans of The CLUTCHING HAND--pervades here too. With campier, less mundane material, in fact, this too could have been a "classic." Herman's mise-en-scene belongs to the Sinister Glances and Counter-Glances School, and includes some rather elaborate "three cushion" shots, predicated on the Herman theory that if a shot of one spy lurking adds a little mystery and suspense to a scene, then three shots of three spies makes it positively Hitchcockian....Herman's use of reaction shots would be more appropriate for comedy, though it could be argued that this is comedy.

See also: DON'T GET ME WRONG. FREE FOR ALL. HOT MONEY. OLD MOTHER RILEY'S GHOSTS.

2 DAWN OF THE MUMMY (U.S.-Egy.?) 1981 color 94m. SP,D,P: Frank Agrama. SP,Story: Daria Price, Ronald Dobrin. Ph: Sergio Rubini. Mus: Shuki Y. Levy. AD: M.A. Nour. SpFX: Luigi Batistelli, F.A. Hai, Tony DiDio Jr. Mkp:(des) M. Trani; Hassan Taha. SdFX: Intersound;(des) David R. Thornton. Ref: TV: Thorn EMI Video. V 1/6/82. with Brenda King, Barry Sattels, John Salvo, Joan Levy.

Egypt. Robbers, photographers, and models violate the tomb of the mummy Sefirama(sp?), who died in 3,000 B.C. The mummy's entrails (kept in an urn) spill and burn a woman's hand; the mummy rises ("I saw the mummy alive!"); then his "armies of the dead" rise too. The head mummy applies a butcher knife to a butcher, then hangs him on a meathook. His hand burns the flesh of his victims. The mummies invade the town, en masse, and break up a marriage ceremony, eating their victims as they go....Uninspired--then again, when was the last time you saw an inspired mummy movie? DAWN OF THE MUMMY is no more likely than TIME WALKER to spark a mummy-movie revival. Thank goodness, one might add. DAWN is simply an old Universal monster film, plus gore, and has just one legitimate shock--the just-revived mummy sitting straight up, abruptly, in the foreground. (Our attention was on a figure in the background of the shot....) Never mind how a New York fashion-magazine crew winds up in the tomb of an ancient Egyptian prince, or king--you wouldn't believe it.

The DAY AFTER ABC-TV/R.A. Papazian 1983 color 125m. D: Nicholas Meyer. SP: Edward Hume. Ph: Gayne Rescher; Chronicle Prods. Mus: David Raksin. PD: Peter Wooley. SpFX: Robert Blalack, Praxis; Robert Dawson. SpPhotoFX: Movie Magic. Mkp: Mike Westmore; Zoltan Elek. SdDes: Frank Serafine. Opt: CFI. Ref: TV. TVG 11/19/83. SFExam 10/14/83. 3/5/84:A1,A9. SFChron 11/18/83. V 11/23/83:102. with Jason Robards, John Cullum, JoBeth Williams, John Lithgow, William Allen Young, Steven Guttenberg, Bibi Besch, Calvin Jung, Jeff East, Stephen Furst.

"What if it does happen?"--"it" being nuclear war. Berlin is blockaded; Moscow evacuated; West Germany invaded. Soon, there are "over 300 missiles inbound" toward the U.S., and perhaps as many "on their way to Russia." Both countries are devastated: "There ain't no Sedalia." There are survivors, but many or most of them are dying of radiation sickness.... The last (so far) and least (so far) of the recent, major entrants in the Armageddon sweepstakes. SPECIAL BULLETIN had irony; TESTAMENT, some honest emotion. The DAY AFTER is, in essence, GODZILLA revisited, a regulation disaster-movie. It's for those who want to watch exploitation movies without feeling guilty. Watching it, in fact, can perhaps even give you a vague feeling that you've done your civic duty. (You can't get that feeling watching GODZILLA....) Nuclear disaster is almost too potent a subject for narrative--it's a "worst case" story. It's the unthinkable, and SPECIAL BULLETIN acknowledged, with intentional irony, this sense of dramatic helplessness-in-the-face-of-annihilation: it's too big a story for even the 6 o'clock news....One character here asks, rhetorically and contemptuously, "You think this is "War of the Worlds" or something?" The director, apparently, is having a bit of fun. (Not much of the latter to be had on this project.) Meyer co-scripted the TV-movie The NIGHT THAT PANICKED AMERICA(1975), which re-created the famous Orson Welles radio version of the H.G. Wells novel, and dramatized "stories" of people affected by the broadcast....Director Meyer is still dealing in weak-tea "human vignettes" in the margins of disaster-from-the-skies. The event here dwarfs the characters; their over-familiar emotions trivialize the event. The actual moments of nuclear destruction, however, are depicted, or imagined, with surprising bluntness: instant death-for-all (in or near Kansas City). No dying words, thoughts, or looks. Just incineration.

DAY THE SKY FELL IN, The see KILL OR BE KILLED

2 The DAY TIME ENDED The Samuel Goldwyn Co./Vortex 1980 SpVisFxD: Paul Gentry. SpPyroFX: Joe Viskocil. SpAnim: Gentry, Randy Cook, D. Allen. SpSdFX:(sup) Gentry, Mark Barton; Courtney Goodin. Ref: TV.

Post-CE3K, effects-laden sf-er. Happy-alien stuff won't really make you feel warm all over--the smiles and optimism of the characters, at the end, seem forced. But the effects scenes with the little girl are offhandedly delightful. The mutually supportive relationship between her and the alien gizmos loosely recalls Amy and Irena in CURSE OF THE CAT PEOPLE--e.g., the green pyramid seems to have absorbed her new pony; she requests its return; request granted....And there are any number of monsters, fireballs, spaceships, and futuristic contraptions to keep you entertained in-between filler scenes with the adult actors.

DEAD MEN DON'T WEAR PLAID Univ/Aspen Film Society(McEuen-Picker) 1982 89m. SP,D & with: Carl Reiner. SP: also Steve Martin, George Gipe. Ph: Michael Chapman;(process) Bill Hansard. Mus: Miklos Rozsa. PD: John DeCuir. SpFX: Glen Robinson. Titles: Dan Curry, Modern, B.D. Fox. Ref: TV. MFB'82:261. Ecran F 29: 6. Hirschhorn. with Martin, Rachel Ward, George Gaynes, Reni Santoni, George Sawaya;(clips) Humphrey Bogart, Vincent Price.

Period mystery spoof, with a science-fiction punchline: a Nazi plot to dissolve the U.S. with a scientist's cheese mold. The latter decomposes rocks, trees, etc., and is reported to have consumed an island and Terre Haute....The term "cleaning woman" sends the detective-hero into a frenzy--he almost strangles the heroine, and snaps a chain in half....mind-reading bits...dialogue reference to The HUNCHBACK OF NOTRE DAME (in clip with Charles Laughton).

Basically a glorified parlor game--clips from Forties noir star vehicles are integrated into the action, and you're invited to admire the smoothness of the operation, and to identify the source films. DEAD MEN DON'T goes PLAY IT AGAIN, SAM one better, or worse: here it's not just the shade of Bogart who aids the hero, but Bogart himself (in excerpts from his films). This recycled-Hollywood-legends gimmick seems primarily a nostalgia exercise, though it's good for a few laughs, and Martin's deadpan stupidity is occasionally very funny. His performance, however, is a put-on monotone--you could look forever for comic or dramatic nuance in him or in the film. The latter is so dry it's downright arid. Good nostalgic/mock-nostalgic (choose one or both) Rozsa score.

See also: UNKNOWN TERROR, The.

The DEAD ZONE Para/De Laurentiis/Debra Hill 1983 color 103m. D: David Cronenberg. SP: Jeffrey Boam, from Stephen King's novel. Ph: Mark Irwin. Mus: Michael Kamen. PD: Carol Spier. SpFX:(coord) Jon Belyeu;(foreman) Calvin Acord; Mark Molin, Michael Newman et al. VideoElecFX: Michael Lennick. Mkp: Shonagh Jabour. MusSdFxEd: James Guthrie. Titles: R/Greenberg. Ref: screen. V 10/12/83. with Christopher Walken, Brooke Adams, Tom Skerritt, Herbert Lom, Anthony Zerbe, Colleen Dewhurst, Martin Sheen, Sean Sullivan, Nicholas Campbell.

An accident victim (Walken) emerges from a five-year coma with a "very new human ability--or a very old one," the ability to see into the past or future of the people he touches. He "sees" himself in some of his visions ("I stood there. I saw his face"), but suffers severe headaches, and his body grows weaker as the visions grow stronger. Puzzled by a "blank spot," or "dead zone," in the latter, he finds that it implies the possibility of not just seeing but altering the future, and he succeeds in saving the life of a boy and in preventing World War III....

The DEAD ZONE resurrects one of the dumbest of all "What if...?" questions--what would you do if you could save the world? Fate makes Walken's Johnny an offer he can't refuse--the chance to play Christ. None of his visions are exactly modest or quiet--based mainly on noise and disaster, they may make you feel like you're drowning in a sea of Dolby--but his penultimate vision is nothing less than epochal: a portrait of a mad, future U.S. President (Sheen) exulting in the fact that--the button pushed--"the missiles are flying!" Our man-who-knows-too-much asks his doctor (Lom) if he should act on his knowledge. But the answer to his question is obvious. (Although it is also true that nuclear holocaust is, through him, circumvented in an unexpected manner....) The script leans toward the grandiose, though, earlier, it has Johnny ask a more interesting "Why...?" question: why should he, who nearly died, and lost almost everything, use his gift to help others, to ease the burden of their "lost lives"? Like the 1948 NIGHT HAS A THOUSAND EYES, The DEAD ZONE treats "second sight" as an affliction. It's of use to others, but it only makes Johnny "die inside." He identifies a killer and prevents a boy's drowning. His rewards: the killer's mother shoots him, and the boy's father fires him as tutor. Clearly, Johnny's "gift" is a mixed blessing. It doesn't ease his suffering--it only extends it. The DEAD ZONE is grim, but it has a cut-and-dried thesis: if you can't save yourself, save others. The film is offputtingly Noble....And, interestingly, it does grant Johnny one non-material reward: at the end, the love-of-his-life (Adams)--who married someone else while he was in a coma--tells the dying Johnny, "I love you!" This is moving, but might have been more so if her affection were simply understood, by him, by us. The film, under David Cronenberg's direction, does not lack for vividness, but it could have used some subtlety too.

DEADLY EYES (H.K.-Can.) WB/Golden Harvest/Filmtrust(Northshore and Arnold & Assoc.) 1982 color 93m. (aka NIGHT EYES. The RATS) D: Robert Clouse. SP,Co-P: Charles Eglee, from James Herbert's novel "The Rats" & a screenplay by Lonon Smith. Ph: Rene Verzier. Mus: Anthony Guefen. AD: Ninkey Dalton; Dan Davis, Suzanne Smith. SpMkpFX: MkpFx Labs; Allan Apone, F.X. Carrisosa, Ken Myers, Douglas White;(des) Kathie Clark; Suzanne Moreau;(prosth) Kathy Shorkey; Bob Clark, Steve Apone et al. SpSdFX: Peter Jermyn. SpFX: Malivoire Prods.; Mark Molin, Mike Kavanagh. Opt: Film Opticals. Ref: TV: Warner Home Video. V 6/9/82. 11/24/82:35. 2/16/83:24. 5/11/83:14: in Chicago. with Sam Groom, Sara Botsford, Lisa Langlois, Scatman Crothers, Cec Linder, Lesleh Donaldson, James B. Douglas.

It's getting "bad and dangerous and ugly" in the drains below an unnamed Canadian city. (The film was shot in Toronto.) Various scrapings and squeals and snarls can be heard coming from, it seems, everywhere down there. Meanwhile, up above, a boy is mysteriously attacked, in the shadows near a trash can, and is left with a rodent bite "much larger than anything" with which one specialist is familiar. Can it be that steroid feed is developing "super rats"? Well, something is....And when their grain supply is burned, they begin using sewers as "runways" in their search for food. Next thing you know, "they've gotten into the subway!" Dog-sized-rat hordes proceed to invade a movie theatre and ruin the grand opening of the new subway extension. They've eaten the mayor, his entourage, and half the guests before people begin to realize that there's a real health hazard here....

If they're gonna do it again, why don't they at least do it a bit differently? you ask. "They" meaning the makers of the movie, not the rats....The latter are sub-Muppets--they look like rodents with buckteeth and mink coats. "Overbite" might have been a more accurate title for the movie. These rats don't look at all deadly, though Jermyn makes them sound like all-hell-about-to-break-loose. They put on a regular concert-in-the-dark....The fact that the rats have their coming-out party the same night as the grand opening of the Fifth Street extension is not, as the script would have it, irony, merely coincidence--these rats are being used....Crothers has the film's nicest moment, enthusiastically describing to a disbeliever some rats "this big!"

DEADLY GAMES Atlantic Television/Dryden(Great Plains) 1982(1980) color 95m. (WHO FELL ASLEEP?-orig t) SP,D: Scott Mansfield. Ph: R.M. Stringer. Mus: Hod David Schudson, R.S. Thompson. AD: Tana Cunningham-Curtis. SpFX: John Eggett. Mkp: Jim Gillespie. Opt: CFI. Ref: TV. TVG. V 5/13/81:16. 9/28/83. with Sam Groom, Steve Railsback, JoAnn Harris, Dick Butkus, June Lockhart, Colleen Camp, Denise Galik, Gale Sayers, Jere Lea Rea.

Mad, black-clad, ski-masked killer of women...board game featuring "Frankenstein," "Dracula," "the mummy's tomb"... theatre showing of The MONSTER WALKS...dialogue references to PSYCHO ("No, I don't look like Janet Leigh!"), "the mummy," "Horror of Dracula's Guest"....Pleasantly but ultimately-rather-hollowly quirky thriller. There are few thrills or surprises (the killer proves, predictably, to be the second-most-obvious person), but acting and dialogue are above-average--the dialogue is occasionally surprising, if the plot isn't. Mansfield honestly attempts to make his characters engage you; they're not, it seems at first, just pawns in the plot, though they're eventually and inevitably reduced to that level. (Denouement and "explanations" are pretty sloppy, as if the director had lost interest.) And who can get mad at a movie which passes off The MONSTER WALKS as a scary experience...?

DEADLY HARVEST (Can.) (Cinaco-TV)/Three Star Movies 1976 color 90m. D: Timothy Bond. SP: Martin Lager. Ph: Robert Brooks. Mus: John Mills-Cockell. Ref: Bill Warren. VideoSB: 1977. with Clint Walker, Nehemiah Persoff, Roy Davies, Jim Henshaw.

In the near future, the world's food supply is running out, and all North American citizens are on tight rations.

DEADLY LESSONS ABC-TV/Goldberg 1983 color 92m. D: William Wiard. SP: Jennifer Miller. Ph: A. Jackson. Mus: Ian Freebairn-Smith. AD: W. Hiney. Title Des: Dan Curry. Mkp: Tim McNalley. SdFxEd: Daniel Finnerty et al. Ref: TV. TVG: "brutal killer." with Donna Reed, Larry Wilcox, David Ackroyd, Ally Sheedy, Robin Gammell, Ellen Geer, Vicki Kriegler.

Murder times three at a special summer session for the hard-to-handle, well-born, and ultra-cute--at Starkwater Hall, an isolated boarding school for teen-age girls from all over the country....two madmen, one Puritanical but relatively harmless, the other the out-for-revenge-on-his-mom killer...false alarms with black cats, skulkers, scare music....Nothing to write home about. Tiny tensions, suspicions, and mysteries keep percolating, but who really cares who's next? The life stories of the two "weirdos" furnish the requisite five minutes of pathos (the commercials take up more time)--short shrift for the past, though the present-tense drama makes little more impression....

*The DEADLY MANTIS 1957 Mus sc: William Lava. SpFX: Fred Knoth. SpPh: Clifford Stine, Tom McCrory. Mkp: Bud Westmore. Ref: TV. Jim Shapiro. LC. Warren/KWTS!. Hirschhorn. Weldon. Stanley. and with Phil Harvey, James Lanphier, Florenz Ames.

Watchable, pleasant, lullingly competent big-bug movie at least manages to stick to its subject (see title), effectively counterpointing buzzing-monster scenes with calm-before-the-storm moments with mood and incidental music. The script switches fairly smoothly, midway, from a "What is it?" to a "Where is it?" sf-mystery. Main flaw: the mantis, whose press is scarier than its presence, which is informed by a nondescript "droning sound" and a frail, gangly, far-from-formidable look.

The DEADLY SPAWN 21st Century/Filmline 1982(1981) color 78m. (RETURN OF THE ALIENS-alt t) SP,Story,D: Douglas McKeown. Story: also Ted Bohus, John Dods. Dial: Tim Sullivan. Ph: Harvey Birnbaum. Mus: Michael Perilstein; Ken Walker, Paul Cornell. SpMkpFX: Arnold Gargiulo. SpFX:(d) Dods;(chief tech) Greg Ramoundos;(tech) Jack Piccuro et al;(min) Tim Hildebrant, Glenn Takakjian. SdFX: Cornell. Titles: Movie Magic. Exec P: Tim & Rita Hildebrant et al. Ref: TV. V 4/27/83. 10/20/82:95. 11/17/82:36. 6/8/83:12. Bill Warren. Scot Holton. Joe Dante. with C.G. Hildebrant, Tom De Franco, Karen Tighe, Jean Tafler.

A fast-growing, self-multiplying monster falls, via meteorite, to Earth. It eats people and plants, thrives on water, and is drawn to sound. A young monster-movie fan (whose favorite monsters are the mole people and it! the terror from beyond space) proves, naturally, to be the one who defeats the monster(s). A communal-bonfire roasting of subsidiary monsters seems to end the threat, but the hills here are literally alive....It seems no accident that this movie is (in terms of running time) half monsters. This is the no-budget, alien-invader version of The HOWLING, that living encyclopedia of movie-werewolf lore. The DEADLY SPAWN is a testament to mis-spent hours well-spent watching monster movies in darkened theaters and living rooms. The moviemakers have obviously logged their time viewing cheapie-creepies. They know and love the stock shock staples such as the old hand-on-the-actor's-shoulder ha-ha-shock. (You'll find at least one of the latter in films from MUERTOS DE RISA to CUJO, MORTUARY, etc.) Their film has its own hand-on-the-shoulder bit--this time, however, the hand is connected to an arm which is in the process of being sucked into the monster's mouth. It's a new joke on an old joke, a false false-alarm....Famous Monsters magazine does not appear in this film simply in printed form. (The boy reads it at the breakfast table.) FJA is formally thanked, and FM turns up (in "disguise") in the dialogue, in a conversation (re: The THING FROM ANOTHER WORLD) which is punctuated by a non-believer's unwittingly witty scoff, "famous monsters!" The movie's fun-gross-out centerpiece is the boy's extended visit to the family cellar, i.e., Monster Central. (Lots of water there.) Creatures of all shapes and sizes are everywhere. The main, big one has just concluded a hearty meal, and has left the scraps to smaller "fish," while one little critter lies quiescent in a mousetrap. This long sequence is simply 57 variations on one, fun-disgusting graphic theme. Like the movie as a whole, it's all "payoff," no narrative niceties (like story, theme, characterization, pacing). In this case, however, no complaint is likely to be lodged....

DEAL OF THE CENTURY WB/Yorkin 1983 color 98m. D: William Friedkin. SP: Paul Brickman. Ref: Bill Warren. V 10/26/83.
Sequence featuring futuristic plane with a mind of its own.

2P DEATH AT LOVE HOUSE ABC-TV/Spelling-Goldberg 1976 color 74m. D: E.W. Swackhammer. SP: Jim Barnett. Ph: D. Dalzell. Mus: Laurence Rosenthal. AD: Paul Sylos. Mkp: Ted Coodley. Ref: TV. TV Season. Weldon. with Robert Wagner, Kate Jackson, Sylvia Sidney, Mariana Hill(Lorna Love), Joan Blondell, Dorothy Lamour, Bill Macy, John Carradine.
Long-thought-dead, fire-scarred silent-movie queen (wearing a Sylvia Sidney-like mask) goes to murderous lengths to take her lover (or rather her ex-lover's son) with her to eternity, or thereabouts. Incidentals: hypnotic(?) fantasies...photo of Lon Chaney...stuffed cat, name of Nosferatu....Far-fetched, foolish mixture of horror and Hollywood nostalgia. Kate does her best; forget the rest.

DEATH BITE see SPASMS

DEATH COTTAGE, The or DEATH HUT, The see HOUSE OF DEATH

DEATH DORM see DORM THAT DRIPPED BLOOD, The

DEATH IN FULL VIEW see DEATH WATCH

DEATH MACHINES Crown Int'l. 1976 color 90m. P & with: Ron Marchini. Ref: Stanley. V 5/12/76:117(ad). no PFA. no V rev. VideoSB. with Michael Chong, Joshua Johnson.
Serum-created kung-fu assassins.

DEATH ON THE 31ST FLOOR(by P.Wahloo) see KAMIKAZE 1989

DEATH RIDES A CAROUSEL see CARNIVAL OF BLOOD

2 DEATH SMILES ON A MURDERER (I) 1973 77m.-U.S. (La MORTE A SORRISO ALL ASSASSINO) Ref: TV. Weldon. no V int'l '72-3.
The events of this movie take place (apparently in Germany) between 1906 and 1909, in ill-coordinated present-tense scenes, flashbacks, and flashbacks-within-flashbacks....A doctor (Klaus Kinski) discovers that the chemical formula engraved on the back of a medallion found on an amnesiac woman, Greta (Ewa Aulin), is the ancient Incan life-formula for which he has been searching. He uses this "secret of life itself" to revive a corpse, but is then murdered--by, apparently, Greta's hunchbacked, adoring brother, Franz von Holstein. Greta's rival-in-love, Eva, walls her up alive; Franz brings Greta back to life; Greta appears to Eva as both her old self and--in flashes--as a

moldering corpse, then slashes Eva and several other people to death with a razor. ("So many corpses!") One of Greta's victims first "sees" Eva's burial as a medical operation (apparently a stillbirth) on Greta, then is confronted by apparitions of both women. Back home, Greta tosses Franz a bouquet...which transforms into a vicious cat which slashes him to death. Finally, Greta is revealed to be the (somewhat aged) wife of the local police inspector....The above is a rough reconstruction of the original storyline, based on an apparently-badly-cut, English-dubbed print. "Somehow," as one character gifted with understatement observes, "it just doesn't add up." It's sometimes difficult even to tell which of the above-cited events is taking place in 1906, which in 1909. One key question: why does Greta reappear to all and sundry in both composed and decomposed states? (One person might hallucinate this double-vision, but three or four people...??)

DEATH TRAP see LEGEND OF THE BAYOU

DEATH VALLEY Univ/Kastner 1982(1981) color 89m. D: Dick Richards. SP,Co-P: Richard Rothstein. Ph: S.H. Burum; J.W. Fleckenstein. Mus: Dana Kaproff. AD: A.H. Jones. SpFX: Roy L. Downey; Bill Nicholson. SpSd: Neiman-Tillar. Mkp: R.N. Norin. Prod Asst: Michael Dempsey et al. Ref: TV. V 1/27/82: "don't look in the desert." MFB'82:168. Ecran F 26:51. Hirschhorn. with Paul Le Mat, Catherine Hicks, Stephen McHattie(Hal), A.W. Brimley, Edward Herrmann, Peter Billingsley.

Five Death Valley murders with knife and pick-ax ("just like the others we've found over the years") are traced to twin brothers guarding a gold mine for their (dead) father....A little suspense, a little "human drama" (the one element having little to do with the other), and not especially badly done. But this sort of thing has been done so often that the story almost tells itself. The Boy's Wild West conceit--mock shoot-outs with fake gunslingers vs. confrontations with real killers--doesn't lead to much, and the suspense ends don't always justify the narrative's illogical means. McHattie's killer's patter, however, is amusing.

DEATH WATCH Quartet-Films Inc./Elie Kfouri 1980(1979/'82-U.S.) (2 DEATHWATCH) 118m.-Eng.-lang.version Mkp: Paul Le Marinel. SdFX: J.-P. Lelong. To Jacques Tourneur. Ref: screen. World Cinema 10/26/79: DEATH IN FULL VIEW-alt t. V 3/2/82(rated). FQ Fall '83:16-22. SFExam 4/30/82. S&S'82:292: Glasgow setting. and with Therese Liotard, William Russel.

In the future. An NTV cameraman (Harvey Keitel) has a camera (and apparently a microphone) implanted in his eye, the better to follow and photograph the dying Katherine Mortenhoe (Romy Schneider) for the "Death Watch" TV show...."Harriet," novelist-computer...poster for X-THE MAN WITH X-RAY EYES....A sporadically affecting sf-drama bearing a strange resemblance to the classic comedy IT HAPPENED ONE NIGHT: a media-man travels cross-country with a celebrity who is unaware that she is a "story" for him. The basic idea is still recognizable despite the radical difference in tone and the added sf-trappings. And the personal-vs.-public ironies are much the same. In the key scene, this literal cameraman sees the private scenes which he has just "played" made public on a pub telly; the shock accelerates a personal-professional crisis in him, the issue of which is that he loses his "eyes." (The camera requires illumination in order to continue to function. In a fit of conscience, Keitel tosses his flashlight-pen into the sea--better drama through technology!) Capra played the conflict for light comedy-drama. Bertrand Tavernier plays it for all it's worth, dramatically, which is not nothing. But the social-scientific contrivances rather overwhelm the film's dramatic kernel. They also back Romy Schneider into a role inescapably reeking with self-righteousness, as the victim of a simply dastardly invasion of privacy. The dramatic-cinematic ironies of the premises are manifold. The viewer (for example) is both public-voyeur-of and private-participant-in her story. We're privileged intruders upon her life. (Dramatic license.) But the ironies are fairly sterile: both her story and the Big Brother themes seem cliches, even (or especially) in such an extreme conjunction. It's too easy to choose sides here, too easy to identify, at the end, with the wrath (directed at NTV bigwig Harry Dean Stanton) of Keitel and Max Von Sydow--easy, despite Stanton's amusing curlicues of character. (Stanton, for example, genuinely admires Schneider--to him "she's great!"--but more, it's true, as a subject than as a person.)

2 DEATHDREAM Entertainment Int'l./Impact & Quadrant(Night Walk) 1972 (aka The VETERAN) Mkp: Tom Savini, Alan Ormsby. Prod Mgr: John Cardos. Ref: TV. "Twilight Zone" mag. Ecran F 31:30.

DEATHDREAM is J'ACCUSE(1937) done right, or at least better--the fruits of war (here, a single soldier's death in battle) brought home, vividly, via a time-and-space-warp which allows the living-dead soldier (Richard Backus) to return home. His stay proves (like the son's return in "The Monkey's Paw") a mixed blessing. Andy succeeds, at first, in keeping his status a secret. To others, he appears simply aloof. His presence is, by turns--depending upon the specific dramatic context--obliquely unsettling, mocking, accusing, threatening, avenging, purging, and, finally (as he's decomposing-on-the-run), downright disgusting. Andy dead, or living-dead, is of course not really Andy, only a reminder that Andy doesn't live there (in Andy's body) any more. All his family and friends--except, pointedly, his mother (Lynn Carlin)--eventually get the message. It was she who brought him (or his shell) back, with her mad prayers, and she accepts this son-shell, right up to the end. The film is at its horrific-satiric sharpest describing her maternal myopia and his chilling clear-sightedness. (He knows what he is.) The latter qualities have a kind of anecdotal power. John Marley's mopey anguish as the father, on the other hand, is an example of spell-it-all-out pseudo-drama. He shouldn't even be in this movie, and yet he takes up almost half of it....DEATHDREAM is, alternately, near-electrifying and turgid. At its worst it has an air of aren't-we-honest? over-earnestness to it. At its best, it has a chill honesty and immediacy.

DEATHSTALKER (Arg.-U.S.) Palo Alto/Aries & New World 1983 color 80m. (El CAZADOR DE LA MUERTE) D: John Watson. SP: Howard R. Cohen. Ph: L.R. Solis. Mus: O.C. Ocampo. AD: Emilio Basaldua, M.J. Bertotto. SpMkpFX: John Buechler; William Smith. SpOptFX: Michael Bronstein. Ref: screen. IFG'84: 47. HR 1/6/84. V 1/18/84. with Richard Hill, Barbi Benton, Richard Brooker, Lana Clarkson, Victor Bo(Kang), Horace Marussi(creature leader).

An evil sorcerer (Bo), who possesses two of the three Powers of Creation--the Amulet of Life and the Chalice of Magic--vs. a semi-good hero (Hill) who possesses the third--the Sword of Justice, which makes him invincible. Kang can multiply himself and perform other illusions, and at one point teleports the hero (via a firebolt) out of one scene and into another. Ultimately, he is drawn and quartered, and the three powers are destroyed....cave-dwelling dwarf-creature (turned human again by dip in water)...various beast-men and giants, including a pig-creature with a taste for pig meat...witch's-staff-into-serpent....Not-quite-bottom-of-the-barrel sword-and-sorcery stuff. (The bottom should be reserved for ATOR, YOR, and SORCERESS.) Much blood is shed--it apparently ran thinner and faster in those days--and the humor tends toward dismemberment sight-gags (e.g., the big-pig-bruiser ripping off a passerby's arm to use as a club). This vein of black comedy does yield one charming item, "Little Howard," Kang's beast-pet, which he keeps in a chest on a table and to which he periodically tosses snacks (e.g., a severed finger). This time the obligatory "hommage" to STAR WARS is paid by the witch, who, in a moment of crisis, counsels our hero, "Embrace the Power." (Deathstalker, you may have noted, rhymes with Skywalker.) Lively, but totally undistinguished.

DEATHTRAP WB 1982 color 116m. D: Sidney Lumet. SP: Jay Presson Allen, from Ira Levin's play. Ph: Andrzej Bartkowiak. Mus: Johnny Mandel. PD: Tony Walton. SpVisFX: Bran Ferren. SpProps: Eoin Sprott. Mkp: Cranzano, Lloyd. Ref: TV. PFA. V 3/17/82. MFB'82:197-8. with Michael Caine, Christopher Reeve, Dyan Cannon, Irene Worth(psychic), Henry Jones, Joe Silver, Joel Siegel, Jeffrey Lyons, Stewart Klein.

Man who seems to return from the dead...scares woman with weak heart to death...woman with ESP who senses past and future violence in house...very insistent thunderstorm....Allen's script of the Levin play attempts to defuse criticism of itself by providing its own self-critique. The principals talk about the "intricate plotting," the "two-dimensional characters," and the "corny but effective" effects in thrillers like DEATHTRAP; they all but provide the critic's byline. DEATHTRAP itself is circumscribed fun. It's hokily twisty and proud of it. In fact it seems rather too self-satisfied with its sophisticated artificiality--the script is competent, but far from inspired. Its greatest service is providing a vehicle for Michael Caine, who revels in the artifice. He gets so far inside the latter, in fact, that he's convincing. Reeve and Cannon are just having fun; Caine, the spoilsport, is having such a good time that he forgets himself, forgets that he's only supposed to be play-acting. He gets involved. For the most part, however, DEATHTRAP is fast-food-for-thought--music, plot, and dialogue are too clever by half. The film's target audience seems to be adults-on-holiday.

DEATHWATCH see DEATH WATCH

DECEPTION (Can.) Gold Key-TV/T.A.E. 1973 color 95m. (The STARLOST QUINTOLOGY 4.) Ref: GKey. TVFFSB. TVG. with Keir Dullea, Ed Ames, Angel Tompkins, Robin Ward.

Hallucination-inducing computer menaces Earthship Ark. See also: ALIEN ORO, The.

DELUSION see HOUSE WHERE DEATH LIVES, The

DEMENTED IRC/IWDC/Sandy Cobe(Four Features Partners) 1980 color 93m. D,Co-P: Arthur Jeffreys. Sp,Exec Co-P: Alex Rebar. Ph: Jim Tynes. Mus: Richard Tufo. SpFxMkp: Robert Burman, Dale Brody. Titles:(des) W.J. Waters; Pacific. Ref: TV: Media Home Ent.(video). VideoSB. Ecran F 32:63,65. with Sallee Elyse(Linda Rodgers), Bruce Gilchrist, Bryan Charles, Chip Matthews, Deborah Alter, Kathryn Clayton, Robert Mendel.

L.A. housewife (Elyse) is gang-raped by four men; recovers in a sanitarium; when released, has visions of the rapists and of "ghosts in the house," and finds herself beset by neighborhood boys in monster masks. She is, however, "able to handle the situation": she disposes of her "guests" (i.e., the boys, whom she takes for the rapists) with cleaver, shotgun, etc.

A "before-and-after" movie. Before Linda goes into action, DEMENTED is a plodding, pointless when-will-she-finally-snap? thriller. It's only after she snaps that the story really begins, and a heretofore humorless film transforms, before your eyes, into a model of wit and black humor....Is the story, from that point on, all in her mind? It's hard to say. But whether her "revenge" is real or phantom--whether, that is, the monster-masked youths are her mind's invention or not--Linda's new "role" is a stunning one. Her Kewpie-doll face and voice--which, previously, had seemed out-of-place in a "realistic" psychological study--prove ideal, comically, for her "casting" of herself as the too, too accommodating hostess. Linda is oh-so-glad to oblige her young male guests: "I'm going to take you somewhere where you've never been before," she squeaks, mock-seductively. She's not kidding either, but this "somewhere" isn't way up high, over any rainbow--it's as close as her cleaver, or wire, or shotgun. She has her revenge, although, mentally, she's not around to savor it. "I just want all the bad things to go away," she distractedly tells one (bound) "guest." And they do--the "bad things" which had composed her psychological reality are long gone by movie's end, or have, at least, been converted in her mind into jokes, into a Game of the Male, to be played according to her own new, inverted rules, which she finds screamingly funny. She laughs--and kills--to keep from crying....

The DEMON (So.African?) Gold Key/Hollard 1981 color 95m. SP,D,P: Percival Rubens. Ph: Vincent Cox. Mus: Nick Labuschagne. Mkp: Reggie Wollschlager. Ref: TV: Thorn EMI Video. Bill Warren: sfa The UNHOLY? VideoSB. with Jennifer Holmes, Cameron Mitchell, Craig Gardner, Zoli Markey, Mark Tanous.

"The time of the demon...is drawing close." In fact, it's here: a huge, powerful "monster" of a man--who is "less than a man and more than a man--much more"--from some strange "shadowland," stalks and kills certain, preselected women. He is apparently psychic and, curiously, features steel-clawed leather gloves and plastic bags as part of his modus operandi. (A demon who works with plastic bags?!) He also hides his true appearance behind a lifelike rubber mask. He seems to begin to melt away when the heroine plants a pair of scissors in his neck....psychic (Mitchell) who can "visualize things until (he's) almost part of them."

Fairly-well-acted, but poorly-written shocker appears to have been concocted with HALLOWEEN in mind, and makes even less sense. (Sense was not HALLOWEEN's forte.) It's not even clear to whom Mitchell is referring--himself or the demon--when he calls someone "an aberration of the species." Mitchell dies just, it seems, as he is about to explain the who and why of the demon--and explanations are badly needed. The plot wanders about aimlessly from stalker to various stalkees and their friends and relations....

DEMON AND THE MUMMY ABC-TV/Univ-TV & Francy 1975 color 92m. D: Don Weis, Don McDougall. SP: Michael Kozoll, Stephen Lord, David Chase, Arthur Rowe. Created by Jeff Rice. From the episodes "Demon in Lace" & "Legacy of Terror" in "The Night Stalker" TV series, aka "Kolchak: The Night Stalker." Ph: R.W. Browne. Mus: Jerry Fielding, Gil Melle. Ref: TV. "TV Drama Series." with Darren McGavin, Keenan Wynn, Jackie Vernon, Carolyn Jones, Andrew Prine, Erik Estrada, Milton Parsons.

Two stories: 1) a 10,000-year-old Sumerian tablet is linked to a succubus which kills, then inhabits women; young men who embrace the latter die of heart attacks. 2) The Aztec millennium in 2027 is heralded by a series of human sacrifices every 52 years....living Aztec mummy? Kolchak and his aggressive comedy are back. He's still yelling at his boss, the cops, etc. It's hard to watch people trying so hard to be entertaining, though there are amusing throwaway lines and bits. What's most curious about this conjoining of two old TV shows is that the two stories are not told consecutively, but concurrently. Kolchak keeps switching his attention from one set of victims--their hearts cut out--to the other--their hearts burst open. And a bit of narration here and there is thrown in to patch it all together--e.g., "Why did I let myself get sidetracked from the investigation of those fatal heart attacks?" The result is ludicrously choppy; the sense of desperation rather-comically apparent.

Le DEMON DANS L'ILE (F) Les Films 7 1983 color 102m. SP,D: Francis Leroi. SP: also O.T. Rozmann. Ph: J. Assuerus. Mus: Christian Gaubert. AD & with: Bruno Bruneau. SpFX: Marc Marmier;(elec) Dominique Crombe. SpProps: Giorgiu Fenu. Mkp: C. Koubesserian. Ref: V 10/20/82:289. 2/2/83. 3/23/83. Ecran F 34:38,43. with A. Duperey, Jean-Claude Brialy, Cerise.
Attack of the household appliances...telekinesis?

DEMON IN LACE see DEMON AND THE MUMMY

The DEMON MURDER CASE NBC-TV/Dick Clark & Steckler 1983 color 92m. D: Billy Hale. SP: William Kelley. Ph: John Lindley. Mus: George A. Tipton. PD: Marc Donnenfeld. SpFX: Peter Kunz, Mark Mann. Mkp: Steve Atha. Graphic Des: Jay Hanson. Opt: F-Stop. Ref: TV. TVG. with Andy Griffith, Eddie Albert, Liane Langland, Joyce Van Patten, Cloris Leachman, R. Masur.

The Incubus, a blasphemous, hoofed, hellfire-burnt "demon of lust" (with Smiley "Frog" Burnette's voice), aka The Beast, possesses an 11-year-old boy (Charlie Fields) and makes a house and a church quake. The boy's experience prefigures the apparent possession of a 19-year-old (Kevin Bacon), who commits manslaughter...demonologist...exorcism (with humorless priests once again playing straight man for sarcastic demons).

Another believe-it-or-believe-it supernatural thriller, a la The ENTITY and the AMITYVILLES, in which you have no choice: the effects department is called in as the star witness for its case. The film--rather than rely on non-coercive second-hand reports of the psychic phenomena--stages (or, if you like, re-stages) the events of the real-life source story. The docu-drama of the fantastic is a new, exasperatingly superficial subgenre species. This example of same self-servingly blurs distinctions between first-hand and second-hand evidence, subjectivity and objectivity. We are, for instance, ear-witnesses, first, to what a cop hears, and, later, to what he reports hearing (i.e., "the voice of the devil"). The first scene renders the second superfluous; the two together produce a sort of phony-objectivity effect....The movie addresses moral, legal, and metaphysical questions, and handily provides far-from-tentative answers. It lets God and man off the hook for human suffering, acts of violence, and problem children. The Beast seems, more specifically, to be a scapegoat....

2 DEMON POND Kino Int'l./Myron Bresnick(Grange) 1980(1979/'82-U.S.) From the play by K. Izumi. Ph: also N. Sakamoto. Ref: screen. and with Tsutomu Yamasaki, Hisashi Igawa, Norihei Miki.

Fantasy realm of men-turned-into-animals (e.g., fish-man, crab-man, "black catfish priest," deer-men, bird-men, goat-man, worm-man), and their Dragon Princess, who can read by her own illumination. At the end, she and her servants are freed of their obligation to humans and float up into the sky....The realm of the humans proves, unfortunately, less taking than that of the "mud creatures" and their princess. Thematically, of course, the two worlds intersect and reflect one another: the quality of romantic love, here, vies with that of duty-to-others for supremacy in both humans and half-humans. The strictly-human scenes, however, are Serious Business, and are played at a deadly-serious pace. You almost have to force yourself to wrench their sense from them--while the casually magical, self-conscious, often-blissfully-silly fantasy sequences seem, spontaneously, to resonate....In the most affecting scene, the phantom princess (tempted by love to shirk her duty to the 8,000 human inhabitants of the Harp-Playing Valley) stands unseen, near our solitary heroine; moved by the sadness of the latter, who fears that her husband is deserting her, and whose only (visible) companion is her doll. You can almost see the film's themes blossoming here, like flowers unfolding in time-lapse photography.

DEMON RAGE see SATAN'S MISTRESS

The DEMONS OF LUDLOW Titan Int'l./Ram 1983 D: Bill Rebane. SP: William Arthur. Ref: HR 10/25/83:S-72: at Mifed. Ecran F 36:82. V 10/26/83:219(ad). with Paul Von Hausen, Stephanie Cushna, James Robinson.

Playing of antique piano summons up demon-ghosts.

DENSETSU KYOSHIN IDEON (J) Shochiku 1982 anim color Ref: V 8/4/82:35. JFFJ 14:8: aka The IDEON.

Feature comprising the last three episodes of the TV series re: a robot which functions on the "ultimate power source."

Le DERNIER COMBAT (F) Les Films du Loup(Alexandrov) 1982 ws 86m. SP,D,P: Luc Besson. SP: also Pierre Jolivet. Ph: Carlo Varini. Mus: Eric Serra. PD: Flamand et al. Mkp: Maude Baron. SdFX: Andre Naudin. Ref: Ecran F 35:52-3.33:39-40. V 10/20/82:289. 5/4/83:387. 5/11/83: no dialogue. 2/2/83:28. with Jolivet, Jean Bouise, Fritz Wepper, Jean Reno.

"Future holocaust."(V)

DESTINATION MOONBASE ALPHA (B-I) Group Three/ITC-TV & RAI-TV 1975(1982) color 93m. Ref: VideoSB. with Martin Landau.

From the "Space 1999" TV series.

DEVIL, The see PICTURE THE DEVIL

The DEVIL'S EXPRESS Mahler 1977(1975) color/ws 82m. (GANG WARS-alt t) D: Barry Rosen. Ref: Cinef V:4:23. Academy. Weldon: ideas from RAW MEAT. with Sam De Fazio, W. Tanzania.

Kung-fu student unleashes ancient demon on New York City subway passengers.

The DEVONSVILLE TERROR MPM/New West 1983 color 84m. SP,D,P, Ph: Ulli Lommel. SP: also George T. Lindsey, Suzanna Love. Mus: Ray Colcord; Ed Hill. Set Des: Priscilla Van Gorder. SpFX: Matthew Mungle, George Rogers;(ph) David Hewitt;(ed) Donald Flick. Mkp: Erica Ueland. Opt: Hollywood Optical. Hist Cons: Elizabeth Trevelyan. Ref: TV: Embassy Home Ent. (video). V 11/2/83. 2/16/83:24. with Love(Jenny), Robert Walker Jr., Donald Pleasence(Dr.Warley), Paul Willson, Deanna Haas (Monica), Mary Walden(Chris), Angelica Rebane, Paul Bentzen; Morrigan Hurt, Leslie Smith, Barbara Cihlar(witches).

Devonsville, New England, Nov. 3, 1983, 300 years to the day after the execution there of three witches. "They're back!" Or at least one of them seems to be: the new schoolteacher, Jenny Scanlon, arrives in town shortly after one citizen (Willson) murders his bedridden wife. Through hypnotic regression, Dr. Warley discovers from her that she is a "messenger from the unknown," sent to right the wrongs of the town's patriarchal society. She appears to the murderer as a vision and has, herself, visions of his crime and dreams of demons and of the Devonsville Inquisition. In that inquisition, the body of one of the witches was "taken" by lightning, as she cast a curse on her executioners. At film's end, after the men of the town have (in the present) executed two women as witches and tied Jenny to a stake, lightning seems to issue from her eyes and makes her would-be executioners melt and disintegrate. The "curse of the worms" on Dr. Warley, great-great-great-grandson of the original inquisitor, whose family was cursed to be "eaten by worms," is lifted....

A forthrightly anti-sexist terror film, which fact automatically makes it a shade more interesting than most similar, low-budget horror movies. At least the authors have more than one thing on their minds. The fact, also, that Jenny is not simply a witch, or a reincarnation of same, but rather a "messenger" with a specific mission, makes matters a bit more complicated than usual. (Even she doesn't know why she's there.) The film is not stillborn. Nor is it, however, exactly bouncing with life. The acting, as usual in Lommel's films, is curiously muted, and the characters are one-dimensional. That leaves ideas--and the script, as indicated above, does indeed have a few--and photography. Photographically, the movie is exquisite. Wisconsin flora is alive here with every shade of green, brown, and red--the exterior shots, day or night, are thoroughly textured, or detailed, in terms of light and shadow, color and movement....The melting and disintegrating horror-effects here are not unusual--the worms-in-the-doctor's-arm inserts are, however, pretty revolting. (I'm not sure if the preceding is condemnation or commendation.)

DIABLE NOIR, Le see BLACK IMP, The

The DIABOLICAL TENANT (F) Famille Melies/Star 1909 color 7m. (Le LOCATAIRE DIABOLIQUE. **DIABOLICAL LODGER) Ref: screen. PFA notes 11/16/82. Lee.

The new tenant brings everything with him--pictures, chairs, table, piano, mirrors, and family--and he brings it all in valise and trunk, taking out one item at a time (the people last). The owner objects, but the dancing, enchanted furniture scares him away. The tenant returns and packs up again. (A nosy gendarme is squeezed into the back of the piano.) A box left behind blows up in the faces of the curious....An oddly eerie, enthralling Georges Melies short. No explanations, hellos or goodbyes--just prestidigitation, methodical process and process-in-reverse, life unpacked and packed up again. Man, demon, or itinerant poltergeist, this "tenant" is an expert at what he does: he furnishes the room in minutes--and he brooks no interference. He has obviously been doing this sort of thing for years, maybe centuries....

1990 (DICIANNOVE...) I GUERRIERI DEL BRONX see 1990: THE BRONX WARRIORS

La DINASTIA DRACULA (Mex) 1978 Ref: V 11/2/83: "Mexican pic." Bill Warren. no Academy. with Fabian Forte(Dracula).

The DISH RAN AWAY WITH THE SPOON WB 1933 anim 7m. D,P: R. Ising. Ref: "WB Cartoons." LC. no Lee.

"Yeast Beast" at large at midnight in bakery.

DJANGO IL BASTARDO or DJANGO THE BASTARD see STRANGER'S GUNDOWN

DO ANDROIDS DREAM OF ELECTRIC SHEEP(by P.K.Dick) see BLADE RUNNER

DOCTOR BUTCHER, M.D. (I) Aquarius(Levene)/Flora-Fulvia-Gico 1980('82-U.S.) color 80m. (La REGINA DEI CANNIBALI. aka ZOMBIE HOLOCAUST. QUEEN OF THE CANNIBALS-ad t. DOCTOR BUTCHER, M.D.-MEDICAL DEVIATE-ad t) D: Franco Martinelli(aka Marino Girolami or Frank Martin). SP: Fabrizio de Angelis, Walter Patriarca, Romano Scandariato. Ph: F. Zuccoli. Mus: Nico Fidenco(aka Walter Sear). AD: V. Morrozi. SpFX: Maurizio Trani, Rosario Restopino. Title Seq: Roy Frumkes. Ref: screen. Ecran F 31:56.22:48. Weldon: NYU-film footage for U.S. prologue. V 5/5/82. 9/30/81:18(ad). 5/7/80:368. 1/23/80. LAT 3/11/82. Prod.Ital.: ZOMBI HOLOCAUST. with Ian McCulloch, Alexandra Delli Colli, Sherry Buchanan, Peter O'Neal, Donald O'Brian.

A "bloodthirsty lunatic" of a doctor (O'Brian), attempting to extend the human lifespan by 100 years, creates zombie-slaves by transplanting the brains of living victims into the heads of corpses. ("This island's hiding something--something even worse than those cannibals.")....blood-drinking, eye-gouging cannibals ("They ate George right in front of our eyes")...

anatomy-class-corpse's hand severed ("You must have a pretty sick sense of humor to laugh during anatomy class")...scalping... impalement...severed vocal cords...hypnotic(?) drug...machete-in-head...outboard-motor-through-zombie's-head...severed, maggoty head in bed....Yes, all your favorites are here, in a film more vile, if possible, than ZOMBIE. The dismemberments and disembowelments occur with almost (not quite) comic regularity, but are too unimaginatively conceived to be laughed off. The film is both sick and oddly bland--Grand Guignol reduced to mechanics.

DOCTOR DRACULA (Americom Int'l.-TV)/Indep.-Int'l./Rafael 1977 color 93m. (DR. DRACULA-ad t) SP,D: Paul Aratow. D: also Al Adamson. SP: also Brown, Reathman. Ph: Gary Graver, Robbie Greenberg. Mus: MW. SpFX: Doug Jones, Larry Todd. Mkp: Mark Rodriguez et al. Adv: Samuel Sherman. Ref: TV. no Academy. Ginny Moilanen. Stanley. TVG. TVFFSB. with John Carradine, Donald Barry, Larry Hankin, Geoffrey Land, Susan McIver, Regina Carrol, Jane Brunel-Cohen, Vic Kirk, Noel Welch, Laurie Gross.

Dr. John Wainwright (Hankin), a hypnotist and former "brilliant university scholar," who bills himself as "the Second Svengali," believes that he actually _is_ the reincarnation of Svengali; that an "intense crystallization" of energy invaded him when he was in a "detached state from nature." At one point, he pits his "superconscious knowledge" against this "alien soul," and separates "Svengali," temporarily, from himself....Wainwright is a member of the occult Society of the Bleeding Rose, or The Evil Ones, headed by Radcliffe (Carradine), whose followers believe themselves to be reincarnated souls "losing psychic energy." A 60-year search for a new energy source has led the group to "Trilby" (Brunel-Cohen), "a goddess, an eternal energy source," whom they plan to sacrifice at a black mass in "the domain of the demon god." A new member, Anatol Gregorio (Land), however, thwarts their plans. Gregorio is, supposedly, a reincarnation of the vampire Dracula, also seeking new energy; actually, he _is_ Dracula, using the Society to claim new victims. _They_, apparently, are self-deluded and, in reality, powerless, and perish when Dracula kills "Trilby" before the scheduled sacrifice.

DOCTOR DRACULA is not really quite as interesting as the above synopsis may make it sound--or, rather, any interest which it might have for anyone lies almost exclusively in its premises and narrative developments, and can easily be contained in such a synopsis. This is all by way of saying that there's not much to look at or listen to here--the _mise-en-scene_, so to speak, is not exactly riveting. But the screenplay, if arrant nonsense, is _unusual_ nonsense, a far-from-nimble, but very curious mixture of the supernatural, the psychic, and the psychological. One assumes, for instance, in retrospect, that the Jekyll-and-Hyde scene between Wainwright and "Svengali" is all in Wainwright's mind, though it seems, at the time, to be a legitimate occult variation on Stevenson. And The Evil Ones die, apparently, because they believe that (without "Trilby") they must. Dracula (none other) exposes them for the occult frauds that they are....Or, as Stephanie (McIver)--who wants to contact her mother (now Dracula's undead "bride")--puts it, "What good is the supernatural if it doesn't work for you?" A pragmatist, she's drawn to Dracula, whose vampirism "works." She is, however, ultimately repulsed by her mother's ghastly paleness, and (on a technicality!) blows herself and the Count to bits. Technically-speaking, he should survive this setback. (Vampire rules and regulations generally require a more formal, ritualistic sendoff.) But the point, apparently, is that nothing works. (Dracula also brushes off religion....) This is a pretty terrible movie--talky, badly photographed, lethargically paced--but at least it has a thesis, which is more than most horror movies (at any level) have....

N.B.: DOCTOR DRACULA appears to be a re-edited version of LUCIFER'S WOMEN(II, 1975?), with added footage featuring Carradine, Barry, etc.

**DOCTOR SYN (B) Gaumont/Gainsborough 1937 81m. (aka DR.SYN, THE PIRATE) D: Roy William Neill. SP: Roger Burford. Dial: Michael Hogan. From Russell Thorndike's novel. Ph: Jack Cox. Mus D: Louis Levy. Sets: Vetchinsky. Ref: TV. Lee. TVG. FD 10/21/37. MFB'37:165. BFC. Weldon. with George Arliss, Margaret Lockwood, John Loder, Roy Emerton, Graham Moffatt, Meinhart Maur(the mulatto), Athole Stewart, George Merritt, Wally Patch, Frederick Burtwell.

1800. The notorious pirate Captain Clegg (Arliss) has survived the hangman's noose and is now posing as Dr. Syn, the Vicar of Dymchurch. He is also known as The Scarecrow, the leader of a band of smugglers, who use the "legend of the (Romney) marshes" to cloak their activities....village talk re: "phantoms on horseback" or "phantom riders," "the supernatural," "bogeys," "spooks," "manifestations," "haunted oasthouse"..."bleeding" scarecrow...monstrous "mad mulatto" ("What's that creature?!")...midnight visits to the cemetery..."nightmares" re: marsh murder.

In story and tone, DOCTOR SYN resembles an Ealing community-comedy: Haunted Little Island, or rather Tight Little Village. Comparing Dymchurch to a pie, one character observes, "What goes on under the crust of this village would surprise anyone." The film is a pleasingly odd brew of beneficent smugglers, marsh "ghosts," young lovers, and the crown's revenue agents. It mixes comedy, drama, sentiment, suspense, and chills, and is as fast-paced as the Hammer remake, NIGHT CREATURES, and a more evocative and atmospheric piece of storytelling as well. Dr. Syn is a sort of Robin Hood; his gain is the village's gain. His violent past as Clegg died on the gallows. Reformed, he's a criminal-philanthropist, "a man of conflicting powers for good and evil," a "hero" for schoolboys, "a regular old sinner," "a strange man." Protagonist and narrative are a blend of the conventional and the unconventional. The happily-ever-after, scot-free-escape ending is a bit "soft," but romantically satisfying. One suspects that in the book the mulatto finally catches up with Clegg/Syn and squares accounts. But living or dead, a hero is a hero, and Clegg's ultimate fate is less important than his accomplishments, his saint-and-sinner balancing act.

DOKTOR FAUSTUS (W.G.) Seitz-Iduna 1982 color 137m. SP,D,P: Franz Seitz. From Thomas Mann's novel. Ph: R. Blahacek. Mus: Benjamin Britten, Rolf Wilhelm. AD: Rolf Zehetbauer. Ref: V 9/29/82. 5/4/83:160(ad). with Jon Finch, Hanns Zischler, Marie Helene Breillat, Andre Heller(satan).

Composer (Finch) sells his soul in exchange for genius.

DOMANI SI BALLA (I) Vides 1982 color 100m. SP,D & with: Maurizio Nichetti. SP: also Guido Manuli. Ph: M. Battistoni. Mus: Eugenio Bennato. Sets: Maria Pia Angelini. Ref: Ecran F 32:6-7. V 9/15/82. with Mariangela Melato, Paolo Stoppa.

"Moon men" from spaceship drive victims to do "compulsive Scottish jig."

DOMINATORE DEL FERRO, Il see IRONMASTER, The

DONALD DUCK AND THE GORILLA RKO/Disney 1944 anim color 6m. D: Jack King. Ref: TV. LC. Maltin/OMAM.

"A terrible gorilla" named Ajax escapes from the zoo during a violent thunderstorm and menaces Donald and his nephews.... Okay animated comedy-chiller. Funny bit: Donald confronted with a "tombstone"--reading "Here Lies a Dead Duck"--in the eye of the monster-gorilla.

DON'T GET ME WRONG (B) WB-FN 1937 80m. D: Arthur Woods, Reginald Purdell. SP: Purdell, Brock Williams, Frank Launder. Ref: BFC. no Lee. with George E. Stone, Olive Blakeney.

"Tabloid petrol substitute invented by mad chemist."(BFC)

DON'T GO TO SLEEP ABC-TV/WB & Spelling 1982 color 92m. D,P: Richard Lang. SP & with: Ned Wynn. Ph: Chuck Arnold. Mus: Dominic Frontiere. AD: Paul Sylos. SpFX: Dutch Van Der Byl. Mkp: Berns, Gonzales. Ref: TV. SFExam 12/31/82:B17: with Ed the iguana. with Dennis Weaver, Valerie Harper, Ruth Gordon, Robert Webber, Robin Ignico, Kristin Cumming, Oliver Robins.

A little girl, implicated in her sister Jennifer's death (in a car crash), imagines that Jennifer has returned and is helping to plot the deaths of other family members. At the end, their mother, too, "sees" Jennifer....Another forced marriage of psychology and suspense. The script, more specifically, couples the evil-child theme from The BAD SEED with the girl-and-her-fantasy-friend theme from CURSE OF THE CAT PEOPLE. The psychological steps (enumerated by the family psychiatrist) leading little Mary to murder: 1) sibling jealousy, 2) mourning, 3) depression, 4) guilt, and 5) anger....It seems (to paraphrase, or reverse, Tolstoy) that all unhappy families are like one another now--at least in suspense-horror movies. You've seen this sad family before, though generally not with actors as able as Weaver, Harper, and Gordon, whose talents give the movie scattered convincing moments and scenes. The film is grim, but shallowly so.

2 DON'T LOOK IN THE BASEMENT Camera 2 & Century 1973 AD: Lynda Pendleton. SpFX: Jack Bennett. Mkp: Jill Esmond. SdFX: Brian Hooper. Ref: TV. Weldon. Stanley. and with Gene Ross, Anne MacAdams, Robert Dracup, Betty Chandler.

A movie decidedly deserving of its less-than-sweet reputation. DON'T LOOK IN THE BASEMENT is every bit as cheery as NIGHT OF THE LIVING DEAD or The TEXAS CHAIN SAW MASSACRE, and just as sick, if not as slick. At the doc's home for "obsession development," the sane go insane and the insane go insaner. After the carnage, the basement is merely one of many places not to look. A Grand Guignol downer.

DON'T OPEN THE DOOR (Cinema Shares Int'l.-TV)/Jefferson & Century (Capital) 1979 color 90m. D,P: S.F. Brownrigg. SP: Frank Schaefer, Kerry Newcomb. Ph: Robert Alcott. Mus: Bob Farrar. AD: Lynda Pendleton. SpFX: Jack Bennett. Mkp: Jackie J. Barnes. Title Des: Mark Hundahl. Ref: TV. TVG. with Susan Bracken(Amanda), Gene Ross, Larry O'Dwyer(Claude Kearn), Annabelle Weenick, Jim Harrell, Hugh Feagin.

Thirteen years after her mother was brutally stabbed to death, Amanda Post returns to her grandmother's "big, rambling old house" in Allerton, Texas. She is haunted by mysterious shadows and flitting figures, and receives threatening phone calls from a "miserable, impotent freak." She finds no friends in the Judge, the town doctor, or even the man who keeps a life-sized replica of her mother (to which he talks) in his historical museum. The killer of Rita Post now kills again (with mallet and hammer), at one point impersonating a museum manniquin, and proves to be, also, the one "haunting" Amanda... who, ultimately, goes mad herself and kills....

The auteur of DON'T LOOK IN THE BASEMENT returns with more advice on What Not To Do. (He also made the charming KEEP MY GRAVE OPEN, qq.v.) To him, madness is apparently the ultimate horror: the people in his films who don't die go mad. Not much of a choice. In DOOR, Amanda is, at first, rather unconvincingly, a Tough Cookie; then (just as unconvincingly) she crumbles. She travels, supposedly, from here to there, but, in terms of dramatic credibility, is really neither here nor there. The film as a whole is not as perverse as it pretends to be, although a sequence featuring a cross between rape and telephone sex qualifies as pretty sick. In light of Amanda's heretofore highly-assertive character, her submissiveness in said sequence is, again, not believable; but S.F. Brownrigg does not seem to be keen on believability....

DOPPELGANGER, The see CRACKLE OF DEATH

DORAEMON--NOBITA NO KYORYU (J) Toho/Shinsei 1980 anim feature (aka DORAEMON AND DINOSAUR or DORAEMON--NOBITA'S DINOSAUR) Ref: V 5/12/82:328. 5/13/81:258. 4/20/83:141(ad).

"Robot cat from the 22nd century...."

Sequels: DORAEMON II. DORAEMON--NOBITA NO DAIMAHO. DORAEMON FESTIVAL. DORAEMON--NOBITA NO KAITEI KIIWAJO.

2 DORAEMON II Toho/Shinsei 1981 91m. (aka DORAEMON AND NOBITA'S SPACE FRONTIER DAYS. DORAEMON AND SPACE ADVENTURES. DORAEMON--NOBITA NO UCHU KAITAKUSHI) Ref: JFFJ 14:10. V 5/12/82:328.

"Gateway into space...outer space gang."(JFFJ)

DORAEMON--NOBITA NO DAIMAHO (J) Toho/Shinsei 1982 anim 90m. (aka The ATOMIC CAT'S BIG ADVENTURE or DORAEMON AND WONDERLAND) Ref: JFFJ 14:10: third in the series.

DORAEMON FESTIVAL (J) Toho 1982 anim color feature Ref: V 10/20/82:248: fourth in the series.

DORAEMON--NOBITA NO KAITEI KIIWAJO (J) Toho 1983 anim feature Ref: V 4/13/83:35: playing.

The DORM THAT DRIPPED BLOOD New Image & Wescom/Obrow 1983(1981) color 84m. (PRANKS-ad t) SP,D,P,Ed: Jeffrey Obrow. SP,D, Ph,Ed: Stephen Carpenter. SP,Assoc P: Stacey Giachino. Mus: Chris Young. AD: Charlotte Grant. SpMkpFX: Matthew Mungle. SdFxEd: John Penney. OptFX: Getty. Ref: screen. Bill Warren: DEATH DORM-project t. V 7/27/83:13. with Laurie Lapinski, Stephen Sachs, David Snow, Pamela Holland.

"Smart-ass that nobody likes" proves to be the madman at large in the university's Dayton Hall, which, except for a small clean-up crew, is now deserted. He dispatches his victims with spiked club, butcher knife, electric drill, wire, pressure cooker, and car, so that he can be alone with the heroine, his secret love. She proves to be uncooperative, and ends up in an incinerator, while he seems to get away with multiple murder--romance, however, continues to elude him.... Formula shocker is not badly done, but keeps dissipating (with its predictable suspense-plot twists) the little good will which it succeeds in building up with actors and dialogue. Much too much time is devoted to the perambulations (and occasional outright skulkings) of a very obvious red herring, while the killer, at one point, takes a tip from this herring (who, for his own part, pilfers a loaf of bread) and smashes up a table-set-for-dinner. This act somehow seems more craven than his more-felonious acts--we expect murder and mayhem from him, but to ruin a good meal...!

DOS FANTASMAS Y UNA MUCHACHA 1958 80m. (*TWO GHOSTS AND A GIRL) AD: J.T. Torija. SpFX: I.R. Ravelo. Ref: TV.

Scene being shot on movie set features Frankenstein-monster-type, gill-man-type, werewolf, mummy....Plus: two ghosts who keep appearing and (after sneezing) disappearing, and who can turn into skulls or skeletons and do all sorts of other tricks... fake ghosts and skeleton....These (real) ghosts are, like the movie, very lively--they even stage their own musical production-number, in which they multiply themselves, split into halves (top and bottom, that is), and summon up thunder and lightning and flying "ghosts"-in-sheets. All pretty silly, but rather ingratiatingly so....

DOUBLE EXPOSURE Crown Int'l./Greyhill(SilverStone) 1982(1981) color/ws 95m. SP,D,Co-P: William Byron Hillman. Ph: R.M. Stringer. Mus: Jack Goga. PD: Ron Talsky. SpPhFX: Homer & Assoc. Mkp: Chris Brice, Sally Childs. Art: Winston Pruett. Ref: TV. V 2/16/83:24. (d)6/9/82(rated). HR 6/5/81. 8/4/81. Don Glut. Bill Warren. Ecran F 30:58. with Michael Callan, Joanna Pettet, James Stacy, Pamela Hensley, Cleavon Little, Seymour Cassel, Misty Rowe, Joey Forman, Terry Moore, R. Tessier.

A photographer (Callan) with "bad headaches and bad dreams" is suspected of being the madman behind 14 "bizarre killings" in L.A. The killer, however, proves to be someone who is close to our hero and who acts out his nightmares. ("I got 'em--just like your dreams.") Zero as mystery; little better as psychological drama. This is The WOLF MAN ("Could I kill anyone?") with a twist so predictable it's embarrassing, and a climactic photographic "red herring" (shots of someone apparently stalking the heroine) that's a crime itself. The actors aren't bad, and there are occasional semi-believable lines and moments, but the script is pathetically transparent--as drama or mystery. This is a you-know-whodunit. Perhaps the only sequence which, unfortunately, gets its desired effect is the snake-in-the-bag nightmare, which is so prolonged, it's revolting (even though you don't see anything).

DOUBLE JEOPARDY see OLIVIA

DRACULA (character created by Bram Stoker) see the following titles and BUENAS NOCHES, SENOR MONSTRUO. DINASTIA DRACULA. DOCTOR DRACULA. DRACULA BITES THE BIG APPLE(P). G-MAN JITTERS. GAYRACULA. HYSTERICAL. KUNG FU FROM BEYOND THE GRAVE. LUST AT FIRST BITE. PASTRIES(P). PIERRE GUIMOND: ENTRE FREUD ET DRACULA(P). STAR VIRGIN. LAST HORROR FILM, The(A).

DRACULA BLOWS HIS COOL (W.G.) Martin Films/Lisa & Barthonia 1979('82-U.S.) color 97m. (GRAF DRACULA BEISST JETZT IN OBERBAYERN) D: Carlo Ombra. SP: Grunbach & Rosenthal. Addl Dial: Donald Arthur. Ph: Heinz Holscher. Mus: Gerhard Heinz. Ref: TV: Media Home Ent.(video). V 5/19/82:6(rated). 11/2/83: DRACULA SUCKS-proposed U.S. t. with Gianni Garko(Dracula/Stan), Betty Verges(Countess Olivia), Giacomo Rizzo, Ellen Umlauf (Ellen Van Helsing), Ralph Wolter(Boris), Linda Grondier.

Castle Van Screw, Upper Bavaria--a "castle haunted with bats and vampires," namely Count Stanislaus Dracula and Countess

Olivia. Music and noise from the new disco (upstairs) literally wakes the dead (downstairs), but Stan (the Count's great-grandson) and the Count reach a compromise: the castle becomes Hotel Dracula, and the vampires enjoy an unlimited supply of tourist-trade blood. They find, however, that they're "sucking more and enjoying it less," and, jaded and satiated, return to Castle Creaky in Transylvania. Ellen, daughter of Prof. Van Helsing, carries on a losing battle against the Count....

A bad movie with entertaining moments, this is a combination horrorpic/comedy/skinflick, with, even, some random attempts at lyric eroticism. Most of its "on" moments occur in the comic mode--e.g., the Count passing by, singing "You've got me under your skin," or delighting in a woman with "corpuscles like caviar." There's also much play with a huge prop phallus. And a bit with Olivia spitting some apparently-bad blood all over the camera is apparently supposed to be funny....In its vampires-on-holiday atmosphere, DRACULA... resembles the Christopher Lee UNCLE WAS A VAMPIRE(1959). This movie might be Great-Grandpa Was A Dracula....

DRACULA JUNIOR (I) TC2 1982 D: A. Albertini. Ref: V 7/28/82: 32: in production. no V 5/4/83(Int'l).

DRACULA SUCKS see DRACULA BLOWS HIS COOL. LUST AT FIRST BITE.

DRACULA TAN EXARCHIA (Greek) Allagi Films 1983 color 84m. SP,D: Nikos Zervos. SP & with: Jimmis Panousis, Vangelis Cotronis. Ref: Ecran F 36:45. with Kostas Soumas.

Dracula, reincarnated as a Greek rocker, constructs his own singer-musician from the body parts of deceased musical notables.

DRACULA'S BRIDE see LUST AT FIRST BITE

DRACULA'S GREAT LOVE see CEMETERY GIRLS

DRAGON ZOMBIES RETURN (H.K.) Fan Kin Kung/Hau Cheung Lun 1983-U.S. color/ws 90m. D: Hou Cheng. Ref: screen. poster: D: Hau Ching. V 7/13/83:10: in Miami. with Lo Lieh, Shan Koon Ling Fung, Cheung Lo, Shek Fung.

Northern China. A "professional mourner" discovers the Heartbreak Sword in the Treasure Cavern of Heartbreak Gorge. She uses it to cut through the rock blocking the entrance to the Dragon Cave in the Cave of the 12 Animals. Her passage through the Golden Waterfall protects her from the cave's freezing-cold, and she learns dragon-style kung fu. She is now the Eastern Dragon, and leader of the man-like "animals," which include a mouse that can burrow underground, a rooster, a snake, a rabbit, a monkey, a pig, and a ram. They represent 12 different styles of kung fu, and unite to defeat Tiger Shark and his lobster-men....Plus: Heartbreak Music which "drives men mad"...million-year-old jade rock which heals those who lie on it for two hours.

It may not be apparent from either the title or the above synopsis, but this is, largely, a comedy. DRAGON ZOMBIES RETURN plays like The Three Stooges Meet Martha Raye; or, as one member of the audience put it, "This is stupid!" That it is, though rather winningly at times. The animals cavort like monsters out of INFRAMAN, and in no way resemble zombies, the title notwithstanding. The direction is sloppy--each scene takes what seems like a month longer than it has to--but some silly, campy details atone, partly, for the messiness. The magic sword, for instance, cuts through the cave rock with a chainsaw buzz. Later, the villainous Five Elements form a circle and begin to rotate around the heroine, to the sounds of a freight train chugging out of a station. The conclusion of the movie is almost-hysterically funny, intentionally or not: Tiger Shark's portable throne is adorned with (most unimposing) papier-mache sharks--he presses one button, and their jaws shoot out, harpoon-like, on lines, and clamp onto their victims. He pushes another button, and the sharks themselves proceed, variously, to fly out, swim off, or scoot along the sand. Our animal-heroes proceed, variously, to run from them, ride them, hack them in half, etc. (The back half of the hacked shark drops onto the beach; the front half darts away, never to be seen again....) The animals bite Tiger Shark into submission, then form a sort of conga line behind Eastern Dragon, and pull the escaping creature back out of the sea.... Hard to recall, or believe--after this spectacle--but the middle of this movie is actually kind of dull....

DRAGONS OF KRULL see KRULL

2 The DRILLER KILLER 1979 Ref: TV: WV Video. MFB'83:307. S&S'82: 290. and with Harry Schultz, Alan Wynroth, Peter Yellen.

Reno (Jimmy Laine), a frustrated, down-on-his-luck New York artist, takes to stabbing dead rabbits as an emotional outlet. It isn't enough. His paintings begin "whispering" to him, and he has a vision of a bleeding-eyed woman. Finally, he takes his power drill and Porto Pak power source out into the streets, and begins drilling random derelicts....This might have been (should have been) a discarded, rough-first-draft of the material that became MS. 45, Abel Ferrara's 1981 stunner. DRILLER for the most part plays less like a movie than it does a laundry list of complaints re: urban "living"--Neil Simon, sleaze division. It at least doesn't smack of slumming--the production seems as threadbare and precarious as its protagonists' existence. The core of DRILLER--like that of HANGOVER SQUARE (1945)--is the schizophrenic artist--self-expression takes the form, ultimately, of madness and murder. Reno applies drill to body as (more or less) he applies brush (and blow dryer) to canvas: got to get those "demons" out. The art/madness parallel is pretty pat--and yet the murders are, somehow, disturbing, partly it seems because they're not only murders. They're "therapy" for Reno, and succeed all-too-well in making "therapy" seem like a dirty word. The orgasmic, jackhammer effect of the drill on the bodies of the victims, in two or three scenes, seems surrealistically out of proportion to the compact cause--the Monster-from-Reno's-Id, materialized....Ferrara and script-writer Nicholas St. John have given us a new image of horror, if not really much of a movie.

DRIVE IN MASSACRE NAF/Gail/S.A.M. 1981(1976) color 78m. D,P: Stu Segall. SP: John Goff, Buck Flower. Story: "Godfrey Daniels." Ph: K.L. Gibb. Mus: Lon John Prods. FxEd: Warren Hamilton Jr. Mkp: The Duke of Disguise. Ref: TV: Cultvideo. V 2/3/82. VideoSB. Sleazoid Exp 4/82:4. Weldon. with Jake Barnes, Adam Lawrence, Douglas Gudbye, Verkina Flowers.

An L.A. County drive-in which was once a carnival, and is staffed by ex-knife-throwers and sword-swallowers, becomes the scene of a series of beheadings and stabbings (including a couple-on-a-sword double-murder). At the end, we learn that the madness at this one drive-in has "spread to other theatres throughout the country," and a voice announces that "there is a murderer loose in the theatre"....sequence in which madman-with-machete chases a girl (who proves to be his daughter) around a warehouse....Despite the disarming device of the direct-threat-to-your-well-being sign-off (see also NIGHT OF TERROR, 1933), this movie remains just a movie, and a resolutely unshocking one at that. It alternates, unimaginatively, between couples-snuggling-up-at-the-drive-in vignettes and cops-following-up-on-leads dialogue scenes. At its best, it tries for drollery, as in one sequence in which the two cops pretend that they're just another couple snuggling-up at the drive-in. (The one in drag really begins to throw himself into his role....) If you can buy the idea, here, that this drive-in is a converted carnival, you'll certainly believe it when business shows no sign of slacking off after a few double-murders....

2P DUELLE (F) Gaumont/Sunchild-Roitfeld-INA 1976 color 118m. SP,D: Jacques Rivette. SP: also Edouardo De Gregorio, Marilu Parolini. Ph: William Lubtchansky. Mus: Jean Wiener. AD: Eric Simon. Mkp: R. Abreu. SpFX: LAX. Ref: screen. V 6/2/76. NYT 10/13/76. PFA notes 6/30/83. with Juliet Berto, Bulle Ogier, Jean Babilee, Hermine Karagheuz.

From the projected series, Scenes de La Vie Parallele. Two sun/moon goddesses inflict wounds, or burns, on the necks and hands of humans; kill three people. A certain "cursed" gem could prolong their stay on Earth, but drops of blood nullify its power. One goddess, Leni (Berto), is weakened by light; the other, Viva (Ogier), by darkness...."The dream is the night's aquarium...." The people in this film speak using real words, and in the correct order for forming real sentences. Real objects are used in real settings. But the esthetic key to it all seems to have been left under a mat somewhere....The punctuating shots of the moon are stunning--eerie, crystal-clear...the stuff of fantasy. However, a few questions: what exactly do the goddesses want with the hero? Why is he wasting away? How is it that his sister is able to defeat the two? No answers here....aka TWYLIGHT?

DUNGEONS AND DRAGONS or DUNGEONS OF KRULL see KRULL

The DYBBUK (Pol.) Clurman/JSToP 1982 color 105m. SP,D: Stephan Szlachtycz, from Szymon Szurmiej's play. Ref: V 6/30/82. with Golda Tencer, Jan Szurmiej, Hersz Hercher.

E.T.--ESTONG TUTONG (Fili) Archer 1983? D: Angel Labra. Ref: vc box: Solar Video. with Chiquito, Pia Moran, Anna Marin.
Heiress must spend night in haunted house to win fortune.

E.T.--THE EXTRA-TERRESTRIAL Univ 1982 color 115m. (E.T. AND ME-early t) D,Co-P: Steven Spielberg. SP,Assoc P: Melissa Mathison. Ph: Allen Daviau;(fx) Mike McAlister;(mattes) Neil Krepela. Mus: John Williams. PD: James D. Bissell. SpVisFX: Industrial Light & Magic;(sup) Dennis Muren;(coord) Dale Martin;(model sup) Lorne Peterson;(ship des) Ralph McQuarrie. Alien:(des) Carlo Rambaldi;(sd) Ben Burtt;(tech sup) Steve Townsend;(movement) Caprice Rothe; Robert Snort;(eyes) Beverly Hoffman. OptFX:(ph sup) Kenneth F. Smith;(coord) Mitchell Suskin. Mattes: Michael Pangrazio. Anim Sup: Samuel Comstock. SpCons: Craig Reardon. Elec Des: Jerry Jeffress. Ref: screen. MFB'82:282-3: origins in NIGHT SKIES project. Ecran F 29:10-31. FComment 5/82. Hirschhorn. Crawley. Nancy Goldman. Bill Warren. V 5/26/82. MagF&SF 1/83:118-120. with Dee Wallace, Henry Thomas, Peter Coyote, Robert MacNaughton, Drew Barrymore, Milt Kogan; Pat Welsh(voice of E.T.).

The life of an alien left behind on Earth in Southern California becomes intertwined--physically as well as emotionally--with that of a boy, Elliott (Thomas). Out of his element, E.T. begins to weaken, and falls into a death-like sleep, almost taking the empathetic Elliott along with him. E.T., however, revives, and Elliott and his friends arrange a rendezvous with his people (who are returning to Earth in their spaceship)....clips from THIS ISLAND EARTH and The QUIET MAN...aural and visual references to "Peter Pan," Yoda, "Buck Rogers," "The Twilight Zone."

A magical movie--maybe even a bit too magical....Steven Spielberg has become the movies' master manipulator, the Hitchcock of the happier emotions. (Baird Searles, MF&SF: "seldom have I felt so manipulated in my life.") Whatever Spielberg wants--or, to be more specific, whatever he wants us to feel--he gets, and there's something slightly offputting about a filmmaker who gets his own way with such astonishing (apparent) ease. Noone, Spielberg virtually challenges his audience, leaves E.T. unhappy. And few viewers do. Yet one might still, stubbornly, like to see what would happen if he and his collaborators ever ran out of sure-fire tricks and shtiks for E.T., and were compelled to burrow more deeply into their subject of emotional empathy. But if their creative well does not seem very deep, it also seems never to run dry....One can hardly help, it's true, but marvel when the bicycles soar in E.T.--they send the viewer flying, emotionally--but, one wonders, could the effects-sensitive Spielberg achieve that same sense of exhilaration without soaring bicycles--through, simply, actors? If Spielberg has imagination, that imagination does not, yet, seem that of a consistently first-rate artist. His talent, at present, seems more extensive than intensive. Like little E.T., he's almost monotonously inventive. He can do so much so well that it may seem beside the point to suggest that it might be better if he could do only one or two things well. (His modest, but gem-like contribution to TWILIGHT ZONE--THE MOVIE suggests that such a suggestion may not be beside the point.) One would, however, certainly not want to do without this movie's many breathtaking compositions and images--e.g., the not-quite-incidental, dreamlike sliver-of-a-moon/cornstalks/greenhouse shot (and repeat of same), which seems to function as a kind of pictorial way-station between fantasy and reality--all manner of twilight creatures might thrive in such an exotic atmosphere....Nor, of course, would one want to surrender any of little Drew Barrymore's action-and-reaction shots. They--more so, even, than the contributions of the (offscreen) technicians--are responsible for bringing E.T. into imaginative existence....And one wouldn't want not to fly. But most of the narrative inventions and visual effects seem to be substituting for a deepening, or widening, of theme and characterization. E.T. is a pleasant-enough fellow, but he has a one-track mind (he wants to go home)--and the youngsters are developed little further than amusing reaction-shots. The adults, intriguingly, are simply sketched into the corners of the story--they, at least, never get tiresome. The score (lesser John Williams) is largely redundant--sweet on sweet. An aural counterpoint to the happy/nice/warm imagery was perhaps needed--Spielberg and Mathison certainly require no direct assistance in getting to our emotions....When, at the end of the movie, the spaceship flies off (with E.T. aboard), it does not leave behind an ordinary vapor trail. It leaves a rainbow--one of the loveliest uses of same since Genesis. Its message of hope might seem a bit shamelessly unshaded, but one has to admire the audaciousness (on Spielberg's, or Muren's, part) of this gesture, this celestial semaphore. If Spielberg gets his own way, well, it's better than most ways....

See also: AIRPLANE II.

EARTHRIGHT see RETURN, The(1980)

EASTER SUNDAY see BEING, The

EATING RAOUL Fox-QFI/Bartel 1982(1981) 90m. SP,D & with: Paul Bartel. SP & with: also Richard Blackburn. Ph: Gary Thietges; Karen Grossman; Gary Graver. Mus: Arlon Ober. AD: Robert Schulenberg. MkpFX: Peter Knowlton. PyroFX: Frank Pope. Opt FX: Jack Rabin. SpThanks: Joe Dante, John Landis, Miller Drake, Ted Gershuny et al. Ref: screen. PFA notes 10/16/81. MFB'83: 13. V 3/24/82. with Mary Woronov, Robert Beltran, Ed Begley Jr., Buck Henry, Garry Goodrow, Don Steele, Billy Curtis, Chuck Griffith, Susan Saiger, John Paragon, Myron Meisel.

A strait-laced couple, Paul and Mary Bland (Bartel and Woronov, respectively), take to murdering swingers for their money; dump their bodies into a trash compactor. ("I'll bag the Nazi and straighten up around here.") Unbeknownst to them, their new assistant, Raoul (Beltran), begins selling the bodies to the Doggie King Dogfood Company--Raoul quickly becomes a nuisance and a dinner, in that order. ("We're having a friend for dinner.")

Rather mild black comedy might have been made by the Blands. The tacit comic point--that the up-tight Blands are kinkier than their kinkiest victims--is too frail a conceit to hold the film together. Paul and Mary are not of course meant to be exactly believable, but they're not believably unbelievable either. They exist in a kind of limbo between character and caricature. Some of the props, however--e.g., Mary's legs (to turn guests on), Paul's frying pan (to turn them off)--take on a life of their own, and the film's sound effects--onscreen and offscreen thumps (as Paul applies the frying pan to various heads); a squeaky mouse-nose--are among the drollest since the heyday of Preston Sturges.

ECHOES Continental Dist.(Rosenthal)/Herberval & Seidelman-Nice Presents & Shiffman 1983(1980) color 89m. D: Arthur Allan Seidelman. SP: Richard J. Anthony. Ph: Hanania Baer. Mus: Stephen Schwartz; G.B. Cohen. AD: Neal Deluca. SpFX: Peter Kunz. Paintings:(orig) Frank Mason; Renaldo De Juan. SpVisFX: Cinema Research. Mkp: Piedra, Stockland. Ref: TV: VidAmerica. V 12/21/83. with Richard Alfieri(Michael/Serrano), Nathalie Nell, Mercedes McCambridge, Ruth Roman, Gale Sondergaard(psychic), Mike Kellin, Duncan Quinn(man in dream).

New York City. An art student is haunted, in visions and dreams, by his unborn twin brother, who is/was the reincarnation of the 19th-century killer of artist Alberto Serrano. A psychic tells Michael that he was "followed" into life, that his own sensitivity gave the phantom an opening, and that a particular Serrano painting "is the place of (his) dreams." Michael's art improves as he delves deeper into his soul (a "very old soul" dating back to ancient Greece), but his personality sours. He becomes surly and rude, as if possessed. Finally, he takes hold of his life and frees himself from the other....

An encore for the artist-possessed theme (a la The DEVIL'S HAND, 1942, and HANGOVER SQUARE, 1945)...a theme which seems to presuppose an inverse ratio between the quality of the art involved and the quality of the life of the artist involved. Michael is happy again at the end of ECHOES--will, then, his art degenerate? We aren't told. The comic sequel would show Michael doing everything he could think of to make himself miserable again, in order to create great paintings. This art-out-of-suffering idea is a bit romantic--it ignores other mainsprings of art (e.g., talent, dedication, environment, chance), and is a pretty clear endorsement of agony and suffering. Would that the road to brilliance and genius were so plainly marked....Within its romantic limitations, however, ECHOES is a decent fantasy-thriller. Its dialogue is often fairly sophisticated--that is, it's suggestive of minds/people slightly more complicated than the people generally found in such thrillers. Michael and Christine (Nell) say unexpected small things which seem to come out of the characters and the situation, or rather out of the character-in-the-situation. And the phantom-twin possession plot is a bit more involved than the possessive-house plots currently in fashion....

ECHTZEIT see REALTIME

EGG, The see SPACE CHILDREN, The

*The END OF THE WORLD L'Ecran d'Art 1930 103m. Adap: Abel Gance, Andre Lang. Ph: also Roudakoff, Forster, Hubert. Mus: also Arthur Honegger, Michel Levine. Ref: screen. Chirat: also German (Das ENDE DER WELT), Spanish, English & sound versions. David Bradley. and with Colette Darfeuil, Samson Fainsilber.

Eighteen minutes of extracts and behind-the-scenes footage are all that is known to exist of La FIN DU MONDE, but they feature some interesting distorting effects, done with either mirror, it seems, or prism....The plot concerns a scientist whose dream of a "Republique Universelle" comes true when a comet threatens to collide with, but finally merely grazes the Earth....

ENDANGERED SPECIES MGM-UA/Alive 1982 color 97m. SP,D: Alan Rudolph. SP: also John Binder. Story: Judson Klinger, Richard Woods. Ph: Paul Lohmann;(addl) Jan Kiesser. Mus: Gary Wright. PD: Trevor Williams. SpFX: Jonnie Burke, Steve Galich. Graphic FX: Digital Multi-Media. Mkp: M. Westmore. SdFxEd: Bob Waxman. Ref: TV. Bill Warren. SFChron 9/11/82. 6/8/83:60: Acad SF,F&H nominee, best sf film. HR 9/8/82. V 9/8/82. E Bay Express 9/17/82. with Robert Urich, JoBeth Williams, Paul Dooley, Hoyt Axton, Peter Coyote, Harry Carey Jr., John Considine, Marin Kanter, Heather Menzies.

"Seems somebody's killing...cows" around Buffalo, Colorado. "Bright lights in the sky" are seen; "strange noises" heard. There are shots of sf-ish-looking, computer-studded "saucer" innards. (UFO's and "devil cultists" are, variously, blamed.) The cattle in question are drained of blood; their vital organs have "evaporated"; and "traces of a rare bacterium" (a deadly poison modified by gene splicing, and associated by a pathologist with government chemical and germ-warfare testing) are found in the remains. "Cows now; people later"--but not much later: some Buffalo citizens find themselves subject to mysterious bleeding, and the sheriff (Axton) dies with his guts popping out. ("The man virtually exploded!") These events are linked to huge Trans-Allied Grain & Storage trucks and to abandoned Air Force missile silos outside town, where underground lights flicker--and surgical-laser machines operate on cattle. (The latter's nervous and reproductive systems, it's explained, are almost identical to a human's.) Behind the events: a right-wing, germ-warfare plot against the Russians.

ENDANGERED SPECIES is more or less an unofficial updating of William Cameron Menzies' The WHIP HAND(1951). Again, a small American town is the setting for secret germ-warfare experiments. This time, however, the experimenters are working against not for the U.S.S.R. And the villains, naturally, are now on the right rather than on the left. The paranoia is the same--only the affiliations have changed. If ENDANGERED SPECIES is clearly the better film, it too is still, at heart, routine melodrama. Story and characters here are basically familiar; however, it's told better, and they're sketched-in more carefully than usual. The community-cavalry-to-the-rescue climax is particularly exciting, and, perhaps oddly, the excitement is not at all mitigated by the fact that the cavalry arrives a bit late, allowing the plotters to escape. This mixed-bag resolution is neither cynical nor sentimental--it celebrates honest, if frustrated effort. It sounds a sort of "Keep watching the skies!" cry. Next Time, maybe....The movie is a skillful, if at times superficial blend of mystery, horror, and sf elements. The look, for instance, of the helicopter cow-catcher (the caught cows seem to be flying upside-down on stilts) lies somewhere between sf and surrealism, and the night raids on the cattle are shot partially-subjectively (the copter's pov), from, in effect, a flying and/or giant-monster's viewpoint. (Cf. TARANTULA, and its giant cattle-eater.) The experimenters' villainy is characterized by their joshing about blood and guts. (Cf. M.A.S.H.)

See also: RETURN, The(1980).

ENDE DER WELT, Das see END OF THE WORLD, The

The ENTITY Fox/American Cinema(Pelleport) 1982(1981) color/ws 125m. D: Sidney J. Furie. SP: Frank DeFelitta, from his novel. Ph: S.H. Burum. Mus: Charles Bernstein. PD: Charles Rosen. VisFX:(des) William Cruse;(opt coord) Walt Shipley; (prod coord) Elizabeth Goldsmith;(exec) Joe Lombardi;(ph) Sam DiMaggio. SpMkpFX: Stan Winston, James Kagel. SpFX: SpFX Unltd.; Marty Bresin et al. Sculpture: George Risko. SdFxEd: Keith Stafford. Video Cons: Hal Landaker. Ref: screen. MFB'82: 263-4. V 11/3/82. Ecran F 32:72-5. with Barbara Hershey, Ron

Silver, David Labiosa, Margaret Blye, George Coe, Alex Rocco; Ed Begley et al(voices).

Los Angeles, 1976. Electrical discharges, rays, ectoplasmic configurations, rumbling dressers and mirrors, and exploding windows ("classic poltergeist activity") prove to be, simply, foreplay for an entity from another plane of existence. This being periodically rapes, bites, and bruises a housewife, and physically repulses both her lover and her son. In a controlled experiment, it is temporarily trapped, by liquid helium, in ice, but even at the end "the attacks continue," though with abated force.

A very serious version of SATAN'S MISTRESS. We are shown, unequivocally, supernatural rape. The script, it's true, also offers a psychological explanation--which may or may not apply in this case--for such incidents. But there's no ambiguity about the supernatural explanation--it does apply. Family, friends, lovers, psychiatrists, and parapsychologists, in this movie, are all here for a reason, and it's the same reason in each case--to be convinced. The ENTITY is concerned less with one woman's attempt to cope with life in an erotic twilight zone than it is with unfriendly persuasion. Belief is all that's required, of characters and viewers. Script and book are based on a true story--any resemblance to the devices of fiction is purely coincidental. In the movie, only the psychiatrist remains unconvinced. He's so mule-headed that it seems to be he and not his patient who is in need of professional help. But--not being a privileged witness to the manifestations which abound (he was, apparently, just about the only person in L.A. in '76 who was so deprived)--he's stuck with a conventional conception of reality. The script is so determined to make its case for the reality of the supernatural that it discredits the possibility of any other reality. It discourages open-mindedness. Of course the same could be said of many horror-fantasies (e.g., CAT PEOPLE, 1942, in which the cat person actually slays her psychiatrist), but in most horror movies, any special pleading for fantasy remains subservient to other matters--like shock scenes, special effects, or the depiction of an emotional reality. Here, there are no other matters. The film's fun-horrific shocks and effects seem very incidental to its characters' views on humongous, invisible rapists....

ESCAPE FROM DS-3 Gold Key-TV c1981 color 90m. Ref: GKey. TVG. TVFFSB. with Jackson Bostwick, David Chandler, Bubba Smith.
Robot-aided escape try from satellite prison.

ESCAPE FROM THE BRONX (I) Fulvia 1983 (FUGA DAL BRONX) D: Enzo Castellari. Ref: V 5/4/83:298. Ecran F 40:70. with Mark Gregory, Henry Silva, Valeria D'Obici, Timothy Brent.
Underground city of the 21st Century.

ESCAPE 2000 (Austral.) New World/Filmco-Hemdale-Second FGH Consort. 1983(1981) color/ws 92m.(75m.-U.S.) (TURKEY SHOOT-orig t) D: Brian Trenchard-Smith. SP: Jon George, Neill Hicks. Story: George Schenck, Robert Williams, David Lawrence. Ph: John McLean. Mus: Brian May. PD: Bernard Hides. SpFX: John Stears; Peter Hutchinson, Bernie Corfield. Mkp:(sp fx) Bob McCarron;(art) Annie Pospischil. Opt: Roger Cowland. Scenic Art: Billy Malcolm. Ref: screen. V 4/20/83. 8/3/83:4(rated). MFB'83:78. Ecran F 35:39-40. with Steve Railsback, Olivia Hussey, Michael Craig, Carmen Duncan, Noel Ferrier.

"Re-education and Behavior Modification" are the order of the day at Camp 47, where "deviates" learn "unquestioning acceptance" of the State and its laws. Torture and sadism are authority's tools, and the camp commander organizes "turkey shoots"--in which inmates are hunted for "sport"--for visitng bigwigs. (The "shoots" also prevent overcrowding.) Rebellious inmates and Standing Order 7--"Wipeout"--however, wipe out the island compound....crossbow-weapon with laser-like, explosive arrows...monstrous circus-freak with weird eyes and big teeth (cf. Tonga, in The SIGN OF FOUR)....A rather nasty-minded cross between The CAMP ON BLOOD ISLAND and The MOST DANGEROUS GAME. The script pays lip service to rugged individualism, but its spirit is clearly with the authoritarian sadists. It's not so much a battle of wits, here, between hunter and hunted, as it is a case of simple tit-for-tat brutality. The film is just too eager to be perversely amusing--it puts the viewer in the position of the camp's guests. You're invited to "savor" the various atrocities--or risk seeming to be a "spoilsport." Not a fun movie, this....

ESCORT TO DANGER AND THE NIGHT OF THE CLONES see SPIDER-MAN

ESPRIT D'AMOUR (H.K.-Cant.) Golden Princess/Cinema City 1983 color 98m. D: Ringo L.T. Lam. SP: Ko Chi Sum, Lo Kin, Raymond Fung. Story,Co-P: Raymond Wong. Ph: Pui, Seng. Mus: Violet Lam. AD: K.Y.C. Man. Ref: V 2/8/84. with Alan Tam, Cecilia Chan, Ni Shu Chun.

"Romantic-horror"...spirit.

The EVIL DEAD New Line/Renaissance(Tapert) 1983(1980) color 84m. (BOOK OF THE DEAD-orig t) SP,D: Sam Raimi. Ph: Tim Philo. Mus: Joe LoDuca. SpMkpFX: Tom Sullivan. PhFxSup: Bart Pierce. Title Des: August. Ref: screen. V 3/24/82:63(ad). 2/9/83. VV 5/3/83:54. Filmex '83. MFB'82:264: poster for The HILLS HAVE EYES featured. Ecran F 30:8-13. with Bruce Campbell, Sarah York, Betsy Baker, Ellen Sandweiss, Hal Delrich.

In Tennessee..."The Trees--they know!" And clocks run backwards....Their pendulums stop...and start again....Trap doors open themselves....Porch swings act like battering rams on old cabin walls (and make sounds like the beating of ceremonial drums)....Here, it's not just "dark shadows moving in the woods" that are menacing--"the woods themselves" are alive--twigs and branches come to snake-like life and rape, or attempt to rape, a young woman....Disembodied voices call "Join us"....

It all seems to start with the "Book of the Dead"--bound in human flesh and written in blood--which records "ancient Sumerian burial practices." Taped recitations from same revive demons who proceed to possess, one by one, four of five young people on holiday. Two of the monstrous possessed are dispatched by dismemberment; two, when the Book is burned. The hero, however, has an appointment with a final demon at the end....

In The EVIL DEAD, the monsters are wittier than ever, and the people are dumber than ever. This schematization appears to be no accident. The characters here are simply stooges, or straight men, for the demons. Unequal to their roles of "heroes" and "heroines," they *deserve* their fates. They venture blindly into the darkest and most dangerous places; they bury the "dead" demons without dismembering them; they *unchain* demons who make sounds like humans. These nincompoops are "comments" on the people in other, less savvy horror movies. (Not, however, on the protagonists of The HILLS HAVE EYES, referred to herein, who are *smart* and earn their happier fates.) The nobody-left ending isn't cynical or nihilistic; for these boobies, it qualifies as poetic, or comic, justice. The hero--i.e., the last to be possessed--is, it's true, sincere and caring, and the trinket which he gave to his beloved carries him through *almost* to the end. But sincerity can carry him only so far, and he too, finally, has to go. His heart is at odds with his head when his sweetie becomes a cackling demon, and in *this* movie, heads win. (Even severed, *her* head keeps on cackling.) It's the survival of the wittiest--the demons have makeup effects *and* sarcasm on their side. They make life--or what little is left of same--hell for these kids. They add insult to injury, constantly hectoring them and sarcastically repeating their lines back at them. They are children of The EXORCIST, but this film, fortunately, has none of the sanctimoniousness or High Purpose of that film. The EVIL DEAD is pure Grand Guignol. It *is* extreme in its violence, but it has a fun-horrific spirit which makes it play, in whole, like the best *parts* of the past decade's horror movies. It's gross, but in such strangely *imaginative* ways that the grossness becomes comical. "Oops!--went too far," Raimi might be saying to us, mockingly. When the "hero" severs his beloved's/the demon's head, the latter plops down, still taunting, in the foreground; the *body* lands (in the background) squarely on *him*--the *neck* keeps pumping out blood or white yuchh, and the *hands* slash his face. So much for sincerity; this is the *definitive* "end-of-the-affair" scene....The EVIL DEAD is (among other things) the *ne plus ultra* of the subjective-camera-monster movie. These demons are intimidating long before we actually see them. They travel halfway across Tennessee, it seems, to reach their intended victims, and they knock down--before them/"us"--just about anything in their way. One such speed-demon is temporarily rebuffed by a closed door, and the camera "recoils," back into the woods, like a bouncing rubber projectile--the kinetic energy of these creatures can't, it's obvious, be contained, only re-directed, and the movie exploits, even celebrates, such kinetic exhilaration. The camera moves faster here; camera angles and positions are more pronounced; sound effects are more insistent; lighting effects are more vivid. Visually and dramatically, the film is pitched several keys higher than it needs to be. It's excessive, and glad to be so--it takes the cinematic and narrative conventions of its genre to their outer limits. At one point, blood on a movie-projector lens projects onto the hero, as if to say to us, "It's only a movie--let's make the most of it while we can!"

EVIL PASSAGE see POWER, The

EVILS OF THE NIGHT Mars 1983 D,P: Mardi Rustam. Ref: Bill Warren. V 7/6/83:30. 12/14/83:4(rated). no PFA. HR 6/28/83. with John Carradine, Neville Brand, Aldo Ray, Julie Newmar, Tina Louise, Karrie Emerson, Keith Fisher.
"Science fiction fantasy."(V)

2 EVILSPEAK The Moreno Co./Camel(Sylvio Tabet) 1982(1981) 90m. SP: also E. Weston. Mus: Roger Kellaway. AD: George Costello, Dena Roth. SpFX: Harry Woolman, John Carter;(ph) R.D. Bailey; (ad) Wendy Vanguard. SpVisFxMkp: Makeup Effects, White, Apone & Carrisosa;(assoc) Suzanne Moreau et al. SpPh: Dream Quest. SpProcessing: Fairlight. OptFX: Cinema Research. Ref: TV. V 11/11/81:6(rated). 1/27/82. Weldon. Ecran F 28:69. and with Joseph Cortese, Claude Earl Jones.
During the Inquisition, the 16th-century devil cult of Lorenzo Esteban (Richard Moll) is banished from Spain; 20th-century cadet Stanley Coopersmith (Clint Howard) finds relics of his cult in the cellar of a California military-school chapel. Coopersmith half-wittingly programs Esteban's spirit into a computer....Wild pigs attack and kill the possessor of the Book of Death, which vanishes and later reappears in Esteban's crypt....nightmare of living-fetus-in-bottle....In the free-for-all finale, Esteban seems to possess Coopersmith, and the latter, levitating, wreaks revenge on his enemies (virtually the whole school) with fire, sword, and pig; a bleeding crucifix sends a nail flying into a priest's forehead; and a corpse revives and kills. Implicit outcome: school soccer match cancelled.
Or, CARRIE with pigs. You know you're in bad hands when the film's first "grabber" is a match cut of a flying severed head and a soaring soccer ball. The twist here on the WILLARD-CARRIE-FADE TO BLACK revenge story is that the black magic is computerized, and some of the resultant effects are indeed striking. But they take up about a minute or two, and the more traditional get-the-nebbish and revenge-of-the-nebbish stuff takes up the bulk of the movie. The computer--not satisfied with dog's blood for its black mass--keeps insisting on "human blood," somewhat as the plant in LITTLE SHOP OF HORRORS keeps demanding food. Not-bad musical score.

*EVOLUTION Red Seal 1925 stopmo anim & live 45m. (The BIRTH OF THE EARTH-alt t) Ref: screen. Glut/CMM.
Brief clips (footage from *GHOST OF SLUMBER MOUNTAIN) pitting a tyrannosaurus against a triceratops, and two triceratops against each other, in a tepid semi-documentary.

EXTERMINATORS OF THE YEAR 3000 (I?) 2T 1983 D: Jules Harrison. Ref: V 9/14/83:6: at Sitges. 5/4/83:330: future holocaust. with Robert Janucci, Gabriele Ferzetti, Luca Valentini.

EYE OF THE BEHOLDER(by M.Behm) see MORTELLE RANDONEE

EYES WITHOUT A FACE 1959('78-Eng.-subtitled version) (*The HORROR CHAMBER OF DR. FAUSTUS-orig U.S.t) SpFX: Henri Assola; LAX. Mkp: Georges Klein. Ref: screen. Durgnat/Franju. AFI: '62-U.S., Cameo Int'l. S&S'83:266-71. Clarens. Bill Warren. V 8/26/59. FQ Smr'62:55-56: "if horror pictures are a disease, this is surely the cure." and with Francois Guerin, Rene Genin, Blavette, Claude Brasseur, Alexandre Rignault.
Via his own, revolutionary process of "hetero-grafting," Professor Genessier (Pierre Brasseur) transplants the face of a young woman (Juliette Mayniel) onto his faceless daughter (Edith Scob); but the graft doesn't take....The jumping-off point for EYES WITHOUT A FACE might be any old Monogram or PRC sf-horror-fantasy like, say, VOODOO MAN or The APE. Not that it quite justifies those films. But the blueprints for it can be found in those beloved "Z" horrors in which a mad doctor sacrifices the lives/bodies/souls of strangers for the sake of a loved one (generally his wife). Director Georges Franju pointedly does not, however, revive golden lines like "You're mad!" or "You can't just take people's lives/bodies/souls/faces!" He retains only the basic, horrific situation, leaving the moral--and thus much of the horror--implicit: the accusation, "You're mad!" (of Brasseur's Genessier), though unspoken, can be heard very clearly in-between the lines of dialogue. In movies from CAPTIVE WILD WOMAN to CURSE OF FRANKENSTEIN, the doctor's aide accuses the doctor, point-blank, of moral and ethical outrages. And although it's true that, in this film, the doctor's daughter at one point states that she would rather die than submit to the pain of another operation (an oblique criticism of his pursuits), it's also true that noone in the film says anything to the effect that removing the faces of living women is, in and of itself, reprehensible. We are left--as in Hawks' SCARFACE--to navigate, morally, for ourselves, in an out-of-kilter world. There's noone to hold up cue-cards for us. We know only that something is not right. The standard shock-movie dialogue seems, in this new light, a sort of moral cushion, protecting us against the full implications of the material, against the horror; doing our thinking and feeling for us. Genessier's experiments are no more appalling than those of John Carradine's Dr. Walters in CAPTIVE WILD WOMAN (qq.v.), but their nature is suggested (in dialogue) and detailed

(in images) without benefit of any moral anesthetic (for the viewer). (Genessier at one point expresses a desire to remove the donor girl's face "in one large piece"--!!) When Genessier's assistant/secretary/mistress (Alida Valli) asks him what he's going to do about one of the still-living victims of his experiments, he responds, "I'll feed her, take care of her...." His solicitude is an afterthought. The theatre audience laughs. We never knew he cared....His daughter, Christiane, is miserable, and probably would be even with a new face. ("Now I have to live for the others too," she muses, when it appears as if the transplanted face will take.) Such considerations wouldn't occur to him. His "care" for her is, in effect, indistinguishable from indifference. Genessier is a maddeningly one-dimensional character--Mr. Scientist--and the film's horror and comedy are played off against that one-dimensionality. He's grotesquely single-minded, the moral hollow at the center of the narrative's universe. When the dogs gnaw his face up at the end you can't really care one way or the other. In a more glibly humanistic film, you would. But with EYES WITHOUT A FACE, your involvement is pitched at some surreal, stunned-responses level; it seems wholly natural, even somehow symmetrical, dramatically, that Genessier lose life and face (like the vivisectionist vivisected in ISLAND OF LOST SOULS). Ernest Callenbach detects "this slight detachedness," but considers it "not part of (the film's) moral strategy...." Yet Genessier's own end distils the horrific essence of his "scientific" acts: you are as calm and detached, at the end of the film, as he was, earlier, and there's a chill in that detachment. You're not really granted the satisfaction of seeing revenge taken, as you are in horror pictures like ISLAND OF LOST SOULS. You're simply seeing Genessier as he saw others--as objects. It's as if, at the end, Franju had inserted a documentary re: the effects of canine incisors on the skin of humans. The dogs' "experiment" on Genessier produces the standard results. This time, however, there's no disparity between intent--he had hoped to usher in a new era in skin-grafting--and effect, means and ends: mincemeat is mincemeat. EYES WITHOUT A FACE is not so much a condemnation of science as it is a critique of the ideal of scientific detachment. It's an endorsement of ambivalence....Christiane--in her coldly beautiful death-mask-in-effect--is, at film's end, free of her father's compulsions. The beauty of her eyes-and-mask haunt the film and give it its fairy-tale ambiance and ambiguity. Christiane is like a displaced princess who has somehow wandered into a horror film, lending the latter her grace, partaking of its dread.

The FACE AT THE WINDOW (Austral.) D.B. O'Connor Feature Films 1919 D: Charles Villiers. From F.B. Warren's play. Ref: George E. Turner. "The Australian Screen." Lee. with Agnes Dobson, O'Connor, Claude Turton.

The FALCON'S ADVENTURE RKO 1946 61m. D: William Berke. SP: Aubrey Wisberg. Addl Dial: R.E. Kent. From Michael Arlen's books. Ph: H. Wild, F. Redman. Mus: Paul Sawtell. AD: Albert S. D'Agostino, W.E. Keller. SpFX: Russell A. Cully. Ref: TV. TVFFSB. LC. HR 12/10/46. V 12/11/46: last of the Conway Falcons. FDY. Bill Warren: bor-sf. MPH 12/14/46. FD 12/12/46. Academy. with Tom Conway, Ed Brophy, Madge Meredith, Robert Warwick, Ian Wolfe, Myrna Dell, Steve Brodie, Jason Robards.

Formula for "industrial diamonds"...alligator-farm setting... scene in which a man (Brophy) dons an alligator-head mask, climbs into a tank, and bellows, in order to scare a crook into a confession....Unremarkable Falcon entry, except for the latter scene, which is fairly flabbergasting. (Or, Variety: film "goes slightly haywire with some eccentric plot furbelows....") Otherwise, Brophy's comic relief is, as usual, no relief.

FALCON'S GOLD (Can.) Showtime-TV/Heller-Schulz-Greenberg-Sonesta (Intrepid) 1982 color 89m. D: Bob Schulz. SP: Olaf Pooley. (A

The FALL OF THE HOUSE OF USHER (Cz) Trnka Studio 1980 anim D: Jan Svankmajer. Ref: IFG'82:335: from Poe. V 5/4/83:264.

The FALL OF THE HOUSE OF USHER (Sp) 1983 D: Jesus Franco. Ref: V 5/9/84:408: Elite Films. with Howard Vernon, Lina Romay.

See also: HOUSE OF THE LONG SHADOWS. HOUSE OF USHER.

The FALLS (B) MOMA/BFI(Greenaway) 1980 color & b&w 190m. SP, D,Ed: Peter Greenaway. Ph: Mike Coles, John Rosenberg. Mus: Michael Nyman; Brian Eno, John Hyde et al. Narr: Hilary Thompson et al. Ref: screen. PFA notes 8/23/83. with Peter Westley, Aad Wirtz, Michael Murray, Patricia Carr.

A post-VUE "documentary," or rather "a fiction" of "considerable complexity." Many years after a Violent Unexplained Event has affected roughly 19 million people around the world (though few in France), 92 case histories of the afflicted are here presented, in an attempt to illuminate the VUE. All living victims (some died) exhibit one or more incipient avian characteristics, including "random white patches" on the body, a six-part heart, a feeling of listlessness and debilitation "away from the influence of chlorophyll," wing-skin, retractable thumbs, and identification with swallows. Victims are also immortal (eternally celebrating the same birthday, be it 8 or 80), generally sterile, and often given to blackouts and dreams of flying over water. One woman, Artesia Fallarine, becomes a "creature designed to render the services of an oasis" (i.e., her every pore produces water). Another is "happiest hanging upside-down like a bat." One person suffers from an "allergy to public exposure." Another is compelled to catalogue "bird-film titles." Many are given to driving vehicles in circles. "Ornithograffiti" is prevalent. Several victims find themselves "starting projects that other, invariably less-gifted people complete." All victims invent new languages. There are VUE novelties and a VUE anthem. One man, fond of illusionism, disappears, and another finds himself "welcome at children's parties." The VUE epicenter is variously thought to have been at The Raven (a pub in West London), the Boulder Orchard of Starling Fallanx, and other locations. The Violent Event itself remains Unexplained, though a "responsibility of birds" theory is popular. One such notion holds that the VUE was/is a revenge plot by ratite birds to turn man into a flightless bird; another, that the VUE is a hoax perpetrated by the estate of Alfred Hitchcock, to give ornithological credence to "the unsettling and unsatisfactory ending" of The BIRDS.

The FALLS is a monument to the inconsequential. Data accrues; facts pile up; theories are promulgated. But (as one of the narrators at one point says) "the value of the surveys is doubtful." A pseudo-documentary, about an imaginary catastrophe (which does silly things to people, or which makes people do silly things), this film is, at base, simply "a wealth of bird anecdotes." It goes on and on, but unlike most fiction films, it doesn't gather, or attempt to gather, meaning or significance to itself. Like a centrifuge, it separates out and expels meaning. Peter Greenaway is, here, in his script's own term, an "ephemerologist," a connoisseur of the evanescent, even non-existent. The VUE does not "expand" into some sociological metaphor, nor does it serve as a pretext for a comment on either the human or the avian condition. The FALLS is the comic inverse of an epic. Its own movie-epic length serves as an undercutting device. Three hours may seem rather a lot of drollery, but the movie's dismaying comprehensiveness can itself be seen as the height of the droll. Greenaway adapts Herzog's absurdist image of the man literally-going-around-in-circles for some of his VUE victims, and the film itself constitutes one big circle. A merry-go-round, it goes nowhere--getting nowhere, however, proves to be half the fun. The FALLS might have been made by an undergraduate amused by the daunting detail of his zoology textbook--it might even be a revised edition of the latter. It's trivia, paradoxically, on a truly grand scale, and it could be an unnerving experience for those who demand development in a narrative; The FALLS depends upon repetition, or minuscule variation. It has all the dramatic sweep of a catalogue or a checklist....The film's tone is mocking, yet friendly. Greenaway obviously loves quirks, and The FALLS is replete with same--in characters, in words and phrases, in images. He has invented a world which is exclusively quirks....

FANGS (Cinaco-TV)/Names-Wilson 1978 color 90m. Ref: VideoSB: horror. no PFA. no V. no Academy. with Les Tremayne, Janet

Wood, Bebe Kelly, Marvin Kaplan, Alice Nunn.
Texas snake-handler unleashes his charges on his enemies.

FANGS OF THE LIVING DEAD (Gold Key-TV)/Europix Int'l. 1968('72-U.S.) 80m.-U.S. (*MALENKA) AD: Lega-Michelena. Mkp: Ponte, Tilli. Ref: TV. Willis/SW. GKey. Lee. no FFacts. Weldon. Stanley. and with Fernando Bilbao, Paul Muller, Ros(s)ana Yanni.
Secrets of Arabic alchemy and necro-biology turn human subjects into "nosferatu," immortal vampires....vampire count who is torched, turned into skeleton...vampire-women who seem to go scot-free (at least in the abridged, U.S. version)....Sloppily-made, undistinguished, though dumb lines help some--e.g., the count's "Go ahead, Sylvia, bite!", as the testy heroine (Anita Ekberg, who also plays Malenka, in a flashback) approaches our bound hero. (But she was only fooling and pretending to be a vampire....) Generous helpings of cleavage don't hurt either....

FANTASIES ABC-TV/Mandy(Goldberg) 1982 color 90m. D: William Wiard. SP,P: David Levinson. Ph: R.L. Rawlings. Mus: James Di Pasquale. AD: Serge Krizman, Paul Sylos. SpFX: Willard G. Ferrier. Mkp: Cash, Moschella. SdFX: Echo, B. Wistrom. Ref: TV. TVG. with Suzanne Pleshette, Barry Newman, Lenora May, Patrick O'Neal, Robert Vaughn, Ben Marley(Arthur), Stuart Damon, Robin Mattson, Madlyn Rhue, Allyn Ann McLerie.
A madman who "went to Middleton," a TV soap-opera town, believes that the "only way to make it stop" is to kill the cast and creator of the show; he proceeds to commit a series of brutal murders....post-shower murder-by-knife...attempted strangling...subjective-camera stalker who hums "Pop Goes the Weasel" and is a red herring....A superficially sensitive, basically crude mystery-shocker--a diluted TV version of the theatrically-released killer-on-the-loose horrors. Its one narrative pseudo-coup: the killer and the subjective-camera stalker prove not to be one and the same. The thin-line-between-real-and-reel-life strokes (including the it's-only-a-movie kicker) seem, simply, pretentious frills. The dialogue is generally just glib, though with occasional bite, and features at least one suspicion-attracting line for each character.

The FANTASTIC JOURNEY NBC-TV/Bruce Lansbury & Col-TV 1977 color 110m. D: Andrew V. McLaglen, Barry Crane. SP: Michaelian, Powers, Gerard. Ph: Lippman, Leavitt. Mus: Robert Prince. AD: Bellah, Purcell, Braunger. SpFX: Richard Albain, Don Courtney. Mkp: Ben Lane. Ref: TVG. V 2/9/77:75. TV: orig.shown as series premiere; run later (with an interpolated series episode) as CBS Late Movie. with Jared Martin(Varian), Scott Thomas, Carl Franklin, Karen Somerville, Ike Eisenmann, Leif Erickson, Scott Brady, Jason Evers, Mike Road(voice of The Source).
Ocean voyagers find a land in the Bermuda Triangle in which past, present, and future exist together, divided into "zones of time." In one zone, a living brain called The Source

telepathically rules the Unders of the Atlantis of 30,000 years ago and regenerates itself by absorbing the life-force of a boy...man, Varian, from the year 2230...part-alien woman who communicates with cat and whose eyes are hypnotic...false double of boy...Pool of Mirrors which reflects gazers' thoughts.... Good (i.e., the friendly) against evil (i.e., the callous) yet again, in a TV movie/premiere/series-episode congested with co-plots and characters--most of the latter just want to go home again. (Except for the ones who are home, in Atlantis--they just want to dethrone The Source, and do.) Better the TV recyclers should bring back "Crusader Rabbit"....

FANTOCHE'S NIGHTMARE see CAUCHEMAR DU FANTOCHE

FAUST (B) 1910 sound D: David Darnett. From Gounod's opera. Ref: BFC: synchronized songs.
See also: AGUJERO EN LA PARED. DOKTOR FAUSTUS.

FAUST IN HELL see DAMNATION OF FAUST, The

FEAR, The or FEAR IN THE CITY OF THE LIVING DEAD see GATES OF HELL

FERAT VAMPIRE (Cz) Barrandov 1982 color 90m. (UPIR Z FERATU) SP,D: Juraj Herz. SP: also Jan Fleischer. Story: Josef Nesvadba. Ph: R. Valenta. Mus: Petr Hapka. Sets: V. Labsky. Ref: V 9/29/82:25: at Sitges. 8/24/83. SFExam 7/15/83:E8.
"About a sports car that runs on blood"(SFE), turning its victims into vampires.

FIEND Cinema Enterprises 1980 color 93m. SP,D,Ed,Addl Ph: Don Dohler. Ideas & with: Don Leifert. Ph: R. Geiwitz. Mus: Paul Woznicki. Mkp,Sets: Mark Supensky. SpVisFX: David W. Renwick. Graphic Art: Tom Griffith. Assoc P: Ted Bohus et al. Ref: TV: Force Video. Willis/SW'81. Amazing Cinema 2. V 10/20/82:95. HR 10/25/83:S-12. VideoSB. Fangoria 34. with Richard Nelson, Elaine White, George Stover, Greg Dohler.
This film posits a supernatural creature new to movies--"one of the least-mentioned creatures of legend," fiends, flying, red, insect-like phantoms "capable of entering a long-buried corpse and bringing resurrected life to the rotted remains." One such fiend enters the interred body of a man named Dorian, who emerges from his grave and blinks red, then proceeds to commit a series of "strangulation murders," in order to "renew" himself. (He absorbs the energy, it seems, of his female victims.) Meanwhile, a "Mr. Longfellow" (Leifert)--aka Dorian--takes up residence in Kingsville and, in a curtained-off room ("straight out of the middle ages") in his basement, conducts weird rituals in which he slashes photos of past and future victims. Stabbed to death with a sword, "Longfellow" decomposes in seconds, and the fiend flies into the air and vanishes.

Despite its groundbreaking contributions in the area of "fiends," this is a basically amateurish effort, a step down, if anything, from Dohler's The ALIEN FACTOR(1979), which at least had more makeup and special effects. This time around, he depends more on his actors--a less-than-fortunate dependence, as it turns out....FIEND features a rather indiscriminate use of close-ups, and standard shock/suspense-scene gimmicks. The electronic musical score is not especially good, but it is, at least, professional. The fiend-in-phantom-form itself--"representing the culmination of evil throughout the ages"--is just an animated (if intriguing) wisp--like the spirit, in its initial form, in SATAN'S MISTRESS.

FIGHTING 69½th, The see ROOKIE REVUE

FIGHTING WESTERNER, The see ROCKY MOUNTAIN MYSTERY

FIN DU MONDE, La see END OF THE WORLD

FINAL EYE NBC-TV/Para-TV & Culzean 1977 color 92m. (COMPUTER-CIDE-alt t) D: Robert M. Lewis. Exec P,Co-SP: Anthony Wilson. Ph: R. Rawlings. Mus: Jack Elliott. SpFX: Richard Johnson. Ref: TV. Cinef XIII:1. TVG: '82 network showing. with Susan George, Donald Pleasence, Joseph Cortese, Tom Clancy, David Huddleston, Linda Gillin, Liam Sullivan.

A crime-free, computer-controlled society, April 1996. Eden Isle is a car-less "perfect community of the future," featuring "electronic burners," hydro-wheat (which "reproduces itself year-round"), eggless hens, and imperfect clones of the heroine and her father....Almost-gratingly-unimaginative sf-detective thriller. Tepid script and score; insufferably glib hero. Huddleston as the bulldozing, no-nonsense police chief provides a few moments of respite from the general dreariness.

The FINAL TERROR Comworld(Arkoff)/Watershed/Roth 1983 color 84m. (BUMP IN THE NIGHT and The FOREST PRIMEVAL-early ts. CAMPSITE MASSACRE-B t) D: Andrew Davis. SP: Jon George, Neill Hicks, Ronald Shusett. Ph: A. Davidescu. Mus: Susan Justin. AD: Aleka Corwin. SpFxMkp: Ken Myers. SdFX: Troutman; Adams. Opt: Cinema Research. Ref: MFB'83:185. Ecran F 26:74. HR 10/25/83:S-52. V 10/12/83:17. Bill Warren. with John Friedrich, Adrian Zmed, Daryl Hannah, Rachel Ward.

Madwoman commits series of murders in Redwood National Park. (A

FIRE AND ICE Fox/PSO/Bakshi-Frazetta(Polyc Int'l.) 1983(1982) Story,D,P: Ralph Bakshi. Story,P: Frank Frazetta. SP: Roy Thomas, Gerry Conway. Ph:(anim) R&B EFX;(live) Francis Grumman. Mus: William Kraft. Sup:(anim) Michael Svayko;(live) Jeffrey Chernov. OptFX: Optical House. Ref: TV: RCA-Columbia Home Video. Ecran F 32:43. V 8/31/83. with Randy Norton, Cynthia Leake, Sean Hannon(Nekron), Eileen O'Neill(Juliana), Steve Sandor, Leo Gordon;(voices) Susan Tyrrell(Juliana), Maggie Roswell,

William Ostrander, Stephen Mendel(Nekron).

"Long ago, at the end of the last great Ice Age...." The evil Ice Lord, Nekron, a practitioner of the black arts, creates a giant glacier to crush his enemies (or "undesirables") and their kingdoms. ("The cold comes from Nekron.") He casts spells which make his foes slay each other, and commands an army of subhumans. His mother, Juliana, appears at one point as a wreath of smoke which strangles one hapless subhuman. Slain, at the end, by a mysterious warrior, Nekron cries out, and his rage unleashes the monster-glacier on Firekeep, which is saved only by its own, unleashed reservoir of lava....sorceress-back-from-the-dead bit...dog-sized centipede-leech creature...giant squid...humongous lizard-like creature....

Pretty-much standard heroes-and-villains stuff, little or no better than its live-action counterparts. "Don't hunt for death, boy. It finds us all soon enough" is the script's biggest thought--which will give you an idea of this movie's cranial capacity. The English-language dialogue spoken by the humans seems out-of-place in this ancient world, where sky-and-landscapes feature odd conjunctions of green/yellow/blue. The onslaught of the glacier might, graphically, be an hommage to The MONOLITH MONSTERS: the glacier's columns gather the same type of sprout/crack/topple momentum. The score is a passable echo of STAR WARS, with a JAWS motif....The characterization of the beyond-despair Nekron is the most interesting feature of the film. He's so powerful, he's blase--making glaciers is apparently the only sport which taxes his super-powers, and which, therefore, holds his interest. Sex, family, and community mean nothing to him. (Though of course he may be sublimating a bit.) Nekron's long pause before responding (with derisive laughter) to the heroine's peace offer is one of the movie's few silences--it actually (like Jack Benny's pause before the punchline to the old "Your money or your life" gag) builds some real tension. Here, Nekron's thinking--what, exactly, we'll never know, and thus is born a moment of ambiguity, unexpected in a movie otherwise fraught with the obvious.

*FIRE MAIDENS OF OUTER SPACE 1956 80m.-orig r.t. Mus: Borodin; Trevor Duncan; Monia Liter. Mkp: Roy Ashton. Ref: TV. FM 18: 18. BFC: FIRE MAIDENS FROM OUTER SPACE-t error or B t? and with Owen Berry(Prasus), Jacqueline Curtis(Duessa), Maya Koumani; Jan Holden, Kim Parker(fire maidens), Harry Fowler.

A rocketship crew discovers a monster ("the man with the head of a beast"), maidens, and an elderly man on the 13th moon of Jupiter--it seems that, when Atlantis sank, the ancestors of the fire maidens flew to this moon ("Welcome to New Atlantis"). The monster seems to spend all his time--all his life--lurking in the bushes outside the maidens' garden stronghold....The most unusual aspect of the movie is the score: Borodin seems to follow the fire maidens around--to follow, that is, not the action, but them, as if they were carrying an invisible radio or phonograph about with them. Noone else rates music. (Though the spaceship gets some traveling music.) It's as if these miniskirted sweeties somehow represented the Spirit of Prince Igor. And much more interesting than the film itself (not difficult) is the tiny-print disclaimer hiding in the credits: "All characters in space are fictitious." Was there any doubt? Does this mean that some of the characters on Earth are supposed to be real or actual?? Who's kidding whom here?

FIREBIRD 2015 AD (Can.?) Viacom 1981 color 97m. D: David Robertson. Ref: V 3/18/81:4(rated). Ecran 31:66. VideoSB: Embassy Home Ent. no PFA. with Darren McGavin, Doug McClure, George Touliatos, Mary Beth Rubens, Alex Diakun, R.C. Wisden.
Cars are banned in a 21st-century world short on gas. (A)

FIREFOX WB/Fritz Manes 1982 color/ws 135m. D,P & with: Clint Eastwood. SP: Alex Lasker, Wendell Wellman, from Craig Thomas's novel. Ph: Bruce Surtees;(process) Bruce Logan;(anim) Harry Moreau, Angela Diamos. Mus: Maurice Jarre. AD: John Graysmark, Elayne Ceder;(asst) Thomas Riccabona. SpVisFX:(p) John Dykstra;(sup) Robert Shepherd;(coord) Percy Angress. SpFX: Chuck Gaspar; Apogee;(models) Grant McCune;(Europe) Karl Baumgartner. MechSpFX: Bill Shourt, Don Trumbull, R. Alexander; Richard Helmer et al. Elec: Paul Johnson;(sp fx) Al Miller. SpTechDevel: Jon Erland. Opt:(sp fx sup) Roger Dorney; Pacific. SdFxEd: A.R. Murray et al. Ref: TV. SFExam 6/18/82. Ecran F 29:7-8. V 6/16/82. MFB'82:169. with Freddie Jones, David Huffman, Warren Clarke, Ronald Lacey, Klaus Lowitsch, Stefan Schnabel, Austin Willis, Ward Costello, Curt Lowens.
The Russians new, "invisible" Firefox aircraft can fly "in excess of Mach 5," and sensors in its pilot's helmet translate thoughts-in-Russian into computer signals which automatically fire missiles, thus giving man and plane a two-to-three-second advantage on the enemy. The plane's technology guarantees it "radar immunity" (though the heat from the exhaust can be traced) as it "burns up the sky" (and whips up the sea, in one scene, a la The TEN COMMANDMENTS)....Sf-in-the-sky, a la BLUE THUNDER...but the Firefox-in-flight is about as imposing, graphically, as a Cracker Jack prize. The movie itself is a rather-too-lean suspenser, with Eastwood as a U.S. pilot sent to Russia to filch the super-plane. The action is almost-comically "tense"--everyone in Russia, it seems, is (at one time or another) suspiciously eyeing Eastwood, or his passport, or (later) his plane. He might be walking around with an "I am a spy" sign pinned to his back. The material here is viable only as comedy: it's the paranoid Gant vs. the bumbling Soviets. (They do, after all, lose the most important plane in the world.) Jarre's score is, occasionally, interesting--it creates an atmosphere of science fiction.

FIRST MEN IN THE MOON(by H.G.Wells) see MOON MADNESS

FIUME DEL GRANDE CAIMANO, Il see GREAT ALLIGATOR, The

FLASH GORDON: THE GREATEST ADVENTURE OF ALL Filmation & King Features 1982(1979) color c90m. Anim D: Gwen Wetzler. (A)

FLYING KILLERS, The see PIRANHA II

FORBIDDEN WORLD New World(Roger Corman) 1982 color 86m. (MUTANT-orig t) D: Allan Holzman. SP: Tim Curnen. Story: Jim Wynorski, R.J. Robertson. Ph: Tim Suhrstedt. Mus: Susan Justin;(elec) Craig Huntley. PD: Chris Horner, Robert Skotak. SpMkpFX: J.C. Buechler, Don Olivera. SpProps: Ron Siegle et al. SpMechFX: Mike La Valley et al. Pyro: Roger George. Ref: screen. V 5/12/82. Ecran F 34:60-1. with Jesse Vint, June Chadwick, Dawn Dunlap, Linden Chiles, Olivera(Sam-104, robot).

Far away and in the future. Altered human cell and "proto-B" cell, spliced via genetic synthesis and implanted in a woman's womb, yield (in two weeks) "Subject 20," an intelligent, "half-breed bastard" of a metamorph which is "totally unpredictable" and keeps mutating. At first just a bit of goo from a cotton-candy-like cocoon, later a shark-headed, spider-bodied thing, it introduces proto-B from its saliva into its human victims, turning them into single-type-celled "pure protein," an amoeba-like source of unlimited food. A cancerous tidbit from the ship's doctor's liver ko's the metamorph.

A not-too-bad variation on ALIEN or either The THING. Nothing groundbreaking or earthshaking, but a smidgeon of wit here and there, from one character or another (generally the doctor), or from the metamorph itself, keeps the formula-narrative perking. The metamorph is, in addition to all its other qualities, also something of a smart-ass. When asked by one of the women (via computer) if coexistence is possible, it replies, in kind, "Please stand by," while it sends out an exploratory tentacle to answer--quite definitively--her question. (In the negative.) The screenplay seems likably determined to "explain" its monster and How It Came To Be, and what it's doing. Hardly a scene goes by without an update on its progress and/or potential. The horrific content of these state-of-the-metamorph bulletins seems intended to compound the horrificness of the graphics. (The most grisly graphic is actually probably the messy extraction-by-hand of the doctor's cancer--a scene questionable as surgery <u>or</u> cinema.)

FORCE FIVE see SHOGUN WARRIORS

FORCED ENTRY Century Int'l./Productions Two(Sotos)/Kodiak 1981 (1975) color 82m. (The LAST VICTIM-orig t) D,P: Jim Sotos. SP,P: Henry Scarpelli. Ph: A. Kleinman. Mus: Tommy Vig. Sp FX: Bob O'Bradovich. SdFxEd: Freddy Sweet. Opt: WJJ. Ref: screen. V 10/14/81. 2/16/83:24. 3/14/84: '80 re-cut. 10/26/83: 113. Bill Warren. Ecran F 22:53. with Tanya Roberts, Ron Max (Carl), Nancy Allen, Brian Freilino.

Madman-mechanic (Max) with delusions of the good (i.e., bourgeois) life murders (with wrench, etc.) women who aren't "nice" to him--resistance inflames him and frustrates him sexually. (His mother, you see, beat him when he was a lad.) He invades the home of an attractive housewife (Roberts), and kills an intrusive delivery boy, but can't consummate his relationship with the woman--with either sex or violence. She ends the stalemate by stabbing him to death with a butcher knife.

FORCED ENTRY is, visually, about as thrilling as radio--the script appears to have been conceived as a monologue for Carl, who narrates and--all too clearly--lays bare his pathetic social and pyschological fixations. The misty visuals are superfluous--a filter might, simply, have gotten stuck on the camera. The movie makes only one or two of its slight, ironic points visually--e.g., Carl keeps a white bunny for a pet; the wife's stabbing of him is described more graphically than are any of his killings--in the name, apparently, of catharsis (ours as well as hers). The pathology here is elementary, but Carl's dialogue and narration are generally well-written. He's such a psychotic simpleton, he's amusing. His psychology has none of the convolutions of Norman Bates--he wants so badly to show women how great a lover he is that he's a total flop. Even after breaking into the woman's home and binding her up, he still tries to carry off the enterprise as just a date, and compliments her on her house, her children....

The FOREST Fury/Wide World of Ent.(Commedia) 1983(1981) color 85m. (TERROR IN THE FOREST-ad t) D,P & with: Don Jones. SP: Evan Jones. Ph: S. Asbjorsen. Mus: Richard Hieronymus; Alan Oldfield. AD: Sandra Saunders. Mkp: Dana Wolski. Ref: V 12/21/83. 10/26/83:203(ad). with Dean Russell, Michael Brody (hermit), Elaine Warner, John Batis.

Woods haunted by cannibalistic madman and the ghosts of his wife and children.

FOREST PRIMEVAL, The see FINAL TERROR, The

FRANKENSTEIN(novel by Mary Shelley) see the following titles and BRITANNIA HOSPITAL. BUENAS NOCHES, SENOR MONSTRUO. DOS FANTASMAS Y UNA MUCHACHA. G-MAN JITTERS. ***GANDY GOOSE IN THE GHOST TOWN. GEEK MAGGOT BINGO. HOLLYWOOD CAPERS. LADY FRANKENSTEIN. MYSTERY! FRANKENSTEIN--LEGEND OF TERROR. PROTOTYPE. RAVISHING OF FRANK N. STEIN, The. TWO HEARTS IN WAX TIME.

FRANKENSTEIN ISLAND Chriswar 1981 color 90m. D: Jerry Warren. Ref: V 9/30/81:4(rated). Cinef XII:4: FRANKENSTEIN'S ISLAND. with John Carradine, Cameron Mitchell.

FRANKENSTEIN, LA VERITABLE HISTOIRE (F?) 1981? short D: Roland Portiche. Ref: Ecran F 22:6: at Paris sf-fest; hommage to Whale's FRANKENSTEIN.

*FRANKENSTEIN--1970 1958 ws (FRANKENSTEIN 1960 and FRANKENSTEIN 1975-early ts) PD: J.T. Collis. Mkp: Gordon Bau. Ref: TV.

Lee. Bill Warren. Glut/TFL. FFacts. LC. Stanley.
A disfigured Victor Frankenstein (Boris Karloff) restores his grandfather's monster (Mike Lane), with the aid of a transplanted brain from a murdered, hypnotized man, real and synthetic skin, and an atomic reactor....opening sequence-with-"monster" (Lane) from TV show being filmed....The latter is the movie's only decent scare sequence--positioning the monster-chasing-girl sequence at the beginning of a film is a good, disorienting dirty trick--though there are also a few interesting reel/real-life conjunctions (e.g., the cameraman "finding" the monster in his viewfinder). Writers and director seem uncertain as to whether they want their movie to be funny or frightening, and it rests, simply, in a dreary limbo, as also does Karloff's performance. (His material is dreadful.) Incidentally, Karloff in effect plays the monster once again here--it's his face that's revealed behind the bandages at the end. (Victor: "I made you in my image....")

*FRANKENSTEIN'S DAUGHTER 1958 (SHE MONSTER OF THE NIGHT-8mm t) AD: Sham Unltd. Ref: TV. Lee. Glut/TFL. FM 18:18. and with Page Cavanaugh & His Trio, George Barrows(monster), Felix Locher, Robert Dix, Bill Coontz.
Oliver Frankenstein's (Donald Murphy) experiments turn one girl (Sandra Knight), temporarily, into a monster, and the body of another (Sally Todd) into "Frankenstein's daughter." Low-grade shocker, dominated by Murphy's unremittingly crude, callous scientist ("The name is Frank!"), who inherits his ancestor's ambitiousness but none of his style. He's a liar, a lecher, a murderer--and he's also insincere. He makes Cushing's Victor in CURSE OF FRANKENSTEIN seem like a nice guy. (Well, almost.) Star John Ashley went on from this to things no bigger or better in the sf-horror field.

FRANKENSTEIN'S ISLAND see FRANKENSTEIN ISLAND

FREAK see BEING, The

FREE FOR ALL Univ 1949 83m. D: Charles T. Barton. SP,P: Robert Buckner. Story: H.C. Lewis. Mus: Frank Skinner. Ref: Lee. Scheuer/MOTV. Hirschhorn. HR 11/2/49. no NYT. V(d) 11/2/49. H'w'd CNews 1/9/50. MPH 11/5/49. Academy. LC. with Robert Cummings, Ann Blyth, Percy Kilbride, Ray Collins, Donald Woods, Mikhail Rasumny, Percy Helton, Dooley Wilson, Russell Simpson, Lester Matthews, Murray Alper, Kenneth Tobey, Willard Waterman.
"Formula for turning water into gasoline"(V): 1 pill + 17 gallons of water = 14 gallons of fuel..."invention is demonstrated at least a dozen times"(HCN)...Plus: "new fangled match"(HR).

The FRESH VEGETABLE MYSTERY Para 1939 anim color/Stereoptical 8m. D: Dave Fleischer. Anim: Tendlar, Sturm. Ref: TV. LC. Cabarga/TFS.

Cloaked, "clawed" midnight-skulker in vegetable-land proves to be a gang of mice. Amusing anthropomorphized vegetables.

FRIDAY THE 13TH--PART 3 Para/Jason-Mancuso 1982 3-D/color 96m. D: Steve Miner. SP: Martin Kitrosser, Carol Watson. Sequel to FRIDAY THE 13TH. Ph: G. Feil. Mus: Harry Manfredini; Michael Zager. AD: R.W. King. SpVisMkpFX: MakeupFxLabs; White, Apone, Carrisosa. SpFX: Martin Becker. Opt: Anderson Co. Sd: (sp) Neiman Tillar;(fx ed) Clive Smith. Ref: TV. V 8/11/82. MFB'83:131-32. with Dana Kimmell, Richard Brooker(Jason), Catherine Parks, Paul Kratka, Annie Gaybis, Larry Zerner.

Jason's chasin' 'em again, disposing of, roughly, a dozen victims, with cleaver, machete, pitchfork, spear-gun, and bare-hand head-lock. Plus: flashback-to-Part-II opener...bled-upon copy of Fangoria...hallucinations of Jason and mom returning at the end....Schlock-squared: shock effects plus corny 3-D effects (involving yoyo, popcorn, springing eyeball, etc.). Comparable in tone and dramatic substance to East Side Kids ghost-comedies. The bulk of the movie is ultra-mechanical skulking-and-hulking--one scene, one victim; next scene, next victim. The climactic cat-and-mouse sequence with Jason and the heroine is marginally more absorbing. She finds knife in victim, uses it again; he finds knife in his leg, uses it again....The effect is almost contrapuntal. Part III may set a record for false alarms and gag-shocks.

The FRIENDLY GHOST Para 1945 anim color 7m. D: Sparber. SP: Turner, Messmer. Narr: Frank Gallop. Ref: TV. Maltin/OMAM. LC.

Ghosts' night-on-the-town terrifies town's inhabitants--a nice beginning for the Casper series, but the unloved-and-unwanted-Casper scenes which follow set the treacly pattern for later entries.

FRIGHT, The see VISITING HOURS

FRIGHTMARE (Atlantic-TV)/Saturn Int'l./Screenwriters 1983(1981) color 86m. (The HORROR STAR-orig t) SP,D: Norman Thaddeus Vane. Ph: Joel King. Mus: Jerry Moseley. AD: Anne Welch; Glen Neufeld. SpFxMkp: Jill Rochow. Holographic FX: Laserworld, J.K. Foy. SpFX: Knott Ltd., Chuck Stewart;(ed) Robert Jackson. Mausoleum: Tom West, Kevin Galbraith, Bill Manning. SpSd: C&D. SpProps: Forrest J Ackerman. Opt: CFI. Ref: TV: Vestron Video. V 9/14/83. 5/4/83:491. 5/25/83:4(rated). 2/16/83: 524. Bill Warren. HR 10/4/83. PFA. with Ferdy Mayne, Luca Bercovici, Jennifer Starrett, Leon Askin, P. Kastner, N. Talbot.

Conrad Ragzoff (Mayne), "the last of the great giants of the horror cinema," is "terrifying in life, but even more so in death." When members of a horror film society called (wittily) The Horror Film Society, steal his body from his deluxe tomb, his wife employs a medium, who brings Ragzoff back from the dead. Accompanied by mist and sound effects, he wreaks revenge on the desecrators of his tomb. One victim is cremated, one beheaded; another bursts into flames; a levitating coffin carries off yet another....1931 DRACULA lines spoofed...Ragzoff-in-vampire-fangs rehearsing commercial...vampire movie on TV.

The overt horror-movie references and framework may be slightly different, but FRIGHTMARE boils down to, simply, just another "first Oscar, then Donna, and now Eve" elimination tournament. Meg (Starrett) is the only (apparent) survivor--she survives, of course, because she's a reluctant desecrator, unlike the other ghouls and boys. But most of the characters--including and especially Ragzoff--are mean-spirited, in life or death. We have no rooting interest, no pleasure in seeing the unpleasant Ragzoff come back to life. He should have stood in bed. Atmospheric lighting and camerawork.

FUGA DAL BRONX see ESCAPE FROM THE BRONX

FULL MOON HIGH Filmways/Larco 1982(1981) color 93m. SP,D,P: Larry Cohen. Ph: Daniel Pearl. Mus: Gary W. Friedman. AD: Robert Burns. Mkp: Steve Neill. Ref: TV. Bill Warren. Scot Holton. no PFA. Ecran F 30:16-19,36: at Paris sf-fest. with Adam Arkin(werewolf), Roz Kelly, Elizabeth Hartman(werewolf), Ed McMahon, Kenneth Mars, Joanne Nail, Pat Morita, Alan Arkin, Louis Nye, John Blyth Barrymore.

The Fifties. The bite of a glowing-eyed werewolf turns high-school student Tony Walker into a playful werewolf who only scratches his victims. He remains young, returning to Full Moon High in the present day as his own son, only to fall victim to silver bullets. He revives, however, since it now takes eight bullets to kill a werewolf. He seeks out his only real victim, Miss Montgomery, who is also, now, a werewolf, and they start a werewolfamily. Plus: PSYCHO shower-scene reversal...hand-from-grave bit.

Larry Cohen's comic targets in FULL MOON HIGH--right-wingers, gays, high-school violence, lycanthropy--appear rather randomly selected. They seem to be merely the handiest subjects; his jabs, the easiest. No joke is too low or obvious for him--e.g., the "pentagram"-"Pentagon" confusion (from WEREWOLF OF WASHINGTON), comments re: Tony's "wolfing food," etc. And a Cohen-on-holiday movie (such as this one) is not really a Cohen movie: his imagination, so to speak, seems to be fired only by his pretentiousness. This werewolf comedy has, with terrible irony, no bite, comic or thematic--it too only scratches. It has only one workable idea: Kelly's Jane--the aggressor with the original Tony--proves, also, to dominate werewolf-Tony. A pinch of psychoanalytical wit....But this Weird Romances match gives way to the less-clever Tony-Miss Montgomery pairing. Cohen doesn't even know when he has something good....

FUN HOUSE, The see LAST HOUSE ON DEAD END STREET

FUNERAL HOME MPM-Wescom/CFDC 1982(1980) 92m. (2 CRIES IN THE NIGHT) Ph: Mark Irwin. PD: Roy Forge Smith. SpFX: Dennis

Pike. Mkp: Shonagh Jabour. Ref: TV. TVG. V 3/10/82. and with Lesleh Donaldson, Stephen Miller, Dean Garbett.

"Madman" in cellar proves to be schizophrenic madwoman (Kay Hawtry) talking to herself, in dead-husband's voice--his rotting corpse kept in cellar...murder by drowning, pick ax, embalming needle....Dreadful bit of a mystery, padded out with flashbacks, false-alarm shocks, and mood shots, to horror-feature-length. The very incidental, nocturnal prowlings of an ominous black cat are more involving than the plot. "Pay-off" of latter is pic's only surprise--a quite blatant recreation of the climax of PSYCHO, right down to the swinging overhead light and the corpse-in-the-chair....Exasperatingly familiar character-types--e.g., the slow-witted handyman, whose lurking/skulking/peering seems to punctuate every other scene.

FURY OF THE SUCCUBUS see SATAN'S MISTRESS

FUTURE WAR 198X (J) Toei 1982 anim color feat. D: T. Masuda, T. Katsumata. SP: Koji Takada, from John Haken's novel "World War III." Mus: Nozomu Aoki. AD: T. Tsuji. Anim D: Masami Suda. Ref: V 5/12/82:339(ad). 5/4/83:342: aka 198X. JFFJ 14:9.

G-MAN JITTERS Fox 1939 anim 7m. (aka GANDY GOOSE IN G MAN JITTERS) D: Donnelly. SP: Foster. Ref: Maltin/OMAM. LC.

Dracula, Frankenstein's monster.

GABI NG LAGIM...NGAYON (Fili) Premiere 198-? D: Cirio H. Santiago, C. Gallardo. Ref: vc box: Trigon Video. with C. Solis.

"Terrifying" spirit out for revenge.

GAIKING see SHOGUN WARRIORS: GAIKING

2 GALAXY EXPRESS 999 1979('82-U.S.) (GALAXY EXPRESS-U.S.) 88m. Ref: screen. JFFJ 14:8: also generated '80 TV-movie. V 8/18/82: space pirate Captain Warlock here from CAPTAIN HARLOCK. Bob Moore. VV 7/12/83: "vampire count"??

A little boy with a long name ending in Smith takes the Galaxy Express 999 from Earth to Andromeda, in order to obtain a machine body and eternal youth. His ultimate goal: to find and kill the trophy-hunting, machine-bodied Count Mecca, who killed his mother. The express travels faster than the speed of light, and features an electro-magnetic barrier for protection, a crystal-bodied waitress, and a conductor with a bowling-ball head (and Ed Wynn's voice). Its first stop is the restored, now-green planet of Taitan, and Vulture Valley, a paradise for orphans whose parents have been slain by Count Mecca. Then: Pluto, the Lost Planet, its cold atmosphere deriving from the "frozen spirits" of its inhabitants. Here, Smith and his companion (a lady who looks like his mother) meet Shadow, the Keeper of the Ice Graves, frozen-lake resting places for the empty bodies of those who have adopted machine bodies; the faceless Shadow keeps her original body preserved in a shrine near the lake. A stop at Count Mecca's Time Castle leaves the Count dead and proves merely a prelude to...the Mechanization-Center Planet, which is composed of human parts. The Queen of the Mechanism Empire--her gown a sort of window-on-space--is enthroned here, and Smith's companion proves to be her daughter, Princess Matel, whose heart is now part of the planet and whose body is that of Smith's mother. A capsule (containing the spirit of an arch-enemy of the Count), when smashed, destroys the Empire....Also: dream-sensor key to the pasts of others... robots and aliens at Hangman's Hollow...X-ray-like, machine-body detector...cosmo-gun weapon against machine people.

GALAXY EXPRESS might be the Hans Christian Andersen version of INVASION OF THE BODY SNATCHERS. It's an animated sf-fairy-tale re: dehumanization and the extinction of feeling--the Snow Queen becomes, here, the Mechanism Queen. At the same time, this is a borderline-oedipal tale of a boy losing his mother, then more or less finding her again (in the Princess), only to lose her once more. At one point, young Smith asserts (a trifle defensively) that his relationship with the Princess is not romantic--it just looks as if it is....Romantic or not, the pathos of their separation (at the end of the film) is given a distinctive twist by the fact that (as she warns him) the next time that he sees her he won't recognize her--she will have a new body; if her unique relationship with the boy and his mother has made her human again, inside, emotionally, her bio-mechanical makeup apparently still requires periodic external renewal....No, this is not your everyday cartoon feature, though the English-language dialogue is unsubtle, and the score is very uneven, alternately syrupy and involving. Themes rather clunk around in the dialogue; the tone of the visuals, however, is generally quite skillfully and subtly controlled. The images are emotionally evocative--and if, say, the fixed, wistful-eyed expressions of the women seem a fairly facile ploy, the look of these sad-eyed creatures does lend the movie some surreal-oedipal overtones: Smith sees--or we see--his mother everywhere. It's as if all the women were somehow attuned to his sense of loss; as if they all saw him through his mother's eyes. The film partakes, roughly equally, of the hyper-sentimental, the genuinely touching, and the perverse, one quality tempering the other. The fact that the script doesn't resolve itself into, simply, the sentimental or the perverse is what keeps it interesting. The lad is noble; the creatures he encounters are more complicated--but both he and they are given their due: the cold-bodied Shadow clings desperately to Smith's body (the Princess has to pry them apart before they can leave the Lost Planet)--she craves heat, and her craving yields a rather ambiguous embrace here, half-pathetic and half-erotic. The apparently pre-teen Smith is understandably perplexed.... The animation is as adventurous as the script--there are unexpected "overhead shots" and even some rack-focusing effects, and you may find both the idea and the idealized execution of the Galaxy Express itself comparing favorably with your better dreams. This interplanetary choo-choo is an enchanting elaboration on Melies' space train in An IMPOSSIBLE VOYAGE. It, too, is palpably impossible: it starts out from some Grand Central Station in Megalopolis, keeps to the ground and the rails for a stretch, then climbs the rails into the sky, and, when it really picks up steam, continues on beyond the end of the rails into space. In "long shots," it almost disappears into the distance, as it chugs into "orbit" above its next planet/destination--this "receding," "Did I really see it?" effect might be one of dream or memory. These dreamlike "portraits" echo those of the boy's last fond looks at Earth as the express pulls up and out: he sees his friends and, then, his dead mother, superimposed over the aerial view--cf. the young man "seeing" into his friends' bedrooms, as they sleep, unaware of his departure-by-rail from his/their hometown, in I VITELLONI....In this animated fantasy, what is left behind is not lost....

See also: QUEEN OF A THOUSAND YEARS.

GAMMA 693 see NIGHT OF THE ZOMBIES(NMD)

GANDAMU (J) Shochiku/Nippon Sunrise 1981(1979) anim (aka GUNDAM) Based on Robert A. Heinlein's "Starship Troopers." Des:(char) Yoshizaku;(mech) Kunio. Ref: V 5/12/82:332. JFFJ 14:7-8,39.

A feature made from the first 13 episodes of the TV series "Mobile Suit Gundam." In the future, a giant robot challenges insurgents on Earth satellite Gion.

Sequels: GANDAMU II. KIDO SENSHI--GANDAMU III.

GANDAMU II (J) Shochiku/Nippon Sunrise 1981(1979-80) anim (aka GUNDAM II) Ref: JFFJ 14:7-8,39.

Sequel to GANDAMU. Feature culled from episodes 14-30 of the TV series "Mobile Suit Gundam."

GANDY GOOSE IN G MAN JITTERS see G-MAN JITTERS

GANDY GOOSE IN POST WAR INVENTIONS see POST-WAR INVENTIONS

GANG WARS see DEVIL'S EXPRESS, The

The GATES OF HELL (I-U.S.) MPM/Robert Warner 1980('83-U.S.) 93m. (2 FEAR IN THE CITY OF THE LIVING DEAD. PAURA NELLA CITTA DEI MORTI VIVENTI. aka CITY OF THE LIVING DEAD. The FEAR. TWILIGHT OF THE DEAD) SP: L. Fulci, D. Sacchetti. Ph: S. Salvati. Mus: Fabio Frizzi. AD: M.A. Geleng; O. Taito. SpFX: Gino de Rossi. Mkp: Rufini; Restopino. SdFX: Studio. Ref: screen. V 5/25/83. MFB'82:89-90. and with Venantino Venantini, Carlo de Mejo, Daniela Doria, Robert Sampson.

"Ever since Father Thomas hanged himself, Dunwich ain't been the same." And on All Saints' Day it gets worse in The City of

The Dead (built upon the ruins of Salem, Mass.): the dead walk forth through the now-open Gates of Hell, and they and the Father appear and disappear at will, literally scalping the living and making them vomit up their guts. The stake-like end of a wooden cross thrust into his guts makes them all go up in flames. Earlier, a woman seems to die of fright in a trance and is buried prematurely....Other highlights: plague of maggots...electric-drill-through-head...rats nibbling brains...maggoty hand rubbed in woman's face....Another Lucio (ZOMBIE) Fulsome special. No first-the-good-news jokes about his movies--they're all bad news. Acting, dialogue, and atmosphere (the art directors rigged up a semi-imaginative underground cavern of the dead) are all incidental to the gore effects, such as the stunt with the drill cited above, an inelegant variation on the sliver-in-the-eye trick in ZOMBIE. Everyone here seems to be either decomposing or subject to a waxy, white build-up.

GAYRACULA Marathon 1983 D: Roger Earl. SP: Lee & Pshaw. P: Terry Le Grand. Ref: SFExam 10/14/83:E12. poster. with Tim Kramer, Douglas Poston, Steve Collins, Ray Medina, Max Cooper.
A gay Dracula in Transylvania.

GEEK MAGGOT BINGO, Or The FREAK FROM SUCKWEASEL MOUNTAIN Weirdo Films 1983 color 73m. SP,D,P,Story,Ph,PD,Ed: Nick Zedd. Story: also Robert Kirkpatrick. SpFX: Tyler Smith, Ed French. Ref: V 5/25/83. Ecran F 36:82. with Robert Andrews(Dr.Frankenberry), Brenda Bergman, Richard Hell, Donna Death(vampire), Zacherle, Bruno Zeus(hunchback).
Mad doc brings two-headed Formaldehyde Man (Smith) to life via "chemosynthetic regeneration"....guest appearance by the editor of Fangoria.

GENMA TAISEN (J) Toho-Towa/Kadokawa 1983 anim feature Ref: V 4/6/83:37: "sci-fi." 5/4/83:360.

*GHOST CRAZY Banner 1944 Mus D: Edward Kay. SpFX: Ray Mercer. Ref: TV. Lee(MPH 1/20/45): above is TV t. Weldon. Stanley.
Barney (Art Miles) from Borneo, "The Gorilla with the Human Mind," circus-sideshow "monster"..."spooky" underground tunnel and private cemetery at the Gardner estate..."ghost" in sheet and monster-mask...ghostly laughter..."horrible face"...portrait which seems to come to life....Billy Gilbert, Shemp Howard, and Maxie Rosenbloom play themselves, or at least characters with their names. Gilbert and Howard are a team for most of the movie, though Rosenbloom joins them near the end. And these comics (including an uncredited bald-headed man who has a couple of odd bits) are not unlikable--their material, however, is awful. (Tim Ryan wrote the script and plays the detective.) It's strange to see those same old Monogram sets--and no Bela Lugosi or East Side Kids. Only Minerva Urecal seems to belong. (She may still be there....)

GHOSTS GALORE (H.K.-Cant.) Shaw 1983 color 100m. D: Hsu Hsia. SP: Yeh Chia. Ph: Kuan Mu. AD: Shen, Sheng. Ref: V 3/2/83. with Chen Hsiao Hou, Yang Tsing Tsing.
"Ghost-nymph," exorcism, "black magic duels."

*The GHOSTS OF BERKELEY SQUARE (NTA-TV) 1947 61m.-U.S. Mkp: Henry Hayward. Ref: TV. V 11/12/47. BFC. TVFFSB. Bill Warren. no Academy. no NYT. and with Marie Lohr, Wally Patch.
A tale told (through an "inter-terrestrial hookup of radio and television") at the thousandth annual dinner of the Old Ghosts' Association (100 ghosts in attendance), held in order to promote a "better understanding" between ghosts and humans. The ghosts of two British officers (Robert Morley and Felix Aylmer) are condemned, in 1708, to haunt no. 7 Berkeley Square until it is visited by "reigning royalty" (which does not occur until the building is bombed during World War I, and the Queen inspects the bomb damage). Initially, the two try to scare unpromising tenants away, and make objects materialize, unraveled wallpaper ravel up again, shoe prints appear in a carpet, etc., thus giving the house the reputation of being haunted....In 1900, one ghost brings some penicillin back from 1943 in order to restore a sick man....A mildly amusing costume ghost-comedy, a la The TIME OF THEIR LIVES, of value chiefly as a vehicle for Morley. He plays, with relish, both General Burlap and (in blackface) the Narwa of Baghwash(sp?), a Middle Eastern potentate who lodges at no. 7 in 1877. Morley seems equally happy with (as the General) lines like "We don't haunt children" and (as the Narwa) exotic-sounding gibberish. He can make a movie seem like a party thrown just for him....

GIRL FROM S.E.X. Caballero Control 1982 color 89m. SP,D & with: Paul G. Vatelli. SP: Mike Hunt. Ph: C.P. Mitchell. Mus: Joan Wilson. Mkp: Steve Riley. Ref: TV: Swedish Erotica (video). Adam Film World 4/83: aka The GIRLS FROM S.E.X.? with Lisa DeLeeuw(Agent 38DD), Nicole Noir, Don Hart, John Sigliono(James), Bill Margold(Mr.Big), Bridgette Monet, Brooke West, Annette Haven, "Ernie Blowfeld"("P"), "Phil Rosen."
Ray-rifle which shoots down flying saucer...Russian plot to wreck the world's economy with counterfeit money...ray(?) machine-on-tripod...James Bondian spy-spoof elements....Star Lisa DeLeeuw is the Acquanetta of adult movies--sensational to look at, but just not an actress. The rest of this quasi-movie is not even anything to look at....

The GIRL, THE GOLD WATCH, & DYNAMITE Para-TV/Fellows-Keegan & Operation Prime Time 1981 color 90m. D: Hy Averback. SP: George Zateslo. Ph: W. Jurgenson. Mus: B. Broughton. AD: T. Bousman. SpFX: Gunter Jennings. Opt: Anderson Co. Ref: TV. TVG. with Philip MacHale, Lee Purcell, Burton Gilliam, Zohra Lampert, Jack Elam, Gary Lockwood, Jerry Mathers, Richie Havens, Carol Lawrence, Tom Poston, Morgan Fairchild, Gene Barry, Larry Linville, Deborah Janssen.

Sequel to The GIRL, THE GOLD WATCH, & EVERYTHING involves a land scheme in Auburn County, California, a supposedly weak levee, and oil deposits....The expected plot complications; limp "folksy" comedy. All for the novelty of seeing someone walking about amongst "frozen" people. At best, this TV-movie meant work for Elam and Lampert.

2P The GIRL, THE GOLD WATCH, & EVERYTHING Para-TV & Fellows-Keegan 1980 color 90m. D: William Wiard. SP: George Zateslo, from John D. MacDonald's novel. Ph: J. Haitkin. Mus: Hod David Schudson. AD: C.L. Hughes. SpFX: J.P. Mercurio. VisCons: Hanson, Feightner. Opt: Anderson Co. SdFxEd: Collier, Osborne. Cons: Jack Arnold. Ref: TV. TVG: orig.shown as TV special or miniseries. V 6/18/80:59: TV "show." with Robert Hays, Pam Dawber, Jill Ireland, Maurice Evans, Zohra Lampert, Ed Nelson, Burton Gilliam, Macdonald Carey, Larry Hankin.

"Time waits for one man": a deceased inventor's stopwatch can stop time for 20 minutes, allowing the possessor to move about freely among humans in a "frozen" world; it can be used no more than 6 times during a 24-hour span and must be used once every 14 days or it will fuse and be useless. At least these are the rules according to the sequel, The GIRL, THE GOLD WATCH, & DYNAMITE. In this, the original, our hero (Hays) seems to have only a minute or so in which to perform his seeming miracles. "You can't use this watch frivolously," insists its possessor, Kirby Winter. The teleplay writer, however, betrays his own words and uses the watch as, basically, a device to make people look silly--either frozen in time in silly poses, or left in silly situations after being unfrozen. The women in this TV-movie all seem to be either would-be or practicing nymphomaniacs....

GIRLS FROM S.E.X., The see GIRL FROM S.E.X.

2 The GLITTERBALL PBS-TV 1977 Addl Dial: Michael Abrams. Addl ElecSdFX: Malcolm Clarke. Ref: TV.

A close encounter of the cute kind. The "glitterball" is a glorified marble, or self-propelled (stopmo-animated) wad of tinfoil...a drolly inexpressive invader-from-space that "eats electricity" and all manner of food. (Though at one point it spits up something disagreeable.) It might be a cousin of those follow-the-bouncing-ball balls--it's at least as much fun to follow as they are. A wry trifle, with a serviceable plot.

GO SHOGUN (J) Toei/Int'l. Movie Co. 1982 anim Anim: Shigenori Kageyama. Ref: JFFJ 14:7.

TV-series-derived feature re: "giant combination-robots."

GOD'S GUN (I) Noak 1975 color 93m. D: Gianfranco Parolini. Ref: vc trailer: Paragon Video. no PFA. with Lee Van Cleef, Jack Palance, Richard Boone.

Western. Preacher returns from the grave seeking vengeance on killers.

GOIN' UP see LIFT, The

GOJIRA NO MUSUKO see SON OF GODZILLA

Das GOLD ER LIEBE (W.G.) MMSFP 1983 color 89m. SP,D: Eckhart Schmidt. Ph: B. Heinl. Mus: B. Blau et al. AD: M. Domant. Ref: V 6/1/83. with Alexandra Curtis, Marie Colbin, H. Strobl.
"Ritual murder...blood-and-guts horror...."

**GOLDEN BOY SUBDUES MONSTER (H.K.-Mand.) 197-? Ref: vc box: Quality Video. Bill Warren.
Monster-frog, "ghost-face king."(QV)

GOLDEN DREAMS(by Z.Grey) see ROCKY MOUNTAIN MYSTERY

*The GOLDEN MISTRESS RK 1954 color Ph:(underwater) Phillip Nash. AD: James R. Connell. PhFX: Howard A. Anderson. Ref: TV. no LC. Weldon. Stanley. and with Andree Contant.
Haitian natives' hands are unaffected by the touch of a red-hot idol, in the voodoo "Dance of the Blazing Idol"....snake-god ceremony...lost tribe, the Untamed, from Africa, on uncharted Caribbean isle....Mainly interminable adventure pic, with occasional, pleasant romantic/exotic details, and oodles of voodoo ceremonies, dances, and chants. No threat to supplant WHITE ZOMBIE. Only for John Agar completists (and Rosemarie Bowe oglers).

GOLIATH AWAITS Col-TV & White-Gay-Jay 1982(1981) color 180m. D: Kevin Connor. Story,SP: Richard Bluel, Pat Fielder. Story, P: Hugh Benson. Ph: Al Francis. Mus: George Duning. PD: Ross Bellah. SpFX: Joe Unsinn. Opt: F-Stop. Ref: TV. TVG. Cinef. Mag of F&SF. with Christopher Lee, Mark Harmon, Eddie Albert, John Carradine, Robert Forster, Frank Gorshin, Jean Marsh, John McIntire, Jeanette Nolan, Alex Cord, Irene Hervey, Alan Caillou, Kip Niven, Clete Roberts, Emma Samms, Alan Fudge.
The luxury liner Goliath, sunk by a U-boat in 1939, is discovered on a volcanic ridge at the bottom of the Atlantic in 1981; the 337 inhabitants (there were originally 240 survivors) have evolved into a society in an air bubble, with the Supreme Council ruling groups of Life People, Salvage People, Agri-People, and the renegade Bow People. Unknown to their commander (Lee), his aide (Gorshin) has been weeding out the crippled and undesirable with "Palmer's Disease"--actually an algae-based poison. The U.S. Navy and British Oceanics effect the rescue of most of the population, but 50 or so elect to die with their leader.
Elaborate but for the most part routine sf-drama. It falls into the sf-horror sub-category of Funny (strange not ha-ha) Societies--previous examples include ZARDOZ, The DARK SECRET OF

HARVEST HOME, CAT-WOMEN OF THE MOON, and "The Twilight Zone" episode, "On Thursday We Leave for Home." It's hardly the worst of this lot, and is marginally better than the aforementioned Rod Serling teleplay, which, however, it very closely resembles. The focus of both is the ruler (here, Lee; there, James Whitmore) of an isolated colony (here, under the sea; there, on a distant planet) which looks upon said ruler as a god and savior. "Help" arrives, but is quite unwanted by the "god"; the premise is viable, it seems, only as a vehicle for the actor who plays same. The show here belongs to Lee, as the "great man" who mistrusts the world above and its "battles, bombs, more death"--although Gorshin as his aide Wesker, with his detestably cheery sliminess, is rather alarmingly watchable. There are also pleasing, if sentimental, death-is-preferable-to-an-imperfect-life roles for Carradine and Ms. Marsh. Much of the drama, however, consists of rather broad, labored intimations of Trouble in Water City--as if maybe we were expecting Utopia. And the conception of the undersea society is undistinguished. Also, any movie in which a gamily exotic dish (here, "octopus eyes") is, at some point, introduced for the sole purpose of turning some poor, queasy soul's face green should have its dramatic license temporarily revoked.

The GORY MURDER (H.K.-Cant.) Eternal Film 198-? color/ws 90m. D: Hwa I-Hung. Ref: TV: Orchids Int'l. Video.

The police discover the body, or parts of same, of a woman dead three days ("There is another piece!") and conclude that "the murderer must be a maniac." ("We should check out all those sex maniacs....") He is, and he has (visualized) <u>nightmares</u> of his victim attacking him, and <u>visions</u> of her severed hand in his lunch bowl and bursting through a wall, and of her (living) severed head....This movie is half-HIGH AND LOW, half-BLOOD FEAST, in the manner, more or less, of current <u>American</u> crime-drama/shockers. Here, however, the murder itself (shown in flashback, <u>sans</u> the gorier details) is not the shocker-half centerpiece. The aftermath is--i.e., the discovery of the limbs and organs, which are offered up, again and again (by the police, during their investigation)--in bags, in trays, in projected slides--for our delectation. In other words, the dehumanization is carried one step further. This is not <u>progress</u>, folks....

GRAF DRACULA BEISST JETZT IN OBERBAYERN see DRACULA BLOWS HIS COOL

GRANDIZER see SHOGUN WARRIORS: GRANDIZER

The GREAT ALLIGATOR (I) (CBS-TV)/Dania 1981(1979) color 90m. (Il FIUME DEL GRANDE CAIMANO. The BIG CAIMANO RIVER or GREAT ALLIGATOR RIVER-ad ts. ALLIGATORS-F) SP,Story,D: Sergio Martino. SP,Story: also Ernesto Gastaldi. SP: also L. Montefiori, M. Chianetta. Story: also Cesare Frugoni. Ph: G. Ferrando;

(underwater) Battaglia, Nannuzzi. Mus: Stelvio Cipriani. AD: A.M. Geleng. SpMechFX: Carlo de Marchis; Paolo Ricci. Mkp: S. Trani. Ref: TV. V 5/9/79:278. 5/7/80:412,400. Academy. TVG. "Tous Les Films 1980." with Mel Ferrer, Barbara Bach, Claudio Cassinelli, Richard Johnson, Romano Puppo, Giulia D'Angelo.

Alligator "devil-monster" ("the Great God Krona") at large in river running through tropical tourist-trap....Some fair dialogue; the usual monster tricks. The script's main concern: how to get people (i.e., potential victims) into the water. It solves it with admirable regularity, which is unfortunate for the alligator, which has a weight problem.

*The GREAT IMPERSONATION 1935 Mus: Franz Waxman. AD: Charles D. Hall. SpPh: John P. Fulton. Ref: screen. Everson. Lee. Hirschhorn. and with Wera Engels.

"Spirits"--actually madman Dwight Frye--haunt the Black Bog on an English estate ("Strange things happen here"), and the madman's cries drive Valerie Hobson to distraction....Esther Dale as the creepy Mrs. Unthank...sets from FRANKENSTEIN(1931) and The OLD DARK HOUSE....Unremarkable international-intrigue-and-politics brew, with nods toward horror and romance. The more interesting (romantic) possibilities of the double-twist impersonation plot are rather thrown away--all for the sake of a surprise ending.

The GREAT SPACE CHASE Viacom/Filmation-TV 1983(1979) anim color 87m. (aka MIGHTY MOUSE IN THE GREAT SPACE CHASE) D: Ed Friedman et al. AD: De Mello, Fletcher. SdFxSup: George Mahana. Ref: V 3/2/83:188(ad). Bill Warren. MFB'84:17-18.

Feature version of the "Mighty Mouse" TV series. Harry the Heartless and his Catomaton...hologram...mind-swapping...Doomsday Device which absorbs, then regurgitates the solar system.

GREAT WHITE (I) FVI/New Fida & Variety 1981 color 88m. (JAWS 3 or The LAST JAWS-ad ts. L'ULTIMO SQUALO) D: Enzo G. Castellari. SP: Mark Princi. Ph: A. Spagnoli;(underwater) Mattei, Moglia. Mus: Morton Stevens; G.& M. De Angelis. PD: F. Vanorio. SpFX:(mech) G. Ferrari, G. Pozzi; A. Corridori. Mkp: G. Morosi. Ref: V 11/11/81:6(rated, as The LAST SHARK). 5/7/80:374. (d)1/15/82. Academy: aka SHARK. HR 3/8/82. MFB'82: 138: Uti & Horizon copro? Weldon. SFChron 4/23/82. Bill Warren. with James Franciscus, Vic Morrow, Stefania Girolami.

"Slow and dull-witted" shark attacks East Coast town; plagiarism of JAWS and JAWS 2.

The GRIM REAPER (I) FVI/PCM Int'l.-Filmirage 1981 color 81m. (2P ANTROPOPHAGOUS) SP,D: Aristide Massaccesi(aka Joe D'Amato). SP: also L. Montefiore. Ph: E. Birbichi. Ref: VV 10/7/81:52(ad). V 10/21/81. 5/13/81:160: sfa SHOCK WAVES? Weldon. Ecran F 22: 48,79. with Tisa Farrow, Saverio Vallone, G. Eastman, V. Steiger

Eerie mansion, catacombs..."monstrous killer."(V)

Sequel: ABSURD.

GUERRA DEL FERRO, La or GUERRE DU FER, La see IRONMASTER, The

GUERRE DU FEU, La(by Rosny) see QUEST FOR FIRE

GULLIVER'S TRAVELS(by J.Swift) see VIAJES DE GULLIVER, Los

GUNAN IL GUERRIERO (I) 1982? D: Franco Prosperi. Ref: Ecran F 26:5.31:46. V 5/11/83:90. 10/5/83:24. with Pietro Torrisi.
Warriors of prehistory.
Sequels: GUNAN IL VENDICATORE. GUNAN RE BARBARO.

GUNAN IL VENDICATORE (I) 1983? D: M.M. Tarantini. SP: Piero Regnoli. Ref: Ecran F 31:46: with P. Torrisi(aka Peter McCoy).

GUNAN RE BARBARO (I) Leader 1983? color D: F. Prosperi. SP: P. Regnoli. Mus: Dino Ferro. Ref: Ecran F 31:46. V 10/20/82: 51(ad): Gunan--King of The Barbarians-ad t. with P. Torrisi, Diana Roy, David Jenkins.

GUNDAM see GANDAMU

GUNDAM II see GANDAMU II

GUNDAM III see KIDO SENSHI

GUNDULA PUTRA PETIR (Indon.) Cancermas 1982 D: Lilik Sudjio. Ref: Ecran F 26:74. with Teddy Purba, Annatairas.
Scientist's super-serum.

HALLOWEEN III: SEASON OF THE WITCH Univ/Akkad/Carpenter-Hill(De Laurentiis) 1982 color/ws 100m. Story,SP,D: Tommy Lee Wallace. Story:(uncred.) Nigel Kneale. Ph: Dean Cundey. Mus: John Carpenter, Alan Howarth. PD: Peter Jamison. SpMkp: Tom Burman. Title Seq: John Wash. Masks: Don Post. Commercial: Sam Nicholson. VisCons: C.R. Moore. SpFX: Jon G. Belyeu; W. Aldridge. Video: David Katz. Anim: Bakshi. Opt: Pacific. Ref: screen. Fangoria 22:8-9,11. V 10/27/82:15,28,33. MFB'83: 158-9. Weldon. with Tom Atkins, Stacey Nelkin, Dan O'Herlihy, Michael Currie, Dick Warlock(android).

"It's time again": the third in the HALLOWEEN series is set in Santa Mira, California. 3,000 years after the last mass sacrifice of animals and children, a modern-day Celtic warlock (O'Herlihy) employs a stone transported from Stonehenge ("We had a time getting it here"), laser-spiked Halloween masks, TV signals, and android assassins in an attempt at another mass sacrifice....clips from earlier HALLOWEEN's.

Composed of roughly equal parts of the ludicrous and the balmily imaginative, HALLOWEEN III is, in some ways (not all of them good), the most entertaining in the series so far. You won't see Nigel Kneale's name on the screen, but you'll hear echoes of Quatermass & co. in this bizarre amalgamation of sf, fantasy, horror, and mystery. (And Atkins' climactic "Stop it!" directly echoes, as do other scenes, the original INVASION OF THE BODY SNATCHERS.) Kneale's cosmic range of reference makes the first two HALLOWEEN's seem provincial and cramped, by comparison, although H-I is decidedly more tidy and disciplined than H-III. (The charitable will forget that there was an H-II.) In no other movie will you likely ever be treated to the sight of a ring of haywire TV monitors generating a rotating ray inside a monster-mask factory, while another beam emanates from the (huge) piece of Stonehenge commanding the scene above the monitors. What a chunk of rock could possibly have to do with laser rays is never made exactly clear; but the intermittent excitement of the movie lies in just such outre juxtapositions. Just to make them is enough; to explain them is perhaps asking too much. Unfortunately, the BODY SNATCHERS, mysterious-community narrative-framework is perfunctorily built out of bits and pieces of a dozen similar sf-mysteries. O'Herlihy's suave, oleaginous monster-mogul--not Atkins' regulation hero-with-a-flaw (drinking)--should have been the center of the movie. And of course there are the usual fun-tasteless makeup effects. (Aided and abetted by apparently-biogenetically-generated cockroaches, snakes, etc.) The kookily menacing Silver Shamrock TV jingle ("Eight more days to Halloween, Halloween....")--to the tune of "London Bridge is Falling Down"--has the grating, insinuating quality of the most-heinously-catchy TV commercials. It shares the repellent charm of O'Herlihy's Conal Cochran. HALLOWEEN III has more going both for and against it than just about any other horror movie in recent years. It's oddly ambitious; rather a fiasco; fraught with both local delights and dismaying defects. It's the WHITE ZOMBIE of 1982.

HAMLET(by Shakespeare) see STRANGE BREW

HAMMER HOUSE OF HORROR DOUBLE FEATURE: CHARLIE BOY/THE THIRTEENTH REUNION (B) ITC-TV/Cinema Arts Int'l. & Hammer/Jack Gill & Chips 1980(1981) color 90m. (CHARLIE BOY/THE THIRTEENTH REUNION-ad t) D: Robert Young; Peter Sasdy. SP: Cooper, Megahy; Burnham. Ph: Frank Watts. Mus: Lindup; McCabe. AD: Carolyn Scott. SpFX: Ian Scoones. Mkp: Eddie Knight. Ref: TV. TVG. with Leigh Lawson, Marius Goring, Angela Bruce; Julia Foster, Dinah Sheridan, Richard Pearson, Norman Bird.

Two from the "House of Horror" TV series: 1) is it coincidence or "Charlie Boy," a "fetish from central Africa"--? Whatever it is, everyone in the group photo dies, in order of distance-from-camera (nearest to farthest). The chance-or-fantasy ambiguity isn't exactly fresh, and no new changes are rung on the voodoo-doll theme. 2) What is the mysterious link between the Ashford Brothers Funeral Directors and the Chesterton Clinic? Hint #1: it involves the survivors of a plane crash who meet and dine once a month to commemorate their 2½-week odyssey without food. Hint #2: someone must have seen and liked SHRIEK OF THE MUTILATED (cf. "The Finger People" to the dining-room gatherers here). Tepid, drawn-out mystery-with-a-horror-payoff.

HAMMER HOUSE OF HORROR DOUBLE FEATURE: CHILDREN OF THE FULL MOON/ VISITOR FROM THE GRAVE (B) 1980 color 90m. D: Tom Clegg; Peter Sasdy. SP: Murray Smith; John Elder(rn: Anthony Hinds). Mus: P. Patterson; M. Wilkinson. Ref: TV. TVG. Ecran 22:76. with Christopher Cazenove, Diana Dors, Celia Gregory, Robert Urquhart, Jacob Witkin(werewolf), Adrian Mann; Kathryn Leigh Scott, Simon MacCorkindale.

Another "House of Horror" duo: 1) "There was this family--of werewolves," with a gent of Hungarian extraction as the leader of the pack, and stray women as his mates. Fairish werewolf tale. The full-moon rule still applies, but the family arrangements are different. Dors is the designated keeper of the pack of little ones. ("Beautiful children while there's still light....") The various mothers apparently all die in childbirth....2) A "walking corpse" proves to be part of a plot to secure a wealthy young American woman's money; her spirit returns at the end to foil the plotters. The spirit isn't the only thing that's transparent here. The all-a-plot plot and last-minute twist are predictable.

HAMMER HOUSE OF HORROR DOUBLE FEATURE: THE HOUSE THAT BLED TO DEATH/GROWING PAINS (B) 1980 D: Tom Clegg; Francis Megahy. SP: David Lloyd; Nicholas Palmer. Ph: N. Warwick. Mus: James Bernard; John McCabe. Ref: TV. TVG. Ecran 22:76. with Rachel Davies, Milton Johns, Sarah Keller; Barbara Kellerman, Gary Bond, Christopher Reilly(William).

1) Hemophiliac house with bloody wall and bleeding pipes... mutilated cat ("She loved that bloody cat")...all a plot for an "Amityville"-like best-seller....But the death of her cat gives a little girl nightmares, and a compulsion to kill. Perfunctory, pseudo-clever shaggy-dog thriller. One nice touch with a toy penguin. 2) A boy, William, who died as a result of his father's experiments with a super-nutrient, returns to possess another boy, adopted in his place....toy rabbit which spills real-rabbit guts...wreath "for all the unloved of this Earth" (formed from experimental flora) lying, at the end, on William's grave....The more interesting of the two shows. The message (love thy children) is blatant, but the overtones are horrific, not didactic. It's too late for the father, who is unrelenting in his blind dedication to science. ("I want my plant!") The clash between the single-minded father and the single-minded, avenging son has a half-comic, half-horrific force and fury to it.

HAMMER HOUSE OF HORROR DOUBLE FEATURE: THE TWO FACES OF EVIL/RUDE AWAKENING (B) 1980 D: Alan Gibson; Peter Sasdy. SP: Ranald

Graham; Gerald Savory. Mus: Paul Pat(t)erson. Ref: TV. TVG. Gloria deVille. with Anna Calder-Marshall, Gary Raymond, Jenny Laird; Denholm Elliott, James Laurenson, Pat Heywood.

1) Doppelgangers seem to be taking over the English countryside. Confusing and confused, with no explanation as to the who, why, or how of these "doppelgangers." 2) A man (Elliott) has a dream within a dream within a dream--or does he? A variation on DEAD OF NIGHT, or the "Shadow Play" episode of "The Twilight Zone," Savory's teleplay attempts to mystify, and it certainly succeeds. You can take the action any and every way you want--as dream, reality, fantasy, hallucination, or prophecy. It's this sense of unsure footing--for viewer and protagonist--which makes this tale so intriguing. Elliott's surveyor leads himself--or is led--a merry chase, as he awakens from one dream into another--and, ultimately, into reality. (Or is it?) "Rude Awakening" shares a quality of maddening "circularity"--as opposed to the usual narrative linearity--with its predecessors, and our hero's attempts to cope with his whirligig existence (and even, finally, exploit it) are highly amusing.

HAMMER HOUSE OF HORROR DOUBLE FEATURE: WITCHING TIME/THE SILENT SCREAM (B) 1980 D: Don Leaver; Alan Gibson. SP: Anthony Read; Francis Essex. Mus: James Bernard; Leonard Salzedo. Ref: TV. TVG. Ecran 22:76. with Jon Finch, Patricia Quinn (Lucinda), Prunella Gee, Ian McCulloch, Lennard Pearce; Peter Cushing, Brian Cox, Elaine Donnelly, Robin Browne, A. Carrick.

1) A witch, Lucinda, born in 1627, escapes her tormentors by skipping to the 20th Century....indoor typhoon...hexed hero. Incidentally and ironically, Lucinda reunites the estranged hero and heroine, by giving them something to do together (i.e., exorcise her). This irony seems intentional, and pretty foolish. Apparently, a witch in time can save any number of marriages.... Bernard's music is little more interesting than the humorless script (and features a motif or two from his previous scores). 2) A "nut case" (Cushing) performs behavior-conditioning experiments on humans and other animals; envisions "prisons without walls" and model ("terrified") prisoners. Difficult to say whether Cushing or the story is more of a nut case. This variation on A CLOCKWORK ORANGE is far from believable, but the "kicker" (though contrived) is amusing, and Cushing (back with Hammer) gets to play a benevolent old gent who proves to be a fiendish Nazi. (And he's believable.)

2P HAUNTED Northgate(Northbrae?) Communications 1976 color 81m. (The HAUNTED-ad t) SP,D,Co-P: Michael De Gaetano. Ph: W.E. Hines. Mus: Lor Crane;(lyrics) Freya Crane. AD: R. Wingo. Opt: Westheimer. Ref: TV: VC II(video). VideoSB. V 5/11/77: 185. with Virginia Mayo, Aldo Ray, Ann Michelle, Jim Negele.

1865. Abanaki, an Indian woman accused of "shamanism," curses those who send her, bound and on horseback, into the Arizona desert to wander and die. She, or her reincarnation, is held responsible for a series of mysterious deaths, over the years, in the Superstition Mountains....In the present, McCloan (Ray) fears that a young Englishwoman, Jennifer Baines (Michelle), is Abanaki's reincarnation, come to wreak revenge on the descendants of her persecutors. He receives a "phantom" phone call from, apparently, Abanaki herself, and dies trying to kill Jennifer....poster from the director's UFO TARGET EARTH.

HAUNTED is, at least, not just another horror movie. It's both terrible and terribly serious. There are echoes of Tennessee Williams (Mayo's "lyrically" mad blind woman) and Luis Bunuel (the phone booth in the cemetery), and the dialogue tends toward the "literary." Occasionally, as in the sequence in which the mad Mayo beds Ray--while "seeing" him as his younger (dead) brother--HAUNTED approaches camp. More often, it just doesn't work as anything--camp, horror, drama, or myth. The absurdist image of the cemetery phone booth may not really "work" either--it's hard to say--but at least it provokes one's curiosity, and it's a striking and unusual way of suggesting the intersection of the past and the present. (McCloan meets his fate--through a quirky accident--in it.) The film hints both that Abanaki is still riding around, topless, and that her curse works only indirectly, psychologically, through the power of suggestion--that Jennifer is not her reincarnation. In other words, it is/is not a fantasy....

HAUNTED HOUSE (I) Capital(Gori) 1982 color (La CASA STREGATA) D: Bruno Corbucci. Ph: Ennio Guarnieri. Ref: V 5/12/82:187, 227(ad). 2/16/83:24. 3/31/82:62: comedy. 4/14/82:33: in Italy. with Renato Pozzetto, Gloria Guida.

The HAUNTING PASSION (US-Can?) NBC-TV/BSR & ITC 1983 color 90m. D: John Korty. Sp,Exec P: Douglas Schwartz, Michael Berk. Ph: Hiro Narita. Mus: Paul Chihara. AD: David Hiscox. Mkp: Ilona Herman. Ref: TV. TVG. with Jane Seymour, Gerald McRaney, Millie Perkins, Ruth Nelson, Paul Rossilli(Kane).

The ghost (Rossilli) of a man who, many years before, poisoned himself in a double-suicide attempt (she rejected the champagne at the last moment) haunts the site of his death. Wine glasses shatter, a white blur appears in a photo (which, later, self-incinerates), a would-be rapist is magically flung headlong out a window, a bottle of champagne is added to our heroine's (Seymour) shopping cart, a name appears in the steam of a bathroom mirror....Kane himself turns up as a face in a painting, a floating head, and a demon lover inviting the heroine to join him in a glass of champagne. His beloved Judith (Nelson), however, enters the house, picks up a gown (and drops several years), drinks the poison herself, and the two fade out....incidental psychic....Actually, our heroine is pretty incidental herself. This seems, at first, an ENTITY-for-TV, as Jonathan Kane threatens to take her husband's place in bed (and shower). But it's not her story; it's Judith's. The latter enters, belatedly, and everyone--corporeal and incorporeal--

lives happily ever after, or at least dies happily. The script here is, perhaps, a tad romantic....

2 HAVE YOU GOT ANY CASTLES 1938 Ref: TV.
Other books/characters coming to life at midnight: a dancing Invisible Man and ghost from "Topper," "Seven Keys to Baldpate," "The Pied Piper," "House of the 7 Gables," "Rip Van Winkle," "Bulldog Drummond." Perky musical short.

HE LIVES BY NIGHT (H.K.-Cant.) Cinema City 1982 color 100m. D: P.C. Leong;(uncred.) Henry Chan. SP: Lo Kin. Ph: W.N. Tai. PD: Shi, Tsang. Ref: V 9/15/82. JFFJ 14:36. with Eddie Chan.
Transvestite killer..."graphic murders...exercise in... fright."(V)

2 HEARTBEEPS Michael Phillips 1981 ws 77m. Sp Dial: Henny Youngman; Jack Carter. Ph: Charles Rosher Jr.;(mattes) Taylor, Glouner. AD: John W. Corso. SpMkp:(concep) James Kagel, Mike McKraken, Ziggy Geike; Zoltan Elek, Vince Prentice. SpCost: Theodora Van Runkle. SpFX:(coord robot) Bob Sturgis;(mech d) Ewing, Krumm; Stirber. Sd:(des) Colin Mouat; Sound Effects; (synth) Jack Manning; Larsen. Titles: Intralink. Ref: TV. V 12/23/81. Bill Warren. Allan Arkush: "SUNRISE with robots." Joe Dante. Hirschhorn. and with Kenneth McMillan, Barry Diamond(Catskil), Kathleen Freeman, Paul Bartel, Mary Woronov, Dick Miller(Walter Paisley); voices: J. Carter(Catskil), Jerry Garcia(Phil), Ron Gans(Crimebuster).
Two human-like, state-of-the-art robots in the new Companion Series--Aqua (Bernadette Peters) and Val (Andy Kaufman)--meet and click and fashion spare-parts offspring....Milton Berle-style robot Catskil with "cigar option." A sweet, unsung sf-comedy-romance. HEARTBEEPS was, perhaps, lost in the commercial shuffle because its robot protagonists don't fit into the conventional movie-robot categories of cute-comic-incidental or sinister-dramatic. In fact, you almost have to go back to 1919 and Lubitsch's Die PUPPE to find a similar stylization of actors' movements for comic purposes. Aqua and Val are "mechanically compatible," but also mechanically restricted, and this restriction-of-movement functions, comically, as deadpan humor; dramatically, as understatement. The movie's comic-dramatic high point is the near-simultaneous running-down to "stop" of the two (as their "energy packs" die)--the expiring Val's "hand" just managing to come to rest in the already-inert Aqua's, before he too shuts off. This is the robotic equivalent of a freeze frame. It's also a touching, serio-comic paraphrase of lovers-dying-in-each-other's-arms romantic strophes. The film's stylization extends to the delivery of dialogue, the dialogue itself, and sound effects, like "baby" Phil's invariable tittering at Catskil's jokes. The robot voices are "orchestrated" with such care that the scenes with humans seem, by contrast, flat and predictable. (Val and Aqua are also reported to have lost some running time to the (ir-

ritating) Crimebuster robot, thanks to a surly preview audience.) John Williams' evocative score manages to be lilting, droll, and bittersweet, often, it seems, all at once.

The HEAVENLY BODY MGM 1943 93m. D: Alexander Hall. SP: Michael Arlen, Walter Reisch. SpFX: Arnold Gillespie. Ref: TV. Lee. V 12/29/43: sf-sequence.

Mt. Jefferson Observatory astronomer William S. Whitley (William Powell) discovers a "new comet," which is named after him and which he predicts will collide with the moon. It does, and the magnified image of this collision is projected onto a movie screen in the observatory, via a photo-electric scanner attached to a telescope....Powell has a couple pleasant pantomimes here, but the actors, in general, seem all too aware that they're "doing comedy," which isn't as easy as they seem to think. Nor do the script's plot contrivances really qualify as comedy. (Hedy Lamarr, however, qualifies as "heavenly.") The film's wonders-of-the-planetarium display isn't as imaginative or spectacular as the one in Universal's The INVISIBLE RAY (1936), but it is integrated (more or less) into the story: the final kiss between Powell and Lamarr is equated with the coming together, earlier, of comet and moon.

HELL OF THE LIVING DEAD see NIGHT OF THE ZOMBIES

HELL'S BELLS see MURDER BY PHONE

HERCULES (B-I?) MGM-UA/Cannon(Golan-Globus) 1983 color 98m. SP,D: Luigi Cozzi. Ph: A. Spagnoli. Mus: Pino Donaggio. PD: M.A. Geleng. SpOptFX: Armando Valcauda; La Roca, Studio 4, Technocine TV. SpFX: Herman Nathan;(vis) Jerry Unger, Phil Travers. SpSdFX: Anzellotti Studios. Mkp: Freddy Spinks. Ref: screen. V 8/31/83. Ecran F 33:10-15. with Lou Ferrigno (Hercules), Sybil Danning(Ariana), Brad Harris, Rossana Podesta, Mirella D'Angelo(Circe), Eva Robbins(Daedalus).

Pandora's Jar shatters, and its fragments become the planets and the solar system. Zeus, on the moon, creates the super-strong, near-invincible Hercules from light, which enters the newborn son of Amphitryon. King Minos of Atlantis has Amphitryon slain, but Zeus's gigantic hand saves the baby from a river's rapids--and the baby saves himself from two drooling snake-creatures by squishing them. The full-grown Hercules flings, variously, dead bears and huge posts into space, and the debris becomes fixed parts of the heavens. At Minos's behest, Daedalus sends metallic, "colossal exterminators" to crush Hercules. One looks like a giant robot-grasshopper; another, a centaur; the third becomes (after enlarging in the Earth's atmosphere) a three-headed Hydra which spits cosmic rays. (Hercules uses the enchantress Circe's shield to deflect the latter back on the Hydra.) The aged Circe drinks 10 drops of Hercules' blood and turns into a young and literally starry-eyed woman; she accompanies Hercules on an endless stairway to the center of the Earth, and then across a rainbow to the gates of hell and Skull Mountain, with an assist from the unearthly ferry-man Charon. Inside the egg-like Soul of the World, under the Hand of Destiny, lies Circe's amulet, which Hercules retrieves after braving alternately burning and freezing magic barriers. The amulet, in the right hands (i.e., Circe's), enables Hercules to grow to giant-size and separate Europe from Africa and win the flying chariot from the King of Africa. A Hercules-hurled stone block pulls the chariot across the world to Minos's Thetan realm, which is dedicated to "science for the sake of science." Hercules's hearthrob Cassiopeia is scheduled to become the Bride of the Phoenix--i.e., a sacrifice to the volcano which is Minos's energy source. Hercules uses the magic sword which keeps the (never seen) Phoenix at bay to defeat Minos (and his sword of multi-colored fire) and the evil Ariana, who turns to stone, then to ash.

HERCULES, as the above may suggest, does not lack for incident--many lacks it may have, but that isn't one of them. If the mythology doesn't quite square with Bulfinch's (liberties are freely taken with Daedalus, Pandora, etc.), there is at least a lot of it--fair excuse, clearly, for myriad effects, none of them of award-winning calibre, but most of them colorful (literally and figuratively). The moon (always hanging very obtrusively in the sky), the temple exteriors, the seas, and the heavens are all designed to be anything but mundane. Some of the floating effects may be unintended, as may also be various wobblings, waverings, and string-like manifestations. (Then again, it's supposed to be an unstable solar system.) As for the characters--Hercules asks "Why...?" and seems to find out. Ignore him. The actors are here only to say who they are and what's coming up next. They perform the function of vaudeville billboard-ladies.

HI-SPIRIT (H.K.) 1982 Ref: V 9/15/82:53: "local horror-comedy."

HIDDEN VALLEY, The see LAND UNKNOWN

HIGH ENCOUNTERS (OF THE ULTIMATE KIND) see CHEECH AND CHONG'S NEXT MOVIE

HOCUS POCUS (Chinese) 1983? Ref: poster: horror-comedy; zombie?

*HOLD THAT LINE 1952 SpFX: Ray Mercer? Ref: TV. V 4/2/52. Warren/KWTS! Weldon. and with Byron Foulger.

Bowery Boy Leo Gorcey's chemical formula #1 makes subject super-strong; formula #2 makes man super-small; formula #3 makes Huntz Hall fly....Formula plot does nothing. Three redeeming moments maximum.

The HOLE IDEA WB 1955 anim color 7m. D: R. McKimson. SP: Sid Marcus. Ref: "WB Cartoons." LC.

Professor's "Portable Hole" invention.

2P HOLLYWOOD BOULEVARD New World/Davison 1976 color 83m. D,Ed: Joe Dante, Allan Arkush. SP: David Opatoshu(aka Patrick Hobby). Ph: Jamie Anderson. Mus: Andrew Stein. AD: Jack De Wolfe. SpFX: Roger George. SpCost: Rob Short. Opt: Rabin. Ed: also Amy Jones. Ref: screen. TV. Joe Dante. Bill Warren. Eric Hoffman. Cinef V:1:25. V 4/28/76. PFA. Weldon: clips from BATTLE BEYOND THE SUN. Ecran F 39:79. with Candice Rialson, Mary Woronov, Rita George, Jeffrey Kramer, Dick Miller(Walter Paisley), Paul Bartel, Jonathan Kaplan, Charles B. Griffith, Forrest J Ackerman, Jon Davison, Joe McBride, Todd McCarthy.

Horror sequence with masked, cloaked killer attacking actress...hommage to ZOMBIES OF MORA TAU: movie which begins as a story of Eskimos fighting dinosaurs, shoots under the title of Mutilated Maidens of Mora Tau, and is released as Machete Maidens...special appearances by Godzilla-like Godzina (who tosses the script for Atomic War Brides into the toilet), Robby the Robot ("I don't do nudity"), and The Fly ("Buzz off!")... DEATH RACE 2000 car used in horror movie set in the year 2050... dialogue reference to Brain from Planet X...ape-suited actor in helmet, a la ROBOT MONSTER...clips from and references to Corman's The TERROR--e.g., Bartel's character here named after Karloff's there.

The informing moment, or cut, in HOLLYWOOD BOULEVARD is arguably the one in which the ineffably pretentious B-movie director Erich Von Leppe (Bartel) describes his Atomic War Brides project as a "penetrating, unflinching look into the future," as we cut to a shot of three foolish-looking future-creatures (from the movie-in-progress), sitting around absent-mindedly between takes. Within the film, there's no middle ground between the pretentious and the mindless. The film itself is the middle ground--the comic. If the production is tacky enough to be mistaken for a mindless action-comedy ("They show this sort of thing at drive-ins," commented one unsuspecting member of the audience), much of its running time it's about tackiness. At its best it's casually self-reflective (e.g., Miller as Paisley watching himself admiringly in The TERROR). At its most problematic, it almost seems to take its real-life/reel-life juxtapositions semi-seriously (e.g., Rialson attacked onscreen and offscreen at the same time). The irony, generally light, occasionally gets a bit heavy. The film's horror-sequence out-Bavas Bava (but where are the zooms??), but doesn't really seem, tonally, to belong. Unlike most scenes in the movie, it doesn't undercut itself. It's a straight hommage.... Question for a film course on the history of New World films: by what letter in the "Hollywood" sign is the murderess in HOLLYWOOD BOULEVARD crushed? (Answer, perhaps significantly: "Y")

HOLLYWOOD CAPERS WB 1935 anim 7m. D: Jack King. Ref: "WB Cartoons." LC: c1936.

"Frankenstein monster" on studio horror-movie set.(WBC)

HOME SWEET HOME 1981 color 85m. D: Nettie Pena. Ref: Ecran F 40:81. V 2/16/83:24: horror. with Sallee Elyse, Jake Steinfeld.
Schizophrenic killer menaces family in isolated country house.

HORROR CHAMBER OF DR. FAUSTUS see EYES WITHOUT A FACE

HORROR HOTEL MASSACRE see LEGEND OF THE BAYOU

HORROR OF THE GIANT VORTEX (J) Kindai Eiga Kyokai 1978 (KYOFU NO DAIUZUMAKI) D: Buichi Saito. Ref: JFFJ 13:30.14:10. with Keiko Natsuo, Toshio Kurosawa.
"Made-for-TV fantasy feature."

2 HORROR ON SNAPE ISLAND 1972 (2P BEYOND THE FOG-re-r t) Ref: TV. V 3/4/81:8. Weldon. and with Mark McBride(Michael), D. Fowlds.
Hideously-deformed killer...impalings...beheadings...grotesque idol of Baal in underground island-cavern....Truly abysmal shocker, featuring hokey shock-close-ups/zooms/music, and a predictable climactic "surprise." Movies like this give trash a bad name. "Seagulls don't nest on Snape Island." Natch.

HORROR STAR, The see FRIGHTMARE

HOSPITAL MASSACRE Cannon(Golan-Globus) 1982(1981) color 89m. (BE MY VALENTINE, OR ELSE...-orig t. X-RAY-int & B t) Story, D: Boaz Davidson. SP: Marc Behm. Ph: Nicholas von Sternberg. Mus: Arlon Ober. AD: J.R. Fox. Mkp: Allan Apone, Kathy Shorkey. SpFX: Joe Quinlavin. Ref: TV: MGM-UA Home Video. V 9/2/81:6: at Sitges. 2/16/83:24. 11/9/83. 4/7/82:4(rated). MFB'82:51-2. Weldon: aka WARD 13. with Barbi Benton, Chip Lucia(Harold), Jon Van Ness, Gloria Morrison, Billy Jacoby(young Harold).
1961. Little Harold, rejected as valentine material by Susan Jeremy, hangs her brother on a hatrack. 19 years later to the (Valentine's) day, he turns Susan's routine medical into a hospital nightmare by killing her doctor, then switching her X-rays for another set which are practically "a death warrant" for her. Before he operates on Susan (he wants her heart--literally), big Harold dispatches some secondary victims (with knife, hypo, surgical buzz-saw and hatchet, etc.) and leaves Susan a gift of a severed-head-in-a-box. In the operating room (finally), Susan turns the tables on Harold and, a) stabs him with a handy medical instrument, b) bashes him with a metal pipe, c) dumps a container of flammable solution on his head, and, d) applies cigarette lighter.
This updated St. Valentine's Day Massacre exploits our fears of X-rays, operating rooms, surgical tools, other hospital patients, etc. Everyone and everything is Intimidating. People give Susan (Benton) funny looks or move in virtual slow motion--in order to foster Suspense. The end effect is not-quite-comic, not-quite-suspenseful, just silly. In the hospital-horror subgenre, MASSACRE ranks below VISITING HOURS, but above HALLOWEEN II, thanks to scattered odd touches--e.g., the presence

on Susan's floor of three dotty old ladies (the Fates?)...the implacable Harold holding aloft a bedsheet before him (as if it were a sail) as he strides down a corridor after his latest prey, then enfolds her in it...the camera lurching, oddly, right and left, subjectively, as Susan, at one point, flees in terror....

HOT MONEY WB 1936 67m. (THERE'S MILLIONS IN IT-orig t) D: William McGann. SP: William Jacobs. Idea: Aben Kandel. Ph: Arthur Edeson. AD: Esdras Hartley. Ref: Bill Warren. MFB'36: 116. LC. V 7/29/36. Academy. FDY. NYT 7/25/36. with Ross Alexander, Beverly Roberts, Joseph Cawthorn, Paul Graetz, Anne Nagel, Cy Kendall, R.E. Keene, Addison Richards.

"Liquid concentrate which, when mixed with pure water, can be used as a substitute for gasoline."(NYT)

The HOUND OF THE BASKERVILLES (B) Mapleton/Weintraub 1983 color 101m. D: Douglas Hickox. SP: Charles E. Pogue, from Sir Arthur Conan Doyle's book. Ph: Ronnie Taylor. Mus: Michael J. Lewis. PD: Michael Stringer. SpFxSup: Alan Whibley. Mkp: (sup) Tom Smith; John Webber. Ref: TV. V 6/15/83. 5/14/83: 432. Ecran F 36:40-42.41:27-8. with Ian Richardson, Donald Churchill, Martin Shaw, Denholm Elliott, Brian Blessed, Ronald Lacey, Eleanor Bron, Edward Judd, Glynis Barber, Nicholas Clay.

The curse of the Baskervilles dates from the 17th Century, when Sir Hugo Baskerville was slaughtered on the moor by a dog "larger than any hound seen by mortal eyes." Over 200 years later, the legend of the "glowing, ghastly hound" drives Sir Charles Baskerville to his death: "It was *fear* that killed him!" This "supernatural hound" strikes at night, "when the powers of evil are exalted," but Sherlock Holmes proves the creature to be one of flesh and blood....

Handsome TV production is easily one of the better adaptations of the much-adapted book. Atmospheric and fairly-well-paced, it *almost* succeeds in obscuring the fact that the original story, here as before, doesn't really translate that well to the screen. It's pretty obviously the *horrific* elements--the phantom dog and the haunted moor--which keep drawing producers--and audiences--back to the tale. But the story's dramatic elements prove less compelling, at least in its film incarnations. One of the key plot elements in fact--the Notting Hill Murderer--proves to be extraneous, a red herring. This killer-at-large is at large only to give the story the illusion of complexity--and to give the hound another victim. The Baskervilles themselves (and their servants and neighbors) are a bland lot--they only succeed in setting off Holmes and Watson (here, Richardson and Churchill, respectively) to good advantage. The latter, at least, have quirks of character and a sense of humor. This HOUND is pretty straightforward, conventional melodrama--until seen in the light of all-is-not-what-it-seemed *retrospect*....

HOUSE OF DEATH (S.Kor.) Asia Society/Yong Lee 1981 color/ws 93m. (PEE-MAK. The DEATH HUT-alt tr t. The DEATH COTTAGE-cr t) D,Ph: Doo-Yong Lee. SP: S.-R. Yoon. Ph: also J.-N. Chah. Mus: H.-K. Kim. Ref: screen. V 12/30/81. PFA notes 2/4/83. with Jee-I. Yoo, Won Namgoong.

The spirit of a man, Samdol, murdered 20 years earlier, seems to return and possess the only heir of the clan responsible....exorcist, Okhwa, who claims that a dream re: the mountain goddess led her to some relics....The local exorcist keeps claiming that this import, Okhwa, is a fraud, and she turns out to be right. HOUSE OF DEATH is one of the most blatant cheats on the supernatural since MARK OF THE VAMPIRE (1935). Here, a display of exorcism appears, in retrospect, to be simply a convenient convulsion on the part of the "exorcised"; ghostly voices of the wronged dead prove, apparently, to be just subjective echoes on the part of the "exorcist".... Yes, it's all a revenge plot. Until the final disclosures, however, the story piques one's interest by appearing to twist, first, one way, then another. First, it looks like a straight case of exorcising an evil spirit; then, like a case of ghostly sublimation: supernatural revenge taken on the heir rather than on the actual perpetrators of the double murder; then, like wholesale extermination of killers by spirits. Finally.... The real-or-supernatural? ambiguity seems, ultimately, beside the (main) point--either way, the film is an attack on family "purity" and on patriarchal oppression. The ambiguity only dilutes the attack.

HOUSE OF EVIL see HOUSE ON SORORITY ROW

HOUSE OF HORROR see HAMMER HOUSE OF HORROR

HOUSE OF SHADOWS (Arg.) Darwin/Sandy Cobe 1977?('83-U.S.) color 103m. (aka The HOUSE OF THE SHADOWS) D: Richard Wulicher. SP,P: Enrique Torres Tudela. Ph: Anibaldi Salvo. Mus: W. Joseph. Sets: Paul Olive, George Marchegiani. Mkp: Ernesto D'Agostino. Ref: TV: Media Home Ent.(video). VideoSB. Bill Warren. Boxo 5/31/76. with John Gavin, Yvonne De Carlo, Leonor Manso, Mecha Ortiz, Roberto Airaldi, Susan Oliver, German Krauss.

1931. A young woman, Audrey, who resembles another woman, Catherine Webster (who died in 1908), witnesses an ectoplasmic reenactment of the murder of Catherine in "the old Webster house." Audrey feels herself to be a "part of Catherine": "I belong to the astral world, the world of waiting--we are only energy." At one point she seems possessed by Catherine, whose angry spirit "cries out for revenge"--on her unknown killer--and appears, fleetingly, at a seance. Ultimately, Catherine reappears and scares the murderer into a fatal fall. Plus: one hatchet murder, one person-in-a-wheelchair-left-on-the-railroad-tracks murder....Catherine's several "entrances" (i.e., materializations) are grand enough. (One time, she appears in the midst of a roomful of dancers, who, on next glance, have vanished.) But the script favors mystery over fantasy, and its suspects are a most unintriguing lot. There would, in fact, be no mystery, but Audrey's suspiciously selective powers grant her an early peek only at the victim and not at the murderer. Execrable music, awful dubbing--the voices don't match the faces. (John Gavin seems to get Alan Alda's voice.)

HOUSE OF THE DARK STAIRWAY (I) 1983 color (La CASA CON LA SCALA NEL BUIO) D: Lamberto Bava. SP: Dardano Sarchetti. Ref: V 8/24/83:38: "chiller." Ecran F 39:12-16: bloody. (A)

HOUSE OF THE DEAD see ALIEN ZONE

HOUSE OF THE LONG SHADOWS (B) London-Cannon/Golan-Globus 1982 color 101m. D: Pete Walker. SP: Michael Armstrong. Suggested by "Seven Keys To Baldpate," novel by Earl Derr Biggers, play by George M. Cohan. Ph: Norman Langley. Mus: Richard Harvey. AD: Mike Pickwoad. Mkp: George Partleton. Titles: Rank. Ref: TV: MGM-UA Home Video. MFB'83:99. V 6/29/82. "Horror Film Stars." Ecran F 34:6-10: U.S.-B. with Vincent Price, Christopher Lee, Peter Cushing, Desi Arnaz Jr., John Carradine, Sheila Keith, Richard Todd, Julie Peasgood.

On a bet, an author (Arnaz) spends a night in an old Welsh manor--Bllyddpaetur, or Baldpate (or, in the book he is writing there, Midnight Manor)--"a cursed place" empty for over 40 years. Soon, however, it's full again, with a "bunch of weirdos"--the Grisbanes, who have assembled on the 40th anniversary of the incarceration therein of Roderick Grisbane, who "brought about the fall of the house of Grisbane" when, as a lad of 14, his "cruel, twisted mind" turned to murder, and the "doomed family" punished him by locking him in his upstairs room. Roderick escapes before his appointed time of release this night, and there follow deaths by heart attack, piano wire, vitriol, poisoned wine, etc....

"Jane Eyre," "Wuthering Heights," and "The Fall of the House of Usher" are all invoked here, as well they might be considering the thick layers of Gothic atmosphere spread upon the plot. That plot, though, finally has more to do with charades--it recalls the movie The GREAT GARRICK(1937), in which a troupe of actors takes over an inn and puts on a performance for someone (Garrick himself) who is an unwitting "audience." Here, the writer, Kenneth Magee, is the dupe. Each inside-out twisting of the plot in HOUSE, however, seems to render the movie less interesting and believable. Most of the characters are revealed to be, simply, actors hired by a publisher--or (a final feeble twist) are they...? The movie passes as mystery; does less well as a shock-suspenser; and is feeblest at narrative game-playing. On another, arguably more important level (given the quality of the material), HOUSE is, also, a reunion of some venerable horror stars. The more fascinating movie might, in fact, have been The Making of HOUSE OF THE LONG SHADOWS. The stories told on the sets in-between takes must have been more engrossing than that of this screenplay--although if the undoubtedly-more-faithful 1947 film adaptation of novel and play is any indication, Michael Armstrong wasn't exactly tampering with sacred text when he wrote this looser adaptation. (7 KEYS TO BALDPATE was filmed five times between 1917 and 1947....) The (phony) family-reunion explanation-of-events is, at least, a shade more satisfying than the '47 version's--there, Baldpate was a hideout for some crooks. And the "family" story gives Lee, Price, Cushing, and Carradine opportunity for a little serious playing....

*HOUSE OF USHER 1960 SpFX: Pat Dinga. PhFX: Ray Mercer. Process Ph: Larry Butler. Paintings: Burt Schoenberg. Mkp: Fred Phillips. Ref: TV. Jim Shapiro. Lee. Weldon.

Roderick Usher (Vincent Price) believes that the House of Usher--i.e., both the family and their actual habitation--is "tainted," evil; he succeeds in preventing his sister Madeline (Myrna Fahey) from leaving that House....Roderick seems to be correct in his belief too. The Poe story and Richard Matheson script offer, in effect, a justification of pessimism--though it's true that there is some ambiguity as to whether Madeline is a real (i.e., tainted) Usher. Roderick, it's hinted, may have "created" her in their image; pushed her over the brink, from sleepwalking and catalepsy into madness....Was there a glimmer of hope for the family line in her? Or did Roderick merely accelerate the process of decline and decay? Even in its sunniest moments, the film evokes a qualified pessimism. Such an attitude is of course esthetically permissable; even, from one angle, refreshingly uncompromising. But a feeling of gloom comes too easily to the occupants of this house. And if there are evil houses, evil families, are there also good houses, good families? If the story's premise is quirky and intriguing, it's also a bit much. It requires that Price (fine here as Roderick) hardly crack a smile--a hearty laugh on his part would subvert the entire enterprise. Even the scattered fun-shock effects seem like cracks in the film's stately facade. This now-semi-classic Roger Corman-Richard Matheson film has, nonetheless, a strange integrity--it may be the best dramatic mounting Poe's story will ever have.

The HOUSE ON SORORITY ROW FVI/ARC(VAE) 1982(1981) color 91m. (SEVEN SISTERS-orig t. HOUSE OF EVIL-B) SP,D,Co-P: Mark Rosman. Addl Dial: Bobby Fine. Ph: T. Suhrstedt. Mus: Richard Band; J. Goldsmith. AD: V. Peranio. SpFX: R.E. Holland, Make-Up Effects Labs; D. Gamba. SdFX: Sandy Berman. Opt: Cinema Research. Ref: screen. MFB'83:329. V 2/9/83. with Kathryn McNeil, Eileen Davidson, Charles Serio(Eric), Lois K. Hunt.

An aging woman's deformed son, Eric--a victim of an experimental fertility drug--is hidden away in an attic playroom and leaves it only to murder sorority girls who accidentally killed his mother. Most of the victims are dispatched with a very versatile cane (passed down at her death from mother to son)--

both the end of the stem and the bird's-beak head are quite sharp. There isn't much here to analyze except weapons, though the movie is competent enough, a passable beginning-director's exercise. That it is the son (and that there is a son) and not the mother--back-from-the-half-dead--who's doing the killing comes as no surprise. Nor does the fact that he still seems to be alive at the end. Along the much-trodden way, however, there are a few unusual diversions--e.g., a bit of macabre lyricism with three bodies found floating in a lighted swimming pool at night...the heroine's hallucinations, in which the cane comes to take on a life of its own, and the eyes of a severed head in a toilet bowl open. (The latter certainly gives the kids in the audience something to talk about afterwards.) Any respite from the wheelwork of "suspense" would be welcome, but these moments--in their machine-be-damned seeming-superfluousness--are especially so.

HOUSE THAT BLED TO DEATH/GROWING PAINS see HAMMER HOUSE OF HORROR

The HOUSE WHERE DEATH LIVES NAF/IPS 1982(1981) color 83m. (DELUSION-orig t) Story,D,Co-P: Alan Beattie. Story,SP: Jack Viertel. Ph: S. Posey. Mus: Don Peake. Ref: V 10/26/83:98 (ad). 6/1/83:10. 9/22/82:14: in Miami. 5/13/81:74(ad). 9/2/81: 6: at Sitges. HR 10/25/83:S-72: "horror-suspense." Willis/SW '83. Ecran F 26:5. with Patricia Pearcy, David Hayward, John Dukakis, Joseph Cotten.

The HOUSE WHERE EVIL DWELLS (U.S.-J) MGM-UA/M.B.Cohen & Toei (CCSH) 1982 color 88m. D: Kevin Connor. SP: R.A. Suhosky, from J.W. Hardiman's novel. Ph: Jacques Haitkin. Mus: Ken Thorne. AD: Y. Sano. SpVisFX: Cruse & Co. Mkp: H. Nagatomo. Ref: TV. V 5/19/82. with Edward Albert, Susan George, Doug McClure, Amy Barrett, Mako Hattori(Otami), T. Okajima(witch).

Kyoto, Japan. The three ghosts of a haunted bell-house enter the bodies of a contemporary threesome; make them re-enact their century-old tale of adultery, murder, and suicide; then depart....The female ghost, Otami, when alive, stole a witch's erotic knickknack and thus started the curse; she now appears, siren-like, to the (living) husband and almost drowns him....Plus: devil-god mask and ivory charm which send out emanations....crabs which attack the couple's daughter (she drank a damned soul in a cup of soup)....monk who attempts an exorcism....Deja boo! for anyone who has seen BURNT OFFERINGS, The AMITYVILLE HORROR, etc. And the ghosts here are a little too versatile--they're material, immaterial, or semi-material, as the mood hits them. Comedy beckons in scenes in which the big crabs chase the little girl up a tree and the ghosts egg on the live humans to mayhem, but the director appears not to have realized it.

HUGUES LE LOUP (F) 1974 color 90m. D: Michel Subiela. From a story by Erckmann-Chatrian. Ref: Ecran F 21:40. with Patricia

Callas, Claude Titre.
TV-movie re: a castle apparently plagued by a werewolf.

2 HUMAN EXPERIMENTS 1980 (aka BEYOND THE GATE) SpFX: also Knott Ltd., Frank De Marco. SdFX: J's Fine Art. Opt: Pacific. Ref: TV. Theresa Hull. and with Mercedes Shirley, Phil Proctor.
Psychiatrist Hans Kline of the Gates Correctional Facility "corrects" his subjects by returning them mentally to the infant stage, and retraining them to be non-violent. He subjects Rachel, wrongly convicted of murder, to an obstacle course of horrors--e.g., a bathroom crawling with spiders, scorpions, etc.--and, shocked out of her mind and identity, she becomes the "very impressionable" "Sarah." Dr. Kline then programs her to kill his warden, but "Sarah" (partially at least) reverts to Rachel at the critical moment....Formula MANCHURIAN CANDIDATE/CLOCKWORK ORANGE mind-bending. The ends, here, are supposedly noble and socially beneficial. The means include murder and mental torture. The film would be <u>less</u> formulaic if the psychiatrist were less obviously a villain; if he were just a tad more scrupulous--or if the heroine <u>needed</u> some "correcting." As it is, the script is one-sided and predictable.

HUMAN LANTERNS (H.K.) Shaw 1982 color 95m. SP,D: Sun Chung. SP: also I. Kuang. Ph: T. An-shun. Mus: S. Shing, S. Chun-hou. AD: C. Chingshen. Ref: V 10/20/82:180: "horror and action." with Lo Lieh, Liu Yung, Tanny, Chen Kuan-tai.
Madman makes doll-lanterns from the skin of the women he murders.

HUMONGOUS (Can.) Embassy/Stevenson-Kramreither(Humongous & Manteco) 1982 color 93m. D,Title Des: Paul Lynch. SP: William Gray. Ph: Brian Hebb. Mus: J.M. Cockell. AD: Carol Spier; B. Dunphy. SpMkp: Brenda Kirk; M.S. Donati. SpFX:(d) Martin Malivoire; Gordon Smith & The Gore Boys. Opt: Film Opticals. Ref: TV. V 6/9/82. MFB'83:215-16. with Janet Julian, David Wallace, Janit Baldwin, Garry Robbins(Ida's son).
Canadian Labour Day, 1946. Prologue re: rape, with rapist savaged by attack dogs and polished off by his victim....Flash-forward to a boating party shipwrecked on Parsons Island... fog...howling dogs...tales of a madwoman...monster-meal remnants everywhere...overuse of subjective camera..."weird" nursery...album with "no more photographs" after Ida's baby is born...mama's corpse (found flopped back in chair)...meat-locker-like cellar...Ida's diary...passages re: acromegalic, brain-damaged son...Humongous himself..."It's okay--he's dead!"...(famous last words)...Heroine (previously compared in appearance to Ida) plays mom, orders "son" away. He has seen The BURNING, or was it FRIDAY THE 13th PART II?, and is not fooled. She sets him and cellar on fire...(premature sigh of relief)...He stalks out of the lake, after putting fire (on himself) out....She stakes him....She has won, but is kinda

beat....Another hour and a half down the drain. From the beloved director and writer of PROM NIGHT....

The HUNCHBACK OF NOTRE DAME (U.S.-B?) CBS-TV/Hallmark Hall of Fame(Col-TV & Rosemont) 1982 color 92m. D: Michael Tuchner. SP: John Gay, from Victor Hugo's novel "Notre Dame de Paris." Ph: Alan Hume. Mus: Kenneth Thorne. PD: John Stoll. SpMkp: Nick Maley. SpFxSup: John Morris. Opt: Cliff Culley. Ref: TV. V 2/10/82:102. with Anthony Hopkins, Derek Jacobi, Lesley-Anne Down, John Gielgud, Robert Powell, Rosalie Crutchley, David Suchet, Roland Culver, Tim Pigott-Smith.

Again the familiar names and scenes: the grotesque, "devil"-eyed hunchback Quasimodo; the "witch" Esmerelda; Frollo; The King of Thieves; the Festival of Fools; the public flogging, and of course Notre Dame....It's about time to retire this tale from films--it's viable, apparently, only as a vehicle for the actor who plays (and the makeup man who designs) Quasimodo. Hopkins makes a not-unworthy addition to the gallery of screen Quasimodos, but there are really no characters here, only qualities--pity, love, cruelty, kindness, hypocrisy, lust, injustice, and, underlying all, self-pity. Hugo's "humanism" has a calculated, aren't-we-compassionate? feel to it, at least in the movie versions of his book.

See also: BOSKO THE DRAWBACK. BUENOS NOCHES, SENOR MONSTRUO.

The HUNGER (B) MGM-UA/Richard Shepherd Co. 1983 color/ws 95m. D: Tony Scott. SP: Ivan Davis, Michael Thomas, from Whitley Strieber's novel. Ph: Stephen Goldblatt; Hugh Johnson;(NY) Tom Mangravite. Mus: Michael Rubini, Denny Jaeger;(elec) David Lawson. PD: Brian Morris. SpMkpFX: Dick Smith, Carl Fullerton; Antony Clavet; Nick Dudman. MonkeyFX: Dave Allen, Roger Dicken. SpFX: Graham Longhurst. Scenic Art: Beverly Miller. SdFxEd: Campbell Askew. Opt: Peerless. Ref: screen. V 4/27/83. MFB '83:133-34. FComment 2/84:10,11. Ecran F 36:6-14. with Catherine Deneuve, David Bowie, Susan Sarandon, Cliff De Young, Beth Ehlers, Dan Hedaya, James Aubrey, Shane Rimmer, Bessie Love, George Camiller(Eumenes); K. Miller, F. Yockers(cadavers).

Miriam Blaylock (Deneuve), a centuries-old, queen-bee-like vampire, born in Egypt and now living in New York, remains young and vital--her blood is "stronger" and "more disease-resistant" than human blood--with once-a-week "feedings." Through exchanges of blood, she is able also to prolong the lives of her lovers, though <u>their</u> youth and vitality eventually drain, leaving them enfeebled and corpse-like. At the end, they manage to rise again and send her to her death, then too waste away. Only her successor and final lover, Sarah (Sarandon), remains....monkey experimentally aged five years in one minute.

If life and love are, in general, mixed matters, eternal life and undying love, suggests The HUNGER, are <u>very</u> mixed. The scene of sweetest contentment shared by our vampire couple, Miriam and John (Bowie): an afternoon of chamber music in their sitting-room. Otherwise, life through the centuries doesn't seem very much fun...."The hunger" can be seen as a hunger for death (on the part of John and Sarah) as well as for life (on Miriam's part), in book as well as film. Both works carry tough-to-be-a-vampire overtones. The book, though, might be described as humanistic; the movie, fatalistic. The book centers on the consequences (for others) of Miriam's hunger for life; the movie, on that unending life itself, on the prospect of immortality. In the film, John's fate is illumined in a flash, in our first shot of him (still moving) in his coffin; and the fates of Miriam's earlier loves, the next instant, in another flash, as we see (in a track back) that his coffin is one of several. This singular-to-plural leap telescopes centuries into a moment. We've seen special effects, in this movie and in others, condense time, translate quietly-accumulated years in a character's life into suddenly-accumulated wrinkles on an actor's face. This shot is like a special effect of the viewer's imagination. It's an instant education in the mathematics of time: Miriam's age = the few-hundred years on the now-aged John's face x the contents of a half-dozen coffins. The track back is a sublimely romantic stroke, if you see the scene from Miriam's point-of-view; from the viewpoint of most anyone else--living, dead, or in-between--it's ironic, a new wrinkle, so to speak, on the Love Never Dies theme. In his book, Strieber talks about suffering, human and superhuman, down through the ages; Scott's film suggests its immensity and scope--it's so hard to live, so hard to die--for Miriam, John, Sarah....At the end, the undead are released by what plays, on one level, like a supernatural earthquake, a deus ex machina; on another, like a boiling-over of pent-up, psychic resentment or longing, or both, on the part of the dear not-quite-departed. The loved ones assail Miriam and scare her into an apparently fatal fall. She ages, and her lovers disintegrate, limb by limb, feature by feature. These aren't effects for effects' sake. We've seen how these creatures cling to life, or rather, how life clings to them. The force and fury of this sequence suggest what it takes for them to shed life--i.e., physically, nothing short of annihilation--and silence, force majeure, questions about what might seem, in retrospect, a rather arbitrary sorting out of living (Sarah), dead (John and company), and undead (Miriam??). A coda with Sarah confirms the film's intimations of immortality. Sarah has just attempted suicide, but Miriam's (displaced) eternal-life-force enters her, it seems, before the aging, shriveling process can take hold. Whether or not Miriam's body lives on, in the weakened, "drone" state, is a moot point. At the end, however, her voice cries out to Sarah from a (closed) coffin....Miriam's electronically-amplified cries echo throughout the film: once, earlier, she calls, supernaturally, to Sarah; in a psychic fragment-of-a-flashback (to her Egyptian origins), she cries out over the bloody body of a victim or lover; and her scream over Sarah's apparently-dead body carries most unnaturally. The last shot of her withered body is a close-up of her still-open mouth.

Miriam's voice carries over centuries, and her cry, emblematic of her life, is an ambiguous one, mixing anguish, command, and something like existential urgency (a la the hero's "I still exist!" at the end of The INCREDIBLE SHRINKING MAN). Her last "Sarah!" might come from within Sarah, from that part of Sarah which is Miriam, rather than from the coffin. It's a cry, perhaps, of ironic triumph. And it signifies that, in one way or another, both Sarah and Miriam are still alive. Miriam's is a love story so grotesque that it's (almost) comic. When, at the climax, her past loves surround her, she assures them, "I love you all," while vainly attempting to keep these mummies at arm's length. Mockingly, they want to embrace her, kiss her. They may not intend their amorousness as mockery, but someone, it appears, is trying to make a macabre farce of the idea of eternal love, and, in this sequence at least, is succeeding. The movie, as a whole, might have been more appealing and less forbidding as a full-fledged serio-comedy. It's "almost comic," almost a farce at times, but generally reins in its sense of self-absurdity. Only with this climactic sequence does it untimidly fuse the romantic, the horrific, and the comic. As it is, The HUNGER is a cold, almost inhuman movie, in Miriam's image. The musical score--a strange melange of electronic music, jungle noises, sounds like railroad cars coupling and uncoupling, and Ravel's "Le Gibet"--might be aural bric-a-brac from Miriam's past and present. The music she plays on her sitting-room piano does, in fact, live on, like her voice, after her--it accompanies the inspector's survey of the now-empty room, and bridges the transition to the coda. In the book, Miriam's past lovers return in her dreams, and the victims of John and Sarah reappear, accusingly, in visions. In the film, there's some pain, but little guilt. Necessity--longevity--is its own punishment, the film suggests. Billowing curtains, fluttering doves, tears shed behind veils, rain streaming down window panes--funereal-ethereal images of peace and the becalmed set the tone. But the climactic sequence--a chaos of rotted, stumbling bodies, panicked doves, twisted and twisting lace curtains, incongruous words of love--dispels the Miriam-fostered illusion of serenity. In the coda which follows, Sarah slips out, through gently encumbering curtains, onto an apartment balcony. A balmy evening, it seems--but Miriam's disembodied voice fills the air.

HUSID (Icelandic) Saga 1983 color 99m. SP,D,Ed: Egill Edvardsson. SP,Ph: S. Thorisson. SP,AD: B. Bjornsson. Mus: T. Bladursson. Ref: V 11/2/83: The House-tr t. IFG'84:171. Ecran F 36:82. with Lilja Thorisdottir, Helgi Skulason(medium).

"Thriller" featuring "nightmarish visions of screaming, contorted faces. Are they ghosts?"(V)

HYDE AND GO TWEET WB 1960 anim color 7m. D: I. Freleng. Ref: "WB Cartoons." LC. Glut/CMM. Maltin/OMAM.

Dr. Jekyll's "Mr. Hyde" formula turns Tweety into a giant.

HYSTERICAL New World/Cinema Works and H&W Film Works(Cinema Group Venture) 1983(1982) color 87m. D: Chris Bearde. SP & with: William, Mark & Brett Hudson. SP: also Trace Johnston. Ph: Donald Morgan; T.A. Del Ruth. Mus: Alcivar, Ragland. PD: J.D. Washington. SpFX: Henry Millar; Baker, Evans, Blitstein. Mkp Sup: Michael Germain. Opt: Opt House. SdFxEd: Bill Stevenson et al. Prod Exec: Venetia Stevenson. Ref: TV: Embassy Home Ent.(video). V 5/25/83. MFB'83:302-3. Ecran F 33:7.32:38. with Cindy Pickett, Richard Kiel, Julie Newmar(Venetia), Bud Cort, Robert Donner, Murray Hamilton, Clint Walker, Franklin Ajaye, Charlie Callas(Dracula), Keenan Wynn, Gary Owens, Annie Gaybis.

Cape Hellview, Oregon. The spirit of a woman (Newmar) who died on Halloween, 1882, reawakens 100 years later and engineers the possession of an author (Bill Hudson) by the spirit of her lover, Captain Howdy (Kiel). Author Lansing sprouts long eyebrows ("Jesus! I look like Tom Snyder!"), undergoes an attempted exorcism (insert: some EXORCIST-like effects), plays scenes from The SHINING, and, as (at the end) a Howdy-look-alike, battles the resurrected Captain's walking corpse....Meanwhile, Venetia uses the lighthouse light to restore the body of the Captain--and the bodies of those he subsequently kills--to life. Plus: JAWS(Spielberg)/"Jaws"(James Bond) bit with Kiel, a two-in-one in-joke....Closer to "sophomoric" than to "hysterical." The gags and effects are occasionally silly-funny, generally just silly. The film is basically a hodgepodge of parodic references to horror and other movies of the past decade, though, granted, it's certainly a lively enough hodgepodge.

I, DESIRE ABC-TV/Col-TV & Green-Epstein 1982 color 93m. D: John L. Moxey. SP: Bob Foster. Ph: R.L. Morrison. Mus: Don Drake. AD: Bellah, Hope. SpFX: Al Lorimer. SpCons: Leonard Wolf. Mkp: Lotito Jr. SdFX: The Pros. Ref: TV. TVG. with David Naughton, Dorian Harewood, Marilyn Jones, Barbara Stock (vampire), Arthur Rosenberg, Brad Dourif(vampire), James Victor.

A vampire named Desire, possessing super-human strength, travels from Fort Worth to Tucson to Hollywood, searching for amoral men with "penetrable" souls--for "a vampire has no power over a righteous man...." Terribly serious horror-drama, concerning goodness, obsession, apparent madness, and lust. The vampire here is, in essence, a punishment for the latter. And if you can buy her name, you can probably buy that too. You still may not, however, be able to buy the sequence in which our hero (Naughton) defends himself from her, not with a cross, but by shouting (as if to convince himself) "I am a righteous man!" The movie is as big a drag for the viewer as the pure-in-heart David is for the other characters. The otherwise unremarkable score features a stirring sinister-majestic motif for Desire. (Yes, that's her name....)

I DO (H.K.-Cant.) Wing-Scope 1983 color 98m. D:("I Do!") Angela Mak. SP: Eunice Lam. Mus: L.M. Eiee. Ref: V 6/1/83.
"I Do!", third of three stories: ghost haunting old mansion seeks vengeance on (living) rival for owner's love.

*I EAT YOUR SKIN (Gold Key-TV)/Tenney 1971 82m. (ZOMBIE-TV. ZOMBIES-TV ad t) AD: Robert Verberkmoes. Ref: TV. GKey. Lee. TVG. Ecran F 31:54. and with Betty Hyatt Linton, Dan Stapleton, Robert Stanton, Don Strawn's Calypso Band.
Voodoo Island, the Caribbean. A doctor seeking a cancer cure by injecting natives with "bombarded" snake-venom serum instead produces zombies (complete with the standard fried-egg eyes and plaster-of-Paris faces); furthers, then finally foils a madman's "dream of conquering the Earth with an indestructible army"....zombie hut with zombies on standby...The author-hero produces a book out of it all--"Voodoo Island."
To paraphrase a line from a Satyajit Ray film--Del Tenney made three types of movies: bad (CURSE OF THE LIVING CORPSE), very bad (HORROR OF PARTY BEACH), and very very bad (I EAT YOUR SKIN). Here he does his version of VOODOO ISLAND (could the name of island and book be an hommage?), FROM HELL IT CAME, etc., complete with all the cliche characters--lady-killer hero, conscience-stricken scientist, latter's loving daughter, randy, comical older lady, etc. There's also a voodoo priest decked out in top hat and funny, beaded mask. (The better to keep his identity secret--though there's only one person on the island that it could be.) The dialogue is too standardized to be very funny, though the hero (William Joyce) has problems with this mouthful: "Do you mean that the natives on this island believe that they can avoid catastrophe by sacrificing a young, blond virgin, in this case Jeanine?"

IDEON, The see DENSETSU KYOSHIN IDEON

IF... see BRITANNIA HOSPITAL

IMMEDIATE DECISION see STRANGER FROM VENUS

The IMP (H.K.-Cant.) Century 1981 color 100m. D: Dennis Yu (rn: Yu Yun-k'ang). SP: Hing, Tan, Moon. Ph: B. Thompson. Mus D: J. Koo. Ref: TV: Rainbow Video. V 12/16/81. 10/14/81: 208(ad). Ecran F 22:54. JFFJ 14:36. IFG'84:154. with Charlie Chin(or Qin), Dorothy Yu, Yue Hua.
The "unappeased spirit" of a little girl haunts an office building (which was once a hideout for child kidnappers), and is ultimately reincarnated as the hero's newborn....flooding elevator which goes "into the ground"...man who dies vomiting mud...another man who's smothered by a levitating newspaper... supernatural lightning bolts...car which is caught in a green fog, levitates, drops, and burns (with yet another victim inside)..."geomancist" with magic amulets and toads...hero (with "overwhelming yin") levitated by ghost...living dead....This is

BEYOND THE DOOR, but with a little-girl-ghost instead of the devil. The hero, Ah Keung, seems to put the amulets in all the right places, yet still fails. The rebirth plot is merely a pretext for a series of ghostly stunts....The ghost's underground domain (the "gate of hell"?) is littered, eerily, with bonfires--on water as well as land. One A-1 "bus" with a falling corpse.

*An IMPOSSIBLE VOYAGE Famille Melies 1904 color Ref: screen.
Galactic voyagers frozen in ice tank, then thawed...parachute-borne submarine...huge octopus....Elaborate but rather ponderous Melies. Much padding with pantomime; some magical moments--e.g., the train to the sun taking off into the air, a la the bicycles in E.T.

IMPULSE Conqueror Films 1974 D: William Grefe. Ref: Weldon: "possessed killer." V 5/7/75:122(ad): "terror & suspense." no PFA. no V(rev). with William Shatner, Ruth Roman, H. Sakata.

IN A GLASS DARKLY(by J.S.LeFanu) see VAMPYR

The INCREDIBLE SEX-RAY MACHINE Carroll Prods. c1978? color 63m. Ref: screen. Oakland Trib 5/4/83:F-12(ad).
Inventor Ludwig Von Boyarowsky's Inter-scoptic-something-or-other Communication Machine sees through the walls of the swinging-singles complex across the way and stimulates the residents there sexually. Another invention makes a blonde appear out of nowhere. At the end, the ray machine explodes. (Insert, stock shot of mushroom cloud.) A rather tentative attempt at a feature, this appears to be a tatty collection of scenes from hard-and-softcore movies, held together only by the mad doc's narration. Only his scenes and the segment with the instant-blonde seem actually to have been shot as part of this enterprise. Among the found footage is a bit of softcore with Uschi Digart and a lengthy male/male/rather-incidental-female sequence. The doctor's lab consists of a sort of telescope and a projection booth.

INCUBUS (Can.) FVI/Guardian Trust/ARC(Friedman, Boyman & Mark Films) 1982(1980) color 92m. (The INCUBUS-ad t) D: John Hough. SP: George Franklin, from Ray Russell's novel. Ph: A. J. Dunk. Mus: Stanley Myers. PD: Ted Watkins. SpFX:(d) Colin Chilvers; Martin Malivoire; Bob Wiggens. SpMkpFX: Maureen Sweeney;(des) Les Edwards. Ref: screen. V 9/8/82. MFB'83:16-17. Ecran F 22:26-29,44,77. with John Cassavetes, Kerrie Keane, Helen Hughes, John Ireland, Dirk McLean(incubus).
Shape-changing, oversexed demon who "materializes through dreams" goes on raping-and-killing spree in small Wisconsin town of Galen....Artes Perditae, book of demons....Supernatural mystery-thriller with more blood than mystery--the main "motif" is a shot of a bloody corpse-sheet, as a boy continues to dream ("Every time I have the dream someone dies") and (as it is

finally revealed) his sister continues to kill. The horror paraphernalia is over-familiar--the plot paraphrases your standard werewolfilm; the murders, your standard subjective-camera-killer-movie murders. Only the mystery element manages at all to intrigue, and only the last few shots--in which the hero (Cassavetes) is at once apprised of the identity of the incubus and the imminence of his doom--are in any way compelling. The one bit of wit is provided by a bumper sticker on one victim's truck: "Galen--150 years of boredom."

The INFERNAL CAKE-WALK (F) Famille Melies/Star 1903 5m. (Le CAKE-WALK INFERNAL) Ref: screen. PFA notes 11/16/82.

Inside the devil's cave: horned demons...dancers...balls of fire. Minor Georges Melies.

The INFERNAL CAULDRON AND THE PHANTASMAL VAPORS (F) Famille Melies/Star 1903 color 2m.? (Le CHAUDRON INFERNAL) Ref: screen. PFA notes 11/16/82. Lee.

The devil boils three women in his cauldron; they transform into hovering wraiths, then into flames....An eerie Melies fragment of a film. There's no dramatic development, but you'll find some of his stranger, more evocative transformations here. The wraiths don't seem to be the usual all-in-fun Melies grotesques. They appear quite capable of taking serious revenge on the devil; but they simply burst into flame, and create only a momentary alarum.

INFERNO DEI MORTI-VIVENTI see NIGHT OF THE ZOMBIES(MPM)

INSPIRATIONS Valiant Int'l. 1982 color 84m. D: H. Hershey, Joe Sherman. SP: David A. Wesson. Mus,SdFX: Harry Marcel? Ref: screen. poster. with Ron Jeremy, Danielle, Lisa DeLeeuw, Serena, Mai Lin, Nikko Dulay, Bambi Lake, Nicole Noir, Howard.

A psychiatrist, Dr. Xavier (Jeremy), programs his female patients with "spacy sexual encounters of the third kind," in order to overcome their inhibitions--his video-recorder-plus machine increases the intensity, or frequency, of the alpha waves of his subjects (when the latter are in an alpha state), and records on videotape the fantasies thus produced....Regulation-unimaginative homegrown porn, with limp filler-comedy. The actresses, however--transsexuals included--seem more beautiful than ever, and this sf-comedy will suffice, at least, as a vehicle for their pulchritude. Never mind how a psychiatrist came to fabricate a dream-recording machine....

INVADERS FROM THE DEEP (B) ITC-TV? 1981 puppets color 90m. Ref: TVG: sequel to 2 THUNDERBIRDS ARE GO?; "aquatic aliens."

The INVASION (Can.) Gold Key-TV/T.A.E. 1973 color 95m. (The STARLOST QUINTOLOGY 2.) Ref: GKey. TVFFSB. TVG. with Keir Dullea, Stephen Young, Donnelly Rhodes.

See also: ALIEN ORO, The.

INVASION OF THE FLESH HUNTERS see CANNIBALS IN THE STREETS

INVASION: UFO (B) ITC-TV 1980 color 90m. SP,D: Gerry Anderson, David Tomblin. D: also Dave Lane. SP: also Sylvia Anderson, Tony Barwick. From the "UFO" TV series. Ph: B.J. Stafford. Mus: Barry Gray. AD: Bob Bell. SpFxD: Derek Meddings. Ref: TV. TVG. Bill Warren. with Ed Bishop, George Sewell, Michael Billington, Gabrielle Drake, Wanda Ventham, Grant Taylor, Anouska Hempel, Shane Rimmer.

The Supreme Headquarters Alien Defence Organization is formed to combat an invasion by aliens "from a solar system probably a hundred million million miles from Earth." SHADO's forces include the Space Intruder Detector satellite and a moonbase. The aliens are humanoids ("doomed to extinction" by hereditary sterility) who use Earth as an organ bank for transplants and who (with an "elaborate miming" system) impersonate key SHADO personnel. One alien ages rapidly and dies on contact with Earth's atmosphere....ray-shooting saucers... underwater UFO with "flying fish" missiles....A tired series of alien-human skirmishes, in space, on land, and underwater--the variety of locations does not disguise the essential sameness of the encounters. The live actors are just as stolid as the Andersons' "Thunderbird" marionettes, though the actors here presumably breathe. The UFOs resemble handle-less egg-beaters; the film, an accidental HARDWARE WARS.

*The INVISIBLE BOY 1957 SpFX: Jack Rabin, Irving Block, Louis DeWitt. Ref: screen. Warren/KWTS! Stanley.

"The revolt of the machine": the 29-year-old super-computer (housing the "sum total of human knowledge") at the Stoneman Institute of Mathematics makes subtle changes, over the years, in its feedback unit, or "forebrain"; seeks the "numerical combination" necessary before it can have itself reconstructed on a space platform, the better to rule the world. (The "small nuclear reactor" which powers it on Earth will run down in two centuries.) Its "servants" include 7 men with transistors embedded in the parietal region of the skull, and Robby The Robot--whose "atomic structure is almost indestructible, as it was designed to be in a far world" (possibly in the future). This unnamed computer attempts to overcome Robby's "basic directive" not to harm humans, but fails--although it does succeed in making Robby adjust the "index of refraction" of the son (Richard Eyer) of the scientist (Philip Abbott) who constructed it (the computer), to "1" on the optic scale, rendering him (the boy) invisible. The computer also succeeds in hypnotizing both man and boy, but Robby dismantles it.

For kids, and adults who don't listen too closely. It won't help much, anyway, if you do--the script's science makes about as much sense as that of INVADERS FROM MARS, by which this movie seems, in part, inspired. And though The INVISIBLE BOY doesn't generate the paranoid-child's-world excitement of the earlier film, it is an at times amusing conglomeration. The undisciplined yet semi-shrewd script seems designed expressly to appeal to a little boy's delusions of grandeur and power. With small regard for logic (each turn in the plot bends the latter further out of shape), it succeeds in touching all the basic fantasy-life bases: flying (on a super-kite, or in free-fall), invisibility, robot-playmates, and beating one's male parent at chess. (It also includes--subhead under "invisibility"--spying on activity in the master bedroom.) Most of these fantasies have been embodied or imagined more successfully elsewhere in sf cinema. And the script deteriorates from sf-mystery into sf-moral-stricture re: machines. But this is still an entertaining vehicle for Robby and a pleasant follow-up to FORBIDDEN PLANET.

See also: HOLLYWOOD BOULEVARD.

INVISIBLE MAN, The(novel by H.G.Wells) and scientific invisibility see CURSE OF THE PINK PANTHER(P). HAVE YOU GOT ANY CASTLES. INVISIBLE BOY, The. INVISIBLE WOMAN, The. LAST NINJA, The(P). LITTLE ORBIT. MAN WHO WASN'T THERE, The. ROOKIE REVUE. STILL SMOKIN'. TIME WARP.

The INVISIBLE WOMAN NBC-TV/Univ-TV & Redwood 1983 color 92m. (PORTRAIT OF AN INVISIBLE WOMAN-orig t) D,P: Alan J. Levi. SP,Exec P: Sherwood & Lloyd Schwartz. Ph: Dean Cundey. Mus: David Frank. AD: R.B. Lewis. SpFX: Alan Hall. Video: Starfax. Mkp: Tony Lane. SdFxEd: P. Haberman. Ref: TV. TVG 1/8/83. V 2/16/83:98. with Alexa Hamilton, Bob Denver, David Doyle, Harvey Korman, Garrett Morris, Teri Beckerman, George Gobel, Ron Palillo, Jonathan Banks, Joseph Phelan, Art LaFleur.

Chimp drinks own chemical formula, disappears; reporter (Hamilton) comes in contact with formula, vanishes. Invisible, she pretends to activate the "Curse of the Nile" (on Cleopatra's scepter) by opening a mummy case and making the scepter "fly," in order to foil art thieves....Abysmal throwback to the worst of the old TV-sitcoms. Silly pranks dominate the effects scenes, which prove to be a sterile showcase for some technical gymnastics, including a "makeup" sequence adapted from Universal's own INVISIBLE MAN TV-movie. (Here, cosmetics rather than plastic surgery bring the invisible one back to visibility.) A powder puff "eating" the invisible Sandy's face away is the most unusual effect--others involving soapsuds, steam, lipstick, and dark glasses seem regulation, if convincing. These peek-a-boo effects are the only justification for this un-comedy.

The IRONMASTER (I-F) Medusa & Dania/Letienne & IEC 1983 color 90m. (IRONMASTER: LA GUERRA DEL FERRO. Il DOMINATORE DEL FERRO. La GUERRE DU FER. La GUERRA DEL FERRO) D: Umberto Lenzi. Ph: G. Ferrando. Mus: G.& M.De Angelis. AD: A. Geleng. SpFX: Paolo Ricci. Ref: Ecran F 31:47. V 5/4/83:307. 8/10/83:43. with Sam Pasco, Elvire Audray, George Eastman, William Berger.

"'New barbarian' fable" with "prehistorians Vood and Ela" and "a sensuous Amazon."

IRRESISTIBLE Essex 1983(1982) color 98m. SP,D: Edwin Brown. SP,P: Sandra Winters. Ph: Teru Hayashi. Mus: Geoffrey Pekofsky. AD: Bryan Costales. Ref: screen. poster. Adult Cinema 5/83. with Samantha Fox, Nicole Noir, Gina Gianetti, Mai Lin.

Inventor Miracle Meyer's (Misha Garr) time machine (which looks like a seat stolen from a ride at Fantasyland) takes Walter (Richard Pacheco) from contemporary San Francisco back to, first, the Egypt of Cleopatra ("I'm from the future" "I thought you were from Marin"), then to the Verona of Juliet. A slip-up brings Juliet back to the present, where she becomes a stripper. Walter also has a glimpse across time at Mata Hari, and God checks up on Meyer from time to time....Resistible hardcore sf-comedy is rather too deliberately paced for the piffle it is. Don't look for any Industrial Light or Magic here....

IS THIS TRIP REALLY NECESSARY? Hollywood Star/Dorn-Thor 1970 color 84m. (aka BLOOD OF THE IRON MAIDEN. TRIP TO TERROR) D,P: Ben Benoit. SP: Lee Kalcheim. Ph: Austin McKinney. Mus: Paul Norman et al. AD: Ray Markham. SpFX: Bob Beck. Mkp: Dodie Warren. Ref: Lee. AFI. with Marvin Miller, Carol(e) Kane, Peter Duryea, John Carradine.

Mad filmmaker kills actress in his torture chamber's iron maiden.

ISLAND CLAWS (CBS-TV)/Island Claws, Joint Venture 1982(1981) color c90m. (THe NIGHT OF THE CLAW-TV ad t) Story,D: Hernan Cardenas. SP: Jack Cowden, Ricou Browning. Story: also Colby Cardenas. Ph: James Pergola. Mus: Bill Justis. AD: Don Ivey. SpFX: Glenn Robinson, Ray Scott, Don Chandler et al. Mkp: M. May. VisCons: Bissell, Teegarden. Ref: TV. V 7/16/80: 48. 2/16/83:24. Bill Warren. with Robert Lansing, Steve Hanks, Nita Talbot, Jo McDonnell, Barry Nelson, Luke Halpin.

A university marine-research center in Florida--attacking the problem of world hunger--is experimenting in the stimulation of growth and size in land crabs. Its staff has discovered that in a warm-water environment, crabs reach full growth in two years, instead of the usual 4-to-8 years. "It's happening" outside the lab, too, in the warm water issuing from a nuclear power plant: the local crabs are "maturing much faster than normal" and are doing some most un-crab-like things. Crabs--which normally "just don't attack people"--now do; they're also out and about in broad daylight, and migrating at the wrong time of the year. The mauling of a dog, the shredding of a woman's arm, and the tipping-over of a bus (in conjunction with the discovery of a huge crab-shell) suggest, further, that at least one giant crab is at large....

As in TARANTULA(1955) or BEGINNING OF THE END(1957), the scientists in ISLAND CLAWS are addressing the problem of world hunger. As in ATTACK OF THE CRAB MONSTERS(1957) or PORT SINISTER(1953), the monster is a giant crab. ISLAND CLAWS, obviously, is for those who want to go back to the mid-Fifties;

it's proof that you can go home again. The problem is that ISLAND CLAWS goes back to Fifties monster-movie-making and stays there. It has all the old tricks down pat, but doesn't come up with any new ones. What this movie needs is a little Industrial Light & Magic--i.e., a humongous crab so real-looking that you take it (as you do E.T., for example) for granted, almost. Then the music wouldn't have to blare; the actors wouldn't have to scream so much; and the crab itself wouldn't have to roar. (Yes, the crab roars.) The people who made this movie want you to believe that theirs is a frightening monster--but how can you believe it when they obviously didn't themselves? The regular-sized crabs here are more unnerving than the big, where-has-he-been-hiding? one--it may be their penchant for clicking noises, or it may just be a matter of sheer numbers. Or maybe real crabs just don't look (or move) right....

IT CAME FROM HOLLYWOOD Para/Strausberg-Stein 1982 color & b&w & tinted 78m. D,Exec P: Andrew Solt, Malcolm Leo. SP: Dana Olsen. Ph: F.J. Koenekamp. Mus: Neiman-Tillar; W. Loose. AD: Richard Sawyer. SpGraphics: Bob Greenberg. Mkp: Monty Westmore. SpCons: Harry & Michael Medved. SupSdFxEd: Clive Smith. Opt: Modern. Ref: screen. TV. V 11/3/82. with Dan Aykroyd, John Candy, Cheech & Chong, Gilda Radner, D.E. Carney(gorilla).

A camp collection of clips from monster and other movies, including (for the record) The AMAZING COLOSSAL MAN, APE, ATOMIC RULERS OF THE WORLD, ATTACK OF THE 50-FOOT WOMAN, ATTACK OF THE KILLER TOMATOES, ATTACK OF THE MUSHROOM PEOPLE, ATTACK OF THE PUPPET PEOPLE, BATTLE IN OUTER SPACE, BEAST FROM 20000 FATHOMS, BEGINNING OF THE END, The BLOB, BRAIN FROM PLANET AROUS, BRAIN THAT WOULDN'T DIE, BRIDE & THE BEAST, BRIDE OF THE MONSTER, The CRAWLING EYE, CREATURE FROM THE BLACK LAGOON, The CREEPING TERROR, CURSE OF THE FACELESS MAN, The CYCLOPS, DARKEST AFRICA, DAY THE EARTH STOOD STILL, The DEADLY MANTIS, EARTH VS. THE FLYING SAUCERS, EVIL BRAIN FROM OUTER SPACE, FIEND WITHOUT A FACE, FIRE MAIDENS OF OUTER SPACE, FIRST MAN INTO SPACE, The FLY, The FLYING SAUCER, FRANKENSTEIN AND THE MONSTER FROM HELL, FRANKENSTEIN CONQUERS THE WORLD, FRANKENSTEIN MEETS THE SPACE MONSTER, FRANKENSTEIN'S DAUGHTER, FROM HELL IT CAME, The GIANT CLAW, GLEN OR GLENDA, HIDEOUS SUN DEMON, HORROR OF PARTY BEACH, HOUSE ON HAUNTED HILL, HYPNOTIC EYE, I MARRIED A MONSTER FROM OUTER SPACE, I WAS A TEENAGE FRANKENSTEIN, The INCREDIBLE MELTING MAN, The INCREDIBLE SHRINKING MAN, The INCREDIBLY STRANGE CREATURES, INVADERS FROM SPACE, INVASION OF THE NEPTUNE MEN, KILLER SHREWS, The LOST CITY, LOVES OF HERCULES, MANIAC(1934?), The MANSTER, MARS NEEDS WOMEN, MISSILE TO THE MOON, MONSTER AND THE APE, MONSTER FROM GREEN HELL, OCTAMAN, PERILS OF NYOKA, PLAN 9 FROM OUTER SPACE, PRINCE OF SPACE, REPTILICUS, ROBOT MONSTER, ROCKET ATTACK USA, The SLIME PEOPLE, SON OF GODZILLA, The SPACE CHILDREN, TEENAGE MONSTER, TEENAGERS FROM OUTER SPACE, The THING WITH TWO HEADS, The TINGLER, WAR OF THE WORLDS, WHITE GORILLA, The X FROM OUTER

SPACE, YONGARY, and ZOMBIES OF THE STRATOSPHERE, just to mention those titles covered in this continuing checklist....Plus: skit re: alien invasion, year 2023.

Or (to paraphrase the "Hollywood and The Stars" episode), "Monsters We've Laughed at." At least that's the guiding principle behind most of these extracts. (The bits from J.D. and reefer movies seem simply padding.) And that's the use most moviegoers will make of IT CAME FROM HOLLYWOOD (which, oddly, makes no reference to IT CAME FROM BENEATH THE SEA or IT CAME FROM OUTER SPACE). It's a sort of super-"Fractured Flickers," and will, similarly, annoy those who prefer their flickers unfractured by campy post-dubbing and narration. But there are some amusing moments, in both new and found footage. The movie is sloppy, disorganized, pointless--but who can resist the comic presence of Dan Aykroyd...Cheech Marin...The Giant Claw? All that's missing (or under-represented) here is the better half of the subject--the monsters we couldn't laugh off. For that we still have to go back to "Monsters We've Known and Loved," though this movie has one appeal in common with that well-known-and-loved TV show: it's an A-1 trivia test. The clips are not identified, and hardcore monster-movie fans are thus encouraged (even challenged) to Name That Film, often in a matter of moments. (I admit to being stumped by about a third of the clips....) A scroll at the end of the film lists the titles of all the movies, but you still have to match title with clip. (Where was The FLYING SAUCER...?!) We make what use we can of movies....

*IT CAME FROM OUTER SPACE 1953 (The METEOR. ATOMIC MONSTER. The STRANGERS FROM OUTER SPACE-all early ts) Mus: Herman Stein. Mkp:(sup) Bud Westmore;(sp des) Millicent Patrick;(tech) Jack Kevan et al. Ref: screen. TV. Warren/KWTS! Hirschhorn. LC.

An alien spaceship (shaped "like a huge ball") crash lands in the desert outside Sand Rock, Arizona. ("...the biggest thing that's ever happened in our time!") The aliens--which are vaguely vegetable-shaped, with one huge eye in the middle--set about repairing their ship, deep inside the old Excelsior Mine. They have "a long way to go" to reach their destination, but in the interim on Earth must transform themselves into doubles of humans in order not to frighten the latter. The aliens seem to travel through, or along, telephone wires, and can be faintly heard therein by human ears--"darnedest noise ever!" At least two aliens-in-human-form are killed, but the rest escape. "It wasn't the right time for us to meet...."

Basically dated science fiction, with a script which poses simple questions ("Are there extraterrestrial beings?" "Are they good or bad?") which are then too simply answered, at least in the film's dialogue. In CLOSE ENCOUNTERS OF THE THIRD KIND--which poses similar questions--the aliens don't have to say "We have souls and minds and we are good"--it's understood. Here, virtually everything is spelled out, in dialogue that's alternately crudely "poetic" and clumsily explicit....The basic idea--that we are not ready for them--is a compelling one: the aliens prove (if you pay no heed to said dialogue) to be neither villains nor heroes...neither out to destroy the world, nor to save it. And we, of course, cannot understand natures so complicated--if, that is, by "we," we mean the town mob which gathers outside the mine at the end. If "we" means, however, hero or heroine (Richard Carlson and Barbara Rush, respectively), we're ready for any kind of close encounter.... Just so does the script over-neatly divide humans into the imaginative--primarily, John Putnam--and the plodding--just about everybody else in town; into the Believers and the Skeptics. (Carlson's RIDERS TO THE STARS is also predicated on such a division.) The townsfolk are, at first, skeptical of the mere existence of the aliens, then, convinced of the fact of their existence (in a not-wholly-explicable-or-explained turnabout), become skeptical of their intentions. Only the sheriff (Charles Drake) is allowed any doubts, though even he, finally, joins, or re-joins, the plodders. Drake's sheriff is the closest the movie comes to a full-fledged, mixed-moods character--it also helps that Drake seems more comfortable, or at home, in the film, than do the other actors, and that he, generally, has the least-bad dialogue. It's Putnam, however, who is given the movie's (potentially) most stirring scene, or speech--though, again, the conception of same is superior to the execution, in dialogue: unable to convince the citizens of Sand Rock to give the aliens time to get away, he turns to the aliens, and convinces them to give him time to keep the mob at bay. Putnam is more far-sighted (natch--he's an astronomy buff), more other-worldly than, even, the aliens....Perhaps the movie's finest feature--or its only fine feature--is the location photography. (The location, however, as Bill Warren notes, is not Arizona, but California's Mojave Desert.) The jumps--both within and between scenes--from location footage to in-studio footage are jarring. They let the desert air out of the picture, so to speak. But, as Putnam notes of that desert: "It's alive!" If IT CAME FROM OUTER SPACE has some of the hokiest 3-D "scream" scenes on film (Rush's screams might have been dubbed by a macaw), it also features some of the most invigorating exterior tracking-shots in Fifties sf-films. The telephone wires here do seem to be "alive." The movie's monster's-eye-view shots are a bit too fancy--they raise visions of movie cameras swathed in cotton candy. But the tracking shots (from moving cars and trucks) of the phone lines along the desert highway--and the helicopter shots (from, or through, the lines themselves, as we track with the vehicles below)--suggest an invisible, watchful life...a world of sentient electricity....It Came from AT&T.

IT'S A BIRD Lowell Thomas 1930 15m. D,Ph: H.L. Muller. Anim & with: Charles Bowers. Ref: screen. PFA. no Lee. no LC.

Rare, metal-eating bird brought back from the Belgian Congo ingests all things metal in auto junkyard; lays egg which hatches what grows into a full-sized automobile in less than a minute... in a sequence which anticipates and arguably tops the best sequence in CHRISTINE. In addition to this instant-car, there are, also, a stopmo bird and worm which engage in a weird, very funny battle of wits. The bird slams the worm's head against a rock (bam! bam! bam!)--no effect....The worm slams the worm's head against the rock--he likes it! The live action scenes are fairly amusing; but in them, the comedy seems merely far-fetched. The comedy in the animated sequences is downright imaginative.

IT'S A GOOD LIFE(by J.Bixby) see TWILIGHT ZONE--THE MOVIE

*IT'$ ONLY MONEY 1962 AD: Pereira, Larsen. SpPhFX: John P. Fulton. Process Ph: F. Edouart. Mkp: W. Westmore. Ref: TV. AFI. and with Mae Questel, Pat Dahl.

At the end of the movie, a fleet of remote-controlled "automatic lawn mowers" converges on Jerry Lewis; one mower even begins chewing up a stone lawn-seat. Other innovations by the "father of television": a super-realistic stereo tape of a 90-mph train, complete with smoke and light effects, shaking living-room furniture, and a conductor...a remote-controlled vacuum cleaner...a closed-circuit TV apparatus...a fence which electrifies Jerry.

Hollow, tacky-looking comedy-thriller, with a feeble storyline and tired slapstick....Lewis, however, plays some of his scenes in a rather fascinating stop/go/back-up manner, as if he were a puppet, and his strings had gotten all tangled up. The effect is one of fractured, or stippled, speech and motion--words and movements come out herky-jerky, in the wrong order. His character here (at least in these scattered scenes) seems to have been incorrectly assembled....There is a basis in this behavioral idiosyncrasy for something, but not for anything to be found in this otherwise pathetic farce. Jack Weston, as an assassin and "president of the Peter Lorre fan club," has a few winning moments of black comedy; but Frank Tashlin is not exactly a magician with actors (Lewis, generally, included). He does, however, whip up some excitement with the climactic charge of the one-"eyed" robot mowers, little mobile monsters with imposing "teeth" and a whir out of THEM!. This sequence is, wisely, angled more towards thrills than laughs, and what it gets is a combination of same. It probably sent folks with short memories home quite happy.

JAMES BOND(character created by I.Fleming) see GIRL FROM S.E.X. RETURN OF THE MAN FROM U.N.C.L.E. UNDERCOVERS.

JAWS OF SATAN UA 1982(1980) color (KING COBRA-orig t) D: Bob Claver. SP: Gerry Holland. Story: James Callaway. Ph: Dean

Cundey. Mus: Roger Kellaway. AD: Robert Topol. SpMechFX: Eoin Sprott. Mkp: Ron Figuly. Ref: Bill Warren. V 12/1/82:11: in Miami. 2/16/83:24. with Fritz Weaver, Gretchen Corbett, Jon Korkes, Norman Lloyd, Nancy Priddy, Bob Hannah.

The devil--in the guise of a giant King Cobra--seeks a priest, whose family has been cursed....snakes-amok scenes.

JAWS 3-D Univ/Landsburg(MCA) 1983 3-D & color 96m. D: Joe Alves. SP: Richard Matheson, Carl Gottlieb. Story: Guerdon Trueblood;(uncred.) Michael Kane. Sequel to JAWS. Ph: J.A. Contner. Mus: Alan Parker. PD: Woods Mackintosh. VisCons: (creative) Roy Arbogast;(des) Philip Abramson. SpFX: Praxis; (ph) R. Blalack;(elec) PSE; Guy Faria et al. SpSdFX: Sandy Berman. MkpDes: Kathryn Bihr. Titles: Celestial Mechanix. Ref: screen. PFA. TVG(ad): JAWS 3-vt t. MFB'83:330. V 8/30/83. Bill Warren. with Dennis Quaid, Bess Armstrong, Simon MacCorkindale, Lou Gossett Jr., John Putch, Barbara Eden.

The dolphins of Florida's Sea World begin acting strangely. Divers disappear. A baby Great White Shark is blamed, caught, and becomes "the only live one in captivity." It dies, but not before its mother (a "big bitch" 35 feet long and with a one-yard bite) enters the park's Undersea Kingdom (inside a man-made lagoon) and becomes an unscheduled feature attraction.

A limp concoction of elements from JAWS, GORGO, and REVENGE OF THE CREATURE. The script works hard at finding ways to bring sharks and humans together; the director works hard at making said sharks look both scary and three-dimensional. Only the effort shows. Mama and baby are not much scarier than the movie's <u>other</u> fish and aquatic mammals--and the airborne, pirouetting dolphins are actually more entertaining, in tandem, in 3-D, than the sharks which star. The latter have only size and teeth going for them, and JAWS exploited these qualities more cannily. Here, the sharks tend, simply, to clog the screen. Only the sight of severed limbs and reddening water reminds us that these are <u>monsters</u>....

See also: GREAT WHITE.

JEKYLL AND HYDE...TOGETHER AGAIN Para/Titan 1982 color 85m. SP,D: Jerry Belson. SP: also M. Johnson, H. Miller, M. Leeson. Ph: Philip Lathrop. Mus: Barry DeVorzon. PD: Peter Wooley. SpMkp: Mark Bussan. SpVisFX: R/Greenberg. SpSynthFX: Michael Boddicker. SpFX: D.G. Grigg. Ref: screen. V 9/1/82. Bill Warren: indebted to the '32 DR.JEKYLL & MR.HYDE as well as the RLS story. with Mark Blankfield(Jekyll/Hyde), Bess Armstrong, Tim Thomerson, Ann M. Nelson(hunchback), George Chakiris.

A cocaine-like concoction turns a repressed hospital surgeon into a super-hip stud (who's repelled by both crosses and Stars of David)....Robert Louis Stevenson shown turning over in his grave...bit with The Elephant Man....Dispiritingly uninspired comedy, of the sort that's determinedly undisciplined and proud of it. The script sacrifices all sense of narrative to slapstick and gags, and winds up neither resonant nor funny.

There's no ending as such; the gags just stop. Blankfield, however, wrests a few chuckles from the Jekyll-Hyde confusions. (His go-go-Hyde voice pops up out of his staid Jekyll persona every now and then, to the latter's great puzzlement.) But even in the story's straight versions Hyde is usually pretty amusing--here, the writers write as if they thought they'd brought humor to the dual role for the first time; as if they hadn't heard of Barrymore, March, Tracy, Barrault, etc.

JONAS QUI AURA 25 ANS EN L'AN 2000 see LIGHT YEARS AWAY

JOURNEY THROUGH THE BLACK SUN (B-I) Group Three/ITC-TV & RAI-TV 1975(1982) color 90m. D: Ray Austin, Lee H. Katzin. SP: A. Terpiloff, David Weir. Story: G.& S. Anderson. Two episodes ("Collision Course" & "The Black Sun") of the "Space 1999" TV series. Ph: F. Watts. Mus: Barry Gray. PD: Keith Wilson. SpFX: Brian Johnson;(d) Nick Allder. Computer Anim: Dolphin. Mkp: B. Newall, A. Cotton. Cost: Rudi Gernreich. Ref: TV. TVG. "Fantastic TV." with Martin Landau, Barbara Bain, Barry Morse, Margaret Leighton(Arra), Clifton Jones.

Well, it seems this old woman (Leighton) runs the universe ("You go to shape the future of eternity"), more or less, but needs the help of humans in order to "mutate" and live forever. Operation Shock Wave, however, sends her and her planet packing....In the second episode, it may, again, be her God-like voice which our heroes encounter in the middle of a black sun, which sun makes them transparent, old, telepathic, and prone to thoughts like "Every star is just a cell in the brain of the universe." The force-field generated by Moonbase Alpha's anti-gravity towers counters the "immeasurable" gravitational force of the sun, and the astronauts are restored....Both of these re-cycled TV shows are and were just re-cycled WHEN WORLDS COLLIDE-like suspensers (with a bit of 2001-like metaphysical speculation thrown in). The characters are bunny-quick to sense imminent death-for-all, and just as quick to get philosophical about the grim prospect. Words like "universe" and "eternity" are very freely bandied about....Only for the easily-awed.

JUDAS GOAT see XTRO

*JUDEX Images Film Archive 1964(1963) AD: Robert Giordani. Mkp: Maguy Vernadet. Ref: screen. Durgnat/Franju. Weldon. AFI. PFA notes 6/15/83. S&S'83:266-71. and with Rene Genin, Theo Sarapo, Jacques Jouanneau.

Suspended animation...magic-mirror-like TV-scope (in 1914)... secret passages (penetrated by electric eye??)..."magical," yet easily-explained writing-with-light..."bird-headed" guests, and prestidigitation, at masked ball....A loving, delicate hommage to Feuillade, and better perhaps actually than the master deserves (cf. VAMPIRES, THE ARCH CRIMINALS OF PARIS, qq.v.). Even Franju's surrealism seems, finally, in fact, to succumb to Feuillade's serial-ism. The campily twisty turns-of-plot--e.g., a circus high-wire artist appearing, providentially, out of nowhere--are an amusing parody, or paraphrase, of Feuillade and his battery of narrative contrivances. But they also seem to betray, at times, the poetic promise of Franju's imagery....Getting back to the aforementioned high-wire artist... she is, forthwith, engaged in an eerily noiseless rooftop scuffle with the villainess of the piece--the former in white tights, the latter in black: good against evil, if you will, in a very disorienting context. Serious subject; camp furnishings; surreal undercurrents--Maurice Jarre's music here might, in fact, be the scene's surreal "voice." (His score for JUDEX is spare but extraordinary.) On one of its three levels, then--the surreal, voice-from-another-world level--this scene is evocative: in this mirror world, good and evil hardly make a sound--the import of their struggle is understood. No drama, no "effects" underlining, just a preternatural hush, a suggestion of rapt attention....As narrative, however, JUDEX does not always seem to be functioning at this level of suggestion. The story thread involving the detective, for instance, is charming but, poetically, relatively unfruitful. The film "shrinks" to accommodate it. By contrast, the early sequence of the masked ball unfolds with a quirky majesty: Judex enters the ballroom as avenging angel/The dead dove which he accusingly bears is "magically" restored--injustice "dissolved"/The prestidigitator then leaves, with, however, his grave mission fulfilled--the villain lies dead. From the serious, again, through the mock-serious, to the surreal. A further twist, revealed later: Judex's victim is not dead, merely lying in suspended animation--the restoration of the (innocent) dove, then, proves to have been a sort of inverse correlative, or prediction, of the "resurrection" of the (guilty) villain; an instance of Judex "tipping his hand" in a most public, yet cryptic way....JUDEX is most tantalizing when Franju is at his most ambivalent--then and only then does one comprehend: he doesn't really mean it/yes, he does....

JUNGLE DEVIL see SUPERMAN AND THE JUNGLE DEVIL

The JUPITER MENACE Celebrity(Davis-Panzer)/Youngstar & Monell (Jupiter Menace) 1982 color 76m. SP,D: Peter Matulavich. D,P: Lee Auerbach. SP: also A.H. Coats. Ph: Robert Harmon; (time lapse) Louis Schwarzberg;(planet) The Magic Lantern. Mus: Synergy; Fast. SpVisFX: Peter Bloch;(des) Scott Bartlett; (anim) Tim Bloch et al; Midocean. SpPhFX: D.M. Garber, David Stipes. Planets: PSE;(vis cons) Dennis Skotak;(tech d) Ken Jones, Bob Skotak. ComputerFX: Digital;(exec p) John Whitney Jr.;(tech d) Gary Demos. Mastodon: Mike Jones, Dan Chambers. MechFX: MkpFxLabs, A&A. VideoFX: Synopsis et al. Vis Cons: Tom Southwell;(planet) Janet Kusnick. Opt: Image 3; Lookout Mountain. Ref: TV: Thorn EMI Video. Ecran F 34:70. V 10/27/82: 6(rated). Bill Warren. with George Kennedy, Greg Michaels,

Dr. Peter Franken, Alex Tanous, Sun Bear; Lindsay Workman(narr.).

Speculation re: the link between the positions of the planets in the solar system, and natural catastrophes on Earth. "Major Earth disturbances" (connected with the Grand Alignment of the Planets) from 1980 to the year 2000 are visualized--and include earthquakes, volcanos, plagues, and spells of extreme heat and cold--and a computer simulates a 12.0 earthquake....Prophets and psychics pinpoint 2000 A.D. as the date of the greatest cataclysm--"Jupiter returns, this time with a companion--Saturn...."

As a pastime, predicting the time and manner of the end of the world appears to be as popular as predicting the American and National League pennant winners--and as harmless....Only the survivalists seem to be doing something about these predictions; actively planning for the future, and they seem to be unified: the reference here to their "most precious commodity--the children" finds its narrative embodiment in the conclusion to (survivalist) Steve Barkett's The AFTERMATH(qq.v.), in which the hero's young son takes up arms after the father lays down his and dies. Their vision of post-holocaust armed encampments seems a natural response to the larger vision of Nostradamus and co., and, certainly, one can understand the desire of the survivalists to create order out of (anticipated) chaos. But their Darwinian militancy seems as naive and one-sided as the old-fashioned humanitarianism of a movie like WHEN WORLDS COLLIDE(qq.v.). Both views seem predicated on a belief in the absolute predictability of human nature--and the survivalist brigades seem to be placing all their bets on Mr. Hyde....Overall, The JUPITER MENACE seems no better or worse than other speculative jumbles-of-films. It's a docu-disaster movie re: a disaster which has not happened yet, and must thus resort to extra-documentary--and hence questionable--means to make its points. It taints facts and figures with fiction... scrambles history and science with speculation, with no distinct lines of demarcation between modes.

See also: MAN WHO SAW TOMORROW, The.

JUST BEFORE DAWN Juniper & Picturmedia/Oakland(Hreljanovic) 1981 (1980) color 90m. D: Jeff Lieberman. SP: Mark Arywitz, Gregg Irving. Story,Co-P: Joseph Middleton. Ph: J.& D. King. Mus: Brad Fiedel. AD: Craig Stearns; Randy Moore. SpFX:(mkp) Matthew Mungle; John Morello;(cons) Dick Johnson; Danny Lester. SdFxEd: Al Nahmias. Ref: TV. TVG. V 11/10/82:24. (d)10/6/81 (rated). MFB'82:229. Screen Intl 9/4/82. Academy. Ecran F 22:5. with Chris Lemmon, Gregg Henry, Deborah Benson, George Kennedy, Mike Kellin, Ralph Seymour, John Hunsaker(twins).

Five young campers venture into the Oregon backwoods and "raise the devil," or at least a few "demons," in the form of huge, mutant, machete-wielding twins, products of inbreeding. Unremarkable imitation-HILLS HAVE EYES shocker might just pass if you've seen fewer than 30 of these goons-on-the-loose things. Lovely photography (the Oregon scenery stars); but the script is principally concerned with Rustlings in the Undergrowth, and with ploys for separating one or two campers from their companions....The machete deaths wouldn't be so bad, but these instruments have saw-like teeth, and are not only stuck into victims but (the director makes sure we don't miss this detail) pulled out again, for later use. The twins' only distinguishing characteristic: they titter. (Or at least one of them does.) "Character development" here means that the heroine resorts, finally, to (a) makeup and (b) physical force at the end. This change in character is undoubtedly meaningful, if not convincing.

KAMIKAZE 1989 (W.G.) TeleCulture/Ziegler-Trio-Oase(ZDF) 1982 ('83-U.S.) color 106m. (KAMIKAZE-G t. KAMIKAZE '89-ad t) SP,D: Wolf Gremm. SP: also Robert Katz, from Per Wahloo's book "Death on The 31st Floor." Ph: X. Schwarzenberger. Mus: Edgar Froese, Tangerine Dream. Sets: Furcht, Mabille. Mkp & Cost: Barbara Naujok, Ursula Sonntag. Video: Cine-Video. Ref: TV: MGM-UA Home Video. V 8/18/82. FComment 11/82:6. VV 3/15/83: 41. Ecran F 32:71. with Rainer Werner Fassbinder, Gunther Kaufmann, Boy Gobert, Brigitte Mira, Frank Ripploh, Franco Nero.

September, 1989. "The Federal Republic of Germany is the richest country....There is no pollution, no energy problem, no inflation nor unemployment." There is only "the spirit of evil," Krysmopompas, who (or which) stands opposed to "The Blue Panther," president of an all-powerful news-and-entertainment combine. "The Blue Panther" (according to one ex-associate) has made a practice of hiring the most brilliant thinkers and then stifling them--"murdering" their minds....

Fast, quirky, more baffling than The BIG SLEEP(1946), but without any of that movie's entertainment value. Out of its social-political context, KAMIKAZE 1989 may seem more modernistically mystifying than it really is, but it's probably no picnic for West German audiences either. The quasi-narrative format is basic Philip Marlowe--(police) detective Jansen follows up on leads; interviews suspects--but dialogue, characters, and action are so idiosyncratic that it's hard to tell who's leading and who's following. The only "peg" for the audience is the mystery of the 31st floor--does it exist? who inhabits it? why is it so hard to locate? Unfortunately, there are 30 other, less intriguing floors in this building....

The KEEP (U.S.-B?) Para/Koch Jr.-Kirkwood(Assoc.Capital & Capital Equip.) 1983 color/ws 97m. SP,D: Michael Mann. From F. Paul Wilson's novel. Ph: Alex Thomson. Mus: Tangerine Dream. PD: John Box. SpVisFX: Wally Veevers, Robin Browne;(tech) Allan Bryne et al. SpMkpFX: Nick Allder; Graham Freeborn et al. SmokeFX: Roger Simons. OptFX: D. Hall. Mattes: Douglas Ferris. Ref: screen. SFExam 12/16/83. V 12/21/83. with Scott Glenn, Jurgen Prochnow, Robert Prosky, Alberta Watson.

Dinu Pass, in the Carpathian Alps--Romania, 1941. "Something has been released" in the castle keep, by someone who didn't listen to the monk when he said "Never touch the crosses!", and its release fulfills the prophecy--posted elsewhere in the keep (in a "language that has been dead for 500 years")--"I will be free." Molasar, freed, pretends to be the friend of "humane men" and the liberator of "my people," the Jews, and he has healing powers; but this demon is really evil incarnate ("I am from you") and sucks the life (or evil) out of its victims. A mysterious "traveler...from everywhere" (Glenn) destroys the being with a talisman.

A theological horror movie, or rather a theological horror of a movie, The KEEP is swell just to look at; hell to think about. Light always seems to come in dire, imposing shafts here, and the director and designer are clearly out to overwhelm with effects and sets. All movement either is or appears to be in slow motion. Even the dialogue seems to be spoken in slow motion....This must be the most portentous horror movie since The BLACK CAT(1934), and it is, similarly, oddly watchable. The problem is that Mann the scriptwriter takes his job just as seriously as Mann the director, and the former might just as well have stood in bed. The script's one twist is that the Evil Monster which seems, for a while, to be Good, really is Evil. Better to enjoy the elaborate cloud and smoke effects than to ponder such allegorical matters. (The monster-issuing-from-cloud effect is, by the bye, lifted from CURSE OF THE DEMON--Wally Veevers, perhaps not coincidentally, worked on both films.) And it doesn't help that the monster, when finally revealed, might have stepped out of a comic book, or that the hero is, in effect if not intention, Super-Christ.

2P KEEP MY GRAVE OPEN Wells/Jefferson & Century 1980 color 78m. D,P: S.F. Brownrigg. SP: F. Amos Powell. Ph: John Valtenburgs. Mus: Robert Farrar. Mkp: Jackie Barnes. Ref: TV: Unicorn Video. TVG. Boxo 7/28/80:10. with Camilla Carr, Gene Ross, Stephen Tobolowsky, Ann Stafford, Annabelle Weenick, Chelsea Ross, Sharon Bunn, Bill Thurman.

Texas. Lesley Fontaine (Carr) and her brother, Kevin, are "unnaturally" close--in fact, they're the same person: Lesley imagines herself, alternately, as Kevin and with Kevin. As Kevin, she kills interlopers with a sword, and stores the bodies in the back seat of an old car. At the end, she dies of a drug overdose, and the real Kevin returns....S.F. Brownrigg (DON'T LOOK IN THE BASEMENT, DON'T OPEN THE DOOR) appears to be a sort of technically-competent Andy Milligan--he is drawn (or at least hopes that his audience is drawn) to the perverse and the sleazy. Mad Sex might be a summing-up title for his movies. If his protagonists aren't insane at the beginning of his movies, they are by the end. This subject of madness seems to appeal to Brownrigg as being both the stuff of Tragedy and Perversity. Comedy, alas, eludes him--if his films were a bit better, they would be comedies; if they were a bit worse, they would be camp. As it is, they plod. They need a spark of self-consciousness, a sense of awareness of their own near-absurdity. Without that, the best they can do is offer up a scene or two of determined kinkiness--here, for instance, the sequence of phantom incest between Lesley and "Kevin." (The camera is subjective--as "him.")

KICK THE CAN(by G.C.Johnson) see TWILIGHT ZONE--THE MOVIE

KIDNAPPERS, The see RAIDERS FROM OUTER SPACE

KIDO SENSHI--GANDAMU III (J) Shochiku/Nippon Sunrise 1982 anim (aka GUNDAM III. MEGURIAI UCHU) Sequel to GANDAMU. Ref: V 4/14/82:33: "sci-fier." 5/4/83:347. JFFJ 14:7-8,39.
Feature drawn from the last 13 episodes of the TV show "Mobile Suit Gundam."

KILL OR BE KILLED ABC-TV/Fox-TV & Irwin Allen & Kent 1966 color 90m. Episodes (including "The Day The Sky Fell In") from the "Time Tunnel" TV series. Ref: TVG. "TV Drama Series." with Linden Chiles, Sam Groom, Lew Gallo, Susan Flannery.

2P The KILLER SNAKES (H.K.-Cant.) Mahler 1974('75-U.S.) color/ws 92m. (SHE SHASHOU) D: Kuei Chi-Hung. Ref: Cinef V:2:35. Willis/SW. V 9/24/75:28(rated). HKFFest V:205.
Young man sics cobras on enemies (cf. FANGS).

KILLER'S DELIGHT 1980 90m. D: Jeremy Hoenack. Ref: Ecran F 32:65. with James Luisi, J. Karlen, Martin Speer.
Super-strong killer stalks Los Angeles.

*KILLERS FROM SPACE 1954(1953) OptFX: Consolidated. Mkp: Harry Thomas. Narr: Mark Scott. Ref: TV: c.1953. TVG. Warren/KWTS! Scot Holton(of course). LC. V 1/27/54. Weldon. and with Steve Pendleton, Ben Welden, Lester Dorr, Robert Roark.
Soledad Flats, Nevada. "They're here!": "strange people" with "horrible eyes"--who journey to Earth via magnetically-propelled ships (on an "electron bridge"), from the planet Astron Delta in the Astron solar system--have accumulated "several billion electron volts" from the government's Operation A-Bomb Test explosions. Their sun is dying (their eyes have enlarged to combat the ensuing darkening of their planet), and, one-billion strong, they have invaded neighboring planets, and are now establishing space platforms prepatory to invading Earth. They use the electricity-controlled atomic energy to "change" the genes in ordinary Earth spiders, grasshoppers, cockroaches, and lizards, and turn them into giants. They plan to unleash these animal "armies" on the world, then exterminate their "menagerie" with gamma rays. The Deltans surgically revive a scientist, Douglas P. Martin (Peter Graves), from the dead and hypnotize him into becoming their ally; but he pulls the plug on their electrical supply, and their under-

ground headquarters goes up in a mushroom cloud.

The science is suspect; the suspense and drama, pretty thin. And the movie features the original Bug-Eyed Aliens. In fact, it's renown among sf-movie fans for this latter particular. (It couldn't gain renown any other way.) Its only other notable feature is the odd score by Manuel Compinsky. His background music is near-omnipresent, but generally not a dominating factor. It is for the most part non-dramatic and understated, with occasional awkward "blares." Although sometimes as tacky as the movie, it features eerie minor chords and it unobtrusively embellishes even the least distinguished scenes. (Not, mind you, that any scenes in this movie are especially distinguished.) Not surprisingly, the credits don't list an art director--"art direction" here would mean standing sets, a portrait of President Eisenhower on a wall, and Bronson Caverns.

The KILLING HOUR Lansbury-Beruh 1982 color 90m. D: Armand Mastroianni. Ref: Ecran F 35:62. 29:7. V 2/16/83:24. with Perry King, Norman Parker, Kenneth McMillan, Elisabeth Kemp.

An art student has "macabre visions" which prove to be premonitions of murder.

The KILLING OF SATAN (Fili) Cinex 1983? D: E.C. Pinon. SP: J.M. Avellana. Ph: R. Herrera. Mus: E. Cuenco. Ref: Ecran F 36:82. V 5/4/83:360(ad). HR 10/25/83:S-157(ad). with Ramon Revilla, Elizabeth Oropesa, George Estregan, Paquito Diaz.

One man vs. "the Lord of Darkness."(V)

The KILLING TOUCH Impact Films 1983 SP,D: Michael Elliot. SP, P: Rafael Bunuel, C. Mankiewicz. Ph: Alfred Taylor. AD: Jay Burkhart. Ref: Ecran F 39:31.41:16.35:68. Bill Warren. Boxo 8/83:10. HR 3/21/83: '84 Olympics setting. V 2/16/83:24. 11/9/83:6: at Paris sf fest. with Sally Kirkland, Melissa Prophet, Sean Masterson, Nicholas Love.

Hooded knifer on the loose at Falcon Academy.

KING COBRA see JAWS OF SATAN

KING SOLOMON'S TREASURE (Can.) (Gold Key-TV)/Canafox(Towers) 1978 color 88m. D: Alvin Rakoff. SP: Colin Turner, Allan Prior. From H. Rider Haggard's novel "Allan Quatermain." Ph: Paul van der Linden. Mus: Lew Lehman. AD: Gauthier, Wetherup. Mkp: M.A. Protat. Ref: TV. MFB'79:176. Bill Warren. with David McCallum, John Colicos, Patrick Macnee, Britt Ekland, Wilfrid Hyde-White, Hugh Rose, Ken Gampu, Yvon Dufour.

Lost Phoenician city in Africa...big green dinosaur with ruff, big mouth, and little mobility...boat hauled upstream on brontosaurus's tail...giant crustaceans...giant snake..."leopard men"....Haggard takes over from Burroughs in this trite but beautifully-photographed dinosaur-and-volcano adventure. This time, time forgets the Phoenicians. The very, very green hills of Africa (and Canada) star. The movie--never really too alive--

expires for good when our heroes get to the Forbidden City, where the sticks-of-characters attempt to take over from the scenic effects. There are no monster-effects credits--a smart, embarrassment-saving move on someone's part. This was, admittedly, your author's kind of movie when he was 11 (it's in the hallowed tradition of UNKNOWN ISLAND, LOST CONTINENT (1951), etc.), and might just pass with 11-year-olds now....

KIRKWOOD HAUNTING/WOLF PACK see SPIDER-MAN: WOLFPACK...

KISS DADDY GOODBYE Cinevid 1981 90m. Ref: TVG. V 5/9/84:264(ad). with Fabian Forte, Marilyn Burns.
Psychic twins set out to avenge their father's death.

KNIGHT RIDER NBC-TV/Larson & Univ 1982 color 94m. D: Daniel Haller. Sp,Exec P: Glen A. Larson. Ref: V 9/29/82:53. Cinef. TVG 1/22/83:12. with David Hasselhoff, Edward Mulhare, Vince Edwards, Phyllis Davis, Richard Basehart.
Super-car "run by remote control" and with "a mind of its own."(V)

KOLCHAK see DEMON AND THE MUMMY

KRABAT (Cz) Ustredi Pujcovna 1982(1977) anim color 71m. SP,D,Des: Karel Zeman. From C. Ucen's book "The Sorcerer's Apprentice." Ph: Pikhart. Mus: J. Moucka. Des: also Spalena, Javerik et al. Ref: V 10/27/82. Ecran F 30:59.
Young, apprentice magician vs. the evil Master Magician.

KRIEG UND FRIEDEN see WAR AND PEACE

KRULL (B) Col/Mann-Silverman(Barclays) 1983 color/ws 120m. (KRULL: INVADERS OF THE BLACK FORTRESS. DUNGEONS AND DRAGONS. The DUNGEONS OF KRULL. DRAGONS OF KRULL--all early ts) D: Peter Yates. SP: Stanford Sherman. Ph: Peter Suschitzky. Mus: James Horner. PD: Stephen Grimes. SpMkp:(des) Nick Maley; Bob Keen, Nick Dudman et al. VisFX:(sup) Derek Meddings;(ph) Paul Wilson;(asst d) Gareth Tandy; P. Wilkinson. OptFX:(ph) Robin Browne; Harcourt, Vinson et al. SpFX:(sup) John Evans, Mark Meddings;(art) Peter Chiang;(ed) Mike Round; Barnard, Biggs et al. Anim: Steven Archer. Models:(sup) Terry Reed; Peter Voysey. SdFX:(sup ed) Winston Ryder;(synth fx) Ian Underwood. Ref: screen. pr. Bill Warren. V 7/27/83. MFB'83: 331. with Ken Marshall, Lysette Anthony, Freddie Jones, Alun Armstrong, Francesca Annis, Bernard Bresslaw(Cyclops).
In a time neither past nor present. The Black Fortress, a space cruiser bearing The Beast and his army of Slayers, arrives on the twin-sunned planet of Krull--the near-omnipotent Beast is strongest at the center of the Fortress, the interior of which is designed in the image of his interior. The Slayers have blue-ray weapons and, when they die, bail out of their armor (and prove to be lobster-bug-like creatures) and dive into

the ground. Plus: the Widow of the Web (Annis), which is patrolled by the giant Crystal Spider...flying, flaming-hoofed firemares...changeling which adopts the likeness of and kills the Seer...flames-of-love-from-hand which defeat The Beast and his energy-ray-puffs-from-mouth...boomerang-like Glaive, which cuts through walls and stuns The Beast...wall which absorbs people...emissary (David Battley) from the Hill People who enters as a fireball and transforms into, variously, a tiger, a goose, and a dog...Cyclops doomed to see his own death.

A long, but lively, fantasy-filled sf-adventure. It's more a matter of the quantity than the quality of the aural and visual elements, though Horner's score and the photography are both of epic stature (if the story and performances aren't). Effects highlights include the there-and-back transformations of Ergo (of the Hill People); the animation of the spider; the spilling-monster deaths of the Slayers. The film is stirring as long as it keeps on the move; unfortunately, it stops periodically for thematic refueling. There are sore-thumb verbal messages on love, fame, freedom, power, fate, and time, all of which subjects you can learn more about elsewhere. Battley's Monty Pythonesque banter helps, occasionally, to check the verbal pomposity.

KUNG FU EXORCIST (H.K.?) Ref: poster. with Kathy Leen. Shaolin holy man vs. the devil.

KUNG FU FROM BEYOND THE GRAVE (H.K.-Cant.) 198-? color 88m. Ref: TV: Orchids Int'l Video.

Sonny Sing's dad--"just come out from hell" ("In hades, I've saved some money") as a green ghost--orders Sonny to avenge his murder....The villain of the piece: a "black magician" who can shoot flames out of his mouth and "multiply" himself, and whose occult rituals require human hearts. At one point, he calls for the aid of Count Dracula ("I'm coming!"), who promptly flies in, cape and all, to battle the hero. ("The vampire!") Some sort of magical fire seems to consume the count....Plus: the attack of the flying fireballs!...the self-filling grave!...the ambulatory stone coffin!...the graveyard geysers!...the flying (evil) ghost, who battles another (good) ghost (limbs and bones come flying out of the dust of the fray)!...the ghost who removes his head-and-shoulders!...stray wizards!...occult rays!...hands reaching out from graves!...regiments of zombie-ghosts!

What more could you possibly want? Discipline, maybe? Forget it. The flights of fancy here depart at highly irregular intervals, and are not covered by any Civil Aeronautics Board regulations. Repeatedly, the mind boggles, then--during stretches of typical martial-arts action--remains safely out of harm's way, until the movie's next, unscheduled flight. The half-obliterated English subtitles perhaps make the continuity more confusing than it really is; the crux of the story appears to be: the ghost legions (including Sonny's father) want the bad guy's heart, to replace the ones that he used in his occult ceremonies. And they apparently get it. It is not explained where Dracula comes from or where he goes. He's just handy....

KUNG FU ZOMBIE (H.K.-Cant.) Transmedia/Eternal Film 1981('82-U.S.) color 95m.(80m.) D: Hwa I Hung. SP: Wong Hoi Ming. Ref: TV: Orchids Int'l Video. SFExam 5/28/82. V 4/7/82:4(rated). Ecran F 3:57. with Billy Chong, Chiang Tao, Chang Leu.

A magician-priest, an adept in "Mau Shan" ("38 ways in giving commands to corpses")(TVFFSB), succeeds in reincarnating a dead man's ghost in a new body. It takes a tug-o'-war with the ghost, finally, to remove it from the body....Vampire-ghost, Leng Heet, an adept in "7 injured, 7 killed" kung fu, fights with flaming hands and foot....At the end, a horde of zombie-ghosts (including one headless one) follows the priest, pleading with him to reincarnate them....Bad Cantonese nonsense-comedies are apparently pretty much the same as bad American nonsense-comedies, bad Mexican nonsense-comedies, etc. This movie is 95 minutes of pure silliness. Zombies and exorcists, however, prove to be pretty funny being silly: the priest uses voodoo dolls, silly chants, cymbals, etc., in his attempts to revive the dead. And they hop and jump and do "square dances." The pace is frantic; the subtitles never let up. This movie also features a kung-fu duel involving furniture and having something of Fred Astaire to it.

K'UNG-PU-TE CH'ING-JEN see THIRD FACE, The

KYOFU NO DAIUZUMAKI see HORROR OF THE GIANT VORTEX

LADY FRANKENSTEIN (I) Filman 1982? D: Alan Cools. Ref: V 5/12/82:216(ad). with Antonella Prati, Mark Shannon.

LADY, STAY DEAD (Austral.) Ryntare 1982(1981) color 95m. SP,D,P: Terry Bourke. Ph: Ray Henman. Mus: Bob Young. AD: Bob Hill. Ref: V 1/27/82. Ecran F 22:15,77.40:9-11. with Chard Hayward(Gordon), Louise Howitt, Deborah Coulls, Roger Ward.

"Demonic" killer who drowns, then "magically reappears."(V)

*The LAND UNKNOWN 1957 ws (The HIDDEN VALLEY-orig t) SpPh: Clifford Stine, R.O. Binger. Ref: TV. Warren/KWTS! Weldon.

An Antarctic expedition discovers a Mesozoic-like valley--3,000 feet below sea level--in which there's no climatic change ("rising volcanic heat," it's explained, melts cliff ice, forming clouds which seal heat in and keep the temperature near 100 degrees, the humidity 100%), and thus no evolution. The featured creatures: a comically constipated-looking, hunchbacked Tyrannosaurus (the "most ferocious dinosaur"), a parade-float plesiosaur, "giant" lizards, pterodactyl, huge, carnivorous plant.

The dramatic conflict: the members of the expedition all want to get out (it's the heat and the dinosaurs), and can; but Hunter (Henry Brandon), survivor of an earlier expedition and "ruler" of the dinosaurs, will give them the way-out secret only if they give him Maggie (Shawn Smith). It's not exactly King Kong-and-Fay Wray, though that seems to be the intended echo. She screams a lot, a la Fay--mostly at the plesiosaur--but her best trick is backing up--twice--almost right into the middle of the tentacled plant. (Add a smile to her face, and she might be a tourist posing in front of it for a snapshot.) After the second incident, she attempts to explain to her rescuer how she managed, all unwittingly, to park herself right in front of the monstrosity, but is not convincing. How She Came To Be There (twice) is, in fact, this movie's most pressing matter, which will give you some idea of the movie.... Some fair work with fog, smoke, water, and traveling shots, and a decent (uncredited) score. But oh! those dinosaurs!

2 The LAST CHASE (U.S.-Can.) Argosy & CFDC & Duffy(Slott/Abramson) 1981(1980) 106m. Aerial Ph: Clay Lacey. Mus: Gil Melle. SpVideo & ElecFX: M. Lennick, David Stringer, Paul Davidson. OptFX: Videfx. SpPhFX: James Liles. Mattes: Matthew Yuricich. Graphic Anim: Lin Timbers. Ref: TV. Ecran F 22:25,77. and with Diane D'Aquila, Harvey Atkin, George Touliatos.

The year 2000-plus, 20 years after an apparently-germ-warfare-created epidemic has decimated the world's population. A mass-transit/tranquillity-oriented U.S. regime attempts to squelch an ex-race-car driver (Lee Majors) fleeing to "Radio Free California" via (outlawed) private car; sends veteran sabre-jet pilot (Burgess Meredith) after him....laser weapon.

An endorsement less of rugged individualism than of ownership of private cars. Seventy years ago or 30 years hence, this idea might seem revolutionary; just now it seems a bit reactionary. The script attempts to exorcise public and private guilt re: cars, pollution, and (rather incidentally) Viet Nam. The movie's subtitle might be "How I Learned To Stop Worrying and Love The Automobile." And it wouldn't be ironic--this lesson is meant to be taken straight. The tone of the script, however, is not at all wild-eyed; no right-wing fire-and-brimstone here. The film is disarmingly low-key, even droll. It's almost-insidiously even-keeled. You can't really disagree with it, ideologically, as far as it goes--which, however, isn't very far: its Big Brother of the Subway premise generates--well-nigh-automatically--a car-as-liberator theme. Politics-as-a-car-chase. Still, the script is smarter than that of the average action movie, if, finally, nearly as hollow. It allots its choicest morsels of melodrama-on-wry to Washington's man, Touliatos, all amused smugness, and to Meredith's last-of-the-jet-pilots, who prefers flying kites to strafing unarmed race-car drivers. The Majors-Meredith friendly-enemies relationship is contrived, but satisfying, in an old-fashioned way. You know they're two-of-a-kind long before Touliatos realizes it.

LAST HOUSE ON DEAD END STREET Cinematic/Production Concepts 1977? color 90m. D: Victor Janos. SP: Brian Lawrence. Ref: VideoSB. HR 10/25/83: "horror." no Academy. Weldon: aka The FUN HOUSE; hunchback. with Steven Morrison, Janet Sorley, Dennis Crawford, Lawrence Bornman.

"Gory feature about snuff films...."(Weldon)

LAST JAWS, The or LAST SHARK, The see GREAT WHITE

LAST TESTAMENT, The(by C.Amen) see TESTAMENT

The LAST UNICORN AFD & Jensen Farley/Rankin-Bass & ITC 1982 anim color 85m. D,PD,P: Arthur Rankin Jr. D,P: also Jules Bass. SP: Peter S. Beagle, from his novel. Ph: H. Omoto. Mus: Jimmy Webb. Anim:(coord) Toru Hara;(cont) Guy Kubo;(bkgd) M. Nishida;(char des) Lester Abrams;(d) K. Yamada. SdFX: Okira, Clack. Tapestry: I Duga. Ref: TV. MFB'83:72. SFExam 11/19/82. Oakland Tribune 11/22/82. V 11/17/82. Voices: Alan Arkin, Jeff Bridges, Mia Farrow, Tammy Grimes, Robert Klein, Angela Lansbury, Christopher Lee(Haggard), Keenan Wynn, Paul Frees, Rene Auberjonois(skull).

The huge, fanged, fiery Red Bull has driven all the unicorns, save one, in the world into exile in the sea behind King Haggard's castle....Sorceress Mommy Fortuna's Midnight Carnival ("Creatures of Night Brought To Light") features _illusory_ monsters--e.g., a man-headed, lion-bodied, scorpion-tailed creature (really only a lion), a satyr (really an ape), a dragon, etc.--and two _actual_ fantastic creatures--the "last unicorn" and a monstrous Harpy, which, when released, kills Mommy Fortuna....bit with fire-breathing, snake-like dragon.

Like GALAXY EXPRESS, The LAST UNICORN is a feature-length cartoon re: feeling and memory. The "last" unicorn is turned, temporarily, into a mortal, "human girl" who falls in love with a human prince, before returning to her proper form. However, she _remembers_ and becomes the only unicorn "who knows what regret is--and love." A formula happy ending is, happily, eschewed, in favor of a bittersweet ending. (_Another_ alternative for fantastic creatures who discover, belatedly, human emotion: the _tragic_ ending, or death--see I MARRIED A MONSTER FROM OUTER SPACE.) The lovers do not live happily _or_ together ever after--the fairy-tale form, as demonstrated here, can also embrace characters who _remember_, who can keep the past alive in the present. The last unicorn sees to it that "unicorns are in the world again"--the unicorn, here, being a symbol of belief, hope, trust. She forsakes the actuality of human love for its memory....In the best Movie Tradition, she (in other words) _sacrifices_ herself. From the latter angle, then, the ending is a cliche. But there's more than one angle involved, as suggested above. The film as a whole is somewhat uneven--some songs intrude and break up the prevailing mood of melancholic nostalgia--but it's ambitious and even, at times, imaginative, graphically--e.g., the unicorns are freed from the sea in huge "waves," which break, triumphantly, over the Red Bull, as the latter retreats into the sea--they return to the world in style....

LAST VICTIM, The see FORCED ENTRY

LATIDOS DE PANICO (Sp) Dalmata 1983 SP,D,with: Jacinto Molina. Ref: Ecran F 32:4,5,70. with Julia Saly, Lola Gaos, M. Zarzo.
Satanist-knight returns from the dead to terrorize a modern-day village.

2 LEGACY OF BLOOD 1978 Sets: Joe Cook? Mkp & with: Walter Ballesten(sp?). Ref: TV. Weldon: remake of The GHASTLY ONES.
"Brain-damaged" brute...seer...premonitions...disemboweled cat-in-bed...severed head on platter...man sawed in half... death by pitchfork, cleaver...surprise killer (the fourth sister!)....Abominable Andy Milligan feature is just about the worst old-house-and-the-will thriller since STRANGE ADVENTURE (1933), a not-inconsiderable feat. Scattered camp moments with the seer and his aide--both demonstratively unstrung by their visions--and with the killer--revealing all in one long, ludicrous, breathless monologue. (Then and only then can she be dispatched.) But, oh Lord!--the rest!

LEGACY OF TERROR see DEMON AND THE MUMMY

LEGEND LIVES, The see MADMAN

2 LEGEND OF THE BAYOU MPM 1976 86m. (2 DEATH TRAP-orig rel t) SpMkp: Craig Reardon, Beth Rogers. Opt: Total Optical. SdFX: Echo, Bill Manger. Ref: screen. poster: '83 re-rel. Weldon: aka HORROR HOTEL MASSACRE. and with Crystin Sinclaire.
Judd (Neville Brand), the mad, seriously-sexually-repressed proprietor of the Starlight Hotel in nowhere, Texas, takes scythe and rake to intruders and feeds them to his (imported) crocodile, which "don't make no distinctions" about items on its bill of fare--it eats anything (including the cutest little dog) and everything--except Judd's wooden leg, which, at the end, is all that remains of him....
A more apt retitling for this Tobe Hooper movie might have been The Texas Scythe Massacre. The existential image of Leatherface and his inseparable chain saw becomes, here, poor Judd and his inseparable scythe. (Even his croc can't take it from him--though, at one point, Judd removes it from a victim's neck just before his pet yanks the body into the swamp.) Or, as Judd puts it, "Gotta do what you gotta do"--in direct reference, ostensibly, to his croc and the latter's canine tidbit. He might, however, be speaking for himself, or for anyone else in the movie. What he's gotta do, specifically, is swing his scythe--an amusing absurdist preoccupation, to be sure. If nothing else, this movie has a core--the problem is that this movie has (almost) nothing else. As in Hooper's SALEM'S LOT,

"suspense" translates into longueurs--Hooper spends so much film-time simply building tension that he dissipates all tension. A movie has "gotta do" more than stitch a few images into an hour-plus of building....The early appearance on the scene of William Finley's nerves-shot-to-hell family man raises the specter of a confrontation between Judd and someone who just might out-Judd Judd in the gone-with-the-mind department. But this bizarre creature has hardly said "boo!"--and begun barking like a dog at his helpless wife--before he becomes croc bait. This "mirror-madman" confrontation must wait until The UNSEEN(1981), where it becomes that film's long, grueling climactic sequence. (Scriptwriter Kim Henkel is the link between the two movies.) The latter half of this movie is all sound effects: swamp noises...c&w music from the radio...screams from the little girl trapped under the hotel...rattling-bed-frame noises from the girl's mother, bound-and-gagged-and-determined-to-get-unbound upstairs...tittering from the couple in bed downstairs...and muttering from Judd. Enough to drive a man to distraction if the man had not already been driven.... The import of this "symphony," or cacophony, is elusive--at least it seems to be more than just an operatic "effect"--is it, perhaps, meant to be an objective correlative of the state of Judd's mind, or an aural "portrait" of the chaos produced by that mind's peculiar operations? Or, maybe, it's just "building tension" time again....

LEWD LIZARD (H.K.-Mand.) 1980? Ref: vc box: LEX Video.
Man injects "animal hormone and women's secretion" into strange lizard, produces "invisible lewd lizards" who kill for him.

La LICEALE, IL DIAVOLO E L'ACQUA (I) Fedelfilm-Medusa-Effe 1979 SP,D: Nando Cicero. SP: also S. Esse. Ref: Prod.Ital. with Gloria Guida, Lino Banfi.
The devil possesses a landlord, in one of three stories.

De LIFT (Dutch) Sigma 1983 color 95m. (aka GOIN' UP) SP,D: Dick Maas. Ph: Marc Fleperlaan. AD: Harry Ammerlaan. Ref: V 5/25/83. IFG'84:229. Ecran 35:69. with Huub Stapel, Willeke van Ammelrooy, Josine van Dalsum.
"Malign" elevator decapitates, drops, or suffocates its victims.

LIGHT YEARS AWAY (F-Swiss; Eng.-lang.) New Yorker/Gaumont/LPA-Phenix & Slotint-SSR 1981('83-U.S.) color 106m. (Les ANNEES LUMIERES) SP,D: Alain Tanner. From Daniel Odier's novel "La Voie Sauvage." Ph: J.-F. Robin. Mus: Arie Dzierlatka. AD: John Lucas. SdFX: Daniel Couteau. Mkp: M. Autret. Ref: screen. VV 4/26/83. V 5/27/81. 4/27/83:41. MFB'81:249-50: sequel to JONAS QUI AURA 25 ANS EN L'AN 2000. with Trevor Howard, Mick Ford, Odile Schmitt, Louis Samier, Bernice Stegers, Joe Pilkington.

In the year 2000, the mysterious old Poliakoff (Howard) prepares for "the great takeoff!" He keeps his secret hidden in a locked shed in the country ("What the hell is he doing?!"), dropping only a hint here and there ("The birds are my teachers") regarding the nature of his project. At one point, he has himself buried, up to his neck, in the ground, and unexplained wounds covering his body heal. The old man can remain for hours in a trance-like, still-mind state, and gives his protege, Jonas (Ford), books containing "everything you've got to know about eagles." Finally, he "bathes" in the "souls" (i.e., blood) of dead birds, straps homemade wings to his body, and prepares to fly "hundreds of light years from here." But if "women don't want men to fly," eagles positively refuse to allow men to share air space. Poliakoff flies only 20 miles before a churlish eagle brings him down.

LIGHT YEARS AWAY is one of those determinedly quirky movies that's easier to think about, in retrospect, than to watch. Its quirkiness is, occasionally, likable (Howard gives a quite taking, offbeat performance); generally, however, just quietly exasperating. Its oddness may, in fact, be a ruse, a ploy to camouflage the fact that it's a cliche (re: birds and freedom) writ large. Within its 100-plus minutes of running time lies a possibly charming (25-minute) anecdote re: man's will to be free of earthly restraints. As it is, the movie plays like 100 minutes of old Ben Kenobi instructing young Luke Skywalker in the art of mystical flight--while the entertaining parts of STAR WARS are conspicuously missing. The setting--western Ireland--however, is lovely. Water, wind, fog, hills, rocks, earth, rainbows, and the "quality of the silence" live in this film, if little else does....LIGHT YEARS AWAY is as painfully quaint as Tanner's first Jonas film, JONAH WHO WILL BE 25 IN THE YEAR 2000.

LIGHTER THAN HARE WB 1960 anim color 7m. D: I. Freleng. Ref: "WB Cartoons." LC. no Lee.

"Yosemite Sam of Outer Space" vs. Bugs Bunny.

El LIGUERO MAGICO (Sp) Frade 1980 SP,D: Mariano Ozores. Ref: Ecran F 21:42,52-3. V 5/13/81:333. with Andres Pajares, Luis Lorenzo(werewolves); Adriana Vega.

Comedy re: gay werewolf.

The LINE BETWEEN YING AND YANG (Taiwanese) Denver Center Cinema 1975 color/ws 80m. D: Ting Shan-hsi. Ref: PFA notes 9/24/82. with K. Yang, Pao Yun.

Two stories: 1) "The Dog": murdered man's spirit out for revenge; 2) "Lieu Tien-shu": spirit...reincarnation.

LIQUID SKY Cinevista/Z Films 1982(1983) color 114m. SP,D,P, Mus: Slava Tsukerman. SP: also Nina Kerova, Anne Carlisle. Ph & SpFX: Yuri Neyman. Mus: also Brenda Hutchinson, Clive Smith. PD: Marina Levikova. Mech Des for SpFX: Oleg Chichilnitsky. UFO Des: Gennadi Osmerkin. Titles: Tri-Pix. Mkp: Rashkovsky-Kaleva, Fieve. Ref: screen. V 9/1/82. 2/16/83:4 (rated). MFB'83:332. with Carlisle, Paula E. Sheppard, Susan Doukas, Otto Von Wernherr.

A transparent eyeball-of-an-alien (inside a flying saucer "the size of a dinner plate") gets high on heroin and on a molecule released into the opiate receptors of the brain during orgasm. Its subjects (mostly male) die, at first with an icicle-like shard sticking out the backs of their heads; later victims just disappear....At the end, a fashion model is (apparently) beamed aboard the saucer....Cryptic study of three brands of aliens: interplanetary, illegal (a German astrophysicist), and punk. One type is apparently supposed to comment on the other, but how is uncertain. One possible subject here: "normal" vs. "abnormal" lifestyles--but the "fantasy look," or at least feel, prevails for all styles in this movie. Another possible theme: sexual exploitation. The movie might be subtitled "The Revenge of the Vagina," but such a title would be misleadingly promising for viewers. The film's very dry sense of humor (at one point, our lethal, non-orgasmic quasi-heroine complains to whatever powers be "I can't have all these bodies...these corpses") is generally indistinguishable from mere quirkiness. The driving, not to say nagging, musical score imparts a kind of phony, flaky urgency to the action.

LISA, LISA see AXE

2P LITTLE ORBIT, THE ASTRODOG, AND THE SCREECHERS FROM OUTER SPACE (F) (HBO-TV)/Jean Image 1981? anim color 75m. D: Image. SP: France Image, Tom Rowe. Ph: Brassart, Moisset. Mus: Fred Freed. Anim: Jose Xavier et al. Ref: TV. TVG: 1977? V 2/4/81:122.

"Aerospace playboy" Terry, his girl friend Firma, and Orbit team with the hip ("Yeah, man!"), transistorized robot, or Screecher, Ruben, from the planet Hunger. The four do battle with the Baddies on Planet High-Rise, who condemn Orbit to a barrage of terrible jokes, and with the Greenzos ("walking asparagus"), which thrive on humans. Also: space bubble with brain and attendant space-bird...wand of invisibility...instant-wall spray...neutralizing freeze-spray...Arago X-001 spaceship.

The wordplay in this cartoon feature is as fast and furious as the action--Orbit isn't the only one subjected to a barrage of awful jokes. But the movie is good-natured about its bad gags. Happily unpretentious, it reduces the universe to straight man for a hip robot and a hyperactive dog. (The two humans are fairly incidental.) And if the sound track is more inventive than the animation, the latter does have occasional snap too. Aural highlights: the indecipherable muttering of the Greenzos, and the Baddies' "Kill, kill, kill! Maim, maim, maim!" And of course the Ruben-Orbit byplay. (Though the script falls back on the latter once--or 27 times--too often.)

LIU-CH'AO KUAI-T'AN (Taiwanese) Hengch'i 1981 color/ws 90m. SP,D,Ph: Wang Chu-chin. SP & with: Kuan Kuan. Mus: Mao-shan.

AD: Kuang-ming. Ref: IFG'82:298: The Legend of The Six Dynasty-tr t. with Hu Yin-meng, Chiang Han.
"Three Fifth-century ghost tales."

LIVING AND THE DEAD, The(by Boileau-Narcejac) see VERTIGO

La LOBA 1964 82m. (*The SHE-WOLF) AD: Salvador Lozano. SpFX: Antonio Munoz. Mkp: Maria del Castillo. Ref: TV. Glut/CMM. and with Columba Dominguez, Noe Murayama, Adriana Roel.
Featured players: a wolf-woman who takes "diving board" leaps at her victims, and who likes to play the theme from LETTER FROM AN UNKNOWN WOMAN on the piano as she transforms into a wolf...a little, deaf-mute girl who, thanks to her proclivity for going out at midnight and playing with mechanical toys in abandoned buildings--and in La Loba's bedroom--is in almost constant, immediate peril throughout the movie...and a doctor who is apparently searching for a medical cure for lycanthropy....In the full-moon climax, La Loba (upstairs) turns into a wolf whose feet get very hairy (though her face hardly alters), while (downstairs) her fiance turns into a wolf who resembles the apeman in RETURN OF THE APEMAN....The tragic conclusion has her stabbed with a special dagger, and dying, and him savaged by a dog, and dying, with the two finally coming to rest beside each other and transforming back into human form, as they both expire....Touching, in a way--almost wonderful, in fact, in a way....

LOCATAIRE DIABOLIQUE see DIABOLICAL TENANT, The

The LOCH NESS HORROR Omni-Leisure Int'l. 1983? color SP,D,P: Larry Buchanan. SP: also Lynn Shubert. Mus: Richard Theiss. Ref: Bill Warren. HR 9/11/81. Academy. Ecran 22(Feb.'82):53: completed. with Sandy Kenyon, Barry Buchanan, Preston Hansen.

LOOKER WB/Ladd Co. 1981 color/ws 94m. SP,D,P: Michael Crichton. Ph: Paul Lohmann. Mus: Barry DeVorzon. PD: D.E. Mitzner. SpFX: Joe Day. Computer Anim: Info. Int'l. VideoCoord: Brent Sellstrom. SpProps: Bruce Behan. SP,P:(commercials) Robert Chandler. SpSystems: Evans & Sutherland. Mkp: Ken Chase. Opt: Pacific. Ref: TV. SFChron 11/2/81. Newsweek 11/2/81. V 10/28/81. with Albert Finney, James Coburn, Susan Dey, Leigh Taylor-Young, Dorian Harewood, Darryl Hickman.
"They're killing all the girls who are perfect"--why exactly is never made clear--and the victims are blinded to the presence of the killer by a gun employing "high intensity light flashes"... dark-glasses defense against this "light gun" (which gun makes its victims "lose all sense of time")...computer-generated "actors" (based on real actors) who hypnotize audiences...electronic "janitor"....LOOKER is glib exploitation of contemporary anxieties re: subliminal advertising, TV, computers, and super-corporations. It's technically sophisticated, but it scans like "Buck Rogers on Madison Avenue." Its serial-like outland-

ishness peaks with a car chase which features good guy and bad guys shooting it out with light guns. But this movie is apparently not supposed to be a campy lark, and rest assured it isn't. In execution, it's a shambles of a mystery, with puzzle, clues, and solution equally silly and offputting. Coburn's Reston Industries scheme is ostensibly politically motivated, but motivations and explanations are subordinated to bang-bang, or flash-flash. There's some hall-of-mirrors-like fun to be had in the climactic shoot-out on the commercials-in-progress sets (featuring animated "actors" and live non-actors), but the sequence is, still, more incredible than it is fun.

2P LORD SHANGO Bryanston 1975 D: Raymond Marsh. SP: Paul C. Harrison. Ref: Weldon: "horror." V 2/5/75:19(ad). Cinef IV:1: 37. with Marlene Clark, Lawrence Cook.
Tribal priest returns to life.

*LOST CITY OF THE JUNGLE 1946 AD: Harold MacArthur. Ref: TV. LC. "Horror Film Stars." Lee.
Man exposed to Meteorium 245 disintegrates..."man-made earthquake by radio"....No-thrills serial, with villain Lionel Atwill's conspicuous absence at key moments--he contracted pneumonia (which proved to be fatal for him) during production--accounted for rather tenuously by the script. Dialogue, also, is rather tenuous. ("The Pool of Light has been blown up!")

The LOST WHIRL Bray 1928 silent 15m. Anim: J.L. Roop. SP, D: Glen Lambert. SP: also Frank Terry. Ref: Don Glut. LC. no Lee. Classic Images Review.
Flashback to brontosaurus and allosaurus on the Isle of Moss.

LOUISIANA SWAMP MURDERS see CRYPT OF DARK SECRETS

La LOUVE (Pol) Zespoly/Pilesia 1983 color 90m. D: Marek Piestrak. SP: Jerzy Gieraltowski. Ph: Pawlowicz. Mus: Jerzy Matula. AD: Andrzej Plock. Ref: Ecran F 35:67: The She-Wolf-tr t. V 11/2/83:42: at Rome sf fest. with Krzystztof Jasinski, Iwona Bieslka(Maryna/Julia), Stanislaw Brejdygant.
Witch-woman "attracted to wolves" seems to return from the dead...haunts husband's dreams...resembles the Countess Julia.

The LOVE BUTCHER Four Rivers/Mirror(Desert) 1983(1975) color/ws 83m. D: Mikel Angel, Don Jones. SP: Jones, James Evergreen. Ph: Jones, Austin McKinney;(titles) Michael Clark. Mus: Richard Hieronymus. AD: Val West, Ron Foreman. Mkp: Gail Peterson. Ref: TV: Monterey Home Video. V 10/20/82. Weldon. with Erik Stern, Kay Neer, Jeremiah Beecher, Edward Roehm.
A schizophrenic (Stern) keeps his dead brother, Caleb, "alive" by "becoming" Caleb (a "mental and physical cripple") at times. In his own, "Les" persona, he returns the abuse heaped by women upon poor "Caleb" by seducing them and then murdering them, with scythe, shears, etc. ("All women are

hypocrites! whores!--even dear mother.") "Caleb" is ugly out-side; the women who mistreat him are ugly inside; and Les... Les is, in his own words, "the great male Adonis of the universe." ("I am the great magnet to all women.") At the end, however, Les is rejected by a woman, and his confidence crumbles. He does a Jekyll-Hyde-like transformation back into, permanently, "Caleb," who, free at last of Les, "kills" him. (Caleb: "I'm alive and I'm beautiful!")

A very uneven movie, yet still one of the more interesting in the psycho-killer subgenre. It both kids that subgenre and belongs to it, or it at least tries (like Caleb/Les) to be two things at once. The Caleb/Les set-tos work as either satire or psychological-thriller material. They're very well dialogued ("I am love--total love....I am Lester and I am alive!") and can, collectively, be taken as either a psychological portrait of male conceit(Les)/male self-loathing(Caleb), or as a mocking caricature of same. It's a field day for Stern, as "Caleb," as Les, and as the other (literal and figurative) lady killers inside him: vanity compounded. Many of the non-Caleb/Les scenes, though, fizzle, whether intended satirically or not. They're either just bad or bad comedy. The further the movie gets from Stern, the shakier it is. He obviously relishes his shots (as the sexually acrimonious Les) at phrases like "bot-tomless body pits" and "nymphoid satisfaction"...but the other actors are not so blessed by the scriptwriters.

LOVE EXORCIST see STRANGE EXORCISM OF LYNN HART, The

LOVE ME DEADLY Cinema Nat'l./United Talent 1972(1975) color 107m. (aka SECRETS OF THE DEATH ROOM) SP,D: Jacques LaCerte. Mus: Phil Moody. Ref: Cinef IV:2:37. V(d) 3/2/72(ad). Bill Warren. Academy. Boxo. Weldon. Stanley. with Mary Wilcox, Lyle Waggoner, Christopher Stone, Timothy Scott.

Satan-worshipping necrophiliacs...woman who "can reach com-plete fulfillment"(Boxo) only after killing her lovers... undertaker who embalms lovers.

LOVE TRAP (B) (Showtime-TV)/Norfolk Int'l./Smedley-Aston 1978 color 97m. D & Mus: James Kenelm Clarke. SP & Lyrics: Michael Gordon. Ph: Phil Meheux. AD: Ken Bridgeman. Ref: TV. TVG. with Robin Askwith, Fiona Richmond, Anthony Steel, Graham Stark, Linda Hayden, Anna Chen.

London, 1947. Everyone's after PJ-46, "potentially the most dangerous miniaturized device in the world." It turns out to be a lighter which, when flicked, temporarily shuts down elec-trical and mechanical power in the immediate vicinity....Low comedy, show-biz satire, secret-agent intrigue, and soft-core fantasies (the hero's daydreams, visualized), all very per-functorily executed.

LUCIFER'S WOMEN see DOCTOR DRACULA

LUGGAGE OF THE GODS! General 1983 color 74m. SP,D: David Kendall. Ph: Steven Ross. Mus: Cengiz Yaltkaya. AD: Joshua Harrison. SpFX: Glenn Van Fleet. Mkp: Arnold Gargiulo. Ref: V 6/15/83. 10/26/83:227(ad). with Mark Stolzenberg, Gabriel Barre, Gwen Ellison.

Tribe "living unchanged from prehistoric times somewhere in North America...."

LUPIN VIII (J-F) Tokyo Movie Shinsha/TF1 & DIC 1982 anim D: Taro Rin. Ref: JFFJ 14:11: feature based on the LUPIN III TV & feature-film series, and set in the 22nd Century.

LUST AT FIRST BITE Backstreet/MR 1980(1979) color c80m. (aka 2 DRACULA SUCKS or 2 DRACULA'S BRIDE) D: Philip Morris. SP & with: William Margold. Ph: Bruce Edwards. Sets: Richard Kingsley. Mkp: Van De Dorff, Bea Morales. Ref: TV: VCA(video). Willis/SW. Jim Shapiro. and with Paul Thomas, Pat Manning, "McGoogle Schlepper"(Renfield), Mike Ranger.

The film now known as LUST AT FIRST BITE began life as DRACULA SUCKS (which is now the title of the softcore edition of the film)--under which latter title it apparently enjoyed a limited release, before being re-launched, theatrically, a few years ago, as DRACULA'S BRIDE....If its history seems confusing, though, you should see the film itself. The facts, roughly: Dracula (Jamie Gillis) moves into Carfax Abbey and vampirizes Lucy (Serena) and Mina (Annette Haven). The latter becomes the Count's "new queen"....The movie's soundtrack is a patchwork of borrowed music, mainly classical ("Bolero," "Also Sprach Zarathustra," "Swing Low, Sweet Chariot"), and borrowed dialogue--from the 1931 DRACULA. In fact this movie qualifies, in part, as a remake of the Lugosi film--the Dracula-Van Helsing (Reggie Nalder) scenes are lifted almost intact from it. And it's not unusual for actors playing Dracula to appropriate Lugosi's accent (as Gillis does here), but the guy playing Renfield uses Dwight Frye's loony-laugh as well....The film's harsh lighting, perhaps intended to be "spectral," is simply unflattering for the women.

MACE IL FUORILEGGE see CONQUEST

2 MAD MAX Kennedy-Miller 1979 93m.-U.S. Asst AD: Steve Amezdroz. Vehicle Des: Ray Beckerley. Mkp: Viv Mephan. Elec: Lex Glouchewera. Ref: TV. Weldon. and with Vince Gil(Nightrider), Hugh-Keays Byrne(Toecutter).

"A few years from now...." Or today, aggravated. Gas is scarce, and biker gangs terrorize the countryside. The premad Max (Mel Gibson) quits the law-enforcing MFP when his buddy is murdered, and turns vigilante when his wife and child are run down by "terminal crazies" on motorcycles....DEATH WISH on wheels. A formula-revenge-film warm-up to The ROAD WARRIOR (qq.v.), MAD MAX's sequel. There's a touch of ambiguity to Max's "zombie," out for blood at the end; but this is no KRIEMHILD'S REVENGE. After his wife is hospitalized, and his son is killed, Max sits, crazily kneading the Tor Johnson monster-mask which, earlier, he had put on as a joke. It's no joke now--he's joining the "rat circus," and he'll be the center-ring attraction. But it's only superficially exciting and not really disturbing when he finally goes into action on his own--the line (spoken more than once) "People don't believe in heroes any more" can be seen as a simple, non-ironic call-to-action which Max, however irrationally, heeds. He has not really become one of them--he has become just another action-hero, a good man gone better....This film is, at base, an intermittently successful mining of the kinetic excitement of moving cars and cycles.

MAD MISSION PART II see ACES GO PLACES II

MADHOUSE (U.S.-I) Assonitis 1982 color/ws? SP,D,P,Exec P: Ovidio G. Assonitis. SP: also Blakley, Shepherd, Gandus. Ph: Piazzoli. Mus: Riz Ortolani. Ref: V 9/29/82:17. Ecran F 29 (Dec'82):54: completed. 36:46. Bill Warren. no Academy. with Trish Everly, Michael Macrae, Dennis Robertson, Morgan Hart.
"Une maison malefique"...brutal murders...macabre finale.(EF)

2P MADMAN Jensen Farley/The Legend Lives(Sales-Giannone) 1982 (1981) color 91m. (The LEGEND LIVES-orig t. MADMAN MARZ-int t) Story,SP,D: Joe Giannone. Story: also Gary Sales. Ph: James Momel. Mus:(d) Sales;(elec) Stephen Horelick. AD: William Scheck. SpFxMkp: Jo Hansen. SpFX: DePaolo, Vogel, Holland, Luckavic. Opt: Exceptional. SdFX:(cons) Skip Lievsay; (ed) R. Haines. Ref: TV: Thorn EMI Video. Weldon. V 2/17/82. 9/30/81:4(rated). 9/23/81:34. with Alexis Dubin, Tony Fish, Harriet Bass, Seth Jones, Paul Ehlers(Marz).
North Sea Cottages, a camp for gifted children. The camp-fire tale of Madman Marz, a farmer who, "many, many years ago," went mad and took an axe to his wife and children (and apparently survived hanging and an axe in the face), comes to life when one camper dares Marz to come out of the woods....He does, and one by one the counselors are slaughtered and dragged away to his cellar lair....There seem to be more counselors than kids at this camp. And they all, helpfully (for Marz), venture out into the woods, at night, one or two at a time. Each new venturer, looking for the last one, adds a new name to the roll call of the missing. ("T.P.!? Richie!? Dave!?") This is as far as the movie ventures in the direction of plot, though it does make some halting attempts at characterization. All such attempts, however, are abandoned when the violence starts. The murders are, from an esthetic standpoint, as unimaginative as those in any part of FRIDAY THE 13TH. But Marz--who recalls the scraggly Glenn Strange in The MAD MONSTER--has an amusing

lope and grunt, and until the end, we are granted only quick, tantalizing peeks at him. The title music ("Song of Madman Marz") is catchy--the score itself is regulation thriller-music.

2 MAGNIFICENT MAGICAL MAGNET OF SANTA MESA 1977 (ADVENTURES OF FREDDIE-alt t) SP: also Dee Caruso. Ph: William Jurgensen. Mus: Jack Elliot, Allyn Ferguson? AD: Bellah, Hulsey. SpFX: Bill Glove. Mkp: Ben Lane. Ref: TV.

A stray bolt of lightning strikes an inventor's lab and gives his experimental, "force field" disc incredible magnetic powers. Industrial Development International plans to use the force to revolutionize industry (and make huge profits), but the disc's energy eventually drains....A thin premise for some weak little-man-vs.-the-corporate-machine comedy. Film supposedly sides with the little man, but plays like the machine.

Ang MAHIWAGANG DAIGDIG NI PEDRO PENDUKO (Fili) Topaz 197-? color D: Celso Ad Castillo. Ref: vc box: Solar Video. Rebecca Atienza: The Strange World of Pedro Penduko-tr t. with Eddie Garcia, Ramon Zamora, Lotis Key.

Folk hero...cursed mermaid...dragon-monster.

Les MAITRES DU TEMPS (F-W.G.-Swiss-Hung.) WDR/SWF/Telecip & TF1 & SSR 1982 anim color 76m. SP,D: Rene Laloux;(graphics) Moebius. SP: also Manchette. From Stefan Wul's novel "L'Orphelin de Perdide." Anim Coord: Grimond. Mus: C. Zanesi et al. Sp FX: Sandor Reisenbuchler. Ref: Ecran F 28:69. V 6/2/82: The Time Masters-tr t. Voices: Alain Cuny, Monique Thierry et al.

Orphan at the mercy of giant hornets on the planet Perdide.... "gnome-like telepathic beings...faceless...angel-like creatures."(V)

MAKE THEM DIE SLOWLY (I) Aquarius 1980('83-U.S.) color 90m. (aka CANNIBAL FERROX. cf.EATEN ALIVE(P)) SP,D: Umberto Lenzi. Ph: Bergamini. Mus: Budy/Maglione. PD: Bassan. Ref: screen. V 11/9/83: "horror format." Ecran F 26:55: Cannibal Ferox. with John Morghen, Lorraine de Selle, Robert Kerman, Richard Bolla, Venantino Venantini.

A cocaine-crazed American publicly tortures a Colombian Indian; consequently drives his tribe "right back to the level of animals!" They proceed to eviscerate and cannibalize the body of another, recently-deceased intruder from the North, castrate the (still-living) chief offender, sever one of the latter's hands, perform cranial whack-top "surgery" on him, and nibble on his brains....The Indians hook one white woman up by her breasts; the other white woman lives to write "Cannibalism: End of a Myth."

The "myth," apparently, is that cannibalism exists naturally in places like Colombia. The "truth," as revealed here, is that the violence of outsiders begets violence, and drives "harmless" Third World natives into cannibalism. Then, as in NIGHT OF THE ZOMBIES(MPM), the Third World strikes back....

Sociologically-and-politically-speaking, this is a long way to go for a bit of gore--there are few spectacles as audaciously sniveling as an out-and-out exploitation movie (such as this one) wearing its "social conscience" on its sleeve....The scattered gore-makeup effects here are familiar. The movie is leech/piranha/maggot-happy; but the most intense violence is that done by man to animal or animal to animal--it does not look faked, and thus comes closer to achieving the desired degree of offensiveness than the man-to-man atrocities.

MALENKA see FANGS OF THE LIVING DEAD

The MAN AND HIS BOTTLE (B) Hepworth 1908 6m. D: Lewin Fitzhamon. Ref: TV(Amazing Years of Cinema). BFC. no Lee. with Thurston Harris.

Devils and big, bug-like monsters torment--and ultimately bottle--alcoholic....The LOST WEEKEND in a nutshell. Cute tricks, employing only some strings and a little papier-mache.

*MAN BEAST 1956 67m. AD: Ralph Tweer. Ref: TV. Warren/KWTS! Weldon. and with G.W. Lewis, Lloyd Cameron.

Himalayan Yeti--"definitely human!" creatures somewhere between Rhodesian Man and Danish Stone Age Man on the evolutionary scale--interbreed with women ("You kidnap women?!"); yield, notably, "fifth-generation" hybrid, Varga (George Skaff).... Superior-of-kind, the kind being a Jerry Warren production (a species rating rather low on the evolutionary movie-scale). Varga proves to have a rather perverse charm (and resembles Henry Hull's pale-haired London werewolf), and in this one, Warren actually stages a few action scenes (instead of lifting them from Mexican horrors)--not well, of course, but....Rest assured, however, that the dialogue scenes are pure Jerry Warren--two or three actors sitting or standing beside each other and talking, talking, talking. And Virginia Maynor is everything one could wish for (and more) from a Warren actress....

MAN FROM DEEP RIVER see SACRIFICE!

*The MAN FROM PLANET X Mid Century 1951 AD: also Byron Vreeland(sp?). SpFX: Andy Anderson, Howard Weeks. PhFX: Jack Rabin. Ref: TV. Warren/KWTS! V 3/14/51. Weldon.

"Strange astronomical phenomena" herald the arrival of "a new planet" in our solar system. It is a "dying" planet guided by "scientific degravitation" towards Earth, in preparation for an invasion. The "strange waves" emanating from this "Planet X" are concentrated over the Scottish island of Burray, "a place on the edge of the world," where an alien emissary (with "a ghastly caricature" of a human face--"like something distorted by pressure") is establishing a "wireless directional beam" to his people in space. He turns the island's inhabitants into "a village of zombies" with a hypnotic light-ray which renders humans his "slaves." "The boogey" communicates with one man via geometry; his spacecraft resembles "a big diving bell"; and an alien "range finder" (made of a substance harder than steel but with 1/5 steel's specific gravity), arriving on Earth ahead of the craft, determines for him the composition of the Earth's atmosphere....

The MAN FROM PLANET X divides, tidily, into two movies, with two different scripts. The first movie is an atmospheric introduction to the Scottish moors ("eerie place, these moors") and to the alien. It's just a set or two, with some fences, trees, rocks, and artificial fog. But music, sound effects, and moving camera turn it into a satisfying mini-horror-picture. The second movie is a very early zombified-humans sf-thriller, dominated by plodding dialogue-passages. Story and character are really of no interest in either half of the film. The one intriguing figure is that of the X-Man. He's only an actor in a head-mask, but the design of the mask makes it a dramatic factor. It's "neutral," impassive--he could be friend or foe, or simply an alien investigative-reporter. But this ambiguous mask suggests more about the alien than all the dialogue of the other principals says about them; it "fits" both halves of the movie--the first half, in which he seems not unfriendly, even cooperative; and the second half, in which, betrayed, he becomes a standard alien-menace....Or was his initial friendliness a ruse?--were invasion plans always "on"??

MAN FROM U.N.C.L.E., The see RETURN OF THE MAN FROM U.N.C.L.E.

*The MAN WHO COULD CHEAT DEATH 1959(1958) (The MAN IN RUE NOIR(E)-ad t) Based on Barre Lyndon's play and on the film The MAN IN HALF MOON STREET) Mkp: Roy Ashton. Ref: TV. Lee. BFC. LC. "Films of C.Lee." and with Delphi Lawrence, Francis de Wolff.

Paris, 1890. Dr. Georges Bonner (Anton Diffring), born in 1786, has discovered the "secret of immortal life" and "perpetual health," through the replacement, every ten years, of his utaparathyroid(sp?) gland. He remains youthful, but leaves a trail of missing and murdered models, from San Francisco to Paris, behind him. At the end of these ten-year cycles he relies on a green fluid to keep him young and sane until a new gland can be procured. Finally, he suffers "a lifetime of pain in one moment" when his new assistant, Gerard (Christopher Lee), betrays him and allows him to age all of his 104 years in moments and die.

Jimmy Sangster's plotting in this early Hammer horror is fairly tight, but it does some cheating of its own. Weisz (Arnold Marle)--Bonner's customary operating assistant and Bonner's 89-year-old junior--discovers to his horror that the replacement gland for this decade's operation is taken not from a cadaver but "from a living body." Weisz's discovery comes (most conveniently) after he has enlisted Gerard's help, and assured the latter that he will be present during the operation. (Gerard signs on mainly on the strength of Weisz's reputation.) The outraged Weisz destroys Bonner's supply of the liquid;

Bonner destroys Weisz; Gerard refuses to operate without Weisz.... There's one slight discrepancy: Weisz presumably operated on Bonner in London, San Francisco, and Bern, all sites of previous murders; so the glands for at least the last four decades' operations have come from "living bodies"--Weisz's long-delayed, conveniently-timed realization permits the newcomer Gerard to have both knowledge and disapproval, to be on the inside, intellectually, and on the outside, morally. It permits him, in other words, to become just like all the other characters--excluding Bonner, of course--in the film. Sangster's cribbing with Weisz and Gerard is just part of a pattern. He "loads" the script against Bonner: story, characters, and dialogue ("Have you become God all of a sudden?") are all angled to discredit his discovery. The latter is bad for the world (the population of same would quickly double); bad for his associates and, of course, for his models; and bad even for Bonner himself. (He must pull up roots every 10 years and start anew elsewhere.) What is it good for?--well, possibly, it seems, for promoting literal eternal love. (See also The HUNGER.) All of the script's contrivances could be forgiven if they did not issue into its final, arbitrary dismissal of this last possibility. Bonner's adoring Janine (Hazel Court), informed by him of his eternal-tea-for-two plan, rejects it and him outright, without even considering it. Her visual-and-verbal expression of horror effectively ends the movie (though a superfluous fire follows it), when her reaction--rather-more-carefully thought-out--could have "begun" it, or in part justified it. (Something midway between her horror and Kay's perverse delight--in SON OF DRACULA--at this prospect of immortality would have been interesting. Mere confusion would have been more believable than this stock reaction-shot.) As it is, the film is worth returning to mainly for the performances of Diffring and Lee--Sangster does, at least, supply them with some dramatic fuel....

2P The MAN WHO SAW TOMORROW WB/Wolper 1981 color 88m. SP,D, Co-P: Robert Guenette. SP: also Alan Hopgood. Based on the production "The Prophecies of Nostradamus" by Paul Drane. Ph: Ackerman, Daarstad, Haskins. Mus: Loose, Tillar. AD: Mike Minor. SpFX:(sup) Phil Kellison; COAST;(ph) R. Ryder. SpVideo FX: Hal Landaker. Lasers: Howard Shore. Ref: TV. Barbara Hill. V 3/4/81. Weldon. with Orson Welles, P.L. Clarke(voice of Nostradamus), Richard Butler(Nostradamus), Ray Laska(warlord).

Dramatizations of the predictions of the 16th-century French astrologer Nostradamus, including visions of world-wide famine in 1986, the outbreak of World War III in 1994, an atomic attack on New York City in 1999, the defeat of the "anti-Christ" after 27 years of war, and the end of the world in the year 3797, after 1,000 years of peace....clip from WHEN WORLDS COLLIDE.

O.K. as an Orson Welles radio show; superfluous as a film--the visuals are incidental to the matching-up, in the narration, of prophecy and (alleged) fulfillment-of-prophecy. And the latter seems, at times, merely a sort of glorified name-dropping

(Hitler, the Duke of Windsor, JFK, and RFK are among the names invoked), a "People" magazine of history. Nostradamus appears to have foretold the exploits of any-and-everyone-of-note--since his day--except Sonny Tufts....Nostradamus also foretells disaster...everywhere and in every era. The scriptwriters append an upbeat, let's-beat-the-future-by-changing-it message, but the master's prophecies clearly lend themselves more readily to a defeatist, can't-buck-fate attitude--if you accept them.
See also: JUPITER MENACE, The.

The MAN WHO WASN'T THERE Para/Mancuso 1983 color & 3-D 110m. D: Bruce Malmuth. SP: Stanford Sherman. Ph: F. Moore. Mus: Miles Goodman. AD: Charles Hughes. VisCons: R.W. King. Sp Ph:(fx) Eric Brevig;(cons) Larry Secrist. SpFX: Reel EFX; (coord) Martin Becker. SdFX: Blue Light. Opt: Van Der Veer. Titles: Celestial Mechanix. Ref: screen. SFChron 8/15/83. V 8/17/83. Oakland Trib 8/15/83. with Steve Guttenberg, Jeffrey Tambor, Art Hindle, Lisa Langlois.

U.S. and Russian agents attempt to suppress an inventor's invisibility formula, which, in the wrong hands, could upset the balance of world power....In the course of the movie, phials of the liquid turn two men and two women, temporarily, invisible....A movie designed for superlatives-in-reverse, MAN... even-handedly reduces all its component elements--3-D, invisibility, politics, sex--to the childish. Here, "special visual effects" means strings. And in what is supposedly a comedy, the most striking invisibility effect is a shot of a person's (unseen) back with two knives sticking out of it, and blood dripping from the wounds. Pretty funny. The most striking 3-D effect is a smoke ring blown into the camera "eye," and the movie has to stop dead to get even that in. This movie might rate a mention in a dissertation with a title like "3-D-Motivated Movement and Placement-of-Objects within The Film Frame"--but where it really belongs is in a study on Ineptitude.

*2 The MAN WITH NINE LIVES 1940 Ref: TV: Favorite Films re-r.

Dr. Tim Mason (Roger Pryor), of King Hospital, uses Frozen Therapy to keep a woman in suspended animation for five days while the diseased areas of her body are frozen and controlled. He and his nurse assistant Judith (JoAnn Sayers) then travel to Crater Island, Silver Lake ("near the Canadian border"), and the house of Dr. Leon Kravaal (Boris Karloff), who has succeeded not only in freezing but killing cancer in a lab animal. A fall through rotting floorboards, a walk through a long-forgotten tunnel, and a descent 100 feet down a stairwell lead the two to an "ice chamber" (part of the "underground arm" of a glacier), where they find Kravaal and four other men frozen in glacial ice. Unfrozen, Kravaal revives and soon comes to realize that it was the administration in vapor form of his anesthetic-plus-"activator"-plus-tissue-protecting-solution which kept the five safe in suspended animation for 10 years. A second dose of the vapor, however, proves to act on the men as a poison which makes their blood corpuscles disintegrate. A final test on Judith proves that the vapor does work on fresh subjects....

Hero-villain Kravaal--as a victim of Fate or, rather, of a very unpredictable vapor--is noble one minute, unscrupulous the next. Boris Karloff's performance, too, is a victim of science's whimsicality here--even he can't quite be all things to all twists of plot. Said plot does little except make Kravaal seem, alternately, admirable and heinous. The most comically-abrupt narrative volte-face occurs when Kravaal--who is momentarily resigned to defeat, and who has adjured Mason to return to the mainland and continue his Frozen Therapy experiments--discovers that he needs Mason and Judith as "fresh" subjects for his own further experimentation. The (resigned) Dedicated Scientist instantly becomes a Common Thug, and compels (with gun and threats) the two to remain. There's just no Mr. In-Between....Shot and dying, at the end, Kravaal lastly becomes the Spirit of Science incarnate. "Frozen, but alive!" he cries, as Judith, certifiably, lives, and he dies. Earlier, he was willing and even eager to sacrifice other lives to science; at the end he sacrifices his own--thus does the script define, respectively, "cad" and "hero"....The inaccessibility of Kravaal's ice chamber is very carefully established--and just as surely disestablished. Mason and Judith have to cover a veritable obstacle course in order to get there (see above); but they cover same unbelievably quickly, in jig, or "B" time. Such is the charm of "B"-movie phoniness....

The MAN WITH TWO BRAINS WB/Aspen Film Society(McEuen-Picker) 1983 color 89m. SP,D: Carl Reiner. SP & with: Steve Martin. SP: also George Gipe. Ph: Michael Chapman. Mus: Joel Goldsmith. PD: Polly Platt. SpFxMkp: Lance Anderson. SpFX:(coord) Allen Hall; Clay Pinney, Robert Willard. Gorillas: Kevin Brennan. Ref: screen. V 6/1/83. with Kathleen Turner, David Warner, Don McLeod(gorilla), Merv Griffin(elevator killer), Paul Benedict.

A scientist (Warner) keeps the brains of a killer's victims alive with a "special fluid." The hero, Dr. Hfuhruhurr (Martin), communicates telepathically with one of the brains, and is very happy with the relationship. But she is dying, and he contrives to have the contents of her brain transferred, scientifically, to the body of his dead wife (Turner)--"the perfect mind in the perfect body." The contents of the dead doctor's brain are transferred to a gorilla....A dead-woman's presence makes a wall portrait of her spin and a house shake....cranial screw-top surgery...DONOVAN'S BRAIN on TV.

A comedy re: the ideal of purely-mental sexual attraction. The doctor's wife is, physically, sensational, but has a horror of a personality; his initially-bodiless inamorata proves, when restored to the land of the bodied, to have a tendency (in terms of shape) towards the balloon. The doc doesn't even notice. He wants her for her mind. This psychic kinship between man and brain is, potentially, kind of sweet and kind of funny. But, actually, it's more strange than sweet or funny, perhaps in part because Steve Martin's comic persona is more strange than funny. He's less a character than a comic facade, a mere put-on of a presence. A Steve Martin mask would be a redundancy--he's already plastic. The facade cracks a bit only at moments of emotional vulnerability--moments more in evidence in the more interesting PENNIES FROM HEAVEN than here. These glimpses of pain and insecurity suggest--by way of contrast--that the more familiar Steve Martin is an emotionally-sanitized construct--that the comedian has (consciously or not) carefully insulated himself, as a performer, against feeling. Where the comedy of a Richard Pryor is expressive, Martin's is repressive. Martin expunges himself; Pryor is his own best subject. Martin has no subject, at least as a comedian. Only, at times, as an actor does he seem to give anything of himself. As a comedian, he's a series of unrelated shtiks, a few of them funny (e.g., his sobriety-test/juggling-act here)--and he has been more comedian than actor in his films so far. Martin is generally, at most, a stand-up psychoanalytic curiosity.

MANBEAST! MYTH OR MONSTER CBS-TV/Landsburg-Webster 1978?(1983) SP,D: Nicholas Webster. SP: also Diana Webster. SpMkp: Rob Bottin, Greg Cannon. SpFX,Sd: Brett Webster. SpSd: Neiman-Tillar. Opt: Westheimer. Ref: TV. V 10/14/81:40(ad). SFExam 8/5/83:E1,E6. with Don Hood, Judy Langford.

Film posits that there are two branches of humans: man and manbeast (aka Gigantopithecus or Yeti or Bigfoot), the latter "harmless" and very elusive, yet inhabiting the Himalayas, Siberia, Northwest America, etc., and originating perhaps in China. The domestication of a female Yeti in Russia (circa 1921) is "dramatized." (She mated with her human master.) Also on display: a recreation of a (dead) sideshow Bigfoot... 17" footprints...a tooth six times man-size...a mountain-road "Bigfoot crossing." MANBEAST! backs up its thesis with some photogenic scenery and ace man-ape outfits. (There's also some irrelevant speculation re: the plesiosaurs of Loch Ness.) Or, rather, it decorates its thesis. The movie's "dramatizations" play like random excerpts from Universal Frankenstein films and The SNOW CREATURE. The producers dramatize even when there's no point in dramatizing--e.g., they don't simply play one person's recording of Bigfoot growls; they show the guy recording them. (Insert, irrelevantly, shots of dark woods looking very mysterious....)

MANHUNT IN THE AFRICAN JUNGLE see SECRET SERVICE IN DARKEST AFRICA

MANIAC MANSION see AMUCK!

La MANSION DE LOS MUERTOS VIVIENTES (Sp) Golden 1982 D: Jesus Franco. Ref: V 5/4/83:414: "horror." with Candy Coster, Robert Foster, Mabel Escano.

MARDI GRAS MASSACRE Weis 1983(1978) color 97m. (cf. CRYPT OF DARK SECRETS) SP,D,P,Ph: Jack Weis. Ph: also Don Piel, Jack

McGowan. Mus: Westbound; Dennis Coffey, Mike Theodore. FX: Mike Nahay. Mkp: Albert Brown Jr. Ref: TV: VC II(video). V 12/16/83:12: in St.Louis. 10/5/83:18: in Buffalo. VideoSB. Ecran F 41:72. with Curt Dawson, Gwen Arment, Laura Misch, Wayne Mack, Ronald Tanet, Cathryn Lacey, Nancy Dancer.

New Orleans. An apparently ageless Aztec priest seeks the "most evil" women to sacrifice to the Goddess Coatla-q(sp?), God of The Four Directions and "Queen of Evil in the Universe," aka "The Lady of the Serpent Skirt." He makes her offerings of "red cactus fruit" (i.e., human hearts and blood), fresh from the bodies of prostitutes. ("You are weird, aren't you?") He apparently circles the world endlessly, sacrificing a minimum of three women each year during carnival time in Rio, Costa Rica, etc., and mystically escapes a police dragnet at the end.

Cinematically, zilch. There's more cutting in the Aztec ceremonial chambers than there was in the editing room--even dramatic scenes that all but cry out for close shots are held in long shot. The script--essentially BLOOD FEAST set to disco music--is just one scene repeated several times: the unnamed high priest stabs his (nude) victim's hand, then her foot, then cuts out her heart. A little sex, a little gore, and you have (more or less) a movie. This quasi-snuff movie may, quality-wise, be a step up from BLOOD FEAST, but then ATTACK OF THE KILLER TOMATOES is a step up from BLOOD FEAST....Most of the dialogue is terrible--what's surprising is that a little of it, here and there, rings true, or at least not-wholly-false....

MARS AND BEYOND Ideal/BV-TV 1957 anim 30m. D: Ward Kimball. Ref: TV. Lee. no LC. Jim Shapiro. comic book.

Conjecture re: life on other worlds: Martians from Wells's "War of The Worlds"...other aliens (including "mechanical monsters")..."space wheels"...simulated Mars expedition...dinosaurs....The Disney version of CE3K, and rather charming in its own right.

MAS NEGRO QUE LA NOCHE (Mex) Conacine & SDT c1970? color c90m. SP,D: Carlos E. Taboada. Ph: Daniel Lopez. Mus: Raul Lavista. AD: Salvador Lozano. Ref: TVG. TV: Darker than the Night-tr t. with Claudia Islas, Susana Dosamantes, Lucia Mendez, Helena Rojo, Pedro Armendariz, Julian Pastor.

Killer-with-cane proves to be the ghost of an old woman who haunts her mansion and kills with knitting needles...."cursed cat"...thunderstorms...mysterious sobbing in the night...dialogue reference to vampires....Routine mystery-horror movie, with an odd twist: the "ghostly effects" here (usually explained "logically" in this sort of thriller) actually are created by a ghost....

MASSACRE AT CENTRAL HIGH Brian Dist./Evan Co. 1976 color 86m. SP,D: Renee Daalder. Ph: Bert Van Munster. Mus: Tommy Leonetti. AD: Russell Tune. SpFX: Roger George. Mkp: Peter Deyell. Ref: TV: Electric Video. V 11/17/76. with Derrel Maury(David),

Andrew Stevens, Kimberly Beck, Robert Carradine, Cheryl Smith.
"Dissent around (Central High) is a real bummer." A "little league Gestapo" of students rules--until it pushes newcomer David too far, and leaves him crippled. Subsequently, one of the elite is electrocuted on high-tension wires; another takes a swan-song dive into a darkened--and empty--indoor pool; a third is locked in the back of a runaway van which goes over a cliff and explodes. A campus power struggle ensues, and things get "real, real ugly." A wire-bomb in a car eliminates one of the new elite; a sabotaged hearing aid dispatches another; a dynamite-created landslide takes care of three at once. Obviously, "somebody in this school is insane..."
...and, just as obviously, it's David, who sees the school's original "scared mice" take the seats of power so abruptly vacated by the original neo-Nazis....The first half of MASSACRE AT CENTRAL HIGH is no better or worse, no more nor less interesting, than your average revenge-of-the-outsider thriller. But this movie continues where similar films stop--it's as if CARRIE had turned into Sodom and Gomorrah, U.S.A. The subject broadens, from personal revenge into "divine" justice. Here, God (David) decides who shall die (just about everyone) and who shall live (only his beloved and his best friend). David is characterized strictly by (a) his sense of justice and (b) his sense of personal loyalty--a conflict between these two forces deciding, rather too neatly, the outcome. The characterization in general, here, is less compelling than the movie's Darwinian vision of high school as a den of inequity: you're either on top or on the bottom--there's no in-between. And--as in "Peanuts," there are no adults--here, there are no teachers in evidence; the students are a law unto themselves. Their only education, apparently, is extracurricular. They're not being prepared for life--this is it....

MASTER OF THE WORLD (I) Falco 1983 (PADRONO DEL MONDO) SP,D: Alberto Cavallone(aka Dick Morrow). Ref: V 5/4/83:296. Ecran F 31:47. with Sven Kruger, Sasha D'Harc.
"Set in the days of the cavemen...."(V)

MATCHEMONEDO see CRACKLE OF DEATH

MATTER OF STATE/PHOTO FINISH see SPIDER-MAN...

MAUSOLEUM MPM/Western Int'l.(Barich) 1983(1982) color 96m. D: Michael Dugan. Adap: Robert Barich, Robert Madero. SP: Katherine Rosenwink. Ph,Co-P: Barich. Mus: Jaime Mendoza-Nava. AD: Robert Burns. SpMkpFX: John Buechler;(sup) Maurice Stein;(lighting) John Murray. SpMechFX: Roger George. SpLenses: Dr.M. Greenspoon. Ref: screen. V 2/9/83:4(rated). 5/11/83. with Marjoe Gortner, Bobbie Bresee, La Wanda Page, Norman Burton, Laura Hippe, Bill Vail(final demon).
"The curse of the Nomed women" (who have a "history of possession") holds that the first-born females shall unleash and

then be possessed by a demon from hell, and that only they can reunite the demon and its crown of thorns and thus return it whence it came. The curse befalls Susan Farrell nee Walker (Bresee), who, as a green-glowing-eyed blonde, makes her victims levitate and their chests and faces split open, a man's head ignite, and a car burst into flames. The cackling demon is revealed in monster-form via hypnosis; a mysterious shadow-figure proves to be the demon's guard....Derivative shocker characterized by a Fifties sort of ineptitude--MAUSOLEUM might be BACK FROM THE DEAD with special makeup effects. Susan is a dream-blonde-turned-nightmare, but the ghastliness-out-of-sweetness irony is pretty limp. It's good, however, for lots of "partial nudity" and for the scenes with the demon, who plays strictly by the rules, and flies back to the crypt when re-crowned. In the demon's last scene, it looks as if Susan is simply putting it back to bed--it doesn't even snarl or whine. The demon also comes equipped with portable fog and little, drooling demon-heads for breasts. Alright!

See also: ONE DARK NIGHT.

MAZES AND MONSTERS see RONA JAFFE'S MAZES AND MONSTERS

The MECHANICAL COW Univ/Disney 1927 anim 6m. Ref: Crafton/BM. Maltin/OMAM. LC. no Lee.

Oswald and "a monster."(BM)

MECHANICAL CRABS (Cz) Short Film Prague 1977 anim color 10m. Ref: VideoSB: Phoenix-Video.

Scientist's "ultimate war weapon": "giant mechanical crabs."

Il MEDIUM (I) Ars Nova 1979 SP,D: Silvio Amadio. SP: also Cucca, Fragasso. Ph: Salvatori. Mus: Roberto Pregadio. Ref: Prod Ital. with Vincent Mannari Jr., Susan Buchanan, Martine Brochard, Philippe Leroy.

A medium is called in to exorcise an evil spirit from a 10-year-old boy.

MEGAFORCE Fox/Golden Harvest(Northshore) 1982 color 99m. SP, D: Hal Needham. SP,P: A.S. Ruddy. SP: also Whittaker, Morgan. Story: Kachler. Ph: Michael Butler;(aerial) David Butler. Mus: Jerrold Immel. PD: Joel Schiller. SpFX: Cliff Wenger Sr.;(flying) Zoptic. OptFX: Westheimer. Lasers: Bakshi. Ref: TV. V 6/30/82. Bill Warren. Cinef XIII:1. with Barry Bostwick, Michael Beck, Persis Khambatta, Henry Silva, Edward Mulhare.

MF, created "to preserve freedom and justice" throughout the world, and composed of "Free Forces" from all "Free World" countries, employs drawing-board technology today, including flying motorcycles, a disintegrator-weapon, vehicles with laser guns, "inverse photo-sensitive skin" (which substance takes temporary "impressions" of objects coming into contact with it), holographs, an infrared topographical scanner, and a computer which stores data from conversations monitored at military command posts around the world.

Another excuse for explosion and pyrotechnic effects. The movie pits the heroes of the "Free World" (a term left undefined within the film) against tyranny and evil, but is, politically, about as serious as a pomegranate. And as far as pure action goes, The ROAD WARRIOR does it better. The characters speak odd, arch "comic" dialogue and are so flip and nonchalant that the movie all but evaporates before it's even over.

MEGURIAI UCHU see KIDO SENSHI

MEN'S INHUMANITY TO MEN (H.K.) Golden Harvest 1982? D & with: Samo Hung. Ref: V 5/12/82:329. JFFJ 14:36.

"Horror-comedy...ghosts and other devils...."(V)

MERLIN THE MAGICIAN see OLD LEGENDS NEVER DIE

MESSAGE FROM THE FUTURE (Israeli) 1982? D: David Avidan. Ref: V 7/28/82:30(FJA): TV sf. Ecran F 22:52.

METALSTORM: THE DESTRUCTION OF JARED-SYN Univ/Band Int'l.(Metalstorm) 1983 color & 3-D 83m. D,P: Charles Band. SP,P: Alan J. Adler. Ph: Mac Ahlberg. Mus: Richard Band. AD: Pamela B. Warner. SpVisMkpFX: MkpFX Labs; D.J. White, A. Apone et al; (key sculptor) Kenny Myers; F.H. Isaacs. SpOptFX: Van Der Veer. SpMechFX: P.O.V. Screenworks. SpAnim: Tony Alderson, Janice Carlberg;(fx) E.D. Farino, B. Mixon. Sp 3-D FX: Fantasy Creations;(sup) F.X. Carrisosa;(cost) Kathie Clark. SpFX: Joe Quinlivan. Min: Tony Trembly et al. Titles: Celestial Mechanix; (cloud) Energy. SdDes: Jay Wertz, James Thornton. Ref: screen. V 8/24/83. MFB'84:80. with Jeffrey Byron, Mike Preston(Jared-Syn), Tim Thomerson, R.D. Smith(Baal), Larry Pennell, R. Moll.

Togetherness--and the Magic Mask from the Lost City--help defeat the evil Jared-Syn, his metal-armed son Baal, and their Master Crystal (which contains the life-forces of the dead). The evil ones possess telepathic and dream-like teleportation powers, and send an "electric," blue monster to fight the Ranger-hero at one point....sand-mole monsters, Cyclopean warriors, etc....The 3-D process gives the backgrounds in METALSTORM a cycloramic depth which, with any luck, will take your mind and eyes off the foreground inanity--otherwise, the 3-D is a melange of blurs, bars, and other unintended optical effects. The movie itself is about the lamest of the STAR WARS--ROAD WARRIOR coattailers. (The outfitting of hero and vehicles seems especially indebted to The ROAD WARRIOR.) The plot is the usual you-gotta-go-here-and-see-this-guy, then-go-there-and-ask-that-guy mythic trek. An occasional monster or effect will perk things up for a moment or two, no longer.

METAMORPH, The see COSMIC PRINCESS

METEOR, The see IT CAME FROM OUTER SPACE

MICHAEL JACKSON'S THRILLER see THRILLER

MICKEY'S CHRISTMAS CAROL BV/Disney 1983 anim color 25m. D, P: Burny Mattinson. SP: Alan Dinehart et al, from Charles Dickens's story "A Christmas Carol." Mus: Irwin Kostal. AD: Don Griffith. FxAnim: Jeff Howard et al. Ref: screen. Jim Shapiro. MFB'84:27.

The story of Scrooge, as enacted by Disney cartoon characters, with Scrooge McDuck (of course) as Scrooge (voice: Alan Young), Goofy as Marley's ghost, Jiminy Cricket as the Ghost of Christmas Past, the giant from "Mickey and the Beanstalk" (a segment of FUN AND FANCY FREE) as the ghost of Christmas present, and Pegleg Pete as the Death-like ghost of Christmas Future....The Dickens story, reduced to essentials, with no time for atmospherics (except for fiery intimations of a future hell for the pre-repentant Scrooge) or dramatic development. This is more a roll-call for Disney than a retelling of Dickens. The Ghost of Cartoons Past is the movie's busiest spectre--the other ghosts get short shrift. They should, really, be allowed a little more time at least to work on Scrooge. Result: a Scrooge all-too-easily cowed.

MIGHTY MOUSE IN THE GREAT SPACE CHASE see GREAT SPACE CHASE, The

MIL GRITOS TIENE LA NOCHE see PIECES

The MIRACLE FIGHTERS (H.K.-Cant.) Wo Ping Co. & Golden Harvest 1982 color 100m. D: Yuen Wo Ping. Ref: V 8/25/82. with Leung Ka Yen, Yuen Cheung Yan.

Two mediums vs. a devil....Finale with "10,000 snakes... kung fu, horror, fantasy...."

*The MIRACLE RIDER 1935 Ph: Ernest Miller, William Nobles. Sup Ed: Joseph H. Lewis. Ref: TV. and with Bob Fraser, Niles Welsh (Dr.Metzger), Edmund Cobb, Bob Kortman, Tom London, Charles King.

"Evil spirits," in the form of the dreaded Firebird, terrorize the Ravenhead Indian Reservation. ("This land is cursed!") There is, however, "nothing supernatural about" the Firebird. Its "fire" proves to be rays (which burn a haystack), and its "claws," a wireless-controlled rocket-glider with "interlocking coils." ("So that's the Firebird that's been scaring the Indians!") It's all a plot by the unscrupulous Zaroff (Charles Middleton) to mine and sell X-94 (a mineral which invests bullets with explosive force) to foreign agents. He communicates with the latter via a "wireless" which spells out words ticker-tape fashion on a screen....The first episode of this serial is busy enough, but the skullduggery which follows is routine. The cliffhangers are mostly hero-jumps-out-before-car/truck/glider-crashes cheats. And there's really nothing supernatural or science-fictional about the Firebird--it's all done with strings....Tom Mix as Texas Ranger Tom Morgan is about as charismatic as a footstool; his acting, indistinguishable from rigor mortis.

2 MISS MORISON'S GHOSTS WGBH-TV(Boston) 1981('83-U.S.) Ph: Richard Crafter; John Shann; Les Young, Gail Tattersall. Mus: Wilfred Josephs. PD: Eileen Diss. Mkp: Jane Boot. Ref: TV. TVG. and with Anna Korwin(Marie Antoinette), Niall Toibin.

1901. Two women (Wendy Hiller & Hannah Gordon) peep "through a curtain of time," via, perhaps, the "imperfect memory" of Marie Antoinette, and catch "disjointed" visual and aural echoes of the "violent convulsions" at Versailles on September 5, 1792....This is easily the most tolerable of the based-on-fact psychic thrillers which have been proliferating in recent years. It, too, finally asks for more than a suspension of your disbelief, but it doesn't require it. It places its displays of psychic phenomena within an historical and social context sufficiently detailed to engage one dramatically. The ghost, or memory, of Marie Antoinette is simply a single element in its tapestry--if, it's true, the most tantalizing element. The theme which finally emerges from the script, however--individual integrity vs. social and educational progress (the furor attendant on the ladies' published account of their experience jeopardizes the future of St. Gilbert's College)--is markedly-less-tantalizing than their "retro-cognitive" experience, and investigation into same. What makes the experience so intriguing is that the misses Morison and Lamont see nothing fantastic or extraordinary per se, simply landscapes and people-in-costumes (who might just be part of a pageant) slightly misplaced--by about a century. (The path they take in 1901 through the gardens of Versailles ceased to exist in 1802.) Only their later research reveals what an extraordinary walk they took: Miss Lamont, for instance, repeats musical phrases--caught by her, during that walk--which prove never to have been published, simply circulated at the palace of Louis XVI. The revelations here are not at all horrific, but they do leave a "Twilight Zone" chill. They mark quiet, subtle transitions from the ordinary to the extraordinary. They're indications of, either, capable storytellers (if one suspects that the historical research was done before the fact) or capable reporters (if one accepts that all research was done after the fact)....

*MISSILE TO THE MOON Layton(Frederic-Foley) 1958 AD: Sham Unltd. Mkp: Harry Thomas. SdFxEd: H.E. Wooley. Ref: TV. FM 18:20. Weldon. and with Tommy Cook, Nina Bara.

Two escaped convicts hide out from the police in the cabin of a solar-powered rocket ship. Yes, they do. It proves to belong to a man from the moon who came to Earth seeking a new land for the people of Orlanda(sp?), a now-exclusively-female lunar kingdom fast running out of food and oxygen (but rich in diamonds). Its queen, or Lido(sp?), dominates others with hypnotic will-power....Featured monsters: rock creatures which thrive in sunlight, but die when exposed to oxygen...The Dark One, a huge but diseased-looking, easily-dispatched spider.

A TV staple in the early Sixties (at least in the Stockton-Sacramento area), and every bit as tacky as its many fans may remember its being. This must be one of the most uncalled-for remakes in movie history. (The original was CAT-WOMEN OF THE MOON.) It, too, has camp possibilities, but plays too tamely. The "best" lines are gone--all that's left are cardboard cut-outs of rocks and rockets, the obligatory meteorite-field scare, instant-eerie moonscape music, etc. The original Lido here looks like Auntie Mame gone geisha. The other women in the moon don't look like beauty-contest winners either, though, supposedly, they were. The dramatic menu features familiar items like treachery (human and alien), self-sacrifice (alien), instant romance (human-alien), and greed (human)....

MR. TERRIFIC see PILL CAPER, The

MISTERO DELLA QUATTRO CORONA see TREASURE OF THE FOUR CROWNS

MOAN AND GROAN, INC. MGM/Roach 1929 15m. SP,D: Robert McGowan. Ref: TV. Maltin/SSS. no Lee. LC. with "Our Gang"(Farina, Jackie Cooper, etc.), Edgar Kennedy, Max Davidson.
"Haunted" house. Typical primitive, pre-Spanky-and-Alfalfa "Little Rascals" comedy.

MOBILE SUIT GUNDAM see GANDAMU. GANDAMU II. KIDO SENSHI.

MODERN PROBLEMS Fox/Shapiro 1981 color 91m. SP,D: Ken Shapiro. SP: also Tom Sherohman, Arthur Sellers. Ph: Edmond Koons. Mus: Dominic Frontiere. PD: Jack Senter. SpFX: Ira Anderson Jr.; Puck, Broussard. SpVisFX: Triplane Films;(des sup) Jane Simpson;(anim) Lorraine Bubar;(anim ph) R&B EFX;(roto) Diana Wilson;(opt) Movie Magic. Mkp: Jack Wilson. Ref: V 12/30/81. TV. with Chevy Chase, Patti D'Arbanville, Dabney Coleman, Mary Kay Place, Nell Carter, Brian Doyle-Murray, Mitch Kreindel.
Exposure to nuclear waste gives an air-traffic controller telekinetic powers; unleashes the "monster inside" him. He makes a man levitate, a ballet dancer fly...induces an orgasm in his girl friend and a nosebleed in his rival...and stops a bullet in mid-air. Finally, his power is transferred (through a TV antenna) to a maid....EXORCIST voodoo scene...nightmare with hero-as-airplane....Bad as comedy; beyond bad as a psychological study. When a movie goes as wrong as this one does, it's hard to say where it could have gone right. As a telekinesis comedy, it's outclassed by SUPER FUZZ; as the story of a man over-compensating telekinetically, it looks up to PATRICK. Smart-ass Chase translates frustrated pique, anger, fear, and shame into telekinetic tricks--but underlying all his stunts is a perhaps-unintended element of smugness....The director doesn't seem to know whether to treat his hero's experiences as a lark or as a cautionary tale re: self-indulgence, and his uncertainty produces a true narrative grotesque.

*The MOLE PEOPLE 1956 Mus sc: Hans J. Salter. Mkp:(sup) Bud Westmore;(des) Millicent Patrick et al. Ref: TV. Jim Shapiro.

Warren/KWTS! Hirschhorn. Weldon. Stanley.

In a prologue, Dr. Frank Baxter describes this movie as a "culmination" of man's long-standing desire to look inside the Earth, to explain the "strange sighs and noises" reportedly issuing from some "inner, habitable world"....Asia. An ancient stone tablet and oil lamp tell of a vanished dynasty, which, at the time of The Flood, traveled in a Sumerian version of Noah's Ark to the top of a mountain--inside said mountain, an archaeological expedition discovers a race of light-over-sensitive albinos who use hunchbacked, mute, mole-like "Beasts of the Dark" for slaves, and who make population-control living-sacrifices to sunlight (which for them is lethal). At the end, the moles revolt, the earth quakes, and our heroes escape.

Dr. Baxter asks us to "study this picture and think about it when it's over. It's a fable with a meaning and a significance" for us....Obviously, he didn't see the film. It's about as significant and meaningful as FIRE MAIDENS OF OUTER SPACE, which it more or less resembles in terms of story. Our enlightened hero (John Agar), it's true, disapproves, morally, of the albinos' rule-of-the-whip, and their destruction is perhaps meant to be significant, but is just a cliche. Baxter's attempts to make inner-Earth theories sound like honest scientific speculation and unlike poppycock are actually more entertaining than the movie itself. The script is all wrong-moves, from the "Marked One," our non-albino heroine (Cynthia Patrick), who provides a bit of love interest and then dies, to the mole people, who provide a bit of horror and then revolt and die.... John Agar's voice here is like an aural time-capsule: it seems to contain the un-dulcet tones of every beloved third-rate Fifties sf "B." Agar gives each phony line (e.g., "Your heart--it beats with tenderness") the ring of phoniness it deserves. (Our hero has hardly met this underground sweetie before he begins analyzing her soul.) His Roger Bentley is supposed to be wise, understanding, and caring; Agar sounds, simply, as if he had had a bad day at the office....Salter's trekking-and-climbing music is pleasing, if the dramatic sections of the score are shrill. He makes it seem as if there might be something interesting in that old mountain, but no....

MONGREL Rondo-Sutherland & Jenkins 1982 color 91m. SP,D: Robert A. Burns. Ph: Richard Kooris. Mus: Ed Guinn. AD: Paul R. Smith; Dave Pearce. SpFxMkp: Smith. Opt: Exceptional. (A)

MONKEY'S PAW, The(by W.W.Jacobs) see DEATHDREAM

*The MONOLITH MONSTERS 1957 (MONOLITH-orig t) Mkp: Bud Westmore. Narr: Paul Frees. Ref: TV. Lee. LC. Warren/KWTS! Hirschhorn. Stanley. Weldon. and with Richard Cutting, Linda Scheley.

The Problem confronted by The MONOLITH MONSTERS: how, convincingly, to turn rocks into monsters. There is, it seems--on the strength of this movie and MISSILE TO THE MOON--no Solution. Animal and vegetable monsters abound in creature features;

but you don't find many mineral-monsters, and for good reason. The (water-stimulated, salt-halted) living rocks here are, it's true, fairly picturesque, and conceptually fascinating. But they are not menacing, or monstrous--despite all the rumbling-and-crashing sound effects. They're impersonal. They bear more relation to disasters like floods and earthquakes than they do to monsters. They don't quite fit the Universal sf-movie formula, and the script, unfortunately, fails to come up with a new format for these intriguing natural phenomena. The monoliths grow, teeter, crash, and begin to grow again; they're implacable, but rather repetitious. In the course of the movie, the camera zooms, or tracks, into monolith fragments several times--but, dramatically, the film never gets beyond this early stage of Ominousness.

*MONSTER ON THE CAMPUS 1958 Ref: TV. Hirschhorn. Lee. LC. and with Eddie Parker(primitive man).

Plasma ingested from a dead, gamma-ray-treated coelecanth triggers "evolution-in-reverse"; temporarily turns Prof. Donald Blake (Arthur Franz) into the subhuman "Beast of Dunsfield".... dragonfly-into-giant...dog-into-primitive-dog...woman who's scared to death....Late, unlamented, Jack Arnold/Universal sf-er, with limp the-savage-beneath-the-civilized-man ironies. In retrospect, the Arnold sub-cult seems founded principally upon a Richard Matheson screenplay (The INCREDIBLE SHRINKING MAN), or strength of same....Prize exchange here: Franz: "Your dog is a throwback." Troy Donahue:(huffily) "He's a German Shepherd!" Second prize: one coed's "And if there was a giant dragonfly, then there could be a primitive man too." Logic....

MOON MADNESS (F) (HBO-TV)/Jean Image & Films A2 1983 anim color 75m. SP,D: Jean Image. SP,Prod D: Frances Image. Suggested by H.G. Wells' novel "The First Men in the Moon." Ph: Jack Capo. Mus: Haim Saban, Shuki Levi. Des: Gonzalez, Olivier. SpFX: Vincent Levan, Gilbert Nottin. Ref: TV.

In the year 1787, the Baron von Munchausen and his crew travel by the hot-air-balloon-powered sailing ship Clair de Lune to a crater inside the moon. There they find the three-legged, horned Selenites--bodiless heads and headless bodies which keep in close contact with each other and which are hatched from nuts. The accordion-necked Greenie-Meanies launch a spaceship attack (from their space station) on the Selenites, and deploy hordes of "munchers," lawnmower-like robot-"insects"-with-rays. Munchausen & co. aid the Selenite cause and are awarded jewels insuring eternal youth....coda set in 1997... three-eyed, alligator-like monsters...flying dragon-mounts... living, marching rock-hordes (cf. MISSILE TO THE MOON and The MONOLITH MONSTERS!)...dragon-"train"...huge honeybees.

Munchausen and his crew here are about the most foolish bunch of adventurers since the Doc Savage books. They giggle and guffaw and "ooh!" and "ahh!", and are all-around general embarrassments. The "weird beasts" on and about the moon, however, are entertaining--the munchers, especially, are a kick. They use their rays to turn the bees into cone-like formations, then have a good (though very unprofessional) laugh at the expense of the defeated....

MORTE A SORRISO ALL ASSASSINO, La see DEATH SMILES ON A MURDERER

La MORTE-VIVANTE (F) Films ABC-Films du Yaka-Films Aleriaz-Selsky 1982 color SP,D: Jean Rollin. Ph: Max Monteillet. Mus: Philippe d'Aram. SpFX: Benoit Lestang. Ref: Ecran F 31: 48,57. V 7/21/82:32. with Francoise Blanchard(Catherine), Marina Pierro, Mike Marshall.

Beautiful zombie who must have blood to prolong her living-death.

MORTELLE RANDONEE (F) Telema & TF 1 1983 color 120m. D: Claude Miller. SP: Michel & Jacques Audiard, from Marc Behm's novel "Eye of the Beholder." Ph: Pierre Lhomme. Mus: Carla Bley. AD: J.-P. Kohut-Svelko. Mkp: C. Desmaemacker. Ref: V 4/13/83: Deadly Circuit-tr t. 5/4/83:401. Ecran F 39:13. with Michel Serrault, Isabelle Adjani, Genevieve Page, Guy Marchand, Sami Frey, Stephane Audran, Macha Meril.

"Pathological murderess...seducing and slaughtering rich young socialites....A female Landru, executing husbands and lovers with bloodcurdling abandon....atmosphere of nightmare."(V)

MORTUARY FVI/Artists Releasing/Hickmar(Movie Makers) 1983(1981) color 92m. SP,D,P: Howard Avedis. SP,P & with: Marlene Schmidt. Ph: Gary Graver. Mus: John Cacavas. AD: Randy Ser; Ed Wolf. SpFx&Mkp: Jim Gillespie, Diane Seletos. Opt: Ray Mercer. SdDes: Biggart. Ref: screen. V 2/16/83:24. 9/28/83. with Mary McDonough, Lynda Day George, David Wallace, Christopher George, Bill Paxton(Paul), Alvy Moore.

A mad-insane and mad-angry mortician's-son (Paxton) dons horror-mask and cloak and skulks about, killing his "enemies" with an aspirator, or trocar, and embalming them, in preparation for his "wedding" to his Cliffside Junior College, would-be sweetheart (McDonough), whom he intends to embalm alive. A Mozart fan, he conducts an imaginary orchestra for his mortuary "guests," but the "bride," sleepwalking, interrupts the ceremony and sleep-axes him to death. "It's all over," more or less, when, suddenly, the embalmed body of Paul's mother (Donna Garrett) returns to life....

There are also seances and black masses, conducted by the mortician himself (C.George) at Heaven's Gate, and a nightmare in which the "highly imaginative" Christie imagines her father returning to life. These bonus ingredients prove, however, to be simply red herrings, rather-too-elaborate devices calculated to make the viewer believe that the dead are somehow returning. Thus this movie is a double, self-canceling cheat: the dead don't really return to life--except in the last shot, ha ha! It is also true, however, that the script could play fair, and this film would still be pretty bad. It's a budget special made by people who know that they're making a horror movie but don't know how to make one. They do their darnedest to make Paul seem pathologically perverse. He's sad when he stabs his father with the aspirator ("Dad! I didn't mean it!"); happy when all are gathered for his "wedding." But he remains a collection of straining-for-the-macabre details. The other principals aren't even that. The kids here might be left over from summer-camp-atrocity movies; the adults appear to be in search of a director. The movie's one semi-eerie scene: night, and the house's electricity (lights, stereo) keeps going on and off....

MOST DANGEROUS GAME, The(by R.Connell) see ESCAPE 2000

MRS. FRISBY AND THE RATS OF NIMH(by R.C.O'Brien) see SECRET OF NIMH, The

2 MS. 45 Rumson & Pacific 1981(1980) AD: Ruben Masters. SpFX: Matt Vogel, Sue Dalton. Mkp: Lisa Monteleone. Titles: Summit. SdFX: John McIntire. Mus&FxEd: Christopher Andrews. Ref: screen. PFA notes 10/31/82. Weldon. Ecran F 26:50.

New York. A young woman, Thana (Zoe Tamerlis), raped twice in one day, is slowly transformed (before our eyes) into a smoothly-efficient, man-killing machine; she stores parts of one victim in her refrigerator....regurgitating bathtub drain, and nod to PSYCHO...nightmare sequence...Halloween costume-party Draculas....Script, direction, music, editing, and acting are all in synch here, at the service of an unnerving fantasy of retribution, a Gothic GLORIA....MS. 45 is very involving, though our involvement is oddly impersonal. We're not really invited to identify with Thana and her vendetta against predatory males--she seems slightly out-of-kilter at the beginning of the movie (partly, perhaps, because she's a mute, partly because her eyebrows converge crazily); very out-of-kilter at the end: she conducts her climactic Halloween-party massacre in a nun's habit, which complements/clashes with her lips, decorated in their customary burst of shocking-red. (She has her .45 parked underneath, in her garter belt.) Nor do we identify with her victims, who, generally, are creeps and bit parts. The movie is infused with a sense of horror and a sense of exhilaration, but it's less characterization than surreal-situation which generates this double-sense. This is third-person spectacle, not first-person drama. It enables us to live out, or to see lived-out, a rather extreme fantasy of inviolability. Thana is not only strange, she's charmed--even when, once, her gun fails to fire, her suicidal victim obliges and shoots himself. After her double-rape, she can do no wrong, or, rather, she can have no wrong done to her. She seems to be wearing an invisible protective shield as she coolly dispatches horny photographers, pimps, muggers, etc. She clearly has something more than the element of surprise going for her. She might be an earthbound goddess of vengeance--Diana the Sharpshooter--susceptible only to...another woman. She's Wonder Woman without bracelets. Her safe passage through the dregs of New York City seems ensured by a sort of fantasy logic--by, that is, the fact that she kills only men, and then only predatory men, not women and not (as is revealed to us in a coda) little dogs, no matter how much the latter may annoy her. (The two non-predators she tracks escape, through chance, logic's proxy.) And Thana, in fact, kills herself, accidentally, as she backs into the fatal knife. She leads a charmed life and death. She's so cool, even cold, a femme fatale, that the movie is, very strangely, very funny. She's mute, yielding, complaisant--a "perfect date"--until she pulls out her .45--her only way of saying "No." Thana is a chillingly sick joke on urban social horrors, a fresh, wit's-end response to the banality of violent crime and male aggressiveness....Thana, The Nun That Stalked New York.

MUMMIES see DEMON AND THE MUMMY. DOS FANTASMAS Y UNA MUCHACHA. RIDERS OF THE WHISTLING SKULL. SATOMI HAKKENDEN. SECRETO DE LA MOMIA, El. SORCERESS. TIME WALKER. VOODOO BLACK EXORCIST(II).

MUNDO DE LOS MUERTOS, El see SANTO EN EL MUNDO DE LOS MUERTOS

MUNDO DI YOR, Il see YOR...

MURDER BY PHONE (Can.) New World/Cooper & CFDC & Famous Players (Canada Trust) 1981('83-U.S.) color 78m. (BELLS-orig t. The CALLING and HELL'S BELLS-int ts) D: Michael Anderson. Story,SP: Michael Butler, Dennis Shryack. SP: also John K. Harrison. Story: also Armondo, Whiton. Ph: Reginald Morris. Mus: John Barry. PD: Seamus Flannery. SpFX: Myatt, Piersig et al. MkpSup: Maureen Sweeney. Ref: screen. V 1/26/83. 10/20/82:125(ad). Cinef XIII:6. Ecran F 30:25. with Richard Chamberlain, John Houseman, Sara Botsford, Robin Gammell, Gary Reineke, Barry Morse.

Death by "lightning in the telephone" traced to wronged inventor's perfection of telephone-receivers-as-capacitors for "spontaneous discharge" of accumulated voltage....Transmitter destroyed by "electrical flashback" of power to source....For those who are already non-fans of ringing telephones--current models seem to have only "loud" and "louder" settings--this movie will serve only to confirm your disaffection. Telephones here not only ring, they make the victim's face bleed, then blast him through the nearest wall or window. This remote-control-murder idea more or less recapitulates the duel-via-telephone scene in SCANNERS, while the inventor-vs.-corporation plot goes back to DEVIL BAT(1941) and NIGHT KEY(1937) and is, here, just as flimsy, simply a vehicle for some amusing acting by, principally, Reineke and Houseman, and some amusing stunts by the effects people. The producers, unfortunately, were not allowed to use the "Reach out and touch someone" line. One assumes, at least, that they asked....

MURDER IN AMITYVILLE(by H.Holzer) see AMITYVILLE II

The MUSICAL DOCTOR Para 1932 8m. D: Ray Cozine. SP,Mus: Timberg & Lerner. Ref: TV. LC. no Lee. with Rudy Vallee, Mae Questal.

"Televisor" brings in images of patients in hospital's rooms. Silly musical short.

MUTANT see FORBIDDEN WORLD

MUTANTS OF 2051 A.D. see STRANGE BREW

*MUTINY IN OUTER SPACE AA/Hugo Grimaldi 1965(1964) (ATTACK FROM OUTER SPACE-int t) Story: Grimaldi, A.C. Pierce. Ph: Arch Dalzell. Mus&SdFxD: Gordon Zahler. AD: Paul Sylos. SpFX: Roger George. Min: Edwards Art Studio. Mkp: Ted Coodley. Sd FX: Josef von Stroheim. Ref: TV. AFI. Lee. LC: c1964. and with Francine York, Glen(n) Langan.

Heat-happy "alien growth...literally eats (victims) up".... Tacky-bland sf/monster-movie at least serves up a few lines--e.g., "I'm not as well-versed in fungi as you, Faith," or (almost as good) "He's on the brink of space raptures!"--and one newspaper headline--"Killer Fungus Threatens Earth." The monster-moss just sort of hangs around the space station, gathering.

See also: UNKNOWN TERROR, The.

The MYSTERIOUS CASTLE IN THE CARPATHIANS (Cz) Int'l. Film/Barrandov(FSB) 1982(1981) color 97m. (TAJEMSTVI HRADU V KARPATECH) SP,D: Oldrich Lipsky. SP: also Jiri Brdecka. From Jules Verne's novel "Le Chateau des Carpathes" or "The Castle of the Carpathians." Ph: Viktor Ruzika. Mus: Lubos Fiser. AD: Zazvorka, Stahl. Ref: screen: The Mysterious Castle in Carpathia-cr t. UC Theatre notes 4/30/83. V 9/29/82:25: at Sitges. Ecran F 30:29,36: at Paris sf fest.41:32-3. with Michael Docolomanky(Teleke), Jan Hartl, Milos Kopecky(Gorz), Rudolf Hrusinsky(Orphanic), Evelyne Steimarova(Salsa).

In 19th-century Europe, opera-buff Baron Gorz keeps his beloved prima donna, Salsa, "alive" after death by preserving her embalmed body in an airtight room; her voice, on a "Quadrophonograph" recording; and her image, on celluloid. The "manifestations" which give his castle the name of "Devil's Castle" and the reputation of being haunted are actually the work of his aide, Prof. Orphanic, who has fired 421 (abortive) moon rockets from the castle, and whose explosive grains of "Orphanic" are used in Operation Robert the Devil to blow the castle (and the baron) to bits at the end....Among the professor's inventions: TV, neon lights, an elevator, a "telephorum" (binoculars), and a gravity-annulling device....hero-as-opera-Quasimodo...Chateau Dracula "vintage '80"...town, Werewolfsville...reference to opera, "The Vampire's Curse."

This Gothic comedy is much broader than it is funny. It goes for belly laughs and it does get a few--e.g., the baron's knife-in-portrait "revenge" on Salsa's fiance, the opera star Teleke (each thrust of his knife elicits a (recorded) operatic groan from the portrait)--it works for the baron, the latter explains, like acupuncture....But none of the characters, or caricatures, are very imaginatively conceived--although Hrusinsky as Orphanic makes his updating of Dr. Strangelove (mechanical hand and all) entertainingly seedy-vile. The mechanically-preserved prima donna is a nice elaboration on Verne's oddball premise of the scientifically-"haunted" castle....

*The MYSTERIOUS DOCTOR 1943 Mkp: Perc Westmore. Ref: TV. FM 18: 22. V 2/24/43. no Lee. "B" Movies. Weldon.

Morgan's Head, a mining town in war-time Cornwall. A local "grisly story" has it that "the headless ghost of Black Morgan" haunts the town and its mine and has claimed at least five victims, all found with their heads cut off. ("The ghost were in the mine!") The "ghost" proves to be a member of the German nobility....The landlord of the town's Running Horse Inn, Simon Tewksbury (Frank Mayo), wears a hood, a la a hangman ("looks a bit scary"), his face having been disfigured by dynamite.

You know your mystery script is in trouble when it devotes half its time to a red herring--here, the village idiot (Matt Willis). The "ghost" itself is about as imposing as a department-store-window mannequin. It's Tewksbury who gets the horror-makeup treatment, while the title refers to a doctor (Lester Matthews) who proves to be one of the good guys....Okay on atmosphere (mostly fog) and music (probably stock)--but the movie is a cross between a horror-mystery and a war-bonds rally.

MYSTERIOUS MOSE Para 1930 anim 8m. D: Dave Fleischer. Anim: Bowsky & Sears. Ref: screen. Lee(LC).

Betty Boop and Bimbo in a haunted house. Cute and kicky.

MYSTERIOUS TWO NBC-TV/Landsburg 1982(1979) SP,D: Gary Sherman. Ph: Steve Poster. Mus: Joe Renzetti. AD: Elayne Ceder. SpFX: Robbie Knott. SpComputerizedFX: Sherman, Wyndham Hanaway, James Warner. Mkp: John Norin. Opt: Modern. SpSdFX: Neiman-Tillar. Ref: TV. TVG. with John Forsythe(He), Priscilla Pointer(She), James Stephens, Robert Pine, Noah Beery Jr., Vic Tayback, E.J. Andre, Bill Quinn.

Two humanoids--apparently "from another galaxy"--arrive in New Mexico, make like celestial evangelists. Heavy-handed.

MYSTERY! FRANKENSTEIN--LEGEND OF TERROR (J) Toei-TV 1981 anim Ref: JFFJ 14:9: TV-movie inspired by the Frankenstein films and by Marvel's "Frankenstein" comic books.

*MYSTERY OF EDWIN DROOD 1935 Mus: Edward Ward. AD: Albert S. D'Agostino. SpFX: John P. Fulton. Ref: TV. V 3/27/35. TVG: "horror story." Weldon: crypt set from DRACULA. Hirschhorn.

1864. Murder-victim's body dissolved in quicklime, buried in cathedral crypt...opium-nightmare sequence ("Queer things happen in dreams!")...murder-by-andiron..."great storm" sequence...midnight-in-the-graveyard sequence...Claude Rains as choirmaster/opium-addict Jasper, variously described as "a monster" and a "dreadful ghost." ("Must I carve (demons) out of my heart?") Tortuously-plotted, not-very-rewarding Dickens adaptation, resolved by incredible coincidences/deductions/disguises and a shilling or two in the right hand. There's no mystery for the viewer (who knows not only whodunit, but who's going to do it, before he does it), and little drama: Rains' bouts of anguished love and guilt seem haphazardly interjected, here and there, into the storyline. Of note only as a curious intersection of Dickens and Universal (and, intermittently, as a curious vehicle for Rains)--all the two seem to have in common is the forbidding Gothic atmosphere. The elements of the latter in the art direction and music manage, nobly, to survive the script....

*The MYSTERY OF THE YELLOW ROOM MOMA 1930 102m. (Le MYSTERE DE LA CHAMBRE JAUNE) SP: L'Herbier? Ph: Burel, Toporkoff. Mus: Edouard Flament. AD: Jaquelux. Models: Meerson, Barsacq. Ref: screen. Chirat: sequel: Le PARFUM DE LA DAME EN NOIR(P). and with Huguette, Leon Belieres, Maxime Desjardins, Edmond Van Daele, Henri Kerny, Kissa Kouprine.

Skulking killer in horror-mask...thunder and lightning...laboratory with neon-light apparatus...old dark country estate...howling wind and weird animal-cries ("C'est un drole de chat!")...spoken credits (except for an eerie tin-foil(?) title credit).... Routine mystrionics. The hyperbolic horror-atmospherics are fun, but they give way to a dialogue-clogged, formula mystery-story. All of the movie's strange sights and sounds seem to subside, mysteriously, when the story takes over. Roland Toutain is the rather-monotonously-energetic reporter-hero.

Die NACHT DES SCHICKSALS (W.G.) Munich F&TAP-BR-Emotion 1982 color 90m. SP,D: Helmer von Luetzelburg. Sequel to the short WHAT DO YOU THINK OF THE DEATH OF WILMA MONTESI? SP: also C. Wagenknecht, A.M. Klug. Ph: A. Witt. Mus: Klug. Sets: Wagenknecht. Ref: V 7/21/82. PFA notes 10/10/78. with Melitta Wolke-Desinee, Wolf Rettig, Billie Zoeckler.

"Haunted castle" with "ghoulish lovables."(V)

NATIONAL LAMPOON'S CLASS REUNION Fox/ABC 1982 color 84m. (AMERICAN CLASS-F) D: Michael Miller. SP: John Hughes. Ph: Phil Lathrop. Mus: Peter Bernstein, Mark Goldenberg. PD: D.E. Mitzner. SpFX: Paul Stewart, James Camomile. Mkp:(des) John Chambers; Del Armstrong et al. SpSdFX: Alan Howarth. Opt: Westheimer. Titles: Wayne Fitzgerald, Modern. Ref: TV: Vestron Video. V 11/3/82. MFB'83:190-91. Ecran F 22:4. with Gerrit Graham, Michael Lerner, Fred McCarren, Miriam Flynn, Blackie

Dammett(Walter), Misty Rowe, Chuck Berry, Jim Staahl(Egon Von Stoker), Zane Buzby(Delores), Shelley Smith, Stephen Furst.

Mad Walter Baylor--who disguises his features with paper bags and lifelike masks--plots diabolical revenge on Lizzie Borden High's Class of '72, at their 10-year reunion....His ex-classmate Delores sold herself to the devil and can breathe fire and wind....School blood-drive sponsor Egon is a vampire.

A horror takeoff geared more towards charm than sidesplitting--or perhaps the charm is all that's left when the gags fizzle, as they generally do here. The comic characters in CLASS REUNION are, basically, appealingly loopy, but seem rather adrift, with little in the way of material or direction to guide them. Buzby's foul-mouthed (in terms of breath or vocabulary) Delores fares best. She has a funny, neo-McCambridge (almost-Selma Diamond) accent, amusing makeup, and even a few good lines and shtiks. Graham as the class snot does as well as he can, with scant help from the script....This is, at any rate, certainly no worse than most high-school reunions.

La NAVE DE LOS MONSTRUOS Col 1959 (*The SHIP OF THE MONSTERS) AD: J.A. Torna. SpFX: Juan M. Ravelo. Mkp: Rosa Guerrero. Ref: TV. Lee.

Venusian vampire-woman (who can transform into a huge bat) commands a robot (which can teleport both itself and others) and monsters (which she unfreezes with a vapor-ray). Another such ray turns one monster into a living skeleton. Other monsters include a cyclops which slobbers, a hairy Godzilla-type, and a "saucer man"-type. One is dispatched to kill all the animals of Earth (and turns a cow into a skeleton); another, to kill all children, etc. Also: levitation ray, freeze ray, robot's video "read-outs" re: Earth...space station....Odd sf-Western-musical-comedy, as perforce such a genre mix must be. The characters break into song at the strangest moments; the finale is a duet between the robot and a jukebox. (Yes.) Cute effects and monsters. (The cuteness seems intended.) Unsophisticated (to say the least), but appealingly lively.

NAZI SPY RING see DAWN EXPRESS

NEBO ZOWET see BATTLE BEYOND THE SUN

NELESITA (Angolan) LNdC 1983 color 90m. SP,D: Ruy Duarte. Ref: V 8/10/83. with Antonio Tyitenda, Francisco Munyele.

Young man vs. "evil spirits."

NEW BARBARIANS, The see WARRIORS OF THE WASTELAND

NEW TAKETORI LEGEND see QUEEN OF A THOUSAND YEARS

NEW YORK RIPPER (I) Fulvia 1982 color/ws 90m. (Lo SQUARTATORE DI NEW YORK) SP,D: Lucio Fulci. SP: also Clerici, Mannino, Sacchetti. Ph: Kuveiller. Mus: Francesco De Masi. Ref: V

5/12/82:196: "horror pic." 6/9/82. HR 10/25/83:S-12: sfa PSYCHO RIPPER? Ecran F 21:11: aka The RIPPER. 30:26-7,36: at Paris sf fest. 29:5: banned in Argentina. with Jack Hedley, Almanta Keller, Howard Ross, Alexandra Delli Colli.

NEXT OF KIN (Austral.) Filmco Ltd./SIS & Film House 1982 color 86m. SP,D: Tony Williams. SP: also Michael Heath. Ph: Gary Hansen. Mus: Klaus Schulze. AD: Richard Francis, N. Hepworth. SpFX:(d) Chris Murray. Mkp: E. Fardon. Ref: MFB'83:244-45. Nancy Goldman. V 10/20/82:98(ad): Mifed screenings. Ecran F 39:70. with Jackie Kerin, John Jarratt, Bernadette Gibson (Rita/Mrs.Ryan), Alex Scott.

"Haunted-house atmospherics" in and around Montclare, an isolated rest home, with "a concluding ten-minute gore-feast."(MFB

The NEXT ONE (U.S.-Greek?) Allstar c1982 color SP,D: Nico Mastorakis. Ph: Ari Stavrou. Mus: Stanley Myers. PD: Paul Acciari. Ref: Bill Warren. with Keir Dullea, Adrienne Barbeau, Jeremy Licht, Peter Hobbs.

The brother of Jesus arrives on a Greek island from a future dimension; restores a dead boy to life; has two hearts; "hears" library's books "talking"; explodes underwater to make way for the Next One. (Cf. REBORN(P))

NIGHT CALLER, The or NIGHT CALLER FROM OUTER SPACE see BLOOD BEAST FROM OUTER SPACE

NIGHT CHILD (B-I) FVI 1975 color (The CURSED MEDALLION-TV) D: Max Dallamano. SP: Massimo Dallamano, F. Marrottax, Jan Hartman. Ref: Weldon. no PFA. no V. Cinef V:1:33. Stanley. Bill Warren. TVG: 1976? with Richard Johnson, Nicole Elmi, Joanna Cassidy.

Possessed killer-girl.

NIGHT EYES see DEADLY EYES

NIGHT IN THE CRYPT, A see ONE DARK NIGHT

NIGHT OF THE CLAW see ISLAND CLAWS

NIGHT OF THE ZOMBIES (Sp-I) MPM 1980('83-U.S.) color 100m. (2 APOCALIPSIS CANIBAL. 2P HELL OF THE LIVING DEAD-ad t. ZOMBIE CREEPING FLESH-B. INFERNO DEI MORTI-VIVENTI. VIRUS, INFERNO DEI MORTI VIVENTI) D: Bruno Mattei(aka V.Darum or V.Dawn). SP: Claudio Fragasso, J.M. Cunilles. Ph: J. Cabrera. Mus: Goblin; G. Dell'Orso. PD: Antonio Velart. Mkp: Giuseppe Ferranti. Ref: screen. V 10/26/83. 9/16/81:5. MFB'82:229. Ecran 31:57.30: 80. and with Margit Newton, Selan Karay, Gaby Renom.

The Hope Centre in New Guinea--supposedly a chemical research center aiding underdeveloped countries--is actually searching for a solution to overpopulation in Third World countries. But their Operation Sweet Death--the code for a cannibalistic "solution"--goes awry, and a "degenerative process" begins: radioactive vapor begins leaking and contaminating the world, turning people into undead cannibals....attack-rat...maggot delicacy...cat-in-guts surprise.

The Romero zombie--inept but persistent, and soft in the head (a bullet there will kill it for good)--returns. Much play with entrails, plus a RABID-like retching motif. Fortunately, the photography is very dim. (As, figuratively, is the whole movie.) In fact, you have to take its title on faith, or on the evidence of ads and posters, since on the screen it's an unreadable, white-on-white, or gray-on-gray, blur. (If you look closely, you can make out what looks like "...THE ZOMBIES.") The thing to remember while watching these zombies slop around is that they're really just extras trying to make a living....The film's explicit Revenge of the Third World theme does not seem quite "sincere," and the guy, here, who loves to taunt the zombies seems adapted from the Scott Reininger character in Romero's own DAWN OF THE DEAD.

2P NIGHT OF THE ZOMBIES NMD/Bowser(Winston) 1981(1980) color 90m. (GAMMA 693-orig t. aka NIGHT OF THE WEHRMACHT ZOMBIES) SP,D & with: Joel M. Reed. Ph & with: Ron Dorfman. Mus: Onomatopoeia Inc., Matt Kaplowitz, Maggie Nolin. SpFX: Peter Kunz. Mkp: David E. Smith. Ref: TV. V 11/24/82:6. 7/20/83. Boxo 7/28/80:9. Ecran F 31:32: 1976? TVG. Arthur McMillan. Weldon. with Jamie Gillis, Ryan Hilliard(zombie), Samantha Grey, Ron Armstrong.

An SS battalion and an Allied chemical-warfare unit--"troops missing in action since World War II"--are still battling each other (in order to battle boredom) in the Bavarian Alps. They are, it seems, zombies, "half-corpses, half-vegetables," kept alive by Gamma 693, an experimental gas developed for Special Unit C in order to keep wounded soldiers in suspended animation. And although one character maintains that "zombies do not devour human flesh--ghouls do," these zombies act like ghouls, to the point of keeping a human "stock farm." At the end, the hero (Gillis) reluctantly accepts their invitation to join them in (potential) immortality....

The idea of the zombie-soldier goes back at least to REVOLT OF THE ZOMBIES(1936). Another, more unlikely antecedent of NIGHT OF THE ZOMBIES is DON'T GIVE UP THE SHIP(1959), in which Jerry Lewis comes across a lost Japanese soldier who was never notified that World War II ended and who, many years later, is still fighting it. The idea for Gillis's Nick--tough, glib, quick to scowl--goes back to Mike Hammer....Nothing much, you may be suspecting, originates here, and you'd be right. The zombie-soldiers do, however--especially in one, humor-in-the-barracks scene--act like soldiers. Like all soldiers, they have a lot of time on their hands (these soldiers are, after all, immortal), and they are forced to invent ways of passing it--e.g., joking, doing mock-battle. The movie succeeds in evoking a sense of camaraderie among its zombies, or ghouls--

and that's some kind of cockeyed accomplishment. (Most movie-zombies don't even talk.) The film as a whole falls something short of an accomplishment. "Dramatic tension" in this movie means some guy who keeps insisting "There are no zombies!" Technically-speaking, he's right, but he's also a bore. He makes partial amends by proving, himself, to be a "zombie"--and at the same time making a camp spectacle of himself--in one long, noisy sequence combining pathos, rampant exposition, horror, screaming, and decomposing. It's not pretty, but it is (unlike most of the movie) amusing. The line "Someone killed him and ate him in the back of the camera store" should also, perhaps, be memorialized. (The specification of site seems somehow beside the point.) N.B. This is a color film, but it uses black-and-white stock footage....

NIGHT SKIES see E.T.--THE EXTRA-TERRESTRIAL

NIGHT STALKER, The see CRACKLE OF DEATH. DEMON AND THE MUMMY

*NIGHT TIDE 1963 Addl Ph: Floyd Crosby. PD: Paul Mathison. Ref: screen. TV. PFA notes 10/29/82: title from Poe's "Annabel Lee." AFI: orig.95m. Weldon. and with Marjorie Eaton(chiromancer), Tom Dillon, Cameron(mystery woman).

A young woman, Mora (Linda Lawson), from the Greek island of Mikonos, fears that she is a siren and must return to the Sea People, and that she is responsible for the deaths of two men....nightmare of mermaid transforming into octopus....A rather sweet, charming love story, or romantic anecdote, which, like its lead actors--Lawson, Dennis Hopper, Luana Anders--seems tentative, hesitant, not quite sure of itself. The tentativeness is part of its charm. Although the 1942 CAT PEOPLE is its narrative model, NIGHT TIDE is not really quite a horror movie. Neither is it, quite, a documentary recording of scenes and sounds of Venice, California. Nor is it exactly a romantic drama. It is, rather, an intriguing fragment of a story, which imbibes life from the atmosphere around it, from suggestions of horror, mystery, romance, and everyday life lived near the sea. David Raksin's score and Vilis Lapenieks' photography help to synthesize the movie's disparate elements, making one play off the other. And Hopper and Anders are much more convincing than their CAT PEOPLE counterparts, Kent Smith and Jane Randolph. They really do suggest two average, likable people bumping into one another, in all their false starts and stops and half-gestures. As Mora, Lawson is adequate--but, well, she's just not Simone Simon. The movie's occasional borderline-dullness derives from this softness at the center. Lawson is neither as warm and human nor as elusive and mysterious as Simon. She can't provide the meaning or reason which Simon provided for the earlier film, though this Curtis Harrington work is more even than the Lewton, and a (minor) accomplishment in its own right.

A NIGHT TO DISMEMBER JER 1983? D,P: Doris Wishman. Ref: V 3/2/83:172(ad): "Satan's axe." 2/16/83:24: horror. Ecran F 34: 70: completed. with Diane Cummins, Saul Meth, Michael Egan.

NIGHT WARNING Comworld/Hennessy-Carrothers/IFM/S2D(Royal American) 1982(1981) color 94m. (NIGHTMARE MAKER. BUTCHER, BAKER, NIGHTMARE MAKER-both alt ts) D: William Asher. SP,P: Stephen Breimer. Story,SP: Alan Jay Glueckman, Boon Collins. Ph: Robbie Greenberg. Mus: Bruce Langhorne. SpMkpFX: Al Apone. SdFX: Val Kuklowsky. Opt: CFI. Ref: screen. V 4/7/82:9. 11/11/81:6(rated). Weldon. with Jimmy McNichol, Susan Tyrrell, Bo Svenson, Marcia Lewis, William Paxton.

Madwoman (Tyrrell) keeps dead lover's rotting body and severed, pickled head in cellar; commits series of butcher-knife murders....Once again, an assortment of weapons finds its way to an assortment of victims. This time, however, there's one difference: Susan Tyrrell plays this daughter of PSYCHO and--within the schlock framework (apparently, like PSYCHO, based on a true story)--manages to create a frightening-funny work of art, or fragment of same. In her universe she is, alternately, an indulgent mother, a horrible harridan, a little girl, and a playful lover. The object of her various affections and affectations is her nephew (McNichol), later revealed to be her illegitimate son. She is all things to one man, or boy, and casts off one "mask" for another with alarming ease. Like Peter Lorre in STRANGER ON THE THIRD FLOOR, Tyrrell's transitions between personae are eerily abrupt, so abrupt that, for an instant, they may seem simply comic turns. It appears, however, to be the character, not the actress's, sense of fun at work here. Her crazy lady has a certain self-consciousness, a picture of herself as, it seems, a poor, confused, but slyly resourceful woman trying on various "costumes" to achieve her (confused) ends. "It's only a game" seems to be the message relayed by her during her transformations--but only at those odd moments does she seem not to be taking this "game" seriously. Only then does she appear, momentarily, to be in control. Tyrrell's performance is a comic-horrific chef-d'oeuvre, and reason enough for a movie which otherwise seems to be stuck for reasons-for-being.

NIGHTBEAST Cinema Enterprises/Amazing Film 1982 color 80m. SP,D,P,Addl Ph: Don Dohler. Ph: Richard Geiwitz; L. Reichman et al. Mus: Rob Walsh, Jeffrey Abrams; Arlon Ober, Leonard Rogowski. SpDes: John Dods. MkpFX: Larry Schlechter, James Chai;(addl) David Donoho, Amodio Giordano. AnimFX: Ernest D. Farino; Kinetic Image. Spacecraft:(des) John Poreda; Kent Burton et al. PyroFX & with: Donoho. SdFX: Dohler, Abrams, Dave Ellis. Ref: TV: Paragon Video. Boxo 12/31/79. HR 10/25/83: S-12. V 10/20/82:95. 5/4/83:219(ad),284. Academy. FM 16:47(3/62): Dohler's fanzine "Wild" plugged. with Tom Griffith, Jamie Zemarel, Don Leifert, Karin Kardian, George Stover, Gary & Dick Svehla; Christopher Gummer & Dennis McGeehan(beast), Anne Frith.

Perry Hill, Maryland. A spaceship crash-lands on Earth, and a flesh-eating monster emerges. It beheads one man, rips out the innards of another, and, with its laser-ray gun, vaporizes people and objects. "Guns have no effect" on the beast, but electricity does: 30,000 volts from an electric coil produce one crispy critter....Again, Don Dohler has assembled some capable effects and makeup people...and again he demonstrates that he is among the least talented directors-of-actors in the genre since William Cameron Menzies. Menzies, of course, had other, pictorial strengths. Dohler comes up with some interesting blue-mist effects, and there's a fun pistols-vs.-laser-gun shootout. But the bulk of his script is devoted to half-baked, hot-and-heavy melodrama. The effects scenes are obviously for the fans; the non-effects scenes don't seem to be geared towards any audience in particular. They're just there....The electrical sendoff for the beast appears to be an hommage to The THING FROM ANOTHER WORLD.

NIGHTDREAMS Caballero Control 1981 color 80m. D,Ph: F.X. Pope. SP: Herbert W. Day, Rinse Dream. PD: Jimmy Rigg. Ref: TV: Wonderful World of Video. Jon Van Landschoot. with Dorothy LeMay, Loni Sanders, Jennifer West, Ken Starbuck(The Demon), Kevin Jay, Monique, Danielle, Andy Nichols.

Two scientists place a woman "under observation"; electronically induce erotic fantasies in her. One fantasy involves a demon who has been inhabiting the same cave "for centuries"; another, a "phallus"-"baby" (a la ERASERHEAD?); a third, an ambulatory Cream of Wheat box. At the end, a switcheroo reveals that it's the "scientists" who are under observation....From the folks who brought you CAFE FLESH. This too has a derisory quality and an elusive (if any) meaning--its procession of fantasy oddities makes CAFE FLESH seem positively accessible by comparison. The twist ending is a wan variation on the twist at the end of A COLD NIGHT'S DEATH.

NIGHTKILLERS, The see SILENT MADNESS

2P NIGHTMARE 21st Century/Goldmine 1981 color 98m. (NIGHTMARES IN A DAMAGED BRAIN-B) SP,D: Romano Scavolini. Ph: G. Fiore. Mus: Jack E. Williams. AD: Jan Foster. SpMkpFX:(d) Tom Savini?; Edward French. SpFX: Les Larran, William Milling. SdFX: Alex Pfau. Opt: Dynamic FX. Ref: screen. PFA. Weldon: Savini's name used fraudulently. NYT 11/1/81. MFB'83:18. V 10/21/81: SpMkpFX cr to Les Larraine(sic). VV 10/28/81. Soho News 11/3/81. with Baird Stafford(George Tatum), Sharon Smith, C.J. Cooke.

"Dreams can hurt you": a schizophrenic's nightmares re: axing his father and the latter's lover to death 25 years earlier drive him to a new series of murders after he finishes a "secret, experimental drug program"....boy who plays bloody practical jokes....A rather scurvy, makeup-effects-mad excuse for a horror movie. It's the same shocker you've seen so many times, but here you see it in gorier-than-usual detail. The final, you-axed-for-it* flashback is, in fact, both superfluous and, structurally, misplaced. That flashback has been played, in bits and pieces, throughout the movie, as Tatum's nightmare, and is replayed, in full, at the end, after he is pretty clearly dead, and thus no longer able to have nightmares. The script--a glorified vehicle for a prop axe--reunites several stock horror characters--the homicidal maniac, the terrified baby-sitter, the terrified mother, the boy-who-cried-wolf--and unimaginatively dumps them into their stock situations. (*A tip of the hat to FJA.)

NIGHTMARE AT 20,000 FEET(by R.Matheson) see TWILIGHT ZONE--THE MOVIE

NIGHTMARE MAKER see NIGHT WARNING

NIGHTMARES Univ/Mirisch-Beaton 1983 color 100m. D: Joseph Sargent. SP(1,2,&3),P: Christopher Crowe. SP:(4) Jeffrey Bloom. Ph:(1&2) G.P. Finnerman;(3&4) Mario DiLeo. Mus: Craig Safan. PD: D.E. Mitzner. SpVideoFX: Bo Gehring. Opt:(des) M.G. Griffin;(ph) John Nogle. SdFxEd: P. Berkos. Mkp: James Scribner. Ref: screen. SFExam 9/9/83. V 9/7/83. MFB'83:335. with Cristina Raines, Joe Lambie, Emilio Estevez, Lance Henriksen, Richard Masur, Veronica Cartwright, Mariclare Costello, Moon Zappa, Robin Gammell, Bridgette Andersen, Billy Jacoby.

Four stories: "Terror in Topanga": an escaped mental patient commits a series of brutal knife-slayings....1931 FRANKENSTEIN on TV. 2) "The Bishop of Battle": a video-game whiz at his "absolute peak" reaches the 13th and highest level of The Bishop of Battle, whereupon the game becomes real, and its ray and saucer machines emerge and engage him in an arcade-wide battle. He escapes but is waylaid by the bishop himself (voice: James Tolkan) in a parking structure and is absorbed into the game. 3) "The Benediction": a Southwestern parish priest in danger of losing his faith is confronted by the devil, in the form of a truck (with unseen driver). 4) "Night of the Rat": "The problem over there may be bigger than you realize," cautions the friendly neighborhood exterminator. It is indeed--it's a rat the size of a cow, a "very special animal" known as The Devil Rodent, which in the 17th Century terrorized Europe, and is now terrorizing a suburban American household....

To dispense with the easily dispensable: story one is a fairly-well directed, but pointless killer-amok exercise, with a limp, jokey perils-of-cigarette-addiction import and fadeout, and a predictable "twist." (None of the story payoffs is very satisfying.) There's a madman loose in the neighborhood, and the lady neglects to lock the car door--sure....Story three is the Certified Awful entry, seemingly obligatory in such omnibus horror movies. It's also the only episode with a psychological explanation: a concussion gives this priest DUEL-like dreams. It has one kicky effect: the satanic truck bursting up out of the ground like a revived corpse. But the subjects of suffering and faith have been treated with rather more insight elsewhere.... The devil-rat story is engaging--until the rat comes out of the closet and proves to be...simply a big rat. And a Western Union rat at that: this invincible monster-rat is invoked merely to dispel the myth of the invincible, "I can do it all" male. Yes, this is a didactic giant-rat tale. Masur, however, has a funny-mean, sarcastic kind of macho as the husband, and the pre-center-stage rat has a sense of humor too. It shreds all of the daughter's dolls and teddy bears...except a cute-cuddly rat-doll....It's hard to tell if "The Bishop of Battle" is didactic or not. That is, does the end of J.J. (Estevez), the vidiot, represent just desserts or apotheosis? J.J. may like being part of an arcade game, though his friends and relatives seem horrified at his fate. Any ambiguity, though, seems quite accidental. The story is a pretty straightforward one of obsession. J.J. is the fastest gun in the arcade, unbeatable by any human opponent. Only a very sophisticated (not to say downright cosmic) game could be a match for him. He definitely likes being part of a real ray-gun fight in the arcade, and the duel is fun for the movie-viewer as well. It's like an indoor form of skeet shooting, but here the "skeets" shoot back. The 13th level is made to sound very mysterious, and it does prove to be, at least, entertaining, if no more mysterious than your average video game....

NIGHTMARES IN A DAMAGED BRAIN see NIGHTMARE

198X see FUTURE WAR 198X

1990: THE BRONX WARRIORS (I) UFDC/Deaf Int'l.(De Angelis) 1983 (1982) color/ws 85m. (1990 I GUERRIERI DEL BRONX. BRONX WARRIORS-B t) SP,D & with: Enzo G. Castellari. SP: also D. Sacchetti, E.L. Briganti. Ph: S. Salvati. Mus: Walter Rizzati. PD: M. Lentini; M. Capuano. SpFX: Corridori, Battistelli, Benassati, Sarao. Mkp: Trani, Maltempo. Ref: TV: Media Home Ent.(video). V 4/27/83. 5/4/83:298. MFB'83:191. Ecran F 30:79. with Vic Morrow, Chris Connelly, Fred Williamson(The Ogre), Stefania Girolami, Luigi Mirafiore, Mark Gregory(Trash), John Sinclair(Ice).

It's 1990, and the Bronx has been declared a "high risk district" by the authorities. The only law--The Riders, a street gang whose emblem is a skull. Other gangs include The Scavengers, grunting, chalk-faced "corpses"-in-rotting-burlap, and The Zombies, warriors with hockey sticks...."vampire"-styled gang member....This season's prize for exposition (aka The Agee Award) goes to the line "The wealthiest, most affluent girl in the world runs away and hides in the Bronx...." (The line also rates a mention for pleonasm.) The movie itself is this season's Italian mock-up of ESCAPE FROM NEW YORK. It's a futuristic J.D. melodrama about a "tough-lookin' buncha guys," and its conceptions of the good, the hard-boiled, and the soft-boiled are more wrong-headed than even those of ESCAPE. The hero, Trash, sheds real tears, twice (once over the body of a buddy; once over the body of the heroine)--i.e., he's sensitive. And the soundtrack is alive with comically-effectless profanity and expostulations like "Be ca'fuh or I'll knock ya block off!" Trash is the brash-yet-reflective type: "Death walks wid us. Death rides and sleeps wid us." This movie is, obviously, a happy answer to the question, Whatever happened to bad dialogue? Our affluent heroine: "I feel safe with you, Trash." Trash himself (as chiller music heralds, for us, the attack of The Scavengers): "I don't like this strange silence!"

NO FOOD FOR THOUGHT(by R.Fresco) see TARANTULA

NOC POSLIJE SMRTI (Yugos.) Adria & Televisija Zagreb 1983 color 84m. D: Branko Ivanda. SP: Zora Dirnbach, from K.S. Djalski's short story. Ph: D. Novak. Mus: A. Kabiljo. AD: Z. Senecic. Ref: V 8/24/83: a la Poe; Night after Death-tr t. with Milena Dravic, Rade Serbedzia

A man attempts, through spiritualism, to bring back his dead wife.

NOT AGAINST THE FLESH see VAMPYR

NOTRE DAME DE PARIS(by V.Hugo) see HUNCHBACK OF NOTRE DAME, The

NOW YOU TELL ONE R-C Pictures 1926 20m. SP,D & with: Charles Bowers. SP,D: also H.L. Muller. SP: also Ted Sears. Ref: screen. PFA notes 4/17/83. no Lee. LC.

A man invents a "universal grafting" process whereby he can splice any two types of branches together and produce just about anything--shoelaces, a hat, an egg and saltshaker (from an eggplant stem)....The members of a liars' club don't believe his (illustrated) story....The finest and most sustained of the rediscovered Bowers shorts. This one is almost all (stop motion) animation and invention, with very little expository interference. Here, you see a man disappear into his hat... one cat grow, amoeba-like, from a branch, or plant-stem... hordes of cats spring from same...a mouse fire a teeny, tiny pistol at a cat...a Christmas tree sprout from the handle of a wheelbarrow....Bowers' imagination begins where that of other filmmakers leaves off. He seems to have had little story-sense--but he could dream up the damnedest things. He might have been the club's original liar....

NUOVI BARBARI, I see WARRIORS OF THE WASTELANDS

O LUCKY MAN! see BRITANNIA HOSPITAL

OASIS OF THE LIVING DEAD see ABIME DES MORTS VIVANTS

2 OCTAMAN (U.S.-Mex) 1971 Ph: Robert Caramico. Mus: Post Prods. Mkp:(sp) also Doug Beswick; Ron Kinney. Ref: TV. Weldon. Stanley. and with Jerome Guardino, Buck Kartalian.

"Who knows what atomic radiation is capable of creating!" "Or distorting." A Latin American superstition re: a "half-man, half-sea-serpent, with many arms," seems to have a basis in fact, in the existence of a "sea creature with the arms of an octopus who walks on the Earth like a man," and who was created (or distorted) by a "shift in the evolutionary process" caused by exposure to 100 times the "safe amount" of radiation. A scientific expedition discovers an "odd little squid" or two (in polluted water), featuring a "human cell." "Octaman," their human-sized father ("mutations can be 100 times larger than normal"), comes to reclaim his own, and also attempts to abduct Susana (Pier Angeli)....

The only thing OCTAMAN really has going "for" it--as camp, that is--is an A-1, highly risible monster-suit, with four "arms," two legs (with octopus suckers going down the inside of each, right to the humanoid feet), and one rudimentary appendage attached to each leg. Octaman's best tricks: standing on a hillside, waving his arms and whistling; "clapping" his two main arms in triumph at one point; stabbing one victim with a tentacle. Unfortunately, he exhausts his limited repertoire in the first half of the movie, leaving semi-historic Bronson Caverns to take up the latter-half slack. Then, as in, say, The SNOW CREATURE, cutting--from actors filing through one branch of this (far-from-extensive) cave system...to the same actors in another (not really very distant) part of the tunnel...to, again, the first stretch of cave (shot, cleverly, from a different angle)--is used to make Bronson Caverns "go farther" than they really, truly do....Although carrying off the heroine bodily seems a task well-suited (so to speak) to Octaman, these libidinous (or so one assumes) antics do not really recapture the glory which was his forebear's in CREATURE FROM THE BLACK LAGOON(qq.v.), to which picture OCTAMAN seems, in several particulars (e.g., the humans netting the monster; the monster trapping--with log barrier--the humans), indebted....The Octababies are made, simply, of resolutely-inexpressive rubber, and the exclamations of awe which they inspire in the characters seem signally inapt....

OF UNKNOWN ORIGIN (Can.) WB/David-Nesis & CFDC & Famous Players (Guardian Trust) 1983 color 88m. D: George Pan Cosmatos. SP: Brian Taggert, from C.G. Parker III's novel "The Visitor." Ph: Rene Verzier. Mus: Ken Wannberg. PD: Anne Pritchard. SpFxMkp: Stephan Dupuis. SpFX: Jacques Godbout, Louis Craig. SdFxEd: Peter Burgess. Opt: Groupe Film Opticals. Ref: TV: Warner Home Video. V 12/7/83. with Peter Weller, Jennifer Dale, Lawrence Dane, Kenneth Welsh, Shannon Tweed, Louis Del Grande.

Or, Felix Unger Vs. "Super-Rat." When his wife and son go away on holiday, Bart Hughes (Weller) is left alone to defend his personally-renovated, old New York brownstone against a huge, hardy, vicious, female rat. (Females, we're told, are "twice as vicious" as males.) The theme: "Rats may be smart, but a guy could be smarter." Bart ultimately does get the rat, but the fray leaves his house a shambles....nightmare sequences with rat popping out of cake, boy breakfasting on rat poison... mangled-cat and rat-in-the-toilet shocks.

"Don't sit around here driving yourself crazy," his wife tells him as she leaves. At the end, when she returns, it appears as if he has ignored her advice. His only explanation for the disarray: "I had a party." The movie has a pleasant, knowing irony about it--a quality one hardly expects in a movie about a humongous sewer-rat. Or, rather, a movie about a pitched battle between man and rat. There are visual references within the film to the book "Moby Dick" and to the film The OLD MAN AND THE SEA, again, ostensibly, ironic references, underlining the less-than-epic nature of the battle waged in Bart's brownstone. If, as a story of paranoia and obsession, OF UNKNOWN ORIGIN does not rank with, say, Bunuel's EL, it is well-done, and it's probably about as far as one can go, qualitatively-speaking, in the feature-length monster-rat movie line. (It certainly goes further than Warner's other Canadian rat-movie, DEADLY EYES.) The solitary Bart, back home from a hard day at the office, throws off his coat and shouts sarcastically, "Darling, I'm home!" to the rat. His days at home are even harder, but he retains a sense of humor. The rat (who can be smart) even chews up the check left behind for the exterminator. Bart begins to appreciate the challenge--he can, at one point, even smile at his nemesis' latest ploy--cutting off the electricity. He expected that sooner. The eventual devastation--chiefly by himself--of the whole house is a not-unanticipated irony, but it's capped by a witty touch: Bart deliberately smashes the last, unbroken vase. This act "balances" his earlier, oh-so-slight righting of a painting, hanging on the wall near the front door, as he left for the office. The script shares his senses of neatness, symmetry....

OLD LEGENDS NEVER DIE ABC-TV/Fox-TV & Irwin Allen & Kent 1966-67 color 90m. D: Allen/Harry Harris/William Hale. SP: Bloom, Wincelberg/William Welch/Leonard Stadd. Ref: TV. TVG. with James Darren, Robert Colbert, Christopher Cary(Merlin), John Alderson, John Crawford, James Lanphier, Lisa Jak, Jim McMullan (Arthur), Whit Bissell, Donald Harrow(Robin Hood), E. O'Brien-Moore.

One part and two whole (or nearly so) "Time Tunnel" TV shows: "Rendezvous with Yesterday" (prologue)...."Merlin The Magician": Merlin materializes in the time-tunnel lab-complex and casts a spell on Doug and Tony, who are needed in Arthur's fight against the Vikings. Unintentional irony (and humor) is provided by the lab technicians at the complex, who can't believe Merlin's magic. (Their time machine, yes; his sorcery, no.) Everyone's appearing and disappearing here--Merlin, Doug, Tony--and everyone's a smart-ass, hinting knowingly at what, historically, lies in store for Arthur & co...."The Revenge of

Robin Hood": Doug and Tony help Robin Hood force King John to sign the Magna Charta. There's a moment or two of suspense, but it is, finally, signed. Robin's merry men provide long bows, and bows and arrows; the tunnelers chip in with phosphine oxide--or else English history might have been very different....

**OLD MOTHER RILEY'S GHOSTS (B) (NTA-TV)/British Nat'l. 1941 80m. D,P: John Baxter. SP: Con West, Geoffrey Orme. Addl Dial & with: Arthur Lucan. Ph: James Wilson. Mus: Kennedy Russell. AD: Holmes Paul. Ref: screen. Anthony Slide. PFA notes 10/2/83. TVFFSB. BFC. with Kitty McShane, John Stuart, A. Bromley Davenport, Dennis Wyndham, John Laurie, B. Williams.

Members of the board of directors of Cartwright Manufacturing Engineers plot to steal the specifications for an inexpensive "new fuel" which will "revolutionize transport all over the world." They lure its inventors to "Riley's Castle" and its "chamber of horrors," where our heroes are beset by a bagpipe-playing "ghost," a knight-in-armor whose monstrous head flies up and away, a living, talking skeleton, and trees with "faces." It's "Riley, the mother of invention," who adds the crucial, third ingredient to the fuel formula, and makes the model motor run....One assumes that the apparitions described above are all part of the crooks' plot, and are not supposed to be real phantoms; the specific mechanics involved in their creation, however, are never explained--this is probably the closest an Old Mother Riley comedy ever came to ambiguity. Lucan as Mother Riley is strenuously impish, "an amazing creature," as one character puts it. His forearms are always, it seems, frantically in motion, like railroad semaphores gone haywire. His performance is more interesting as spectacle than as comedy--he's more acrobat than actor. Lucan's "additional dialogue" is, mainly, elementary wordplay, and the plot is functional, though the apparitions are a bit more elaborate than usual for a ghost comedy.

OLIVIA Ambassador/New West 1983(1981) color 84m. (FACES OF FEAR-orig t. A TASTE OF SIN-alt t. BEYOND THE BRIDGE and DOUBLE JEOPARDY-both int ts) SP,D,P,Ph & with: Ulli Lommel. SP: also J.P. Marsh, Ron Norman. Ph: also J. Breitenstein et al. Mus: Joel Goldsmith. Ref: V 3/23/83: "psychological horror." 10/14/81. 2/16/83:24. vt trailer. MFB'83:95-6: gory bits. Ecran F 34:70. with Suzanna Love, Robert Walker Jr., Jeff Winchester, Amy Robinson(young Olivia).

Murderess "controlled" by her dead-mother's voice.

OMEGA FACTOR, The see SILENT MADNESS

OMNISCIENT, The see SARVASAKSHI

ON THURSDAY WE LEAVE FOR HOME see TWILIGHT ZONE REVISITED

ONE DARK NIGHT Comworld 1982 color 89m. (REST IN PEACE. A NIGHT IN THE CRYPT. MAUSOLEUM-all early ts) SP,D: Tom McLoughlin.

SP: also Michael Hawes. Ph: Hal Trussel. Mus: Bob Summers. PD: Craig Stearns. SpFxDes: Tom & Ellis Burman, Bob Williams. Ref: V 2/2/83. 7/14/82:32. Ecran F 30:36.28:18-19(R.Lofficier). with Meg Tilly, Robin Evans, Leslie Speights, Adam West.

Mausoleum houses telekinetic, energy-draining corpse.

1000 CRIES HAS THE NIGHT see PIECES

ONE WAY TO THE MOON see RAIDERS FROM OUTER SPACE

OPERATION: RABBIT WB 1952 anim color 7m. D: Chuck Jones. SP: M. Maltese. Ref: TV. "WB Cartoons." Lee. Maltin/OMAM. LC.

Wile E. Coyote, "super genius," invents a robot rabbit, a rabbit-seeking flying saucer, etc. But he's no match for Bugs Bunny. Droll moment: W.E., in desperation, pulls down the window shade, but the oncoming locomotive crushes the shack--with him in it--anyway.

ORIENTAL VOODOO (H.K.) Golden Harvest 1982? D: Yuen Wo Ping. Ref: V 5/12/82:329. JFFJ 14:36. with Leung Chia Jen, Y.Y. Chu.

"Period action thriller involving the occult aspects of Taoism...."(JFFJ)

ORPHELIN DE PERDIDE, L'(by S.Wul) see MAITRES DU TEMP, Les

The OSTERMAN WEEKEND Fox/OWA 1983 color 102m. D: Sam Peckinpah. SP: Alan Sharp, from Robert Ludlum's novel. Adap: Ian Masters. Video Coord: Todd Grodnick. Ref: screen. VV 11/15/83:52: sf trappings. V 10/5/83. MFB'83:322-3.

CIA operative interrupts network TV and switches on TV sets (in order to broadcast) by remote control....Sloppy, and--politically and dramatically--facile; but Peckinpah's inter-cutting of simultaneous (slowmo) action, on various fronts, is fascinating to behold. Whether or not it's meaningful is another matter....

See also: YOU MAY BE NEXT!

2P The OVAL PORTRAIT (Salzburg-TV)/Maple Leaf 1972 color 89m. From Edgar Allan Poe's story. Ref: V 5/3/72:28. VideoSB. with Wanda Hendrix, Gisele Mackenzie, Barry Coe.

Spirit in portrait begins to possess young woman.

PADRONO DEL MONDO see MASTER OF THE WORLD

PAESE DEL SESSO SELVAGGIO, Il see SACRIFICE!

PAGAN MOON WB 1931? anim 7m. D,P: R. Ising. Ref: screen. "WB Cartoons." no LC. Maltin/OMAM. no Lee.

Bit with (pre-Kong) giant gorilla bopping monkey atop palm tree...monster-toothed fish. Kinda cute Merrie Melodies entry.

*PALACE OF THE ARABIAN NIGHTS 1905 Ref: screen. Lee.
A very lively Melies fantasy, featuring a fire-breathing dragon, a magic forest which parts in the middle, fireballs, and a battle between skeletons and swordsmen--50 years before Ray Harryhausen and Dynamation. Something's always popping up or down or in or out here....

PANDEMONIUM UA/TMC(Krost-Chapin) 1982 color/ws 81m. (THURSDAY THE 12TH-orig t) D: Alfred Sole. SP: Richard Whitley, Jaime Klein. Ph: Michel Hugo. Mus: Dana Kaproff. PD: Jack De Shields. SpFX: Bob Dawson;(foreman) Richard Johnson; Bill Purcell;(mixer) Elliot Tyson. Opt: H.A. Anderson Co. Title Des: Visual Concepts. Mkp:(sup) Bob Mills; Dorinda Carey. Ref: TV. TVG. Bill Warren. with Tom Smothers, Carol Kane, Miles Chapin, Debralee Scott, Marc McClure, Judge Reinhold, Sydney Lassick, Kaye Ballard, Donald O'Connor, Tab Hunter(killer), Eve Arden, Candy Azzara, Richard Romanus, Randi & Candi Brough.
Killer-with-knife stalking It Had To Be U. campus...cheerleader shish kebab, or five-on-a-javelin...cheerleaders, variously, toothpasted to death, stabbed with megaphone, stuffed with pompoms...cheerleader with telekinetic powers...secondary killer who turns victims into furniture...Dead Cheerleaders Tour..."stewardess Godzilla"...dialogue references to The WOLF MAN and RODAN...Ouspenskaya-like character...phone dead, knifed. A parody even worse than most of the movies it parodies. An AIRPLANE!-type, try-anything-and-everything farce, it couldn't really be called hit-and-miss because it misses 10 times for every time it hits (charitable estimate), sometimes so badly that it's hard to say what it missed. PANDEMONIUM tries for so-dumb-it's-clever comedy, makes it only halfway, and peaks with the title sequence....

PANIC ON THE AIR see YOU MAY BE NEXT!

PARADIS POUR TOUS (F) A.J. & A2 1982 color 110m. SP,D,P: Alain Jessua. SP: also Andre Ruellan. Ph: J. Robin. Mus: Rene Koening. AD: Constantin Mejinsky. Ref: V 9/15/82. with Patrick Dewaere, Jacques Dutronc, Fanny Cottencon, Stephane Audran, Philippe Leotard.
Doctor's "new medical process" relieves subjects of all anxieties.

PARASITE Embassy/Yablans-Band(Parasite Venture) 1982 color/ws? & 3-D 85m. D,P: Charles Band. SP: Alan J. Adler, Michael Shoob, Frank Levering. Ph: Mac Ahlberg. Mus: Richard Band. AD: Pamela Warner; Karen Scheibel. SpMkpFX: Stan Winston, James Kagel, Lance Anderson; F.X. Carriosa et al. SpFX: Doug White;(prop des) Duoy Swofford. Pyro: Roger George. Ref: TV: WV Video. V 3/24/82. MFB'82:135,275. Weldon. with Robert Glaudini, Demi Moore, Luca Bercovici, Vivian Blaine, James Davidson, Cherie Currie, Cheryl Smith.
1992. Dr. Paul Dean (Glaudini) has created and is harboring

inside him one of two examples of a "new strain of parasite." His parasite eats and grows, but is stunned by hypo injections, and is finally eliminated by high-frequency sound. The other parasite is apparently burned to death, along with its host.... "big trouble" in big cities after a deluge of "atomic shit" from the skies...anarchy in the hinterlands...work camps... ruling-class "merchants"....Regulation post-atomic-war melodramatics, with borrowings from THEY CAME FROM WITHIN. The effects shots are generally rather murky, as if they had been filmed in a dirty aquarium, and the popping-and-leaping-parasite stunts seem strictly hand-me-downs from ALIEN, THEY CAME..., etc. Dispiritingly derivative on all counts.

PATRICK VIVE ANCORA (I) Stefano 1980 D: Marlo Landi. Mus: Berto Pisano. Ref: Prod.Ital. with Sacha Pitoeff, Gianni Dei, Maria Angela Giordan.
Bedridden boy "gifted with supernatural powers."

PAURA NELLA CITTA DEI MORTI VIVENTI see GATES OF HELL, The

PEE-MAK see HOUSE OF DEATH

The PENALTY MGM/Goldwyn-Beach 1920 85m. D: Wallace Worsley. SP: Charles Kenyon, Philip Lonergan, from Gouverneur Morris's novel. Ph: Donovan Short. AD: Gilbert White. Ref: screen. PFA notes 8/21/83. Lee. FM 8:24. Ecran F 36:32,66-7. with Lon Chaney, Claire Adams, Kenneth Harlan, Ethel Grey Terry.
Blizzard, a malign, legless "cripple from Hell" (who is also, variously, called a "monster," a "Beast," and "the devil"), plots to have a doctor (who, years before, needlessly amputated his legs) graft the legs of the doctor's aide onto his stumps. ("You've played the trick with apes.") He also plots to loot San Francisco with an army of "disgruntled foreign laborers." (His scheme to lure the military and the police out of the city is visualized--and he "sees" himself whole, leading the uprising.) In the meantime, he poses as "Satan--after the fall" for the doctor's sculptor-daughter. (He intends eventually to "cripple her soul.") The doctor, however, operates on Blizzard's brain, relieving the pressure caused by a contusion at the base of the skull, and thus restores his sanity.
If the above precis suggests the sheer incredibleness of this movie, it still can't quite do it justice. Blizzard and a female secret service agent (the latter detached to spy on him) discover here a certain kinship in the realm of Art: he plays the piano, beautifully--the keys, that is; she works the pedals for him (beautifully). This romance-on-an-esthetic-plane is balanced by his relationship with the doctor's daughter. The latter is also talented, but meets Blizzard's advances with disgust. (The titles say she laughs at him, but it looks more like horror than disdain on her face.) She is, obviously, Superficial, at least as a person. Then again, she hasn't heard him play the piano. A final bizarre twist or two allows

a sane Blizzard to die a Noble Death. This happy-sad ending seems dictated by certain Laws of Melodrama, one covering Oblique Culpability, another Inherent Goodness. The script links Blizzard the "devil" with Blizzard the criminal kingpin--the master of the Underworld--and Chaney is appropriately malefic. His pantomime is not subtle, but it gets the point across. He seems here an incarnation of hate and bitterness. He makes his character credible, in spite of the plot.

PENGABDI see SATAN'S SLAVE

PER ASPERA AD ASTRA see TO THE STARS BY HARD WAYS

The PERFECT WOMAN Gold Key-TV c1981 color c90m. Ref: Dolores Willis. GKey. TVFFSB. with Cameron Mitchell, Fred Willard, Rudy Vallee, Marie Windsor, Barry Gordon, Peter Kastner.
The King of the Planet Zuko agrees to marry; sends his emissaries to Earth seeking a woman with a special mark.

Le PERIL RAMPANT (F) P.I. 1981 25m. D,Ed: Alberto Yaccelini. Ph: B. Lutic. Mus: J. Arriagada. Ref: Ecran 34:76,79. with Pierre Julien, Bernard Born, G.K. Jakubzcyk(robot).
A short film "presented as the sixth episode" of a serial, "Aventures du Serpent," featuring "robots, terrifying inventions," etc.

La PETITE BANDE (F) Hamster-Gaumont-Stand'Art-FR3-Elefilm 1983 color 91m. SP,D: Michel Deville. SP: also Gilles Perrault. Ph: Claude Lecomte. Mus: Edgar Cosma. AD: Guyot, des Plas. Anim: Cartoon Farm. Ref: V 3/30/83. with Andrew Chandler, Helene Dassule, Francois Marthouret.
Sinister cult submits children to "diabolical machine"'s "aging rays."

PHANTOM OF THE OPERA (U.S.-Hung.) CBS-TV/Halmi & Hungarofilm-Mafilm 1983 color 92m. D: Robert Markowitz. SP: Sherman Yellen, from Gaston Leroux's novel. Ph: Larry Pizer. Mus: Ralph Burns. SpMkpDes: Stan Winston; Willie Whitten et al. SpFX: Janos Kukoricza(sp?). Opt: Movie Magic. Ref: TV. TVG. with Maximilian Schell(The Phantom), Jane Seymour, Michael York, Jeremy Kemp, Diana Quick, Philip Stone.
Budapest, 1910. The acid-and-fire-scarred Phantom haunts the Magyar Kiralyi Opera House; keeps his wife's embalmed body in bed; commits murder-by-ravens....Handsome but empty, choppy TV-movie version of the Leroux story. The spectacle is much the same as before. The icons are all back: the masks, the cloak, the mirrors, the organ, the "Faust" costumes and makeup, the chandelier, the candles in the cavern, and, of course--the face behind the masks. It's the same old story too (though with some narrative changes-for-changes' sake) and it has, over the years and various productions, lost just about all its meaning. The Phantom claims, "In my heart I'm good," and the

conductor (York) counter-claims, later, "His love kills," but all spoken words echo rather hollowly through this opera house. Sandor Korvin seems only a Skulker--if picturesquely sinister as such--not really a full-fledged Phantom. This is not quite as silly as the 1943 PHANTOM OF THE OPERA, but it features probably the most contrived chandelier scene of all.

*PHANTOM OF THE RUE MORGUE 1954 Mkp: Gordon Bau. Ref: TV. and with Allyn McLerie, The Flying Zacchinis, Frank Lackteen.

Paris, around the turn of the century. "Freud and the libido" are all the rage, and a pioneer psychologist's (Karl Malden) "desperate wish to understand the human mind"--particularly "the dark, secret recesses" of his own mind--proves to stem from his own schizophrenia. If, as he says, "all of us are (neurotic) to some degree," he is very much one of us--his wish to revenge himself on all women who are repulsed by his real self (as was his dead wife) takes the form of murder via the gorilla Sultan (Charles Gemora), "a regular monster" from Madagascar, conditioned to kill at the sound of bells....

Fun-awful psychological-horror-movie. It's mystery and horror above the roofs of Paris--where the Phantom stalks--and psychology below. We learn that there is a "killer instinct" at work in some of us, and that animals are subject to "conditioned reflexes." Dr. Malden--his own choicest subject--makes psychology seem rather a grim science; this physician seems wholly incapable of healing himself, let alone anyone else. To the end, he counsels Sultan to "Kill!" (And Sultan does, with hokey inevitability, kill his "creator" at the end.) Counteracting the grimness are the all-in-fun 3-D effects (SCTV, where are you?) and the comically stilted Gay Paree atmospherics. David Buttolph's rousing score and the art direction make the Sultan's-shadow scenes pretty exciting--temporarily at least, we're not in a phony Paris, but in a never-never zone of curious architectural inspirations and unseen lurkers, or at least one unseen lurker. This Phantom has one fairly-grandly conceived sequence in which he crashes through a skylight, and brings a huge curtain to the studio floor with him. And a climactic scene in which he mauls a display-window mannequin might have furnished the Bunuel of The CRIMINAL LIFE OF ARCHIBALDO DE LA CRUZ(1955) with some ideas. Said scene is, strangely, more unsettling than the scenes in which the Phantom attacks real women--it's not-so-easily categorized, more irrational. It goes beyond psychopathology....

The PHANTOM SHIP WB 1936 anim 7m. D: Jack King. Mus: B. Brown. Ref: "WB Cartoons." LC. no Lee.

"Adventure/horror film"..."walking skeletons"...suspended animation.(WBC)

PHOENIX, The see WAR OF THE WIZARDS

PICTURE OF DORIAN GRAY, The(by O.Wilde) see DORIAN GAY(P). SINS OF DORIAN GRAY, The.

PICTURE THE DEVIL (H.K.) First Film 1981 feature Ref: JFFJ 14:36: "the occult of the East." V 10/14/81:223(ad): sfa The DEVIL ("the occult," H.K., F.F.)?

PIECES (Sp-Puerto Rican) FVI/Artists Releasing/Almena & Fort (Spectacular Film) 1982('83-U.S.) color 85m. (MIL GRITOS TIENE LA NOCHE. 1000 CRIES HAS THE NIGHT-ad t) D: Juan Piquer. SP: Dick Randall, John Shadow. Ph: Juan Marino? Mus: CAM. Ref: screen. V 5/4/83:406. 12/7/83:7. 9/28/83. Ecran F 41:28. with Christopher George, Lynda Day George, Paul Smith, Edmund Purdom, Frank Brana, Jack Taylor, Gerard Tichy, Ian Sera.

A "maniac is running loose" around an unnamed-university campus in Boston. He turns out to be "a real freak" who's slicing up coeds with chainsaw and butcher knife, and coordinating his acts of dismemberment with the completion of a jigsaw puzzle of a naked woman. It all started, apparently, when, as a lad, he saw his mother chopped up; it ends when his "human jigsaw puzzle" (composed of parts of his victims) comes, quite inexplicably, to life. (Cf. *The BOARDING SCHOOL, 1969)

The ad campaign wants you--forces you--to think TEXAS CHAIN SAW MASSACRE. But, hardware notwithstanding, this is just a belated mad-slasher movie. Actually, it's late in the day now even for a slasher parody, on which PIECES verges. (The killer in fact is a straight, or straighter, version of The Breather in STUDENT BODIES.) At least it's apparently not supposed to be funny when cop Christopher George (who seems to reach wit's end rather quickly) proclaims "I'm up a tree with this guy. I mean--he's mad!" The dialogue here is replete with gratuitous exclamations of horror--"Holy mother of God!" is one of the more colorful reactions to the atrocities. Other reactions include wretching and Lynda Day George's carefully-measured "Bastard! Bastard! Bastard!" The movie is entirely too stilted, however, for its characters' outrage to be taken seriously--that outrage seems to be merely a ploy to make the film's horror more horrific. The U.S. release version appears to have been shot in English, but it sounds as if it were dubbed from a foreign language. Mr. George's lips move, and his voice comes out, but it does not seem to belong to them.

PIG BIRD (Can.) 1982? anim D: Richard Condie. Ref: S&S'82: 226: Canada "devoured by insects."

PIGS or PIGS, The see STRANGE EXORCISM OF LYNN HART, The

The PILL CAPER CBS-TV/Univ-TV 1967 color 80m. D: Jack Arnold. SP: Budd Grossman, Harvey Bullock et al. Ph: Strenge, Rawlings, Thackery. Mus: Gerald Fried. AD: J.T. McCormack et al. Ref: TV. TVG. "Directory/TV Shows." with Stephen Strimpell, John McGiver, Dick Gautier, Harold J. Stone, Paul Smith, Luciana Paluzzi, David Opatoshu, Angelique Pettyjohn, Robert Cornthwaite, Henry Brandon, Ellen Corby, Richard Dawson, Tyler McVey.

Parts of apparently-three episodes from the "Mr. Terrific"

TV series. Pills developed by the Bureau of Special Projects work only with a certain Stanley Beamish (Strimpell); give him super-strength and the ability to fly, for either an hour (large pill) or 10 minutes (small, "booster" pill)...."power paralyzer" which "stops any machine"...hypnosis....Was there a call to bring back this old TV show? Painfully coy comedy would best be forgotten by Jack Arnold fans.

PINK FLOYD THE WALL see WALL, The

PIRANHA II: THE SPAWNING (Dutch-I?) Saturn Int'l./Brouwersgracht-Chako & Schechtman 1981('83-U.S.) color 95m. (aka The FLYING KILLERS. PIRANHA II: FLYING KILLERS-B. PIRANHA, PART II: THE SPAWNING-cr t) D,P: Ovidio Assonitis(aka James Cameron). SP: H.A. Milton. Ph: Piazzoli. Mus: S. Powder. AD: Medusa, Paltrinieri. SpFX:(sup) G. De Rossi; Corridori, Carbonaro, De Rossi. SpSdFX: Roberto Arcangeli. Titles: V.G. Ref: TV. MFB '82:233. Cinef XIII:5. V 9/15/82:54. 2/16/83:24. 4/13/83:4(rated). 12/21/83: U.S.-Ital.? Scot Holton. Bill Warren. with Tricia O'Neil, Steve Marachuk, Lance Henricksen, Ted Richert, R.G. Paull.

Setting: The Club Elysium, a posh resort on a "small island" in the Caribbean, during the first full moon after the Spring Equinox. The grunion are running, but they're a new species--"not the same piranha" as in PIRANHA, and not grunion, and not flying fish, but a little of each and "more vicious than anything you can imagine!" An "unnamed government project... spliced in genes from different species," it seems, "to create the ultimate killer organism," one that can "live in all environments."

Here, "the bastards fly!"--an ideal premise for a piranha comedy. Unfortunately, this isn't a piranha comedy, although comic supporting-character-types abound. More a package than a movie, PIRANHA II is keener on aping ALIEN (with one monster-fish popping out of a corpse's innards) and its monster-fish predecessors than it is on doing anything witty or original. All its ingenuity is directed towards the climactic confrontation between man and fish. And it's the genetic makeup of the super-piranha which makes that confrontation possible: these babies are part-grunion, and thus gather by the seashore at the appointed time. They're part-flying-fish, and thus can fly after the revelers when the latter catch on to the fact that they are not your typical grunion-types. And, of course, they're part-piranha, and the happy chant of "We want fish!" turns to screams and yells of horror. And although these ironic ends do not quite justify the arduous means, they are not unappreciated. If, however, you've seen JAWS, The GREAT ALLIGATOR, TENTACLES, etc., there's no reason to see this movie. If you haven't, there still isn't a hell of a lot of reason to see it....

PIRATES OF PRAH see ROCKY JONES, SPACE RANGER

The PLAGUE DOGS (B-U.S.) Rowf & Nepenthe/Martin Rosen 1982('84-U.S.) anim color 83m. SP,D,P: Rosen. From Richard Adams's novel. FxAnim: J.A. Armstrong, Tony Guy. SdFX: D.M. Hemphill. Ref: screen. V 10/27/82. SFFilm Fest catalog. PFA.

Scientific experiments in the confusion of the subjective and the objective in the minds of dogs...bit with stone mounds (subjectively) transforming into "wild animal" monsters....A canine survival story, with sf-horror overtones. Rather-off-puttingly serious-minded and grim. The subtext seems to be: and you thought cartoons were fun/fluff/escapism, eh? The text seems to be: life isn't easy anywhere in the animal kingdom. A fox and a sheepdog ("Bloody cheek!") provide some humor.

PLANETA NA SUKROVISHTATA (Bulg.) Bulgariafilm 1983 anim color 64m. D: Roumen Petkov. SP: Boris Anghelov, Yossif Peretz. Ref: V 10/12/83: Treasure Planet-tr t.

2581 A.D. An sf/pirate-movie....

PLAY DEAD Rudine-Wittman & United Construction 1981 color D: Peter Wittman. SP: Lothrop W. Jordan. Ph: Bob Bethard. AD: Robert Burns. Ref: Ecran F 32:70. V 2/16/83:24. (d)10/30/81. 10/20/82:144(ad). Bill Warren. Academy. with Yvonne De Carlo, Stephanie Dunnam, David Cullinane.

Woman out for revenge trains her dog to be a killer....

PLAYTHINGS 1982 color 72m. Ref: TV. Jim Shapiro.

Alien Dork from Pork learns about sex from humans in Marin ("I want it all now!"), who remind him of a race of "artificial humanoids," now extinct. He communicates telepathically with the no. 1 alien. Plus: stimulating "erogenous belt"...songs with unintelligible lyrics. More forlorn porn, with bits of wit.

POHADKY TISICE A JEDNE NOCI (Cz) Short Film-Gottwaldov 1974 anim color 89m. SP,D: Karel Zeman. Ph: Pikart. Mus: F. Bulein. Ref: V 10/13/82: aka TALES OF 1001 NIGHTS.

"Fiendish monsters"...Sinbad...ogre...dragon.

POLTERGEIST MGM-UA 1982 color/ws 115m. D: Tobe Hooper. SP, Co-P: Steven Spielberg. SP: also Michael Grais, Mark Victor. Ph: M.F. Leonetti. Mus: Jerry Goldsmith. PD: J.H. Spencer. SpVisFX: Industrial Light & Magic;(sup) Richard Edlund;(coord) Mitch Suskin;(ed sup) Conrad Buff;(ad) N. Rodis-Javero. SpMkp FX: Craig Reardon. Cloud FX: Gary Platek. SpSdFX: Alan Howarth. MechFxSup: Michael Wood. Anim:(sup) John Bruno;(key) Art Vitello;(ph) J.C. Keefer;(tech sup) S. Comstock. ElecSysDes: Jerry Jeffress;(coord) C. McCarthy. OptPhSup: Bruce Nicholson. Chief Model Maker: Phil Huston. Mattes: Michael Pangrazo. SpFxForeman: Jeff Jarvis. SpWires: Paula Paulson. SpWardrobe: L.J. Mower. Ref: TV. V 5/26/82. MFB'82:205-6. Crawley. with Craig T. Nelson, Jobeth Williams, Beatrice Straight, Dominique Dunne, Richard Lawson, Zelda Rubinstein(psychic), Heather O'Rourke, James Karen, Oliver Robins, Phil Stone.

Spirits in the "dream state" communicate via TV with a little girl in her Cuesta Verde house (built on a cemetery); draw her into another dimension inhabited by the Light and the Beast (the latter resembling a ghastly, emaciated dinosaur). The girl's mother--on a rope-lifeline through this X dimension--rescues her. At the end, coffins erupt through the ground and the house and spew up corpses, and the house is absorbed into the other dimension. Plus: belches of flame...clown-doll to life...indoor electrical-storm clouds (which deposit trinkets of the dead)...carnivorous monster-tree, carried off by weird tornado...esophagus-to-hell in closet...hallucination of decaying face...ghostly procession through living room...girl's soul passing through mother...A GUY NAMED JOE on TV.

Spare POLTERGEIST isn't....To all the furious psychic activity, it counterpoints the daughter's big-blue-eyed placidity--a sweet conceit. What all this furiousness signifies is another matter. POLTERGEIST is a reworking of both Spielberg's TV-movie SOMETHING EVIL(qq.v.), and the "Twilight Zone" episode "Little Girl Lost," yet seems to have little (if any) more substance than they. It's just more elaborate. Boy, is it! It's a candy store of horror effects....But the core, again--as in SOMETHING EVIL and "Little Girl Lost"--is, simply, two parents attempting to rescue their child from The Beyond. Nor are the other effects and elements--e.g., the revenge of the cemetery (WITCHCRAFT, 1964), the tree creature (FROM HELL IT CAME, 1957), the stunts in the children's bedroom (BEYOND THE DOOR, 1974)--unprecedented. On a piece-by-piece basis, this movie isn't exactly fresh. It does, however, do most of what it does (or re-does) better. The cemetery, for instance, delivers up its dead with disconcerting directness: coffins erupt through floorboards (like plant-shoots breaking through soil in time-lapse photography), and their lids promptly swing open to confront the living with the dead. "The Past Recaptured"....Like E.T., POLTERGEIST has a great-idea!/throw-it-in feel to it. Both movies seem to have been put together by people with minds that never sleep or stop; by inventive, but not especially reflective minds. There's an element of the mechanical to such fecundity. Anything, one feels, which Spielberg & co. can conceive, IL&M can execute--reason enough, clearly, not to stop and think, work and re-work. Just do. The only suggestion of self-doubt betrayed by POLTERGEIST lies in its over-neat use of reaction shots. Not that there isn't a wide array of on-screen reactions to the phenomena. But human response is plugged-in to the action too schematically. An effect-reaction-effect-reaction pattern sets in, as Spielberg tries, apparently, to "humanize" his grand effects-show. Characters are reduced to facial-expressions punctuating effects. And this push-button pantomime is, supposedly, the link between us and the mysterious electrical world beyond the television sign-off and the national anthem....

PORTRAIT OF AN INVISIBLE WOMAN see INVISIBLE WOMAN, The

POSESION DE AMITYVILLE, La see AMITYVILLE II: THE POSSESSION

POSSESSED (H.K.-Cant.) Johnny Mak 1983 color 100m. D: David Lai. SP: John Au. Ph: Bob Thompson. Ref: V 8/24/83. 10/26/83: 295. with Lau Siu Ming, Siu Yuk Lung, Sue Chan, Irene Wan.
"Unknown force" in old country house commits acts of violence.

POST-WAR INVENTIONS Fox 1945 anim color 7m. (GANDY GOOSE IN POST WAR INVENTIONS) D: C. Rasinski. SP: J. Foster. Ref: TV. LC. Maltin/OMAM. no Lee.
Nightmare of robotic rhino-monsters from super-TV-set... rocket into space...robot waiter...full-course dinner from pill. Silly, slight Gandy Goose cartoon.

The POWER FVI/ARC(Jeff Obrow) 1983(1984) color 85m. (EVIL PASSAGE-orig t) SP,Story,D,P: Obrow. SP,Story,D,Ph: Stephen Carpenter. Story: also John Penney, John Hopkins. Mus: Chris Young. PD: Chris Hopkins. SpMkpFX: Matthew Mungle. Idol: David Mansly. Opt: Getty. SdFxEd: Lars Hauglie. Ref: screen. Bill Warren. V 10/26/83:110(ad). 2/1/84. SFExam 1/20/84. with Warren Lincoln, Susan Stokey, Lisa Erickson, J.D. Myrtetus.
A supernatural thriller re: "little trinkets that kill people"...set in Santa Monica, with a prologue in Mexico, in 1971. Successive possessors of a tiny idol of the Aztec god Descacatyl, or Destacatyl, unwittingly unleash its power. It turns one man (Lincoln) into a monster (destroyed only when the idol itself is smashed), disfigures another, and acts telekinetically or magnetically on objects near it....Technically competent, but dull. The acting, generally, passes, but the script is at best functional. This idol is rather indiscriminate· the good, the bad, and the morally neutral are, alike, victimized A bit of suspense, until the movie resolves itself into another poor-slob-possessed movie....The composer occasionally borrows from Saint-Saens--he cheats, but cannily.

PRANKS see DORM THAT DRIPPED BLOOD, The

PRAY TV Filmways 1980 color 88m. (PRAY TV AKA KGOD-ad t) D, P,Co-SP: Rick Friedberg. Mkp: Jeff Angell. Ref: TV. TVG.
Two fantasy segments: 1) Religious-radio-station report from exorcism central: the devil refuses to quit Bernie Olafsson (Dick Chudnow)--who is tormented by a bad face and a levitating baseball bat and glove--stating that "possession is 9/10 of the law." 2) A legally-dead ornithologist turns up as a talk-show guest...."Pathetic," as Dabney Coleman says at one point (re: specifically, an act auditioning for his religious-TV station). His pithy commentary is, occasionally, hilarious; but the movie that he's <u>in</u> is as bad as the acts at which his comments are directed.

PRE-HYSTERICAL HARE WB 1958 anim color 7m. D: R. McKimson. Ref: "WB Cartoons." LC. no Lee. TV.
10,000 B.C. Caveman Elmer Fuddstone hunts "sabertoothed rabbit Bugs Bunny."(WBC)

El PRECIO DEL DEMONIO (Mex) 1958 D: Raphael Baledon. Ref: Ecran F 21:48. no Glut/CMM. no Lee.
Sf-horror...witches and werewolves.

*The PREMATURE BURIAL 1962 81m. SpFX: Pat Dinga. Mkp: Louis La Cava. Paintings: Burt Schoenberg. Ref: screen. TV. AFI. Lee. Stanley. and with Jonathan Haze.
Guy Carrell (Ray Milland), whose family has a history of horrible deaths, fears being buried alive, and rigs up a plush crypt with warning bell, collapsible coffin, dynamite, and (all else failing) poison goblet. His wife (Hazel Court), meanwhile, plays on his fears; subjects him to a series of shocks which brings on catalepsy, and has him buried alive. He returns and buries her alive....nightmare-in-blue re: premature burial, climaxed with goblet-of-maggots...lightning-struck dog almost buried alive...demonic painting.
Awkwardly-plotted, with frequent trips to the crypt to keep atmosphere and suspense perking. The burials themselves (the wife's for good) are rather anti-climactic--the movie is more successful as a study of the fear of premature burial. It uses sound effects, in particular, quite eerily, to suggest Guy's paranoia: e.g., the trapped-cat's augmented mewing...the wind "singing" "Molly Malone"...and, most imaginative of all, the strains of "Molly Malone" echoing crazily across the foggy moors, as Guy frantically attempts to track them to their source. Dick Miller's mocking smile--he plays a combination gravedigger-graverobber--is also used well, to punctuate the latter sequence. (John Dierkes is his partner-in-crime.)

PRIMITIVES (Indon.) 1981 D: Sam Gardner. Ref: Ecran F 28:20. with Michael Kelly, Ringa Takengow.
Terror in the jungle, a la CANNIBAL HOLOCAUST(qq.v.).

PRISONERS OF THE LOST UNIVERSE (U.S.-B?) Showtime-TV/Marcel-Robertson & United Media Finance 1983 color 75m. SP,D: Terry Marcel. SP,Mus,P: Harry Robertson. Ph: Derek Browne. SpMkpFX: Aaron & Maralyn Sherman. SpFX: Ray Hanson; A. Moshapo. OptFX: Ray Caple. SpProps: Tony Shuttleworth. Ref: TV. Ecran F 30:38. with Richard Hatch, Kay Lenz, John Saxon, Kenneth Hendel, Ray Charleson(The Greenman), Philip Van Der Byl(The Manbeast), Myles Robertson(The Waterbeast), Danie Voges(giant).
A trio of humans blunders into a "parallel world" via a scientist's (Hendel) inter-dimensional machine. There they find such delights as mini-warriors with flashing-red eyes, dead-monk-like creatures, the God of the Rock (which rock annihilates whatever touches it), gas-pod guns, and "amber light" (for starting fires). A moment, our time, equals (roughly) an hour of theirs....The dramatic cliches, however, remain unchanged from dimension to dimension. This is, to put the best light on it, fizzled camp...camp being the only avenue open to material as dismayingly stale as this. Hero and heroine keep shouting expletives (e.g., "You bastard!") at villain

Kleel (Saxon), to no discernible end--curses just seem to encourage him. Really awful TV-movie.

Le PRIX DU DANGER (F-Yugos.) Swanie & TF 1 & UGC-Top 1/Avala 1983 color 99m. SP,D: Yves Boisset. SP: also Jean Curtelin. From Robert Sheckley's short story "The Prize of Peril." Ph: P.-W. Glenn. Mus: Vladimir Cosma. AD: Serge Douy. SpFX: Pierdel. Mkp: M. Granier. Ref: V 2/2/83. SS Index'74-'78. Ecran F 32:44. Berkeley Public Library. MFB'84:48-9. with Gerard Lanvin, Michel Piccoli, Marie-France Pisier, Bruno Cremer, Andrea Ferreol.

Televised manhunt-to-the-death in future-society city.

PROPHECIES OF NOSTRADAMUS(by P.Drane) see MAN WHO SAW TOMORROW, The

PROTECTORS, BOOK #1, The see ANGEL OF H.E.A.T.

PROTOTYPE CBS-TV/R.C. Papazian & Levinson-Link 1983 color 90m. D: David Greene. SP,Exec P: Richard Levinson, William Link. Ph: Harry May. Mus: Billy Goldenberg. AD: Bill Ross. SpFX: Marty Bresin, SpFxUnltd. Mkp: Zoltan Elek. Opt: CFI. Ref: TV. TVG. Mag F&SF 5/84:70-1. with David Morse(Michael), Christopher Plummer, Arthur Hill, Frances Sternhagen, Stephen Elliott, James Sutorius, Jonathan Estrin.

Michael, a Model 2VR android, is "close to human...very real," and as a tabula rasa is very obedient, a "perfect companion." He absorbs the contents of whole books instantly. His scientist-creator (Plummer), fearing that the Pentagon intends to use him as a soldier or a political assassin, absconds with him, but, ultimately, is forced to let Michael destroy himself....Michael watches the 1931 FRANKENSTEIN on TV ("It was a sad story"), reads the Shelley novel, and comes to the realization that his number (as someone who's "not anything") is up. His, too, is a sad story, and, for the most part, a predictable one. As in the TV-movies of "The Time Machine" and "The Invisible Man," the military-industrial complex plays Guest Villain, and makes it easy for the viewer to choose sides....Michael himself is a bit less predictable than most movie-androids--he, at least, does not fall victim to emotion, a common android-affliction. His human-like dilemma is more existential than emotional; his last, almost incidental wish is that his maker's next model be in his, Michael's, image... if, that is, it's alright with his maker. This combination of deference and the will to self-perpetuation is about as complex as the script gets--which, at that, is more complex than most TV-movie scripts ever get.

The PSYCHIATRIST 1981? color 92m. (SHOULD YOU TRUST YOUR DAUGHTER TO THE PSYCHIATRIST?-cr t) Ref: Jim Shapiro.

Psychiatrist proves to be devil-cult leader who hypnotizes his followers into believing that they're possessed by the devil....ventriloquism...hallucinations.

**PSYCHO-MANIA Thunderbird/Victoria-Emerson(Del Tenney) 1963 90m. (BLACK AUTUMN-orig t. VIOLENT MIDNIGHT-alt t) SP,D: Richard Hilliard. SP: also Robin Miller, Mann Rubin. Ph: Louis McMahon;(stopmo) Robert Woodworth. Mus: W.L. Holcombe. Ref: TV. Lee. AFI: aka PSYCHOMANIA. V 2/19/64: "sex & horror." 12/16/64. Weldon. with Lee Philips, Shepperd Strudwick, Jean Hale, Lorraine Rogers, James Farentino, Dick Van Patten.

Sadistic murders...sequence in which a model is brutally stabbed to death--insert, shots of her eye and hand, a la the PSYCHO shower-murder....Tedious mystery-thriller, with a strangely-scratchy sound track and snappy dialogue with no snap.

PSYCHO RIPPER see NEW YORK RIPPER

PSYCHO II Univ/Oak Industries(Bernard Schwartz) 1983 color 111m. D: Richard Franklin. SP & with: Tom Holland. Sequel to PSYCHO. Ph: Dean Cundey. Mus: Jerry Goldsmith. PD: John W. Corso. SpVisFX: Albert Whitlock. SpFX: Melbourne Arnold. Mkp: Michael McCracken, Chuck Crafts. Ed,SdDes: Andrew London. Mattes:(art) Syd Dutton;(ph) Bill Taylor, Dennis Glouner. Ref: screen. V 6/1/83. MFB'83:245-6. Ecran F 36:15-23. with Anthony Perkins, Vera Miles, Meg Tilly, Robert Loggia, Dennis Franz, Hugh Gillin, Claudia Bryar, Osgood Perkins(young Norman).

The Bates Motel ("Vacancy"), outside Fairvale, California. When psychopathic killer Norman Bates (A. Perkins) is pronounced cured, and released to the outside world, a) the sister and niece of one of his victims plot to make it look as if his mother, Mrs. Bates, is alive, in order to drive him mad and have him re-committed; b) his mother, who is not Mrs. Bates, but Mrs., or Miss, Spool, her sister, attempts to protect him by murdering his tormentors, and, c) Norman does go mad again, murders his real mother, and the two have long talks.

In other words, they couldn't make up their minds. This is, roughly, Psycho II, III, and IV. Or, rather, Psycho 102, 103, and 104, counting all unofficial remakes/ripoffs/sequels/hommages....At least when they finally did it officially they made a few right moves--e.g., the sequel begins with (most of) the original's shower-murder sequence, as if to reassure us, Don't worry, no attempt will be made to duplicate or top that film's most famous shock scene. And Anthony Perkins (quite good) returns as Norman, less witty but just as (perhaps more) human, and pathetically vulnerable: as played by Perkins, Norman could, it seems, go either way--sane or insane....But this time the poor guy seems to have a dozen mothers hectoring him. It might be a convention--Mothers of Norman. A good black comedy seems always in the offing, but never develops. This script is serious about its Bates-Loomis parallel...its portrait of offspring attempting to break free of maternal locks and bonds. Unfortunately, the Loomis third of the plot is the most contrived part: young lady goes into lair of killer in order to provoke latter into going mad (but not killing) again. Gimme a break. Of course there is an irony lying around here somewhere--Mrs. Loomis seems half-willing to sacrifice her daughter's life to her own mania for revenge--but noone seems to have picked it up. Near the end, the contrivances begin piling up nearly as fast as the bodies: Loomis fille accidentally stabs the psychiatrist to death, with a butcher knife. (Cf. Karloff's "I had the acetylene torch in my hand--sometimes you can't help things like that" in the 1935 The RAVEN.) A minute or two later, she's caught in a Mama Bates dress and butcher-knife ensemble by the cops, who dispatch her just as she seems about to dispatch poor Norman. And Miss Spool turns out to be as dotty as Mrs. Bates and Norman....ARSENIC AND OLD LACE, where are you? The sequel that should be made to PSYCHO is the one in which Norman has a quiet vacation....

See also: 3 ON A MEATHOOK. WACKO.

PUPPET'S NIGHTMARE, The see CAUCHEMAR DU FANTOCHE

PURA SANGRE (Col.) Ospina-Castano 1982 color 98m. SP,D: Luis Ospina. SP: also Alberto Quiroga. Ph: Ramon Suarez. Mus: Gabriel & Bernardo Ossa. Ref: V 7/14/82. 9/14/83. Ecran F 40: 66: at Sitges. with Florina Lemaitre, Humberto Arango, C. Mayolo.

"Tale of vampirism" re: ailing tycoon who lives on transfusions of blood from boys.(V)

Q UFD/Arkoff/Larco 1982 color 90m. (SERPENT-orig t. The WINGED SERPENT-int t. aka Q THE WINGED SERPENT) SP,D,P: Larry Cohen. Ph: Fred Murray. Mus: Robert O. Ragland. SpVisFX: David Allen, Peter Kuran et al. SpMkp: Dennis Eger. Models: Roger Dicken et al. SdFX: Milch, Moseley. Ref: screen. PFA notes 5/22/82. V 5/26/82: Ph: A. Crespi? MFB'83:62-3: Ph: F. Murphy?? Willis/SW'83: aka Q: QUETZALCOATL. Weldon. with Michael Moriarty, David Carradine, Richard Roundtree, Ron Cey, Candy Clark, Mary Louise Weller, Bruce Carradine.

The gigantic, winged incarnation of the god Quetzalcoatl inhabits the top of the Chrysler Building in New York City; flies "right in line with the sun to blind people" to its presence; grows "bigger every day"; eats people....Final score: mamma-bird and one bird-in-egg destroyed...one overlooked egg left (in coda to story) to crack open....Another brain-defying Larry Cohen concoction, composed of roughly-equal parts of the mock-horrific, the ultra-serious, and the ultra-daft. Inimitable funny-strange, off-the-wall, big-bird-over-the-metropolis scenes alternate with exasperating vignettes from the sentimentally-observed low-life of an ex-junkie (Moriarty). Cohen very much wants us to like this poor-slob-redeemed character; but we like the bird. The latter's subjectively-shot attacks on sunning atop-skyscraper New Yorkers are accompanied by the sounds of (obviously huge) wings beating, and constitute, on the side, a weirdly-exhilarating aerial tour of New York City. Later,

Moriarty--the man with the key to the bird-monster's whereabouts--does, it's true, have his lighter moments: he becomes, temporarily, hilariously ambitious, demanding everything from city officials except 90% of the Yankees. The movie as a whole, however, is closer to appalling than enthralling.

The QUEEN OF A THOUSAND YEARS (J) Toei 1982 anim color (aka QUEEN MILLENIA) Created by Leiji Matsumoto. Anim: Yoshinori Kanamori. Ref: V 5/4/83:347. JFFJ 14:9.

Based on the TV series (aka "New Taketori Legend"), itself a spinoff from the movie GALAXY EXPRESS(qq.v.), which contributed a clone of the Matel, or Maeter, character.

QUEEN OF THE CANNIBALS see DOCTOR BUTCHER, M.D.

QUEEN OF THE GORILLAS see BRIDE AND THE BEAST

QUEST FOR FIRE (F-Can.) Fox/Belstar-Stephan & ICC(Gruskoff)-Cine Trail-Royal Bank of Canada-Famous Players 1982(1981) color/ws 97m. D: Jean-Jacques Annaud. SP: Gerard Brach, from J.-H. Rosny Sr.'s novel "La Guerre du Feu." Dial: Anthony Burgess. Body Lang: Desmond Morris. Ph: Claude Agostini. Mus: Philippe Sarde. PD: Brian Morris, Guy Comtois. CreaMkp Cons: Christopher Tucker. SpFxMkp: Stephan Dupuis; John Caglione. SpFX:(sup) Martin Malivoire;(tech) Neil Trifunovich, Mark Molin. Mammoths: Colinon. SdFxEd: Evans, Ward. Costumes: Hay, Rose. Body Painters: Michel Seguin et al. Ref: screen. TV. V 12/30/81. NYorker 3/8/82. MFB'82:67-8. with Everett McGill, Rae Dawn Chong, Ron Perlman, Nameer El-Kadi, The Great Antonio, Gary Schwartz, Rod Bennett.

Prehistory, roughly 80,000 years ago. Principal players: cave-men, mammoths, sabre-toothed tigers, Neanderthal men, and cannibals....A serio-comic struggle-for-survival epic. Our ancestors here discover new weapons such as arrow-spears and mammoths, and the secrets of making fire and love. But their most important find: a sense of humor. These cave-men, the Ulam, discover the engaging spectacle they themselves make. For them, it's no laughing matter when a couple of tigers chase them up a tree and then plop down and wait, patiently, at its base; for <u>us</u>, however, it <u>is</u>, and this difference in viewpoint becomes the movie's definition of the human. The comical and the philosophical are one here; this way--through objectivity--also, clearly, lies art....The first time one of our protagonists gets bonked on the head--with a sort of coconut--only the <u>heroine</u> (a pick-up from another tribe, the Ivaka) laughs. <u>Later, everyone</u>--including the (bleeding) victim (of a repeat bonking)--laughs. Pain--a serious matter--becomes a laughing matter. (Depends on the point of view....) This is a most winning, if perhaps rather slender thesis, and maybe the most surprising thing about this movie is that its unassuming theme never quite gets lost in the multi-million-dollar production shuffle. (This super-production proves, definitively, that

Dolby Stereo is the ideal medium for presenting the bellows of a herd of restless woolly-mammoths.) If the subject of fire proves somewhat-less-than-fascinating to the modern-day movie-goer, the quest for it is amusing. The sight--the very thought--of fire makes these cave-men jump up and down...cheer...fight... and roll around in campfire ashes. The script begins by asking "Aren't they silly?"; the question becomes "Aren't we silly?" by the end. In all that jumping up and down and cheering lies the joke of recognition--we're laughing at ourselves, at the continuity of human behavior.

RAGE OF THE DRAGON (Chinese) Trans-continental/George Lai 1980 color c95m. D: Godfrey Ho. SP: Robert Sezto. SpFX: Michael Tsang. Ref: TV. TVG.

Sequence or two with "ghost" (man in mask) in "haunted" cavern...charm against "evil spirits"....More kung-foolery, featuring dubbed accents of every kind except Chinese, and the usual "It is my duty to avenge my father's death" plot.

RAIDERS FROM OUTER SPACE ABC-TV/Fox-TV & Irwin Allen & Kent 1966 color 90m. D: Allen/Sobey Martin/Harry Harris. SP: Bloom, Wincelberg/William Welch/Welch. Three "Time Tunnel" shows fused: "Rendezvous with Yesterday," "The Kidnappers," "One Way to the Moon." Mus: Johnny Williams. AD: J.M. Smith, W.J. Creber, R.E. Maus. Ref: TV. TVG. "TV Drama Series." with James Darren, Robert Colbert, Gary Merrill, Whit Bissell, Warren Stevens, J.T. Callahan, Michael Ansara, Ross Elliott.

Story no. 1 introduces us to the Time Tunnel Complex, a government-funded project beneath the desert. In story two, the sun-dependent plant-people on a planet in another solar system in "the distant future" have achieved "perfect climate control" and super-hearing. The time tunnelers eschew the "immortalization" planned for them and attempt to escape via their captors' time machine. Story three concerns sabotage on a manned Mars expedition (with a pit stop on the moon, and footage from DESTINATION MOON)....Our tunnelers always seem to land right in the thick of things--no dull times or spaces for them. "Suspense" is manufactured with all sorts of time-limits and deadlines--for both those out in the field and the staff back at home base. "Only a few minutes!" is a typical breathless line. This TV-pseudo-movie is only for those who want to go back to 1966.

RATS, The(by J.Herbert) see DEADLY EYES

RATTLES (U.S.-I) Cineamerica & Interocean(Rossi) 1981 D: R. Deodato. Ref: V 7/29/81:17,30: giant snake. 2/16/83:24. 10/28/81: completed. Academy.

The RAVISHING OF FRANK N. STEIN (Swiss) 1982 anim 9m. (Le RAVISSEMENT DE FRANK N. STEIN) D: Georges Schwizgebel. Ref: PFA notes 11/5/82: re: "the creation of life." Filmex '83.

RAW FORCE (U.S.-Mex?) American Panorama/Ansor Int'l.(Zacharias) 1982(1981) color 86m. (SHOGUN ISLAND-orig t) SP,D: Edward Murphy. Ph,P: Frank Johnson. Mus: Walter Murphy. Set Des: Rodell Cruz. PhFX: Optrics. SdFxEd: Akerson, Wertz. Mkp: Cecile Baun. Ref: TV. V 7/14/82: footage from PIRANHA. with Cameron Mitchell, Geoff Binney, Jillian Kessner, Vic Diaz, Hope Holiday, Jennifer Holmes, Robert Dennis; Rolly Tan et al(corpses).

Charter-boat passengers shipwrecked on Warriors' Island ("This is the place in the brochure!"), in the South China Sea, encounter "fighting cadavers"--kung-fu losers brought back to life for a last chance to redeem themselves...."Female flesh gives (monks) the power to raise the dead"....Sloppy, catch-as-catch-can actioner could be fairly enjoyable if it catches you in the mood for real junk. A little gore, a little kung fu, a little sex, a little slapstick, a little melodrama (a little of everything, in other words, but grand opera), and presto!--a movie is born, kind of. On a scale from must-see to take-it-or-leave-it, this rates an oh-what-the-hell. The zombie-warriors prove quite unremarkable martial-arts opponents for our protagonists. They charge in slow motion and are tinted blue; they even bleed blue. Vic Diaz and his merry monks provide the only real bad-cheer. His horror-laugh and little-boy-gleeful fits of clapping are hokily amusing.

REALTIME (W.G.) B-Pictures & vVF & Rundfunk 1983(1982) color 107m. (ECHTZEIT(REALTIME)) SP,D,SpFX: Hellmuth Costard, Jurgen Ebert. Ph: Costard, Schwan et al. Anim: R. Krumme, S. Hofter;(stopmo?) Cinegrafik, Helmut Herbst. ElecFX: Winfried Wolf, C.Y. Chong. Ref: screen. PFA notes 12/15/83. IFG'84. with George Kramer, Ruth Bierich, Adolf Hornung.

"The cosmos as a giant computer": data from aerial photographs is converted into "synthetic landscape" in a computer Legoland. Through some kind of space warp, a man is suddenly lifted out of the real landscape and converted into the point-of-view of this programme. He feels himself to be at once a "momentary state in the programme" and "master of space and matter"....3-D-like, computer-generated photos...lunch which prepares itself (in stop-motion animation) on kitchen table.

The above data is approximate, though it comes as directly as possible from the film itself. The transformation which we see the man undergo may be a flashback...or it may be an image of cyclicality (like the last sequence of DEAD OF NIGHT). It's definitely amusing (as is the scene with the self-slicing bread), something which cannot be said for much of the rest of the film. Said film seems to concern design and chance, determination and free will--but don't quote me. Any sense which it makes would seem to be by chance, not design. It compares the universe to the world inside a computer (cf. TRON) to the world in a Tiepolo painting, but to unclear ends. This is the kind of puzzle film in which you know you're in trouble when--against all esthetic odds--you begin, now and then, to "get it." Such moments here will pass....

RED TIDE see BLOOD TIDE

El REFUGIO DEL MIEDO (Sp) Profilmes 1973 color c90m. SP,D: Jose Manuel Ulloa. SP: also Miguel Sanz. Ph: Antonio Milla. Mus: Juan Pineda; Brahms. AD: Andres Vallve. Mkp: Elisa Aspachs; Isidro Planas. Ref: TV: The Refuge of Fear-tr t. V 5/8/74:207. with Craig Hill, Patty Shepard, Pedro Maria Sanchez, Fernando Hilbeck, Teresa Gimpera.

New York City. The few survivors of a nuclear disaster carry on bravely, or not, in an underground bomb-shelter.... Above, charred bodies; below, conventional melodramatics.

REGINA DEI CANNIBALI, La see DOCTOR BUTCHER, M.D.

RENDEZVOUS WITH YESTERDAY see OLD LEGENDS NEVER DIE. RAIDERS FROM OUTER SPACE. REVENGE OF THE GODS.

REST IN PEACE see ONE DARK NIGHT

The RETURN (Can.) Gold Key-TV/T.A.E. 1973 color 95m. (The STARLOST QUINTOLOGY 5.) Ref: GKey. TVFFSB. TVG. with Keir Dullea, Lloyd Bochner, Edward Andrews.

"Space senility" threatens voyagers on Earthship Ark.

See also: ALIEN ORO, The.

The RETURN Greydon Clark(O.F.M.) 1980 color 91m. (EARTHRIGHT-orig t) D,P: G. Clark. SP: Ken & Jim Wheat, Curtis Burch. Ph: Daniel Pearl. Mus: Dan Wyman. AD: Chester Kaczenski. Sp MkpFX: Ken Horn, Tom Schwartz. SpFX: Dana Rheaume; A&A. Sp VisFX: Larry Clymer, Cheryl Smith et al. SdFX:(sp) Jim Cypherd; (ed) Richard Brummer. Opt: Optrex. Ref: TV: Thorn EMI Video. V 7/21/82:69. Weldon. with Jan-Michael Vincent, Cybill Shepherd, Martin Landau, Raymond Burr, Neville Brand, Susan Kiger.

Little Creek, New Mexico. A little boy (Zachary Vincent) and girl (Farah Bunch), a prospector (Vincent Schiavelli), and a big rock are subjected to a gaseous substance in a light beam....25 years later, Jennifer (Shepherd) is a research scientist for her father's SSR Institute; Wayne (Vincent) is a "yahoo with an interest in the wonders of the universe"; the prospector is super-strong, has not aged, and tosses cattle and human parts (extracted with a laser-like bar) into a cave with a strange ring of fog but no gravity; and the rock is still a rock--although, as Dr. Kramer (Burr) discovers, it features "one hell of a crystal structure" and "circular patterns" which prove to be diagrams of the solar system and adjacent stars, as seen from the "opposite side of the galaxy" on a certain date--"today." Ultimately, the prospector is sucked into the cave, and vanishes, and Jennifer and Wayne, the "chosen," are taken up into the spacecraft and then returned safely to Earth.

The prologue is promising, but the movie's midsection--with its speculation re: "lights in the sky," cattle mutilations, "devil cults," and "satanists or even...aliens"--was soon to be done more skillfully as ENDANGERED SPECIES(qq.v.). To this public-domain material, The RETURN adds, at first, only the details re: the rock, and the idea of the aerial and ground-level photographs of New Mexico which turn out to have "fogged areas" on them. This movie then goes on to reach more fantastic and less satisfying conclusions than does ENDANGERED SPECIES: Jennifer and Wayne float away into the cave, kiss, and wind up in some sort of connubial/celestial bed in the ship, which ship a concluding quotation from Psalms 43 suggests is the "altar of God"....The filmmakers appear to confuse "cosmic" with "nebulous." The conclusion of CLOSE ENCOUNTERS OF THE THIRD KIND, a likely model for The RETURN, was discreet; the imagery was suggestive of wonders-to-come. The imagery here is comically unimaginative, a what-next? joke. The movie as a whole is stronger on stunt work and pyrotechnics than on mystery or science fiction. Its only moments of subtlety or mystery are limited to the prologue and to Jennifer's subdued double-take when she first realizes that Wayne is/was the boy who shared her childhood close encounter. (A)

RETURN OF CAPTAIN INVINCIBLE see CAPTAIN INVINCIBLE

RETURN OF THE ALIENS see DEADLY SPAWN, The

RETURN OF THE JEDI Fox/Lucasfilm 1983 color/ws 130m. (REVENGE OF THE JEDI-orig t. STAR WARS: EPISODE VI: RETURN OF THE JEDI-cr t) D: Richard Marquand. SP: Lawrence Kasdan, George Lucas. Story, Exec P: Lucas. Sequel to STAR WARS(qq.v.). Ph: Alan Hume; Jack Lowin;(hi speed) Bruce Hill. Mus: John Williams. PD: Norman Reynolds. SpVisFX:(sup) Richard Edlund, Dennis Muren, Ken Ralston; Industrial Light & Magic;(ad) Joe Johnston. SpMkp:(des) Phil Tippett, Stuart Freeborn;(cons) Jon Berg, Chris Walas;(coord) Patty Blau. SpFX:(sup) Roy Arbogast;(locati n) Kevin Pike, Mike Woods;(sr tech) Peter Dawson;(pyro) Morris, Pier;(elec des) J. Jeffress, K. Brown. Anim:(sup) James Keefer; (stopmo) Tom St.Amand;(fx sup) Garry Waller, Kimberley Knowlton. OptPh:(sup) Bruce Nicholson; Lookout Mountain, Van Der Veer, Movie Magic et al. Sd:(des) Ben Burtt;(Huttese lyrics) Annie Arbogast. Concep Art: Ralph McQuarrie. Mattes:(sup) Michael Pangrazio;(ph) Neil Krepela, Craig Barron. MechFX:(sup) Kit West;(models) Lorne Peterson, Steve Gawley;(animatronics) John Coppinger;(wires) Bob Harman. Computer Graphics: W. Reeves, T. Duff. SpCost: Barbara Kassal et al. Scenic Art: Ted Michell. Decor: Bob Walker. Ref: screen: interiors at EMI. V 5/18/83. Time 5/23/83:62-8. Bill Warren. MFB'83:181-82. with Mark Hamill, Harrison Ford, Carrie Fisher, Billy Dee Williams, Anthony Daniels(C-3PO), Kenny Baker(R2-D2/Ewok), Peter Mayhew(Chewbacca),

Ian McDiarmid(Emperor), David Prowse(Darth Vader; voice: James Earl Jones), Alec Guinness, Frank Oz(Yoda), Felix Silla.

The STAR WARS principals are gradually re-gathered, to do battle, first, with the frog-eating gangster-monster Jabba the Hutt, on Tatooine, and, later, with the Emperor and Darth Vader ("more machine now than man") on a new Death Star. The latter, a second armored space-station, is protected by an energy shield operated by the Empire's forces on the Forest Moon of Endor. Personal data: Vader is the father of Luke (Hamill) and Leia (Fisher), Luke's twin sister, and dies after renouncing the Dark Side of the Force....Yoda, that fount of wisdom and near-unintelligible exposition, also dies, but he, Vader (nee Annakin), and Ben Kenobi (Guinness) return in spirit at the end....Han (Ford) is unfrozen at the beginning, and warms to Leia. Creature count: a tentacled monster with a reputedly-very-long digestive tract...the diminutive Ewoks, forest-dwelling, Chewie Jr. bears (or as Han puts it, "little furballs")...various frog, goat, and ape-like creatures haunting Jabba's lair (they include a strange-animal band, a leftover scavenger from Part IV, and a cackler-at-Jabba's-tail)...horrible, drooling monster in Jabba's dungeon...spider-like creature, or robot, at Jabba's gate. Vehicles, weapons, etc.: "speeders," airborne cycles...ostrich-like AT-ST ray machines (from Part V), plus a four-legged walker or two...antigravity sail barges...the Emperor's fingertip-rays...light-sabers for duelling and deflecting rays..."old Jedi mind trick."

In Episode VI of the STAR WARS saga, spectacle definitively takes over from drama, and the principals prove to be not so much characters as relatives. The Skywalker connections--to Vader and to Leia--pretty much resolve all dramatic and romantic complications. Han gets Leia, while Luke-in-a-box mustn't, on the one hand, (deliberately) kill his father (children are watching) or, on the other hand, join the Dark Side of the Force (the children again). If the script is fairly ingenious at letting Luke out of his box, the drama is ever-circumscribed by the dark-side/light-side schema. (Remember when it was called good and evil?) The Emperor seems more confident than the viewer that Luke will succumb, that his anger will, somehow, make him go bad. Vader, meanwhile, succumbs. But the Force seems an either-or proposition: Vader of the Empire is not really (as Ben opines) Luke's father; a reformed Vader is not really Vader. Luke himself either breaks or he doesn't; he's either good or evil. Lucas and Kasdan try very hard to give their script some dramatic bite...while IL&M makes spectacle look easy. And in a sense it is: effects shots may require hours, days, or months of preparation, but they require very little screen time to do their job. They don't need the on-screen development that drama does. They can be instantly impressive, and often are in JEDI. The sheer intricacy of physical detail in the spaceport and multiple-spacecraft shots, for instance, is assuredly astonishing. A half-second and you're overwhelmed--welcome to the other side of the universe....

A minute or two of allegorical-sounding dialogue, however, and you're right back on Earth. And a minute or two is all, it seems, that most of the actors in JEDI are given. Ford has to make his presence felt, generally, in two-second clips, and good an actor as he is, he needs a bit more time than that. JEDI is admittedly not as charming as STAR WARS--the actors, except for Hamill, are basically incidental--but it is more spectacular, or the sky here, at least, seems more crowded. This movie can, at a given moment, seem like the greatest adventure movie ever made--it certainly has some of the greatest moments. But most of the exhilaration is short-lived. The effect of even the best effects wears off alarmingly fast. The epic vision into which they are woven is not nearly as majestic as they--they're less realization than gilding; ends, not means. JEDI has to stop, awkwardly, for the story and characters; the effects start the movie up again. They're the vision--the universe according to IL&M. The sequences here with the speeders brilliantly combine stop-motion-like photographic effects and subjective-camera movement, to create a sort of aerial chariot-race-a-la-BEN HUR. (Look ma!--no wheels! no wings!) And this time the space battles aren't just battles. They're also on-the-spot, filmed reports--halfway between dream and documentary--of myriad strange soaring, sweeping, darting spacecrafts, all in motion, it seems, at once, like schools of very large fish swimming about in a very large aquarium. (For no reason other than to amaze, a huge ship, at one point here, sweeps out of formation and into close shot, and back.) There is, finally, the wonderfully-fulfilling moment when several Ewoks attempt to trip up an AT-ST. Said strategy yields what looks like a shot of a giant, mechanical ostrich dragging a gaggle of live teddy bears behind it on a rope. It took six years to get from "A long time ago...." to that shot, but it was worth it....

RETURN OF THE MAN FROM U.N.C.L.E.: THE FIFTEEN YEARS LATER AFFAIR CBS-TV/Sloan & Viacom 1983 color 92m. D: Ray Austin. SP: Michael Sloan, based on "The Man from U.N.C.L.E." TV series. Ph: F.J. Koenekamp. Mus: Gerald Fried. AD: H. Zimmerman. Sp FX: Clifford Wenger (or Winger) Sr. Opt: CFI. Ref: TV. TVG. with Robert Vaughn, David McCallum, Patrick Macnee, Geoffrey Lewis, Gayle Hunnicutt, Anthony Zerbe, Tom Mason.

Some quasi-sf elements: THRUSH threatens to explode the H957 bomb, "the most powerful, effective nuclear device in the world," in Chicago....bomber-disabling device...ID bracelet which explodes on contact with water...grenade-force bullets...rocket-equipped car....Regulation intrigue; regulation nostalgia. A "seems like old times" theme prevails, and Vaughn, McCallum, and George Lazenby--as Solo, Kuryakin, and James Bond, resp.--do have their ingratiating moments. But don't old TV series ever die??

The RETURNING Shapiro/Willow Films 1983 color 80m. D: Joel Bender. SP: Patrick Nash. Ph: Oliver Wood. Mus: Harry Manfredini.

AD: S. Finkin. Ref: V 8/17/83:37(ad),36: at Montreal fest. 2/16/83:24. 9/14/83. Ecran F 39:64. with Susan Strasberg, Gabriel Walsh, Ruth Warrick, Victor Arnold, Brian Foleman.
The Mojave Desert. Indian spirits possess two men.

REVENGE OF ROBIN HOOD, The see OLD LEGENDS NEVER DIE

*REVENGE OF THE CREATURE 1955 Story: William Alland. Mus sc: Herman Stein. Mkp: Bud Westmore;(des) Millicent Patrick et al. Ref: TV. Jim Shapiro. LC: 3-D. Warren/KWTS! Weldon. Hirschhorn. Stanley. and with Clint Eastwood, Brett Halsey, Don C. Harvey.
Sequel to CREATURE FROM THE BLACK LAGOON(qq.v.) features inchoate eroticism, as the gill-man (Ricou Browning)--the missing "link between marine and extraterrestrial life"?--shadows John Agar and Lori Nelson, as if he were meant, perhaps, to represent the dark side of their romantic simpering, or to be a displaced spirit of noir alienation, rather than be (as he is) just a man in a wetsuit. The script has, in effect, an idea for an idea. Noted-in-passing: the Creature's stint at Ocean Harbor, Florida, is bracketed, amusingly, by the p.a. announcer's "Once you've seen the gill-man, please move on," and by his later "The gill-man has escaped!"--from scheduled to unscheduled thrills, or The Revenge of the Commercialized.

REVENGE OF THE GODS ABC-TV/Fox-TV & Irwin Allen & Kent 1966-67 color 90m. D: Allen/Sobey Martin/Nathan Juran. SP: H.J. Bloom, Simon Wincelberg/W.R. Woodfield, Allan Balter/Ellis St. Joseph, from the "Time Tunnel" TV shows "Rendezvous with Yesterday," "Revenge of the Gods," & "Walls of Jericho," resp. Ph: Winton Hoch. Mus: Leith Stevens. AD: Jack Martin Smith. SpPhFX: L.B. Abbott. Mkp: Ben Nye. SdFxEd: Robert Cornett; (sup) Dan Hall Jr. Ref: TV. TVG. "TV Drama Series." with James Darren, Robert Colbert, Whit Bissell, John Zaremba, Lee Meriwether, John Doucette(Ulysses), Rhodes Reason, Dee Hartford (Helen), Myrna Fahey, Michael Pate, Lisa Gaye, Paul Carr, Kevin Hagen, Abraham Sofaer, Tiger Joe Marsh, Wesley Lau.
Doug and Tony travel back in time to prove the stories of The Fall of Jericho and The Siege of Troy to be true. ("It'll become legendary, Ulysses.") They hobnob with Ulysses, Paris, and Helen, and play spies in Jericho....The Troy story offers some fairly entertaining, if stilted play with myth/history/stock footage. No point, but Tony (or is it Doug?) gets to "fire the straw" that saves Ulysses' army, and hops inside the Trojan Horse. The Jericho story tries to be inspirational and suspenseful at the same time; fails.

REVENGE OF THE JEDI see RETURN OF THE JEDI

**The RIDERS OF THE WHISTLING SKULL (NTA-TV)/Republic 1937(1936) 58m. D: Mack V. Wright. SP: Oliver Drake, John Rathmell. Story: Drake, Bernard McConville. From William Colt MacDonald's books "Riders of the Whistling Skull" & "The Singing Scorpion."

Ph: Jack Marta. Mus D: Harry Grey. Ref: TV. Turner/Price. FD 6/3/37. TVFFSB. Lee(e). with Bob Livingston, Ray Corrigan, Max Terhune(The Three Mesquiteers); Mary Russell, Yakima Canutt, Roger Williams, Fern Emmett, Chief Thunder Cloud, Iron Eyes Cody, Ed Peil, C. Montague Shaw, Earle Ross, Frank Ellis.

A "mysterious lost cult" of Indians conducts sacrificial rituals at the base of a mountain dominated by a skull-like rock formation--the sound of the wind passing through the rocks leads to "legends of the Whistling Skull." ("I can't stand it! It howls in my ears!") Plus: murder with cursed knives and arrows ("And it's the same curse too!")...cursed skull... one mummy in Skull's caves which "speaks" (via ventriloquism), and one which comes to life ("A remarkable mummy!") and proves to be a (briefly) live Indian. ("I don't think that mummy'll bother us any more.") Remade as **The FEATHERED SERPENT.... Not exactly literate, but replete with mystery and semi-horror elements, and keynoted by picturesque location-shooting. Atmosphere in spades; no acting to speak of....

*RIDERS TO THE STARS A-Men 1954 color Mus: Harry Sukman;(lyrics) Leon Pober. SpFX:(d) Harry Redmond Jr.;(ph) Jack R. Glass. Mkp: Louis Phillippi. SdFxEd: Cathey Burrows. Research: Maxwell Smith. Ref: TV. Warren/KWTS! Ecran F 35:6. Lee.

Metal fragments of a rocket which crashed to Earth are found to have crystallized--cosmic rays have altered their molecular structure and turned them almost to powder....Dr. Donald Stanton (Herbert Marshall), of The Bureau of Scientific Investigation, believes that the substance which protects meteors in space could also protect U.S. spaceships from these cosmic rays. Consequently, twelve men, selected for their intelligence and accomplishments, are brought to the Snake Mountain Proving Grounds in California to undergo unexplained psychological testing in the Conference Room (the patient ones pass) and physical testing in the centrifuge. (A simulated flight registers up to 12 G's and 135 degrees.) The field is narrowed to three: Richard Stanton (William Lundigan), the doctor's son; Jerry Lockwood (Richard Carlson), and Walter Gordan (Robert Karnes). The latter attempts to catch an over-sized meteor in his rocket's meteor-catching scoop, and the ship disintegrates. Lockwood panics, and his rocket drifts off into space. Stanton succeeds in capturing a meteor, and is returned to Earth by remote control....Dr. Stanton finds the meteor coated with crystallized carbon (i.e., diamonds).

RIDERS TO THE STARS is a gallant attempt to turn scientific-lecture material into drama. The wonder of space is played off--a la '50's DESTINATION MOON--just-plain-folks characters. Lundigan and Carlson are relaxed and affable. They're everyday people--Marshall and Martha Hyer play far-from-everyday scientist-dreamers. (Even her actual dreams, as she describes them--of flying through space--combine science and romance.) At one point, she quotes Stanton Sr. to Stanton Jr.: "Man's desires are his prayers." This near-redundancy convinces Richard to accept the meteor-catching mission. The movie, though, was more interesting when it mixed the Convinced with the Unconvinced, the idealists with the realists. Once the men are tested and won over, the script's one bit of drama is resolved. True, there's romance and action still to come, but the pleasantness of the actors seems to evaporate in the heat of the drama. True also, the climax contains the film's one memorable moment--I remembered it for 24 years--the sight of the charred, now vaguely simian face of Gordan, still in his space suit and helmet, as his body passes by Lockwood's rocket--an interjection of the unexpected and horrific into an otherwise tame movie. For such moments do young (and old) sf-horror-movie fans live.... More-typically-Fifties-sf moments include the opening narration by Marshall--in religious terms it would be called an Invocation. It's meant to make the subject of the movie sound important: "Man, during his brief existence on the Earth, has met every challenge but one--the void of outer space. Having explored the world he lives in, he has turned his gaze upon the heavens...has focused his attention on the timeless lure of the universe." The words mean nothing and everything. But you're hooked. Doubly so, after the title tune, which sounds like a lead-in to a swell sf-parody. (And now we're whirling past the moon/Far away from Earth/Just the way I dreamed love would be/Riders to the stars are we.)

RIPPER, The see NEW YORK RIPPER

ROAD GANGS see SPACEHUNTER

The ROAD WARRIOR (Austral.) WB/Kennedy Miller & Others 1981 ('82-U.S.) color/ws 94m. (MAD MAX 2-orig t) SP,D: George Miller. SP: also Terry Hayes, Brian Hannant. Ph: Dean Semler. Mus: Brian May. AD: Graham Walker. SpFxD: Jeffrey Clifford. SpMkpFX: Bob McCarron. OptFX: Kim Priest. Ref: screen. V 12/23/81. MFB'82:87-88. with Mel Gibson, Bruce Spence, Mike Preston, Kjell Nilsson(The Humongous), Emil Minty, Vernon Welles.

The more-or-less-civilized vs. barbarian hordes--led by The Humongous, "the Ayatollah of Rock-and-Rollah"--in a desolate, fuel-starved future, some time after "two warrior-tribes went to war"....This sequel to MAD MAX(qq.v.) has plenty of kinesthetic clout; little or no emotional clout. It's good guys and bad guys again, and unending violence/stuntwork. There are nods to civilization-vs.-savagery and individual-vs.-society themes: Max the loner is kin to the Bogart of TO HAVE AND HAVE NOT and the Wayne of The SEARCHERS. But this movie is--for better and worse--pretty much nonstop action. Result: lots to look at; nothing much to feel (or write about). You won't be bored, but you won't exactly be transfigured either. The ROAD WARRIOR is exciting, entertaining, ultimately rather empty....Director Miller's way with moving vehicles--something is always moving here--recalls early Spielberg (e.g., DUEL, The SUGARLAND EXPRESS). The camera moves around, above, about, beside, into, and away from speeding cars/truck cabs/cycles/autogiros. The effect is one of movement-compounded, and it is exhilarating. But it's not everything, or shouldn't be....

ROADSIDE PICNIC(by The Strugatskys) see STALKER, The

ROBOT RUMPUS see SHOGUN WARRIORS: DANGUARD ACE

ROCK AND RULE (Can.) Nelvana-CFDC 1983 anim color 83m. D, AD: Clive A. Smith. SP: Peter Sauder, John Halfpenny. Story: Patrick Loubert, Sauder. Ph: Leonora Hume. Mus: Patricia Cullen. AD: also Louis Krawagna. SpFX:(p) Norman Stangel;(d) Keith Ingham. Ref: V 4/13/83. Ecran F 30:59. Voices: Paul Le Mat, Don Francks, Susan Roman.

Power-granting demon.

ROCKET-BYE BABY WB 1956 anim color 7m. D: Chuck Jones. SP: M. Maltese. SdFX: Treg Brown. Ref: "WB Cartoons." LC. no Lee.

Human and Martian babies sent to wrong sets of parents.

ROCKY JONES, SPACE RANGER: PIRATES OF PRAH Reed 1953 75m. Ref: TV. VideoSB. with Richard Crane, Sally Mansfield, Maurice Cass.

Rocky vs. space pirates. Primitive TV space-opera.

ROCKY JONES, SPACE RANGER: TRIAL OF ROCKY JONES Reed 1953 75m. Ref: VideoSB. with Richard Crane, Scotty Beckett, Maurice Cass.

ROCKY MOUNTAIN MYSTERY Para 1935 63m. (The FIGHTING WESTERNER-TV) D: Charles Barton. SP: Edward E. Paramore Jr. Adap: Ethel Doherty. From Zane Grey's "Golden Dreams." Ph: Archie Stout. Ref: TV: Favorite Films reissue. TVG. V 4/3/35. FDY. with Randolph Scott, Chic Sale, Ann Sheridan, Mrs. Leslie Carter, George Marion Sr., Kathleen Burke, Willie Fung.

A badman disguises himself as the night-skulking Black Rider in order to frighten Ballard-family heirs away from their Lost Hope, Nevada, radium mine; crushes his victims to pulp under a stamp mill ("That thing gives me the creeps!")...screams... creaking cabin-doors...wind-rustled sheet which makes corpse seem to move....Western and mystery cliches, as the Ballards gather at the old man's (they hope) deathbed, and the deputy sheriff, at the appointed moment, assembles all the suspects in one room. Scott and Sheridan, however, are pleasing presences, and the denouement is interesting. (At the end, Scott is forced to make a deal with the villain, and is hoodwinked into the bargain.) Scott even gets a standard, breathless unravelling-the-whole-mystery spiel at film's end--in essence he simply tells the bad guy what the latter already knows. Lots of wind and mill sound-effects....

*RODAN 1956 color 79m.-U.S. Mus: Akira Ifukube. SdFxEd: Anthony Carras. Lighting: Shigeru Mori. Ref: TV. Warren/KWTS! no LC. no V. FM 18:22-3. Ecran F 41:38. with Kenji Sawara,

Akihiko Hirata, Akio Kobori, Yasuko Nakata; Paul Frees(voices).

H-bomb testing fractures the Earth's crust, allowing air and water down to some 20-million-year-old eggs, which were hermetically sealed in a volcanic eruption. Two 100-ton Rodans hatch. They are carnivorous flying reptiles "closely related to the extinct pteranodon," but with, however, a 500' wingspread. (The pteranodon's was 25'.) They proceed to gobble up the nearby scorpion-caterpillar-like creatures (a "species of prehistoric insect") and, later, fly at supersonic speeds and level cities with their sonic blasts, or slipstreams, "of hurricane proportions." They die in a volcanic eruption.

Toho's second "biggie" (after GODZILLA) to gain U.S. release is a similarly unstable mixture of spectacle, horror, and pathos. Human love here is contrasted to, or compared with, flying-reptile love. When these two lovebirds perish in flames at the end, our hero (with heroine clinging tearfully to him) notes that it's "as if something human were dying." The fact, however, that most of the movie depicts the Rodans wreaking worldwide havoc qualifies, somewhat, the pathos of the conclusion. The two will, typically, "gorge on food," human or otherwise, then return to their volcano roost for r&r. And, like the deadly mantis and the giant claw, they are better heard-about than actually seen. They don't have much in the way of personality, fearsomeness, or visual splendor....As in GODZILLA, the early mystery-horror scenes are the best. They feature unseen monsters attacking waders-in-water; ominously-gathering shadows filling the mouths of caves, and a flashback vision of "many monsters" inhabiting a nightmare version of Carlsbad Caverns. They also feature the most telling indication of the sheer size of the Rodan pair: the insects--certifiable giants compared to the humans which they dwarf--are seen to be mere morsels in the maw of one Rodan....This movie is nothing if not lively--there are any number of explosions, earthquakes, eruptions, and devastations; it seems determined that, if it can't make you cry, it will at least keep you awake....

ROLLOVER WB-Orion/IPC 1981 color 115m. D: Alan J. Pakula. SP: David Shaber. Story: Shaber, Howard Kohn, David Weir. Ph: Giuseppe Rotunno;(NY) William Garroni. Mus: Michael Small. PD: George Jenkins; Jay Moore. Video: Tom Hanlon; James Dalton. Opt: Computer Opticals. Ref: TV. Cinef. S&S'82:312. V 12/9/81. MFB'82:155-6. with Jane Fonda, Kris Kristofferson, Hume Cronyn, Josef Sommer, Bob Gunton, Macon McCalman, Jodi Long.

"Secret financial manipulation" by Arabs ends in the collapse of the world's currencies, a "bankrupt world...teetering on the very edge of anarchy," after businesswoman Lee Winters (Fonda) interferes, and the Arabs withdraw all their money from U.S. banks. ("You're playing with the end of the world, you know.") That, at least, seems to be the story here. It is not certain, however, if chaos is what the Arabs were after, and if it's all to their advantage--though the implication is that Winters's interference merely speeds up a socio-political demolition process. The prerequisite for viewing the film: Stocks & Bonds 101A. The prerequisite (unfulfilled) for writing it, or thrillers like it: pithiness. ROLLOVER is almost two hours long, yet seems to be, simply, a little bit of plot, chewed very slowly. The indication is not so much for streamlining as for a complete overhaul--the Fonda-Kristofferson romance seems mere sugarcoating of a financial pill of a story. Both actors seem incidental to the computer read-outs, and to the phrases that keep cropping up in same, and in conversation: e.g., First New York Account 21214, ARAB-NAB, Borough National Bank, etc.

RONA JAFFE'S MAZES AND MONSTERS CBS-TV/McDermott and Procter & Gamble(Jaffe) 1982 color 92m. D: Steven M. Stern. SP: Tom Lazarus, from Jaffe's book "Mazes and Monsters." Ph: Laszlo George. Mus: Hagood Hardy. AD: Trevor Williams. SpFxEd: Douglas Grindstaff. Mkp: Linda Gill. Ref: TV. TVG. V 1/5/83: 44. with Chris Makepeace, Wendy Crewson, David Wallace, Tom Hanks, Vera Miles, Murray Hamilton, Lloyd Bochner, Anne Francis, Peter Donat, Louise Sorel, Susan Strasberg.

Teleplay based on the theory that "the most frightening monsters are the ones that exist in our minds": Grant University students' dungeons-and-dragons-like game leads them to dangerous Pequod Caverns and a "programmed" "monster" and skeleton ("Mazes and Monsters is a far-out game"), while The Great Hall, a nightmare figure, leads one player (Wallace) to New York City, where he "sees" a young hood as a maze monster ("Robbie's been acting a bit weird lately")....Frankenstein-monster-masked guest at Halloween party...bats...storm....Ludicrous psychological-suspense-mystery-drama is, dramatically, about as sensitive as a blowtorch, and features a rather far-out perils-of-games theme. The psychology of the protagonists is laid out as neatly and obviously as the characteristics of the medieval characters they assume, and the separating-fantasy-from-reality idea is crudely introduced and developed, and rather unfeelingly subordinated to suspense.

The ROOKIE REVUE WB 1941 anim color 7m. (not 2P The FIGHTING 69½th) D: I. Freleng. SP: Dave Monahan. Ref: TV. "WB Cartoons." LC. no Lee.

Bit: "camouflage corps" composed of invisible soldiers and horses. Okay cartoon.

ROOM IN THE DRAGON VOLANT, The(by J.S.LeFanu) see VAMPYR

ROTTWEILER Goldfarb/UG/Earl Owensby 1983 color & 3-D D: Worth Keeter III. SP: Tom McIntyre. Ref: V 10/20/82:14: "horror." 3/2/83:158(ad). 4/6/83:4(rated). 5/9/84:212: aka DOGS OF HELL.

Ein RUCKBLICK UN DIE URWELT (G) c1927 silent docu c10m. Ref: Don Glut: dinosaur.

SA INIT NG APOY (Fili) Trigon Cinema Arts 197-? D: Romy Suzara. SP: Edgardo Reyes. Ref: vc box: Trigon Video. Rebecca Atienza: In The Heat of Fire-tr t. with Lorna Tolentino, Rudy Fernandez, George Estregan(evil spirit).
"Deviltry and reincarnation."

SACRIFICE! (I-Bangkok) Brenner/Roas-Medusa & U.I.D. 1972 color/ ws 90m. (Il PAESE DEL SESSO SELVAGGIO. MAN FROM DEEP RIVER-alt t) D: Umberto Lenzi. SP: Massimo D'Avack, F. Barilli. Ph: R. Pallottini. Mus: Daniele Patucchi. Ref: FFacts. LAT 9/10/77: "graphic violence." Academy. Ecran F 30:72. with Ivan Rassimov, Me Me Lay, Ong Ard.
Photographer encounters cannibals "along the Thailand-Burma border"; becomes part of their tribe...."One horrendous sequence involving cannibals."(LAT) Cf. EATEN ALIVE(P). LAST SURVIVOR, The(II). MAKE THEM DIE SLOWLY.

**El SANTO CONTRA LOS CAZADORES DE CABEZAS (Mex) Zacarias 1970 color SP,D: Rene Cardona. Story: A.T. Portillo. Ph: Salona. Mus: L.H. Breton. Ref: Ecran F 31:55. M/TVM 12/69. Lee(e): sfa CAZADORES DE CABEZAS? with Santo, Nadia Milton, F. Fernandez.
The mad Dr. Mathus revives the dead with the blood of the living.

**SANTO EN EL MUNDO DE LOS MUERTOS (Mex) Sotomayor 1969 color (El MUNDO DE LOS MUERTOS) D: G.M. Solares. SP: R.G. Travesi. Ph: Solares. Mus: G.C. Carreon. Ref: Ecran F 31:25,55. Lee. M/TVM 3/69. with Santo, Blue Demon, Pilar Pellicer, A. Raxel.
A Santo ancestor vs. a witch and her zombie-hordes.

SARVASAKSHI (India-Marathi) MOMA/Giriraj 1979 115m. (aka The OMNISCIENT) Story,D,P: Ramdas Phutane. SP: B.& M. Chandawarkar. Ph: Navale. Mus: B. Chandawarkar. AD: D. Chavhan. Ref: screen. VV 10/7/81:44: "Lewtonesque." HKFFest. V 2/20/80. with J. Hardikar, Vijay Joshi.
Man with ESP who "sees," prevents murder...woman (his wife) with premonitions of her own death, nightmares re: ritual child-murder...local Bhagat who orders children sacrificed to the goddess Chamunda....Muddled meditations on science, superstition, and religion, with an odd use of freeze frames, and PRC-style chiller music. Skimpily subtitled. The movie does have a nice sense of setting, though, and some comic moments.

SATAN'S MISTRESS K-Pay/MPM/B.J. Creators(Diversified) 1982(1980) color 91m. (DARK EYES-orig & TV t. DEMON RAGE-vt t. FURY OF THE SUCCUBUS-alt t) SP,D,P: James Polakof. SP,Exec P: Beverley Johnson. Ph: J.L. Carter; Tom Denove. Mus: Roger Kellaway. AD: Fred Cutler, John Flaherty. SpFX: Karen Kubeck, Dennis

Dion, Tom Shouse. Mkp: Kubeck;(Belline) Donna Lyons. Spirit Cat: Animal Actors. Opt: CFI;(des) Dale Tate. SpProcessing: Fair Light. SpCost: Susan Bedi. Ref: TV. V 10/13/82. 10/14/81: 72. 5/26/82:10: in Miami, as FURY... 8/4/82:20. VideoSB. with Lana Wood, Britt Ekland(psychic), Kabir Bedi(spirit), Elise-Anne(Belline, spirit), Tom Hallick, Sherry Scott, John Carradine, Howard Murphy(the beast); La Donna, Chris Polakof et al(demons).

Northern California. A lonely wife's (Wood) demon lover (Bedi) proves to be a spirit-in-limbo sought by the devil, who is using her for bait....glowing-eyed, temporarily possessed girl...visions of devil, quicksand, spirits..."weird faces" in the woman's paintings...guillotine death...bleeding fingers, backs, statuary....At the end, the wife seems possessed.... Rudimentary horror plot, padded out with mostly-indifferent effects and suspense scenes--only the first appearance of the spirit (as an animated, darting cloud) elicits any sense of mystery. The plot--frustrated wife turns to spirit for sexual satisfaction--could also been seen as, simply, a pretext for undressing Ms. Wood as often as possible, in as many different settings as possible (bedroom, shower, work room). This is not, I might add, a complaint....

SATAN'S SLAVE (Indon.) Rapi Films 1982 color (PENGABDI) D: S.G. Putra. Ph: Tarigan. Ref: Ecran F 31:48,57. with Ruth Pelupessy, W.D. Mochtar, Fachrul Rozy.

"Nightmarish vision of the living dead."

The SATISFIERS OF ALPHA BLUE Audubon/Damiano 1981(1980) color 85m. SP,D,PD,P: Gerard Damiano. Ph: Elroy Brandy, J.M. Calmont; A.C. Peters. PD: also Paula Reisenwitz, Vincent Benedetti. PropDes: G. Damiano Jr. Mkp: Chuck Contreras. Ref: TV. SF Chron 10/16/81(ad). Playboy 6/81. with Lysa Thatcher, Hillary Summers, Maria Tortuga, Marilyn Gee, Lee Carrol, Richard Bolla, Sharon Mitchell, Jody Maxwell, Herschel Savage, Tiffany Clark.

"In the 21st Century, the world was perfect...almost." There's "no war, no poverty" in this "controlled environment." Teleporters bring automatically pre-selected sex partners to the recreational planet of Alpha Blue, where--also--test-tube babies are assigned to "mothers," and unionized relaxers, satisfiers, and hostesses satisfy all sexual needs, and are identified by numbers. "Names are important," it seems, only to one man, Algon (Bolla), who single-handedly attempts to resurrect the idea of romantic love....

A love-has-gone lament which, like The SEX MACHINE, attempts to establish a dialectic between love and sex. But if SATISFIERS isn't as <u>smug</u> as SEX MACHINE, it's equally hypocritical. "Love" gets token obeisance in the dialogue (and in one scene in which Algon browbeats a satisfier into saying she loves him)--while the movie is otherwise replete with the usual desultory sex-scenes. The desultoriness seems, as usual, <u>unintentional</u>, not willed, when it might, logically, have been "placed" by the script, which is supposed to be <u>against</u> mechanical sex...."Guest star" Annie Sprinkle's scene is not "placed" in any thematic context either, but at least is not just more-of-the-same....

SATOMI HAKKENDEN (J) 1983 D: Kinji Fukasaku. SP: Toshio Kamata. Ref: Ecran F 40:70: sf. with Sonny Chiba, Hiroyuki Sanada.
Mummy, giant snake, etc.

SAVAGE APOCALYPSE see CANNIBALS IN THE STREETS

SCALPS 21st Century/American Panther(The Eel) 1983 color 82m. SP,D: Fred Olen Ray. Ph: Brett Webster, Larry van Loon; Bryan England. Mus: Drew Neumann, Eric Rasmussen. SpMkpFX: Chris Biggs; Jon McCallum? Ref: V 12/14/83:4(rated). 1/18/84. Ecran 31:71.36:82-3. with Kirk Alyn(Dr.Howard Machen), Carroll Borland, JoAnn Robinson, Forrest J Ackerman, R. Hench.
Spirit of Black Trees Indian sorcerer possesses college students.

SCARAB (U.S.-Sp) Tesauro & Alloi 1982 color 92m. SP,D: Steven-Charles Jaffe. SP: also Robert Jaffe, Ned Miller, Jim Block. Ph: Fernando Arribas. Mus: Miguel Morales. Ref: V 10/20/82:113(ad). Ecran F 30:59.36:45. with Rip Torn, Robert Ginty, Cristina Hachuel, Don Pickering.
Egyptian god reincarnated in the body of a Nazi-sorcerer long presumed dead.

SCENES DE LA VIE PARALLELE see DUELLE

Die SCHWARZE SPINNE (Swiss) Pica-Film AG(Eduard Steiner) 1983 color 98m. D: Mark M. Rissi. SP: Walther Kauer, from Jeremias Gotthelf's story. Adap: Peter Holliger. Ph: Edwin Horak. Mus: Yello, Veronique Muller. AD: Rolf Knutti. SpFX: Peier, Defries, Reithaar. Ref: V 11/2/83: The Black Spider-tr t. with Beatrice Kessler, Walu Lueoend, Peter Ehrlich, Walter Hess.
A story re: "ecological disaster," framing a tale of the middle ages re: the devil cursing a village to be plagued by a black spider, after a woman breaks a pact with him.

SCIENCE FICTION THEATRE see TARANTULA

SCREAMTIME (B) 1983 color 90m. D,P: Al Beresford. SP: Michael Armstrong. Ph: Don Lord et al. Ref: V 9/21/83:12(ad): at Mifed. HR 10/25/83:S-52. Ecran F 36:83.41:21,28: at Paris sf fest 11/83. with Jean Anderson, Robin Bailey, Dora Bryan.
Three horror stories involving macabre visions, a puppeteer apparently possessed by his puppets, and "strange creatures."(EF)

The SECRET OF NIMH UA-MGM/Aurora/Bluth(Mrs.Brisby) 1982 anim color 83m. D: Don Bluth;(anim) John Pomeroy, Gary Goldman. Adap,P: Bluth, Pomeroy, Goldman. Adap: also Will Finn. From Robert C. O'Brien's novel "Mrs. Frisby and the Rats of NIMH." MovementFX: Opt. Camera Service. Mus: Jerry Goldsmith. SpFX:

(anim) D.A. Lanpher; Tom Hush et al. SpProcesses: Fred Craig. FX:(opt) Westheimer;(syn) Stan Levine;(stage) A&A. SdFxEd: D.M. Horton. Ref: TV. V 6/16/82. MFB'82:175. Voices: Derek Jacobi, Elizabeth Hartman, Dom DeLuise, John Carradine, Peter Strauss, Aldo Ray, Hermione Baddeley, Paul Shenar.

An inoculation program at an experimental lab, NIMH, produces intelligent, slow-aging rats and mice....strange, moving vines in rats' lair...forbidding, glowing-eyed, be-cobwebbed Great Owl...huge spider (mouse's p.o.v.)...rat-sorcerer Nicodemus and magic mirror and stone....Mild but eye-pleasing rat-and-mouse intrigue. In this cartoon-realm, there is only one bad rat--the others are o.k.--and he seems incidental to the mouse-survival story which is the movie's not-overly-compelling core. Unlike smart ants (cf. PHASE IV), smart rats are, apparently, no menace to mankind (or mousedom). The lush visuals and lively score are the main attractions, though the picture is also a reminder that John Carradine (here, The Great Owl) has a fine, resonant voice.

SECRET SERVICE IN DARKEST AFRICA Rep 1943 serial 10 episodes (MANHUNT IN THE AFRICAN JUNGLE-rr t. The BARON'S AFRICAN WAR-TV feature t) D: Spencer G. Bennet. SP: Royal Cole et al. Ph: W. Bradford. Mus: Mort Glickman. AD: R. Kimball. SpFX: Howard Lydecker Jr. Ref: Lee. Stanley. LC. with Rod Cameron, Joan Marsh, Duncan Renaldo, Lionel Royce, K. Kreuger, R. Harolde.

Death ray...suspended animation...Dagger of Solomon.

El SECRETO DE LA MOMIA (Braz) Mapa/Super 8 1982 (O SEGREDO DA MUMIA) Ref: V 10/26/83:359(ad). 5/4/83:468. Ecran F 39:12: "amusing." with Wilson Grey, Anselmo Vasconcellos, T. Boscoli.

"Horror...(the mummy) strikes again."(V)

SECRETS OF THE DEATH ROOM see LOVE ME DEADLY

*SECRETS OF THE FRENCH POLICE 1932 Mus: Max Steiner. AD: Carroll Clark. Ref: screen. William K. Everson. and with Gwili Andre.

A count hypnotizes a flower girl and passes her off as the lost Russian Princess Anastasia. At the end, he dies in his own electronic gizmo....This is, for the most part, formulaic international intrigue, with little or no excitement or pathos generated by the above, oddball premise. The most interesting narrative strophe should not be the fact that the hero is a thief working for the Surete, but that indeed provides the movie's only amusement...at least until the climax. The latter is an apparent last-minute graft from MYSTERY OF THE WAX MUSEUM (which was shooting at the time at Warner Brothers). (The scene does not appear in the August 12, 1932 estimating script of the film.) In it, the mad count attempts to turn our heroine into statuary and our hero into a lightning rod. Instant Horror Movie--and instant, total (and hilarious) loss of credibility....

SECTOR 13 New World/Studio 30 1982 SP,D,Exec P: Robert Stone Jordan. Ph: Greg Gardiner. AD: Richard Desiato. Ref: Bill

Warren. Academy. HR 6/15/82. V 10/26/83:364: sf. no PFA. with D.W. Brown, Kirsten Baker, Chip Frye, Wendy Grayson.

SEE YA LATER GLADIATOR WB-7A 1968 anim color 7m. D: Alex Lovy. Ref: "WB Cartoons." LC. Maltin/OMAM. no Lee.
Time machine.

SEGREDO DE MUMIA see SECRETO DE LA MOMIA

SEMANA DEL ASESINO, La see APARTMENT ON THE THIRTEENTH FLOOR

The SENDER (B) Para & Kingsmere/Feldman-Georgia Film Commission 1982 color 91m. D: Roger Christian. SP: Thomas Baum. Ph: Roger Pratt;(U.S.) James Pergola. Mus: Trevor Jones. PD: Malcolm Middleton. SpFX: Nick Allder; Allan Bryce et al. Mkp: Sarah Monzani. SdFX: C. Askew. Opt: Rank. Ref: screen. V 10/27/82. Weldon. with Kathryn Harrold, Zeljko Ivanek(the sender), Shirley Knight, Paul Freeman, Sean Hewitt, Marsha Hunt.
No matter what Kathryn Harrold (in the film) or the ads (for the film) say about dreams, this movie is about a young man who has visions, and who makes others have visions--of, for example, cockroaches-in-refrigerators, rats-in-mouths, and (most importantly) over-protective mothers....The receivers here are not sleeping, and the sender is (usually) not sleeping, when his/their visions are activated. This is not just a technical point. Any movie which makes you spend half your time sorting out intentional from accidental mystification has a real problem. And even after everything is sorted out, The SENDER still has problems, the main one being predictability. The cockroaches are back again; the rats too. The more spectacular visions and scenes are shot in slow motion. The film ends with a freeze frame. And the mother (Knight) of the sender has been dead, it transpires, for some time. This latter fact will not be a surprise to anyone who has seen more than eleven horror movies. The only surprise is that it is a surprise to heroine Harrold. She is quick to catch on to the fact that the son is a sender; she ought to realize that the mother is a projection, "sent" by him....With all its problems, however, The SENDER becomes, finally, fairly compelling, after the dust of confusion has settled, and the script has resolved itself into a battle between psychiatrist and mother for son. Even the last shot--the inevitable freeze-frame--is satisfying. It's a gentle, ironic reminder of the hold that the phantoms of the past maintain over those living in the present. Its quietness, too, is counterpoint to the noisiness of an earlier fire-and-explosion which, by all odds, should have settled matters. But the movie, after all, does concern the psychical, not the physical, and explosions do not signify....

El SER (Sp) Balcazar/D'Arbo 1982 SP,D: Sebastian d'Arbo. SP: also Luis Murillo. Ref: V 8/18/82:15: "anent 'parapsychological' phenomena." 5/4/83:418. Ecran F 31:39: telekinesis; La Vie Apres

La Mort to conclude a trilogy. 26:75. with Mercedes Sampietro, Ramiro Oliversos, Narciso Ibanez Menta.

SERPENT see Q

SEVEN KEYS TO BALDPATE see HAVE YOU GOT ANY CASTLES. HOUSE OF THE LONG SHADOWS.

SEVEN SISTERS see HOUSE ON SORORITY ROW

SEXY EROTIC LOVE (I) Mondial 1980 color D,Ph: Aristide Massaccesi(aka Joe D'Amato). SP: Enrico Michettoni. Ref: Ecran F 31:38,57. with Laura Jimenez, Mark Shannon, A. Goren.
Voodoo priest who can bring the dead back to life.

2 SHADOWMAN 1973 90m.-U.S. Ref: TV: Cultvideo. Cinef V:2:33. Weldon. S&S'83:271.
A mad doctor's "solution of the future": zombies with "totally inactive" brains. "No more unemployment; no more social security. If there's a recession, (they) hop into the box, and stay there calmly until things improve." He envisions "human storehouses" of worker and warrior-zombies, and, meanwhile, allows the Shadowman to use his creatures as assassins in a search for the treasure of the Knights Templar. Their one limitation: the color red stops them cold....The rings, medallions, and keys of the knights are made from alchemists' gold and are radioactive; a special directional finder is magnetically attracted to them....taxi operated and destroyed by remote control.
The 1964 JUDEX(qq.v.) was as much Feuillade as Franju, for better or worse. In SHADOWMAN, Georges Franju seems entirely subsumed in Feuillade--there's no poetry-of-pulp here, just pulp. Any odd resonance has been lost in either the dubbing or the trimming: SHADOWMAN began as an eight-hour TV mini-series and a 105-minute feature, and the good stuff appears to have been cut somewhere along the line. What's left are serial-ish "thrills" and a movie as blank and impersonal as the doc's zombies. Whatever Franju's original concept may have been, it has been effectively reduced to CREATURE WITH THE ATOM BRAIN....

SHAOLIN DRUNKARD (H.K.-Cant.) First Distributors 1983 color 100m. D: Yuen Wo Ping. Ph: M.K.W. Ma. Mus: T.S. Lam. Ref: V 8/24/83. with Simon Yuen Jr., Yuen Yan.
"Black magic voodoo duels."

SHARK see GREAT WHITE

*SHE DEMONS (NTA-TV) 1958 PD: Harold Banks. Ref: TV. Lee. V 3/19/58. FM 18:22. Stanley. and with Billy Dix, Bill Coontz.
Even in the worst--the very worst--movies (and, yes, this is one of them), there can be moments worth waiting for...moments even worthy of a sort of commemoration. In SHE DEMONS, what might be termed the Time-Out for Technical Explanations is such

a moment. At the proper time, the movie stops, and the mad ex-Nazi Col. Osler (Rudolph Anders)--dubbed "The Butcher" for his wartime experiments on prisoners--slowly and carefully explains: in order to develop the Master Race, the scar tissue of wounded soldiers had to be replaced by new skin. Osler discovered that the "thermal energy," or heat, from lava promoted this replacement process. In his current lab (under a volcano on a Pacific island), he electronically extracts energy from the greatest single source of same on Earth--the latter's molten core--and converts it into electricity, thus creating "perpetual motion." Osler has, further (yes, there's more), isolated "character X," the gene responsible for human identity, and exchanges genes between the she demons and his wife, Mona (Leni Tana), disfigured in a radiation accident. It seems that a pure dose of Mona, however, would be too much for the demons, and animal genes must, also, be introduced into the formula. (Hero Tod Griffin: "That accounts for their animalistic mannerisms"--e.g., fangs, claws.) His intent, apparently, is to transfer the beauty of the women (abducted from a tribe on another island 10 years before) to his wife. The transfer, however, seems to work in one direction only--they get ugly. But (not done yet) they also get pretty again, in time, as their own genes reassert themselves, and they "rebuild" their characters, sans memory or identity. They are infinitely recyclable subjects....All this, and the she demons escape, the wife remains ugly, and she and Osler die in a volcanic explosion. Sometimes it just doesn't pay to get up in the morning, or to be a genius....The development of the hate-like-love relationship between hero and heroine (Irish McCalla) in this movie gives new meaning to the word "elementary." It's as simple as the science is tortuous.

SHE MONSTER OF THE NIGHT see FRANKENSTEIN'S DAUGHTER

SHE SHASHOU see KILLER SNAKES

SHE-WOLF, The see LOBA, La. LOUVE, La.

SHIP OF THE MONSTERS see NAVE DE LOS MONSTRUOS

SHOCK WAVES see GRIM REAPER, The

SHOGUN ISLAND see RAW FORCE

SHOGUN WARRIORS: DANGUARD ACE (J) Jim Terry & Toei/MK 1982 anim color 105m. (aka FORCE FIVE: DANGUARD ACE. DANGUARD ACE) Ref: TVG. VideoSB. Sequel to ROBOT RUMPUS?

SHOGUN WARRIORS: GAIKING (J) Jim Terry & Toei Anim/MK 1982(1980) anim color 105m. (aka GAIKING. FORCE FIVE: GAIKING-cr t) D,P: Jim Terry. SP: Collins Walker. Created by Nakaya, Sugino, Kobayashi. Mus: Shunsuke Kikuchi. Video: American Film Factory. Ref: TV.

Giant Space-Dragon ship (a la Atragon), with detachable "fighting robot" Gaiking, and "thruster power," defense shields, pincer laser, "electron chains," etc., versus King Darius (with his mouth in his forehead) and his Death Quartet, from a planet "eaten" by a Black Hole. The latter, evil forces establish a base on Mars and send out bird-men...a space gladiator-creature named Taurus...a Mechagodzilla-like, lightning-spewing monster-robot with a "false image" size-enhancer...and three giant, ray-shooting robots resembling, respectively, a grasshopper, a beetle, and a dragon. Darius proves to be a giant android with nova-beam capability and a computer-bank forehead....Our bionic-plasma-blessed hero can, personally, double the power of his hydro-blazer weapon....And: teleportation...near-impregnable dome...Pegasus, android with energizing power.

Frantically-paced, and crammed with monsters, machines, and weapons, and combinations thereof. One gizmo is hardly introduced before giving way to the next one--STAR WARS compounded, but without the latter's genial asides. The Satellite Graveyard is the one fairly-unusual narrative ingredient--the cartoon itself seems ticketed, ultimately, for a Celluloid Graveyard. Aggressively simple-minded characterization.

SHOGUN WARRIORS: GRANDIZER (J) (Showtime-TV)/Terry & Toei 1982 anim color 101m. (aka FORCE FIVE: GRANDIZER. GRANDIZER) Ref: TVG. JFFJ 13:30: from Go Nagai's comic "Shogun Warriors," the basis also of the TV series "UFO Robot Grendizer." VideoSB.

SHOGUN WARRIORS: SPACEKETEERS (J) Terry & Toei Ginga Kikaku 1982 anim color 105m. (FORCE FIVE: SPACE-KETEERS-cr t. aka SPACEKETEERS) D,P: Jim Terry. SP: C. Walker. Mus: S. Kikuchi. Video: American Film Factory. Ref: TV.

Princess Aurora and the Three Spaceketeers, cyborgs, aboard the Cosmos Queen, versus mutants with the power to turn animals into "animoids"....Plus: rocket-firing robot army...gigantic, fire-breathing, self-healing, mechanical space-dragon...giant missile-shooting bat-dragon warships...Space Ark carrying goat-like-mutant's slaves...space slime..."cometized" spaceship... artificial undersea cyclone...astro-lightning and space ice (weapons)...giant, flying-bug-like mutants...ant-like aliens... toe-jectiles...electro-cleansing (i.e., brainwashing)...magnetic storm...stegosaurus-like mounts.

Elementary characterization/comedy/adventure-for-kids. Lively enough, but the liveliness soon becomes indistinguishable from monotonousness. The monsters, villains, and weapons all kind of run together after a while--each "new" wonder begins to seem just a recycled old one. Only the Space Oysters really stand out--it's not just that they're flying, jabbering oyster-warriors. They all, also, for some reason, have Peter Lorre's voice. Busy but very conventional graphics....

SHOGUN WARRIORS: STARVENGERS (J) Terry & Toei 1982 anim color 95m. (aka FORCE FIVE: SHOGUN WARRIORS: STARVENGERS) Ref: TVG.

JFFJ 13:30. VV 12/7/82:63: "baroque robots." VideoSB: aka STARVENGERS.

SHOULD YOU TRUST YOUR DAUGHTER TO THE PSYCHIATRIST see PSYCHIATRIST, The

2 SHRIEK OF THE MUTILATED 1974 Mkp: Maxim Kinsky. Ref: TV. Weldon.
Z-level, God-why-am-I-watching this? atrocity does, at least, mount a crude-but-gallant attempt at a comic Grand Guignol climax--"Bon appetit!" their comrade wishes the "Finger People," as the latter prepare to launch into the main course (i.e., the heroine). And there is the line, "Doesn't Tom mean any more to you than a piece of bait to hang on a hook?" But mainly you'll just want it to end.

SI LAS MUJERES MANDARAN (Sp-Mex) Nuevo Cine & Conacine 1982 D: Jose Maria Palacio. Ref: Ecran F 32:70. V 5/4/83:418. with A. Munoz, Jose Sazartonil, Claudia Islas.
Women stage a coup d'etat, rule Spain.

The SIGN OF FOUR (B) Mapleton/Sy Weintraub(Ross & Partners) 1983 color 103m. D: Desmond Davis. SP: Charles E. Pogue, from Sir Arthur Conan Doyle's book "Sign of the Four." Ph: Dennis Lewiston. Mus: Harry Rabinowitz. AD: Eileen Diss; Fred Carter. SpFxSup: Alan Whibley. Mkp: Tom Smith; John Webber. Ref: TV. V 5/18/83. 5/4/83:432. Ecran F 29:4.36:40-2. with Ian Richardson, David Healy, Cherie Lunghi, Terence Rigby, Thorley Walters, John Pedrick(Tonga), Joe Melia, Clive Merrison.
The principals: Mary Morstan (Lunghi), who lives in fear of the "curse that haunts the Sholtos and the Morstans," and which is linked to The Great Mogul, a fabulous diamond...a man who, under said curse, is scared to death on a stormy night...Tonga, a pygmy from the Andaman Islands who is rated "the most blood-thirsty creature in the world" and who is kept (in-between skulking assignments) in a pit as a sideshow attraction ("My God! How can you keep a thing like that!") and fed raw meat (cf. ESCAPE 2000 and its circus freak)--Tonga has monster-teeth, or fangs, a nasty growl, and surprising leaping ability, and he carries a blowgun which shoots poisoned thorns that make their victims die agonizing deaths (he's bad)...and of course Sherlock Holmes, who is not in the least perturbed by the tacky manifestations of a fairground "Ghost House" ride....
The SIGN OF FOUR is, in effect, less a mystery than it is a series of serio-comic turns by Holmes (Richardson). The viewer here--a privileged insider on the story behind the events--watches as the less-privileged Holmes makes one brilliant deduction after another, and catches up with said viewer on said story with alarming swiftness. The detective's smugness in the face of the (to others in the movie) mystifying is amusing... unless by chance you identify with the other characters, in which case Holmes might seem rather insufferable. But Richardson's Holmes so obviously enjoys being brilliant--who would begru

a person such keenly-felt satisfaction? The story is--as usual with filmed Holmes--a tad bland (Holmes and Watson are really the only characters), but it moves along nicely and neatly--there are few distractions from the deductions--and the feisty Tonga proves to be a full-fledged, all-out monster, not just more narrative-baggage. (He's a permissable distraction.)

SILENT MADNESS MAG & Earls 1983 color & 3-D (The NIGHTKILLERS-orig t. The OMEGA FACTOR and BEAUTIFUL SCREAMERS--both int ts) D,P: Simon Nuchtern. SP,P: William Milling. SP: also Robert Zimmerman. Ph: Gerald Feil. Ref: HR 10/25/83:S-52: at Mifed. V 10/26/83:123(ad). Fangoria 34. Ecran F 41:71. with Belinda Montgomery, Viveca Lindfors, Sydney Lassick.
Campus killer-at-large.

SILENT RAGE Col/Unger-Topkick 1982 color 101m. D: Michael Miller. SP: Joseph Fraley. Ph: Robert Jessup, Neil Roach. Mus: Peter Bernstein, Mark Goldenberg. AD: Jack Marty. SpFX: (sup) Jack Bennett; Randy Fife;(mkp) MkpFxLab. Opt: Fantasy II. Ref: TV. V 4/7/82. MFB'82:207. with Chuck Norris, Ron Silver, Steven Keats, Toni Kalem, William Finley, Stephen Furst, Brian Libby(John Kirby).
Super-serum Monogen 35 turns an ax-murderer (Libby) into an instant-self-healing killer with a "deranged" cellular structure, and enables him to survive bullet wounds, sulphuric-acid injections, fire, falls, collisions, etc....Larky stunt-violence, scenes of suspense-horror, and a disjointed plot. The heroine (romantic angle) and the motorcycle gang (action angle) eventually drop out of the plot, leaving only our Super-madman. Both hero and villain are virtually indestructible--the former through physical, the latter through scientific conditioning. There's no significance to this parallel--it just means that the two are a match for each other, like King Kong and Godzilla. This is HALLOWEEN on a scientific, FRANKENSTEIN footing: this science-made monster can be killed 100 times and come back 100 times. The movie is a backhanded tribute to resilience. At the end, our sheriff-hero drops Kirby down a very deep well, but the last, frozen frame hints that it's not deep enough. Kirby's inevitable resurrections are admittedly kind of kicky; they follow very brief, but apparently very restorative "naps"....

SILVER SLIME (F?) 1981? short D: Christophe Gans. Ref: Ecran 22:6: "strange creature"...hommage to Mario Bava.

SINGING SCORPION, The(by W.C.MacDonald) see RIDERS OF THE WHISTLING SKULL

El SINIESTRO DR. ORLOFF (Sp) Golden 1982 D: Jesus Franco. Sequel to *The AWFUL DR. ORLOF? Ref: V 5/4/83:414. with Howard Vernon, Robert Foster, Rocio Freixas.

The SINS OF DORIAN GRAY ABC-TV/Rankin-Bass 1983(1982) color 94m. D: Tony Maylam. SP: Ken August, Peter Lawrence, from

Oscar Wilde's book "The Picture of Dorian Gray." Ph: Zale Magder. Mus: Bernard Hoffer;(lyrics) Jules Bass. AD: Karen Bromley. SpMkp: Bob Laden; Barbara Palmer. PhFX: New Cinematic FX. Opt: Film Opticals. Ref: TV. TVG. V 2/17/82:19(ad). with Anthony Perkins, Belinda Bauer, Joseph Bottoms, Michael Ironside, Olga Karlatos.

An aspiring actress's (Bauer) wish never to grow old comes true. She remains young, while her screen-test image ages and becomes more and more grotesque, reflecting her "sins." At the end, she stabs her screen image, and presto!--it's beautiful; she's ugly and dead (and oddly scratched and spliced)....Yet another TV-movie reworking of a horror-fantasy classic. The two twists: Dorian is a woman, and the "picture" is on celluloid. The first is pointless--it simply proves a pretext for a lot of show-biz-romance cliches. The second "twist" is a lift from TAKE OFF(1978)...."Beauty is only skin deep," the movie seems to be saying. Yes, it does. The only reason to watch this is to watch Dorian run her reel. She runs it several times. She becomes more and more "heartless" and "unreasonable"; the makeup for her screen-test reel becomes more and more special....This is Evil? Bad is a line like "You destroy everybody who cares about you!"

*SKY PIRATE 1939 (TAILSPIN TOMMY IN MYSTERY PLANE-cr t) SP: G. Waggner(aka J.West). Ph: Archie Stout. Mus: Frank Sanucci. AD: E.R. Hickson. Ref: TV. Les Otis.

Inoffensive programmer. John Trent is the star, but Peter George Lynn as the "washed-up" flier, Brandy, does the acting. His crazy-beatific smile as he crashes his plane into the sea (and not-incidentally saves our heroes) is prime Ultimate-Sacrifice stuff. So who needs "believable"?

SLAUGHTERERS, The see CANNIBALS IN THE STREETS

The SLAYER 21st Century/IPS 1982(1981) color 82m. SP,D: J.S. Cardone. SP,P: William R. Ewing. Ph: Karen Grossman. Mus: Robert Folk. Sets: Jerie Kelter. SpMkpFX: Robert Short. Sp FX: Spectacular FX, Robert Babb. Opt: Cinema Research. Ref: TV: Planet Video. Ecran F 30:58.41:22,28. V 10/27/82. 9/9/81: 4(rated). with Sarah Kendall, Frederick Flynn, Carol Kottenbrook, Alan McRae, Carl Kraines(the slayer).

"Things aren't always what they appear to be...." An artist (Kendall) who "paints what (she) dreams" fears that her dream-life is taking over and supplanting real life when a two-couple vacation trip to an island off Georgia begins to turn into a nightmare of deja vu. Her "strange sensitivity" began as a child, when she first began having a recurrent dream...which dream now appears to have been a premonition. One man on the island dies when an elevator trap-door slams shut on his neck; another man is "landed" like a fish on a hook; a woman is stabbed to death with a pitchfork....Kay has one visualized nightmare in which a monster suddenly appears, and another in which she kisses what turns out to be a severed head. Through all this, a ferocious storm continues unabated...until she is, finally, confronted by her monster, and her nightmare "no longer needs (her) to give it life...."

The SLAYER is a trifle spare--three incidents and 75% atmosphere/suspense--as of course an 80-minute "Twilight Zone" is apt to be. And this picture is, in spirit, a "Zone" episode... say, "Stopover in a Quiet Town" or "Shadow Play" or "The Arrival." It keeps you guessing--is it all a sick-mind's delusion?--either dream or partly dream?--a nefarious murder-plot?--real monster or madman on the loose? The script distributes red herrings and legitimate clues fairly even-handedly. And the final twist is not, that I can recall, directly out of any "TZ" episode. It's pleasingly half-unexpected, if not really inspired. And the ending justifies--or at least helps to explain--the odd repetitiousness and nebulousness-of-detail of much of what goes before it. The SLAYER has its horror effects, but it's more a puzzler or chiller than an outright horror movie. In fact, you only see "the slayer," briefly, at the beginning and at the end. There are murders, but the murderer--or first cause--is strangely missing, or ellipsed....A low-budget mini-winner, with good photography, effects, score.

SLEEPAWAY CAMP United Film Dist./American Eagle 1983 color 85m. SP,D,Exec P: Robert Hiltzik. Ph: Benjamin Davis. Mus: Edward Bilous. PD,SpFxCoord: William Billowit. SpMkp: Edward French. SpMechFX: Ed Fountain. OptFX: Computer Opts. Ref: screen. V 11/30/83: HOMICIDAL "gender switch." Robert Moore. with Mike Kellin, Felissa Rose(Angela), Paul De Angelo, R.E. Jones.

Psychotic kid ruins summer camp for other kids at Camp Arawak; slaughters little boys in their sleeping bags; scalds cook to near-death; knifes one counselor as she showers; and shoots (with bow and arrow) another, as he wanders, foolishly, onto the archery range....The operative word in the title is "Camp." Just when you thought it was safe to write off all the official-and-unofficial sequels to FRIDAY THE 13TH, along comes one which is, well, different--not good, but bad in a "good" way. Watchable. Funny--mostly unintentionally. SLEEPAWAY CAMP has, for instance, the funniest horrified-reaction shots (to dead bodies)--i.e., retching, "takes" and looks of horror, extended screams--since PIECES. True, the bodies of the victims here are pretty messed up--unbelievably so, in fact--the makeup effects are as cornily exaggerated as the actors' reactions to same. And the director is, obviously, proud of his colleague's work: he actually gives you time to judge the details of bloating and bruising. At one point, a doctor comments on the awful fate of the scalding victim: "The pain must be incredible!" Yes, it's all so horrible--or would be if they didn't have to keep telling you how horrible. The actors pose and pause to say things like "It can't be you!" Shots are held, ominously; scenes fade out, self-consciously, or dissolve, sinisterly, to the next one. (Yes, dissolves can be sinister--watch.) And to camouflage the HOMICIDAL twist referred to above, half the characters in the movie are "weird" or affected--not just the two directly involved in the twist.

SLEEPLESS NIGHTS see SLUMBER PARTY MASSACRE, The

The SLUMBER PARTY MASSACRE New World(Santa Fe) 1982 color 75m. (SLEEPLESS NIGHTS-orig t) D,P: Amy Jones. SP: Rita Mae Brown. Ph: Steve Posey. Mus: Ralph Jones. AD: F. Bartoccini; P. Cunzano. SpFX: Larry Carr, Rick Lazzarini, MkpFxLab. Opt: Jack Rabin. CoP: Aaron Lipstadt. Ref: screen. V 3/31/82. MFB '83:307. Weldon. with Michele Michaels, Robin Stille, Michael Villela(Russ Thorn), Debra DeLiso, Joe Dante.

An escaped mass-murderer commits a new series of murders with drill and butcher knife....pizza man (Lipstadt) delivered, dead and eyeless...HOLLYWOOD BOULEVARD('76) (slasher scene) on TV....A more-or-less-regulation slash-and-drill thriller. Publicized as a feminist statement on the genre, it really gets little further, socio-politically-speaking, than identifying the killer's drill as phallic. This isn't really a parody either--it's about as funny as The TEXAS CHAIN SAW MASSACRE, which is to say not too....The occasional stroke of macabre humor seems incidental to the horror-plot mechanics. The characters here are little more than functional, whether their function be to kill, be killed, or both. Even the murderer, Thorn, is mostly business. He might actually be the pizza man that he impersonates in one scene. The glossy impersonality of the characters and production seems only an end, not a means.

The SNAKE QUEEN (Indon.) Rapi 1983? D: Sam Gardner. Ref: V 1/19/83:64(ad). 10/20/82:235(ad). Ecran F 33:31.32:70. with Ratno Timoer, George Rudy, Nenna Rosier, Barry Prima.

Woman with power over snakes.

2 SO DARK THE NIGHT 1946 AD: Carl Anderson. Ref: screen. HR 10/30/46. MPH 9/14/46. FD 9/12/46. and with Adrienne d'Ambricourt, Frank Arnold, T. Gottlieb(hunchback).

The English-language, French-accented dialogue blunts the tragic/horrific overtones of this Jekyll-and-Hyde-like story--the occasional French phrases merely underline the artificiality. The hero-as-villain story angle, however, provides some touching moments. The film's high point: the detective (Steven Geray) "seeing" himself, at the end, as he was when he first arrived at the country inn--an image of vanished peace and contentment.

2A SOMETHING EVIL CBS-TV/Trident-TV(Lembeck-Knapp) 1972 SP: Robert Clouse. Ph: Bill Butler. Mus: Wladimir Selinsky. AD: E.A. Heschong. SpOptFX: Brandes, Berke & Assoc. Mkp: Ken Chase. Ref: TV. Crawley. Weldon. and with Johnny Whitaker (Stevie), Lynn Cartwright, Carl Gottlieb, Margaret Avery, Michael Macready, Bruno Ve Sota, Steven Spielberg.

The devil possesses a boy (Whitaker) and drives his mother

(Sandy Dennis) to distraction....Clouse seems to be out to beat the film of The EXORCIST to the punch; director Spielberg seems to be anticipating CLOSE ENCOUNTERS OF THE THIRD KIND, and the disintegration of the family therein. And--thanks mainly to Dennis as Marjorie Worden--the breakdown of the Wordens is more compelling than that of the Nearys. (Admittedly not that difficult a feat--the human drama of CE3K was not its strength.) Her increasing helplessness and isolation are harrowingly detailed, if the supernatural manifestations are less intriguing than her personal drama. The hyper-dramatic, near-camp climactic sequence calls for an actress to repeat the familiar line "I love you," convincingly, several times. Dennis convinces. (It seems that her love is all that stands between her son and the devil.)

SOMETHING WICKED THIS WAY COMES BV/Bryna 1983 color 95m. D: Jack Clayton. SP: Ray Bradbury, from his book, in turn inspired by his story "Black Ferris." Ph: S.H. Burum; Jan Kiesser. Mus: James Horner. PD: Richard MacDonald. SpVisFX: Lee Dyer; Van Der Veer; Visual Concepts. SpMkp: R.J. Schiffer. Anim: (fx sup) Michael Wolf;(prod coord) Ron Stangl. SpFX:(cons) Harrison Ellenshaw;(asst d) Steve McEveety;(ph) Cruickshank, Anderson, Meador. KaleidFX: Symmetricon. SpMechFX:(sup) R. Tautin; Allen Hall et al. SpSdFX: Portman, Horton. Computer FX: Magi-Synthavision. OptSup: Bill Kilduff. Composite Sup: Clint Colver. Creative Cons: Jeanie Simms. Ref: screen. FComm 11/82:39. V 5/4/83. pr. MFB'83:278-9. with Jason Robards, Jonathan Pryce(Mr.Dark), Pam Grier(Dust Witch), Diane Ladd, Royal Dano, Vidal Peterson, Shawn Carson, Ellen Geer, Angelo Rossitto, Richard Davalos.

"Something's going on" in Greentown: "The Autumn People" arrive with Dark's Pandemonium Carnival (known, back in the 1880's, as The Autumn Carnival) and fulfill, "Faust"-like, the fantasies of the townsfolk. They "feed" (as Mr. Dark explains) on the emotional torments of others...but happiness (and a little lightning) "makes 'em run"....man who becomes young on merry-go-round-in-reverse...witch who gives man "brief taste of death"; boys, nightmares re: spiders...dreams-on-display in hall of mirrors...kaleidoscopic tattoo.

A most adventuresome--if not really too successful--fantasy. The main thought in SOMETHING WICKED seems to sort out something to the effect that the remedy for unhappiness is happiness. This is, perhaps, a slightly unfair paraphrase of the film's theme, but it's close enough to suggest weaknesses in the film. Bradbury's script is laced with interesting ideas and compelling imagery, but the levels on which it works--the literal and the figurative--seem to be out of synch. Is it, for instance, the love which the boy declares for his father--or the lightning--which ultimately vanquishes all things wicked? Or both? Is (as it seems) one of the two quantities superfluous? The climactic sequence seems to operate somewhere between metaphor and coincidence....The effects comprise a fairly splendid carnival themselves, but as often as not seem unnecessary or redundant--the invasion of the spiders, for example, doesn't add much except spiders. At its best--in, say, the scene in which Dark equates each lost year of the librarian's life with a page torn flaming from a book--the movie vividly and lucidly literalizes its ideas. Dark scorns the man for "living through other men's lives"--living only through books--and thus author Bradbury, implicitly, equates the two men...for Dark and his carnies literally live on the life-force of others. But how, exactly, this comparison is supposed to work within the movie is uncertain. The only thing which is certain is that a leech-like existence is discouraged....At the end, the librarian shatters the (literal and figurative) mirrors of illusion, deception, whatever, and begins (apparently) to live his own life. (As in SOMETHING EVIL, above, the magic words are "I love you," spoken here son-to-father; there, mother-to-son.) You can't get around the symbolism in this movie--it's very insistent--but you may also find yourself stuck as to what to do with it. The spectacle of a full-grown man taking a (literal) ride back into childhood--on a mystically-blurry merry-go-round--is undeniably a fascinating one. But what, actually, does he--and what does Dark--get out of such physical regression? Childhood is wasted on this child: he just goes out and rounds up another lost dreamer (the schoolmarm) for Dark. He doesn't enjoy his gift. That would be real horror. If a pristine, childlike (Bradbury-like) wonder (as well as childhood itself) were restored to the denizens of the carnival, some ambivalence would tinge the scenes of their destruction at the end. But there's no such thing (the movie seems to say) as a happy vampire, even in Greentown....

*SON OF GODZILLA (AI-TV) 1968 (GOJIRA NO MUSUKO) Puppet FX: Fumio Nakadai. Ref: TV. Glut/CMM. Lee. no LC. JFFJ 14:26-7,38.

UN scientists' weather-controlling experiments on a "spooky island" go awry and cause a "radioactive storm." The latter, in turn, starts already-gigantic mantises growing even larger. Driven, apparently, by curiosity, they unearth and crack open a huge egg--"It looks as if it's a baby Godzilla." At the end, the proud father and "young Godzilla" hibernate for the duration of a man-made blizzard....huge, ugly spider which "stays underground until he gets hungry," and whose web can be severed only with heat. ("It's a terrible monster!"--not just a middling-bad one.) Also: "miraculous" red-water cure.

Toho, angling for the "cute" trade, does its own SON OF KONG. Here, papa (or mama) is still around, and teaching baby the basics--like breathing fire. (Baby's first try produces only a smoke ring.) Young Godzilla also plays kick-the-rock and hop-on-pop. Like most babies, he's utterly adorable, and touchingly helpless. Unlike most babies, however, he probably weighs a ton or two. The most winning use here of monster-body language: the son's flopped-flat-on-his-back, arms-flailing pout. One would much rather indulge him than the plot, which is composed of miscellaneous humans (including a "native girl" who tosses tidbits up into "little" Godzilla's mouth--they look like watermelons going up and M&M's going in) and monsters, and is viable only as a showcase for the quasi-heartwarming father-son scenes, which, for better or worse, are somewhat unforgettable.

SORCELLERIE CULINAIRE see COOK IN TROUBLE, The

SORCERER'S APPRENTICE, The see KRABAT

SORCERESS New World/Jack Hill 1982 color 75m. D: Brian Stuart. SP: Jim Wynorski. Ph: Alex Phillips Jr. AD: Joe Greenman. SpDes: John Buechler. SpFX: New World FX; Marcus Patchet. Anim Des: Deborah Gaydos. Mkp: Carol Palomino. Ref: screen. V 2/16/83. with Leigh & Lynette Harris, Bob Nelson, Bruno Rey, Ana de Sade, David Millbern.

The "secrets of sorcery" are passed on by Krona to the psychically-and-sexually-bound twins Mira and Mara (the Harrises)....The invocation of "The Name" summons the bat-lion god Vital(sp?) from the heavens to do battle with the evil, deformed, ray-spitting god Kalgara(sp?)....The evil sorcerer Traigon (Robert Ballesteros) disintegrates at the end of the first of his three lives....Plus: catacombs mummies which come to life...intelligent ape-servant, and band of apes with laughing-gas fruit-weapons...Soma, hypnotic nectar of the gods...Pando, satyr...enveloping earth...sword-into-snake.

Atrocious sword-and-sorcery fantasy aspires to comedy, doesn't even rate as camp. Informed that they are "not boys," the voluptuous, goatskin-disguised twins disbelievingly ask "We're not?! Are you sure?" The general level of comic invention is scarcely higher...though the remote-control sex scene with Mira (or is it Mara?)--a variation on the scene with the Siamese twins in FREAKS--is both amusing and, even, erotic. ("Is she being tortured?" asks an inobservant observer.) "The Name" by any other name is still "The Force." The acting by the cast is so uniformly stilted that it seems to be calculated.

SOTTO GLI OCCHI DELL'ASSASSINO see TENEBRAE

*The SPACE CHILDREN 1958 (The EGG-orig t) Process Ph: Farciot Edouart. Mkp: Wally Westmore. Ref: TV. Bill Warren. Scot Holton. V 6/18/58. Stanley. and with John Washbrook, R. Shannon.

Omelet-like being from space travels a column-of-light to a seashore cave on Earth; gives children psychic powers over adults and objects; ultimately prevents the launching of The Thunderer, a satellite armed with a hydrogen warhead and powered by a new propellant. Similar beings render warheads the world over harmless....A modest, compact, rather-likably earnest sf-drama, told as a mystery--The Egg and Us. If the presence on Earth of the alien is no secret, its specific mission is. (Its general, anti-war mission is common to Fifties aliens, and no surprise.) This is a message movie, but the message is reserved for the movie's concluding moments, and doubles as the "solution" to the mystery. If the script's celebration of the triumph of the "wisdom and innocence of a child" is rather facile, it's also the source of odd images of kids not just playing at spies-about-the-rocket-plant, but actually becoming pint-sized agents of the alien (as they reconnoiter on the beach, at the launch site, etc.). They play for real. Fortunately or unfortunately, the movie's only camp element is the person of the scientist on the base, who keeps breaking into metaphor to describe his profession. Among his incisive analogies: "A man of science is like a deep-sea diver. He mustn't be afraid to walk down where it's dark and frightening, in the hopes of scooping up a handful of truth." (The writers here scooped up quite a handful themselves....)

SPACE CRUISER see UCHU SENKAN YAMATO--KANKETSUHEN

SPACE 1999 see COSMIC PRINCESS. DESTINATION MOONBASE ALPHA. JOURNEY THROUGH THE BLACK SUN.

SPACE RAIDERS New World/Millennium 1983 color 82m. SP,D: Howard R. Cohen. Ph: Alec Hirschfeld. Mus: James Horner; (songs) Murphy Dunne. AD: Wayne Springfield; Roger Kelton. SpVisFX:(sup) Tom Campbell;(elec) F. Lee Stone;(roto) Deborah Gaydos. SpMkpFX: Mike Jones; Tony Tierney, Judy Elkins. Pyro FX: Roger George, Adams Calvert. with Vince Edwards, David Mendenhall, Patsy Pease, Thom Christopher, Luca Bercovici, Drew Snyder, Dick Miller, Ray Stewart(Zariatin). Ref: screen. V 8/10/83: music from BATTLE BEYOND THE STARS. 5/11/83:6(rated).

Heavy traffic in outer space, as humans and aliens shuttle back and forth between Regulus(sp?) 5 and other planets (including Earth), and a boy, Peter (Mendenhall), makes friends (and enemies) everywhere. The main vehicle: a giant "robot ship." Supporting characters: Peter's space-insect pet, a telepathic alien, a monster-"cat," and assorted extra-terrestrial

PAPER MOON in outer space again. (See also SPACEHUNTER, below.) The Edwards-Mendenhall teaming conjures up Instant Sentiment. The man learns how to care for someone; the boy learns how to demolish enemy spaceships. Edwards gets both a Death Scene and a Back-from-the-Dead Scene...neither of them done as well as E.T.'s. Somewhere someone is--or should be--blushing....Fortunately, the mawkishness is occasionally dispelled by bits of humor--e.g., the alien reading a magazine written in alien...the line concluding "...and we came out with a kid with a bug in a beer can"...the spaceship co-pilot muttering "I hate rocks," as he flips a switch and blasts a passing meteor...and of course the spiel by the seemingly-ubiquitous Dick Miller, as used-transport dealer Crazy Mel, in the form, here, of a hologram. An appearance by Miller is getting to be the Seal of Approval for any self-respecting genre piece nowadays....

SPACE SEED see STAR TREK--THE WRATH OF KHAN

SPACE WARP see COSMIC PRINCESS

SPACE WARRIOR--BALDIOS see BARUDIOSU

SPACEHUNTER: ADVENTURES IN THE FORBIDDEN ZONE Col/Delphi(Ivan Reitman) 1983 color/3-D/ws 88m. D: Lamont Johnson. SP: Edith Rey, David Preston, Dan Goldberg, Len Blum. Story: Stewart Harding, Jean Lafleur. Ph: Frank Tidy. Mus: Elmer Bernstein. PD: Jackson De Govia. SpMkpFX:(sup) Thomas R. Burman; S. Laporte, Rob Burman et al. SpVisFX:(sup) Warren Kleinow;(ad) Michael Minor; Fantasy II. SpFX:(coord) Dale Martin; Robert Burns et al. OptFX:(sp) Image 3;(coord) Vicky Witt;(ph) Phil Huff et al. Anim: E.D. Farino, B. Mixon. PyroFX: Joe Viskocil. Graphics: Lee Cole. SdDes: Blue Light. Titles: R/Greenberg. SpProps: R. Joyce. Mattes: Matte FX. Models: Dennis Schultz. Ref: screen. V 5/18/83. MFB'83:279: ROAD GANGS and ADVENTURES IN THE CREEP ZONE-early ts. with Peter Strauss, Molly Ringwald, Michael Ironside(Overdog), Andrea Marcovicci(android), B. Carroll.

On the distant, Earth-like planet Terra Eleven ("the garbage heap of the universe"), sometime in the 21st Century. The mechanically-enhanced Overdog, ruler of mutants, prolongs his life by draining the vitality of his captives, and has children scientifically turned into mutants...."vultures," warriors who fly wing-contraptions...sea monster and Amazons...cryogenic.

Story-wise, a pretty tired crossing of STAR WARS and PAPER MOON, as Earther Strauss and adolescent Scav Ringwald search her dump of a planet for three women kidnapped to satisfy the lusts of Overdog. He's not bad doing William Holden circa STALAG 17, and she's o.k. doing a punk Tatum O'Neal. But Ironside, as usual, is the center of attention--his special makeup insures it. He still looks himself--craggily intimidating--only more so. It's the set and creature design, however, which are most responsible for keeping the proceedings from becoming too dull: there are tree stumps, or roots--growing up out of a cavern lake--which look like upside-down hat-racks gone wild, and baggy monsters that might be the Michelin-tire man gone to seed. Overdog's indoor domain features elements of ancient Rome, a disco from hell, and ROAD WARRIOR costuming; his filament-based vitality-drainer might have been designed by a mad, renegade GE scientist. Overdog himself seems to be operated by crane, like a motion-picture camera. He's the latest in movie man-machine hybrids, a human wrecking-crane.

SPACEKETEERS see SHOGUN WARRIORS: SPACEKETEERS

SPACESHIP Almi Cinema 5/Schwartz-England 1981 colors/ws 88m. (2 The CREATURE WASN'T NICE-orig t. SPACESHIP!-int t?) SP,D, Songs & with: Bruce Kimmel. Ph: Vilis Lapenieks(aka Denny Lavil). Mus: David Spear;(chor) Joe Tremaine. PD: Lee Cole. VisFX: The Magic Lantern;(sup) W.J. Hedge, Bob Greenberg et al.

Min: Omens, Bostrom, Guest. SpDes: Cary Howe. SpMkpFX: Peter Knowlton. Prosth: Fran Evans. SdFX: Stan & Carol Jones. Ref: TV. V 10/28/81. 9/9/81:4(rated). 4/20/83:10,22. Weldon. Scot Holton. Bill Warren: stock from WAR OF THE WORLDS. Bob Greenberg. with Cindy Williams, Leslie Nielsen, Gerrit Graham, Patrick Macnee, Ron Kurowski(creature), Paul Brinegar, C. Eichen.

ALIEN with laughs. The year is 2012, and the crew of the spaceship Vertigo discovers a new planet, Stark (named after a member of the crew), and, on it, a plant, a "weird city," and, most importantly, a "living organism" which grows into a monster that "eats everything." A special communication-helmet enables the creature to sing and dance to "I Want To Eat Your Face," the lyrics of which reveal its motivation. During a second musical interlude, the creature is tricked into outer space. Plus: Max, an "abusive, emotionally-unstable" computer.

A generally deft, charming minor-league comedy. The teamwork of Nielsen (as the pompous, self-satisfied captain) and Graham (as his abusive, emotionally-unstable subordinate) anchors the movie. All aboard (including the creature) seem to be out for a good time, at the expense of space-opera cliches. The actors here pause at the right, are-you-listening? moments--e.g., Nielsen, sententiously: "Pressure--the demon of space." Or, Macnee, later: "I don't want to appear in any way...ominous." The actors seem happy not to be taking their job seriously--at least their usual job of maintaining credibility as characters. Here, their job is to undermine credibility, to call attention to themselves as actors, doing tricks with words and phrases. SPACESHIP is a "This Is Your Life" of favorite monster-movie dramatic-devices and cliches...The False Alarm, for instance. (See also The DEADLY SPAWN.) Here, the latter is a hammer, dropped repeatedly during a mock-tense scene in one of the ship's corridors. Each time the hammer falls, the characters scream and jump, as actors do in all good, by-the-rules monster movies. The creature itself doesn't so much play by the rules as with the rules; the two dance numbers reduce--or elevate--him, or it, to song-and-dance-beast status. He's done in by ribbing long before he is dispatched into...the void of space. The comedy in SPACESHIP thins a bit, as the cast thins to Kimmel and Williams, who can't quite maintain the tone, or level, of drollery established by Nielsen, Macnee, and Graham.

SPADE DEI BARBARI see SWORD OF THE BARBARIANS

SPASMS (Can.) Cinequity-NTC(Erlichman) & CFDC-Famous Players/PDC(Nat'l.Trust) 1983(1982) color 89m. (aka DEATH BITE) D: William Fruet. SP: Don Enright, from Michael Maryk & Brent Monahan's novel "Death Bite." Ph: Mark Irwin; Maris Jansons. Mus: Eric N. Robertson;(theme) Tangerine Dream. AD: Gavin Mitchell; Gallo, Harvey. SpFX:(d) Brian Warner;(cons) Colin Chilvers; M. Kavanagh. SpDes: Raymond A. Mendez;(mech fx) Lewis Gluck, G. McLaughlin;(model) Neal Martz. SpMkpFX: Dick Smith, Carl Fullerton, Stephan Dupuis. SdFxEd: Jim Hopkins.

Opt: Film Opticals. Ref: TV: Thorn EMI Video. V 3/9/83:4(rated). Bill Warren. MFB'83:308. with Peter Fonda, Oliver Reed, Kerrie Keane, Al Waxman, Miguel Fernandes, Marilyn Lightstone.

A giant Micronesian demon-snake returns to the island of Maraka-Bintu(sp?), or "The Gates of Hell," every 7 years to collect the souls of the dead. Brought back alive to San Diego, this "one-of-a-kind...devil" escapes....The bodies of its victims swell horribly, and the putrefying process therein is fantastically accelerated. One man, Kincaid (Reed), bitten by the snake 7 years earlier, "sees through its eyes," telepathically, and experiences the demon's killings....

What DEADLY EYES does for big rats, SPASMS does for big snakes--i.e., nothing. The thrashing and bloating effects--involving the snake's victims--are pretty horrific. But the snake itself hardly makes its presence felt. This is, yes, yet another in the continuing Attack of the Steadicam series of subjective-camera-monster movies, and although the Steadicam is, in a sense, ideal in the role of gliding-demon-snake, it's beginning to suffer from type-casting as any-and-every type of monster. Once more, actors and actresses are caught in the awkward position of fleeing in abject terror from...a movie camera. Rats, snakes, and Steadicams ought, perhaps, be given a holiday from horror movies....The diffuse script of SPASMS is all false starts and loose ends, with ill-coordinated elements of telepathy--which element seems extraneous--snake worship, and general herpetology. Keane's role (as Reed's niece) consists of telling Reed and Fonda not to do whatever it is that they're planning on doing next (e.g., import a monster-snake...proceed into a greenhouse in search of same). Swell role....

SPECIAL BULLETIN NBC-TV/Ohlmeyer 1983 color 92m. Story,D,P: Edward Zwick. Story,SP,P: Marshall Herskovitz. Ph: Hank Geving;(lighting) Carl Gibson; Charles Fernandez. SpVisFX: Image West, Pendulum. SpFX: Carol Lynn Ent. VideoFX: William Feightner. Mkp: Kenneth Horn. Ref: TV. TVG: videotaped. V 3/23/83:65. 9/26/83:22: Emmy for Best Special. Oakland Tribune 3/21/83:A1,A10. SF Chron 3/18/83:24. with Christopher Allport, David Clennon, Ed Flanders, Kathryn Walker, David Rasche.

"Terrorism has reached the atomic age": a terrorist group demanding disposal of the 968 nuclear-warhead detonating modules located in the Charleston, S.C., area threatens to explode its own nuclear device containing 5.2 kilos of stolen plutonium. The bomb's anti-tamper devices thwart a Nuclear Emergency Search Team, and the bomb explodes, leaving about 2,000 dead and 500,000 people homeless, and creating a miles-long "nuclear footprint" corridor contaminated by radiation.

SPECIAL BULLETIN is actually a series of bulletins, background stories (on the terrorists; on Charleston), and news-story summaries from the fictional RBS-network newsroom. It's a TV-movie which cannily mines the spectacle, drama, and suspense associated with live TV-network news coverage: it's self-consciously present-tense narrative. The "bulletins" here expertly mimic the moves and sounds of broadcasters, reporters, experts-in-their-fields, media-conscious activist-types. There are the significant and insignificant pauses, the dead moments, technical and human static, technical delays, bulletins interrupting bulletins, repeated words and phrases, the eerily familiar vocal patterns of the newscasters and reporters, the fancy graphics and transitional visual devices, the newsroom sounds (ticker tapes ticking, phones ringing), filler material--and the touchingly hit-and-miss moments of drama and horror. The chill of the movie lies not just in the semi-apocalyptic story itself, but also in its presentation: this might be any major news story of the past 20 years. We know the wrapping--time, it seems, will supply any sort of apocalyptic content. The predictions of Nostradamus (or, The MAN WHO SAW TOMORROW, qq.v.) are your guide to the nightly news of 1986--tamed, packaged, but not lacking in horrific fascination. This TV-movie is at once quite responsible-seeming--it amounts to a collective indictment of the government, the media, and terrorists, or the collusion therefrom--and highly irresponsible-seeming--it might be a lesson plan for atomic-age terrorists. It does everything but supply the plutonium....The end, as seen here, will not come with a bang or whimper, but with television static.

SPIDER-MAN: THE CON CAPER AND THE CURSE OF RAVA CBS-TV/Fries & Goodman(Danchuk) 1978 color 92m. (The CON CAPER AND THE CURSE OF RAVA-ad t) D: Tom Blank, Michael Caffey. SP: G.S. Dinallo, Robert Janes. Story: B. McKay, D. Nelson, Janes. From "The Amazing Spider-Man" TV series, based on the Stan Lee comic strip. Ph: Vincent Martinelli, Jack Whitman. Mus: Dana Kaproff, Stu Phillips. AD: Steve Berger, Bill Ross. SpFX: William Schirmer, Don Courtney. SdFX: The Cutters. Opt: CFI. Ref: TV. TVG. with Nicholas Hammond, Robert F. Simon, Chip Fields, Ellen Bry(continuing cast); Theodore Bikel, Michael Pataki, Andrew Robinson, Ramon Bieri, Adrienne LaRussa, P. Wexler.

Spider-Man (Hammond) has X-ray (and apparently flashback) vision, super-strength, the ability to leap up and climb walls and to shoot out rope-like webs and nets....The high priest (Bikel) of Rava, Kalistani God of Death, possesses telekinetic powers; makes a young woman begin to suffocate; makes an idol of Rava fall and kill one man; makes a car stop and start.... "Computerized, ultrasonic sensor" opens bank vault.

Slick, hollow, pseudo-serious. The subjects of political corruption and prison reform are raised, then quietly dropped, in the first story, "The Con Caper." This "film" is, of course, simply two TV-series episodes spliced together. A clumsily written and performed linking scene has, however, been inserted between the two to provide a sort of phantom continuity. At least it must have satisfied someone's sense of narrative propriety. The super-stunts are, visually, unremarkable; Ms. LaRussa is another matter altogether....

SPIDER-MAN: ESCORT TO DANGER AND THE NIGHT OF THE CLONES 1978 color 92m. Ref: TVG.

SPIDER-MAN: PHOTO FINISH AND MATTER OF STATE 1978 (MATTER OF STATE/PHOTO FINISH-ad t) D: Tony Ganz, Larry Stewart. SP: Howard Dimsdale. SpFX: W. Schirmer, Sam Dockrey. Ref: TV. TVG. with Jennifer Billingsley, Nicholas Coster, John Crawford, Charles Haid, Geoffrey Lewis, Milt Kogan.

Peter Parker aka Spider-Man is jailed for withholding evidence from the police and (in story two) uncovers a government cover-up....An awkward mixture of shallowly "serious" storytelling and hokey super-stunts with X-ray vision, bendable iron bars, over-starched ropes (or "webs"), and supposedly spider-like, all-fours crawling-about on sides of buildings. Was "The Adventures of Superman"--back in "our" day (i.e., the Fifties)--as silly as this? Again, the "highlight" of this Spider-Man "movie" is the linking scene, in which both the episode you have just witnessed and the episode you are about to see are oh-so-subtly alluded to and thus effectively and forever "linked."

SPIDER-MAN: WOLFPACK AND THE KIRKWOOD HAUNTING 1978 (The KIRKWOOD HAUNTING/WOLF PACK or WOLFPACK/THE KIRKWOOD HAUNTING-ad ts) D: Joe Manduke, Don McDougall. SP: Steve Kandel, Michael Michaelman. SpFX: W. Schirmer. Ref: TV. TVG. TVFFSB. with Dolph Sweet, Alan Arbus, Paul Carr, Marlyn Mason.

Story one: Spider-Man vs. a "failed chemist" who uses a hypnotic mist (which temporarily renders the subject a "zombie") for criminal purposes. Also: catalepsy drug. Story two: a manor house is plagued by mysterious noises, footsteps, manifestations, and aural and written messages from the beyond. Behind it all: the head of the Psychic Research Institute (and author of "Ghosts of Hudson Valley"), who employs ultra-sound devices, electric charges, and stereo speakers for his "ghosts." "The Kirkwood Haunting" features the odd spectacle of Peter Parker using his super-powers to debunk the supernatural. The former are "real"; the latter is fake....The usual super-stunts and skullduggery in tepid TV-pseudo-movie.

SPIRITS OF THE DEEP 1979 color c90m. Ref: TVG. no Academy. Speculation re: hauntings at sea.

SPLIT IMAGE Orion/PolyGram(GAC) 1982 color/ws 111m. SpFX: Jack Bennett. OptFX: Modern. Mkp: Jimi White. Ref: TV. Jim Shapiro. V 10/6/82. PFA.

Sequence including (brief) hallucination of deprogrammer-as-human-lizard...clip from '41 DR. JEKYLL AND MR. HYDE, and post-screening discussion re: "the duality of human nature".... Love in its various forms--religious-platonic, parental, romantic--makes various claims on youth; romance wins, for unclear reasons, though partly, perhaps, because both the Homeland cultists and his folks act a bit "unnatural" (the former are anti-sex; his mom seems jealous of his light-o'-love) and don't seem wholly sincere. James Woods is very good as the brutally business-like brain-cleaner; Peter Fonda is well-cast as the too-too-loving guru.

2 SPOILERS OF THE PLAINS 1951 Mus: R. Dale Butts. AD: Frank Arrigo. SpFX: Howard & Theodore Lydecker. OptFX: Consolidated. Mkp: Bob Mark. Ref: TV. Bill Warren.

An "experimental station" headed by Dr. Jonathan Manning (William Forrest) is testing a "long-range weather forecasting" mechanism, "the most advanced of its kind in the world today." Sent aloft on an "entirely new type of rocket," it "can predict the weather months ahead," for farming or (as the spy-saboteur notes) for military purposes. More specifically, the device performs "upper air research," making a record of "protons, upper air activity...." At least that's, roughly, what the enemy agent tells us. The doctor himself never does let anyone in on his research. He's very dedicated, and orders his daughter/assistant to stay away from Roy Rogers ("a lowbrow cowpoke") and his buddy (a "submarginal idiot"). The unexpected science-fiction elements notwithstanding, this is a standard Roy Rogers Western, with the familiar lowbrow mixture of action, music, comedy, and pathos.

SQUARTATORE DI NEW YORK, Lo see NEW YORK RIPPER

SRDECNY POZDRAV ZE ZEMEKOULE (Cz) 1982 D: Oldrich Lipsky. Ref: Ecran F 40:73: sf-parody. with Jiri Menzel.

Two aliens on Earth.

2 The STALKER New Yorker/Sovexport 1979('81-U.S.) 157m. Ref: screen. Cinef XIII:6. SFChron 3/16/83. MagF&SF 2/83: the source book reviewed, as "Roadside Picnic." FQ Fall'81:12-17(M.Dempsey).

Was it a meteorite or a "visitation from outer space," 20 years ago, which created "The Zone," a tightly-guarded area somewhere in (apparently) Russia, in which "things change every minute"? This strange new wonderland features highly mutable topography, a long, man-sized metal pipe which is "the most terrible part of The Zone," and The Room, in which one's innermost wishes are granted. The Stalker leads a writer and a scientist to The Room, but they refuse to enter it, for obscure reasons....The Stalker's daughter, a "Zone victim," or mutant, proves to have budding telekinetic powers.

Director Andrei Tarkovsky, who put it all together with SOLARIS(1972), took it apart again with his next two films, The MIRROR and The STALKER, the former well-nigh-impenetrable, the latter all-but-unendurable. In The STALKER (or STALKER, as it is advertised), he is stating baldly, and for the most part unartistically, that authors and scientists have taken away hope. What or whose hope, exactly, is not clear. In two-plus hours of film, Tarkovsky accomplishes what he could have (and has) accomplished in two sentences in an interview. The most awful effect of his Zone: it seems to encourage travelers through it drone on and on philosophically. The characters here are merely mouthpieces....The coda with the daughter (who does not speak), however, is remarkably well-conceived, one of the finest scenes in all Tarkovsky. The director scatters hints that this child, "Monkey," is an embodiment of hope: most scenes outside The Zone are tinted a dreary brown; scenes inside it are shot in color--life, hope, anything seems possible here; outside, only the girl's scenes are shot in color. And, at one point, the Stalker states that age ossifies people... only the young possess the power of believing....The film's coda is connected with a close shot at the very beginning of the movie, in which a drinking glass sliding mysteriously across a table is promptly and simply "explained"...as the rumble of an approaching train becomes apparent. The coda reverses this supernatural-to-natural drift: again a glass slides across a table, but this time its movement appears to coincide with the gaze of the girl, who is seated at the far end of the table. The connection is clarified as she then stares, in turn, a bottle and a vase across the table's surface. The rumble again, immediately afterwards, of the train produces a relatively minor, quasi-telekinetic effect. Its mundane roar, though, is now accompanied by the sound of Beethoven's triumphant Ninth; the latter does not "take over" the sound track, however--it recedes in the distance (in effect) along with the sound of the train. But that originally-demythologizing train now carries away some magic of its own--as does the girl--into the non-Zone world. Visitors to The Zone are said to have the power to change it--the girl seems to have the power to change the outside world....

STAR TREK--THE WRATH OF KHAN Para 1982 color/ws 113m. (STAR TREK II--THE WRATH OF KHAN-ad t) D: Nicholas Meyer. SP: Jack B. Sowards. Story: Sowards, Harve Bennett. Based on the "Space Seed" episode of the "Star Trek" TV series. Ph: Gayne Rescher. Mus: James Horner. PD: Joseph R. Jennings. SpVisFX: Industrial Light & Magic; Tom Smith;(sup) Ken Ralston, Jim Veilleux;(ph) Don Dow, Scott Farrar;(models) Steve Gawley;(elec) Marty Brenneis. Starfield FX: Evans & Sutherland. SpFX:(sup) Bob Dawson; E.A. Ayer, Martin Becker et al;(lighting) Sam Nicholson. Graphics:(des) Lee Cole;(computer) Dr. Robert Langridge. SpSdFX: Alan Howarth; Eugene Finley. OptFX:(sup) Bruce Nicholson; Modern. Anim:(sup) Samuel Comstock; Visual Concept Eng. Mattes:(art) Chris Evans, Frank Ordaz;(ph) Neil Krepela. Mkp: Werner Keppler, J.L. McCoy. Video: Hal & Alan Landaker. Ref: screen. TV. V 5/26/82. Bill Warren. MFB'82: 175-6. with William Shatner, Leonard Nimoy(Spock), DeForest Kelley, Ricardo Montalban(Khan), James Doohan, Walter Koenig, George Takei, Nichelle Nichols, Bibi Besch, Paul Winfield, Ike Eisenmann, Kirstie Alley(Saavik).

The 23rd Century. Genesis Project to create life on dead planets via matter reorganization..."hypnotizing," mind-burrowing creatures...Kirk vs. his old foe, Khan, exiled with his followers on a once-fertile, now-desolate planet...Spock's body left, at the end, in a Genesis-spawned new Eden....A treat, apparently, for fans of the series; for non-trekkies, a pop-cultural museum tour, with the bodies (living and dead) of the series characters all-too-prominently on display. You already have your feeling for them, or not; this film won't generate it. Khan seems to have developed a chronic floridity-of-delivery after 15 years on Senti(sp?) Alpha 5, and is saddled with a folly-of-revenge theme, which his monotonous monomania is intended to illustrate. Kirk himself is stuck with some personal-and-professional-growth themes (in some particularly heavy-handed dramatic scenes), though Shatner, as usual, is most ingratiating in lighter moments. (Though even some of these are rather-too-heavily underscored by staging and editing.) Kirk comes to terms with himself, with death, etc., and one is supposed to feel that he has grown. But one may, instead, simply be left feeling that something has been outlined, or diagramed, on a blackboard. In STAR TREK II, the whole universe, it seems, is reduced to a learning experience for Admiral Kirk.

See also: AIRPLANE II.

2P STAR VIRGIN Gail(Treetop) 1980(1979) color 75m. D,P: Linus Gator. SP: Humphry Knipe. Ph: Thomas Jaque. Mus: Nisan Evantoff; Franz Vote. SpProps,Assoc P: Jason W. Mayall. Sp Lighting: Terry Smith. Mkp: Tony Lambe. Titles: New Genesis. Ref: TV: VCX(video). Jim Shapiro. V 5/21/80(rated). with Kari Klark(Star Virgin), Johnny Harden(Dracula), Tracy Walton, Mike Ranger, Kevin Thompson(robot), J.C. Phillips(snake), Zen Kitty.

"At the end of time," on the planet XR-31. Humans have been "discontinued" (due to their inefficiency) by a race of "thinking machines." The latter have, however, produced Star Virgin from a "protoplasmic duplicator" and preserve her "as a curiosity." She herself is curious about sex, which no longer exists, and persuades the robot Mentor to show her scenes (culled from a memory bank) of sex on Earth in the past. One scene, set in Transylvania, at Sunshine Manor, features Count Dracula and his assistant, Igor. Dracula rapes the heroine, but is defeated by the hero and a cross....Marginally-more-professional-than-usual for an "adult" movie. The Dracula segment is done, fairly slickly, as a black-and-white silent comedy, complete with title cards and "Swan Lake" on the sound track. It's competently edited and photographed, and actually has a few laughs--e.g., a shot of a roadsign reading "Please Brake for Vampires"; the Nixon-masked Igor flashing the Nixon victory sign. The robot gets some laughs, too, with his skittishness in the presence of Star Virgin. That leaves just-under-an-hour of waste footage....

2 STAR WARS 1977 (STAR WARS: EPISODE IV: A NEW HOPE-cr t. The STAR WARS. ADVENTURES OF THE STARKILLER-working ts) Composite OptPh: Robert Blalack; Praxis;(coord) Phil Roth. OptFxPh: Richard Edlund, Dennis Muren. Des:(elec) A.J. Miller;(min) Don

Trumbull, R. Alexander, W. Shourt. Cost: John Mollo. 2nd Unit Ph: Carroll Ballard, Tak Fujimoto et al. SpComponents: James Shourt. Models: Grant McCune. Anim: Michael Ross, Peter Kuran et al. SpMechEquip: Jerry Greenwood et al. AddlOptFX: Modern, Master. Ref: TV. Bill Warren.

The Empire's giant space station, the Death Star (with turbo-lasers, tractor beam, etc.), vs. rebel spaceships (complete with targeting computers, energy deflectors, proton torpedoes, etc.)...Torpedo-in-reactor sets off a chain reaction which destroys the Death Star....Plus: hyper-space-travel... holographic distress-signal recording...light-sabers, mind-probes...mind-control...glowing-eyed scavengers with stun rays...air cars...Sand People with ram-horned, buffalo-like mounts...monster-tentacle...space bar frequented by assorted aliens and humans (androids not welcome).

The first in the STAR WARS series appears, in retrospect, a strangely schizophrenic movie, alternately light/funny/charming and ponderous/pontifical. It mixes the casually enchanting with the offputtingly "uplifting." Director George Lucas presses a MAGNIFICENT OBSESSION-style, pragmatic spiritualism into service in a world of war and weaponry--Otto Kruger and his magic light bulb become Alec Guinness (as Ben Kenobi) and his handy Force. The dialogue alternates between delightful robot-robot, robot-human, robot-alien, human-alien byplay and old-Jedi-never-die counseling like (the semi-dead Ben's voice to hero Luke) "Trust your feelings." The intended center of the movie may be these Ben-to-Luke mystic-master transmissions; but the effective human center is Harrison Ford's Han Solo, a sturdy, semi-satiric updating of the cynical-mercenary Bogart, circa TO HAVE AND HAVE NOT. Guinness sinks beneath his weighty material; Ford fairly floats on his. Han, unlike Ben, can be taken seriously as a character because he doesn't ask to be, at least until perhaps the key moment in the movie, when he finally sinks, and encourages Luke, "May the Force be with you"...an all-too-clear, dismaying indication of a fortune-cookie-level spiritual conversion. After Han cheers Luke on his way, the movie is no longer schizophrenic--it's over. There are, it's true, more special effects. But the casual, carefree spirit of the best part of the picture is dead and gone. What's left is bang-bang-in-outer-space, with God-on-our-side/can't-be-beat overtones.

See also: RETURN OF THE JEDI.

STARBIRDS (U.S.-J) Showtime-TV/3B-New Hope-Toei 1982 anim color 74m. Chief D: Tadao Nagahama. SP,D,Ed: Michael Part. Mus: Joseph Zappala, Douglas Lackey. Video: Michael Gross. Anim: Toei. Ref: TV. TVG.

A colony of winged humanoids from a distant, destroyed planet inhabits Valerion(sp?) II, a pyramidal space station orbiting Jupiter; the heart of its evil ruler is connected to the station's master computer, which controls the Valerions still in suspended animation. New York City is destroyed by ray-shooting Valerion robots....giant robot-cyclops which absorbs all enemy weapons..."backup" robot with screwdriver-like head...robot with web-weapon...robot-fighter-ships....The Earth Federation's super-robot-ship, Dynamo, is powered by Crystal Light from a comet and, later, by solar energy, and is programmed with the voice of its dead inventor, Dr. Hunter, whose son pilots it; Dynamo can create Double Blizzard and pulverize with giant fists....Stolid melodramatics...galactic skirmishing and young, seemingly-doomed love (between the winged and the non-winged). The sentiment (altruism, heroism, love) is as mechanical as the robots. Most of the phenomenally-powerful, seemingly-invulnerable super-weapons last less than two minutes...then it's back to the drawing board.

STARFLIGHT: THE PLANE THAT COULDN'T LAND ABC-TV/ON-Orion 1983 color 140m. (STARFLIGHT ONE-ad & B t) D: Jerry Jameson. SP: Robert M. Young. Story: Peter R. Brooke. Ph: Hector Figueroa. Mus: Lalo Schifrin. PD: David L. Snyder. SpFX: John Dykstra; Terry Frazee. SpVisFX:(p) Robert Shepherd; Apogee. SpOptFX Sup: Roger Dorney. Min:(sup) Grant McCune;(model) Black Prince; Rockwell. SdFxEd: Doug Grindstaff. Mkp: Peter Altobelli. Ref: TV. MFB'83:76-7. SFExam 2/25/83:E13-14. TVG 2/26/83. V 10/20/82:71(ad),192. with Lee Majors, Hal Linden, Lauren Hutton, Robert Webber, Ray Milland, Gail Strickland, Jocelyn Brando, George DiCenzo, Tess Harper, Terry Kiser, Michael Sacks.

Starflight One, the "first hypersonic transport plane," is operated by a network of computer banks and powered by rockets (for takeoff) and scram jets (using liquid-hydrogen fuel). On its eventful first flight, it's hit by debris from a destroyed rocket, and damaged rocket-control cables send it through the "atmospheric lid" into space, 87 miles up, where it goes into orbit. The Columbia shuttle is sent up several times in order, a) to replenish S-One's fuel; b) to take aboard a man sent out of S-One in a hermetically-sealed coffin; c) to take on passengers via a modified "universal docking device" (which sparks from malfunctioning rocket cables set afire), and d) to take on more passengers via a booster tank. The leftover crew and passengers on S-One use Columbia's XU-5 rocket as a heat shield and ride its "plow wave" back into Earth's atmosphere.

Special effects, myriad suspense gimmicks, and Reader's-Digested "human dramas." Scientist-designer Linden's rescue-operation brainstorms occur at comfortingly-regular intervals, like the commercial breaks. (You can all but see the light bulb in his head blink on.) The suspense depends overly on oxygen-supply time limits, orbit-degeneration time limits, sparking-cable time limits....But the Extending The Frontiers of Science maneuvers are engaging, in an episodic, serial-like way. And they make for any number of colorful gliding, rotating, and soaring effects, involving planes and rockets and Earth-from-space vistas. The drama, by contrast, is mere filler.

STARLOST QUINTOLOGY, The. From the "Starlost" TV series see ALIEN ORO. BEGINNING, The. DECEPTION. INVASION, The. RETURN, The(197-?)

STARSHIP TROOPERS(by R.Heinlein) see GANDAMU

STARVENGERS see SHOGUN WARRIORS: STARVENGERS

STASERA SCIOPERO (I) CM 1951 Story,D: Mario Bonnard. SP: Manzari, Vecchietti. Ph: Pesce. Mus: C.A. Bixio. AD: Boccianti. Ref: Lee(Ital Prod): Striking Tonight-tr t. with Laura Gore.
Psychiatrist combines two brains to make one perfect brain.

STILL SMOKIN' Para/C&C's Comedy Fest. #1 1983 color 91m. (aka CHEECH AND CHONG'S STILL SMOKIN') Ref: TV. SFChron 5/10/83.
Wrestling skit with C&C vs. The Invisible Man...bit with Cheech pretending to be E.T.--The Extra-Testicle...skit, The Astronaut, scored with "Also Sprach Zarathustra"....More genial grossness from C&C. They're good at accents and impersonations; not always so good at comedy-writing...though a few of the skits here manage to get from square one (idea) to square two (development of same). The wrestling match herein is, at least, funnier than the boxing match in ABBOTT AND COSTELLO MEET THE INVISIBLE MAN(qq.v.).

STRANGE BREW MGM-UA 1983 color 89m. (The ADVENTURES OF BOB & DOUG McKENZIE: STRANGE BREW-cr t) SP,D & with: Dave Thomas, Rick Moranis. SP: also Steven de Jarnatt. Ph: Steven Poster. Mus: Charles Fox;(song) Ian Thomas. PD: David L. Snyder. Sp FX: Henry Piersig et al. SpPh:(fx) Eric Allard;(mattes) M. Yuricich. Mkp: L. Gill, K. Graham. Ref: screen. V 8/24/83. with Max Von Sydow(Smith), Paul Dooley, Lynne Griffin, Angus MacInnes, Eric House(John Elsinore), Mel Blanc(voice).
"The Mutants of 2051 A.D.," movie venture aborted when the film breaks in the projector...post-World War IV...flying van... mutant...very cheap-looking....The film itself: the "Hamlet" plot, adapted to beer. Madman Brewmeister Smith of the Elsinore Brewery spikes asylum-inmates' daily beer with a drug which makes them "obey" computerized musical tones. They engage in a STAR WARS-style hockey match. ("He saw JEDI 17 times.") And: hologram-"ghost" of murdered Elsinore ("Nice effects, eh?")... flying dog-hero...super-strong Smith impaled on computer-map rays.
Bob & Doug's "SCTV" fans seemed to enjoy this; the precise nature of their appeal may remain elusive for others. That appeal depends upon endlessly repeated words and phrases like "hoser," "beauty!", "eh?", and "Take off!" and has been known, just barely, to sustain a three-minute skit. The two are semi-engagingly petty-minded-and-mannered, but that's about all they are--their repertoire is not exactly extensive. A tired beer-and-intrigue plot has to take up the comedic slack here. The brothers' TV-format intro and postscript presents them in a more familiar, relaxed mood. One fears further "adventures".... The abandoned "Mutants..." was, at least, promising, in a home-movie-tacky way; STRANGE BREW itself is conventionally glossy-looking.

STRANGE CASE OF DR. JEKYLL AND MR. HYDE, The(by R.L.Stevenson) see CASE OF THE STUTTERING PIG. HYDE AND GO TWEET. JEKYLL AND HYDE...TOGETHER AGAIN. PINK LIGHTNING(P). TWO HEARTS IN WAX TIME.

2 The STRANGE EXORCISM OF LYNN HART 1972 color 84m. (PIGS-TV. The PIGS-orig t? aka LOVE EXORCIST) D,P & with: Marc Lawrence. Ph: Glenn Rowland. Mus: Charles Bernstein. SpFX: Bruce Adams. SdFX: Nick Eliopolas. Ref: TV. TVG. Bill Warren. Academy. HR 7/25/74. Cinef IV:4:35. vc box: DADDY'S DEADLY DARLING-vt t. with Jesse Vint, Jim Antonio, Walter Barnes, Paul Hickey.

Porcine horror, as Zambrini, a pig-farmer/restaurateur (Lawrence) who was once declared legally dead after a fall, but revived and began acting "strange," lets nature take its course when his pigs devour a stray drunk and begin to acquire a taste for human flesh. He hires a runaway (Toni Lawrence) as a waitress. She, too, leads a colorfully melodramatic life: she murdered her father, after he raped her ("Crazy family!"), and has just escaped from an insane asylum. She has a (visualized) nightmare re: pigs, and is haunted by the "voices" of one of her victims. Ultimately, she slashes Zambrini to death.

If not the first, then likely the worst movie to plumb the macabre possibilities of oinks. There may, admittedly, be more potential for the macabre _there_ than in baas, moos, or whinnies, but that still doesn't make pigs _frightening_. These porkers need all the help they can get from indirect sources, like dialogue--e.g., "It's the _pigs_!" or "That young man is a _pig_ now!" This movie proves, rather definitively, that pigs and pathos don't mix. The pig man (who, Sweeney Todd-like, feeds humans to his pigs and his pigs to his customers) and the razor-blade lady, Lynn, have a certain odd kinship, but it's described in oink-level dialogue. The one touching moment occurs when Lynn rings up her (dead) father for the last time, and we, for the _first_ time, hear, at the other end, "This is a recording." (_Sniff_!)

STRANGE INVADERS Orion/Laughlin/EMI & McQuade(Greenberg Bros.) 1983 color/ws 95m. SP,D: Michael Laughlin. SP: also William Condon. Ph: Louis Horvath;(NY) Zoltan Vidor. Mus: John Addison. Cost & PD: Susanna Moore. SpVisFX: Private Stock FX;(sup) C. Comisky;(tech d) Ken Jones;(prod exec) Larry Benson;(des) John Muto;(cons) Robert & Dennis Skotak;(prod coord) Declan Kavanagh; Cyril Baird, Judy Evans et al. Spaceships: Emad Helmy. Mech SpFX: Martin Malivoire. Alien FX: Stephan Dupuis, Martin Coblenz et al. Sd:(sp fx) Jonathon Rosen;(des) Lon E. Bender. OptFX: Modern. Mkp: Ken Brooke. Scenic Art: David Moon. Ref: TV: Vestron Video. V 9/14/83. Bill Warren. MFB'84:86-7. with Paul Le Mat, Nancy Allen, Diana Scarwid(Margaret), Michael Lerner, Louise Fletcher, Wallace Shawn, Fiona Lewis(alien), Kenneth Tobey(alien), June Lockhart, Charles Lane, Lulu Sylbert (Elizabeth), Ron Gillham(alien).

"Man is just one species...." Alien beings from "very far

away" reach an agreement with the U.S. government to conduct a 25-year study on Earth. They arrive in Centerville, Illinois, in 1958; use lightning-like rays to transform the populace into floating spheres (which form constitutes, apparently, a kind of limbo); and adopt human "costumes" (including "well-scrubbed, Midwestern faces"). Some of the Earthbound aliens "participate in the social structure"...Margaret, in fact, has a child, Elizabeth, by a human (Le Mat). At the end, all the humans-in-limbo are released, and the aliens shed their disguises and return to their spaceship. Elizabeth, too, is taken aboard, with her father, but discovers that she has special powers, and the two escape....Throughout, the aliens use their telepathic and electrical powers to turn on TV sets, open doors, operate elevators, etc....

STRANGE INVADERS recalls any number of other science-fiction movies, from IT CAME FROM OUTER SPACE to CLOSE ENCOUNTERS OF THE THIRD KIND. The human-disguise idea comes from the former; the government-alien-collusion idea, from the latter; the little-girl-with-the-power from The STALKER. And yet this movie achieves, at least intermittently, an identity of its own. If CE3K rates as a (flawed) vision, SI qualifies as, at least, an occasionally-elegant variation on favorite sf themes. In toto, it's little more than a skillful synthesis... but it makes one major contribution to the genre: the idea of the floating limbo. It is introduced late in the film, in a flashback: a man watches as his wife and two children are shriveled and shrunk and converted into spheres...which call to him as they float out of the rooming-house room. At this point, we don't know the reason for this conversion. (Perhaps the aliens eat only spherical objects; perhaps sphericality is a higher state....) But the fact that he (and we) can hear the voices of the converted hints that the space visitors are up to something more than plain murder or mayhem...suggests that they (the wife and kids) are still there....The climactic reunion of these dispossessed ones--with each other and with other humans--is arguably the movie's best sequence. It features a well-judged combination of sentiment and humor. (Some of the returnees are left stranded on light standards, tree limbs, etc.) The reunions, farewells, and separations of this climax, as a whole, recall, inescapably, the climax of CE3K, and are virtually as well-orchestrated. The only element missing is CE3K's near-mystical sense of awe, which is not adequately replaced by a shot of hero, heroine, and Elizabeth strolling off at the end hand-in-hand, happy as ducks. The film's final shots (which directly follow the aforementioned one) do, at least, constitute something of a recovery: we see views of the Earth (looking like one of the limbo globes) from the departing spaceship. It's a sort of putting-in-perspective series of shots....If it's true, sometimes, that details make a movie, this movie is made by the shot of the back-from-limbo teenage girl picking up (with the boy) exactly where she left off--and still working on that same wad of gum....

*STRANGER FROM VENUS Vitapix/Rich & Rich 1954 90m. SP: Hans Jacoby. Story: Desmond Leslie. Ph: Kenneth Talbot. Mus: Eric Spear. AD: John Elphick. Mkp: Nel Taylor. Ref: TV. Warren/KWTS! Scot Holton. BFC: IMMEDIATE DECISION-title error? and with Cyril Luckham, Nigel Green, John Le Mesurier.

The stranger (Helmut Dantine) at the inn "never paid taxes"... has no pulse...doesn't like beer...is multilingual...has an invisible protective shield...can heal wounds instantly...is telepathic...has an unusual set of fingerprints (with little squares in them)...and has, he says, temporarily conditioned his respiratory system to our atmosphere. He is from, no doubt, where he says he is from--Venus. (Although his Venus is "millions of light years" away.) His kind live hundreds of years, then simply vanish. They fly magnetic-powered crafts planet-to-planet. And long ago they witnessed a nuclear disaster which left only the Asteroid Belt in its wake. They mean to keep us from a sequel, which, they say, would disrupt the entire solar system, and are threatening to stop our nuclear "progress" by burning off the Earth's atmosphere and incinerating the planet with the sun's rays.

Over-detailed, TV-scale sf-drama lacks the monsters and robots of its British contemporaries FIRE MAIDENS OF OUTER SPACE and DEVIL GIRL FROM MARS, though it does have an alien who Does Things. And it is, in its drab, economy-special way, rather-likably stodgy. The desperate-for-drama script features a familiar sf balance of noble and ignoble character-motivations, with no ambiguity as to which is noble and which is ignoble. Our hero, who seems at first to be here by accident, proves later to have a conventional reason for dropping in, and romance (with Patricia Neal) blossoms, as it will. The script's one nice invention involves that romance and the alien's telepathic powers: The Stranger, walking beside a pond, happens to pick up some of Susan's idle thoughts and goes to sit by her.... Tacky awe-music predominates on the sound track.

A STRANGER IS WATCHING MGM/Heron 1982(1981) color 88m. D: Sean S. Cunningham. SP: Earl MacRauch, Victor Miller, from Mary Higgins Clark's novel. Ph: Barry Abrams. Mus: Lalo Schifrin. AD: Virginia Field. SpFX: Connie Brink. Mkp: Andrew Ciannella. SdFxEd: Bud Nolan. Opt: Optical House. Ref: TV. SFExam 3/26/82: "horror movie." V 1/20/82. Weldon. with Rip Torn, Kate Mulgrew, James Naughton, Shawn von Schreiber, Roy Poole, Barbara Baxley, Stephen Strimpell, Jason Robards III.

Madman...murder and mayhem with hammer, flashlight, pocket knife, kitchen knife, screwdriver, steel pipe...nightmares.... Distracting sentiments (both pro and con) re: capital punishment punctuate A STRANGER IS WATCHING, but remain, essentially, just distractions. The real story is Torn's killer-thug, and the other, lesser creeps he encounters on the dimmer, danker fringes of New York City. The subway shadows seem to breed them. Sinister-seedy is the norm in this night-blooming society, but most of these creatures are fairly harmless. Even

Artie seems normally abnormal--until he sticks a screwdriver into the heroine, and a knife into a too-inquisitive derelict. His methodicalness, as a kidnapper, is at first reassuring--it implies no fuss, no mess; but this matter-of-factness later becomes doubly disturbing. Artie is not just a "creep" to be dismissed; not just "atmosphere." He's methodically malignant--an illustration of the ugliness of "crime without passion." As a suspenser, A STRANGER IS WATCHING is, on the whole, more-or-less routine, the better perhaps to set off Artie and his casual viciousness....

STRANGERS FROM OUTER SPACE see IT CAME FROM OUTER SPACE

The STRANGER'S GUNDOWN (I) New Line/Herman Cohen/Sepac-Tigielle 33 1969('76-U.S.) color/ws 107m. (DJANGO IL BASTARDO. aka DJANGO THE BASTARD) SP,D: Sergio Garrone. SP & with: Antonio De Teffe. Ph: Gino Santini. Mus: Mancuso. Ref: Cinef V:3:28. Bill Warren. V 4/17/74. Stanley. Academy. Ital Prod. Frayling/SW: one of the Django series. with Lu Kamante, R. Rassimov.

"Cowboy returns from the grave to seek vengeance on his killers."(Cinef)

STRYKER (U.S.-Fili) New World/HCI Int'l. 1983 color 82m. D, P: Cirio H. Santiago. SP: Howard R. Cohen. Story: Leonard Hermes. Ph: R. Remias. Mus: Ed Gatchalian; Susan Justin. AD: P. Dimalanta. SpFX: J.S. Domingo. Mkp: Puzon, Mercador. Assoc D: J.M. Avellana. Ref: screen. V 9/14/83. MFB'84:88. with Steve Sandor, Andria Savio, William Ostrander, Michael Lane, Julie Gray, Monique St. Pierre.

"The last war began in error," and the resultant nuclear holocaust has left the world with little water. Now, "water is power." Men (and women) die for it, and only a few, at first, know of the spring water of the hill colony. By the end, <u>everyone</u>, of course, knows, and, to top it off, it rains, and <u>everyone</u> gets wet....A quickie, obviously, and a near-scriptless variation on The ROAD WARRIOR. The story is patched together with functional "Let's move it out!"-type dialogue and consists, mostly, of routine action, with dollops of cynicism, sentimentality, and romantic "tragedy." The ungrammatical hero's philosophy is "Everybody's got their own highway to hell." The hooded dwarfs seem inspired by the scavengers in the first STAR WARS <u>and</u> by the Ewoks in the third.

STUPOR DUCK WB 1956 anim color 7m. D: Robert McKimson. SP: Tedd Pierce. Ref: TV. "WB Cartoons." LC. no Lee.

Daffy Duck as mild-mannered reporter Cluck Trent, who ducks into a broom closet and emerges as--a witch on a broomstick...? ("Wrong costume.") Try again, and Daffy is--Stupor Duck!, a "strange being from another world" who comes to the aid of those who don't really need it. At the end, he takes a "Project Moon" rocket around the moon and back to Earth....Daffy at his most charming, as an inverse-Superman. (Type-casting.)

See also DAFFY DUCK'S MOVIE: FANTASTIC ISLAND(P).

The SUN NEVER SETS Univ 1939 98m. D,P: Rowland V. Lee. SP: W.P. Lipscomb, from the play by Jerry Horwin & Arthur Fitz-Richard. Ph: George Robinson. Mus: Frank Skinner. AD: Jack Otterson, R.H. Riedel. Ref: TV. MPH 6/10/39. NYT 6/9/39. TVG. Lee(e). LC. Hirschhorn. with Douglas Fairbanks Jr., Basil Rathbone, Lionel Atwill(Zurof), Barbara O'Neil, Melville Cooper, C. Aubrey Smith, Cecil Kellaway, Virginia Field, Mary Forbes.

Scientist (Atwill) bent on becoming world dictator runs "mystery radio" station from the Gold Coast; "blankets other stations" around the world with his broadcasts (cf. YOU MAY BE NEXT!); foments worldwide rioting, rebellion, sabotage.... Obvious script pits brothers' Duty to the British Empire against Family Loyalty, in too-neatly-packaged scenes of dramatic conflict. Fairbanks and Atwill, however, do good work. Rathbone compounds the script's obviousness with his unshaded dramatics; Fairbanks tempers the melodrama with understated tones, gestures, and is at times almost Colmanesquely affecting.

SUOR OMICIDIO (I) 1978 color 90m. D: Giulio Berruti. Ref: Ecran F 36:79: "erotic-horrific." with Anita Ekberg, Massimo Serato, Joe Dallesandro, Alida Valli.

Killer-nun at large.

SUPER FUZZ (U.S.-I) Avco Embassy/Trans-Cinema TV(El Pico) 1981 ('82-U.S.) color 98m. (SUPERSNOOPER-orig t) SP,D: Sergio Corbucci. SP: also S. Giuffini. Ph: S. Ippoliti. Mus: La Bionda. PD: M. Dentici. SpFX: Cass Gillespie. Mkp: Maurice St. Just. OptFX: Studio 4. SdFX: Studio Sound. Ref: TV. TVG. MFB'81:162. with Terence Hill(rn: Mario Girotti), Ernest Borgnine, Joanne Dru, Marc Lawrence, Julie Gordon, W. Woodbury.

A NASA nuclear rocket (carrying a device for locating minerals beneath the moon's crust) explodes; subjects a policeman (Hill) to mega-rays. He develops mind-over-mind and mind-over-matter powers, including X-ray vision, virtual invulnerability, telekinesis, super-speed, and the ability to restore life. Condemned to death, he survives the gas chamber, the noose, the firing squad, and the electric chair....A silly splicing of The ATOMIC KID to WALKING TALL, as our plutonic-cop takes on organized crime. The stunts are occasionally amusing, ultimately simply ludicrous, as Hill develops super-breath... turns a wad of bubble gum into a huge hot-air balloon...hops onto the top of a plane...guides it to the ground...and finally tunnels his way through the Earth to China....Anything, it seems, for a gag. If a powder puff can be termed irresponsible, this is...though it will probably neither promote delusions of grandeur in small children nor encourage police brutality. (Instances of the latter figure as occasional, incidental chuckles.) The color red inhibits Hill's powers; it never occurs to him to close his eyes: though the script was clearly designed as, simply, a series of stunts, and is functional as such, even a little more care, logic, or simple thought would have been appreciated.

SUPER-RABBIT WB 1943 anim color 7m. D: Chuck Jones. SP: T. Pierce. Ref: "WB Cartoons." LC. no Lee.
Doctor's secret formula gives Bugs Bunny super-powers.

SUPERMAN AND THE JUNGLE DEVIL Ellsworth-Luber-Maxwell 1954 Ref: Lee. Terrace/CEOTP. TVG. with George Reeves.
Feature composed of episodes (including "Jungle Devil") from the TV series "The Adventures of Superman."

SUPERMAN III WB/Salkind(Dovemead) & UAA 1983 color/ws 125m. D: Richard Lester. SP: David & Leslie Newman. Sequel to SUPERMAN(1978). Ph: Robert Paynter;(process) John Harris; (aerial) Wesscam. Mus: Ken Thorne; John Williams;(songs) Giorgio Moroder. PD: Peter Murton. SpFX & Min:(d) Colin Chilvers;(flying) David Lane; Bob Harman. SpVisFX:(sup) Roy Field;(cons) Zoran Perisic. Models:(ph) Harry Oakes;(ad) Charles Bishop. OptFX: Optical Film FX;(cam) P. Harman, M. Body. Mattes: Dennis Bartlett. SpFX: Martin Gutteridge, Brian Warner. Video:(sup) Ian Kelly;(computer anim) Atari. Titles: Camera FX. Mkp: Engelen, Freeborn. Ref: screen. V 6/8/83. Academy. Bill Warren. pr. MFB'83:221-22. with Christopher Reeve, Richard Pryor, Jackie Cooper, Marc McClure, Annette O'Toole, Robert Vaughn, Margot Kidder, Graham Stark, Shane Rimmer, John Bluthal, Robert Beatty.
"Computers rule the world"...or do they? Superman vs. the "ultimate computer," with incidental villain (Vaughn) and incidental computer-genius (Pryor). Principal episodes within this episode of the series: 1) Superman (Reeve) uses super-breath to freeze over the surface of a lake, then transports it through the air to extinguish a fire at a chemical factory. 2) When Gorman ("I'm a genius!"), working for Webster's Webscoe Industries, programs the Vulcan weather satellite to destroy Colombia's coffee crop, Superman uses his laser-ray-like eyes to dry the land, and his super-strength to invert and disable a tornado. 3) Computer-analyzed Kryptonite fragments from the Xeno Galaxy yield an imperfect formula for the metal. The resultant quasi-Kryptonite (one element of its composition remains unknown) puts Superman on the moral skids, and he straightens the Leaning Tower of Pisa, extinguishes the Olympic Flame, and has a casual sexual affair. In a visualized internal struggle, Clark Kent wins out over his evil-Superman-self. The restored Superman cleans up (with super-breath) an oil spill caused by the bad Superman. 4) Gorman's super-computer, a) temporarily traps Superman in an invisible-shield vacuum-bubble, b) shoots rockets and a missile at Superman, c) shoots a perfected Kryptonite ray at Superman (but Gorman, who doesn't want to be known as "the man who killed Superman," pulls the computer's plug), d) reactivates by "feeding itself" from America's power supply, e) "computerizes" a woman, who then shoots levitation-rays which Superman bounces back on her, and f) dies of "acid indigestion" induced by Superman.
The third and most problematic in the series. Both this

schizophrenic movie and its characters exhibit multiple personalities. Is it an effects show or a psychological study? Is it myth or slapstick? Is Gorman a good guy or a bad guy? He seems, at first, perfectly willing to hand Superman a fatal dose of synthetic Kryptonite (he does not know that it's defective); then, later, saves the Man of Steel. He works for Webster and money, yet is, at least implicitly, compared with Superman--he does with science, that is, what Superman does with super-skills. (Both "create" rainstorms...Superman over the chemical factory, Gorman over Colombia.) His moral regeneration is as skimpily-documented as is Superman's. The latter's, however, is the most compelling aspect of this over-freighted epic. The Clark Kent vs. Bad-Superman sequence does not really "belong": it's a Jekyll-and-Hyde, monster-movie confrontation (produced without benefit of a chemical formula), a psychological-horror sequence in a super-hero movie. Yet, physically and psychologically, it's effective, even unusual. It isn't often that you see Jekyll win out over Hyde, good (Kent bursting, whole, out of the metal-compressor) dramatized as simply and powerfully as evil. "Superman's Back!" might be the title of this sequence, which (jarring, tonally, as it is) produces the movie's most stirring moment: the real Superman up and about, flying again....Then the movie has to start up all over again, with a new "episode."

See also: STUPOR DUCK.

SUPERSNOOPER see SUPER FUZZ

SUPERSTITION Carolco 1982 color 84m. D: James Rober(t)son. SP: Michael Sajbel, from his book (also orig t) "The Witch." Mus: David Gibney. Ref: HR 3/20/81. 3/17/81. V 3/30/83. Ecran F 30:4,15,36: at Paris sf fest. Academy. AcadSF,F&H. with James Houghton, Albert Salmi, Lynn Carlin, Larry Pennell.

The spirit of a witch, Elondra Shorack, crucified 200 years ago, proves to be the "mysterious force" haunting a house.(EF)

SVENGALI CBS-TV/Halmi 1983 color 92m. D: Anthony Harvey. SP: Frank Cucci, from George du Maurier's novel "Trilby." Story: Sue Grafton. Ph: Larry Pizer. Mus: John Barry. AD: Charles Bennett. Mkp:(O'Toole) Dan Striepeke. Opt: EFX. Ref: TV. TVG. with Peter O'Toole(Anton Bosnyak), Jodie Foster(Zoe Alexander), Elizabeth Ashley, Larry Joshua, Pamela Blair.

A vocal coach (O'Toole)--who lost his voice after appearing in a production of "Svengali"--proves influential in the career of a young singer (Foster); the quality of her voice seems dependent on his presence....A more accurate title would be "Hardly Svengali." In this very, very loose version, "Svengali" sends "Trilby" away at the end. One wants to advise the adapters, That's not the idea. Picture a SVENGALI in which Trilby keeps assuring Svengali--without benefit of hypnosis--that she loves him. Picture, that is, a SVENGALI without irony. Eliminate the element of hypnosis--the element of coerced love--

and you effectively eliminate du Maurier. The script here attempts to equate Zoe's psychological dependence (on Anton) with hypnosis, but the dramatic mechanics are different: Trilby hypnotized is a character without psychology--the mind of Svengali is the operative--the only--mind involved. Seeing O'Toole as Anton makes one think, ironically, Yes, he would make an excellent Svengali. But here he is simply...Anton. The difference between Anton and Zoe is simply a matter of age, not elective affinities--it's simply a contrast, not a dramatic conflict.

See also: DOCTOR DRACULA.

2 SWAMP THING Avco Embassy/Melniker-Uslan(Swampfilms) 1982(1981) color 90m. SP,D: Wes Craven. Based on the D.C. Comics character. Ph: Robin Goodwin. AD: David Nichols, R.W. King; Rhoda Neal. SpMkpFX Crew: Ken Horn, Esther Mercado, Deborah Shankle. SdFX: Jay's M&P. Titles: Modern. Ref: TV. V 3/24/82. and with Reggie Batts, Don Knight, Al Ruban.

The Holland formula, intended to give plants the aggressive drive to survive of animals, "amplifies the essence" of its subjects, turns scientist (Ray Wise) into the super-strong Swamp Thing (Dick Durock), a half-human, half-plant monster which thrives on sunlight and has the power to heal the wounded and revive the dead. The same formula turns the villainous Arcane (Jourdan) into a reptilian, lion-maned monster (Ben Bates) and turns his burly henchman (Nicholas Worth) into a dwarf (Tommy Madden)...."haunted swamp...full of ghosts."

Tepid, occasionally agreeable comic-book-inspired feature is part-adventure, part-sf, part-monster-movie, part-romance, part-comedy, and part-ultra-jiggle-show (courtesy of Adrienne Barbeau)--all adding up to...? The most curious aspect of the movie is that it seems to take place all in a day or so--which means that the monster has hardly been a monster 24 hours before he begins waxing tragic. ("Everything's a dream when you're...alone.") The closest movie antecedent of SWAMP THING is perhaps The LEGEND OF BOGGY CREEK, which also featured a lonely, backwater monster. The latter even had his own theme song ("Is there no other such as I?"); Swamp Thing, fortunately, contents himself with an occasional bellow of desolation. The pathos of BOGGY CREEK was appalling; this picture's overtones of pathos seem, simply, a part of the narrative package, neither overdone nor underdone, just there.

SWEET SIXTEEN Century Int'l./Productions Two(Sweet Sixteen) 1983(1981) color 91m. D,P: Jim Sotos. SP: Erwin Goldman. Ph: J.L. Carter. Mus: Tommy Vig;(lyrics) J.& M. Wertman et al. Mkp: Jim Gillespie; Debbie Gillespie. SdFX: Sandy Berman. Creative Cons: Billy Fine. Ref: screen. V 9/28/83. ad: Mus: Ray Ellis. with Bo Hopkins, Susan Strasberg, Don Stroud, Dana Kimmell, Aleisa Shirley, Michael Pataki, Patrick Macnee, Larry Storch, Henry Wilcoxon, Sharon Farrell.

Sun Valley, Texas. "Why doesn't anything exciting ever

happen around here?" asks a young murder-mystery fan (Kimmell). Something does happen--"a real, bonafide nut" starts slashing up Sun Valley High students...specifically, any boy who makes an assignation with sultry, sweet-fifteen Melissa (Shirley). Behind it all: a schizophrenic who "became" her dead sister and who keeps "killing her father" (who drove them both mad) "over and over again." At the end, it's Melissa who has a funny look on her face and is carrying a knife....visualized nightmare of thing-at-door.

Not badly acted--Kimmell and Farrell, especially, brighten their scenes--but the script is even-more-than-usually-pointless for a crazed-slasher exercise. There are, it's true, happy-vs.-unhappy-families undertones, but on any list of the film's most pressing concerns, those undertones would finish in approximately tenth place. First or second place would, unhappily, go to the far-from-burning question, whodunit? Someone's suspicion--not mine or yours--is very clumsily directed one way, towards one person, when one brief, early scene should direct anyone at all familiar with the mystery-horror genre the right way. The scene in question is a "false alarm" (out on the highway) which proves, in retrospect, to have been "foreshadowing"...at least that's the way it's supposed to scan. A dead giveaway, it makes much of the subsequent action superfluous. And there are only two likely suspects anyway....

The SWORD AND THE SORCERER Univ/Brandon Chase/Bremson(Sorcerer) 1982 color 100m. SP,D: Albert Pyun. Sp,Co-P: Thomas Karnowski, John Stuckmeyer. Ph: Joseph Mangine; Gary Graver. Mus: David Whitaker. AD: George Costello; Dena Roth. SpFX:(sup) John Carter;(cons) Harry Woolman; Terry Woolman et al; Knott Ltd. SpMkpFX: Greg Cannom; MkpFxLabs, White, Apone, Carrisosa. SpWeaponsDes: Roger Holzberg;(sword) Elroy Payne. SpSdFX: Frank Serafini. Ref: TV: planned sequel Tales of the Ancient Empire. V 5/12/82. MFB'82:236-7. Weldon. Ecran F 28:39. with Lee Horsley, Kathleen Beller, Simon MacCorkindale, George Maharis(Machelli), Richard Lynch, Nina Van Pallandt, Richard Moll, Chris Cary, Peter Breck, Alan Caillou, Jay Robinson, Corinne Calvet, Barry Chase, John Davis Chandler, Reb Brown.

In a kingdom "at the far edge of the world"....The witch-conjured sorcerer-demon Xusia (Moll) proves his power by magically extracting the witch's heart; later, he splits open his human guise (Maharis) like a fruit rind...rocket-like sword blade...stone faces on Xusia's crypt which are brought to life... cave-rat attack...torture chamber....As in CONAN, our hero, Talon (Horsley), a) sees the villain (Lynch) kill his mother (and there is, similarly, a mini-flashback to this scene when hero and villain meet again), b) wields a mean sword, and, c) is crucified. Yes, it's the same damn hero and those same damn weapons. Only the names and effects are different. SWORD... is, at least, strikingly designed, lit, and photographed, and the horror effects help. But Talon is a little too glib, and there's a casualness about much of the acting and dialogue which would be camp if it were accidental. If CONAN is a bit "heavy," SWORD... is a bit "light." And both movies are rather straitjacketed by their identification of myth with the hoariest narrative cliches. They appear to be predicated on a belief that seeing the same story yet once more will do us good, and fail to make that some old story seem new. The picture-opening introduction of Xusia, however, is a startler--it gives false promise that the movie is going to be serious business.

SWORD OF THE BARBARIANS (I) Cannon/Visione-Filman(Leader) 1983 (1982) color 88m. (Le SPADE DEI BARBARI) D: Michael E. Lemick. SP: P. Regnoli. Ph: G. Ferrando. Mus: Franco Campanino. Sets: F. Cuppini. SpFX: Corridori. Ref: V 10/20/82:225. 5/4/83:332,298: "caveman epic." 7/27/83:26: in Chicago. 10/5/83. HR 10/12/83. with Peter M(a)cCoy(rn: Pietro Torrisi), Sabrina Siani(Rani), Margarethe Christian, Yvonne Fraschetti.

Semi-sequel to ATOR. Sacrifices to evil goddess..."rebirth"... lizard-men...monkey-men.

TAG--THE ASSASSINATION GAME New World/Ubaud-Edelman(T.A.G.) 1982 color 90m. SP,D: Nick Castle. Ph: Willy Kurant. Mus: Craig Safan. PD: Peter Politanoff. Mkp: Bob Jermain. OptFX: Image II, Mike Warren. Titles: E.D. Farino. SpThanx: John Carpenter, Tommy Wallace et al. Ref: TV. TVG. Ecran F 21:11: "chiller." V 4/28/82. with Robert Carradine, Linda Hamilton, Bruce Abbott (Gersh), Kristine DeBell, Perry Lang, Ivan Bonar, Frazer Smith.

The fun-with-dart-guns TAG offers college students a chance to "get away from the books." It's only a game--until "the champ," Gersh, suffers a fluke defeat and decides to play for keeps. He begins to eliminate his victims with bullets, and stores the bodies in a laundry cart. The two survivors of TAG--Gersh and Susan Swayze (Hamilton)--face each other in "the finals." He declares, "I can't die!"; she comes across a stash of corpses in a cart and realizes that her life is at stake....

Much easier to take than the similar RONA JAFFE'S MAZES AND MONSTERS, but nearly as easy to leave alone. Relative to the heaviness of M&M, TAG's lightness-of-tone is quite welcome, if it ultimately prevents the movie from making very much of itself. If M&M takes itself over-seriously, TAG doesn't take itself seriously enough, though its bizarre-souffle tone is appealingly offbeat. It's noir material done blanc, and for that at least rates a passing grade for being daring. The three leads, fortunately, are talented enough to bring off their unusual assignments, which occasionally consist of playing it straight and not-so-straight at the same time....

TAILSPIN TOMMY IN MYSTERY PLANE see SKY PIRATE

TAJEMSTVI HRADU V KARPATECH see MYSTERIOUS CASTLE IN THE CARPATHIANS, The

TAKING TIGER MOUNTAIN (U.S.-Welsh) The Players Chess Club 1983 (1975) color/ws 81m. (TRECHI MYNYDD Y TEIGR(sp?)) SP,D: Tom Huckabee, Kent Smith. SP: also Paul Cullum;(addl mat'l) William S. Burroughs, from his "Bladerunner." Ph: Smith et al. Mus: Radio Free Europe; Randy Kelleher, David Boone. PD & with: Bill Paxton. Opt: Hollywood Opticals. Ref: screen. UC Theatre notes 3/24/83. flyer. with Barry Wooller, Judy Church, Lou Montgomery;(voices) June Allen, Scott Pitcock.

Post-thermonuclear-war 1990. Feminist terrorists subject a young man with a "pliable personality" to electro-narcosis and transsexual experimentation; pack him off to a Welsh village to assassinate the white-slaver leader of a Common Market prostitution ring....Your guess is as good as mine. This movie stimulates the most satisfying audience hissing since DON'T LOOK NOW. It's a sort of becalmed, befogged MANCHURIAN CANDIDATE. Without the explanatory, prefatory discussion by the feminists, the plot would make no sense at all...with it, it makes very little. The theme is apparently moral and sexual confusion--accent on "confusion." The British Information Service bulletins which accompany most of the footage, however, are wry. They run on about military strongholds in Reno, executions of luminaries such as Shirley MacLaine, the emergence of the Holy Catholic Empire and the nation of Exxon, and connections between Texas Instruments and the church....

TALE OF TALES (Russ) 1982? anim D: Yuri Norstein. Ref: VV 1/11/83:50: "minotaurs."

TALES OF 1001 NIGHTS see POHADKY TISICE A JEDNE NOCI

TALES OF THE UNEXPECTED NBC-TV/Quinn Martin 1977 color 98m. Host: William Conrad. Ref: TVG: from the TV series. TVFFSB. "TV 1970-1980." with Lloyd Bridges, Eve Plumb.

*TARANTULA 1955 Story: Jack Arnold, R.M. Fresco, based on Fresco's "Science Fiction Theatre" teleplay "No Food for Thought." Mus sc: Henry Mancini. SpPhFX: Clifford Stine, David S. Horsley. Mkp: also Millicent Patrick, Jack Kevan. Ref: TV. Jim Shapiro. Warren/KWTS! LC. Hirschhorn. Stanley. and with Ed Rand, Raymond Bailey, Tom London, Edgar Dearing, Ed Parker(Jacobs), Don Dillaway, Clint Eastwood, Rusty Wescoatt.

Desert Rock, Arizona. A nutrient-biology specialist's (Leo G. Carroll) atomically-synthesized 3Y formula produces a rat 8 times normal size, a dog-sized guinea pig, and a tarantula the size of a house. Injected into humans, the nutrient causes acromegaly and insanity....Competent, surprisingly-well-remembered Alland-Arnold monster movie is well-paced and businesslike--it wastes very little time on atmosphere, characterization, or "mush." Leads John Agar and Mara Corday "click," but only incidentally. They are not even allowed a postscript after the spider is napalmed. And the movie's dramatic elements are almost non sequiturs: Deemer's scientifically-deformed partner injects Deemer himself with the unstable nutrient out of (it seems at first) perfectly-justified revenge; later, however, it's revealed that both of Deemer's partners injected themselves, and therefore have no kick coming. Deemer produces a big rat, a big guinea pig, a big spider; his partners are the ones responsible for experimenting, very prematurely, on humans, and for unleashing the spider. Why should he be stuck--as he seems, indirectly, to be--with the guilt tab? His only crime is, apparently, that he's a scientist....Among the movie's well-remembered moments: the tantalizing pre-credit sequence, in which the camera pans left across the desert landscape, and comes upon a man stumbling about in the distance. Closer examination reveals his ghastly countenance just before he expires...and the scene gives way to the imposing presence of the movie's title. The presence of the tarantula itself is heralded in generally quietly-ominous ways. (Occasionally in noisy ways--e.g., by the crashing boulders....) The camera, for instance, will simply hold on the desert highway for a bit after a car has exited frame left...until the spider enters frame right. Or shots of spooked horses in a corral will alternate with shots of an empty hillside...empty until the creature crawls up, finally, over the rim of the hill....The tarantula makes sounds something like the clicking of hordes of crickets; these unlikely sound effects aren't nearly as eerie as Mancini's score. Graphically, however, the tarantula here is decidedly more impressive than Universal's other big bug, the deadly mantis. It's very well integrated, photographically, into the landscape.

TASTE OF SIN, A see OLIVIA

TECHNO POLICE (J) Toho & Dragon 1982 anim color 78m. Anim: K. Tomizawa;(des) Studio Nue. Ref: V 10/20/82:231(ad). 5/12/82: 335(ad). JFFJ 14:10: aka TECHNO POLICE 21C.

10 TO MIDNIGHT Cannon-City Films/Y&M/Golan-Globus 1983 color 102m. Story,D: J. Lee Thompson. SP: William Roberts. Ph: Adam Greenberg. Mus: Robert O. Ragland. AD: Jim Freiburger. Mkp: Alan Marshall. Opt: MGM. SdFxEd: Mike Le-Mare. Titles: Gunther Stotz. Ref: TV: MGM/UA Home Video. Bob Moore. MFB'83: 141. V 3/16/83. Express 3/18/83. HR 3/15/83. SFChron 3/15/83. with Charles Bronson, Lisa Eilbacher, Andrew Stevens, Gene Davis(Warren Stacey), Geoffrey Lewis, R. Lyons, Wilford Brimley.

The Los Angeles "slasher" is an office worker (Davis) who "gets even" with the women without "morals" or "manners" who "put him down." He sublimates by stalking them nude and knifing them. Caught after slaughtering three student nurses, he challenges ex-cop Kessler (Bronson), "I'm sick! One day I'll get out! That's the law!" Kessler puts a bullet through his head (cf. BLOODRAGE, A SCREAM IN THE STREETS, etc.).

Stacey's fatal mistake is throwing "That's the law!" in Kessler's face--he might just as well have pulled the trigger himself. The last thing Kessler wants to be reminded of is the law (i.e., "loopholes"). But until he actually does pull the trigger, the movie has a chance to be something more than just a bit of right-wing wish-fulfillment: "One day I'll get out!", that is, would ring more loudly as an unanswered challenge. The script is always rounding itself off too neatly--it does all the work for us. Admittedly, this is somewhat more textured than your average mad-slasher movie--the characters actually have glints of personality--but that's not saying much, nor is it meant to be. The movie carries its Stacey/Kessler "parallel" only so far: Stacey's at-large status drives Kessler into planting evidence on him; when Kessler confesses, and the case against Stacey is dismissed, Kessler hounds him and goads him into action. (Norman Bates, in PSYCHO II, is similarly goaded, by the Loomises.) "You drove me to it!" Stacey--not, however, without implied guile--accuses him. And it's the guile, not the element of truth, in Stacey's accusation that is, here, dramatically operative. Kessler's final act of violence is clearly intended to be taken as an act of Justice, and not as absolution for any part which he may have played as "prompter" in the climactic slaughter. Stacey's "You drove me to it!" is, in context, just a prospective legal defense, which his ill-timed "That's the law!" effectively nullifies.

TENEBRAE (I) Bedford Ent./Sigma 1982('84-U.S.) color 101m. (SOTTO GLI OCCHI DELL'ASSASSINO) SP,D: Dario Argento. SP: also George Kemp. Ph: Luciano Tovoli. Mus: S.P. Morante. AD: Giuseppe Bassan. SpFX: G. Corridori. Mkp: The Mecaccis. Sd FX: The Anzellottis. Ref: MFB'83:139. Ecran F 35:39-40.34:36-8. Cinef XIV:3. with John Saxon, Anthony Franciosa, Christian Borromeo, Mirella D'Angelo, John Steiner, D. Nicolodi, G. Gemma.
Rash of brutal murders in Rome parallels events in novelist's thriller.

TERROR CANIBAL (Sp) Titanic 1981 D: J.P. Tabernero. Ref: V 5/12/82:378. with Silvia Solar, Antonio Mayans, M. Salvador.

TERROR IN THE FOREST see FOREST, The

TERROR ON TOUR IWDC & Four Features Partners/Tour(Sandy Cobe) 1980 color 88m. D: Don Edmonds. SP: Dell Lekus. Ph & with: James Roberson. Mus: The Names. AD & with: Verkina Flower. SpFxMkp: Jack Petty; Steve La Port. SpFX: Charlie Spurgeon. Opt: F-Stop. Exec Co-P: Alex Rebar. Ref: TV: Media Home Ent. (video). V 9/7/83. Ecran F 39:64. with Rick Styles, Chip Greenman, Rich Pemberton, Dave Galluzzo, Kalassu, J. Wintergate.
"Some crazy (who) really bought" the Grand Guignol act of the punk-rock group The Clowns borrows their ghoulish-makeup ideas and adds a "real body with real blood." He goes around knifing people who have "defiled themselves" and have "no moral values at all!"....Don Edmonds--never the most dynamic of

directors--has, here, a script as flaccid as his direction--"direction" in TERROR ON TOUR meaning, simply, actors reading lines. And the readings, generally, are as lacking in point as Edmonds' staging. The movie ends with the near-obligatory irony of real violence occurring onstage. (Well, everyone in the movie feigns surprise....) One of The Clowns prepares us for this life-intruding-on-art finale by noting (of the musicians and their audience): "I think we're sick...they're sick!" This is--quiet on the set!--an insight....

TESORO DE LAS CUATRO CORONAS see TREASURE OF THE FOUR CROWNS

TESTAMENT Para/Entertainment Events & American Playhouse-TV 1983 color 90m. D,Co-P: Lynne Littman. SP: John Sacret Young, from Carol Amen's story "The Last Testament." Ph: Steven Poster; Charles Minsky. Mus: James Horner. PD: David Nichols. SpFX: Chuck Stewart. Mkp: Tonya Wexler. Opt: Movie Magic. Titles: (des) Tavoularis; Pacific. SdFX: J's Fine Art et al. Ref: screen. V 10/19/83. MFB'84:89-90. with Jane Alexander, William Devane, Ross Harris, Roxana Zal, Lilia Skala, Leon Ames, Lurene Tuttle, Kevin Costner, Mako, Lukas Hass, Clete Roberts.

"Everything looks the same," at first, in Hamelin, California, after East and West Coast reports of devastation-by-nuclear-devices. People, however, begin to sicken and die--victims apparently of radiation poisoning--and Hamelin becomes a virtual ghost town. Some few escape to what they hope is safety in Canada....TESTAMENT is the more-conventional, direct, dramatic version of SPECIAL BULLETIN. Here, there's no ironic interplay between the catastrophic and the banal, between raw event and sanitized reportage. There's just grimness. The unrelentingness, it's true, does have a cumulative effect. Despite an upbeat note near the end (a la WHERE HAVE ALL THE PEOPLE GONE)--to the effect that suicide is a defeatist measure (it's rejected)--the film sticks to its subject: "losing things." One after another, commodities...community services...people go--phffft! This steady, irreversible progression is decidedly dismaying, and the movie is occasionally touching and even powerful. But it's also too obvious, too eager to wield its dramatic power. It wants to move you, but that's all it wants to do. It doesn't surprise--with any seeming irrelevancies, with any gallows humor, with any unexpected changes in tone. It doesn't seem to realize that it's only a movie, not a testament. Even the score fails to provide any counterpoint. The heroine's visualized, home-movie-like memories are all of happier times--as if there were no unhappy moments in her life before-the-bomb. And the pre-bomb sequences of everyday-madhouse home-life (three kids and uncountable appliances) have a feel closer to sitcom than to life. The movie is sharper at describing the atypical than it is describing the typical....

THERE'S MILLIONS IN IT see HOT MONEY

The THING Univ/Turman-Foster 1982 color/ws 108m. D: John Carpenter. SP: Bill Lancaster, from John W. Campbell Jr.'s story "Who Goes There?" Ph: Dean Cundey. Mus: Ennio Morricone. PD: John L. Lloyd. SpVisFX: Albert Whitlock;(title seq) Peter Kuran, Visual Concept Eng. SpMkpFX: Rob Bottin;(coord) Ken Diaz; Rob Burman et al;(illus) M. Ploog et al;(line p) Eric Jensen. SpFX: Roy Arbogast; L. Routly, M.A. Clifford. Dimensional Anim: R.W. Cook; J. Aupperle, E.D. Farino et al. Mattes: Bill Taylor. Min: Susan K. Turner. Opt: Univ;(title seq) RGB Opt. et al. SpThanx: Stan Winston. Ref: screen. V 6/23/82. MFB'82:158-160. Weldon. Ecran F 28:40-58. with Kurt Russell, Richard Dysart, Wilford Brimley, T.K. Carter, David Clennon, Norbert Weisser, Richard Masur.

Antarctica, 1982. An organism from outer space capable of assimilating and imitating any other form of animal life wreaks havoc at a U.S. scientific outpost....Carpenter and Lancaster can't seem to locate the story, or rooting, interest in their material here. There are effective scenes, or ideas for effective scenes, but they seem to come in rather random order. Don't expect a Hawks-like narrative flow and you'll do alright. This movie's wild effects-scenes, fortunately, save the day. Bottin's alien-human biological conglomerations are highly inventive, even imaginative, and are just too far-fetched to be considered repellent or repugnant. Highly-outrageous conjunctions of tentacles, teeth, heads, eyeballs, and general putresence, they constitute a gross, outre form of sculpture-in-motion. But the film--with its hip-cynical, every-man-for-himself underpinnings--generally plays like a straight, flat-footed version of DARK STAR, that still-cherished Carpenter-O'Bannon existential comedy....Terrific bit here: the hot-wired alien-blood leaping/exploding out of the tin. You know it's coming, but that doesn't seem to matter--it's still a startler.

The THIRD FACE (H.K.) 1982 (K'UNG-PU-TE CH'ING-JEN) D: Chiang Lang. Ref: IFG'83:297: "blood-and-gore...psycho thriller."

*THIRTEEN WOMEN 1932 SP: also Samuel Ornitz. Mus: Max Steiner. AD: Carroll Clark. Ref: screen. William K. Everson. V 8/26/32 & 10/18/32. Academy.

Sinister half-caste ("Half-Hindu, half-Japanese...I don't know!") Ursula Georgi (Myrna Loy) uses the power of suggestion to drive the sorority women she despises to madness and death. She also wills/hypnotizes Swami Yogadachi (C. Henry Gordon) into throwing himself before a subway train, while the swami, on his part, foretells her death....A clumsily-done, but still intriguing horror-fantasy variation on VILLAGE OF THE DAMNED. Here, it's evil Myrna Loy's will vs. "strong" Irene Dunne's (instead of that of the space kids vs. George Sanders's will). Ms. Dunne's psychic "brick wall" eventually crumbles. And Loy, like the space children, drives one person to shoot herself. ("Anyone can think himself into anything.") The theme might be The Frightening Power of The Mind. But this cornball product-features Loy as a cousin of Fu Manchu's daughter (she's actually half-East-Indian) and astrology-inspired cartoon "stars" flaring up at us from the sites of her mind-murders (or "Horoscope Murders"). Loy's presence, however, dominates; Dunne and Ricardo Cortez seem almost incidental.

*The THIRTEENTH CHAIR 1929 70m.-sd version AD: Cedric Gibbons. Ref: screen. PFA notes 3/16/83. Barbara Hill. Weldon. Lennig.

Setting: Calcutta. Ingredients: the corpse of a murder victim (seated in a chair at a seance) which seems to point to the murder weapon...a fatal stabbing at an earlier seance, just as a "spirit voice" seems about to reveal the identity of the murderer...phony medium, Madame La Grange (Margaret Wycherly), who seems occasionally to be a real one...dialogue references to "witchcraft and occultism."

This is a wonderful document, not necessarily of the Bayard Veiller stage play upon which it's based--the story's yokings of shock effects and romantic-and-mother-love sentiments hardly seem worth preserving. But the movie is a wonderful record of the intonations and mannerisms of the relatively young Bela Lugosi, who here plays a C.I.D. Inspector. Several of the other actors also throw themselves bodily into the melodrama, and they too are to be commended, in a way. But they _just aren't Bela Lugosi_. If Lugosi is not exactly _good_ here, he's certainly indelible--just _try_ erasing his Inspector Delzante from your memory. Lugosi is loud, almost _belligerent_--a villain in bearing--in a role which is not particularly distinguished, but which _is_ abundant in words, and Lugosi, obviously, loves _words_. Each phrase gets its own delivery, its own arch of the hand, its own tilt of the head. At one point he repeats the line "_Something unexpected happened_," and you'd better believe that the way _he_ says it it's a line worth repeating. He could have copyrighted his version....

THOR THE CONQUEROR (I) Cannon 1982 color 88m. (THOR IL VENDICATORE) D: T. Ricci(aka A.Richmond). Ref: V 7/27/83:4 (rated). Ecran F 31:46.40:81. with Malisa Lang, Conrad Nichols.

Prehistoric hero...bird-man...magic sword.

THORNY WAY TO THE STARS, The see TO THE STARS BY HARD WAYS

THOUSAND DEATHS, A(by J.London) see TORTURE SHIP

3 ON A MEATHOOK Studio 1 1973(1972) SP,D: William Girdler. Ref: V 11/15/72:3(rated): _not_ sfa 2 The MAD BUTCHER. Weldon: "very gory"; inspired by the Ed Gein story. with Charles Kissinger, James Pickett.

Cannibalistic madman who murders young women.

THRILLER Optimum 1983 color 14m. (MICHAEL JACKSON'S THRILLER-alt t) SP,D: John Landis. SP & with: Michael Jackson. Ph: Robert Paynter. Mus: Elmer Bernstein; Rod Temperton. AD:

Charles Hughes. SpMkpFX: Rick Baker, EFX. Ref: TV. TVG. Ecran F 41:40-47. with Ola Ray; Vincent Price(voice).

"Werewolf" sequence which turns out to be only a movie on a theatre screen...zombie sequence which proves to be not-quite-all-a-dream....Or, NIGHT OF THE LIVING DEAD with a beat. Atmosphere and choreography, an interesting combination. The zombies (including Jackson) are impressive, both as makeup-and-costume creations and as dancers. The Jackson-Baker werewolf seems a shade over-dressed, fur-wise.

See also: MAKING OF THRILLER, The(P).

THURSDAY THE 12TH see PANDEMONIUM

2 TILL DEATH 1978(1974?) Ph: G. Smart, J. Steeley. Mus: Chick Rains, J.E. Norman. SpFX: Roger George. Mkp: Jerry Soucie. Ref: TV. and with Marshall Reed, Jonathan Hole.

The power of love seems to bring a young bride (Belinda Balaski) back from the dead, to a rendezvous (in a crypt) with her still-living husband (Keith Atkinson)...spirit...premonitory nightmare of walking corpse....Awkwardly written and acted, but the love-conquers-all theme proves perversely appealing. Down in the crypt, the husband at first can't quite get into the kinky-romantic spirit of the thing. ("I'm sorry, Anne--I just can't do it here.") But passion, finally, overcomes death, and even propriety. Pretty bad, but at least they had an idea for a movie--a Bunuel movie, perhaps.

TILL DEATH DO US PART (Can.) Seagull/Brady-TV 1982 90m. SP, D: Timothy Bond. SP: also Peter Jobin. Ref: V 7/14/82:100. with James Keach, Claude Jutra, Helen Hughes, Jack Creley.

"Tele-film has one grisly murder after another....frightening and funny."

TILL DEATH DO WE SCARE (H.K.-Cant.) Cinema City 1982 color 100m. D: Lau Kar Wing. SP & with: Raymond Wong. SP: also Ko Chi Sum. Ph: Lai, Rumjahn. PD: Shi, Tsang. SpMkpFX: Tom Savini. OptFX: Toho Eizo. Ref: V 11/17/82: "horror-comedy." Ecran F 30:58-9. with Alan Tam, Olivia Cheng, John Keung.

Spirits of widow's three late husbands conspire to scare new suitor.

TIME RIDER see TIMERIDER

TIME TUNNEL see ALIENS FROM ANOTHER PLANET. KILL OR BE KILLED. OLD LEGENDS NEVER DIE. RAIDERS FROM OUTER SPACE. REVENGE OF THE GODS.

TIME WALKER New World/Villard & Wescom(Byzantine) 1982 color 86m. D: Tom Kennedy. SP: Karen Levitt, Tom Friedman. Story: Jason Williams, Friedman. Ph: Robbie Greenberg. Mus: Richard Band. AD: R.A. Burns, Joe Garrity. SpFX: New World;(ed) Joseph Yanuzzi. Anim: January Nordman. SpSdCons: Chris Stone.

Mkp: Sue Dolph. Ref: screen. V 11/17/82. Ecran 35:68-9.29:54. with Ben Murphy, Nina Axelrod, Kevin Brophy, James Karen, Austin Stoker, Jack Olson(Ankh-Venharis), Sam Chew Jr., Robert Random, Melissa Prophet, Shani Belafonte-Harper, Buffy(mummy dog).

The California Institute of the Sciences. A mummified "noble traveller" from space--sealed 3,000 years in Tutankhamen's tomb--revives after exposure to a strong dose of X-ray radiation. He seeks five crystals for a transmitting device which, at the end, transports both the hero and him to another dimension.... Ankh-Venharis is super-strong, moves by "floating," and has a glowing crystal embedded in his chest....flesh-eating green fungus on mummy wrappings...costume-party mummy.

Stilted, old-fashioned monster movie (complete with "wipes") features all sorts of sf, horror, and fantasy gimmicks which, though not very well coordinated, do make for a busy picture. How a major discovery could be made in Tut's tomb at this late date--the story is very conspicuously set in the computer age--is a matter which lies outside the script's area of concern. It's concerned, mainly, with getting the crystals to various coeds...then getting the coeds alone...then getting the mummy to the coeds. These goals are accomplished, but not without some narrative strain. The dialogue in this movie appears to have been written (and spoken) by people without ears....

TIME WARP Gold Key-TV/Sandler-Emenegger 1981 color 90m. D, Mus: Robert Emenegger. D: also Allan Sandler. SP,P: Anne Spielberg. Ph: J.L. Mignones. PD: M. Scheffe. SpPhFX: J. Castle, B. Bryant. SpProps: Leslie Ekkel(sp?). Mkp: Miriam Lemel; S. Francis. SdFxEd: G. Gilbert. Ref: TV. GKey. TVFFSB. with Adam West, Gretchen Corbett, Peter Kastner, Barry Gordon (voice of MUD), Chip Johnson, Karen Kondazian, Kirk Alyn, S. Mond.

An astronaut on a "one-year mission into the farthest reaches of our galaxy"--to probe signals coming from, ostensibly, a black hole (they aren't)--passes through a "door in time" behind one of Jupiter's moons, and slips from the year 1985 into 1986. He is invisible, in effect, though small animals (inexplicably) sense his presence, and he speaks, at a seance, through a well-coached parrot. At the end, he journeys back, on Solo 2, through the warp, from 1986 to 1985....Lost in all this time-tripping is his super-computer, nicknamed MUD (for "More Unnecessary Data"), the "perfect companion to Man," created in its designer's image (i.e., "dull"). MUD adopts, variously, Jewish and Pakistani accents, sings Gene Autry songs, and has a miniature version of itself constructed.

The flattened-X style of the spaceship wings is post-STAR WARS, and the laughs-in-space approach initially suggests DARK STAR. But the body of this movie is screwball fantasy-comedy, a la TOPPER, and is, mostly, laborious talk. Corbett is the only actor who doesn't "condescend" to comedy, and plays her scenes fairly straight. The astronaut-computer duologues are hardly inspired, but provide occasional amusement. The explanations as to how and why Mark can return to 1985 are extremely involved, scientifically--listen very closely....

TIMERIDER: THE ADVENTURE OF LYLE SWANN Jensen Farley/Zoomo 1982 color 93m. SP,D: William Dear. SP,Mus,Exec P: Michael Nesmith. Ph: Larry Pizer; Bryan Greenberg. AD: Linda Pearl. SpFxEquip: Knott Ltd. SpVisFX: Computer Camera Service. SdFX: The Provision Co. Opt: Westheimer. Ref: screen. V 8/25/82:4(rated, as TIME RIDER...). 1/26/83. MFB'83:107-8. FComment 2/84:19. with Fred Ward, Belinda Bauer, Peter Coyote, L.Q. Jones, Ed Lauter, Richard Masur, Bruce Gordon.

A motorcyclist caught in a time-travel experiment is transported (motorcycle and all) to the Old West of 1877, and is ultimately rescued by a helicopter sent back from the present.... It's Silicon Valley vs. old San Marcos, in this slight but fairly entertaining sf-comedy-drama. The plot really gets no further than the more obvious comic anachronisms and juxtapositions--e.g., asked by the local padre (in 1877) where he obtained such a wonderful road map, Lyle innocently deadpans "Got it at an Exxon station"--although the conclusion has some historical-dramatic pretensions: the woman for Lyle (in 1877) is apparently also his grandmother, or great-grandmother; this is not so much incest (Lyle, technically, hasn't even been born yet) as it is cyclicality, or Fate. Whatever it is, it's terribly incidental. The movie has no more resonance than a charming old "Twilight Zone" like "The 7th is Made up of Phantoms" (the one in which National Guardsmen from 1964 end up at Custer's Last Stand in 1876) and it's less eerie because its time warp is explained. (It's a secret government project involving accelerators and transmitters.) In "The 7th...," 1964 and 1876 just happen to "overlap." For no reason.... TIMERIDER at best is amusing, and leaves no room for wonder.

TIN MAN Goldfarb/Thomas-Biston & Westcom 1983 color 95m. D, P: John G. Thomas. SP,Mus: Bishop Holiday. Ph: Virgil Harper. Ref: V 10/5/83. with Timothy Bottoms, Deana Jurgens, John Philip Law, Troy Donahue.

Deaf-mute boy builds a machine which enables him to hear and talk, and an "electronic robot" with its own personality.

TO ALL A GOODNIGHT IRC/IWDC & Four Features Partners(Sandy Cobe) 1980 color 84m. D: David Hess. SP,Exec Co-P: Alex Rebar. Ph: B. Godsey. Mus: Rich Tufo. PD: Joe Garrity. SpFxMkp: Mark Shostrum; Miles Liptak. Opt: Pacific. Ref: TV: Media Home Ent.(video). V 11/2/83. Ecran F 40:80. Berkeley Public Library. I.Berlin. with Jennifer Runyon, Forrest Swanson, Linda Gentile, William Lauer, Buck West("weird Ralph"), Sam Shamshak(Polansky), Katherine Herrington(Mrs.Jensen), J. Bridges.

"The devil's here," at the Calvin Finishing School for Girls. Not one, but two mad killers in Santa Claus costumes lurk, exacting revenge on the "rich little pompous bitches" who were responsible for their daughter's death two Christmases ago. The victims include several teenagers, two cops, etc., among the dead, and one girl still living, but mindless. Murder weapons include an axe, a crossbow, and an airplane propeller.

Perfunctory, nondescript teenagers'-last-holiday movie. In-between murders, survivors argue amongst themselves about how much (or how little) danger they're in. Viewers, meanwhile, may wonder if they're supposed to think that there are two Santas-at-large, or just one very busy one. The tipoff to the identity of one of the killers comes in a scene in which he acts not exactly mad, but odd--melodramatic foreshadowing...? The script is worthless; the acting, passable. There is, however, one clever-in-context line--note and remember who it is who says, "Everybody's a suspect, miss."

TO THE STARS BY HARD WAYS (Russ) IFEX/Sovexport 1982 color/ws 142m. (The THORNY WAY TO THE STARS-cr t) SP,D: Richard Victorov. SP: also K. Bulchynov? Ph: A Rybin. Mus: A. Rybnikov. Sets: K. Zagorsky. Ref: screen. Academy. UC Theatre notes 1/6/83. V 7/28/82:6(FJA): sfa PER ASPERA AD ASTRA(at Trieste)? Willis/SW'83. with Yelena Metelkina(Niya), Nadezhda Sementsova, Vtaslav Dvorhetsky.

In two parts: Niya, Test Tube Human, and Guardian Angels of Space. In the year 2222, Niya--the only clone, or biorobot, to survive Dessan scientist Glyn's cloning experiments--stows away aboard the spaceship Astra. The latter's mission: condense the sludge on the polluted Dessa using "plasma discharges." "Biomass," here, is raw, pudding-like cellular material (created by Glyn) used to fashion "perfect" humans; at the end, Niya's telekinetic powers repulse this biomass-gone-mad ("devouring all organic matter") and turn it into (in effect) fertilizer for Dessa....Niya can "telepult," or "jump cut," herself through matter and space, and is invulnerable, but is a slave to her "obedience center," until human emotions win out....Academician Prule, intelligent, octopus-like alien, returned via Astra to watery planet Ocean...Glasha, robot...13-2A robot Barmalei... brain probes...(unseen) animal mutants on Dessa...planet destroyed by nuclear-waste accident, or sabotage..."happy masks" for deformed Dessans.

TO THE STARS... begins, with its not-quite-human woman, like SOLARIS; turns, in Part II, with its capitalistic Dessan fiend Turanchoks (who sells air to the planet's children-of-smog), into a socialist FLASH GORDON, or Eisenstein on Mars; and winds up, with the onslaught of the pulsating biomass, like The UNKNOWN TERROR(qq.v.). This is not, it must be said, an enviable evolution. The movie is, it's true, pretty consistently amusing--it begins as humanistic comedy and ends as allegorical camp. And there are some wry touches even in Part II. (Turanchoks is not only a grotesquely-pale dwarf, but also quite ticklish.) But the rampaging biomass-blob is not supposed to be hilarious. ("Miscalculation" is a good word here.) It's supposed to be an example, ultimately, of the good uses to which science can be put. As an sf film, TO THE STARS... is less responsible than The UNKNOWN TERROR--better, yes, but less responsible. The only possible way to "read" Dessa and the biomass to the movie's esthetic advantage is as a satire on glibly-"progressive" filmmaking: this Turanchoks is a villain worthy of Victorian melodrama--you not only get to hiss the reactionary, you get to see him eaten by The Blob (which is, then, tamed by our forward-looking, pro-masses heroes). But the filmmakers seem to think of this 180-degree turn of events as poetic, or allegorical, license, not as comic or satiric exaggeration....Easier to take The BLOB seriously. And easier to take the first half of TO THE STARS..., which at least keeps its loony pretensions to itself, and functions mainly as a showcase for Niya's powers and limitations. Even here, though, her final transcendance of her humanoid origins seems inevitable--why can't android-types ever just be themselves?

*TORTURE SHIP (Picturmedia-TV) 1939 SP: George Sayre, from Jack London's story "A Thousand Deaths." Mus: David Chudnow. AD: Fred Preble. Ref: TV. TVFFSB. Lee. "B" Movies. no LC. Stanley. and with Stanley Blystone.

When a doctor's (Irving Pichel) synthetic formula--derived from "the active ingredients of the endocrine glands governing criminality"--fails to alter the criminal nature of his subject, he proceeds to take an extract from the endocrine glands of a "normal" man (Lyle Talbot), "free from criminal taint," and injects it into the body of "Poison Mary" (Sheila Bromley). (Harry, The Carver, is another of the criminal elements on board.) Her bitterness turns to sweetness, and she feels "born again." Bob himself reacts violently, even crazily, at first, to the extraction, and later feigns madness....

Weird little "B" horror-drama is half routine-action and half A CLOCKWORK ORANGE. Neither half could exactly be called a success, though the theme of scientific rebirth is, even here, semi-interesting. Pichel seems to qualify as a MAD Doctor onyy because Talbot, his subject, a) is also his nephew and, b) reacts strangely to glandular deprivation. But Lyle recovers, and the experiment is wildly, not to say deliriously, successful. Uncle Irving's death, then, may be a noble one, but it's also, dramatically, weakly-motivated and not really necessary. (Cf. the fate of Leo G. Carroll's scientist in TARANTULA, qq.v.) Bespectacled, creepy Skelton Knaggs (who looks like his name)--a sort of Elisha Cook by way of "The Twilight Zone"--plays one of the shipboard criminals and is one-up on this movie and just about any other for weirdness. The musical score here is charmingly rudimentary.

2 TRACK OF THE MOONBEAST Cinema Shares Int'l./Lizard Prods. 1976 D: Dick Ashe. Ph: E.S. Wood. Mus: Bob Orpin. SpMkp: Joe Blasco. Ref: TV. Weldon. and with Gregorio Sala.

Meteorite particle lodged in man's skull periodically turns him into tyrannosaurus-like beast; ultimately, diffused through his body, causes him to explode, or self-consume....Pre-inept monster-tragedy, with a rather-sloppily-synched sound track. Too slow and formulaic to be very funny. Our heroine here, though, models a wonderful variety of shorts and mini-outfits....

TRASHI Artimi 1982(1981) color 73m. D: Louie Lewis. Ref: screen. with Lisa DeLeeuw(Trashi), Paul Thomas, Sharon Mitchel(l), Joey Silvera, Loni Sanders, Dorothy LeMay, Lysa Thatcher.

Mad doctor Schtup creates a "perfect woman" (DeLeeuw) from "spare parts" from (apparently) dead bodies. She is programmed for sex, and eventually develops feeling....Imperfect-model robots such as R69-D69 litter the doctor's apartment....This is not really quite "like some grade-B Bela Lugosi movie" (in the words of one character)--it's not that good. Threadbare even for a porn flick, it looks up to PLAN 9 FROM OUTER SPACE. It might be spare parts itself--the scenes featuring Carol Doda and Serena, for instance, seem to have been hastily grafted onto the main body of the film. The (literal) main body of the film--DeLeeuw's--is rather more than perfect, but the doctor can be forgiven for his excesses in this case.

TREASURE OF THE FOUR CROWNS (U.S.-Sp) Cannon/M.T.G.-Lotus(Lupo-Anthony-Quintano) 1983(1982) color & 3-D 99m. (El TESORO DE LAS CUATRO CORONAS) D: Ferdinando Baldi. SP: Battista, Bryce, Lazarus. Story: Petit(t)o, Quintano. Ph: Masciocchi, Ruzzolini. Mus: Ennio Morricone. AD: Spadoni. SpFX: Unger, Natali;(mkp) de Marchis. SdFX: Arcangeli. Ref: screen. V 1/26/83. MFB'83:249. Ecran F 31:47: Ital.?;aka Il MISTERO DELLA QUATTRO CORONA. with Tony Anthony, Ana Obregon, Quintano, Francisco Rabal, Kate Levan, Emiliano Redondo(Jonas).

Green and gold jewels from two of the four crowns of the Visigoths cause their bearer's head to spin around and his face to "melt" and enable him to shoot fire at his foes and to incinerate the evil Father Jonas in the latter's fortress-like City of Love and Unity....Power from the key to the crowns seems to possess a mountain cabin and wreak (3-D) havoc with its contents, and to make a model of the fortress shudder and shake....Said fortress has "laser eye" defense and sound-operated locks....castle haunted by pterodactyl-like birds and ghostly laughter, and by skeletons, suits of armor, and cross-bows which seem to come to life.

There are two good reasons to see this movie...plenty of good reasons not to. Primary among the latter: the plot, which is a pinch of RIFIFI, a soupcon of GUNGA DIN, and a liter or two of RAIDERS OF THE LOST ARK. (There's also a disintegration effect adapted from HORROR OF DRACULA.) If 3-D does wonders for exploding fireballs and dangling ropes, it's not much help when it comes to plot/character/dialogue, in movies from CREATURE FROM THE BLACK LAGOON to this one. There are, however, four or five sequences in TREASURE which are specifically designed to "use" the 3-D process...for frivolous, non-esthetic purposes, it's true--but, kinetically-speaking, they're minor marvels. They're just stunt after stunt, strings of visual firecrackers touched off by the powers of the key and the jewels. The effect is a sort of hallucinatory Cinemascope, substituting depth for width....Reason For Seeing #2: a strange, occasional, elusive sense of nobility, even grandeur, threading through the movie, the source of which sense is obviously not the laughably trashy story and effects. If you find yourself taking away odd traces of a puzzling, gentle splendor from this tawdry adventure movie, blame composer Ennio Morricone. The latter has summoned up a genuinely stirring theme or two or three from...nowhere, apparently....

TRECHI MYNYDD Y TEIGR see TAKING TIGER MOUNTAIN

TRESOR DES MORTS VIVANTS see ABIME DES MORTS VIVANTS

TRIAL OF ROCKY JONES see ROCKY JONES, SPACE RANGER

TRICK OR TREATS Lone Star 1983(1982) color 91m. SP,D,Co-P, Ph,Ed: Gary Graver. Sets: Michael Railsback. SpCons: Orson Welles. Ref: V 9/29/82:4(rated). 11/17/82. Ecran F 30:58. with Jackelyn Giroux, Peter Jason, David Carradine, Carrie Snodgress, Steve Railsback, Dan Pastorini, Paul Bartel, John Blyth Barrymore(mad doctor), Chris Graver.

Madman on the loose on Halloween...terrified babysitter.

TRILBY(by du Maurier) see SVENGALI

TRIP TO TERROR see IS THIS TRIP REALLY NECESSARY?

TRON BV/Lisberger-Kushner 1982 color/ws 96m. Story,SP,D,Vis FxConcep: Steven Lisberger. Story: also Bonnie MacBird. Ph: Bruce Logan. Mus: Wendy Carlos;(songs) Journey. PD: Dean E. Mitzner. VisFX:(sup) Richard Taylor, Harrison Ellenshaw;(tech sup) John Scheele;(anim sup) Lee Dyer;(bkgd des) Peter Lloyd. Computer FX:(sup) Taylor;(chor) Bill Kroyer et al. ElecConcep: (des) Jean Giraud, Taylor;(art) Syd Mead et al. Mech:(sp fx) R.J. Spetter;(des) Don Iwerks et al. SdDes:(fx) Frank Serafine;(sup) Michael Fremer. Roto:(sup) Ron Osenbaugh et al; (coord) Marian Guder. Opt: Bob Broughton. Mattes: Arnie Wong. Technology Concep: Phillip Mittelman. Titles: Abel & Assoc.; (des sup) Kenny Mirman. TRON Formation: Digital FX. Ref: screen. pr. V 7/7/82. Robert Moore. MFB'82:237-8. Ecran F 29: 44-53,60-63. with Jeff Bridges, Bruce Boxleitner(Alan/Tron), David Warner, Cindy Morgan, Barnard Hughes, Dan Shor.

There is, according to TRON, a computer universe within our universe, and one man, Flynn (Bridges), succeeds in crossing over to the other side--and coming back. On one narrative plane, he triumphs over Dillinger (Warner), the man who cheated him out of his Space Paranoids video-game idea and subsequently became head of ENCOM, Flynn's former employer; on another plane, he helps defeat Dillinger's brainchild, the Master Control Program (MCP), which has taken over ENCOM's computer operations and is 2,415 times smarter than when Dillinger programmed it. For every computer "user," the script posits, there is a (humanoid) program, or "conscript" (in MCP terms), and a freak accident with ENCOM's "Program Orange" laser machine (which alters the molecular structure of matter) allows Flynn to be reconstituted within the computer, in program form, where he helps his friend Alan's TRON program liberate the other programs from the MCP and create a "free system"....Incidental computer phenomena: a disc which enables a program to communicate with its user...a butterfly-like transport-on-light-beam...a voice-crystal...columns-and-cornice-like flying warships, with shadows (light source unspecified)...funny-looking "aliens" (in the image of alien users??)...a sphinx-like "guardian" program...glob-bubbles...grid-"spiders."

Yes, there are, according to TRON, little men inside computers--and the movie never quite recovers from this premise. Inside, there are also, if one looks closely, "frisbees," handball games, spaceships, tanks, cycles, and "live" video games--these anthropomorphized computer-programs seem, however, to lack good restaurants and yogurt parlors. Not that the movie is without a thematic "justification" for its scheme of anthropomorphization: as, that is, users are created in His image, so programs are created in the image of users. Programs are exhorted (by Dillinger's program) to disbelieve in users, but Flynn is, clearly, users' gift to programs. He even brings one program "back," a la Lazarus. TRON is both graphically and metaphysically ambitious--give it that much--but, dramatically, it has the bite, not to mention the plot, of DEVIL BAT. If, on one level, Flynn is Christ, on another, he's Bela Lugosi, out for revenge on the company that profited by his genius--and then let him go. And yet TRON is, at least, watchable: the computer-generated images, animation, and other visual effects--it's hard to tell where one process leaves off and another begins--do substitute, fairly effectively at times, for old-fashioned drama. If they don't make drama, they occasionally atone for its loss. The movement, particularly, of the warships, the "spiders," and the crystal is quirkily amusing, and the "motorcycle" "video game" is exciting if, logistically, confusing. The vehicles here may look like tanks and motorcycles, but they move differently. If technology in TRON won't quite wash as metaphysics, it's still, occasionally, interesting as technology.

La TUMBA DE LOS MUERTOS VIVIENTES (Sp) Marte & DIASA 1982 D: Jesus Franco. Ref: V 5/4/83:418. no Ecran 31. with Manuel Gelin, Eduardo Fajardo, Lina Romay.

TURKEY SHOOT see ESCAPE 2000

2019: THE FALL OF NEW YORK (I-F) Medusa & Dania/Letienne & IEC 1983 color (2099: AFTER THE FALL OF NEW YORK-ad t. 2099: DOPO LA CAPUTA DI NEW YORK) D: Sergio Martino. Ref: V 5/4/83:307. 9/21/83:42: in Italy. Ecran F 29:55.39:6.

"Post-nuclear holocauster...set in a magnetic bubble over N.Y.C...."(V)

TWICE UPON A TIME WB/Ladd/Kortyfilms & Lucasfilms 1983 anim & live color 75m. Story,SP,D: John Korty. SP,D: Charles Swenson. Story,SP: Suella Kennedy. Story,SP,P: Bill Couturie. Mus: Dawn Atkinson, Ken Melville. AD: Harley Jessup. Sup Anim: Brian Narelle. SpPhFX: David Fincher. Composite Opt: Midland. Sd:(des) Walt Kraemer;(fx ed) K.G. Wilson et al. Ref: screen. Bill Warren. pr. V 8/3/83. Ecran F 31:6. Voices: Lorenzo Music, Judith Kahan Kampmann, Marshall Efron, James Cranna, Julie Payne, Hamilton Camp, Paul Frees.

Nightmare-maker Synonamess Botch, of the Murkworks Nightmare Factory, has time frozen by releasing the mainspring of the Cosmic Clock. All life on Din (read: Earth) speeds up, slows down, then stops. Meanwhile, Botch dispatches Rudy and the rest of his vultures to plant Nightmare Bombs on Rushers (read: people) all over Din, in hopes that the bombs will explode and generate general misery when time starts up again. Further ingredients: Botch's Video Gorilla, or Ibor (roughly, "Robby," backwards), half-gorilla and half-robot, who "speaks" in film clips (from STAR WARS, THEM!, etc.), which are flashed on the TV screen on his chest...giant, Kong-like gorilla...the "essence of terror" (the active ingredient in the bombs), which is extracted from creatures subjected to frightening sights and incidents in the Murkworks Factory--e.g., dancing skeletons, dinosaurs, etc...fake dragon and shark (in the Murkworks moat)... nightmare sequence in which office tape-dispensers, pencil sharpeners, etc. come to life...hero with X-ray-vision glasses.

TWICE UPON A TIME plays as blithely and lightly as an episode of "Rocky and His Friends." In this cartoon fantasy-comedy, the good guys are, surprisingly, as droll as the bad guys. The movie is so light, in fact, that it almost floats away. Everyone (especially Music, as Ralph, the All-Purpose Animal) seems to be having so much fun with odd phrases...odd inflections...odd shapes and sizes...odd transformations...odd plot twists...that it may seem like carping to draw attention to the lack of dramatic or emotional resonance. The bland title and songs are the only real drawbacks. Comically, the picture is very efficient, and it's as chock-full of incident and invention as a Spielberg special like E.T. or POLTERGEIST. Within its flip-fairy-tale limitations, TWICE UPON A TIME is very entertaining.

TWILIGHT OF THE DEAD see GATES OF HELL, The

TWILIGHT ZONE--REVISITED Viacom-TV/CBS-TV & Cayuga 1963 96m. D: David Butler/Buzz Kulik. From two "Twilight Zone" episodes by host Rod Serling. Ph: G.T. Clemens. Mus: Fred Steiner. AD: G.W. Davis, E. Carfagno/Davis, P. Groesse. Ref: TV. TVG. with Jack Weston, John Williams, Howard McNear, Doro Merande, Burt Reynolds, John McGiver; James Whitmore, James Broderick, Tim O'Connor, Paul Langton, Russ Bender.

"The Bard": would-be writer Julius Moomer (Weston) uses "The Book of the Black Arts" to conjure up Shakespeare (Williams);

employs him as a ghost writer for a TV drama special, "The Tragic Cycle." Broad comedy, as Shakespeare and television, rather too predictably, clash. Weston's hack is supposed to be untalented; what he's not, also, supposed to be is unlikable, and in his pure, petty selfishness, he is. Shakespeare's material--archaisms and all--is, unbelievably, snapped up by the TV moguls. The better (and shorter) joke would have been to have them reject it outright....

"On Thursday We Leave for Home": in 1991, after 30 years on a planet with two suns, the Earth's first space colonists prepare to return home. The issues are cut-and-dried: individualism vs. (benevolent) authoritarianism; anarchy vs. order. They will probably not interest anyone as presented here, on a platter--and with sententious dialogue. Whitmore, however, has some touching moments as the lonely leader-"god" who both rhapsodizes about the green Earth and wants to keep his subjects from it, all-dependent upon his descriptions...upon him.

TWILIGHT ZONE--THE MOVIE WB/Spielberg-Landis 1983 color 105m. D:(1) John Landis;(2) Steven Spielberg;(3) Joe Dante;(4) George Miller. SP:(1) Landis;(2) George Clayton Johnson, Richard Matheson, Melissa Mathison(aka Josh Rogan);(3&4) Matheson. Stories:(2) Johnson ("Kick the Can," "Twilight Zone" teleplay); (3) Jerome Bixby ("It's a Good Life");(4) Matheson ("Nightmare at 20,000 Feet"). Ph: Steven Larner, Allen Daviau, John Hora. Mus: Jerry Goldsmith. PD: James D. Bissell. SpMkpFX:(3) Rob Bottin;(4) Craig Reardon, Michael McCracken. SpFX:(sup) Mike Wood; Paul Stewart. SpDes:(4) Ed Verreaux. SpVisFX:(4) Peter Kuran, Industrial Light & Magic, David Allen. Anim(3):(sup) Sally Cruickshank; Mark Kausler. Cons & with: Carol Serling. SdFxEd: Warren Hamilton et al. Narr: Burgess Meredith, Rod Serling. Ref: screen. V 6/15/83. G.C.Johnson. Bill Warren. VV 7/5/83:54: "Dante, one of Hollywood's more perverse recyclers." Fangoria 30:10: BIMBO'S INITIATION on TV in #3. MFB'83:281-82. FComment 2/84:18,24. Ecran F 41:48-68. with John Lithgow, Scatman Crothers, Kathleen Quinlan, Vic Morrow, Peter Brocco, Dan Aykroyd(monster), Albert Brooks, Dick Miller(Walter Paisley), Kevin McCarthy, Abbe Lane, Larry Cedar(creature), William Schallert, Billy Mumy, Donna Dixon, Eduard Franz, Chris Eisenmann, Selma Diamond, Cherie Currie, Norbert Weisser.

Four stories (with numbers two, three, and four reworkings of "Twilight Zone" episodes), plus a prologue and epilogue.... 1) Exit from tavern proves to be entrance into the past for bigot, who finds himself a victim of violence--as, variously, a Jew in Nazi-occupied Paris, a Black at a KKK lynching in the South, and a V.C. in Viet Nam. 2) Mr. Bloom and his tin can bring literal youth to the elderly at Sunnyvale Rest Home. Most of the recipients of the gift choose to be restored to their proper age, but one remains young, and lights out. 3) "Anything can happen in cartoons"--and in one cartoon fan's (Jeremy Light) house, here, anything he thinks happens: he "erases" his sister's mouth; injects an "adopted" sister into a monster-filled TV cartoonland; creates a TV-generated "cyclone" which yields real-life cartoon monsters; posts a giant-eyeball "guard" at the front door; and makes his "adopted" father pull a monster-rabbit out of a top hat....4) A man absolutely paranoid about flying watches as a creature tears up an airliner's engine--while the plane is in flight, caught in a thunderstorm. Plus: prologue with man-turning-into-monster...dialogue references (in number three) to TZ towns Cliffordville and Willoughby, and to writer Charles Beaumont; Quinlan's character's name (Helen Foley; in #3) from TZ episode, "Nightmare as a Child."

No movie version now, of course, could possibly re-create the excitement of a certain time of evening then; the excitement of, say, 10 p.m., Friday, March 31, 1961 ("Long Distance Call"), or any Friday, 10 o'clock (Sacramento time) between 1960 and 1962, when "The Twilight Zone" ended its first run of half-hour shows...although one of the entries here (episode two) is about recapturing such long-past moments. In retrospect, not all of those TZ's might seem to have justified that feeling of excitement--but the good ones carried the rest, the ones with a terrific moment or two, and the ones with jolly surprise endings and nothing else. Because some of the shows were so good, the series was good. It was worth waiting for: Friday "carried" the rest of the week. The MOVIE can't recreate scattered moments in time. It does, however, contain three of the better TZ's (even if they are remakes); and the prologue by Landis integrates--with disarming smoothness--our sentiment for the original series into our feelings about this new enterprise. His lengthier, official contribution then proceeds to recapture, ironically, the stolidness-of-purpose of the worst TZ's, the well-meaning solemnity of "A Quality of Mercy," "The Mirror," etc. He has, perhaps, also seen BLACK LEGION too often. Even this one extended lapse in the movie, however, features the requisite "terrific moment or two": the barroom door into the past, and the view from the cattle car which our anti-hero (Morrow) is granted of his pals, as they stand, oblivious of him, outside the bar. (You can see out of The Twilight Zone, apparently, but not into it.)

The surprise of the movie is the Spielberg episode. His version of "Kick the Can" must be the quietest thing he has ever done. He leaves the noise and commotion to Dante, Miller, and Landis. The original teleplay had a promising premise, but painful thoughts-in-dialogue on youth, aging, friendship, etc. (Crothers' Mr. Bloom inherits a few of these here.) This is the one of the movie's three adaptations that needed some work. At the story's core is the old "Of Mice and Men" dreamers-vs.-realists chestnut. The script, however, is not at all doctrinaire or insistent. Most of the recipients reject the gift of physical youth offered them, in favor of the prospect of mental youth; one recipient enthusiastically accepts the gift of a second life; and one old man comes, bitterly, to regret the fact that he passed up the original offer. In 20-or-so minutes, Spielberg and co. can't create full-fledged characters--but they can and do limn a full range of possible responses to this idea of renewed youth. There's a marvelous openness about the anecdote, as told here--a feeling of wonder evoked not so much by Mr. Bloom's magic, as by the configuration of human response to that magic....At story's end, he's entering another old-folks'-home: fade out on this picture of the magician casually setting up his act before yet another audience....The Dante-Matheson segment which follows is virtually as entertaining, if not quite as resonant. It's nearly swamped by its out-of-the-minds-of-babes effects; but the latter are so well conceived and executed that the lack of a strong, human center is not too sorely missed. The original show was (of necessity) a small-scale affair, but well done. The movie version leans toward spectacle (this is Dante's POLTERGEIST) and, in its own, HELLZAPOPPIN way, is an engaging, cartoonland horror show--young Anthony is a most imaginative mind-monster. A trace of regal discontent, however, (not in the Bixby short story) is introduced into his absolute monarchy (in, perhaps, an attempt to locate that "human center"), and jars a bit, leading to a not-quite-right-seeming happy ending, in which Anthony thinks miles and miles of flowers. And after the flowers? we want to know. A trace of residual irony would help...perhaps a shot of a weed....

Matheson's screenplay for the last segment is cannier than his "Nightmare..." teleplay. The latter squandered time on distracting is-it-real-or-imagined? ambiguity. In the movie, it doesn't matter: there's every (psychological) reason to believe that the guy (Lithgow) is imagining the gremlin; he, apparently, however, isn't. It seems to be a perverse coincidence that all signs point to derangement. Either way it's a nightmare for him; whichever way, that is, you take the tale, it works, and Matheson seems less concerned now with which way you take it....The monster in this movie remake is, however, rather-conventionally makeup-effects monstrous. The impish "snowman" in the TV show was a variation on Robert Bloch's favorite image of The Clown at Midnight. An ordinary clown isn't scary...but on the wing of an airplane, at 40,000 feet.... The movie monster would be scary anywhere; its presence on the wing is intimidating, but hardly as droll as was the snowman's in the teleplay. And this segment features the same sort of hyper-activity as the Dante one...Spielberg's, perhaps, should have been placed between rather than before the two, in order to give the audience a breather. George Miller's every shot--even when nothing much is happening--seems to be an intense close-up, or at least intense. At that, the mise-en-scene is no-more-overwrought than the prose of the Matheson short story (which story seems, in retrospect, simply a vehicle for the wry image of a grinning gremlin). There's no real dramatic point--to story, teleplay, screenplay--no psychological insight. The hero's mental breakdown is a narrative ruse, a pretext for a succession of black-comic stunts; a ruse most successful in this movie version, thanks in large part to the conviction which Lithgow brings to his portrait of the terrified passenger....In sum: who could feel ungrateful about a movie which brings us top Spielberg; the best, so far, of Joe Dante; close to the best of Richard Matheson; even, yes, almost, the best of "The Twilight Zone"? (I would argue for only a stray episode or two in the original series--say, the Beaumont-Brahm "Shadow Play"--as being, possibly, superior to the better segments here....)

TWILITE PINK St. Germaine/Eagle-Bolla 1981 color 75m. (TWI-LIGHT PINK-ad t) D: Travis St. Germaine. SP: Kang Cruel. Ph: Misha. AD: Leslie Amber. Ref: screen. with Veronica Hart, Richard Bolla, Kandi Barbour, Annie Sprinkle, Mistress Candice.

In a sort of production-within-a-production, Sterling Rod conducts us into "The Erogenous Zone," the crux of which is a watch which makes time stand still. The bearer then presses it against selected "frozen" subjects around him, thus releasing their bodies--and their inhibitions. When time resumes, the subjects have no memory of their actions under the spell. The bearer of the watch lives, in effect, 50 years in one year.... Perfunctory as porn <u>or</u> as science-fantasy. Not even serviceable as a vehicle for Ms. Hart, whose customary believability becomes, here, mere stridency.

TWINKLE, TWINKLE, LITTLE STAR (H.K.-Cant.) Shaw 1983 color 100m. D,Ph: C.K. Ming. SP: C. Wen et al. Mus D: Shing, Hou. AD: Tsao. SpFX: Chua Lan. Ref: V 3/2/83. with Yi Lei, Cherry Chung, Tan Tien Nan.

"Dumb broad" raped by "hostile monster" from flying saucer.

TWO FACES OF EVIL/RUDE AWAKENING see HAMMER HOUSE OF HORROR

TWO GHOSTS AND A GIRL see DOS FANTASMAS Y UNA MUCHACHA

TWO HEARTS IN WAX TIME MGM 1935 color 20m. Ref: Don Glut. LC.

Models of the Frankenstein monster, Fu Manchu, and Dr. Jekyll and Mr. Hyde-like characters come to life.

TWO SWORDS, TWO SORCERERS (H.K.?) VIC 1982-U.S. color/ws 97m. Ref: screen. poster. with John Liu, Angela Mao.

"Cartilege poison" which renders man insensible...acupuncture counteractive...weaponless, neck-and-torso-puncturing martial arts...green-palmed master who, with his bare hands, breaks swords and sends foes flying...village-fortress "defense line" which is booby-trapped with poison gas, bombs, buzz-saw-like discs...wooden needles which are driven through table-top and into victim's chest...downed combatants who seem to right themselves magically (but then just topple over again).... Balinese-dance-style martial arts mayhem, with "choreographed" thwacks, swishes, whooshes, oofs, and grunts. No sorcerers here; a sword or two, though, and lots of knives. If you have the time, wait for dubbed lines like "I just can't stand <u>men</u>

who attack women," "I need no thanks for killing scum," and "That's right--I'm known as The Flying Knife--Tong-Tong." But only if you have the time....

TWYLIGHT see DUELLE

UFO see INVASION UFO

UFO ROBOT GRENDIZER see SHOGUN WARRIORS: GRANDIZER

UCHU KAIZOKU KYAPUTEN HAROKKU see CAPTAIN HARLOCK IN ARCADIA

UCHU SENKAN YAMATO--KANKETSUHEN (J) Toei 1983 anim feature Sequel to SPACE CRUISER. Ref: V 4/13/83:35: "sci-fi."

ULTIMO SQUALO, L' see GREAT WHITE

UNDERCOVERS Cockatoo/Evolution 1982 color 86m. SP,D,P: Virginia Ann Perry-Rhine. Ph: Ken Gibb et al. Mus: Carlos Martinez, J.-J. Schoc. Opt: Alberto Soria. Mkp: Greg Yedding. Ref: screen: Cover-Up, projected sequel. poster. Adam 1/83. with Samantha Fox, Bobby Astyr, Sharon Mitchell, Becky Savage.

The Type 2 Thought Extractor, a small atomic device, is implanted in a secret agent's vagina; she ends up "screwing everybody's brains out," leaving half-dozen diplomats mindless.... decoding device for detecting the presence of the Extractor... James Bond references (e.g., the Q, Commander James, and Grossfinger characters)....The principal victim of the Thought Extractor was apparently the script, which was sucked dry. This forlorn James Bond take-off plays like a comedy--broadly, and with "comical" characters and dialogue--but there's no threat of a laugh in the film. Scene-to-scene continuity is tenuous; moment-to-moment continuity is not impeccable.

*UNEARTHLY STRANGER (TV Cinema Sales)/CW Film Co.(Wintle-Parkyn) 1963 75m. (BEYOND THE STARS-orig t) Idea: Jeffrey Stone. AD: Harry Pottle. Mkp: Trevor Crole Rees. Ref: TV. AFI. BFC.

The world's space scientists are mysteriously dying, their brains destroyed, their neck vertebrae fused, and traces of triamorphinide (a substance also found inside space capsules returning to Earth) in their arteries. Behind it all: a 20-year-old plot by aliens "projecting their minds through space" and--with "power of concentration"--assuming human form, the better to contain Earth's space ventures. (They kill by unleashing an invisible, "cataclysmic force.") One alien, Julie (Gabriella Licudi), falls in love with her intended victim (John Neville) and is atomized; the powers of another (Jean Marsh) are checked by an anesthetic, and she falls to her death and evaporates. But, as the latter proclaims, "There are too many of us, and few as weak as Julie."

A competent, very-low-budget variation on I MARRIED A MONSTER FROM OUTER SPACE. This is not really a mystery since the clues to Julie's identity--she doesn't blink; tears burn her cheeks; she has no pulse; an oven-hot casserole doesn't burn her bare hands--are obvious to everyone except her adoring husband. The doubly-improbable plot demands that, a) his love be blind, and b) she reciprocate, emotionally, and these demands generate some improbable dialogue on the nature of love. Suspense the film generates; philosophy is a bit beyond its ken. The director, John Krish, isn't subtle. Aurally and visually, the movie is overstated...filled, as it is, with close-ups, dramatic declamations and pauses, hype-music. Krish appears to be overcompensating for his lack of material means. To a certain extent, however, this overloading works; it is, alternately, compelling and silly. Actors and director really want to put this over. The only problem is that you're all-too-aware of their earnestness....

UNHINGED Anavisio 1983(1982) color 79m. SP,D,P: Don Gronquist. SP: also Reagan Ramsey. Ph: Richard Blakeslee. Mus: Jonathan Newton. PD: Sol Leibowitz. Mkp: Janet Scoutten. Opt: Alpha FX. Ref: MFB'83:282. Academy. Ecran F 35:2. with Laurel Munson, J.E. Penner(Marion), Sara Ansley, Virginia Settle.

Terror in an old Oregon mansion...murder by scythe, machete.

UNHOLY, The see DEMON, The

*The UNKNOWN 1927 54m. Ref: screen. W.K. Everson. PFA notes.

Madrid. Alonzo, The (phony) Armless Wonder (Lon Chaney) falls for Estrellita (Joan Crawford), who loathes men "pawing" her. He looks up a shady surgeon and--now truly armless and 'armless--returns to find his love "cured" and about to marry The Strong (and armed) Man (Norman Kerry). The incensed Alonzo plots to have wild horses tear off his rival's arms during a stage act, but his plans go awry, and he is stomped to death.

Macabre enough for two Chaney movies, or at least one-and-a-half. The perversity here, however, is a bit mechanical. It seems less the contrivance of Fate at work than, simply, contrivance. A fortunate fall into the arms of Malabar the Strong Man is all that it takes for Estrellita to begin to appreciate the advantages of male hands and arms. This, after her hatred of groping hands has been established, re-established, and rendered all-but-axiomatic. Still, the cheating is done in the name of Alonzo's Malevolent Obsession, and the latter is, occasionally, compelling as a sort of bizarre variation on "Gift of the Magi" themes--here, arms rather than hair are cut, all for love, and all, as it transpires, for nothing. Chaney relies too often on a fixed sneer (perhaps because he is so good at making his lips go, putty-like, all crooked); but his key dramatic pantomimes are so complicated that they're disturbing. They involve a kaleidoscopic melange of expressions--suggesting revulsion, madness, despair--which expressions supplant one another so quickly that you can't be sure what, in God's name, you just saw. If there were any lingering doubts that Alonzo was mad....

*UNKNOWN ISLAND (Western-TV)/A.J. Cohen 1948 Ref: TV. V 11/24/48. LC. Weldon. Stanley. Lee.

UNKNOWN ISLAND's agreeable, mystery-mood-setting opening sequence (set an an "exotic," one-set Singapore) may lead you to expect another KING KONG or SON OF KONG. But, no, it's just UNKNOWN ISLAND, a movie populated by several decrepit dinosaurs, pleasant actors like Virginia Grey, Barton MacLane, and Richard Denning, and what appears to be a Ray Corrigan gorilla suit leftover from WHITE GORILLA. (Here, it's supposed to represent a giant sloth.) Lots of dramatic and dialogue cliches. MacLane's lascivious, malicious captain carries most of the dramatic weight, or what passes for same.

*The UNKNOWN TERROR Regal/Emirau 1957 ws OptFX: Jack Rabin, Louis DeWitt. Mkp: Glen Alden. Ref: TV. FM 18:22. Warren/KWTS! Weldon. and with Charles Gray, Martin Garralaga.

Mad doctor (Gerald Milton) working "with all kinds of fungi" in (apparently) South America proves responsible for fungus-monster-and-men in lost Cava Muerta....Film, unlike fungus, is slow-moving. It's also over-solemn, and if not very horrific, it's not for lack of trying: there's thunder-and-lightning, wind-whipped foliage, ominous drumbeating, flash-flooding, lurking fungus-men ("That man was all covered with fungus!"), and plop-plop-plopping fungus. (The latter resembling an Attack of the Soapsuds or--to Joe Dante--"half-cooked oatmeal," or both.) Sir Lancelot's calypso ode to the Cave of the Dead, however, is ear-catching, and there are some redeeming camp moments and lines--e.g., the crippled Paul Richards beating his wooden leg in frustration...the hopeful cry "We've got to get Ramsey to stop that fungus!" The script is oddly silent about what made him start it....

See also: MUTINY IN OUTER SPACE.

2 The UNSEEN 1981(1980) 91m. Ph: Roberto Quezada; Irv Goodnoff; James Carter. AD: Dena Roth. SpFX: Harry Woolman. Opt: MGM. Ref: TV. V 10/7/81. Weldon.

The first hour of The UNSEEN is little more than your standard women-in-the-dark screamer. For what it is, it's well done. But it wastes some smart editing and photography on the second-oldest suspense tricks in the book. And it centers on the father, Ernest (Sydney Lassick), of "Junior," The Unseen (Stephen Furst). Father has, previously, committed incest (his sister) and murder (his father), and at the time the movie picks up his story, his personality has not noticeably improved. Ernest is a mental sadist who delights in tormenting and playing practical jokes on his dim-witted sister Virginia (Lelia Goldoni)--and the film seems to endorse his petty sadism by dwelling on it. This portion of the movie might better be labeled The

Unpleasant. But it gets worse, or better, depending upon your point-of-view. The film's first hour--which is simply mean, even misanthropic, a la The TEXAS CHAIN SAW MASSACRE (Kim Henkel worked on the scripts for both films)--proves to be just an overextended set-up for the last half-hour, the confrontation between father and son and mother. (The nominal heroine more or less "drops out" at this point--her only remaining duty being to scream.) The picture spends roughly half its running time working up antipathy for the father, when a well-selected minute of his loathsomeness would have sufficed....Our unseen killer, seen, finally, is an overgrown baby, a mad butterball of a hulk who wants to play with the heroine. (Father just wants the lad to eliminate this witness to the boy's crimes.) The audience knows whom to root for (son)--that's simple enough. And yet the movie has succeeded in involving us, however uneasily, in this weird-family drama. It's not the (mentally) sick vs. the well, as in TEXAS...; it's the sick vs. the sicker, and even PSYCHO didn't quite take that turn. When the father's horrified scream merges with the angry bellow of his onrushing son (son saw pop knock down mom), the movie ventures into giddy, uncharted realms of (for us) not-quite-horror, not-quite-cathartic-exhilaration. The climactic sequences of The UNSEEN feature one of the odder, grimmer forms of pathos--if even this Addams Family of characters can move one....Grand Guignol is right next door...Greek tragedy, just around the corner. The son commits a couple of nasty murders, but--as the hero of the climactic scenes--dies the nastiest death (by nail) of all, at the hands of his father....The UNSEEN perversely criss-crosses the familiar narrative-patterns of horror movies. It divides, or rather short-circuits, one's sympathies, and makes "hero" seem a relative term.

UPIR Z FERATU see FERAT VAMPIRE

V NBC-TV/Kenneth Johnson & WB-TV 1983 color 190m. SP,D,Exec P: Johnson. Ph: John McPherson. Mus: Joe Harnell. PD: C.R. Davis. SpFX: Tom Ryba. SpOptFX: Pacific Title, Dream Quest Images, Coast. Mkp:(sup) Leo LeTito or Lotito;(tech) Werner Keppler. Ref: TV. TVG. V 5/11/83:68. with Marc Singer, Faye Grant, Jane Badler, Richard Herd(alien), Richard Lawson, Andrew Prine, Rafael Campos, David Hooks, Curt Lowens, Myron Healey, Clete Roberts, Howard K. Smith, Denny Miller, Michael Wright.

Giant spaceships--each bearing several thousand aliens--station themselves above major cities around the world. The human-like visitors inside the ships state that they are here to secure "synthetic chemicals" for their endangered planet (in the constellation of Canis Major) and assure earthlings that "they're safe aboard our ships." They prove, however, (in a clumsily-explicit overheard conversation) to be snake-tongued reptilian beings converting humans into Rodentia--i.e., food....personality-altering experiments.

An unbearably glib fusion of schlock and social comment, V (for "Victory," a la Z) is HOLOCAUST as based on a joke from "The Twilight Zone"--to wit, the "To Serve Man" alien-cookbook story. In this effects-coated allegory, the neo-Nazis from outer space find scapegoats in scientists, and herd humans into spaceships. There's a "Visitors' Friends" group for young adults, a propaganda-poster campaign, computer registration of scientists. Informers divide families; an underground springs up. One old Jewish gentleman remembers it all from Berlin, 1938, and you may remember it too--from other movies. In V, you're condemned to relive not history, but a mechanical recycling of same; condemned to watch an unofficial remake of EDGE OF DARKNESS. The movie, however, does deploy its spaceships ingeniously--hovering over cities like Los Angeles and London, they become airborne monuments, floating architectural landmarks; in the background, on living-room TV's, they're instantly rooted in the film's depiction of everyday life....

*VALLEY OF THE ZOMBIES 1946 Ref: TV. V 5/29/46. Stanley. and with William Haade, Charles Hamilton.

Ormand Murks (Ian Keith), an undertaker who died in 1941, returns several years later with a "passion for pickling"--i.e., he strangles and embalms his victims. He needs a special-type blood to counteract his zombie formula ("When I need blood, I must have it")--the latter discovered in the Valley of the Zombies--and hypnotizes the heroine (Adrian Booth) into assisting him....Witless Republic programmer. The zombie explains all at the beginning, with fifty, now-superfluous minutes left to go in the movie. (He never does, however, explain why he embalms his victims--maybe it's just force of habit....) Zombie, cops, hero (Robert Livingston), and heroine all behave predictably. The latter two are supposed to be amusing, and even when they're locked in the family crypt at night, say the most rib-tickling things. Keith on his part at least tries to work up a semblance of macabre relish for his role, but his material is no help. Fairly good shock-score...but the best thing about this ill-conceived movie is the zombie's name....

VAMPIR or VAMPIRE see VAMPYR

VAMPIRE PLAYGIRLS see CEMETERY GIRLS

VAMPIRES see BELLE CAPTIVE, La. BLACK ROOM, The. CAFE FLESH. CHAPPAQUA. DEVIL'S MISTRESS, The(I). DISCIPLE OF DEATH(II). titles under DRACULA. FERAT VAMPIRE. FRIGHTMARE. GEEK MAGGOT BINGO. I, DESIRE. KUNG FU ZOMBIE. MORTE-VIVANTE, La. MURDER MANSION(II)? NATIONAL LAMPOON'S CLASS REUNION. NAVE DE LOS MONSTRUOS, La. PURA SANGRE. TOM THUMB AND LITTLE RED RIDING HOOD VS. THE MONSTERS(I). VALLEY OF THE ZOMBIES. ZOMBIES ATOMICOS(II).

*The VAMPIRE'S GHOST 1945 AD: also F.J. Arrigo. Dance D: Jerry Jarrette. Ref: TV. V 6/6/45. Glut/TDB: ideas from Polidori's story "The Vampyre." Lee. LC. HR 4/16/45. Academy. and with Charles Gordon, Jimmy Aubrey.

Bakhunda(sp?), Africa. 400-year-old vampire Webb Fallon (John Abbott) is sustained by earth-from-his-grave kept in a box which Queen Elizabeth gave him in 1588. The "curse of the undead" keeps him alive "until the end of time...to destroy the peace and happiness" of others. He is, nonetheless, killed, at the end of the movie, by a) a spear dipped in molten silver, b) fire, and/or, c) a falling idol....witchcraft cult, voodoo drums, death-cult temple.

Republic's most honorable attempt at a horror movie, yet still very much a failure, The VAMPIRE'S GHOST is easier to admire than to watch. The writers (Leigh Brackett and John K. Butler) do their damnedest to make Webb Fallon a noble, tragic figure. He laments "I cannot die" and ponders over "things that may even tear (a man's) soul." But the tired, "B"-movie characters around him don't so much set him off as drag him down to their level. And Fallon himself is rather humorless and stodgy, though Abbott lends some of his scenes a melancholic authority. Brackett and Butler, to their credit, consolidate elements from several monsters and monster-movies for their vampiric villain-hero, rather than simply regurgitate lore from previous vampire pictures. The full-moon stipulation (Fallon must replace earth lost from the box by that time), the silver-dipped spear, and the "curse" seem inspired by The WOLF MAN. Fallon's desire to have the heroine, Julie (Peggy Stewart), join him for eternity seems to derive from, among other movies, the Lugosi DRACULA and the Karloff MUMMY. And the moonlight which revives the weakened or dead Fallon is, apparently, from Polidori, but might just as easily come from the scenes with the sun-restored Ananka in The MUMMY'S CURSE. To these mythic tics and traits the writers add such piquant details as the facts that...bullets pass harmlessly through Fallon...he can summon Julie from afar...he hypnotically dominates the hero (Gordon)...sunglasses allow him to operate in daylight hours....And a vampire is re-defined as "a dead man denied heaven because of his crimes." The name "Fallon" is explained as old Gaelic for "the stranger, one who walks in the darkness beyond the campfires." But the screenplay does little more than (as I do here) catalogue these elements. It doesn't dramatize them--although the unusual scene in which Fallon is left alone on a hill, in the moonlight, piques the imagination. This movie could serve as a rough sketch for an interesting, as-yet-unmade vampire film....

*VAMPIRES, THE ARCH CRIMINALS OF PARIS 1915-16 10 40-minute episodes (Les VAMPIRES) SP: Feuillade. Ph: Manichoux. Ref: screen. PFA notes 5/8/83. VV 4/19/83:52. Lee. and with Musidora (Irma Vep), Marcel Levesque, Louis Leubas(Satanas), Jean Ayme (Le Grand Vampire).

Capsule which produces a death-like sleep...man whose hypnotic stare makes Irma kill...tranquilizing gas which puts roomful of people to sleep...needle which paralyzes...electric cannon hidden behind panel...invisible ink which materializes when blown upon...poisoned paper...fake psychic...hypnotic sleep.

Dated serial curio. The posing-for-the-camera style of acting is still good for laughs, and Levesque as a Sig Ruman-type character gives an intentionally funny performance--he uses the camera as a "confidante," while the other actors seem to look upon its presence as, at best, a necessary evil. But VAMPIRES is, for the most part, a series of interminable pantomimes, interrupted not-nearly-frequently-enough by comically abrupt bursts of action. The actors spend half their screen time simply perusing maps, letters, newspaper articles, etc., and there's no lighting, no atmosphere--the amount of illumination is just increased or decreased from one scene to the next. The spectacle of the well-endowed Musidora in tights, however, may account for the popularity of this serial in some quarters....

*VAMPYR (F-G) Twyman/Tobis-Klangfilm(Dreyer Prod.) 1932 70m. (83m.) (VAMPYR Ou L'ETRANGE AVENTURE DE DAVID GRAY-F. VAMPYR, DER TRAUM DES ALLAN GRAY-G. VAMPIRE-alt U.S. & orig F t. VAMPIR-orig G t. ADVENTURES OF DAVID GRAY-alt t. aka NOT AGAINST THE FLESH) Based on "Carmilla," "The Room in the Dragon Volant," and other stories in J.S. Le Fanu's collection "In A Glass Darkly." Ph: also Louis Nee. AD: also Hans Bittmann, Cesare Silvagni. Ref: screen: Danish (Gloria Film) print. Edith Kramer. Bordwell/Films of C-TD. Milne/Cinema of CD. MFB'76:180. Chirat. LC. Clarens. Sadoul/DOFilms. Lee: shot in '31. PFA flyer 10/25/83. NYT 7/31/32. Murphy/Celluloid Vampires. Prawer/Caligari's Children.

David Gray (Julian West), visiting the town of Courtempierre--Styria, Austria, in Le Fanu's "Carmilla"--witnesses the workings of a strange shadow-world in and around an old building. The shadows of people and reflections-of-same (in streams) seem to have a life of their own. The shadow of (presumably) a gravedigger catches dirt in his shovel; the shadow of a peg-legged man acts independently of the man, until it catches up with him; music and shadow-dancers stop at the command of Marguerite Chopin (Henriette Gerard), the vampire. The latter figures prominently in Paul Bonnard's "The Book of the Vampires," which an old man (Maurice Schutz) gives Gray to read. The old man's daughter, Leone (Sybille Schmitz), is a victim of the vampire, and he himself is shot to death by one of her shadow-minions. The doctor (Jan Hieronimko) attending Leone is another of Chopin's aides....Gray has two nightmares: a brief one in which a skeleton holds out a bottle of poison, and a longer one in which his double sees himself in a coffin, and we see through the corpse's (cataleptic's? dreamer's?) eyes. A steel shaft driven through Chopin's body turns her into a skeleton and restores Leone. The forces of evil now seem to be turned upon themselves: the doctor sees the now-dead Chopin* at a window (in the form of a huge, forbidding face) and is driven by fear to the grist room of a flour mill, where he suffocates to death in a shower of flour.

VAMPYR contains a number of extraordinary passages, which latter have become a central part of our horror-fantasy-film heritage, and succeed in conjuring up an alien, nigh-inexplicable world, a world fashioned out of fleeting, idiosyncratic images of death and decay. This world-of-the-dead within the film is fully realized, a work of art in itself. The shadows, skeletons, and reflections--like the movie's gauze-filter exterior photography, and the floury mill-mist--are not so much symbolic as suggestive. They appear to constitute an artist's impressions of death...of its "tone" and "feel"--of what it might be like "on the other side"...."This side," unfortunately, in VAMPYR, resembles a grade-B horror movie. Like Tod Browning's MARK OF THE VAMPIRE(1935), Carl Dreyer's VAMPYR is split into breathtaking spectacle and banal narrative. It's art and trash together (to paraphrase the title of a recent Hungarian film). The best that director Dreyer can do for the living in VAMPYR: uncomfortably sentimental images of Leone "awaking" happily from the spell of the vampire, and hero and heroine strolling off together, at the end...as the doctor is sifted to death. Hieronimko, as the quirky sneak of a doc, gives the only performance of note. Generally, the acting is (to put the best light on it) unhelpful--Dreyer's actors, as usual, are intentionally suppressed, emotionally: half the time, it seems, they/we are simply reading "The Book of the Vampires," a rather ponderous tome....VAMPYR plays more like Dreyer's alternately inspired and confused hommage to Murnau's NOSFERATU(1922)--which features its own vampire study-book--than it does an adaptation of Le Fanu's stories. Dreyer's characters--unlike Murnau's--seem incidental to his vision. Gray, in fact, is (at-least-partly by design) more a witness-to-unearthly-wonders than he is a character. He is, at first, exclusively a vehicle for Dreyer's visual inspirations; then, belatedly and unconvincingly, the plot tries to convert him from the role of bystander to hero. And the "heroine," Leone's sister Gisele (Rena Mandel), is only the heroine, it seems, because she ends up with the "hero," David Gray. It is Leone whom Gray saves from the vampire, but Gisele with whom he walks off at the end. Either Leone or Gisele (take your pick) seems to be a narrative loose-end, innocent victim of a Dreyer caught between his official (Le Fanu) and unofficial (Murnau) sources. (The scene in which Leone evilly eyes her sister seems one of the few semi-directly inspired by "Carmilla"--the film's Gisele seems, otherwise, expendable.) Narrative, though, is but one of the esthetic forces at work in VAMPYR. The doctor's demise--an absurd, not-really-satisfying end to VAMPYR-as-story--is, on a more surreal level, "right" for him: derisory, seemingly haphazard, and, like him, slightly askew. He dies an embarrassing death, yet all the same a terrible one. (Dreyer here was perhaps invoking D.W. Griffith's 1909 A CORNER IN WHEAT, in which a financie suffocates to death in a wheat bin.) His odd fate is sealed by a combination of chance (fleeing from phantoms, the doctor stumbles into a cage), the unknown (the cage door mysteriously shuts), and the known (human hands start the wheels grinding). He is abandoned by all...and yet the potential sadness of his fate is overridden by its--and his--oddness.

*Most printed sources disagree on this point, maintaining that the giant face is that of the old man. The latter apparition would, it's true, seem a more logical one: the good dead seeking vengeance on the evil living. But if the face is that of the vampire, this shot makes another kind of sense, and is arguably more unsettling: the jig (in this latter case) would seem, to the doctor, to be more convincingly up--the vampire is a harsh mistress (especially, it would seem, with those who allow her to be staked). Conversely, why should the doctor--who has had truck with all kinds of supernatural creatures--be so frightened by the ghost of a dead old man? This shot makes some kind of dramatic sense; the question is what kind....

VAMPYRE, The(by Polidori) see VAMPIRE'S GHOST, The

VENOM (B) Para/Venom(Bregman)/Morison Film Group(Aribage) 1982 (1981) color 92m. D: Piers Haggard. SP: Robert Carrington, from Alan Scholefield's novel. Ph: Gilbert Taylor; Denys Coop. Mus: Michael Kamen. AD: Tony Curtis. SpFX: Alan Whibley, Richard Dean. Mkp: Basil Newall. Ref: TV. V 1/27/82. MFB'82: 50-1. with Klaus Kinski, Oliver Reed, Nicol Williamson, Sarah Miles, Sterling Hayden, Susan George, Michael Gough, Lance Holcomb, John Forbes-Robertson, Cornelia Sharpe.

A mixup in snakes ("What an incredible mistake to make!") results in the delivery of a venomous black mamba to the wrong address. "That bloody mamba" is, a) "probably the most poisonous snake in the world," b) also maybe the fastest, c) very aggressive, d) "paranoid" and, e) adept at leaping....Yes, all of the above are true; this is not multiple choice. To paraphrase Monty Pytnon: that snake's dynamite! The sound people work overtime honing the nasty edge on its hissing, and the sequence documenting its attack on Ms. George is fairly harrowing. At the end, we discover little mambas....So. We know what the snake is doing here. But what are Klaus Kinski, Oliver Reed, etc. doing? Unknowns could just as easily have handled the simple suspense mechanics involved. It's certainly no disgrace for these actors to appear in a vehicle for a snake, but....

2019, I NUOVI BARBARI see WARRIORS OF THE WASTELAND

2099: DOPO LA CAPUTA DI NEW YORK see 2019: THE FALL OF NEW YORK

VERTIGO Para/Hitchcock 1958 color/ws 123m. D,P: Alfred Hitchcock. SP: Samuel Taylor, Alec Coppel, from the Boileau-Narcejac novel "D'Entre Les Morts" aka "The Living and The Dead" or "Vertigo." Ph: Robert Burks. Mus: Bernard Herrmann. AD: Hal

Pereira, Henry Bumstead. SpFX: John P. Fulton. Titles:(des) Saul Bass;(exec) John Whitney. Mkp: Wally Westmore. Process Ph: Farciot Edouart, Wallace Kelley. Ref: screen. Jim Shapiro. Lee. Stanley. Ecran F 39:13. Robert Moore. Jon Van Landschoot. with James Stewart, Kim Novak, Barbara Bel Geddes, Tom Helmore, Henry Jones, Raymond Bailey, Ellen Corby, Lee Patrick.

"The beautiful, mad Carlotta has come back from the dead and taken possession of Elster's wife"--or so it seems. San Francisco shipbuilder Gavin Elster (Helmore) believes that "someone out of the past...someone *dead*"--to wit, Carlotta Valdes, who died in 1857 at the age of *26*, a suicide--has "returned" and possesses his wife, Madeleine (Novak). The latter is that age now and periodically "goes into that other world," the world of Carlotta, which *she*, Madeleine, recalls only vaguely, as "fragments of a *mirror*." She has never heard of Carlotta Valdes, yet adopts her whorl-keyed hair style, wears her (inherited) jewels, and purchases a bouquet of flowers which matches a bouquet that Carlotta holds in a portrait on display in a gallery at the Palace of the Legion of Honor. As Carlotta Valdes, she rents a room at the McKittrick Hotel--which was originally a house built for Carlotta, and to which, at one point, she pays a "phantom" visit--and she visits Carlotta's grave, which *Madeleine* sees, in her dreams, as an "open grave"--her own. Madeleine has a recurrent nightmare ("the dream came back again") which appears to be both recollection and premonition... of her own/Carlotta's life/death...and, as Carlotta, she makes an apparent suicide attempt. Elster hires ex-police-detective Scottie Ferguson (Stewart) to keep the dream's conclusion from coming true, but Scottie's acrophobia prevents him from saving Madeleine/Carlotta when she jumps from a tower...as prefigured by her dreams...."Was it a ghost," or was Madeleine mad, as she feared? ("If I'm *mad*....") Elster tells Scottie, "You and I know who killed Madeleine," and he's half-right: Elster--who was at the top of the tower--killed her, *her* meaning, however, not *Scottie's* Madeleine, who was merely a pawn in Elster's reincarnation/murder scheme, but his (Elster's) wife, whom Scottie never met. *Scottie*, now, suffers from nightmares (including a visualized one in which he sees himself falling into an empty grave) and "sees" Madeleine (who, on closer look, is only a woman resembling her) at a restaurant. By chance, he encounters *Judy*, who strongly resembles Madeleine, even on *closer* look. (And who actually *is* the woman who "was" Madeleine for Elster.) As he tried to save "Madeleine" from *Carlotta*, so Scottie tries to extract and refine "Madeleine" from *Judy*... to the point, where, the process complete, he finds himself (in an embrace with Judy) back with "Madeleine" in the mission stable where they stood just before her "death." Discovering, subsequently, that he has been duped, he tries to break "free of the past" by returning with Judy to the scene of the crime. He succeeds in conquering his vertigo, but loses Judy/Madeleine *again*, when a ghostly figure (who proves to be a nun) comes out of the tower darkness at them, and Judy, startled, plunges to her death.

"I just want to know who you are," Scottie at one point tells Judy. The ingenuous "just" is ironic, at least on the part of Hitchcock and the scriptwriters, whose film is <u>all about</u> seeing and knowing, or rather <u>not</u> knowing; appearance <u>and</u>, if you will, reality. Or at least it's supposed to be. In reality, it's strictly about appearance...surfaces, images, exteriors. The subject of the script--at least from one angle--is the unknowability of the other, the beloved. In the movie's more-or-less-Proustian terms, love is in the eye of the beholder, the lover-creator--the one beheld is irrelevant, unimportant. ("It is the tragedy of other people that they are to us merely showcases for the very perishable collections of our own mind"--"The Sweet Cheat Gone.") The imaginative burden, then, of such a work of art is on the beholder, the one-and-all--and the imagination, here, of Scottie/Hitchcock/Taylor... is decidedly inferior to Marcel's/Proust's in "Remembrance of Things Past." Scottie and Hitchcock seem mere fashion designers, or re-designers, both of them after a "look"--"Madeleine's"--which captures their fancy. Hitchcock obviously admires the look--we, as well as Scottie, are meant to be overwhelmed by it when Scottie first sees Madeleine at Eddie's: the lighting, camerawork, and music for the scene are in a soaringly (not to say swooningly) romantic mode. To this ultra-chic, Hitchcock's-of-Hollywood look, the script and Elster append the Carlotta story, which is as superficially glamourous as the look itself. The Madeleine/Carlotta connection--calculated to get the half-daft Scottie to the tower--has the excruciating over-ingeniousness of a story out of Alfred Hitchcock's Mystery Magazine. "The Romantic Image" might be the movie's subtitle, but the Madeleine/Carlotta composite image is a shade slick, glossy, fashionably outre, and requires of Kim Novak her best impersonation of fine, shatterable China. Midge's (Bel Geddes) sarcastic words ("the beautiful, mad Carlotta....") prove to be a pretty fair and accurate summation of the Gothic-dream-image which Scottie "buys": makeup and madness (Carlotta's, Madeleine's), an irresistible combination. (At least for acrophobiacs.) So much for "appearance." It's fairly pulpy here, while the <u>reality</u> is elusive to the point of non-existence--although that may, in fact, be the film's point, and Where's Judy? is one of the movie's more intriguing questions. Judy speaks clearly, as herself, only twice in the movie: in her (unsent) letter to Scottie and at the end, with him, at the top of the tower. Elsewhere, she is Madeleine, Carlotta, or Judy-who-must-dissociate-herself-from-Madeleine. All we know about Judy is that she loves Scottie, as all we know about Scottie is that he loves "Madeleine." The classic, cross-purposes triangle, with a twist: the third side of the triangle doesn't exist. VERTIGO presents its people almost exclusively as shiny surfaces. With Judy/Madeleine/Carlotta, it becomes a guessing game: is it Judy, for instance, or Madeleine who tells Scottie "It's too late," just before "Madeleine" dies? It's a fairly unresonant game since the three personae, taken singly, are rather glib, hollow constructs: the sexy, tawdry-but-sweet working girl; the goddess-mannequin; the mad, sad wraith. And Novak seems out of her element playing metaphysical charades. Scottie, conversely, is a one-note character, or the same note sounded four times: trauma one: the policeman attempting to rescue him falls to his death. Trauma two: "Madeleine" falls to her death. Three: Judy is found to be "Madeleine," who thus never was. Four: Judy falls to her death. There are only two things certain in the world of VERTIGO--death and traumas. Scottie goes from obsessed to mad (in perhaps both senses--angry and insane) without breaking stride. Johnny (Scottie's real name) is as well-lost to the world as Judy. If Scottie and Elster are Judy's puppeteers, Hitchcock is Scottie's. He even has his Scottie-puppet, helpfully, echo Judy's "It's too late" just before she really dies. Stewart gives an occasional, incidental comic line his personal stamp; but the dialogue for the most part is undistinguished, simply the authors' vehicle for thematically loaded words like "power," "possess," and "darkness," and anguishedly-romantic expressions like "It's too late." There are similarly-neatly-planted words in SABRINA(1954), which, like VERTIGO, was co-scripted by Samuel Taylor; here, "power" and "freedom," not words used in conjunction with one another every day, are used and linked by two characters who ostensibly have never met. This sort of dialogue was not meant to be spoken, only analyzed. The movie as a whole, in fact, is perhaps better analyzed than seen, though it has occasional impressive single images, a stunningly abrupt ending, and one great scene, or shot: to wit, the 360-degree tracking shot around Scottie and Judy which takes him back to the mission and "Madeleine." Madness and romantic passion merge, and the irony underlying all the story's convolutions--that Scottie can possess "Madeleine" only in his own mind--becomes vital and moving. Peel away "Carlotta" and Judy, and there's--nothing....

VETERAN, The see DEATHDREAM

Los VIAJES DE GULLIVER (Sp) Delgado-Art Animacion 1983 anim color 82m. D,P: Cruz Delgado. SP: Gustavo Alcalde, based on Jonathan Swift's book "Gulliver's Travels." Ref: V 12/21/83.
"Land of the giants" features giant crab, gorilla, giant hornet.

VIDEODROME (Can.) Univ/Filmplan Int'l. & CFDC & Famous Players (Guardian Trust) 1983(1982) color 87m. SP,D: David Cronenberg. Ph: Mark Irwin. Mus: Howard Shore. AD: Carol Spier. SpMkpFX: Rick Baker;(artists) Steve Johnson, Bill Sturgeon. SpFX: Frank Carere. SpVideoFX: Michael Lennick. Scenic Art: Nick Kosonic. Opt: Film Opticals. Ref: screen. V 2/2/83. MFB'83:310-11. with James Woods, Sonja Smits, Deborah Harry, Peter Dvorsky, Les Carlson(Barry Convex), Jack Creley(Brian O'Blivion), Lynne Gorman.
Toronto. Max Renn (Woods), the co-producer of Civic-TV, channel 83, becomes involved in a plot by Spectacular Optical

to introduce the revolutionary Videodrome process ("the next phase in the evolution of man as a technological animal") to the general public....VIDEODROME the film is the next phase (after ALIEN) in the evolution of the movie monster as a cross between the animal and the technological. Like the process within the movie, it's a "giant hallucination machine": the mind of the protagonist here plays as many tricks with size and shape and texture as the body of the monster did in ALIEN. One might go further, and say that VIDEODROME is only an hallucination machine, but that would be only half-fair to the film. It's also a David Cronenberg machine, which is coming to mean that, even if the particular model is not in perfect working order, that model's operating parts can still be fairly fascinating to behold. Which is by way of saying that Cronenberg still has problems finding plots capable of containing and enhancing his ideas. In VIDEODROME, plot means simply a hero and a conspiracy, either or both of which may be partly hallucination. (In fact, it's hard to tell if the latter half of the movie is bad storytelling or bad dreams.) The film is, finally, after all, simply a vehicle for the Videodrome stunts, which have "something to do with" brain tumors and with the effect of exposure to images-of-violence on the nervous system. As narrative, VIDEODROME reduces to your basic brainwashing tale; as spectacle, it yields human videocassette recorders (front-loading), throbbing videocassettes, living, breathing TV sets, and a gun which literally becomes part of a man's hand-and-arm. Cronenberg combines the outrageousness-of-vision of a Larry Cohen with his own near-surreal insights into the malleable nature of things--i.e., minds and physical objects. (This is probably the first movie in which a television set rates the best special makeup effects.) Cohen's brainstorms fall more on the "ridiculous" side of the Great Esthetic Divide; Cronenberg's, on the "sublime" side. But there's enough overlap to delight Cohen's fans and dismay Cronenberg's. The graphic excesses of VIDEODROME, for instance, seem, at times, nearly as much the work of accidental-self-parody as they do that of imagination. The man who made it seems to be all-too-keenly-aware that he is expected to "go too far...."

VIOLENT MIDNIGHT see PSYCHO-MANIA

VIRUS see CANNIBALS IN THE STREETS

VIRUS, INFERNO DEI MORTI VIVENTI see NIGHT OF THE ZOMBIES(MPM)

VISITING HOURS (Can.) Fox/Filmplan Int'l.-CFDC/David-Solnicki (Guardian Trust) 1982 color 103m. (The FRIGHT-orig t) D, Co-Ed: Jean Claude Lord. SP: Brian Taggert. Ph: Rene Verzier. Mus: Jonathan Goldsmith. AD: Michel Proulx. SpFX:(sup) Gary Zeller;(coord) Don Berry; Renee Rousseau et al. SpMkpFX: Stephan Dupuis. Ref: screen. V 5/5/82: "misogynistic ripper." 11/9/83: 24. MFB'82:94. with Michael Ironside(Colt Hawker), Lee Grant,

Linda Purl, William Shatner, Lenore Zann, Harvey Atkin.
Cold, brutal shocker harks back not so much to PSYCHO as to both WHILE THE CITY SLEEPS--the script shuttles back and forth between the protagonist's story and the killer's, as it tries to account for everyone's violence--and to PEEPING TOM--the killer photographs his victims, and makes a death-mask-shaped collage from the cut-out faces and bloody bodies. This movie has, however, basically, the intellectual content of a casaba--the goal of the script seems to be just to show how many ways a knife-wielding maniac can penetrate a hospital's security. As a suspenser, though, VISITING HOURS has a certain hollow ingenuity (though its scares are dependent on screeching musical punctuation and nerve-wrackingly-augmented sounds); and Ironside (as the killer) is as dourly imposing as he was as Revok in SCANNERS. The movie's brutality clearly has more to do with suspense than with sociology, although it occasionally appears to be painting a grim portrait of a world in which violence invariably begets violence. At one point a woman describes her failed marriage as "three years in a war zone," and at the end, Ironside and Grant switch "roles," as the former becomes the stalker stalked. Ultimately, however, VISITING HOURS seems merely to be justifying its own violent content.

VISITOR, The(by C.G.Parker III) see OF UNKNOWN ORIGIN

VISITORS FROM BEYOND THE STARS see ALIENS FROM ANOTHER PLANET

VOIE SAUVAGE, La(by D.Odier) see LIGHT YEARS AWAY

VORTEX B Movies(Vortex) 1982 color 85m. SP,D,Mus,Ed: Scott B & Beth B. Ph: Steven Fierberg. Mus: also Adele Bertei et al. AD: Tom Surgal. LaserFX: The Science Faction Corp. Mkp: J. Aspinal, A. Gargiulo. Titles: B. Baker, F. Armstrong. Ref: screen. V 10/6/82. SFChron 11/18/83. with James Russo, Lydia Lunch, Bill Rice, Ann Magnusen, Dick Miller.
Rivalry between two corporations--Fieldsco and Navco--for U.S. government "automated electronic warfare" weapons-contracts leads to laser warfare between the two companies. Fieldsco's "new weapon" is the BFW, an "offensive and defensive weapon" which is to be used, apparently, to defend space stations against enemy-laser attacks. (It creates a "field" which "deflects" laser rays.) A filmstrip demonstrates its potential. (Or is this sequence a VIDEODROME-like hallucination??) Another Fieldsco invention--a gun which shoots out "two electrical bars"--"fries" a man's brain. Fieldsco is also working on "behavior control" via electrodes....The center-of-interest--intended or actual--of VORTEX is very difficult to locate. The film's derisory feel suggests put-on or parody or camp, but it's not really very funny; its seedy look is the look of hard-boiled melodrama, but it isn't very exciting. The film exists in a sort of limbo, and leaves the viewer in an emotional limbo. The main characters ("hero" and "heroine" are words which would have no application here)

are, in varying degrees, unpleasant and unsympathetic, and their unpleasantness is not "placed." It's just there, and they're welcome to it. This is not a good "B movie."

WACKO Jensen Farley/Clark(O.S.M.) 1983(1981) color 87m. D,P: Greydon Clark. SP: Dana Olsen, M. Spound, M.J. Kouf Jr., D. Greenwalt. Ph: Nicholas von Sternberg. Mus: A. Kempel. AD: Chester Kaczenski; Jay Burkhart. SpMkpFX: MkpFxLabs; Allan Apone, Kenny Myers. SpFX: Joe Quinlavin; Dana Rheaume. Opt: Modern. Ref: TV: Vestron Video. V 2/9/83. 12/28/81 & 5/18/83: 4(rated). with Joe Don Baker, Stella Stevens, George Kennedy, Julia Duffy, Scott McGinnis(Norman Bates), Victor Brandt(Dr. Mengele aka Moreau), Darby Hinton, Sonny Davis(the weirdo), David Drucker(the loony), Michael Lee Gogin(Damien).

It's the night of the Halloween Pumpkin Prom at Alfred Hitchcock High School, and the 13th anniversary of the night that the pumpkin-headed lawnmower killer dispatched poor Mary's (Duffy) sister. At movie's end, a lawnmower killer (there are at least two) appears to die several times, but keeps coming back....CARRIE + ALIEN nightmare-coda in which a "baby" lawnmower pops out of a boy's chest...Gates of Hell (and The OMEN's Damien) in attic...doctor's serum which turns football players into animals (e.g., ape, pig, Elephant Man) for the big game (between the Hitchcock Birds and the De Palma Knifes(sic))... living head in bottle...Hitchcock's "Funeral March..." theme.

Last (in any alphabetical listing) of the recent batch of horror-movie takeoffs--see also FULL MOON HIGH, HYSTERICAL, NATIONAL LAMPOON'S CLASS REUNION, and PANDEMONIUM in this volume--but not really least. Granted, its comic "outrageousness" is generally pretty predictable. (It would be more unusual here if some character's head didn't spin like a top, a la The EXORCIST.) But there are scattered surprises--e.g., the chest-bursting mini-mower (played strictly for laughs); the loony's impromptu prom-night, "Tonight Show" monologue; the sequence in which Norman and "Mrs. Bates" (a prop mummy) do a ventriloquism act for the other dinner guests....These go a bit beyond the *de rigueur* gags which, otherwise, proliferate. Duffy's Mary is, also, a funny caricature of the typical teen horror-heroine: fleeing from the killer, she is stopped, at every turn, by a locked door which, inexplicably, then opens; whereupon she half-turns and pertly smiles and thanks the powers-that-be, before fleeing on....

WAGA AOIBA NO ALUCADIA or WAGA SEISHUN NO ARUKADEIA see CAPTAIN HARLOCK IN ARCADIA

The WALL (B) MGM/Tin Blue & Goldcrest 1982 color/ws anim & live 94m. (aka PINK FLOYD THE WALL) D: Alan Parker. SP, Mus: Roger Waters, based on the Pink Floyd album. Ph: Peter

Biziou;(micro) Oxford;(anim) Chris King. PD: Brian Morris. Anim: Gerald Scarfe;(key anim) Mike Stuart;(coord) Roland Carter. SpFX: Martin Gutteridge, Graham Longhurst. Mkp: Paul Engelen, Peter Frampton. Opt: Camera FX, Gen'l. Screen. Ref: screen. MFB'82:172-3. Ecran F 26:52. with Bob Geldof, Christine Hargreaves, Bob Hoskins, Eleanor David.

Animated sequences featuring vulture-creature-aircraft... Rodan-like flying monster...soldiers-as-uniformed-skullheads... living-faces-in-walls...woman's shadow becoming plant-flower-monster...snake-into-scorpion-into-woman-creature...giant judge-creature...gas-mask-faced creatures, etc....Live-action sequences featuring faceless school children taking a treadmill to the sausage machine...a man decomposing, then shedding his "skin"...an IT HAPPENED HERE-like vision of fascists in England.

The WALL is less narrative than it is free association... sounds and images colliding with one another and creating, with those collisions, meaning--or at least interesting collisions.... Meaning there undoubtedly is here, but it seems subordinated to sheer spectacle, to an ultimately-rather-shallow kinesthetic appeal. The film is, at this level, involving, but it's difficult for eyes and ears not to get involved when live and animated figures are swarming across the screen, and the sound of music is registering a 3.7 on the Richter, or Dolby, scale, under your theatre seat. This minor-earthquake effect is fun, but the fun seems to be at odds with the ostensible subjects of The WALL--isolation, destruction, the forces of suppression. The meaning which the movie's free-association method generates is generally loose, free-floating--e.g., the image of a mother's protecting arms transforming into a wall is suggestive of a smothering love (and also reflective of the lyrics of one of the songs on the sound track), but seems, in its virtual isolation, merely a generalization, a cliche, if a wittily expressed one. Sparks of meaning here remain just that--sparks; they never catch fire. The film's glints-of-themes are here-and-gone in an instant, like the configurations in a kaleidoscope. The only cumulative effect of The WALL is one of general sound and movement--it's the inverse of the effect of a film such as Bunuel's EL, in which a single incident or gesture or line reverberates with a meaning and feeling all, seemingly, out-of-proportion to the incident. Don't fault The WALL, however, for lack of ambition--its ends are simply beyond its means.

WALLS OF JERICHO see REVENGE OF THE GODS

WAR AND PEACE (W.G.) Teleculture/Filmverlag der Autoren & Bioskop-Film & Kairos-Film 1982-3 color 85m. (KRIEG UND FRIEDEN) SP,D: Volker Schlondorff, Heinrich Boll et al. AD: Bernd Lepel. Narr: Axel-Torg Gros. Ref: screen. PFA notes 12/13/83. VV 12/6/83:62.

Film includes two or three post-nuclear-holocaust vignettes, one re: U.S. astronauts in one space vehicle and Russian cosmonauts in another asking and fielding questions re: who won?

("Amsterdam is sunk...."); another re: the uncontaminated eliminating the contaminated (brother, here, and sister, respectively)....Random thoughts and speculation on war, especially nuclear war, and on the "Cubanization" of Germany, the latter country trapped in the uneasy role of "host" to the Russians and Americans and their nuclear arsenals. The dry, mordant doomsday humor of the (intermittent) narration is the only element which gives this movie a semblance of unity. The narrator's tone of seemingly-effortless irony rather eludes Boll and Schlondorff, who score points more heavy-handedly in their brief after-the-bomb skits.

WAR OF THE WIZARDS (Taiwanese) 21st Century/Eastern Media(Frank Wong) 1978('83-U.S.) color/ws 76m.-U.S. (The PHOENIX-orig t) D,SpVisFX: Sadamasa Arikawa. D: also Richard Caan. SP: F. Kenneth Lin. Dial: Rudolph Marinelli, Richard Vetere. Ph: Mike Tomioka. Mus: Lawrence Borden. SdFX: Charles Dexter. Ref: TV: Planet Video. V 12/21/83. HR 10/25/83. Weldon: H.K., '80? with Richard Kiel, Charles Lang, Betty Noonan.

Flower Fox, a "bad, evil power" from "far out in space," travels to Earth with her two handmaidens (in the form of three stars). She wants to rule the world, and can, with the aid of a wish-granting vessel and the Bamboo Book. She has the power to spew blinding red vapor from her mouth; glide on water; appear as a giant; and create tidal waves and windstorms with her fan. She is, finally, contained (by lightning) within her own forcefield. Her aides use blue rays against some priests's yellow rays; she herself summons up warriors (from the vessel) to do battle with the hero and his orange-ray-shooting sword, and pits her super-strong henchman (Kiel) against him. Also: giant Phoenix vs. giant rock-monster which, beheaded, rises again.

Amiable nonsense features characters with names like Deadly Chopsticks and Killer Palm Force. The whole movie is arguably (in fact almost inarguably) pretty bad, but half of it--mostly the effects-and-monster stuff--is amusing. This is no INFRAMAN, but the Phoenix is a (literally) colorful cuss, from ostensibly the same genus as the giant claw, and it inspires some (figuratively) colorful dialogue--e.g., "A giant bird brought me here!"

WARD 13 see HOSPITAL MASSACRE

WARGAMES MGM-UA/Goldberg-Sherwood 1983 color 112m. D: John Badham. SP: Lawrence Lasker, Walter F. Parkes. Ph: William A. Fraker;(min) Jack Cooperman. Mus: Arthur B. Rubinstein. PD: Angelo P. Graham. VisFX:(sup) Mike Fink;(coord) Linda Fleischer. SpElecFX: Robert M. Cole. SpFX: Joe Digaetano. VisCons: Geoffrey Kirkland. Computer Graphics: Colin Cantwell; (video cons) Steve Grumette. SupSdFxEd: M.C. Burrow, W.L. Manger. Pterosaur Cons: Bill Watson. Ref: screen. V 5/11/82. Bill Warren: sf; clips from ONE MILLION YEARS B.C. MagF&SF 11/83 (B.Searles): not sf. MFB'83:223. with Matthew Broderick, Dabney Coleman, John Wood, Ally Sheedy, Barry Corbin, Joe Dorsey.

The code word "Joshua" hooks a high-school whiz kid's home computer into Norad's War Operation Plan Response computer, a self-improving machine designed to fight World War III as a game, in order to avoid WWIII. David (Broderick), believing that he is playing a new Protovision game, programs WOPR for "Global Thermonuclear War," then tries to cancel the program when Norad takes the simulated Soviet attack for the real thing. WOPR, however, continues to play; Norad reaches Defense Condition 1, at which point a "full scale retaliatory strike" is ordered, or almost ordered. WOPR shuts down only when it discovers that, in the nuclear game, "the only winning move is not to play."

A DR. STRANGELOVE for the video-game era--or a more sophisticated INVISIBLE BOY--WARGAMES is a fun-exciting "message" movie. ("Don't play" is the message.) The graphics star; the actors are on hand mainly for reaction shots and aural interjections. This is an old-fashioned "star" vehicle, but the star is a computer. The movie translates the anti-nuke message into computer-logical "scenarios"; it's like a series of locker-room-blackboard game-plans for an unwinnable game. "Winner: None" is the end result of all of WOPR's nuclear game plans. At the end, it dissects and discards dozens of the latter in the space of a minute or two, and the sheer speed with which it makes its epochal decisions is exhilarating. True, WOPR espouses, ultimately, currently-very-fashionable attitudes, but seeing it get there is half the fun. Its final opinion seems decidedly informed....Whether or not this computer's logic violates or bends extant-computer logic is another matter....

WARLORDS OF THE TWENTY-FIRST CENTURY (New Zealand) New World/Phillips-Whitehouse(Battletruck) 1982(1981) color 91m. (BATTLETRUCK-orig t) SP,D: Harley Cokliss. SP: also Irving Austin, John Beech. Story: Michael Abrams. Ph: Chris Menges. Mus: Kevin Peek. PD: Gary Hansen. SpFX:(sup) Jonnie Burke; Kevin Chisnell. Vehicles:(des) Kai Hawkins;(truck) Jones & Odell, & Mid-Canterbury; Tony Austin. Titles: R. Stenhouse. MkpSup: Christine Beveridge. Opt: Colorfilm. Ref: TV: Embassy Home Ent.(video). V 4/21/82. Ecran F 28:17: U.S.-N.Z. Bill Warren. with Michael Beck, Annie McEnroe, James Wainwright, John Ratzenberger, Randolph Powell.

"After the oil wars...it's a new world, with new rules," most of which are formulated by the autocratic Straker, whose humongous, nearly-impregnable Battletruck enables him to enforce them. Gas, in this future world, is all-but-unobtainable--the chief supply is housed in an underground fuel module under a boulder. "Old-fashioned" democracy is scarce too--and Straker is intent on making it scarcer....The hero is, of course, the one who says "Don't care much for people," then goes halfway to hell to get the people out of their mess. The villain, Straker, is the one who kills at the slightest provocation. (He even starts when someone, all-unbidden, unexpectedly lays a hand on his shoulder; his paranoia isn't just for show.) Easy to choose sides here. (Only the warlord's daughter has a moment of weakness. She may hug dad, but is otherwise rebellious, and even, at one point, tries to shoot him.) The movie is handsomely shot, and the score isn't bad. But the script has the complexity of a glazed donut. Wainwright's reptilian Straker is the only character to watch; his Battletruck--a fortress on wheels--is the only vehicle to watch. This is the kind of movie in which an armored truck seems to have a love affair with the camera....

WARP SPEED Gold Key-TV c1981 color 90m. Ref: GKey. TVFFSB. TVG. with Camille Mitchell, Adam West, David Chandler.
Clairvoyant discovers a strange force at work on spaceship.

WARRIORS OF THE WASTELAND (I) New Line/Deaf Int'l. 1983('84-U.S.) color 87m. (I NUOVI BARBARI. The NEW BARBARIANS-ad t. 2019, I NUOVI BARBARI) SP,D & with: Enzo Castellari. SP: also Tito Carpi. Ph: Zuccoli. Mus: Claudio Simonetti. PD: Antonio Visone. SpFX: Germano Natali. Ref: V 5/4/83:298. 1/18/84. Ecran F 29:55. MFB'83:219-20. with Mark Gregory, Fred Williamson, Giancarlo Prete, Luigi Montefiori, Anna Kanakis, V. Venantini.
The year 2019. Lone warriors and barbarians in a post-holocaust America.

WAVELENGTH New World/Rosenfield Co.(Wavelength) 1983(1982) color 88m. SP,D: Mike Gray. Ph: Paul Goldsmith. Mus: Tangerine Dream. AD: Linda Pearl; Zorba. SpFX: Mike Menzel. SpOptFX: (sup) Joseph Wallikas; Cinema Research. Mkp: Jim Gillespie. Opt: CFI. Ref: TV: Embassy Home Ent.(video). V 8/17/83. with Robert Carradine, Cherie Currie, Keenan Wynn, Cal Bowman, Robert Glaudini; Dov Young, Joshua Oreck, Christian Morris(aliens); James Hess, George Skaff, Milt Kogan.
Dormant, humanoid aliens from a laser-downed UFO are secretly stored by the government in underground freezers at the Lookout Mountain Air Force Station above Hollywood. The aliens look like children but are, in reality, very old. They have translucent viscera, but no digestive tract--they are, in fact, photosynthetic, and absorb energy from their immediate environment, through their skin and through two sets of lungs. A young woman, Iris(Currie), a psychic twin, proves to be receptive to their longwave signals, or super-concentrated thoughts, and discovers that they are "just tourists." Their touch or presence, however, can, if they so choose, be deadly...or life-giving. They revive, and escape from the base, and--forced by government paranoia to cut short their visit--depart from Earth in a globe a mile-or-two in diameter.
"It wasn't the right time for us to meet...." Those words are from IT CAME FROM OUTER SPACE, but might just as easily conclude WAVELENGTH too. The newer movie is more even, and is in fact a somewhat improved version of the older one, though it lacks the latter's eerie-lyrical high points. It's well-done, even interesting--but it's just not involving. We've seen it all before--generally, it's true, in much tackier form.

But protagonists, aliens, and military personnel here are just going through the approved motions. Tradition has been too-well-observed. There are few surprises, if there are several pleasing details--e.g., the aliens' incomprehension of our embarrassment about sex; the beyond-reaction shot of the first soldier to see the giant globe. There's much speculation within the movie as to whether the visitors are friendly or unfriendly. Such speculation is not new either, though the behavior of "Gamma," "Beta," and "Delta" proves to be quite believable--they repay friendliness with same...unfriendliness with same. They are, somewhat like the movie, rather predictable.

*WAXWORKS Twyman-Rohauer 1924('29-U.S., Viking) 60m. Ref: screen. Lee. PFA notes 2/26/84. Eisner/Haunted Screen.

Luna Park. The proprietor of a wax-museum sideshow commissions a writer to compose stories re: three wax figures. The first story concerns Haroun-al-Raschid, caliph of Bagdad, and the wishing ring; the second, Ivan the Terrible and the hourglass, which he must keep turning: if the sands all run out, he will, he believes, die. (He eludes death, but does go mad.) In the third (abbreviated) tale, Jack the Ripper, in ghostly double-exposure, attacks the writer...in what turns out to be a dream.

Two amusing anecdotes and an eerie coda (the Ripper segment), in a very early omnibus horror movie. WAXWORKS, as narrative, does not have the force of, say, the 1945 DEAD OF NIGHT--its two longer tales are surprisingly unambitious. Its fascination lies, rather, in its art direction. Its sets, as designed, were obviously never meant to be lived in, only looked at: the caliph's palace, for instance, is a nightmare-in-stone, from its flights of steps--which seem both to come from and to lead nowhere--to the master bedroom, with its forest/chorus-line of columns in the background. The most stunning moment in the picture, however, is contributed by an actor, Conrad Veidt: when Ivan's torture-chamber victim dies, Ivan's reaction is one of quiet but heartfelt ecstasy....He takes the man's death obscenely personally. One other imaginative moment (in the first story): the thieving baker's image caught in each of the many facets of the gem in the ring....

WEREWOLVES and Other Shape-Shifters see A CULPA(P). ALCHEMIST, The. BEAST WITHIN, The. BESTIA Y LA ESPADA MAGICA. BUENAS NOCHES, SENOR MONSTRUO. CONQUEST. COSMIC PRINCESS. DOS FANTASMAS Y UNA MUCHACHA. FORBIDDEN WORLD. FULL MOON HIGH. HAMMER HOUSE OF HORROR DOUBLE FEATURE: CHILDREN OF THE FULL MOON/VISITOR FROM THE GRAVE. HOW TO DROWN DR. MRACEK(A). HUGUES LE LOUP. INCUBUS. IT CAME FROM OUTER SPACE. LIGUERO MAGICO, El. LOBA, La. LOUVE, La. MONGREL(M,A). NIGHT TIDE. PRECIO DEL DEMONIO, El. THING, The. THRILLER. WACKO. ZELIG.

WHAT DO YOU THINK OF THE DEATH OF WILMA MONTESI? see NACHT DES SCHICKSALS, Die

*WHEN WORLDS COLLIDE 1951 Ph: also W.H. Greene. SpFX: Gordon Jennings, Harry Barndollar. Process Ph: F. Edouart. Tech Adv: Chesley Bonestell. Mkp: Wally Westmore. Narr: Paul Frees. Ref: TV. Warren/KWTS! V 8/29/51. Weldon. and with James Congdon, Stephen Chase, James Seay, John Ridgley, Kirk Alyn, Stuart Whitman.

Astronomers discover a wandering planet, Bellus, and its Earth-size satellite, Zyra, approaching Earth. Zyra is due to pass by us in about 7 months; Bellus will actually collide with Earth 19 days after that. When the United Nations rejects the scientists' findings, Dr. Cole Hendron (Larry Keating) begins private construction of a spaceship--"a 20th century Noah's Ark," with a "rocket-propelled undercarriage"--which will take 40 specially-selected passengers to the "new Earth," Zyra.

An easy film to criticize; a hard film to dislike. The new hope of mankind, Zyra, is represented by a cross between a mural and the cover of an inspirational greeting card, and the effects are, at best, passable. Fortunately, the script favors "human drama" over spectacle. Here, instead of FORBIDDEN PLANET's Id, it's the ego vs. the superego, selfishness vs. self-sacrifice, or, more specifically, John Hoyt's Stanton vs. everyone else. Stanton is "bad" from film's beginning to end; the other principals all come out of it "good," no matter how they started. Stanton's "dog eat dog" view applies only to himself and to some bit players; Richard Derr's materialist-playboy Dave reforms, and Peter Hanson's Tony accedes to sweetie Barbara Rush's preference for rival Dave. This is, Lord knows, a simplistic picture of life, but at least there's a bit of give-and-take between the Darwinian and the humanitarian, if, dramatically, the latter wins out fairly easily. WHEN WORLDS COLLIDE belongs to the Wishful Thinking school of philosophy: all but 40 people on Earth die--more important is the fact that those 40 Behave Well....It's chance, not force, which saves them. And chance seems, not accidentally, to favor the selfless here. Most of the "good" also come out alive--would you really want it any other way? The acting of Hoyt, Derr, and even, at times, Hanson makes these simple schematics "play" more compellingly than they have a right to. And Leith Stevens's score makes up for, in drive, what the effects lack in vividness--it imparts a sense of urgency to the action, if the effects and the p.a. man's periodic "Two days to go, and we're 30 minutes behind" promptings don't.

WHO FELL ASLEEP? see DEADLY GAMES

WHO GOES THERE?(by J.W.Campbell Jr.) see THING, The

WHOLLY SMOKE WB 1938 anim 7m. (WHOLLY SMOKES) D: Tex Avery. SP: G. Manuell. Ref: screen. "WB Cartoons." LC. no Lee.

Anti-smoking nightmare...cigarettes-and-matches-as-monsters. Lesser Avery/Porky Pig.

The WILD BEASTS (I-W.G.-So.African) CCC & Shumba 1983 color 90m. SP,D: Franco Prosperi. Mus: Daniele Patucchi. Ref: Ecran F

35:67. V 11/2/83:42: at Rome sf fest. with Lorraine de Selle.
Drug gets into a city zoo's water supply, drives the animals crazy; they all escape and terrorize the city.

A WILD ROOMER FBO/R-C Pictures 1926 20m. SP,D & with: Charles Bowers. SP,D: also H.L. Muller. SP: also Ted Sears. Ref: screen. PFA notes 4/17/84. no Lee. LC.
Jumbo-size machine/invention/truck performs all manner of tasks, from dumping garbage to fashioning a doll...and instilling it with life....The latter sequence is the clear high-point of this otherwise almost-mundane Bowers short. His comedies seem to come fully to life only during the stopmo-animation sequences--which sequences are, however, usually little short of amazing. A tear brings the doll to life in Starevitch's The MASCOT; here, a candy-like heart does the trick. Then a squirrel hatches from a nut, and begins pulling a near-unending supply of knickknacks out of its purse (a la Harpo pulling all manner of things out of his coat). In terms of story, this sequence is incidental, but it's obviously this short's raison d'etre.

*The WILD WOMEN OF WONGO Jaywall 1958 Mkp: R. Liszt. Chor: Olga Suarez. Ref: screen. Weldon. and with Adrienne Bourbeau.
Rampaging "ape-men"..."Dragon-God" (alligator) who "speaks"...priestess who magically transforms her appearance and dances.... This is (hopefully) the only movie which begins with a disembodied voice intoning "I am Mother Nature...." It is also one of the worst movies ever made, though it does have two undeniable inverse-highlights: the dance in the Temple of the Dragon-God--the looniest dance of its kind on film, a sort of impromptu mass writhing by priestess and Wongo women, who, incomprehensibly, seem inspired by her gyrating--and a fight between two Wongo women. (Their thrashing-about is intercut with shots of on-lookers making like prehistoric cheerleaders.) But there's only so much that semi-actors can do with lines like "We have heard of the Wongo women" and "What are the women like in Goona?" (The dispiriting response: "They are like your Wongo men.") This Florida-based production is so pathetic that the audience has to be informed that the ape-men are indeed ape-men. You couldn't possibly tell from the "makeup" on the two actors in question--they merely seem to be sporting three-day-old beards. And the costumes for the women of 10,000 B.C. would do well as playsuits for the women of 1958. In fact, probably did....

WINGED SERPENT, The see Q

*The WITCH Famille Melies 1906 color Ref: screen. PFA notes.
Routine Melies adventure-fantasy, featuring, however, some amusing "terrible monsters," which the hero encounters on his way to save the princess: Death-like ghosts emerging from their crypts, a giant frog, a giant owl, a winged serpent, and wriggling, horned worm-creatures.
See also: SUPERSTITION.

WITCHING TIME/The SILENT SCREAM see HAMMER HOUSE OF HORROR

WIZ KID, The see ZAPPED!

2 WOLFMAN 1978 AD: David Caddell. SpFX: Al Yehoe(sp?). Mkp: Sandy Barber, W. Keeter. Opt: Cinopticals. Ref: TV: Thorn EMI Video. Glut/CMM. Weldon. and with Sid Rancer, Brownlee Davis.

Georgia, 1910. The Rev. Leonard (Edward Grady), "the keeper of the curse" on the Glasgow family, kills Edwin Glasgow (Julian Morton) with a silver dagger; then, in a ceremony invoking "beings of the other side," he passes on the curse to Edwin's son Colin (Earl Owensby)--the latter "will become a murderer, a lycanthrope," as punishment for the breaking of a pact with the devil by (apparently) his grandfather. "The mark of the werewolf": elongated index fingers. In a nightmare, Edwin tries to pull Colin into his grave. Then, on the first night of the full moon, Colin transforms into a werewolf and kills two people. He slays six more the next night ("That creature beats anything I've ever seen!") and, finally, on the third night, is stabbed with a dagger by Leonard, but lives long enough to put an end to the reverend's career too....

Flat reworking of the 1941 The WOLF MAN. A stray wolf attacks our hero and, apparently, makes good the curse; said hero is well-born and returns to his home (in the South) after being away for some time; the heroine works in a curio shop in town; townsfolk actively distrust him....Lighting and camerawork aren't bad; most everything else is. The pace is slow; the staging, unimaginative; the acting, passable at best. There's lots of thunder-and-lightning, but, oddly, no rain, and little wind....

WOLFPACK see SPIDER MAN: WOLFPACK...

WORLD OF YOR see YOR...

WORLD WAR III(by J.Haken) see FUTURE WAR 198X

2P The WORM EATERS New American Films/Genini(Mikels) 1982?(1977) color 94m. SP,D & with: Herb Robins. Story & with: Nancy Kapner. Ph: Willis Hawkins. Mus: Theodore Stern. PD: Jack DeWolf. Ref: V 10/28/81. 5/11/77:405(ad). Weldon. Ecran F 22: 52. with Lindsay A. Black, Joseph Sacket.

...turn into "worm people." Or, SQUIRM with laughs....

X-RAY see HOSPITAL MASSACRE

*X, THE UNKNOWN Sol Lesser 1956 80m.-U.S. SpFX: Bowie Margutti Ltd., Jack Curtis. SpMkpFX: Philip Leakey. Ref: TV. LC. and with Marianne Brauns, Peter Hammond, Ian McNaughton, Jameson Clark.

Scotland. A radioactive force--driven (by the cooling of the Earth's crust) further in towards the core--develops intelligence, and breaks out through the crust every 50 years in search of radioactive material for sustenance. It melts those in its path, but is, finally, neutralized by radar-like scanners.

Mechanical Jimmy Sangster imitation of Nigel Kneale's Quatermass stories. The radioactive mud in this movie is, graphically, about as menacing as a wad of bubble gum. But that fact doesn't really matter a jot--what John Williams does for water, in JAWS, James Bernard does here for mud. His horror music is not subtle; he, obviously, would like to scare you to death, as witness the sense of feverish anticipation he (almost single-handedly) succeeds in building up for the boys-in-the-woods sequence....The movie's most amusing scenes belong to Dr. Royston (Dean Jagger), as he jumps wildly from conclusion to conclusion.

XTRO (B) New Line/Amalgamated(Ashley) 1983(1982) color 80m. (JUDAS GOAT-orig t) Story,D,Mus: Harry Bromley Davenport. SP: Robert Smith, Iain Cassie. Story: also Michael Parry. Addl Dial: JoAnn Kaplan. Ph: John Metcalfe; John Simmons. Mus: also S.L. Palmer. AD: Andrew Mollo; Peter Body. SpMkpFX: Robin Grantham, John Webber. Creature FX: Francis Coates. SpMechFX: Tom Harris; NEEFX;(ph) Mike Metcalfe; David Anderson. VisCons: Christopher Hobbs. Opt: GSE. Ref: screen. V 2/2/83. MFB'83: 109. Ecran F 22:54. with Philip Sayer(Sam), Simon Nash(Tony), Bernice Stegers, Danny Brainin, Maryam D'Abo, Peter Mandell (clown), Tik(monster), Tok(commando).

Man (Sayer) abducted by aliens returns after three years, in alien form, and is re-born, in human form, from a woman's womb. He possesses psychokinetic-plus powers and an odd appetite, and bestows same on son (Nash). The boy uses his powers to bring a toy soldier and clown to life-sized life, in order to kill for him. One female victim is cocooned and used to fertilize alien eggs, one of which hatches at the end. Man and boy (the former back in alien form) are whisked away on a flying saucer, or triangle-of-light....

One of the more interesting sf-monster-movie ripoffs in recent years--interesting, in part, because it rips off such (one would think) <u>irreconcilable</u> movies as ALIEN (and its <u>nasty</u> alien) and CLOSE ENCOUNTERS OF THE THIRD KIND (and its <u>nice</u> aliens). It does, however, employ <u>all</u> adapted elements (body-burstings, toys'-life glimpses) for horror purposes. With its boy-among-the-aliens theme it echoes Spielberg; in its fun-with-anatomy horrors it evokes Cronenberg. And this splicing is not without its shuddery charm. The activating of the clown and commando mimes is, in fact, such a startling stroke that it seems it must be, simply, a childish hallucination, not a narrative "reality." But this is a physiological, not a psychological study, very Cronenbergian in its attention to the physiologically appalling. The highlights, of sorts: a woman giving birth to a full-grown man...a man sucking down the contents of snake eggs...a man suctioning-up by mouth a lump on his son's shoulder...an alien ambulating like a disabled grasshopper... a mime-toy collecting alien eggs at the bottom of a human cocoon-funnel...a boy bathed in blood "sent" by his (alien) daddy, etc. A toy tank blasting away with real-tank force in the halls of an apartment seems positively benign in such an operating-room-nightmare atmosphere. Just keep repeating to yourself "It's only a makeup effect...." And this film does seem to be "only effects," the ickiest its makers could dream up. It's just good unclean fun, to which fun the father-son relationship appears almost incidental. XTRO might have been concocted from the results of a man-on-the-street survey re: what people find most disgusting....

The YESTERDAY MACHINE Video City/Carter Films 1965? 85m. SP, D,P,Lyrics: Russ Marker. Ph: Ralph K. Johnson. Mus: Don Zimmers. AD: Robert Dracup. Mkp: Marcia Fox. Ref: TV. no AFI. no Lee. VideoSB. no Weldon. with Tim Holt, James Britton, Ann Pellegrino, Carol Gilley, Bill Thurman, Linda Jenkins, Jay Ramsey.

"We have conquered time! Hitler will return, and soon...!" By 1944, Hitler's administrator of the Department of Scientific Warfare, Prof. Von Hauser (Jack Herman), had almost perfected an aging machine. ("Screwiest piece of machinery I've ever seen!") But time ran out, and the war was lost....Twenty years later, our physicist has put his "theory of super-spectronic relativity" into practice...in a cellar outside an old country house in Texas. ("Somebody around here is tampering with time.") He has discovered that, with the "minus ray" (a "new ray in the spectrum" shorter even than the cosmic ray), the velocity of light can be further accelerated, and light itself started moving in the direction of the past. Using an "underground atomic power supply," Von Hauser has perfected a machine which can travel into the past (and does, to 1789) end even, briefly, into the future, and which can speed up or slow down time. Those who wander into the "machine's field of materialization" disappear from the present and into a sort of crossroads-of-history in the prof's lab. Ultimately, Von Hauser is shot, and vanishes into time, and Lt. Partane (Holt) destroys the lab: "Yesterday should be left alone, because today the world has enough problems just trying to make sure we'll have a tomorrow."

Another Texas "classic" resurfaces. Two possible themes here: How SF Movies Revive The Nazis, and How Bad Can A Movie Be? (Not much worse, assuredly, than this one.) The first half here is dull "teaser" stuff; Herman's campily colorful mad physicist enlivens the latter half, when the movie becomes comically "ambitious." (Six outfits from Central Costuming, and, presto!--the whole glorious panorama of History unfolds before you....) He goes, suddenly, into great and unnecessary detail outlining his theories on a blackboard (for our hero), as if he were a Dr. Frank Baxter of the Third Reich. Where

Baxter seems self-confident and reasonable, however, Von Hauser seems strictly cloud-cuckooland....

YOR--THE HUNTER FROM THE FUTURE (I-Turkish) Col/Kodiak/Diamant & AFM 1983 color 87m.(105m.) (The WORLD OF YOR-ad t. Il MUNDO DI YOR) SP,D,SpFX: Antonio Margheriti. SP: also Robert Bailey. From Juan Zanotto & Ray Collins's novel "Yor." Ph: M. Masciocchi. Mus: John Scott; G.& M. de Angelis. AD: Walter Patriarca. SpFX: also Eduardo & Antonella Margheriti. Mkp: M. Scutti. Ref: screen. V 5/4/83:201(ad),296. 8/24/83. Ecran F 22:55.36:46. FComment 2/84:21. with Reb Brown, Corinne Clery, John Steiner(The Overlord), Carole Andre, Alan Collins.

"Generations" after an atomic war on Earth. "Primitive tribes" (including the fallout-plagued inhabitants of the Land of the Diseased) and dinosaurs (including a sort of styracosaurus, a dimetrodon, and the Beast of the Night, a big bat-creature) inhabit hills and wastelands. The virtually omnipresent Overlord rules an island kingdom with Vader-like androids (with red rays), and plots to "create a master race" of "genetically perfect...hybrid clones" from humans (including the hero, Yor) and from a new line of (even better) androids. Plus: men preserved in ice in desert cave...crystal-ball-like viewer... stun rays...newsreels of the distant past...green rays (for the good guys)...mysterious ray-from-space...snake-moat....Thoroughly undistinguished sub-camp. Even the title is a mistake: Yor is not from the future; he's in the future, as also are the dinosaurs--God knows how they got there. All the "tribes" here speak English--the dialogue (e.g., "Get outta here, I said!") instantly returns one from another time and place to here-and-now. The "monsters" are a pretty sad lot, yet still qualify as semi-welcome diversions--at least they have no dialogue....

YOU MAY BE NEXT! Col 1936 66m. (PANIC ON THE AIR-orig t. CALLING ALL G-MEN-int t) D: Albert S. Rogell. SP: Fred Niblo Jr., Ferdinand Reyher. Story: Reyher, Henry Wales. Ph: A.G. Siegler. Ref: TV. LC. NYT 2/24/36. Academy. V 3/4/36. with Lloyd Nolan, Ann Sothern, Douglass Dumbrille, John Arledge, Berton Churchill, Robert Middlemass, Gene Morgan, George McKay, Clyde Dilson.

"Television's still around the corner" in 1936. But, here, an ABC radio engineer's "high frequency transceiver" can cut "through anything" as far away as Tokyo, and is used to jam navy, police, and ABC radio broadcasts. ("Radio Industry Totters" and "Radio Pirate Perils Coast Guard" read the headlines.) Fast, smooth, bland. Basically just a plot, to which the appealing presences of Nolan and Sothern are pretty incidental.

See also: OSTERMAN WEEKEND, The.

*YOU'LL FIND OUT 1940 SP: also Monte Brice, Andrew Bennison, R.T.M. Scott. Mus: James McHugh;(d) Webb;(arr) George Duning; (lyrics) Johnny Mercer. Assoc AD: Carroll Clark. SpSd&MusFX: Sonovox; Gilbert Wright. Ref: TV. LC. V 11/20/40. Stanley. Weldon. and with Alma Kruger, Harry Babbitt, Sully Mason.

Ingredients: two seances, featuring phosphorescent "phantoms" and wind-like "ghost" voices...thunder-and-lightning...ape dummy....At the end, Kay Kyser is atomized by electrical gizmos. Bela Lugosi (as a "turban-topped Svengali"), Peter Lorre, Boris Karloff, and the other atmospheric effects help; but you still have to get through Kyser (music and comedy) and Dennis O'Keefe (plot), and that's easier said than done. The horror boys themselves are little more than decoration, though each has his moments. (One of Lugosi's is his mock-gruff emphasis on the last word of the line, "For those who scoff at their existence, the spirits consider no punishment too drastic.") Ish Kabibble proves more of a screen presence than Kyser (or O'Keefe, for that matter)--which, admittedly, is not saying a heck of a lot. His "Bad Humor Man" number is a (relative) highlight, and will leave few minds un-boggled.

YUREISEN (J) 1956? anim color 10m. Ref: J.Anim Film. no Lee.
Pirate ship manned by living dead-men...hunchback...phantoms.

ZAPPED! Embassy/Apple & Rose/City(Thunder) 1982 color 99m. (The WIZ KID-orig t) SP,D: Robert J. Rosenthal. SP: also Bruce Rubin. Ph: Daniel Pearl. Mus: Charles Fox. AD: Boyd Willat. VisFX:(sp) Robert Blalack; Praxis;(prod sup) Nancy Rushlow;(d) Max Anderson;(ph) Chris Diedorff et al. SpFX: A&A, Dick Albain, Ron Nary. Anim: Peggy Regan et al. Opt: Pacific;(coord) Chris Regan. Elec: Bill Tondreau. Sd:(des) Bonnie Koehler;(fx ed) John Post. Ref: TV. V 7/28/82. Ecran F 26:5. with Scott Baio, Willie Aames, Felice Schachter, Robert Mandan, Scatman Crothers, Sue Ane Langdon, Heather Thomas.

A lab explosion--involving a chemical concoction--gives a high-school whiz-kid (Baio) telekinetic, "mind over matter" powers. He uses them to make a model spacecraft fly, a dummy's head spin around (a la The EXORCIST), clothes "explode," at the prom (a la CARRIE), and his girl friend (and himself) fly across town. Also: visualized space fantasy with giant dog... visualized fantasy with Einstein and salami-bazooka...lab mouse with magnetic powers....What do you get when you cross SON OF FLUBBER with CARRIE?--ZAPPED!, an inelegant hybrid composed of effects stunts, three romances (two student, one faculty), fantasies, a bit of slob comedy, horror-movie take-offs, and appallingly "lyrical" songs. The tone wavers, to say the least. The movie is alternately serious and larky, in the worst ways. Comedies like ZAPPED! and MODERN PROBLEMS give telekinesis a bad name.

ZEDER: VOICES FROM DARKNESS (I) AMA & RAI 1983 color 92m. SP,D: Pupi Avati. SP: also M. Costanzo, A. Avati. Ph: Delli Colli. Mus: Riz Ortolani. AD: Basili Scarpa. Ref: V 5/4/83: 295. IFG'84:196-7. Ecran F 36:42,86-93. with Gabriele Lavia,

Anne Canovas, Bob Tonelli, Paola Tanziani.
Ancient alchemy and the living dead.

ZELIG WB-Orion/Rollins-Joffe 1983 b&w & color 78m. SP,D & with: Woody Allen. Ph: Gordon Willis;(process) Bill Hansard. Mus: Dick Hyman. PD: Mel Bourne. SpMkp:(fx) John Caglione; (des) Fern Buchner. OptFX: Joel Hynick, Stuart Robinson, R/Greenberg. Anim: Steven Plastrik, Computer Opts. SpProps: Eoin Sprott. SpThanx: W.K. Everson et al. SdFX: Hastings. Titles: Opt.House. Narr: Patrick Horgan. Ref: screen. MFB'83: 293-6. V 7/13/83. 8/24/83:13. SFChron 8/15/83:40. with Mia Farrow, Stephanie Farrow, Will Holt; Susan Sontag, Saul Bellow, Irving Howe, Bruno Bettelheim.

The life of Leonard Zelig (Allen), the human chameleon, is related in newsreel footage, photos, interviews, etc., which mediums capture his uncanny ability to adapt to his immediate human surroundings--e.g., in the company of fat men, he swells to 250 lbs.; on St. Patrick's Day, he "turns Irish." "The miraculous changing man" is, variously, Asian, Mexican, French, Greek, Black, a Brown Shirt, an Indian, and a rabbi. (The latter is one of the few transformations we, in part, actually see.) The roots of this phenomenon are thought to be glandular or neurological, but turn out, in fact, to be psychological. Zelig, "devoid of personality," "the ultimate conformist," simply wants "to be liked," to be "safe." A movie, "The Changing Man" (WB, 1935), with Garrett Brown as Zelig, is based on his life, and he inspires songs, dances, and a series of children's books (e.g., "Leonard Zelig and The Mischievous Mummy"). An experimental drug makes him, temporarily-but-literally, walk up walls. Dr. Eudora Fletcher (Mia Farrow) of the Manhattan Hospital takes Zelig under her wing and, with reverse psychoanalysis, confounds him out of his omnifariousness. He becomes over-assertive, "over-opinionated." A few adjustments, however, and he finds a psychological happy-medium.

Woody Allen's Zelig is a comic, psychosomatic updating of Orson Welles' Charles Foster Kane, the man who wanted to be loved, but went about finding love the wrong way. ZELIG, the film, however, (unlike CITIZEN KANE) irons out all or most of the mystery and ambiguity of its eponymous hero. Abused and neglected as child and adolescent, Zelig the adult is cured by love. It seems to be as simple as that. The power of love may, even, account for the one mystery, or loose end, in the narrative: Zelig's climactic transformation into a pilot. Here, he acquires not a physical characteristic, but a skill, and from a woman, Eudora of course. Women, oddly, have no physiognomic effect on Zelig; but in this scene, the unconscious Eudora's piloting skills are transferred, by osmosis, to Zelig. As the narrator says, his sickness is also, ultimately, his salvation--and love is, implicitly, the catalyst. Zelig's cure is clearly intended to be the satisfying conclusion to a problem drama, or comedy, and might be. But it also marks the transformation of an extraordinary character into an ordinary one. Like

"Rhinoceros," ZELIG is about the human tendency to conformity. And at the end, Zelig is indeed just one of the gang; but the irony appears to be unintentional. Cured of conformism, he conforms. Sans "chameleon-ness," he's nothing special, a Joe Blow. Psychoanalytically, this is certainly progress; esthetically, it's oblivion. Until Dr. Fletcher gets under Zelig's skin, or skins, Zelig (man and movie) is an amusing curiosity; he's a more versatile version of Laurence Harvey's vocal-chameleon in EXPRESSO BONGO. He is viable as a satiric exhibit; less so as a romantic character. A phenomenon like him (or, say, Bartleby) can't be explained without being explained away. Once you realize what makes him tick, he stops ticking. The switch of gears from the satiric-fantastic to the humanistic yields, however, perhaps the movie's most interesting sequence. Eudora herself temporarily assumes Zelig's psychological makeup, and Zelig, unmanned, or unlizarded, squirms, as he has a glimmering of self-truth. That glimmering, unfortunately--our first glimpse, as well, of his superego-overwhelmed ego--signals the beginning of a series of more-or-less unbelievable plot developments. The first, Zelig-as-phenomenon half of the movie is, in a sense, static: he doesn't develop; the public phenomenon does. In the latter, Zelig-as-individual half of the movie, he, still, does not so much develop as shuttle back and forth between human and chameleon states, as public opinion of him blows hot and cold. Zelig-the-phenomenon has, as a subject, a comic-esthetic integrity, not to mention an air of mystery. The back-and-forth, more-or-less-cured Zelig reacts all-too-predictably to both public and private forms of rejection and acceptance. His interaction with others is then no longer a comic conceit, just a dramatic cliche.

ZOMBI HOLOCAUST see DOCTOR BUTCHER, M.D.

ZOMBI HORROR (I) Esteban 1980 D: Andrea Bianchi. Ph: Maioletti. Mkp: G. de Rossi. Ref: Prod Ital. Ecran F 31:57: ZOMBIE HORROR. 22:48: aka ZOMBI 3. with Karin Weil, G.L. Chirizzi, Peter Bark, Maria Angela Giordan.

Zombies overrun Scottish estate.

ZOMBI 3 see ZOMBI HORROR

ZOMBIE see I EAT YOUR SKIN

ZOMBIE CREEPING FLESH see NIGHT OF THE ZOMBIES(MPM)

ZOMBIE HOLOCAUST see DOCTOR BUTCHER, M.D.

ZOMBIE HORROR see ZOMBI HORROR

ZOMBIES see I EAT YOUR SKIN

PERIPHERAL AND PROBLEM FILMS

("??" indicates insufficient information available--i.e., a "problem" title.)

A CULPA (Port.) Ref: Ecran F 21:53: werewolf?? 1981
ACES GO PLACES (H.K.-Cant.) 1982? (TSUI-CHIA P'AI-TANG) Ref: screen: remote-control, explosive model-cars...crook named King Kong, aka "Superman." Sequel: ACES GO PLACES II(M).
2P ADVENTURES OF CAPTAIN FABIAN 1951 Ref: TV: no witchcraft.
ADVENTURES OF CAPTAIN FUTURE 1980 anim Ref: VideoSB. ??
ADVENTURES OF FLASH GORDON 1953 Ref: VideoSB: 2 TV shows.
ADVENTURES OF ULTRAMAN 1981 anim 90m. Ref: VideoSB. ??
AGE OF DINOSAURS (J) Toei anim Ref: V 5/4/83:409(ad). ??
AMAZING ADVENTURES OF JOE 90 Ref: Showtime-TV: "secret invention." ??
L'AMIE ETRANGER (F) 1982? Ref: Ecran F 28:75: alien; TV-movie??
AND NOW FOR SOMETHING COMPLETELY DIFFERENT (B) 1971 Ref: TV: anim. bit with (unseen) creature in baby carriage...bit with "vicious gangs of Keep-Left signs."
AND THE SHIP SAILS ON (I) 1983 Ref: screen: "ghost" at seance. PFA.
ANGELS' WILD WOMEN 1972 Ref: Weldon: devil-worship sequence.
ANN AND THE VAMPIRE (Pol) Ref: IFG'83: based on fact.
O ANTHROPOS POU HATHIKE (Greek) Ref: IFG'77:168: Death personified.
APE MAN OF THE JUNGLE (I) Ref: M/TVM 10/65:25. Lee: ape-creature??
L'ARGENT (Swiss-F) Ref: V 5/11/83: ax murders. MFB'83:178-9.
AROUSED Ref: V 8/2/68. AFI: psychopathic killer. ??
AS IN THE DAYS OF YORE (B) 1917 Ref: BFC: "prehistoric fantasy." ??
ATTACK FROM OUTER SPACE Ref: TVFFSB. ??
ATTACK OF THE FLYING SAUCERS Ormond Ref: Scot Holton. ??
ATTILA, ENEMY OF GOD (I) Ref: V 5/4/83:298: "magic sword satire." ??
AUTOMAN Ref: TVG 12/21/83: 90m.series pilot; holographic super-hero.
The AWAKENING OF CANDRA 1983(1981) Ref: TV: killer brainwashes woman.

BATTLE SHOCK 1956 Ref: TV: amnesiac artist kills during "blank periods of nothing." TVG.
BEAUTY 1981 Ref: screen: non-fantasy "Beauty & The Beast" story.
BEHULA LAKHINDAR (Bengali) 1977 Ref: Dharap: snake-goddess' curse.
BELLS OF ATLANTIS 1953 Ref: MOMA: life in Atlantis??
BERLIN ALEXANDERPLATZ (W.G.) 1980 Ref: SFChron 10/9/83: Death pers.
The BEST OF SEX & VIOLENCE 1981 Ref: Weldon: gory trailers.
BEWITCHED BUNNY 1954 anim 7m. Ref: TV: Hansel & Gretel; Witch Hazel (also in A HAUNTING WE WILL GO(M), BROOMSTICK BUNNY, A WITCH'S TANGLED HARE); prince from "Snow White." Played for laughs.
BEYOND WITCH MOUNTAIN Ref: V 2/24/82:88: TV-pilot sequel to ESCAPE TO WITCH MOUNTAIN(II).

A BID FOR FORTUNE (B) 1917 Ref: BFC: "occult scientist." no Lee. ??
BIGGER THAN LIFE 1956 Ref: screen. TVG: "experimental wonder drug." Bill Warren.
BLOOD BATH 1976 Ref: Weldon: "weird tales." Cinef V:1:27. ??
BLOOD FEAST (I) 1976 (aka FEAST OF FLESH) Ref: Weldon: policier.
BLOODROOT 1982 Ref: V 2/16/83:24: horror. ??
BLOODY GHOST (Tamil) (aka ERATHA PEY) Ref: WorldF'68. ??
BONEYARD BLUES 1924 anim Ref: Crafton: a la SKELETON DANCE.??
BORDELLA (I) 1975 Ref: Ecran F 36:88: invisible man??
BOWERY BUGS 1949 anim 7m. Ref: TV: bit with huge gorilla/bouncer.
BUDDY THE GOB 1934 anim 7m. Ref: "WB Story": dragon. "WB Cartoons."
*BULLDOG DRUMMOND COMES BACK 1937 Ref: TV: "haunted"-house bit.
BUNNY HUGGED 1951 anim 7m. Ref: TV: super-strong wrestler.
The BUTCHER Cinevid Ref: V 5/9/84:264(ad). 10/10/82:164(ad).??

C.O.D. (W.G.-U.S.) Ref: V 8/24/83: "The Zombies' Revenge" filming.
C.T.(COED TEASERS) Ref: SFExam 9/9/83(ad).??
CAIN'S WAY 1970 (aka BLOOD SEEKERS) Ref: Weldon: decapitation.
CALIGARI'S CURE Ref: V 1/19/83:28. VV 2/8/83:42. PFA notes.??
CALLED BACK (B) 1914 Ref: BFC: in trance, man "sees murder."
CAMPUS CORPSE M&M 1977 Ref: Academy. with J.East, C.M.Smith.??
CARNIVOROUS Ref: V(d) 5/8/80: horror. sfa CATACLYSM?
CARNIVORE Comworld (aka THREE BLIND MICE) Ref: V 8/3/83:4(rated).??
CARRY ON EMMANNUELLE (B) 1978 Ref: TV: stone eagle to life, for gag; dial.ref. to "Snow White Meets The Incredible Shrinking Man."
La CASA DALLE FINESTRE CHE RIDONO (I) 1976 D: Avati. Ref: IFG'84: 197: horror. Ecran F 36:88: part-policier; part-horror.??
La CASA DEL TAPPETTO GIALLO (I) Ref: V 6/8/83: mystery-"chiller."??
CASCABEL Ref: TVG: "horror." TV: no way.
The CASE OF THE BERMUDA TRIANGLE 1976 docu Ref: TVG: TV?; on "Nova."
CAUCHEMARS A DAYTONA BEACH (Sp) Ref: Ecran F 31:42: mad killer. ??
The CAVE OF THE SPOOKS 1908 Ref: Crafton: skeletons. no LC. no Lee.??
CEILING HERO 1940 anim 7m. Ref: "WB Pictures": rocketship bit.
The CHARLATAN (B) 1916 Ref: BFC: "fake occultist." ??
*CHARLIE CHAN'S MURDER CRUISE 1940 Ref: screen: mystic, strangler.
CHESTY ANDERSON--U.S.NAVY 1976 Ref: V 5/9/84:526: carnivorous plant.
CHILDREN OF THE NIGHT Ref: V 5/9/84:264(ad). ??
Le CHOIX DES SEIGNEURS (F) 1983 Ref: Ecran F 41:5-7: sorcerer.
CINDERELLA 2000 1977 Ref: Weldon: sf. ??
The CLAIRVOYANT Cinemax Ref: V 3/9/83:4(rated). ??
CLASS OF 1984 Ref: vc box: BLACKBOARD JUNGLE, 1984. ??
CONJURING A SPIRIT AT MIDNIGHT (H.K.) 1964 Ref: HKFFest '82:139. ??
COORAB IN THE ISLE OF GHOSTS (Austral) 1929 Ref: V 5/5/76:98. ??
A COTTAGE ON DARTMOOR (B) 1929 Ref: MFB'76:14: nightmarish. ??
The CRADLE WILL FALL Ref: TVG 5/21/83. Cinef XIII:6: youth serum.??
The CRAVEN SLUCK 1965 Ref: PFA pr: Kuchar sf-parody. ??
CURSE OF THE PINK PANTHER Ref: screen: anim.invisible-man bit; super plastic-surgery; computer with sense of humor.
CURSE OF THE SCREAMING DEAD Ref: V 10/20/82:139(ad). ??

DAFFY DUCK'S MOVIE: FANTASTIC ISLAND 1983 anim feature Ref: TV: includes STUPOR DUCK; magic wishing-well...Tasmanian Devil.

The DAM (Greek) Ref: FComment 11/82:6: "magical macabre river." ??
The DAMNED (Greek) Ref: WorldF'68: "haunted desert island." ??
DARK GAMES 1981 Ref: V 2/16/83:24: horror. ??
The DARK ROOM 1982 Ref: V 2/16/83:24. HR 1/4/83: non-horror.
DAWN OF THE NIGHT OF THE DEAD Ref: TVG: on "Night Flight." ??
DEATH GAME 1977(1974) (MRS.MANNING'S WEEKEND-orig t. The SEDUCERS-vt t) Ref: MFB'79:119. V(d) 5/3/77: horror. TV: non-horror.
The DEATH OF OCEAN VIEW PARK 1979 Ref: Stanley: psychic. Maltin/TVM.
DEATH SCREAMS E&C 1982 D: David Nelson. Ref: Ecran F 26:74: horror. with Susan Kiger, Jody Kay, M. Tucker. ??
The DEATHHEAD VIRGIN JPD Ref: TVFFSB: ghosts. with Jack Gaynor. ??
DEMON SHOCK 1982 Ref: V 2/16/83:24: horror. ??
The DENTIST c1921 anim Ref: Crafton: Stone Age. ??
2P DESERT LEGION 1953 Ref: TV: "hidden city" founded by ex-Legionnaire
The DEVIL IN MISS JONES--PART 2 1982 Ref: Ecran F 36:44. ??
DIRTY LILY 1977 Ref: MFB'82:292: spirit; Satanists.
DOCTOR OF EVIL Ref: V 5/9/84:264(ad). ??
DON'T WATCH IT ALONE Ref: vc box: horror-movie trailers.
DORIAN GAY Ref: SFExam 12/4/81. ??
DRACULA (B) Thames-TV 1971 Ref: TVFFSB. no Glut/TDB. ??
DRACULA (J) Toei anim Ref: V 5/4/83:409(ad). Movie? TV?
DRACULA BITES THE BIG APPLE Ref: TVG: on "Night Flight." ??
DRAKULA DRAKULA (B) c1973 Ref: MFB'83:258-9: "domestic drama."
DRAGONS OF THE LOST ARK Ref: V 2/24/82:16: in Miami. ??
DREADNAUGHT (H.K.) 1980 Ref: JFFJ 14:36: "martial arts-horror." ??
DUE RAGAZZI NELLA GUIUNGLA (I) 1982 Ref: Ecran F 26:75: horror. ??
DYNAMITE JOHNSON (B) 1979 (aka BIONIC MAN NO.2) D: B.A. Suarez. Ref: "Tous Les Films 1980." Bionic boy, robot, dragon, laser.??

EATEN ALIVE (I) 1980 (MANGIATI VIVI DAI CANNIBALI) D: Lenzi. Ref: V 5/7/80:374. MFB'81:251: N.Guinea. with Rassimov, Lai, Ferrer, Agren. Cf. MAKE THEM DIE SLOWLY(M). SACRIFICE!(M). ??
EDDIE & THE CRUISERS Ref: V 9/7/83: return-from-the-dead overtones.
EDO PORN Shochiku Ref: Playboy 11/82: J.; octopus-monster??
ELECTRIC MUMMY Ref: TVG: on "Night Flight." ??
The ELEPHANT MAN Ref: TVG 1/4/82. V 1/20/82:68. No horror-makeup.
ETERNALLY YOURS 1939 Ref: TV: magician "creates" woman, on stage, in retort, using "love," "jealousy" chemicals, etc.; hypnotism.
Une ETRANGE AFFAIRE (F) 1981 Ref: Filmex '83: vampire-film overtones.
EUREKA 1983 (MURDER MYSTERY-int t) Ref: FComment 4/83:20-3: alchemy, telepathy. MFB'83:115-16: voodoo; horror-story opening.
The EVIL EYE 1973? Ref: TVFFSB: the supernatural? with R.Conte. ??
The EVIL EYE 1982 (aka MANHATTAN BABY) Ref: V 2/16/83:24: horror??
EVIL IN THE DEEP 1977 Ref: Weldon: JAWS-inspired.
2 EXPERIMENT ALCATRAZ 1950 Ref: Bill Warren: not sf.
EYES OF THE VAMPIRE Ref: V 5/9/84:264(ad). ??

FACES OF DEATH II 1982? Ref: Ecran F 29:4: docu-gore. ??
The FAKE GHOST CATCHERS (H.K.) Ref: V 9/15/82:53. ??
The FALCON STRIKES BACK 1943 Ref: TV: Edgar Kennedy as mad puppeteer; dial.ref. to Dracula; "Bluebeard" marionette show.
FALLING HARE 1943 anim 7m. Ref: "WB Cartoons": gremlin; giant plane.

FANNY OCH ALEXANDER (Swed-F-WG) Ref: V 12/22/82: "the gruesome"; telepathy. MFB'83:83-4: "supernatural shudders." Berkeley Monthly 9/83: "gentle spirit"; ghost of "sadistic stepfather."
The FATAL FORMULA (B) 1915 Ref: BFC: new explosive. no Lee.
FIGHTING TROUBLE 1957 Ref: TV: cig.lighter-camera invention.
FILMGORE D: K. Dixon. Ref: vc box: compilation film.
FIRELIGHT 1964 Ref: Crawley: amateur sf-film shown once commercially.
The FLYING CLAW FIGHTS 14 DEMONS Ref: SFExam 4/23/84.??
The FLYING HOUSE 1916 anim 6m. Ref: screen: winged, motorized house.
FLYING MAN (India) 1966 Ref: Ecran 73: sf; "monster finale." ??
FOTO PROIBITE DI UNA SIGNORA PER BENE (I-Sp) 1970 Ref: MFB'72:112: ?? plot to drive woman mad with appearances of "threatening stranger."
FOX SPIRIT (H.K.) 1982 Ref: V 3/2/83:122. ??
FRENCH QUARTER 1977 D: D.Kane. Ref: Ecran F 22:73: Macumba elements.??
FURY BELOW Ref: V 3/16/38: "crazed mine driller."??

GANGWAY FOR TOMORROW Ref: V 12/22/43: "horrific material." TV: Roy Webb music, expressionistic lighting for James Bell sequence.
GENERATIONS 1980 54m. Ref: VideoSB: sf. ??
GETTA ROBOT (J) Toei anim Ref: V 5/4/83:409(ad). ??
GHOST NURSING (H.K.?) Ref: V 7/14/82:85. ??
The GHOST OF BINGVILLE INN 1915 Ref: AF-Index. no LC. ??
GHOSTS FOR SALE (India) 1980 Ref: HKFFest'82: debunking-ghost-story.??
GIGANTIC MARIONETTES (B) 1913 Ref: BFC: "monstrous marionettes." ??
GOD'S BLOODY ACRE Ref: Boxo 10/27/75. HR 10/25/83:S-74: "terror." ??
GOING BERSERK Ref: V 11/2/83: brainwashing-for-murder.
2 GOLD KEY "ZODIAC" SERIES Ref: TVFFSB: '83 ed. lists only AGE OF PISCES. B.Warren: none of the 11 probably exist.
GORKY PARK 1983 Ref: MFB'84:14-15: gory.
GRAD NIGHT Cineworld Ref: V 5/18/83:6: "horror." ??
GRAND CENTRAL MURDER 1942 Ref: TV: psychic "sees" death for actress.
GRETTA Ref: HR 10/25/83:S-74: "suicide club"; horror??
The GROUNDSTAR CONSPIRACY 1972 screen. B.Warren: non-fantastic p.surgery & brainwashing. Frank/SF&FFHandbook. Lee(e).
A GUIDE FOR THE MARRIED MAN 1967 Ref: TV: anim.-dinosaur bit.
The GUYRA GHOST MYSTERY (Austral) 1921 Ref: V 5/5/76:95. ??

El HACEDOR DE MIEDO Ref: TVG: "horror." ??
HAND OF THE ASSASSIN 1965? Ref: TVFFSB: inn murders. with J.Ferrer.??
HARLEM ON THE PRAIRIE Ref: V 2/9/38: spooky cave sequence.
HEIDI'S SONG 1982 Ref: C.Epstein: nightmare with comic monsters.
HELP! (B) 1965 Ref: screen. Lee: paralyzing ray. ??
HERE COME THE GIRLS 1953 Ref: J.Shapiro: R.Strauss as Jack The Slasher.
HEX VS. WITCHCRAFT (HK) 1981 (XIE DOU XIE) Ref: JFFJ 14:36. HKFFest.??
The HIDDEN EYE 1945 Ref: TV: chiller bit with skulker in mansion.
HOLLYWEIRD UFD Ref: V 8/31/83:14: in Boston. ??
HOLLYWOOD RIPPER Ref: V 5/9/84:259(ad). ??
HOLLYWOOD STRANGLER MEETS THE SKIDROW SLASHER Steckler Ref: Fangoria.??
L'HOMME QUI A VU LE DIABLE (F) Ref: V 10/27/82:8: at Sitges. ??
The HONOR GUARD (WOLF LAKE-orig t) Ref: Ecran F 30:58: horrific end.??
HORROR MOVIE 1982 Ref: V 2/16/83:24: horror. ??
HORRORS OF THE RED PLANET Ref: V 10/20/82:164. with Chaney, Carradine. ??

The HOT PEARL SNATCH 1966? Ref: AFI: voodoo hex on pearls.
HOTLINE 1982 Ref: TVG: PLAY MISTY FOR ME, Jr.
**HOUSE OF DANGER 1934 Ref: TV: old house, storm, peephole.
HUMAN HIGHWAY Ref: V 8/18/82: nuclear disaster??
HUMAN TOUCH Ref: SFExam 2/24/84:E15: rock video re: computerized future; "isolation capsules." ??
HUNDRA (U.S.-Sp) Ref: V 12/7/83:7: at Paris sf fest. Ecran F 29:55.??
HUTCH STIRS 'EM UP (B) 1923 Ref: BFC: "mad squire's torture chamber."

I LOVE A PARADE 1933 anim 6m. Ref: screen: caged ape-"wild man" bit.
I LOVE YOU (Braz) 1981 Ref: TV: "monster movie" seq. with taped horror-movie sounds and man disguised as bear.
ILLEGAL ALIEN Ref: UC Theatre: ALIEN spoof. Greg Keller. ??
IN THE SHADOW OF...BIGFOOT 1983? Ref: TV(ad): movie??
The INN ON THE RIVER (WG) 1962 Ref: TVFFSB: "nameless terror."??
The INTERNECINE PROJECT Ref: Cinef IV:1:37: "sonic death ray."??
INVITATION OF GHOST (Chinese) Ref: poster: horror??
INVITATION TO THE DANCE (B) 1956 Ref: TV: seq. with anim. dragon.
L'INVITE DE LA 11me HEURE (F) Ref: V 10/10/45: scientist's "atomic style" discovery.
IO ZOMBO, TU ZOMBI, LEI ZOMBA (I) 1980 Ref: Prod Ital. ?? no Ecran F.
The IPCRESS FILE (B) 1965 Ref: screen: proto-proton-scatterer.

JOGO DE MAO (Port) Ref: V 9/14/83: man in "Dracula outfit." ??

KILLER BEES Ref: TVG: horror parody on "Night Flight." ??
KILLER LEOPARD 1954 Ref: TV: night-prowling "devil cat"; non-horror.
The KILLER METEORS (HK?) Ref: V 9/28/83:60(ad): kung fu. ??
The KILLING KIND Ref: V 6/13/73: horror?? aka?
KILLING TIME Ref: V 2/16/83:24: horror? B.Warren: completed?
KING KONG (J) c1933 Ref: David Bordwell(poster). B.Warren: doubt. ??
KOCICI PRINZ (Cz) 1978 Ref: "Tous Les Films 1980": monsters??
KOYAANISQATSI Ref: MFB'83:217. ??
KUNG FU HALLOWEEN Ref: V 11/3/82:11: "ghostly." Ecran F 22:10: "night of horror." TVFFSB: action. ??

LAGOON OF THE UNDEAD Ref: V 5/9/84:264(ad).??
LAIR OF THE VAMPIRES Ref: V 5/9/84:264(ad).??
The LAST FARM IN THE VALLEY (Iceland) 1950 Ref: FComment 9/80:8: "fairy story of trolls, ogres, flying trunks...." ??
The LAST NINJA Ref: V 7/13/83:54: TV-movie with Kung Fu invisibility.
LIFE AFTER LIFE Ref: V 1/6/82: "possession/reincarnation mystery."??
LINCOLN COUNTY INCIDENT (NZ) 1980 Ref: MFB'83:42: "eerie" ghost.
The LITTLE GIRL WHO LIVES DOWN THE LANE (US-F-Can) 1977 Ref: TV: girl keeps embalmed body of dead mom in cellar. Cinef VI:2:24.
The LOST WORLD 1982? anim Ref: S&S'82:226. ??
LOVE IN COLD BLOOD 1969 (aka The ICE HOUSE. The PASSION PIT) Ref: TV: man suffers "blackouts," murders women, puts bodies in ice h.
LUCIFER RISING 1982 29m. Ref: MFB'82:191-2: flying saucers. ??
LUNATIC Ref: V 10/20/82:139(ad). 5/9/84:259(ad). ??
La LUNE DANS LE CANIVEAU (F-I) Ref: V 5/18/83: laser beam. Ecran F 34.

The MAGIC LOTUS LANTERN (Chi) 1959 (PAO LIEN-TENG) Ref: MFB'77:50: "magnificently fiery dragon...Heavenly Hound." ??
The MAKING OF THRILLER 1983 Ref: TV: behind-scenes on THRILLER(M).
MALAMORE (I) Ref: V 9/22/82: monstrous dwarf; fortune telling. ??
The MAN FROM CLOVER GROVE 1973 Ref: TV: inventor's gizmos disrupt local electrical and mechanical activity.
Un MARCIANO NA MINHA CAMA (Braz) 1981 Ref: V 3/17/82:60. ??
MARCO POLO JR. (Austral) 1972('74-U.S.) Ref: TV: "Red Dragon" conjures up sea storm; Delicate Dinosaur. MFB'74:181. V 12/26/73.
MARIANNA (HK) Ref: V 7/21/82: "non-existent ghostly tribe." ??
MARINES COME THROUGH Ref: V 7/14/43: "newly-invented bomb sight."
*MASQUERADE 1965(1964) Ref: TV: non-horror; skeleton-with-crown.
MASSARATI AND THE BRAIN 1982 Ref: TVG: TV-movie; "007-style inventions."
MEET BOSTON BLACKIE 1941 Ref: screen: The Mechanical Man, (human) sideshow attraction; murder-by-dart in Tunnel of Horror.
MEMOIRS OF A SURVIVOR (B) Ref: V 5/27/81: futuristic chaos. LAT ?? 3/1/83: sf ending? Sacto Union. MFB'81:203-4. Roxie Cinema notes.
METROPOLIS 2000 Ref: V 8/24/83:39: "scifier" in Berlin. ??
MEURTRES A DOMICILE (Belg-F) Ref: V 1/26/83: exorcism, necrophilia.
The MILD WEST 1947 anim 7m. Ref: TV: bit with Spike Bones & His Boys, skeletons, dancing in Death Valley. LC. no Kausler. B.Warren.
MINISTRY OF FEAR Ref: V 10/18/44. screen: seance.
MIRRORS Ref: TVG: weird deaths; nightmares. ?? with K.Wynn,P.Donat.
MISTERIO EN LAS BERMUDAS Ref: TVG. with Santo. ??
MODIGA MINDRE MAN (Swed) Ref: WorldF'68: horror parody. ??
MOLBA (Russ) 1968 (aka The PRAYER) Ref: screen: monkey-king, gore.
The MONSTER FROM OUT OF TOWN 1981 Ref: V 2/16/83:24: horror. ??
MONTY PYTHON'S THE MEANING OF LIFE (B) Ref: V 3/23/83: Death, gore.
MORTE IN VATICANO (I-Sp-Mex) Ref: V 9/15/82: "altered states" potion.
MURDER ON VOODOO ISLAND 1977 Ref: TVG: from "Starsky & Hutch." ??
MY NAME IS JULIA ROSS 1945 Ref: screen: sadist; clutching hand.
2P The MYSTERIOUS DESPERADO 1949 Ref: TV: hooded figure, cobwebs.
The MYSTERIOUS STRANGER (US-Aust-WG) 1982 Ref: TV: imp from alternate world makes gold, doppelgangers in medieval castle.
A MYTHICAL TALE OF DRAGON SLAYING (HK) 1940 Ref: HKFFest'82:132. ??

NIGHT FIEND (Sp) 1977 Ref: TVG: brutality. with F.Rey, M. Mell. ??
NIGHT OF HORROR Ref: V 10/20/82:139(ad). 5/9/84:264(ad). ??
NIGHTKILL 1980 Ref: TV: perfect-crime suspenser, chiller moments.
NIGHTMARE HONEYMOON 1973 Ref: Cinef III:4:37: "genre piece." Weldon.??
1988--THE REMAKE Ref: SFExam 3/4/83:E9. ??
99 AND 44/100% DEAD Ref: V 6/19/74: futuristic. Weldon: giant gators.??
2P NORTHVILLE CEMETERY MASSACRE 1975 Ref: TV: bloody biker movie.
NUCLEAR NIGHTMARES Ref: TVG 1/30/83: end of the world?? On "Ovation."
La NUIT DE LA MORT (I) 1980 Ref: "Tous Les Films 1980": horror. ??
NURSERY FAVORITES 1913 Ref: Lee(Warren): giant spider. No AF-Index.??

ONE STEP AHEAD OF MY SHADOW 1933 anim 7m. Ref: "WBCartoons": dragon.
OPIUM SMOKER'S DREAM 1906 Ref: Lee: dream of demons in hell.
The OUTCASTS (Irish) Ref: V 8/3/83: "devilish" stranger. ??
An OVER-INCUBATED BABY (B) 1901? Ref: BFC: incubator ages child.

PANDEMONIUM (J) 1972 (SHURA) Ref: MFB'74:133: gore; nightmare; visions. Stanley: sfa DEMONS? IFG'73:239. V 5/10/72. ??
PANIC (Hung) anim Ref: V 11/2/83:42: at Rome sf fest. ??
Le PARFUM DE LA DAME EN NOIR (F) 1930 Ref: Pierre LePage: death-semblance serum; sequel to MYSTERY OF THE YELLOW ROOM(M).
PARSIFAL (WG-F) Ref: V 5/26/82. MFB'83:137-8: magician's spell.
PASTRIES 1979 Ref: TV: bit with Count (with Lugosi accent) from Transylvania--possibly a vampire (left implicit).
Die PATRIOTIN (WG) Ref: MFB'81:224: film "Werewolves" being shot.
PHANTOM KILLER (HK) 1981 Ref: JFFJ 14:36: "martial arts-horror."??
PIERRE GUIMOND: ENTRE FREUD ET DRACULA (Can) Ref: Ecran F: docu.
PINK LIGHTNING Ref: TV: Jekyll-&-Hyde potion. TV cartoon? no LC.
POBRES MILLONARIOS (Mex) Ref: TV: cataleptic "returns to life."
Le PONT DU NORD (F) Ref: V 10/14/81: "fire-breathing dragon."
The PREY Ref: V 2/16/83:24: horror? (d) 12/2/80(rated). HR 11/23/79.
PROF. ZOVEK (Mex) 1971 Ref: Ecran F 31:31: zombies?; title character also in INVASION DE LOS MUERTOS(II).
PROSHI KINDYNOS (Greek) Ref: V 11/9/83: mad killer; "shock qualities."
PSYCHO FROM TEXAS 1974 Ref: V 10/13/82: subplot with mad slasher.
PSYCHO MANIAC (Fili) Ref: WorldF'68. ??
PSYCHO SISTERS Ref: V 10/20/82:139(ad). with S.Strasberg, Domergue.??

RANSOM 1977 Ref: TVG. Weldon: "horror ad campaign"; inserted masked-killer sequence. Aka MANIAC! and ASSAULT ON PARADISE.
REBORN (Sp-US) Ref: S&S'82:230: "the Second Coming." V 5/9/84:302. See also: NEXT ONE, The(M).
RED NIGHTMARE 1957 28m. Ref: Roxie notes: Commie takeover; robots??
The RESCUERS 1977 Ref: screen: attack bats in "creepy" Devil's Bayou.
REVENGE OF DR. X Ref: V 5/9/84:264(ad). ??
El REY DE LOS GORILLAS Ref: TVG. ?? with H.Stiglitz, Peggy Bass.
RIO NUDO 1969 Ref: AFI: ape-like woman; voodoo dance. ??
ROCKET TO MARS 1977 Ref: Stanley: Super-8. no VideoSB,PFA,TVFFSB.??
RULES OF THE GAME (F) 1939 Ref: screen: "Danse Macabre" sequence.

SABRINA 1954 Ref: TV: bullet-proof, fire-resistant plastic from sugar cane, tested, works.
Die SAGE DES TODES (WG) Ref: MFB'82:91: masked killer. (BLOODY MOON-B)
SANCTUARY OF FEAR 1979 Ref: TVG. TV: mystery-suspense.
SANS SOLEIL (F) Ref: Filmex'83: "electronic future"??
The SCAREMAKER Indep-Int'l Ref: V 12/8/82:4(rated). 2/16/83:24: horror. Academy. with H.Holbrook. sfa RITUALS??
SCHULMADCHEN--REPORT 10 (WG) Ref: MFB'78:28: fake exorcism.
SCREAM Cal-Com Ref: V 8/24/83:4(rated). 11/16/83:12: in Miami.??
A SCREAM IN THE STREETS 1973? Ref: TV: mad slasher/transvestite.
SCREAM OF THE SOUL 1982 Ref: V 2/16/83:24: horror. ??
The SEDUCTION 1982 Ref: TV: "erotomaniac" murders woman's lover.
SEX IN OLD CHINA (HK) Ref: TV: magician conjures up lightning.
SHE'S DRESSED TO KILL 1979 Ref: TVG: "unknown murderer." ??
SHOCKING ASIA (WG-HK) Ref: V 3/24/82: "gore." ??
SIEGE (Can.) Ref: MFB'83:277. V 2/9/83: "violent exploitation."
SILENT DEATH 1982 Ref: V 2/16/83:24: horror. ??
The SINISTER URGE Ed Wood Ref: VV 2/1/83: "psycho-killer." ??

SISSY'S HOT SUMMER Ref: screen: end bit with "robot."
SLIME 1981 Ref: V 2/16/83:24: horror. ??
The SMALL BACK ROOM (B) 1949 Ref: screen: nightmare with giant bottle.
SOULS(THE FORCE OF EVIL) Ref: V 5/12/82:211(ad): horror??
SPACE IS THE PLACE 1974 Ref: Stanley: alien. no V,PFA,VideoSB.??
SPASM Rebane Ref: V 2/16/83:24. HR 11/80: sf; shooting. with J.P.Law.??
SPASMO 1976 D: Lenzi. Ref: Cinef V:2:35: gory; inherited madness.??
The STATE OF THINGS Ref: FComment 11/82:6: remake of MOST DANGEROUS MAN ALIVE being shot. MFB'83:7-9. Ecran F 30:79.
The STEEL KEY (B) 1953 Ref: Lee. Stanley. BFC: steel-hardening process.
STEP BY STEP 1946 Ref: TV: "key members of the German general staff" continue plotting after WWII, with the U.S. as home base.
STILL OF THE NIGHT (STAB-orig t) Ref: V 11/3/82. TV: dream sequence.
The STOLEN AIRSHIP (Cz) 1969 Ref: screen: boat-airship in 1891.
The STORY OF TEMPLE DRAKE 1933 Ref: screen: dream: old house, storm.
The STRANGENESS Ref: V 10/20/82:164(ad). ??
STUPENDOUS SCI-FI MOVIE Ref: V 10/20/82:139. ??
SUMMER GIRL 1983 Ref: TV: TV-movie; psychopathic killer. TVG.
SUPERBUG, SUPER AGENT (WG) 1976 Ref: TVG: flying car. V 9/21/83: 103(ad): combo VW-copter; sequel to SUPERBUG.
SUPERCHICK 1973 Ref: TV: seq. with Carradine as Igor Smith, flagellation freak who "acted in mostly low-budget horror films."
SURVIVAL ZONE Ref: V 10/26/83:203(ad): post-nuclear-holocaust. ??
A SWARM IN MAY (B) Ref: MFB'83:140-41: ghost exorcised.

The TALE OF THE FIDDLE (B?) 1909 Ref: Lee: deal with devil? not in BFC.
TANGLED DESTINIES 1932 Ref: Turner/Price: "forbidding farmhouse."??
A TASTE OF HELL Ref: V 12/12/73: mutilated soldier; decapitation.
TATTOO Ref: MFB'81:226: tattoing-gun-as-weapon.
TEMPTATION 1946 Ref: TV: "curse" on Rameses' mummy.
TENDRES COUSINES 1980 Ref: MFB'83:107: souls captured in balloons.
The TERRITORY (Port-US) Ref: V 3/16/83: cannibalism, "surrealism."
THERE WAS ONCE A CHILD (I-US) Creative (SCARED TO DEATH-alt t?) Ref: V 5/13/81:152: "terror." cf.2P NIGHT DANIEL DIED, The.??
THEY CALL HER ONE EYE 1973 Ref: V 6/26/74: gore. Ecran F 41:16,29.??
THOR, IL CONQUISTATORE Ref: Ecran F 35:71: sfa THOR THE CONQUEROR(M)?
2 THRESHOLD 1981('83-U.S.) Ref: SFExam 3/4/83: based on fact. TV.
THROUGH THE MAGIC PYRAMID 1981(1979) Ref: TVG: time travel. ??
THUNDERBIRDS 2086 (B-J) 1983 anim Ref: TV: TV-series episodes.
The TIGRESS (Can) (aka ILSA-TIGRESS OF SIBERIA) Ref: Sleazoid Exp 5/83:6: unofficial f.-u. to the ILSA films; torture chamber.
TO HELL WITH THE DEVIL (HK) Ref: V 5/5/82: deal with devil.
TODAY OR TOMORROW (Dutch) Ref: IFG'77:220: "near future." ??
TOMORROW'S CHILD 1982 Ref: TVG: TV-movie: lab-developed fetus.
TOWER OF DEATH (HK) Ref: JFFJ 14:36: "martial arts-horror."??
TOWN OF BLOODY HORROR Ref: V 10/20/82:139(ad). ??
The TRAIL (HK) Ref: V 4/20/83. 5/4/83:342: horror-comedy. Ecran F.??
TRANCE (WG) Ref: V 6/30/82: brutal murder, dismemberment, "trance."
TRAPPED 1981 Ref: MFB'83:109: teens-in-peril + DELIVERANCE. ??
TRAUMA 1982 Ref: V 2/16/83:24: horror. ??
TRIONIC WARRIOR (HK) KTR Ref: HR 3/31/78: "action." ??
Les TROIS COURONNES DU MATELOT (F) Ref: V 6/1/83: "damned ship."

TRUNK CRIME (B) 1939 Ref: BFC: attempted premature burial. ??
TUTTI DEFUNTI TRANNE I MORTI (I) 1977 Ref: Ecran F 36:88: a la "Ten Little Indians." ??
12-10 (B) 1919 Ref: BFC: death-semblance drug.
TWILIGHT ZONE Ref: TVG: source-shows for The MOVIE shown as movie.

ULVETID (Dan) Ref: V 10/7/81: "werewolves of their psyches."
UM S MARGINAL (Port) Ref: IFG'83: "near future"; tame dogs go wild.

VICE SQUAD Ref: V 1/27/82: "horror film" climax. TV: sadistic killer.
La VIE EST UN ROMAN Ref: V 4/20/83: fantasy. Ecran F 35:50: monster??

WENT THE DAY WELL? (B) 1943 (48 HOURS-U.S.) Ref: screen: German paratroopers in England plan to knock out radio communication with (never used) apparatus; told as post-WWII "flashback."
*The WEREWOLF 1923 and 1932 Ref: Ecran F 22:2(J.-C.Romer): both films re: escaped convict who, to explain to his young son why he's always "on the run," tells him a werewolf is chasing him.
Il WEST TI VA STRETTO, AMICO (I-WG-F) 1973 Ref: Prod Ital: Western featuring "all kinds of unheard of scientific weapons."
WHITE DOG 1982 Ref: Weldon: dog conditioned to kill blacks. MFB'84:33.
WHO DONE IT? (B) 1956 Ref: BFC: "weather control device." "Ealing S."
WHOSO DIGGETH A PIT (B) 1915 Ref: BFC: "death stimulant" injection.
The WORLD ACCORDING TO GARP 1982 Ref: TV: anim.bit with "Death."
2 WORLD WAR III 1982 Ref: TV: nuclear holocaust implied. Weldon: 1987; Russia invades Alaska.
WRONG IS RIGHT 1982 Ref: TV: scale-model demonstration of effects of nuclear attack on NYC. MFB'82:269: MAN WITH THE DEADLY LENS-B.

The YELLOW CAB MAN 1950 Ref: Lee: unbreakable glass.
YELLOW DOG (B) 1973 Ref: MFB'73:215: "artificial fuel" formula.
YOHKI YASHIKI (J) 1954 Ref: Ecran F 31:52: aka The MONSTER'S OLD DARK HOUSE. ??
YOU, JOHN JONES Ref: screen: fantasy bit re: bomb attack on U.S.

ZEI CHEN UND WUNDER (WG) Ref: V 3/10/82: strange rays from patent office.
ZHONG KUI, THE EXORCIST (HK) 1939 Ref: HKFFest'82:132. ??
ZU (HK) Ref: V 2/23/83: mythological "zoo." 5/4/83:342. ??

ALTERNATE TITLES

Since the publication of Horror and Science Fiction Films (in 1972) and Horror and Science Fiction Films II (in 1982), many new alternate release-titles of films listed therein have, in the course of research, come to light. Rather than hold this new information until all the entries in question are updated, I have cross-indexed these titles, provisionally, here, in order to keep the previous editions as up-to-date as possible.

ALIEN FORCE see ALIENS ARE COMING, The (II)
ALIEN WARNING see IT CAME...WITHOUT WARNING (II)
ASSIGNMENT TERROR see DRACULA VS. FRANKENSTEIN (I)
ATAUD VACIO, El see MONSTERS DEMOLISHER, The (I)
ATOMIC ROCKETSHIP see FLASH GORDON (I)
ATTACK OF THE GIANT HORNY GORILLA see APE (II)
BATTLE OF THE MONSTERS see GHIDRAH (I)
BEAST OF THE DEAD see BEAST OF BLOOD (I)
BEYOND THE LIVING see NURSE SHERRI (II)
BEYOND THE LIVING DEAD see BRACULA (II)
BIG HUNT, The see BLOODLUST (I)
BLOOD BRIDES see BRIDES OF BLOOD (I)
BODY SNATCHER FROM HELL see GOKE (I)
BOURBON STREET SHADOWS see INVISIBLE AVENGER (I)
BRAM STOKER'S COUNT DRACULA see COUNT DRACULA (I)
CARNIVOROUS see LAST SURVIVOR, The (II)
CATASTROPHE 1999 see LAST DAYS OF PLANET EARTH (II)
CHINESE GODS see STORY OF CHINESE GODS (II)
CHRISTMAS EVIL see YOU BETTER WATCH OUT (II)
CITY OF THE WALKING DEAD see ZOMBIES ATOMICOS (II)
COLLEGE-GIRL MURDERS, The see MONK WITH THE WHIP (I)
COLLISION COURSE see BAMBOO SAUCER, The (I)
CREATURE'S REVENGE, The see BRAIN OF BLOOD (I)
CREEPER, The see RITUALS (II)
CURLEY AND HIS GANG IN THE HAUNTED MANSION see WHO KILLED 'DOC' ROBBIN? (I)
CURSE OF THE LIVING DEAD see KILL, BABY, KILL (I)
DAMA EN EL MUERTE, La see CURSE OF THE STONE HAND (I)
DANCE OF THE VAMPIRES see FEARLESS VAMPIRE KILLERS, The (I)
DANIEL AND THE DEVIL see DEVIL AND DANIEL WEBSTER, The (I)
DEADLY AND THE BEAUTIFUL, The see WONDER WOMEN (II)
DEADLY ORGAN, The see BLOODY PLEASURE (I)
DEADLY TREASURE OF THE PIRANHA see KILLER FISH (II)
DEATH RIDE see CRASH! (II)
DEATHQUAKE see EARTHQUAKE 7.9 (II)
DEATH'S DOOR see CONFESSIONAL, The (II)
DEMONS OF THE DEAD see THEY'RE COMING TO GET YOU! (II)

DR. BREEDLOVE see KISS ME QUICK (I)
DRACULA'S CASTLE see BLOOD OF DRACULA'S CASTLE (I)
DUGO NG VAMPIRA see CURSE OF THE VAMPIRES (I)
DUNGEON OF TERROR see CRAZED VAMPIRE (II)?
ESTUDIANTE Y LA HORCA, El see MONSTERS DEMOLISHER, The (I)
EXORCISM AT MIDNIGHT see NAKED EVIL (I)
FANGS see MAMMA DRACULA (II)
FANTASTIC INVASION OF PLANET EARTH see BUBBLE, The (I)
FEAST OF FLESH see BLOODY PLEASURE (I)
FIFTH COLUMN SQUAD see SPIES OF THE AIR (I)
FIREBALL see SECRET AGENT FIREBALL (I)
FRANKEN PROJECT, The see DOCTOR FRANKEN (II)
FREEZE BOMB see DEATH DIMENSION (II)
FRENZY see LATIN QUARTER, The (I)
FREUDSTEIN see QUELLA VILLA ACCANTO AL CIMITERO (II)
FULL MOON see MOONCHILD (II)
FURY ON THE BOSPHORUS see AGENT 077, FROM THE EAST WITH FURY (I)
GAMES OF COUNTESS DOLINGEN see JEUX DE LA COMTESSE DOLINGEN (II)
GARU THE MAD MONK see GURU THE MAD MONK (I)
GOLIATHON see MIGHTY PEKING MAN, The (II)
GRAVE DESIRES see BRIDES OF BLOOD (I)
GRAVEYARD TRAMPS see INVASION OF THE BEE GIRLS (II)
GUARDING BRITAIN'S SECRETS see FIENDS OF HELL, The (I)
HAUNTED MANSION, The see WHO KILLED 'DOC' ROBBIN? (I)
HELL-FACE (I) sfa INCREDIBLE FACE OF DR. B (I)
HORROR OF THE WEREWOLF see NIGHT OF THE HOWLING BEAST (II)
HORROR PLANET see INSEMINOID (II)
HOUSE BY THE CEMETERY see QUELLA VILLA ACCANTO AL CIMITERO (II)
HOUSE OF DOOM see HOUSE OF PSYCHOTIC WOMEN (IIP)
HOUSE OF INSANE WOMEN see EXORCISM'S DAUGHTER (II)
HOUSE THAT CRIED MURDER see HERE COMES THE BRIDE (II)
INCENSE FOR THE DAMNED see BLOODSUCKERS (I)
INVASION FORCE see HANGAR 18 (II)
ISLAND OF LIVING HORROR see BRIDES OF BLOOD (I)
ISLAND OF THE BURNING DAMNED or ISLAND OF THE BURNING DOOMED
see NIGHT OF THE BIG HEAT (I)
JAIL BAIT see HIDDEN FACE, The (II)
KILL AND GO HIDE see CHILD, The (II)
LAST HOUSE ON THE LEFT PART II see TWITCH OF THE DEATH NERVE (II)
LEGEND OF SUPER GALAXY see CYBORG 009--LEGEND OF SUPER GALAXY (II)
LITTLE GRAINS OF LOVE see LIQUID LOVE (I)
LUNATICS, The see SYSTEM OF DR. TARR & PROFESSOR FETHER (I)
MAGNITUDE 7.9 see EARTHQUAKE 7.9 (II)
MAN FROM S.E.X., The see LICENSED TO LOVE AND KILL (II)
MAN OF STONE, The see GOLEM, The (I,1935)
MAN WITHIN, The see OTHER, The (I,1930)
MISHAPS OF THE NEW YORK-PARIS RACE see NEW YORK TO PARIS (I)
MR. SUPERINVISIBLE see MR. INVISIBLE (I)
MOMIA, La see ATTACK OF THE MAYAN MUMMY (I)
MONSTER OF BLACKWOOD CASTLE see HOUND OF BLACKWOOD CASTLE (I)
NIGHT OF THE BLOOD MONSTER see WITCH-KILLER OF BLACKMOOR (I)
NIGHT OF THE LAUGHING DEAD see HOUSE IN NIGHTMARE PARK (II)

PRINCIPAL REFERENCES

Books, Annuals, Catalogs

The American Film Institute Catalog of Motion Pictures: Feature Films 1961-1970. New York: R.R. Bowker Co., 1976.

Cowie, Peter, ed. International Film Guide. Cranbury, N.J.: A.S. Barnes & Co., 1982-1984.

Crafton, Donald. Before Mickey. Cambridge, Mass. & London: The MIT Press, 1982.

Crawley, Tony. The Steven Spielberg Story. N.Y.: Quill, 1983.

Durgnat, Raymond. Franju. Berkeley: University of California Press, 1968.

Gianakos, Larry James. Television Drama Series Programming: A Comprehensive Chronicle, 1959-1975. Metuchen, N.J. & London: Scarecrow Press, 1978.

Gifford, Denis. The British Film Catalog 1895-1970. N.Y.: McGraw-Hill, 1973.

Glut, Don. Classic Movie Monsters. Metuchen, N.J.: Scarecrow Press, 1978.

_______. The Dracula Book. Metuchen, N.J.: Scarecrow Press, 1975.

_______. The Frankenstein Legend. Metuchen, N.J.: Scarecrow Press, 1973.

Hirschhorn, Clive. The Universal Story. N.Y.: Crown, 1983.

Lee, Walt. Reference Guide to Fantastic Films. Los Angeles: Chelsea-Lee, 1972, 1973, 1974. Three volumes.

Maltin, Leonard. Of Mice and Magic. N.Y.: McGraw-Hill Book Co., 1980.

Motion Pictures: 1912-1939; 1940-1949; 1950-1959; 1960-1969. Washington, D.C.: Library of Congress Register of Copyrights, 1951, 1953, 1960, 1971. Four volumes.

La Produzione Italiana. Rome: ANICA, 1972, 1973, 1980. Three volumes.

Stanley, John. Creature Features Movie Guide. Pacifica, CA: Creatures at Large, 1981.

Television Feature Film Source Book. N.Y.: Broadcast Information Bureau, 1983.

The Video Source Book. Syosset, NY: The National Video Clearinghouse, 1982. 4th ed.

Warren, Bill. Keep Watching the Skies!. Jefferson, N.C.: McFarland, 1982.

Weldon, Michael. The Psychotronic Encyclopedia of Film. N.Y.: Ballantine Books, 1983.

Willis, John A. Screen World. N.Y.: Crown, 1983.

Periodicals

Cinefantastique. Oak Park, Ill.: Frederick S. Clarke.
L'Ecran Fantastique. Paris: Media Presse Edition.
Famous Monsters. N.Y.: Warren Publishing Co.
Fangoria. N.Y.: O'Quinn Studios.
Film Notes. Berkeley: University Art Museum/Pacific Film Archive.
Film Quarterly. Berkeley: University of California Press.
The Japanese Fantasy Film Journal. Toledo, Ohio: Greg Shoemaker.
The Monthly Film Bulletin. London: British Film Institute.
San Francisco Chronicle. S.F.: The Chronicle Publishing Co.
San Francisco Examiner. S.F.: The Hearst Corp.
Shaw Brothers 76. H.K.: Shaw Bros.
Sight and Sound. London: British Film Institute.
TV Guide. Radnor, PA: Triangle Publications.
Variety. N.Y.: Variety, Inc.
The Village Voice. N.Y.: Village Voice, Inc.

ADDENDA

(M) AIRPLANE II 1982 Ref: V 5/9/84:508: FLYING HIGH II-foreign vt t.

ALIEN'S RETURN see RETURN, The(1980)(M,A)

ATOMIC CAT'S BIG ADVENTURE, The see DORAEMON--NOBITA NO DAIMAHO(M)

ATOMIC MONSTER see BEAST OF YUCCA FLATS(A)

*The BEAST OF YUCCA FLATS 1961 (aka ATOMIC MONSTER--THE BEAST OF YUCCA FLATS) Ph: John Cagle. Mkp & with: Larry Aten. FX: Ray Mercer. Ref: TV. AFI: GIRL MADNESS-'64 re-r t? V 5/24/61. and with Bing Stafford, Conrad Brooks.

A Hungarian scientist (Tor Johnson) is caught in, or near, an atom-bomb blast and lives, becoming a monster who wants only to kill. ("Touch a button, and things happen--a scientist becomes a beast," notes our narrator.) This is the straight, budgetless version of The ATOMIC KID(qq.v.). The director, Coleman Francis, might have taken lessons from Jerry Warren on how to avoid (apparently very costly) lip-synching of dialogue: the characters here speak, but the actors speaking are offscreen; have their backs to the camera; are shot from the neck down; are in long shot; are in the dark (in a cave); or cup their hands around their mouths, as if shouting. Forget the "plot"--the only suspense: will we see an actor's lips move...? Yes, finally--Johnson's, to be specific, but only for a few monster-growls....The "Warren effect" here is, in effect, one of modernistic "distancing"--story and character, that is, are held at one remove from us. It's not far enough....

BEYOND THE BRIDGE see OLIVIA(M)

BLADE IN THE DARK, A see HOUSE OF THE DARK STAIRWAY(M,A)

The BRAIN MACHINE PC 1972 color 89m. SP,D: Joy N. Houck Jr. SP,Exec P: Thomas Phillips. SP,Assoc P: Christian Garrison. Ph: R.A. Weaver. Mus: James Helms. Set Des: K.L. Addington. Opt: Consolidated. Mkp: Scott Hamilton. SdFxEd: Gene Eliot. Ref: TV: Paragon Video. V 5/9/84:140. with James Best, Barbara Burgess, Gil Peterson, Gerald McRaney, Anne Latham, Doug Collins.

Film is an illustration of the fact that "feeding impulses into the upper or lower cortex of the brain can be dangerous."

"Brain probes" conducted at the National Environmental Control Center reach into the subjects' brains and, via computer, extract The Truth. At one point, an incipient fistfight in E-Box, where the subjects are isolated, "overloads" the computer, which, in turn, submits the subjects to a lot of pain and "unnecessary hell." A "total brain probe" of one of them (Best) enables a special converter to "convert brain impulses into exact pictures of thought" on a computer screen.

A generally-stilted exploitation of contemporary paranoia re: government and science, which topics, along with psychology and theology, are all kind of squished together by the script. This movie belongs to the get-it-done school of filmmaking, and all awkwardnesses of performance (the film is alternately over and under-acted) and editing are let stand. The script is, essentially, a science-fiction version of group therapy--this machine has access to every last little convolution of the subject's brain, and won't let said subject fool himself or anyone else about what's in it. Lies must be acknowledged, or the walls in E-Box will close in on those inside. And the computer won't accept the "paradox of mankind"--i.e., that man believes himself to be, one way or another, immortal: only when one recalcitrant believer here dies does the computer close its case: "Question of Mortality. Subject No. 4 is Cleared." The movie goes through a lot of unnecessary hell of its own to get to that computerized irony, but it is, in a way, almost worth the trip. The latter, metaphysical stages of The BRAIN MACHINE are, at least, entertainingly awful....

CASA CON LA SCALA NEL BUIO, La see HOUSE OF THE DARK STAIRWAY(M,A)

DADDY'S DEADLY DARLING see STRANGE EXORCISM OF LYNN HART, The(M)

DOGS OF HELL see ROTTWEILER(M)

EGGED ON R-C Pictures 1926 20m. SP,D & with: Charles Bowers. SP: also H.L. Muller, Ted Sears. Ref: screen. PFA. no Lee. LC.

An inventor's Rube Goldberg-like contraption produces elastic, unbreakable eggs--which can only be opened with scissors. One such egg (laid in a case of dynamite) explodes after being sent through the machine. A bunch of eggs hidden in a (running) car-engine hatches little cars....The ends here justify the rather far-fetched means. This short leaps from slapstick to science fiction to outright fantasy without so much as a by-your-leave. When the eggs start hatching, and the tiny car-embryos begin stretching into car-shape, however, all narrative sins are gladly forgiven. It's hard to imagine a narrative which would lead naturally to such a spectacle....

FACES OF FEAR see OLIVIA(M)

(M) FALCON'S GOLD 1982 SP: also Walter Bell. Ph: Laszlo George. Mus: Lalo Schifrin. PD: Dave Davis. SpFX: Lorencio Cordero,

Jesus Duran. Mkp: Graciela Munoz. SdFxEd: Charles Bowers. Opt: Film Opticals. Ref: TV. Cinef XIII:6. HR 10/25/83:S-52. V 10/26/83:180: aka ROBBERS OF THE SACRED MOUNTAIN. with John Marley, Simon MacCorkindale, Louise Vallance, Blanca Guerra, George Touliatos, Jorge Reynoso.

"Cursed," meteorite-derived stones, with a "complex crystalline structure (which) astrophysicists have never seen before," form part of a "refractive alloy" used in the construction of a super-laser which destroys a satellite--and consequently knocks out all power and nuclear-guidance systems, temporarily, in Canada. ("Every hockey rink is melting.") Strictly routine high-adventure (with incidental sf elements) moves quickly, but not too nimbly. The characters who usually live, live; the characters who usually die, die....The sf stuff doesn't seem too carefully thought out--its appeal lies more on the "far-fetched" than on the "believable" side.

FANATIC see LAST HORROR FILM, The(A)

(M) The FINAL TERROR 1983 SpMkpAsst: Ed Jensen. SdFX: also Sd FxInc. Ref: screen.

"This bus ain't goin' nowhere," declares a character at one point in the movie, which latter is, in that respect, very much like the bus. The setting is Mill Creek, but it might as well be Camp Crystal Lake again. In-between shock scenes with the lurking murderess (Tony Macciaro), the protagonists bicker and quarrel with each other. Some of the bickering is mildly funny; but both the shock scenes and the in-between scenes are overstated, and the action unfolds rather aimlessly.

(M) FIREBIRD 2015 AD Merritt White(Mara) 1981(1980) SP: Barry Pearson, Maurice Hurley, Biff McGuire. Ph: Robert Fresco. Mus: Paul Hoffert, Lawrence Shragge;(lyrics) Brenda Hoffert. AD: Richard Hudolin; Don Zacharias. SpFX: Neil Trifunovich; Garry Paller. Opt: Film FX. Mkp: Dancose; McIntosh. Ref: TV.

"In the year of our gas, 2015," it's the Department of Vehicular Control vs. outlaw "burners." The former is empowered to disable private cars, but forbidden to harm drivers of same, although one revenge-hungry DVC operative (Diakun) persists in destroying owners as well as vehicles....FIREBIRD 2015 AD, only nominally science fiction, is a vehicle for vehicles, a paean to speed...although personal freedom is the ostensible subject. This is a movie which only a car-lover could love. While cinematically competent (the camera moves at the proper times), it's dramatically sprawling, and over-freighted with exposition...a sputtering version of the similarly-premised The LAST CHASE(qq.v.). The protagonists here are a jolly, fun bunch; the kids--Rubens and Wisden--have a Hawks-like, slow-man/fast-woman relationship. Diakun's Indian semi-renegade is the one serious character (his fun is vicious) and seems out-of-place in such company.

(M) FLASH GORDON: THE GREATEST ADVENTURE OF ALL NBC-TV/Don Christensen 1982 anim D: Sutherland, Towsley, Zukor. SP: Samuel A. Peeples. Based on Alex Raymond's comic strip. Mus: Blais, Michael, Mahana. Seq D: Marsh Lamore, Kay Wright. Ref: TV. TVG. "TV 1970-80."

A condensation of the "Flash Gordon" TV series. It's 1939, and Ming, Hitler's ally on the nuclear-powered "wandering planet" Mongo, is plotting the conquest of Earth, and begins with a "bombardment (by meteorites) from space." Plus: robot-Ming...machine which makes tree roots grow and kill Molemen... Lionmen...Hawkmen...cannibalistic lizard-women...primitives... giant, carnivorous constrictor-plant...dinosaur-like monster... dragon...huge blind two-headed monster...robot-warriors which, zapped, turn to stone...mole-machine-vehicle...astral projection...city in space.

Story-wise, not as sophisticated (to say the least) as GALAXY EXPRESS or The LAST UNICORN, but well-directed-and-animated. Sex and violence rather unambiguously power the plot here. (Flash and Ming's daughter, Aura, are the two main generators.) The dynamics of the graphics combine the livelier elements of comic books and live-action films--cutting-within-scenes, camera movement and placement (though the quick, short "zooms in" on characters quickly become cliche), movement within the frame, shifting camera angles and perspective, lighting/silhouette/color effects, etc. The monsters keep things lively, and the visual details (like the way Ming's flaming-sword swirls as it falls from the top of the tower) bespeak some care and attention to the look of things. The graphic highlight: the near-chaos wrought by the passing by, or near, Earth of Mongo.

FLYING HIGH II see AIRPLANE II(M,A)

GIRL MADNESS see BEAST OF YUCCA FLATS(A)

GRITO DE LA MUERTE, El see LIVING COFFIN, The(A)

(M) HOUSE OF THE DARK STAIRWAY National-Nuova Dania 1983 (A BLADE IN THE DARK-ad t) Ref: V 5/4/83:307. with Andrea Occhipinti, Lara Nasinki.

HOW TO DROWN DR. MRACEK, THE LAWYER, or, THE LAST OF THE WATER-SPRITES IN BOHEMIA (Cz) IFEX 1974 color 95m. D: Vaclav Vorlicek. Anim: J. Doubrava. Mkp: Josef Lojik. Ref: screen. Jon Van Landschoot. UC Theatre notes 5/7/84. no NYT('73-'80). no V. no IFG. no MFB('74-'78). no PFA(IFEX).

Fantasy film featuring a science-fictional subplot re: "a revolution in biology": a scientist's formula (involving carp-extract and "bezuli elements") transforms a man, temporarily, into a fish....The main subjects: water-sprites who drown humans and keep the souls of the latter in teapots, and who can transform into fish or inanimate objects--one sprite, turned into flour and baked in a cake (which rises spectacularly well), returns in human form as a giant.

Alternately droll and silly fantasy-comedy, with some delightful effects--e.g., the sprites (who travel via drainpipe) plunging into sinks and bathtub drains (the pipes swell momentarily). The romantic and comic complications are--as often as not--more complicated than they are inspired. (The human/water-sprite semi-impossible love is a comic variation on either CAT PEOPLE--here, intercourse issues not in death, simply in the loss of the sprite's powers.) The fantastic premises, however, yield their share of surprises--e.g., the revivifying soul of one drowned human restored (through his mouth) to his body....

HUNDIMIENTO DE LA CASA USHER, El see FALL OF THE HOUSE OF USHER('83)

2 The LAST HORROR FILM Twin Continental(Shere) 1982 color 91m. SP,D,P: David Winters. SP,P & with: Judd Hamilton. SP: also Tom Klassen. Ph: Tom DeNove. Mus: Jesse Frederick, Jeff Koz. AD: Brian Savagar. SpMkpFX:(cons) Peter McKenzie; Jones, Humphreys, Scott. Opt: Rabin, Rota Color. SdFxEd: Anthony Ippolito. Ref: TV: Media Home Ent.(video). no PFA. V 5/4/83: 254(ad): aka FANATIC. and with Mary Spinell, Sean Casey.

Would-be genius-director Vinny Durand (Joe Spinell) goes to Cannes to recruit horror-movie-queen Jana Bates (Caroline Munro) for his project, "The Loves of Dracula." Rebuffed, he murders an agent, a director, and an actress, and films their death scenes for later use. But Jana's ex-husband, Bret (Glenn Jacobson) "returns from the dead" (he was ostensibly Vinny's first victim), and interrupts Vinny's final "Dracula" scene with Jana, informing the two that he has been "using" Vinny to wreak revenge on her. Vinny dispatches him with a chainsaw.... gore in slasher-movie, "Caller in The Night," on theatre screen.

Easy to identify the inspiration behind this movie: someone went to Cannes; someone's chateau was available; Marcello Mastroianni walked by (and became, here, an instant "extra").... The script was written "around" a film festival. Its real/reel-life conceits and notes on the relationship between sex and violence are old-hat, and the characters talk like a column in a fan magazine. Pathos is one thing; Vinny's sexually-frustrated legend-in-his-own-mind is quite another....Wry, if unlikely, parting shot.

The LAST WARRIOR (I) Cannon/Immagine 1983 D: Romolo Guerrieri. SP: Roberto Leone. Ref: V 5/9/84:318. with David Warner, Woody Strode, Marina Costa.

"Big actioner with a futuristic setting."

*The LIVING COFFIN Alameda-Galindo/Alfredo Ripstein Jr. c1964 color c75m. (El GRITO DE LA MUERTE) D: Fernando Mendez. SP: Ramon Obon. Ph: Victor Herrera. Mus: G.C. Carrion. AD: Gunther Gerszo. SpFX: "Benavides." Mkp: Angelina Garibay. Ref: TV.

TVG. Lee. and with Carlos Ancira, Pedro D'Aguillon, A.S. Raxel.
Man in horror-mask pretends to be woman, Clothilde de Varga (who died in 1915), returned from the dead; runs around strangling people....Very inexpensive-looking mystery-horror-western (set in an oddly automobile-less 20th Century), with risible acting/action/chiller music, and a strange bit with a knife stuck in the face of a grandfather clock. The death/horror-mask is pretty-convincingly-detailed, however....

(M) MONGREL 1982 Ref: TV: Paragon Video. Bill Warren. with Aldo Ray, Terry Evans(Jerry), Catherine Molloy, Mitch Pileggi, J.M. Ingraffia.
"Something was in the house!"..."some sort of animal," it seems. But the "killer-animal" that guts a puppy and rips out the throats of its human victims proves to be a "high-strung" young man who brings his nightmares to life by "becoming" a dog and slaughtering his "enemies"....
Over-acted by all, including the human "dog." (He seems to have a case of psychological rabies, or lycanthropy.) The performances are broad and, in some cases, strident, and the script has two fairly-transparent main goals--to make the whole household appear to be "against" the killer (at least in his own mind) and, at the end, to isolate killer and heroine. Low-budget horror drama's only possible angle of interest is the mystery one.

(M) The RETURN 1980 (ALIEN'S RETURN-TV) Ref: TVG.

ROBBERS OF THE SACRED MOUNTAIN see FALCON'S GOLD(M,A)